§sas. | SAS Publishing

MW01273960

SAS® 9.1
Language Reference: Concepts

The Power to Know.

The correct bibliographic citation for this manual is as follows: SAS Institute Inc. 2004. *SAS® 9.1 Language Reference: Concepts*. Cary, NC: SAS Institute Inc.

SAS® 9.1 Language Reference: Concepts

Contents

PART 1   **SAS System Concepts**   1

Chapter 1 △ Essential Concepts of Base SAS Software   3
What Is SAS?   3
Overview of Base SAS Software   4
Components of the SAS Language   4
Ways to Run Your SAS Session   7
Customizing Your SAS Session   9
Conceptual Information about Base SAS Software   10

Chapter 2 △ SAS Processing   11
Definition of SAS Processing   11
Types of Input to a SAS Program   12
The DATA Step   13
The PROC Step   14

Chapter 3 △ Rules for Words and Names in the SAS Language   15
Words in the SAS Language   15
Names in the SAS Language   18

Chapter 4 △ SAS Language Elements   23
What Are the SAS Language Elements?   25
Data Set Options   25
Formats and Informats   27
Functions and CALL Routines   38
ARM Macros   55
Statements   69
SAS System Options   71

Chapter 5 △ SAS Variables   77
Definition of SAS Variables   78
SAS Variable Attributes   78
Ways to Create Variables   80
Variable Type Conversions   84
Aligning Variable Values   85
Automatic Variables   85
SAS Variable Lists   86
Dropping, Keeping, and Renaming Variables   88
Numeric Precision in SAS Software   90

Chapter 6 △ Missing Values   101
Definition of Missing Values   101

Special Missing Values   102
Order of Missing Values   103
When Variable Values Are Automatically Set to Missing by SAS   104
When Missing Values Are Generated by SAS   105
Working with Missing Values   107

Chapter 7 △ Expressions   109
Definitions for SAS Expressions   110
Examples of SAS Expressions   110
SAS Constants in Expressions   110
SAS Variables in Expressions   116
SAS Functions in Expressions   117
SAS Operators in Expressions   117

Chapter 8 △ Dates, Times, and Intervals   127
About SAS Date, Time, and Datetime Values   127
About Date and Time Intervals   137

Chapter 9 △ Error Processing and Debugging   147
Types of Errors in SAS   147
Error Processing in SAS   156
Debugging Logic Errors in the DATA Step   159

Chapter 10 △ SAS Output   161
Definitions for SAS Output   162
Routing SAS Output   163
The SAS Log   163
Traditional SAS Listing Output   167
Changing the Destination of the Log and the Output   170
Output Delivery System   170

Chapter 11 △ BY-Group Processing in SAS Programs   195
Definition of BY-Group Processing   195
References for BY-Group Processing   195

Chapter 12 △ WHERE-Expression Processing   197
Definition of WHERE-Expression Processing   197
Where to Use a WHERE Expression   198
Syntax of WHERE Expression   199
Combining Expressions by Using Logical Operators   207
Constructing Efficient WHERE Expressions   208
Processing a Segment of Data That Is Conditionally Selected   208
Deciding Whether to Use a WHERE Expression or a Subsetting IF Statement   211

Chapter 13 △ Optimizing System Performance   213
Definitions for Optimizing System Performance   213
Collecting and Interpreting Performance Statistics   214

Techniques for Optimizing I/O **215**
Techniques for Optimizing Memory Usage **220**
Techniques for Optimizing CPU Performance **220**
Calculating Data Set Size **221**

Chapter 14 △ Support for Parallel Processing **223**
Definition of Parallel Processing **223**
Threaded I/O **223**
Threaded Application Processing **224**

Chapter 15 △ Monitoring Performance Using Application Response Measurement (ARM) **225**
Introduction to ARM **225**
How Does ARM Work? **227**
Will ARM Affect an Application's Performance? **227**
Using the ARM Interface **228**
Examples of Gathering Performance Data **231**

Chapter 16 △ The SAS Registry **235**
Introduction to the SAS Registry **236**
Managing the SAS Registry **238**
Configuring Your Registry **246**

Chapter 17 △ Printing with SAS **251**
Introduction to Universal Printing **252**
Managing Printing Tasks with the Universal Printing User Interface **254**
Configuring Universal Printing with Programming Statements **273**
Forms Printing **279**

PART *2* Windowing Environment Concepts **281**

Chapter 18 △ Introduction to the SAS Windowing Environment **283**
Basic Features of the SAS Windowing Environment **283**
Main Windows of the SAS Windowing Environment **288**

Chapter 19 △ Managing Your Data in the SAS Windowing Environment **307**
Introduction to Managing Your Data in the SAS Windowing Environment **307**
Copying and Viewing Files in a Data Library **307**
Using the Workspace to Manipulate Data in a Data Set **313**
Importing and Exporting Data **321**

PART *3* DATA Step Concepts **327**

Chapter 20 △ DATA Step Processing **329**
Why Use a DATA Step? **329**
Overview of DATA Step Processing **330**
Processing a DATA Step: A Walkthrough **333**

About DATA Step Execution   337
About Creating a SAS Data Set with a DATA Step   342
Writing a Report with a DATA Step   347
The DATA Step and ODS   354

Chapter 21 △ Reading Raw Data   357
Definition of Reading Raw Data   357
Ways to Read Raw Data   358
Kinds of Data   358
Sources of Raw Data   361
Reading Raw Data with the INPUT Statement   362
How SAS Handles Invalid Data   367
Reading Missing Values in Raw Data   368
Reading Binary Data   369
Reading Column-Binary Data   371

Chapter 22 △ BY-Group Processing in the DATA Step   375
Definitions for BY-Group Processing   375
Syntax for BY-Group Processing   376
Understanding BY Groups   377
Invoking BY-Group Processing   378
Determining Whether the Data Requires Preprocessing for BY-Group Processing   379
Preprocessing Input Data for BY-Group Processing   379
How the DATA Step Identifies BY Groups   380
Processing BY-Groups in the DATA Step   383

Chapter 23 △ Reading, Combining, and Modifying SAS Data Sets   387
Definitions for Reading, Combining, and Modifying SAS Data Sets   389
Overview of Tools   389
Reading SAS Data Sets   390
Combining SAS Data Sets: Basic Concepts   391
Combining SAS Data Sets: Methods   402
Error Checking When Using Indexes to Randomly Access or Update Data   428

Chapter 24 △ Using DATA Step Component Objects   437
Introduction   437
Using the Hash Object   438
Using the Hash Iterator Object   445

Chapter 25 △ Array Processing   449
Definitions for Array Processing   449
A Conceptual View of Arrays   450
Syntax for Defining and Referencing an Array   451
Processing Simple Arrays   452
Variations on Basic Array Processing   456
Multidimensional Arrays: Creating and Processing   457
Specifying Array Bounds   459

Examples of Array Processing   461

PART 4   **SAS Files Concepts   465**

Chapter 26 △ SAS Data Libraries   467
Definition of a SAS Data Library   467
Library Engines   469
Library Names   469
Library Concatenation   471
Permanent and Temporary Libraries   473
SAS System Libraries   474
Sequential Data Libraries   476
Tools for Managing Libraries   477

Chapter 27 △ SAS Data Sets   481
Definition of a SAS Data Set   481
Descriptor Information for a SAS Data Set   481
Data Set Names   482
Special SAS Data Sets   484
Sorted Data Sets   485
Tools for Managing Data Sets   485
Viewing and Editing SAS Data Sets   486

Chapter 28 △ SAS Data Files   487
Definition of a SAS Data File   489
Differences between Data Files and Data Views   489
Understanding an Audit Trail   491
Understanding Generation Data Sets   499
Understanding Integrity Constraints   505
Understanding SAS Indexes   518
Compressing Data Files   537

Chapter 29 △ SAS Data Views   539
Definition of SAS Data Views   539
Benefits of Using SAS Data Views   540
When to Use SAS Data Views   541
DATA Step Views   541
PROC SQL Views   545
Comparing DATA Step and PROC SQL Views   545
SAS/ACCESS Views   546

Chapter 30 △ Stored Compiled DATA Step Programs   547
Definition of a Stored Compiled DATA Step Program   547
Uses for Stored Compiled DATA Step Programs   547
Restrictions and Requirements for Stored Compiled DATA Step Programs   548
How SAS Processes Stored Compiled DATA Step Programs   548

Creating a Stored Compiled DATA Step Program   **549**
Executing a Stored Compiled DATA Step Program   **550**
Differences between Stored Compiled DATA Step Programs and DATA Step Views   **554**
Examples of DATA Step Programs   **554**

Chapter 31 △ DICTIONARY Tables   557
Definition of a DICTIONARY Table   **557**
How to View DICTIONARY Tables   **557**

Chapter 32 △ SAS Catalogs   561
Definition of a SAS Catalog   **561**
SAS Catalog Names   **561**
Tools for Managing SAS Catalogs   **562**
Profile Catalog   **563**
Catalog Concatenation   **564**

Chapter 33 △ About SAS/ACCESS Software   569
Definition of SAS/ACCESS Software   **569**
Dynamic LIBNAME Engine   **569**
SQL Procedure Pass-Through Facility   **571**
ACCESS Procedure and Interface View Engine   **572**
DBLOAD Procedure   **573**
Interface DATA Step Engine   **573**

Chapter 34 △ Processing Data Using Cross-Environment Data Access (CEDA)   575
Definition of Cross-Environment Data Access (CEDA)   **575**
Advantages of CEDA   **576**
SAS File Processing with CEDA   **576**
Processing a File with CEDA   **578**
Alternatives to Using CEDA   **580**
Creating New Files in a Foreign Data Representation   **581**
Examples of Using CEDA   **581**

Chapter 35 △ SAS 9.1 Compatibility with SAS Files From Earlier Releases   583
Introduction to Version Compatibility   **583**
Comparing SAS System 9 to Earlier Releases   **583**
Using SAS Library Engines   **584**

Chapter 36 △ File Protection   587
Definition of a Password   **587**
Assigning Passwords   **588**
Removing or Changing Passwords   **590**
Using Password-Protected SAS Files in DATA and PROC Steps   **590**
How SAS Handles Incorrect Passwords   **591**
Assigning Complete Protection with the PW= Data Set Option   **591**
Using Passwords with Views   **592**
SAS Data File Encryption   **594**

Chapter 37 △ SAS Engines   597
Definition of a SAS Engine   **597**
Specifying an Engine   **597**
How Engines Work with SAS Files   **598**
Engine Characteristics   **599**
About Library Engines   **602**
Special-Purpose Engines   **604**

Chapter 38 △ SAS File Management   607
Improving Performance of SAS Applications   **607**
Moving SAS Files Between Operating Environments   **607**
Repairing Damaged SAS Files   **607**

Chapter 39 △ External Files   611
Definition of External Files   **611**
Referencing External Files Directly   **612**
Referencing External Files Indirectly   **612**
Referencing Many External Files Efficiently   **613**
Referencing External Files with Other Access Methods   **614**
Working with External Files   **615**

PART *5*   **Industry Protocols Used in SAS   617**

Chapter 40 △ The SMTP E-Mail Interface   619
Sending E-Mail through SMTP   **619**
System Options That Control SMTP E-Mail   **619**
Statements That Control SMTP E-mail   **620**

Chapter 41 △ Universal Unique Identifiers   621
Universal Unique Identifiers and the Object Spawner   **621**
Using SAS Language Elements to Assign UUIDs   **623**

PART *6*   **Appendices   625**

Appendix 1 △ Recommended Reading   627
Recommended Reading   **627**

Index   629

x

P A R T *1*

SAS System Concepts

Chapter 1 . . . . **Essential Concepts of Base SAS Software** *3*

Chapter 2 . . . . **SAS Processing** *11*

Chapter 3 . . . . **Rules for Words and Names in the SAS Language** *15*

Chapter 4 . . . . **SAS Language Elements** *23*

Chapter 5 . . . . **SAS Variables** *77*

Chapter 6 . . . . **Missing Values** *101*

Chapter 7 . . . . **Expressions** *109*

Chapter 8 . . . . **Dates, Times, and Intervals** *127*

Chapter 9 . . . . **Error Processing and Debugging** *147*

Chapter 10 . . . . **SAS Output** *161*

Chapter 11 . . . . **BY-Group Processing in SAS Programs** *195*

Chapter 12 . . . . **WHERE-Expression Processing** *197*

Chapter 13 . . . . **Optimizing System Performance** *213*

Chapter 14 . . . . **Support for Parallel Processing** *223*

Chapter 15 . . . . **Monitoring Performance Using Application Response Measurement (ARM)** *225*

Chapter 16........The SAS Registry   *235*

Chapter 17........Printing with SAS   *251*

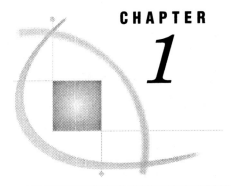

CHAPTER

1

Essential Concepts of Base SAS Software

What Is SAS? **3**
Overview of Base SAS Software **4**
Components of the SAS Language **4**
　　SAS Files **4**
　　SAS Data Sets **5**
　　External Files **5**
　　Database Management System Files **6**
　　SAS Language Elements **6**
　　SAS Macro Facility **6**
Ways to Run Your SAS Session **7**
　　Starting a SAS Session **7**
　　Different Types of SAS Sessions **7**
　　SAS Windowing Environment **7**
　　Interactive Line Mode **8**
　　Noninteractive Mode **8**
　　Batch Mode **9**
Customizing Your SAS Session **9**
　　Setting Default System Option Settings **9**
　　Executing Statements Automatically **9**
　　Customizing the SAS Windowing Environment **10**
Conceptual Information about Base SAS Software **10**
　　SAS System Concepts **10**
　　DATA Step Concepts **10**
　　SAS Files Concepts **10**

What Is SAS?

SAS is a set of solutions for enterprise-wide business users as well as a powerful fourth-generation programming language for performing tasks such as these:

- data entry, retrieval, and management
- report writing and graphics
- statistical and mathematical analysis
- business planning, forecasting, and decision support
- operations research and project management
- quality improvement
- applications development

With Base SAS software as the foundation, you can integrate with SAS many SAS business solutions that enable you to perform large scale business functions, such as data warehousing and data mining, human resources management and decision support, financial management and decision support, and others.

Overview of Base SAS Software

The core of the SAS System is Base SAS software, which consists of the following:

SAS language a programming language that you use to manage your data.

SAS procedures software tools for data analysis and reporting.

macro facility a tool for extending and customizing SAS software programs and for reducing text in your programs.

DATA step debugger a programming tool that helps you find logic problems in DATA step programs.

Output Delivery System (ODS) a system that delivers output in a variety of easy-to-access formats, such as SAS data sets, listing files, or Hypertext Markup Language (HTML).

SAS windowing environment an interactive, graphical user interface that enables you to easily run and test your SAS programs.

This document, along with *SAS Language Reference: Dictionary*, covers only the SAS language. For a complete guide to Base SAS software functionality, also see these documents: *SAS Output Delivery System: User's Guide, SAS National Language Support (NLS): User's Guide, Base SAS Procedures Guide, SAS Metadata LIBNAME Engine User's Guide, SAS XML LIBNAME Engine User's Guide, Base SAS Glossary, SAS Macro Language: Reference*, and the *Getting Started with SAS* online tutorial. The SAS windowing environment is described in the online Help.

Components of the SAS Language

SAS Files

When you work with SAS, you use files that are created and maintained by SAS, as well as files that are created and maintained by your operating environment, and that are not related to SAS. Files with formats or structures known to SAS are referred to as *SAS files*. All SAS files reside in a *SAS data library*.

The most commonly used SAS file is a *SAS data set*. A SAS data set is structured in a format that SAS can process. Another common type of SAS file is a *SAS catalog*. Many different kinds of information that are used in a SAS job are stored in SAS catalogs, such as instructions for reading and printing data values, or function key settings that you use in the SAS windowing environment. A *SAS stored program* is a type of SAS file that contains compiled code that you create and save for repeated use.

Operating Environment Information: In some operating environments, a SAS data library is a physical relationship among files; in others, it is a logical relationship. Refer to the SAS documentation for your operating environment for details about the characteristics of SAS data libraries in your operating environment. △

SAS Data Sets

There are two kinds of SAS data sets:

☐ SAS data file

☐ SAS data view.

A *SAS data file* both describes and physically stores your data values. A *SAS data view*, on the other hand, does not actually store values. Instead, it is a query that creates a logical SAS data set that you can use as if it were a single SAS data set. It enables you to look at data stored in one or more SAS data sets or in other vendors' software files. SAS data views enable you to create logical SAS data sets without using the storage space required by SAS data files.

A SAS data set consists of the following:

☐ descriptor information

☐ data values.

The descriptor information describes the contents of the SAS data set to SAS. The *data values* are data that has been collected or calculated. They are organized into rows, called observations, and columns, called variables. An *observation* is a collection of data values that usually relate to a single object. A *variable* is the set of data values that describe a given characteristic. The following figure represents a SAS data set.

Figure 1.1 Representation of a SAS Data Set

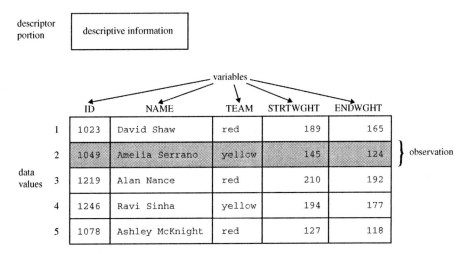

Usually, an observation is the data that is associated with an entity such as an inventory item, a regional sales office, a client, or a patient in a medical clinic. Variables are characteristics of these entities, such as sale price, number in stock, and originating vendor. When data values are incomplete, SAS uses a *missing value* to represent a missing variable within an observation.

External Files

Data files that you use to read and write data, but which are in a structure unknown to SAS, are called *external files*. External files can be used for storing

☐ raw data that you want to read into a SAS data file

       ☐ SAS program statements

       ☐ procedure output.

Operating Environment Information: Refer to the SAS documentation for your operating environment for details about the characteristics of external files in your operating environment. △

Database Management System Files

SAS software is able to read and write data to and from other vendors' software, such as many common database management system (DBMS) files. In addition to Base SAS software, you must license the **SAS/ACCESS** software for your DBMS and operating environment.

SAS Language Elements

The SAS language consists of statements, expressions, options, formats, and functions similar to those of many other programming languages. In SAS, you use these elements within one of two groups of SAS statements:

       ☐ DATA steps

       ☐ PROC steps.

A *DATA step* consists of a group of statements in the SAS language that can

       ☐ read data from external files

       ☐ write data to external files

       ☐ read SAS data sets and data views

       ☐ create SAS data sets and data views.

Once your data is accessible as a SAS data set, you can analyze the data and write reports by using a set of tools known as SAS procedures.

A group of procedure statements is called a *PROC step*. SAS procedures analyze data in SAS data sets to produce statistics, tables, reports, charts, and plots, to create SQL queries, and to perform other analyses and operations on your data. They also provide ways to manage and print SAS files.

You can also use global SAS statements and options outside of a DATA step or PROC step.

SAS Macro Facility

Base SAS software includes the SAS Macro Facility, a powerful programming tool for extending and customizing your SAS programs, and for reducing the amount of code that you must enter to do common tasks. Macros are SAS files that contain compiled macro program statements and stored text. You can use macros to automatically generate SAS statements and commands, write messages to the SAS log, accept input, or create and change the values of macro variables. For complete documentation, see *SAS Macro Language: Reference*.

Ways to Run Your SAS Session

Starting a SAS Session

You start a SAS session with the SAS command, which follows the rules for other commands in your operating environment. In some operating environments, you include the SAS command in a file of system commands or control statements; in others, you enter the SAS command at a system prompt or select SAS from a menu.

Different Types of SAS Sessions

You can run SAS in any of several different ways that might be available for your operating environment:

- □ SAS windowing environment
- □ interactive line mode
- □ noninteractive mode
- □ batch (or background) mode.

In addition, SAS/ASSIST software provides a menu-driven system for creating and running your SAS programs. For more information about SAS/ASSIST, see *Getting Started with SAS/ASSIST*.

SAS Windowing Environment

In the *SAS windowing environment*, you can edit and execute programming statements, display the SAS log, procedure output, and online Help, and more. The following figure shows the SAS windowing environment.

Figure 1.2 SAS Windowing Environment

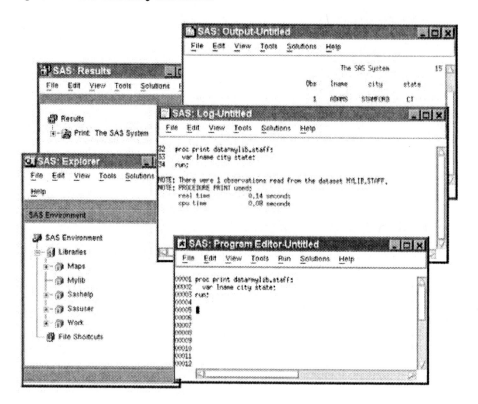

In the Explorer window, you can view and manage your SAS files, which are stored in libraries, and create shortcuts to external files. The Results window helps you navigate and manage output from SAS programs that you submit; you can view, save, and manage individual output items. You use the Program Editor, Log, and Output windows to enter, edit, and submit SAS programs, view messages about your SAS session and programs that you submit, and browse output from programs that you submit. For more detailed information about the SAS windowing environment, see Chapter 18, "Introduction to the SAS Windowing Environment," on page 283.

Interactive Line Mode

In *interactive line mode*, you enter program statements in sequence in response to prompts from the SAS System. DATA and PROC steps execute when
- □ a RUN, QUIT, or a semicolon on a line by itself after lines of data are entered
- □ another DATA or PROC statement is entered
- □ the ENDSAS statement is encountered.

By default, the SAS log and output are displayed immediately following the program statements.

Noninteractive Mode

In *noninteractive mode*, SAS program statements are stored in an external file. The statements in the file execute immediately after you issue a SAS command referencing the file. Depending on your operating environment and the SAS system options that you use, the SAS log and output are either written to separate external files or displayed.

Operating Environment Information: Refer to the SAS documentation for your operating environment for information about how these files are named and where they are stored. △

Batch Mode

You can run SAS jobs in *batch mode* in operating environments that support batch or background execution. Place your SAS statements in a file and submit them for execution along with the control statements and system commands required at your site.

When you submit a SAS job in batch mode, one file is created to contain the SAS log for the job, and another is created to hold output that is produced in a PROC step or, when directed, output that is produced in a DATA step by a PUT statement.

Operating Environment Information: Refer to the SAS documentation for your operating environment for information about executing SAS jobs in batch mode. Also, see the documentation specific to your site for local requirements for running jobs in batch and for viewing output from batch jobs. △

Customizing Your SAS Session

Setting Default System Option Settings

You can use a *configuration file* to store system options with the settings that you want. When you invoke SAS, these settings are in effect. SAS system options determine how SAS initializes its interfaces with your computer hardware and the operating environment, how it reads and writes data, how output appears, and other global functions.

By placing SAS system options in a configuration file, you can avoid having to specify the options every time that you invoke SAS. For example, you can specify the NODATE system option in your configuration file to prevent the date from appearing at the top of each page of your output.

Operating Environment Information: See the SAS documentation for your operating environment for more information about the configuration file. In some operating environments, you can use both a system-wide and a user-specific configuration file. △

Executing Statements Automatically

To execute SAS statements automatically each time you invoke SAS, store them in an *autoexec file*. SAS executes the statements automatically after the system is initialized. You can activate this file by specifying the AUTOEXEC= system option.

Any SAS statement can be included in an autoexec file. For example, you can set report titles, footnotes, or create macros or macro variables automatically with an autoexec file.

Operating Environment Information: See the SAS documentation for your operating environment for information on how autoexec files should be set up so that they can be located by SAS. △

Customizing the SAS Windowing Environment

You can customize many aspects of the SAS windowing environment and store your settings for use in future sessions. With the SAS windowing environment, you can

- change the appearance and sorting order of items in the Explorer window
- customize the Explorer window by registering member, entry, and file types
- set up favorite folders
- customize the toolbar
- set fonts, colors, and preferences.

See the SAS online Help for more information and for additional ways to customize your SAS windowing environment.

Conceptual Information about Base SAS Software

SAS System Concepts

SAS system-wide concepts include the building blocks of SAS language: rules for words and names, variables, missing values, expressions, dates, times, and intervals, and each of the six SAS language elements — data set options, formats, functions, informats, statements, and system options.

SAS system-wide concepts also include introductory information that helps you begin to use SAS, including information about the SAS log, SAS output, error processing, WHERE processing, and debugging. Information about SAS processing prepares you to write SAS programs. Information on how to optimize system performance as well as how to monitor performance.

DATA Step Concepts

Understanding essential DATA step concepts can help you construct DATA step programs effectively. These concepts include how SAS processes the DATA step, how to read raw data to create a SAS data set, and how to write a report with a DATA step.

More advanced concepts include how to combine and modify information once you have created a SAS data set, how to perform BY-group processing of your data, how to use array processing for more efficient programming, and how to create stored compiled DATA step programs.

SAS Files Concepts

SAS file concepts include advanced topics that are helpful for advanced applications, though not strictly necessary for writing simple SAS programs. These topics include the elements that comprise the physical file structure that SAS uses, including data libraries, data files, data views, catalogs, file protection, engines, and external files.

Advanced topics for data files include the audit trail, generation data sets, integrity constraints, indexes, and file compression. In addition, these topics include compatibility issues with earlier releases and how to process files across operating environments.

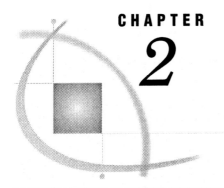

CHAPTER

2

SAS Processing

Definition of SAS Processing **11**
Types of Input to a SAS Program **12**
The DATA Step **13**
    DATA Step Output **13**
The PROC Step **14**
    PROC Step Output **14**

Definition of SAS Processing

SAS processing is the way that the SAS language reads and transforms input data and generates the kind of output that you request. The DATA step and the procedure (PROC) step are the two steps in the SAS language. Generally, the DATA step manipulates data, and the PROC step analyzes data, produces output, or manages SAS files. These two types of steps, used alone or combined, form the basis of SAS programs.

The following figure shows a high level view of SAS processing using a DATA step and a PROC step. The figure focuses primarily on the DATA step.

Figure 2.1 SAS Processing

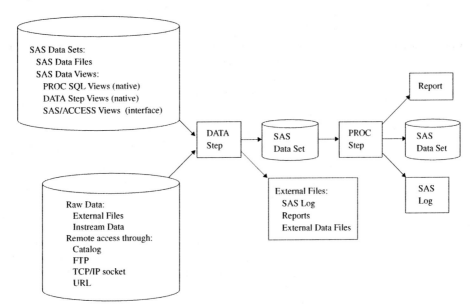

You can use different types of data as input to a DATA step. The DATA step is composed of SAS statements that you write, which contain instructions for processing the data. As each DATA step in a SAS program is compiling or executing, SAS generates a log that contains processing messages and error messages. These messages can help you debug a SAS program.

Types of Input to a SAS Program

You can use different sources of input data in your SAS program:

SAS data sets
:   can be one of two types:

    SAS data files
    :   store actual data values. A SAS data file consists of a descriptor portion that describes the data in the file, and a data portion.

    SAS data views
    :   contain references to data stored elsewhere. A SAS data view uses descriptor information and data from other files. It allow you to dynamically combine data from various sources, without using storage space to create a new data set. Data views consist of DATA step views, PROC SQL views, and SAS/ACCESS views. In most cases, you can use a SAS data view as if it were a SAS data file.

    For more information, see Chapter 28, "SAS Data Files," on page 487, and Chapter 29, "SAS Data Views," on page 539.

Raw data
:   specifies unprocessed data that have not been read into a SAS data set. You can read raw data from two sources:

    External files
    :   contain records comprised of formatted data (data are arranged in columns) or free-formatted data (data that are not arranged in columns).

    Instream data
    :   is data included in your program. You use the DATALINES statement at the beginning of your data to identify the instream data.

    For more information about raw data, see Chapter 21, "Reading Raw Data," on page 357.

Remote access
:   allows you to read input data from nontraditional sources such as a TCP/IP socket or a URL. SAS treats this data as if it were coming from an external file. SAS allows you to access your input data remotely in the following ways:

    SAS catalog
    :   specifies the access method that enables you to reference a SAS catalog as an external file.

    FTP
    :   specifies the access method that enables you to use File Transfer Protocol (FTP) to read from or write to a file from any host machine that is connected to a network with an FTP server running.

    TCP/IP socket
    :   specifies the access method that enables you to read from or write to a Transmission Control Protocol/Internet Protocol (TCP/IP) socket.

URL specifies the access method that enables you to use the Universal Resource Locator (URL) to read from and write to a file from any host machine that is connected to a network with a URL server running.

For more information about accessing data remotely, see FILENAME, CATALOG Access Method; FILENAME, FTP Access Method; FILENAME, SOCKET Access Method; and FILENAME, URL Access Method statements in the Statements section of *SAS Language Reference: Dictionary*.

The DATA Step

The DATA step processes input data. In a DATA step, you can create a SAS data set, which can be a SAS data file or a SAS data view. The DATA step uses input from raw data, remote access, assignment statements, or SAS data sets. The DATA step can, for example, compute values, select specific input records for processing, and use conditional logic. The output from the DATA step can be of several types, such as a SAS data set or a report. You can also write data to the SAS log or to an external data file. For more information about DATA step processing, see Chapter 20, "DATA Step Processing," on page 329.

DATA Step Output

The output from the DATA step can be a SAS data set or an external file such as the program log, a report, or an external data file. You can also update an existing file in place, without creating a separate data set. Data must be in the form of a SAS data set to be processed by many SAS procedures. You can create the following types of DATA step output:

SAS log contains a list of processing messages and program errors. The SAS log is produced by default.

SAS data file is a SAS data set that contains two parts: a data portion and a data descriptor portion.

SAS data view is a SAS data set that uses descriptor information and data from other files. SAS data views allow you to dynamically combine data from various sources without using disk space to create a new data set. While a SAS data file actually contains data values, SAS data views contain only references to data stored elsewhere. SAS data views are of member type VIEW. In most cases, you can use a SAS data view as though it were a SAS data file.

External data file contains the results of DATA step processing. These files are data or text files. The data can be records that are formatted or free-formatted.

Report contains the results of DATA step processing. Although you usually generate a report by using a PROC step, you can generate the following two types of reports from the DATA step:

Listing file contains printed results of DATA step processing, and usually contains headers and page breaks.

HTML file   contains results that you can display on the
                            World Wide Web. This type of output is
                            generated through the Output Delivery System
                            (ODS). For complete information about ODS, see
                            SAS Output Delivery System: User's Guide.

The PROC Step

The PROC step consists of a group of SAS statements that call and execute a procedure, usually with a SAS data set as input. Use PROCs to analyze the data in a SAS data set, produce formatted reports or other results, or provide ways to manage SAS files. You can modify PROCs with minimal effort to generate the output you need. PROCs can also perform functions such as displaying information about a SAS data set. For more information about SAS procedures, see *Base SAS Procedures Guide.*

PROC Step Output

The output from a PROC step can provide univariate descriptive statistics, frequency tables, cross-tabulation tables, tabular reports consisting of descriptive statistics, charts, plots, and so on. Output can also be in the form of an updated data set. For more information about procedure output, see *Base SAS Procedures Guide* and *SAS Output Delivery System: User's Guide.*

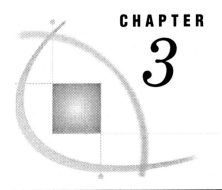

3

Rules for Words and Names in the SAS Language

Words in the SAS Language **15**
> *Definition of Word* **15**
> *Types of Words or Tokens* **16**
> *Placement and Spacing of Words in SAS Statements* **17**
>> *Spacing Requirements* **17**
>> *Examples* **17**
Names in the SAS Language **18**
> *Definition of a SAS Name* **18**
> *Rules for User-Supplied SAS Names* **18**
>> *Rules for Most SAS Names* **18**
>> *Rules for SAS Variable Names* **20**
> *SAS Name Literals* **21**
>> *Definition of SAS Name Literals* **21**
>> *Important Restrictions* **21**
>> *Avoiding Errors When Using Name Literals* **21**
>> *Examples* **21**

Words in the SAS Language

Definition of Word

A *word* or *token* in the SAS programming language is a collection of characters that communicates a meaning to SAS and which cannot be divided into smaller units that can be used independently. A word can contain a maximum of 32,767 characters.

A word or token ends when SAS encounters one of the following:

☐ the beginning of a new token

☐ a blank after a name or a number token

☐ the ending quotation mark of a literal token.

Each word or token in the SAS language belongs to one of four categories:

☐ names

☐ literals

☐ numbers

☐ special characters.

Types of Words or Tokens

There are four basic types of words or tokens:

name

> is a series of characters that begin with a letter or an underscore. Later characters can include letters, underscores, and numeric digits. A name token can contain up to 32,767 characters. In most contexts, however, SAS names are limited to a shorter maximum length, such as 32 or 8 characters. See Table 3.1 on page 19. Here are some examples of name tokens:
>
> □ data
>
> □ _new
>
> □ yearcutoff
>
> □ year_99
>
> □ descending
>
> □ _n_

literal

> consists of 1 to 32,767 characters enclosed in single or double quotation marks. Here are some examples of literals:
>
> □ 'Chicago'
>
> □ "1990-91"
>
> □ 'Amelia Earhart'
>
> □ 'Amelia Earhart''s plane'
>
> □ "Report for the Third Quarter"
>
> *Note:*   The surrounding quotation marks identify the token as a literal, but SAS does not store these marks as part of the literal token. △

number

> in general, is composed entirely of numeric digits, with an optional decimal point and a leading plus or minus sign. SAS also recognizes numeric values in the following forms as number tokens: scientific (E−) notation, hexadecimal notation, missing value symbols, and date and time literals. Here are some examples of number tokens:
>
> □ 5683
>
> □ 2.35
>
> □ 0b0x
>
> □ -5
>
> □ 5.4E-1
>
> □ '24aug90'd

special character

> is usually any single keyboard character other than letters, numbers, the underscore, and the blank. In general, each special character is a single token, although some two-character operators, such as ** and <=, form single tokens. The blank can end a name or a number token, but it is not a token. Here are some examples of special-character tokens:
>
> □ =

□   ;

□   '

□   +

□   @

□   /

Placement and Spacing of Words in SAS Statements

Spacing Requirements

1 You can begin SAS statements in any column of a line and write several statements on the same line.

2 You can begin a statement on one line and continue it on another line, but you cannot split a word between two lines.

3 A blank is not treated as a character in a SAS statement unless it is enclosed in quotation marks as a literal or part of a literal. Therefore, you can put multiple blanks any place in a SAS statement where you can put a single blank, with no effect on the syntax.

4 The rules for recognizing the boundaries of words or tokens determine the use of spacing between them in SAS programs. If SAS can determine the beginning of each token due to cues such as operators, you do not need to include blanks. If SAS cannot determine the beginning of each token, you must use blanks. See "Examples" on page 17.

Although SAS does not have rigid spacing requirements, SAS programs are easier to read and maintain if you consistently indent statements. The examples illustrate useful spacing conventions.

Examples

□ In this statement, blanks are *not required* because SAS can determine the boundary of every token by examining the beginning of the next token:

```
total=x+y;
```

The first special-character token, the equal sign, marks the end of the name token **total**. The plus sign, another special-character token, marks the end of the name token **x**. The last special-character token, the semicolon, marks the end of the **y** token. Though blanks are not needed to end any tokens in this example, you may add them for readability, as shown here:

```
total = x + y;
```

□ This statement *requires blanks* because SAS cannot recognize the individual tokens without them:

```
input group 15 room 20;
```

Without blanks, the entire statement up to the semicolon fits the rules for a name token: it begins with a letter or underscore, contains letters, digits, or underscores thereafter, and is less than 32,767 characters long. Therefore, this statement requires blanks to distinguish individual name and number tokens.

Names in the SAS Language

Definition of a SAS Name

A *SAS name* is a name token that represents

□ variables

□ SAS data sets

□ formats or informats

□ SAS procedures

□ options

□ arrays

□ statement labels

□ SAS macros or macro variables

□ SAS catalog entries

□ librefs or filerefs.

There are two kinds of names in SAS:

□ names of elements of the SAS language

□ names supplied by SAS users.

Rules for User-Supplied SAS Names

Rules for Most SAS Names

Note: The rules are more flexible for SAS variable names than for other language elements. See "Rules for SAS Variable Names" on page 20. △

1   The length of a SAS name depends on the element it is assigned to. Many SAS names can be 32 characters long; others have a maximum length of 8.

2   The first character must be a letter (A, B, C, . . ., Z) or underscore (_). Subsequent characters can be letters, numeric digits (0, 1, . . ., 9), or underscores.

3   You can use upper or lowercase letters. SAS processes names as uppercase regardless of how you type them.

4   Blanks cannot appear in SAS names.

5   Special characters, except for the underscore, are not allowed. In filerefs only, you can use the dollar sign ($), pound sign (#), and at sign (@).

6   SAS reserves a few names for automatic variables and variable lists, SAS data sets, and librefs.

   a   When creating variables, do not use the names of special SAS automatic variables (for example, _N_ and _ERROR_) or special variable list names (for example, _CHARACTER_, _NUMERIC_, and _ALL_).

   b   When associating a libref with a SAS data library, do not use these:
       SASHELP

SASMSG

SASUSER

WORK

c When you create SAS data sets, do not use these names:

NULL

DATA

LAST

7 When assigning a fileref to an external file, do not use:

SASCAT

8 When you create a macro variable, do not use names that begin with **SYS**.

Table 3.1 Maximum Length of User-Supplied SAS Names

SAS Language Element	Maximum Length
Arrays	32
CALL routines	16
Catalog entries	32
DATA step statement labels	32
DATA step variable labels	256
DATA step variables	32
DATA step windows	32
Engines	8
Filerefs	8
Formats, character	31
Formats, numeric	32
Functions	16
Generation data sets	28
Informats, character	30
Informats, numeric	31
Librefs	8
Macro variables	32
Macro windows	32
Macros	32
Members of SAS data libraries (SAS data sets, views, catalogs, indexes) except for generation data sets	32
Passwords	8
Procedure names (first 8 characters must be unique, and may not begin with "SAS")	16
SCL variables	32

Rules for SAS Variable Names

The rules for SAS variable names have expanded to provide more functionality. The setting of the VALIDVARNAME= system option determines what rules apply to the variables that you can create and process in your SAS session as well as to variables that you want to read from existing data sets. The VALIDVARNAME= option has three settings (V7, UPCASE, and ANY), each with varying degrees of flexibility for variable names:

V7

is the default setting.

Variable name rules are as follows:

1 SAS variable names can be up to 32 characters in length.

2 The first character must begin with an English letter or an underscore. Subsequent characters can be English letters, numeric digits, or underscores.

3 A variable name cannot contain blanks.

4 A variable name cannot contain any special characters other than the underscore.

5 A variable name can contain mixed case. Mixed case is remembered and used for presentation purposes only. (SAS stores the case used in the first reference to a variable.) When SAS processes variable names, however, it internally uppercases them. You cannot, therefore, use the same letters with different combinations of lowercase and uppercase to represent different variables. For example, `cat`, `Cat`, and `CAT` all represent the same variable.

6 You do not assign the names of special SAS automatic variables (such as _N_ and _ERROR_) or variable list names (such as _NUMERIC_, _CHARACTER_, and _ALL_) to variables.

UPCASE

is the same as V7, except that variable names are uppercased, as in earlier versions of SAS.

ANY

1 SAS variable names can be up to 32 characters in length.

2 The name can start with or contain any characters, including blanks.

CAUTION:

Available for Base SAS procedures and SAS/STAT procedures only.
VALIDVARNAME=ANY has been verified for use with only Base SAS procedures and SAS/STAT procedures. Any other use of this option is considered experimental and might cause undetected errors. △

Note: If you use any characters other than English letters, numeric digits, or underscores, then you must express the variable name as a *name literal* and you must set VALIDVARNAME=ANY. If you use either the percent sign (%) or the ampersand (&), then you must use single quotation marks in the name literal in order to avoid interaction with the SAS Macro Facility. See "SAS Name Literals" on page 21. △

3 A variable name can contain mixed case. Mixed case is stored and used for presentation purposes only. (SAS stores the case that is used in the first reference to a variable.) When SAS processes variable names, however, it internally uppercases them. Therefore, you cannot use the same letters with different combinations of lowercase and uppercase to represent different variables. For example, `cat`, `Cat`, and `CAT` all represent the same variable.

SAS Name Literals

Definition of SAS Name Literals

A *SAS name literal* is a name token that is expressed as a string within quotation marks, followed by the letter *n*. Name literals allow you to use special characters (or blanks) that are not otherwise allowed in SAS names. Name literals are especially useful for expressing DBMS column and table names that contain special characters.

Important Restrictions

- □ You can use a name literal only for variables, statement labels, and DBMS column and table names.
- □ You can use name literals in a DATA step or a PROC SQL step only.
- □ When the name literal of a variable or DBMS column contains any characters that are not allowed when VALIDVARNAME=V7, then you must set the system option VALIDVARNAME=ANY.
- □ If you use either the percent sign (%) or the ampersand (&), then you must use single quotation marks in the name literal in order to avoid interaction with the SAS Macro Facility.
- □ When the name literal of a DBMS table or column contains any characters that are not valid for SAS rules, then you might need to specify a SAS/ACCESS LIBNAME statement option.
- □ In a quoted string, SAS preserves and uses leading blanks, but SAS ignores and trims trailing blanks.

Note: For more details and examples about the SAS/ACCESS LIBNAME statement and about using DBMS table and column names that do not conform to SAS naming conventions, see *SAS/ACCESS for Relational Databases: Reference.* △

Avoiding Errors When Using Name Literals

For information on how to avoid creating name literals in error, see "Avoiding a Common Error With Constants" on page 115.

Examples

Examples of SAS name literals are

- □ `input 'Bob''s Asset Number'n;`

- □ `input 'Bob"s Asset Number'n;`

- □ `libname foo SAS/ACCESS-engine-name`
     `SAS/ACCESS-engine-connection-options;`
  `data foo.'My Table'n;`

- □ `input 'Amount Budgeted'n 'Amount Spent'n`
     `'Amount Difference'n;`

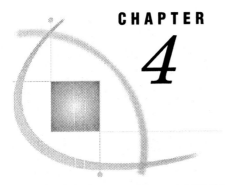

CHAPTER

4

SAS Language Elements

What Are the SAS Language Elements? **25**
Data Set Options **25**
 Definition of Data Set Option **25**
 Syntax for Data Set Options **25**
 Using Data Set Options **25**
  Using Data Set Options with Input or Output SAS Data Sets **25**
  How Data Set Options Interact with System Options **26**
Formats and Informats **27**
 Formats **27**
  Definition of a Format **27**
  Syntax of a Format **27**
  Ways to Specify Formats **28**
  Permanent versus Temporary Association **29**
 Informats **29**
  Definition of an Informat **29**
  Syntax of an Informat **29**
  Ways to Specify Informats **30**
  Permanent versus Temporary Association **31**
 User-Defined Formats and Informats **32**
 Byte Ordering for Integer Binary Data on Big Endian and Little Endian Platforms **32**
  Definitions **32**
  How Bytes Are Ordered **33**
  Writing Data Generated on Big Endian or Little Endian Platforms **33**
  Integer Binary Notation and Different Programming Languages **33**
 Working with Packed Decimal and Zoned Decimal Data **34**
  Definitions **34**
  Packed Decimal Data **34**
  Zoned Decimal Data **35**
  Packed Julian Dates **35**
  Platforms Supporting Packed Decimal and Zoned Decimal Data **35**
  Languages Supporting Packed Decimal and Zoned Decimal Data **35**
  Summary of Packed Decimal and Zoned Decimal Formats and Informats **36**
 Data Conversions and Encodings **38**
Functions and CALL Routines **38**
 Definitions of Functions and CALL Routines **38**
  Definition of Functions **38**
  Definition of CALL Routines **39**
 Syntax of Functions and CALL Routines **39**
  Syntax of Functions **39**
  Syntax of CALL Routines **40**
 Using Functions **40**

Restrictions on Function Arguments **40**

Notes on Descriptive Statistic Functions **41**

Notes on Financial Functions **41**

Special Considerations for Depreciation Functions **41**

Using DATA Step Functions within Macro Functions **42**

Using Functions to Manipulate Files **42**

Using Random-Number Functions and CALL Routines **43**

Seed Values **43**

Comparison of Random-Number Functions and CALL Routines **43**

Example 1: Generating Multiple Streams from a CALL Routine **43**

Example 2: Assigning Values from a Single Stream to Multiple Variables **44**

Pattern Matching Using SAS Regular Expressions (RX) and Perl Regular Expressions (PRX) **45**

Definition of Pattern Matching and Regular Expressions **45**

Definition of SAS Regular Expression (RX) Functions and CALL Routines **45**

Definition of Perl Regular Expression (PRX) Functions and CALL Routines **45**

Benefits of Using Perl Regular Expressions in the DATA Step **46**

Using Perl Regular Expressions in the DATA Step - License Agreement **46**

Syntax of Perl Regular Expressions **47**

Example 1: Validating Data **49**

Example 2: Replacing Text **51**

Example 3: Extracting a Substring from a String **52**

Writing Perl Debug Output to the SAS Log **54**

Base SAS Functions for Web Applications **55**

ARM Macros **55**

Definition of ARM Macros **55**

Using ARM Macros **56**

Overview of ARM Macros **56**

Using Variables with ARM Macros **57**

ARM API Objects **58**

ID Management Using ARM Macros **58**

Complex ARM Macro Call Schemes **61**

Defining User Metrics in ARM Macros **63**

Defining Correlators in ARM Macros **64**

Enabling ARM Macro Execution **65**

Setting the _ARMEXEC Macro Variable **65**

Enabling ARM Macro Execution with SCL **66**

Conditional ARM Macro Execution **66**

Setting the Macro Environment **67**

Using ARM Post-Processing Macros **68**

Statements **69**

Definition of Statements **69**

Executable and Declarative DATA Step Statements **69**

Global Statements **70**

SAS System Options **71**

Definition of SAS System Options **71**

Syntax of SAS System Options **71**

Using SAS System Options **71**

Default Settings **71**

Determining Which Settings Are in Effect **71**

Determining Which SAS System Options Are Restricted **72**

Determining How a SAS System Option Value Was Set **72**

Obtaining Descriptive Information about a System Option **73**

Changing SAS System Option Settings **73**

How Long System Option Settings Are in Effect **74**

Order of Precedence **75**
Interaction with Data Set Options **75**
Comparisons **76**

What Are the SAS Language Elements?

The major language elements of Base SAS software are as follows:

☐ data set options
☐ formats and informats
☐ functions and CALL routines
☐ Application Response Measurement (ARM) macros
☐ statements
☐ SAS system options

For detailed information on each language element, see *SAS Language Reference: Dictionary*.

Data Set Options

Definition of Data Set Option

Data set options specify actions that apply only to the SAS data set with which they appear. They enable you to perform operations such as these:

☐ renaming variables
☐ selecting only the first or last *n* observations for processing
☐ dropping variables from processing or from the output data set
☐ specifying a password for a data set.

Syntax for Data Set Options

Specify a data set option in parentheses after a SAS data set name. To specify several data set options, separate them with spaces.

(*option-1=value-1<...option-n=value-n>*)

These examples show data set options in SAS statements:

```
data scores(keep=team game1 game2 game3);
```

```
proc print data=new(drop=year);
```

```
set old(rename=(date=Start_Date));
```

Using Data Set Options

Using Data Set Options with Input or Output SAS Data Sets

Most SAS data set options can apply to either input or output SAS data sets in DATA steps or procedure (PROC) steps. If a data set option is associated with an input data set, the action applies to the data set that is being read. If the option appears in the DATA statement or after an output data set specification in a PROC step, SAS applies the action to the output data set. In the DATA step, data set options for output data sets must appear in the DATA statement, not in any OUTPUT statements that might be present.

Some data set options, such as COMPRESS=, are meaningful only when you create a SAS data set because they set attributes that exist for the life of the data set. To change or cancel most data set options, you must re-create the data set. You can change other options (such as PW= and LABEL=) with PROC DATASETS. For more information, see "The DATASETS Procedure" in *Base SAS Procedures Guide*.

When data set options appear on both input and output data sets in the same DATA or PROC step, SAS applies data set options to input data sets before it evaluates programming statements or before it applies data set options to output data sets. Likewise, data set options that are specified for the data set being created are applied after programming statements are processed. For example, when using the RENAME= data set option, the new names are not associated with the variables until the DATA step ends.

In some instances, data set options conflict when they are used in the same statement. For example, you cannot specify both the DROP= and KEEP= options for the same variable in the same statement. Timing can also be an issue in some cases. For example, if using KEEP= and RENAME= on a data set specified in the SET statement, KEEP= needs to use the original variable names, because SAS will process KEEP= before the data set is read. The new names specified in RENAME= will apply to the programming statements that follow the SET statement.

How Data Set Options Interact with System Options

Many system options and data set options share the same name and have the same function. System options remain in effect for all DATA and PROC steps in a SAS job or session, unless they are respecified.

The data set option overrides the system option for the data set in the step in which it appears. In this example, the OBS= system option in the OPTIONS statement specifies that only the first 100 observations will be processed from any data set within the SAS job. The OBS= data set option in the SET statement, however, overrides the system option for data set TWO and specifies that only the first 5 observations will be read from data set TWO. The PROC PRINT step prints the data set FINAL. This data set contains the first 5 observations from data set TWO, followed by the first 100 observations from data set THREE:

```
options obs=100;

data final;
   set two(obs=5) three;
run;

proc print data=final;
run;
```

Formats and Informats

Formats

Definition of a Format

A *format* is an instruction that SAS uses to write data values. You use formats to control the written appearance of data values, or, in some cases, to group data values together for analysis. For example, the WORDS22. format, which converts numeric values to their equivalent in words, writes the numeric value 692 as `six hundred ninety-two`.

Syntax of a Format

SAS formats have the following form:

<$>format<w>.<d>

Here is an explanation of the syntax:

$
indicates a character format; its absence indicates a numeric format.

format
names the format. The format is a SAS format or a user-defined format that was previously defined with the VALUE statement in PROC FORMAT. For more information on user-defined formats, see "The FORMAT Procedure" in *Base SAS Procedures Guide*.

w
specifies the format width, which for most formats is the number of columns in the output data.

d
specifies an optional decimal scaling factor in the numeric formats.

Formats always contain a period (.) as a part of the name. If you omit the *w* and the *d* values from the format, SAS uses default values. The *d* value that you specify with a format tells SAS to display that many decimal places, regardless of how many decimal places are in the data. Formats never change or truncate the internally stored data values.

For example, in DOLLAR10.2, the *w* value of 10 specifies a maximum of 10 columns for the value. The *d* value of 2 specifies that two of these columns are for the decimal part of the value, which leaves eight columns for all the remaining characters in the value. This includes the decimal point, the remaining numeric value, a minus sign if the value is negative, the dollar sign, and commas, if any.

If the format width is too narrow to represent a value, then SAS tries to squeeze the value into the space available. Character formats truncate values on the right. Numeric formats sometimes revert to the BEST*w.d* format. SAS prints asterisks if you do not specify an adequate width. In the following example, the result is x=**.

```
x=123;
put x=2.;
```

If you use an incompatible format, such as using a numeric format to write character values, first SAS attempts to use an analogous format of the other type. If this is not feasible, then an error message that describes the problem appears in the SAS log.

Ways to Specify Formats

You can use formats in the following ways:

☐ in a PUT statement

The PUT statement with a format after the variable name uses a format to write data values in a DATA step. For example, this PUT statement uses the DOLLAR. format to write the numeric value for AMOUNT as a dollar amount:

```
amount=1145.32;
put amount dollar10.2;
```

The DOLLAR*w.d* format in the PUT statement produces this result:

```
$1,145.32
```

See the "PUT Statement" in *SAS Language Reference: Dictionary* for more information.

☐ with the PUT, PUTC, or PUTN functions

The PUT function writes a numeric variable, a character variable, or a constant with any valid format and returns the resulting character value. For example, the following statement converts the value of a numeric variable into a two-character hexadecimal representation:

```
num=15;
char=put(num,hex2.);
```

The PUT function creates a character variable named CHAR that has a value of 0F.

The PUT function is useful for converting a numeric value to a character value. See the "PUT Function" in *SAS Language Reference: Dictionary* for more information.

☐ with the %SYSFUNC macro function

The %SYSFUNC (or %QSYSFUNC) macro function executes SAS functions or user-defined functions and applies an optional format to the result of the function outside a DATA step. For example, the following program writes a numeric value in a macro variable as a dollar amount.

```
%macro tst(amount);
   %put %sysfunc(putn(&amount,dollar10.2));
%mend tst;


%tst (1154.23);
```

For more information, see *SAS Macro Language: Reference*.

☐ in a FORMAT statement in a DATA step or a PROC step

The FORMAT statement permanently associates a format with a variable. SAS uses the format to write the values of the variable that you specify. For example, the following statement in a DATA step associates the COMMA*w.d* numeric format with the variables SALES1 through SALES3:

```
format sales1-sales3 comma10.2;
```

Because the FORMAT statement permanently associates a format with a variable, any subsequent DATA step or PROC step uses COMMA10.2 to write the values of SALES1, SALES2, and SALES3. See the "FORMAT Statement" in *SAS Language Reference: Dictionary* for more information.

Note: Formats that you specify in a PUT statement behave differently from those that you associate with a variable in a FORMAT statement. The major difference is that formats that are specified in the PUT statement will preserve leading blanks. If you assign formats with a FORMAT statement prior to a PUT statement, all leading blanks are trimmed. The result is the same as if you used the colon (:) format modifier. For details about using the colon (:) format modifier, see the "PUT Statement, List" in *SAS Language Reference: Dictionary*. △

☐ in an ATTRIB statement in a DATA step or a PROC step.

The ATTRIB statement can also associate a format, as well as other attributes, with one or more variables. For example, in the following statement the ATTRIB statement permanently associates the COMMA*w.d* format with the variables SALES1 through SALES3:

```
attrib sales1-sales3 format=comma10.2;
```

Because the ATTRIB statement permanently associates a format with a variable, any subsequent DATA step or PROC step uses COMMA10.2 to write the values of SALES1, SALES2, and SALES3. For more information, see the "ATTRIB Statement" in *SAS Language Reference: Dictionary*.

Permanent versus Temporary Association

When you specify a format in a PUT statement, SAS uses the format to write data values during the DATA step but does not permanently associate the format with a variable. To permanently associate a format with a variable, use a FORMAT statement or an ATTRIB statement in a DATA step. SAS permanently associates a format with the variable by modifying the descriptor information in the SAS data set.

Using a FORMAT statement or an ATTRIB statement in a PROC step associates a format with a variable for that PROC step, as well as for any output data sets that the procedure creates that contain formatted variables. For more information on using formats in SAS procedures, see *Base SAS Procedures Guide*.

Informats

Definition of an Informat

An *informat* is an instruction that SAS uses to read data values into a variable. For example, the following value contains a dollar sign and commas:

```
$1,000,000
```

To remove the dollar sign ($) and commas (,) before storing the numeric value 1000000 in a variable, read this value with the COMMA11. informat.

Unless you explicitly define a variable first, SAS uses the informat to determine whether the variable is numeric or character. SAS also uses the informat to determine the length of character variables.

Syntax of an Informat

SAS informats have the following form:

<$>*informat*<*w*>.<*d*>

Here is an explanation of the syntax:

$

indicates a character informat; its absence indicates a numeric informat.

informat

names the informat. The informat is a SAS informat or a user-defined informat that was previously defined with the INVALUE statement in PROC FORMAT. For more information on user-defined informats, see "The FORMAT Procedure" in *Base SAS Procedures Guide*.

w

specifies the informat width, which for most informats is the number of columns in the input data.

d

specifies an optional decimal scaling factor in the numeric informats. SAS divides the input data by 10 to the power of *d*.

Note: Even though SAS can read up to 31 decimal places when you specify some numeric informats, floating-point numbers with more than 12 decimal places might lose precision due to the limitations of the eight-byte floating point representation used by most computers. △

Informats always contain a period (.) as a part of the name. If you omit the *w* and the *d* values from the informat, SAS uses default values. If the data contains decimal points, SAS ignores the *d* value and reads the number of decimal places that are actually in the input data.

If the informat width is too narrow to read all the columns in the input data, you may get unexpected results. The problem frequently occurs with the date and time informats. You must adjust the width of the informat to include blanks or special characters between the day, month, year, or time. For more information about date and time values, see Chapter 8, "Dates, Times, and Intervals," on page 127.

When a problem occurs with an informat, SAS writes a note to the SAS log and assigns a missing value to the variable. Problems occur if you use an incompatible informat, such as a numeric informat to read character data, or if you specify the width of a date and time informat that causes SAS to read a special character in the last column.

Ways to Specify Informats

You can specify informats in the following ways:

□ in an INPUT statement

The INPUT statement with an informat after a variable name is the simplest way to read values into a variable. For example, the following INPUT statement uses two informats:

```
input @15 style $3. @21 price 5.2;
```

The $*w*. character informat reads values into the variable STYLE. The *w.d* numeric informat reads values into the variable PRICE.

For a complete discussion of the "INPUT Statement" , see *SAS Language Reference: Dictionary*.

□ with the INPUT, INPUTC, and INPUTN functions

The INPUT function reads a SAS character expression using a specified informat. The informat determines whether the resulting value is numeric or character. Thus, the INPUT function is useful for converting data. For example,

```
TempCharacter='98.6';
TemperatureNumber=input(TempCharacter,4.);
```

Here, the INPUT function in combination with the *w.d* informat reads the character value of TempCharacter as a numeric value and assigns the numeric value 98.6 to TemperatureNumber.

Use the PUT function with a SAS format to convert numeric values to character values. See the "PUT Function" in *SAS Language Reference: Dictionary* for an example of a numeric-to-character conversion. For a complete discussion of the "INPUT Function", see *SAS Language Reference: Dictionary*.

□ in an INFORMAT statement in a DATA or a PROC step

The INFORMAT statement associates an informat with a variable. SAS uses the informat in any subsequent INPUT statement to read values into the variable. For example, in the following statements the INFORMAT statement associates the DATE*w*. informat with the variables Birthdate and Interview:

```
informat Birthdate Interview date9.;
input @63 Birthdate Interview;
```

An informat that is associated with an INFORMAT statement behaves like an informat that you specify with a colon (:) format modifier in an INPUT statement. (For details about using the colon (:) modifier, see the "INPUT Statement, List" in *SAS Language Reference: Dictionary*.) Therefore, SAS uses a modified list input to read the variable so that

□ the *w* value in an informat does not determine column positions or input field widths in an external file

□ the blanks that are embedded in input data are treated as delimiters unless you change the DELIMITER= option in an INFILE statement

□ for character informats, the *w* value in an informat specifies the length of character variables

□ for numeric informats, the *w* value is ignored

□ for numeric informats, the *d* value in an informat behaves in the usual way for numeric informats

If you have coded the INPUT statement to use another style of input, such as formatted input or column input, that style of input is not used when you use the INFORMAT statement.

See the "INPUT Statement, List" in *SAS Language Reference: Dictionary* for more information about how to use modified list input to read data.

□ in an ATTRIB statement in a DATA or a PROC step.

The ATTRIB statement can also associate an informat, as well as other attributes, with one or more variables. For example, in the following statements, the ATTRIB statement associates the DATE*w*. informat with the variables Birthdate and Interview:

```
attrib Birthdate Interview informat=date9.;
input @63 Birthdate Interview;
```

An informat that is associated by using the INFORMAT= option in the ATTRIB statement behaves like an informat that you specify with a colon (:) format modifier in an INPUT statement. (For details about using the colon (:) modifier, see the "INPUT Statement, List" in *SAS Language Reference: Dictionary*.) Therefore, SAS uses a modified list input to read the variable in the same way as it does for the INFORMAT statement.

See the "ATTRIB Statement" in *SAS Language Reference: Dictionary* for more information.

Permanent versus Temporary Association

When you specify an informat in an INPUT statement, SAS uses the informat to read input data values during that DATA step. SAS, however, does not permanently associate

the informat with the variable. To permanently associate a format with a variable, use
an INFORMAT statement or an ATTRIB statement. SAS permanently associates an
informat with the variable by modifying the descriptor information in the SAS data set.

User-Defined Formats and Informats

In addition to the formats and informats that are supplied with Base SAS software,
you can create your own formats and informats. In Base SAS software, PROC FORMAT
allows you to create your own formats and informats for both character and numeric
variables.

When you execute a SAS program that uses user-defined formats or informats, these
formats and informats should be available. The two ways to make these formats and
informats available are

   □ to create permanent, not temporary, formats or informats with PROC FORMAT

   □ to store the source code that creates the formats or informats (the PROC FORMAT
      step) with the SAS program that uses them.

To create permanent SAS formats and informats, see "The FORMAT Procedure" in *Base
SAS Procedures Guide.*

If you execute a program that cannot locate a user-defined format or informat, the
result depends on the setting of the FMTERR system option. If the user-defined format
or informat is not found, then these system options produce these results:

System option	Results
FMTERR	SAS produces an error that causes the current DATA or PROC step to stop.
NOFMTERR	SAS continues processing and substitutes a default format, usually the BEST*w.* or $*w.* format.

Although using NOFMTERR enables SAS to process a variable, you lose the
information that the user-defined format or informat supplies.

To avoid problems, make sure that your program has access to all of the user-defined
formats and informats that are used in the program.

Byte Ordering for Integer Binary Data on Big Endian and Little Endian Platforms

Definitions

Integer values for binary integer data are typically stored in one of three sizes:
one-byte, two-byte, or four-byte. The ordering of the bytes for the integer varies
depending on the platform (operating environment) on which the integers were
produced.

The ordering of bytes differs between the "big endian" and "little endian" platforms.
These colloquial terms are used to describe byte ordering for IBM mainframes (big
endian) and for Intel-based platforms (little endian). In SAS, the following platforms
are considered big endian: AIX, HP-UX, IBM mainframe, Macintosh, and Solaris. The
following platforms are considered little endian: OpenVMS Alpha, Digital UNIX, Intel
ABI, and Windows.

How Bytes Are Ordered

On big endian platforms, the value 1 is stored in binary and is represented here in hexadecimal notation. One byte is stored as 01, two bytes as 00 01, and four bytes as 00 00 00 01. On little endian platforms, the value 1 is stored in one byte as 01 (the same as big endian), in two bytes as 01 00, and in four bytes as 01 00 00 00.

If an integer is negative, the "two's complement" representation is used. The high-order bit of the most significant byte of the integer will be set on. For example, −2 would be represented in one, two, and four bytes on big endian platforms as FE, FF FE, and FF FF FF FE respectively. On little endian platforms, the representation would be FE, FE FF, and FE FF FF FF. These representations result from the output of the integer binary value −2 expressed in hexadecimal representation.

Writing Data Generated on Big Endian or Little Endian Platforms

SAS can read signed and unsigned integers regardless of whether they were generated on a big endian or a little endian system. Likewise, SAS can write signed and unsigned integers in both big endian and little endian format. The length of these integers can be up to eight bytes.

The following table shows which format to use for various combinations of platforms. In the Sign? column, "no" indicates that the number is unsigned and cannot be negative. "Yes" indicates that the number can be either negative or positive.

Table 4.1 SAS Formats and Byte Ordering

Data created for...	Data written by...	Sign?	Format/Informat
big endian	big endian	yes	IB or S370FIB
big endian	big endian	no	PIB, S370FPIB, S370FIBU
big endian	little endian	yes	S370FIB
big endian	little endian	no	S370FPIB
little endian	big endian	yes	IBR
little endian	big endian	no	PIBR
little endian	little endian	yes	IB or IBR
little endian	little endian	no	PIB or PIBR
big endian	either	yes	S370FIB
big endian	either	no	S370FPIB
little endian	either	yes	IBR
little endian	either	no	PIBR

Integer Binary Notation and Different Programming Languages

The following table compares integer binary notation according to programming language.

Table 4.2   Integer Binary Notation and Programming Languages

Language	2 Bytes	4 Bytes
SAS	IB2., IBR2., PIB2., PIBR2., S370FIB2., S370FIBU2., S370FPIB2.	IB4., IBR4., PIB4., PIBR4., S370FIB4., S370FIBU4., S370FPIB4.
PL/I	FIXED BIN(15)	FIXED BIN(31)
FORTRAN	INTEGER*2	INTEGER*4
COBOL	COMP PIC 9(4)	COMP PIC 9(8)
IBM assembler	H	F
C	short	long

Working with Packed Decimal and Zoned Decimal Data

Definitions

Packed decimal   specifies a method of encoding decimal numbers by using each byte to represent two decimal digits. Packed decimal representation stores decimal data with exact precision. The fractional part of the number is determined by the informat or format because there is no separate mantissa and exponent.

An advantage of using packed decimal data is that exact precision can be maintained. However, computations involving decimal data might become inexact due to the lack of native instructions.

Zoned decimal   specifies a method of encoding decimal numbers in which each digit requires one byte of storage. The last byte contains the number's sign as well as the last digit. Zoned decimal data produces a printable representation.

Nibble   specifies 1/2 of a byte.

Packed Decimal Data

A packed decimal representation stores decimal digits in each "nibble" of a byte. Each byte has two nibbles, and each nibble is indicated by a hexadecimal digit. For example, the value 15 is stored in two nibbles, using the hexadecimal digits 1 and 5.

The sign indication is dependent on your operating environment. On IBM mainframes, the sign is indicated by the last nibble. With formats, C indicates a positive value, and D indicates a negative value. With informats, A, C, E, and F indicate positive values, and B and D indicate negative values. Any other nibble is invalid for signed packed decimal data. In all other operating environments, the sign is indicated in its own byte. If the high-order bit is 1, then the number is negative. Otherwise, it is positive.

The following applies to packed decimal data representation:

□ You can use the S370FPD format on all platforms to obtain the IBM mainframe configuration.

□ You can have unsigned packed data with no sign indicator. The packed decimal format and informat handles the representation. It is consistent between ASCII and EBCDIC platforms.

□ Note that the S370FPDU format and informat expects to have an F in the last nibble, while packed decimal expects no sign nibble.

Zoned Decimal Data

The following applies to zoned decimal data representation:

□ A zoned decimal representation stores a decimal digit in the low order nibble of each byte. For all but the byte containing the sign, the high-order nibble is the numeric zone nibble (F on EBCDIC and 3 on ASCII).

□ The sign can be merged into a byte with a digit, or it can be separate, depending on the representation. But the standard zoned decimal format and informat expects the sign to be merged into the last byte.

□ The EBCDIC and ASCII zoned decimal formats produce the same printable representation of numbers. There are two nibbles per byte, each indicated by a hexadecimal digit. For example, the value 15 is stored in two bytes. The first byte contains the hexadecimal value F1 and the second byte contains the hexadecimal value C5.

Packed Julian Dates

The following applies to packed Julian dates:

□ The two formats and informats that handle Julian dates in packed decimal representation are PDJULI and PDJULG. PDJULI uses the IBM mainframe year computation, while PDJULG uses the Gregorian computation.

□ The IBM mainframe computation considers 1900 to be the base year, and the year values in the data indicate the offset from 1900. For example, 98 means 1998, 100 means 2000, and 102 means 2002. 1998 would mean 3898.

□ The Gregorian computation allows for 2-digit or 4-digit years. If you use 2-digit years, SAS uses the setting of the YEARCUTOFF= system option to determine the true year.

Platforms Supporting Packed Decimal and Zoned Decimal Data

Some platforms have native instructions to support packed and zoned decimal data, while others must use software to emulate the computations. For example, the IBM mainframe has an Add Pack instruction to add packed decimal data, but the Intel-based platforms have no such instruction and must convert the decimal data into some other format.

Languages Supporting Packed Decimal and Zoned Decimal Data

Several different languages support packed decimal and zoned decimal data. The following table shows how COBOL picture clauses correspond to SAS formats and informats.

IBM VS COBOL II clauses	Corresponding S370Fxxx formats/informats
PIC S9(X) PACKED-DECIMAL	S370FPDw.
PIC 9(X) PACKED-DECIMAL	S370FPDUw.
PIC S9(W) DISPLAY	S370FZDw.

IBM VS COBOL II clauses	Corresponding S370Fxxx formats/informats
PIC 9(W) DISPLAY	S370FZDUw.
PIC S9(W) DISPLAY SIGN LEADING	S370FZDLw.
PIC S9(W) DISPLAY SIGN LEADING SEPARATE	S370FZDSw.
PIC S9(W) DISPLAY SIGN TRAILING SEPARATE	S370FZDTw.

For the packed decimal representation listed above, X indicates the number of digits represented, and W is the number of bytes. For PIC S9(X) PACKED-DECIMAL, W is `ceil((x+1)/2)`. For PIC 9(X) PACKED-DECIMAL, W is `ceil (x/2)`. For example, PIC S9(5) PACKED-DECIMAL represents five digits. If a sign is included, six nibbles are needed. `ceil((5+1)/2)` has a length of three bytes, and the value of W is 3.

Note that you can substitute COMP-3 for PACKED-DECIMAL.

In IBM assembly language, the P directive indicates packed decimal, and the Z directive indicates zoned decimal. The following shows an excerpt from an assembly language listing, showing the offset, the value, and the DC statement:

```
offset  value (in hex)      inst label      directive

+000000 00001C              2 PEX1          DC PL3'1'
+000003 00001D              3 PEX2          DC PL3'-1'
+000006 F0F0C1              4 ZEX1          DC ZL3'1'
+000009 F0F0D1              5 ZEX2          DC ZL3'1'
```

In PL/I, the FIXED DECIMAL attribute is used in conjunction with packed decimal data. You must use the PICTURE specification to represent zoned decimal data. There is no standardized representation of decimal data for the FORTRAN or the C languages.

Summary of Packed Decimal and Zoned Decimal Formats and Informats

SAS uses a group of formats and informats to handle packed and zoned decimal data. The following table lists the type of data representation for these formats and informats. Note that the formats and informats that begin with S370 refer to IBM mainframe representation.

Format	Type of data representation	Corresponding informat	Comments
PD	Packed decimal	PD	Local signed packed decimal
PK	Packed decimal	PK	Unsigned packed decimal; not specific to your operating environment
ZD	Zoned decimal	ZD	Local zoned decimal
none	Zoned decimal	ZDB	Translates EBCDIC blank (hex 40) to EBCDIC zero (hex F0), then corresponds to the informat as zoned decimal
none	Zoned decimal	ZDV	Non-IBM zoned decimal representation

Format	Type of data representation	Corresponding informat	Comments
S370FPD	Packed decimal	S370FPD	Last nibble C (positive) or D (negative)
S370FPDU	Packed decimal	S370FPDU	Last nibble always F (positive)
S370FZD	Zoned decimal	S370FZD	Last byte contains sign in upper nibble: C (positive) or D (negative)
S370FZDU	Zoned decimal	S370FZDU	Unsigned; sign nibble always F
S370FZDL	Zoned decimal	S370FZDL	Sign nibble in first byte in informat; separate leading sign byte of hex C0 (positive) or D0 (negative) in format
S370FZDS	Zoned decimal	S370FZDS	Leading sign of - (hex 60) or + (hex 4E)
S370FZDT	Zoned decimal	S370FZDT	Trailing sign of - (hex 60) or + (hex 4E)
PDJULI	Packed decimal	PDJULI	Julian date in packed representation - IBM computation
PDJULG	Packed decimal	PDJULG	Julian date in packed representation - Gregorian computation
none	Packed decimal	RMFDUR	Input layout is: *mmsstttt*F
none	Packed decimal	SHRSTAMP	Input layout is: *yyyydddFhhmmssth*, where *yyyydddF* is the packed Julian date; *yyyy* is a 0-based year from 1900
none	Packed decimal	SMFSTAMP	Input layout is: *xxxxxxxxyyyydddF*, where *yyyydddF* is the packed Julian date; *yyyy* is a 0-based year from 1900
none	Packed decimal	PDTIME	Input layout is: 0*hhmmss*F
none	Packed decimal	RMFSTAMP	Input layout is: 0*hhmmss*F*yyyydddF*, where *yyyydddF* is the packed Julian date; yyyy is a 0-based year from 1900

Data Conversions and Encodings

An encoding maps each character in a character set to a unique numeric representation, resulting in a table of all code points. A single character can have different numeric representations in different encodings. For example, the ASCII encoding for the dollar symbol $ is 24hex. The Danish EBCDIC encoding for the dollar symbol $ is 67hex. In order for a version of SAS that normally uses ASCII to properly interpret a data set that is encoded in Danish EBCDIC, the data must be transcoded.

Transcoding is the process of moving data from one encoding to another. When transcoding the ASCII dollar sign to the Danish EBCDIC dollar sign, the hex representation for the character is converted from the value 24 to a 67.

If you want to know what the encoding of a particular SAS data set is, for SAS 9 and above follow these steps:

1 Locate the data set with SAS Explorer.

2 Right-click the data set.

3 Select Properties from the menu.

4 Click the Details tab.

5 The encoding of the data set is listed, along with other information.

Some situations where data might commonly be transcoded are:

□ when you share data between two different SAS sessions that are running in different locales or in different operating environments,

□ when you perform text-string operations, such as converting to uppercase or lowercase,

□ when you display or print characters from another language,

□ when you copy and paste data between SAS sessions running in different locales.

For more information on SAS features designed to handle data conversions from different encodings or operating environments, see *SAS National Language Support (NLS): User's Guide*.

Functions and CALL Routines

Definitions of Functions and CALL Routines

Definition of Functions

A *SAS function* performs a computation or system manipulation on arguments and returns a value. Most functions use arguments supplied by the user, but a few obtain their arguments from the operating environment.

In Base SAS software, you can use SAS functions in DATA step programming statements, in a WHERE expression, in macro language statements, in PROC REPORT, and in Structured Query Language (SQL).

Some statistical procedures also use SAS functions. In addition, some other SAS software products offer functions that you can use in the DATA step. Refer to the documentation that pertains to the specific SAS software product for additional information about these functions.

Definition of CALL Routines

A *CALL routine* alters variable values or performs other system functions. CALL routines are similar to functions, but differ from functions in that you cannot use them in assignment statements.

All SAS CALL routines are invoked with CALL statements; that is, the name of the routine must appear after the keyword CALL on the CALL statement.

Syntax of Functions and CALL Routines

Syntax of Functions

The syntax of a function is as follows:

function-name (*argument-1*<...,*argument-n*>)

function-name (OF *variable-list*)

function-name (OF *array-name*{*})

Here is an explanation of the syntax:

function-name
:   names the function.

argument
:   can be a variable name, constant, or any SAS expression, including another function. The number and kind of arguments that SAS allows are described with individual functions. Multiple arguments are separated by a comma.

   Tip: If the value of an argument is invalid (for example, missing or outside the prescribed range), then SAS writes a note to the log indicating that the argument is invalid, sets _ERROR_ to 1, and sets the result to a missing value.

   Examples:

   - ☐ `x=max(cash,credit);`

   - ☐ `x=sqrt(1500);`

   - ☐ `NewCity=left(upcase(City));`

   - ☐ `x=min(YearTemperature-July,YearTemperature-Dec);`

   - ☐ `s=repeat('----+',16);`

   - ☐ `x=min((enroll-drop),(enroll-fail));`

   - ☐ `dollars=int(cash);`

   - ☐ `if sum(cash,credit)>1000 then`
         `put 'Goal reached';`

variable-list
:   can be any form of a SAS variable list, including individual variable names. If more than one variable list appears, separate them with a space or with a comma and another OF.

   Examples:

   - ☐ `a=sum(of x  y  z);`

   - ☐ The following two examples are equivalent.

```
□  a=sum(of x1-x10 y1-y10 z1-z10);
   a=sum(of x1-x10, of y1-y10, of z1-z10);
```

```
□  z=sum(of y1-y10);
```

array-name{}*
  names a currently defined array. Specifying an array in this way causes SAS to treat the array as a list of the variables instead of processing only one element of the array at a time.

  Examples:

```
□  array y{10} y1-y10;
   x=sum(of y{*});
```

Syntax of CALL Routines

The syntax of a CALL routine is as follows:

CALL *routine-name* (*argument-1*<, ... *argument-n*>);

CALL *routine-name* (OF *variable-list*);

CALL *routine-name* (*argument-1* | OF *variable-list-1* <, ...*argument-n* | OF *variable-list-n*>);

Here is an explanation of the syntax:

routine-name
  names a SAS CALL routine.

argument
  can be a variable name, a constant, any SAS expression, an external module name, an array reference, or a function. Multiple arguments are separated by a comma. The number and kind of arguments that are allowed are described with individual CALL routines in the *SAS Language Reference: Dictionary*.

  Examples:

```
□  call rxsubstr(rx,string,position);
```

```
□  call set(dsid);
```

```
□  call ranbin(Seed_1,n,p,X1);
```

```
□  call label(abc{j},lab);
```

variable-list
  can be any form of a SAS variable list, including variable names. If more than one variable list appears, separate them with a space or with a comma and another OF.

  Examples:

```
□  call cats(inventory, of y1-y15, of z1-z15);
   call catt(of item17-item23 pack17-pack23);
```

Using Functions

Restrictions on Function Arguments

If the value of an argument is invalid, then SAS prints an error message and sets the result to a missing value. Here are some common restrictions on function arguments:

□ Some functions require that their arguments be restricted within a certain range. For example, the argument of the LOG function must be greater than 0.

□ Most functions do not permit missing values as arguments. Exceptions include some of the descriptive statistics functions and financial functions.

□ In general, the allowed range of the arguments is platform-dependent, such as with the EXP function.

□ For some probability functions, combinations of extreme values can cause convergence problems.

Notes on Descriptive Statistic Functions

SAS provides functions that return descriptive statistics. Except for the MISSING function, the functions correspond to the statistics produced by the MEANS procedure. The computing method for each statistic is discussed in "SAS Elementary Statistics Procedures" in *Base SAS Procedures Guide*. SAS calculates descriptive statistics for the nonmissing values of the arguments.

Notes on Financial Functions

SAS provides a group of functions that perform financial calculations. The functions are grouped into the following types:

Table 4.3 Types of Financial Functions

Function type	Functions	Description
Cashflow	CONVX, CONVXP	calculates convexity for cashflows
	DUR, DURP	calculates modified duration for cashflows
	PVP, YIELDP	calculates present value and yield-to-maturity for a periodic cashflow
Parameter calculations	COMPOUND	calculates compound interest parameters
	MORT	calculates amortization parameters
Internal rate of return	INTRR, IRR	calculates the internal rate of return
Net present and future value	NETPV, NPV	calculates net present and future values
	SAVING	calculates the future value of periodic saving
Depreciation	DACCxx	calculates the accumulated depreciation up to the specified period
	DEPxxx	calculates depreciation for a single period

Special Considerations for Depreciation Functions

The period argument for depreciation functions can be fractional for all of the functions except DEPDBSL and DACCDBSL. For fractional arguments, the depreciation is prorated between the two consecutive time periods preceding and following the fractional period.

CAUTION:
   Verify the depreciation method for fractional periods. You must verify whether this method is appropriate to use with fractional periods because many depreciation schedules, specified as tables, have special rules for fractional periods. △

Using DATA Step Functions within Macro Functions

The macro functions %SYSFUNC and %QSYSFUNC can call DATA step functions to generate text in the macro facility. %SYSFUNC and %QSYSFUNC have one difference: %QSYSFUNC masks special characters and mnemonics and %SYSFUNC does not. For more information on these functions, see %QSYSFUNC and %SYSFUNC in *SAS Macro Language: Reference.*

%SYSFUNC arguments are a single DATA step function and an optional format, as shown in the following examples:

```
%sysfunc(date(),worddate.)
%sysfunc(attrn(&dsid,NOBS))
```

You cannot nest DATA step functions within %SYSFUNC. However, you can nest %SYSFUNC functions that call DATA step functions. For example:

```
%sysfunc(compress(%sysfunc(getoption(sasautos)),
   %str(%)%(%')));
```

All arguments in DATA step functions within %SYSFUNC must be separated by commas. You cannot use argument lists that are preceded by the word OF.

Because %SYSFUNC is a macro function, you do not need to enclose character values in quotation marks as you do in DATA step functions. For example, the arguments to the OPEN function are enclosed in quotation marks when you use the function alone, but the arguments do not require quotation marks when used within %SYSFUNC.

```
dsid=open("sasuser.houses","i");
dsid=open("&mydata","&mode");
%let dsid=%sysfunc(open(sasuser.houses,i));
%let dsid=%sysfunc(open(&mydata,&mode));
```

You can use these functions to call all of the DATA step SAS functions except those that pertain to DATA step variables or processing. These prohibited functions are: DIF, DIM, HBOUND, INPUT, IORCMSG, LAG, LBOUND, MISSING, PUT, RESOLVE, SYMGET, and all of the variable information functions (for example, VLABEL).

Using Functions to Manipulate Files

SAS manipulates files in different ways, depending on whether you use functions or statements. If you use functions such as FOPEN, FGET, and FCLOSE, you have more opportunity to examine and manipulate your data than when you use statements such as INFILE, INPUT, and PUT.

When you use external files, the FOPEN function allocates a buffer called the File Data Buffer (FDB) and opens the external file for reading or updating. The FREAD function reads a record from the external file and copies the data into the FDB. The FGET function then moves the data to the DATA step variables. The function returns a value that you can check with statements or other functions in the DATA step to determine how to further process your data. After the records are processed, the FWRITE function writes the contents of the FDB to the external file, and the FCLOSE function closes the file.

When you use SAS data sets, the OPEN function opens the data set. The FETCH and FETCHOBS functions read observations from an open SAS data set into the Data Set Data Vector (DDV). The GETVARC and GETVARN functions then move the data to DATA step variables. The functions return a value that you can check with statements or other functions in the DATA step to determine how you want to further process your data. After the data is processed, the CLOSE function closes the data set.

For complete descriptions and examples, see the functions and CALL routines in *SAS Language Reference: Dictionary*.

Using Random-Number Functions and CALL Routines

Seed Values

Random–number functions and CALL routines generate streams of random numbers from an initial starting point, called a *seed*, that either the user or the computer clock supplies. A seed must be a nonnegative integer with a value less than $2^{31}-1$ (or 2,147,483,647). If you use a positive seed, you can always replicate the stream of random numbers by using the same DATA step. If you use zero as the seed, the computer clock initializes the stream, and the stream of random numbers is not replicable.

Each random-number function and CALL routine generates pseudo-random numbers from a specific statistical distribution. Every random-number function requires a seed value expressed as an integer constant, or a variable that contains the integer constant. Every CALL routine calls a variable that contains the seed value. Additionally, every CALL routine requires a variable that contains the generated random numbers.

The seed variable must be initialized prior to the first execution of the function or CALL routine. After each execution of a function, the current seed is updated internally, but the value of the seed argument remains unchanged. After each iteration of the CALL routine, however, the seed variable contains the current seed in the stream that generates the next random number. With a function, it is not possible to control the seed values, and, therefore, the random numbers after the initialization.

Comparison of Random-Number Functions and CALL Routines

Except for the NORMAL and UNIFORM functions, which are equivalent to the RANNOR and RANUNI functions, respectively, SAS provides a CALL routine that has the same name as each random-number function. Using CALL routines gives you greater control over the seed values.

With a CALL routine, you can generate multiple streams of random numbers within a single DATA step. If you supply a different seed value to initialize each of the seed variables, the streams of the generated random numbers are computationally independent. With a function, however, you cannot generate more than one stream by supplying multiple seeds within a DATA step. The following two examples illustrate the difference.

Example 1: Generating Multiple Streams from a CALL Routine

This example uses the CALL RANUNI routine to generate three streams of random numbers from the uniform distribution, with ten numbers each. See the results in Output 4.1.

```
options nodate pageno=1 linesize=80 pagesize=60;

data multiple(drop=i);
   retain Seed_1 1298573062 Seed_2 447801538
          Seed_3 631280;
   do i=1 to 10;
      call ranuni (Seed_1,X1);
      call ranuni (Seed_2,X2);
```

```
        call ranuni (Seed_3,X3);
        output;
     end;
  run;


  proc print data=multiple;
     title 'Multiple Streams from a CALL Routine';
  run;
```

Output 4.1   The CALL Routine Example

```
                      Multiple Streams from a CALL Routine                  1

   Obs      Seed_1          Seed_2          Seed_3       X1        X2        X3

    1    1394231558      512727191       367385659     0.64924   0.23876   0.17108
    2    1921384255     1857602268      1297973981     0.89471   0.86501   0.60442
    3     902955627      422181009       188867073     0.42047   0.19659   0.08795
    4     440711467      761747298       379789529     0.20522   0.35472   0.17685
    5    1044485023     1703172173       591320717     0.48638   0.79310   0.27536
    6    2136205611     2077746915       870485645     0.99475   0.96753   0.40535
    7    1028417321     1800207034      1916469763     0.47889   0.83829   0.89243
    8    1163276804      473335603       753297438     0.54169   0.22041   0.35078
    9     176629027     1114889939      2089210809     0.08225   0.51916   0.97286
   10    1587189112      399894790       284959446     0.73909   0.18622   0.13269
```

Example 2: Assigning Values from a Single Stream to Multiple Variables

Using the same three seeds that were used in Example 1, this example uses a function to create three variables. The results that are produced are different from those in Example 1 because the values of all three variables are generated by the first seed. When you use an individual function more than once in a DATA step, the function accepts only the first seed value that you supply and ignores the rest.

```
options nodate pageno=1 linesize=80 pagesize=60;

data single(drop=i);
   do i=1 to 3;
      Y1=ranuni(1298573062);
      Y2=ranuni(447801538);
      Y3=ranuni(631280);
      output;
   end;
run;


proc print data=single;
   title 'A Single Stream across Multiple Variables';
run;
```

The following output shows the results. The values of Y1, Y2, and Y3 in this example come from the same random-number stream generated from the first seed. You can see this by comparing the values by observation across these three variables with the values of X1 in Output 4.2.

Output 4.2 The Function Example

```
                A Single Stream across Multiple Variables              1

                Obs       Y1         Y2         Y3

                 1      0.64924    0.89471    0.42047
                 2      0.20522    0.48638    0.99475
                 3      0.47889    0.54169    0.08225
```

Pattern Matching Using SAS Regular Expressions (RX) and Perl Regular Expressions (PRX)

Definition of Pattern Matching and Regular Expressions

Pattern matching enables you to search for and extract multiple matching patterns from a character string in one step, as well as to make several substitutions in a string in one step. The DATA step supports two kinds of pattern-matching functions and CALL routines:

□ SAS regular expressions (RX)

□ Perl regular expressions (PRX).

Regular expressions are a pattern language which provides fast tools for parsing large amounts of text. Regular expressions are composed of characters and special characters that are called metacharacters.

The asterisk (*) and the question mark (?) are two examples of metacharacters. The asterisk (*) matches zero or more characters, and the question mark (?) matches one or zero characters. For example, if you issue the `ls data*.txt` command from a UNIX shell prompt, UNIX displays all the files in the current directory that begin with the letters "data" and end with the file extension "txt".

The asterisk (*) and the question mark (?) are a limited form of regular expressions. Perl regular expressions build on the asterisk and the question mark to make searching more powerful and flexible.

Definition of SAS Regular Expression (RX) Functions and CALL Routines

SAS Regular expression (RX) functions and CALL routines refers to a group of functions and CALL routines that uses SAS' regular expression pattern matching to parse character strings. You can search for character strings that have a specific pattern that you specify, and change a matched substring to a different substring.

SAS regular expressions consist of CALL RXCHANGE, CALL RXFREE, CALL RXSUBSTR, RXMATCH, and RXPARSE, and are part of the character string matching category for functions and CALL routines. For more information on these functions and CALL routines, see *SAS Language Reference: Dictionary*.

Definition of Perl Regular Expression (PRX) Functions and CALL Routines

Perl regular expression (PRX) functions and CALL routines refers to a group of functions and CALL routines that uses a modified version of Perl as a pattern matching language to parse character strings. PRX functions enable you to do the following:

□ search for a pattern of characters within a string

□ extract a substring from a string

□ search and replace text with other text

□ parse large amounts of text, such as Web logs or other text data, more quickly than with SAS regular expressions.

Perl regular expressions consist of CALL PRXCHANGE, CALL PRXDEBUG, CALL PRXFREE, CALL PRXNEXT, CALL PRXPOSN, CALL PRXSUBSTR, PRXPAREN, PRXMATCH, and PRXPARSE, and are part of the character string matching category for functions and CALL routines. For more information on these functions and CALL routines, see *SAS Language Reference: Dictionary*.

Benefits of Using Perl Regular Expressions in the DATA Step

Using Perl regular expressions in the DATA step enhances search and replace options in text. You can use Perl regular expressions to do the following:

□ validate data

□ replace text

□ extract a substring from a string

□ write Perl debug output to the SAS log.

You can write SAS programs that do not use regular expressions to produce the same results as you do when you use Perl regular expressions. The code without the regular expressions, however, requires more function calls to handle character positions in a string and to manipulate parts of the string.

Perl regular expressions combine most, if not all, of these steps into one expression. The resulting code has the following advantages.

□ less prone to error

□ easier to maintain

□ clearer to read

□ more efficient in terms of improving system performance.

Using Perl Regular Expressions in the DATA Step - License Agreement

The following paragraph complies with sections 3 (a) and 4 (c) of the artistic license:

The PRX functions use a modified version of Perl 5.6.1 to perform regular expression compilation and matching. Perl is compiled into a library for use with SAS. The modified and original Perl 5.6.1 files are freely available from the SAS Web site at http://support.sas.com/rnd/base. Each of the modified files has a comment block at the top of the file describing how and when the file was changed. The executables were given non-standard Perl names. The standard version of Perl can be obtained from http://www.perl.com.

Only Perl regular expressions are accessible from the PRX functions. Other parts of the Perl language are not accessible. The modified version of Perl regular expressions does not support the following:

□ Perl variables.

□ the regular expression options /c, /g, and /o and the /e option with substitutions.

□ named characters, which use the \N{name} syntax.

□ the metacharacters \pP, \PP, and \X.

□ executing Perl code within a regular expression. This includes the syntax (?{code}), (??{code}), and (?p{code}).

□ unicode pattern matching.

□ using ?PATTERN?. The ? metacharacter is treated like a regular expression start-and-end delimiter.

□ the metacharacter \G.

□ Perl comments between a pattern and replacement text. For example: s{regexp} # perl comment {replacement}.

□ matching backslashes with m/\ \ \ \/. Instead m/\ \/ should be used to match a backslash.

Syntax of Perl Regular Expressions

Perl regular expressions are composed of characters and special characters that are called metacharacters. When performing a match, SAS searches a source string for a substring that matches the Perl regular expression that you specify. Using metacharacters enables SAS to perform special actions when searching for a match:

□ If you use the metacharacter \d, SAS matches a digit between 0–9.

□ If you use /\dt/, SAS finds the digits in the string "Raleigh, NC 27506".

□ If you use /world/, SAS finds the substring "world" in the string "Hello world!".

The following table contains a short list of Perl regular expression metacharacters that you can use when you build your code. You can find a complete list of metacharacters on the following Perl man page at http://www.perldoc.com/perl5.6.1/pod/perlre.html.

Metacharacter	Description
\	marks the next character as either a special character, a literal, a back reference, or an octal escape: □ "n" matches the character "n" □ "\n" matches a new line character □ "\\" matches "\" □ "\(" matches "("
|	specifies the or condition when you compare alphanumeric strings.
^	matches the position at the beginning of the input string.
$	matches the position at the end of the input string.
*	matches the preceding subexpression zero or more times: □ zo* matches "z" and "zoo" □ * is equivalent to {0}
+	matches the preceding subexpression one or more times: □ "zo+" matches "zo" and "zoo" □ "zo+" does not match "z" □ + is equivalent to {1,}
?	matches the preceding subexpression zero or one time: □ "do(es)?" matches the "do" in "do" or "does" □ ? is equivalent to {0,1}

Metacharacter	Description
{n}	n is a non-negative integer that matches exactly n times: □ "o{2}" matches the two o's in "food" □ "o{2}" does not match the "o" in "Bob"
{n,}	n is a non-negative integer that matches n or more times: □ "o{2,}" matches all the o's in "foooood" □ "o{2,}" does not match the "o" in "Bob" □ "o{1,}" is equivalent to "o+" □ "o{0,}" is equivalent to "o*"
{n,m}	m and n are non-negative integers, where n<=m. They match at least n and at most m times: □ "o{1,3}" matches the first three o's in "fooooood" □ "o{0,1}" is equivalent to "o?" *Note:* **You cannot put a space between the comma and the numbers.** △
period (.)	matches any single character except newline. To match any character including newline, use a pattern such as "[.\n]".
(pattern)	matches a pattern and captures the match. To retrieve the position and length of the match that is captured, use CALL PRXPOSN. To match parentheses characters, use "\(" or "\)".
x|y	matches either x or y: □ "z|food" matches "z" or "food" □ "(z|f)ood" matches "zood" or "food"
[xyz]	specifies a character set that matches any one of the enclosed characters: □ "[abc]" matches the "a" in "plain"
[^xyz]	specifies a negative character set that matches any character that is not enclosed: □ "[^abc]" matches the "p" in "plain"
[a-z]	specifies a range of characters that matches any character in the range: □ "[a-z]" matches any lowercase alphabetic character in the range "a" through "z"
[^a-z]	specifies a range of characters that does not match any character in the range: □ "[^a-z]" matches any character that is not in the range "a" through "z"
\b	matches a word boundary (the position between a word and a space): □ "er\b" matches the "er" in "never" □ "er\b" does not match the "er" in "verb"

Metacharacter	Description
\B	matches a non-word boundary: □ "er\B" matches the "er" in "verb" □ "er\B" does not match the "er" in "never"
\d	matches a digit character that is equivalent to [0-9].
\D	matches a non-digit character that is equivalent to [^0-9].
\s	matches any white space character including space, tab, form feed, and so on, and is equivalent to [\f\n\r\t\v].
\S	matches any character that is not a white space character and is equivalent to [^\f\n\r\t\v].
\t	matches a tab character and is equivalent to "\x09".
\w	matches any word character including the underscore and is equivalent to [A-Za-z0-9_].
\W	matches any non-word character and is equivalent to [^A-Za-z0-9_].
\num	matches num, where num is a positive integer. This is a reference back to captured matches: □ "(.)\1" matches two consecutive identical characters.

Example 1: Validating Data

You can test for a pattern of characters within a string. For example, you can examine a string to determine whether it contains a correctly formatted telephone number. This type of test is called data validation.

The following example validates a list of phone numbers. To be valid, a phone number must have one of the following forms: **(XXX) XXX-XXXX** or **XXX-XXX-XXXX**.

```
data _null_;  ❶
   if _N_ = 1 then
      do;
         paren = "\([2-9]\d\d\) ?[2-9]\d\d-\d\d\d\d";  ❷
         dash = "[2-9]\d\d-[2-9]\d\d-\d\d\d\d";  ❸
         regexp = "/(" || paren || ")|(" || dash || ")/";  ❹
         retain re;
         re = prxparse(regexp);  ❺
         if missing(re) then  ❻
            do;
               putlog "ERROR: Invalid regexp " regexp;  ❼
               stop;
            end;
      end;

   length first last home business $ 16;
   input first last home business;

   if ^prxmatch(re, home) then  ❽
      putlog "NOTE: Invalid home phone number for " first last home;
```

```
      if ^prxmatch(re, business) then   ❾
          putlog "NOTE: Invalid business phone number for " first last business;

   datalines;
Jerome Johnson (919)319-1677 (919)846-2198
Romeo Montague 800-899-2164 360-973-6201
Imani Rashid (508)852-2146 (508)366-9821
Palinor Kent . 919-782-3199
Ruby Archuleta . .
Takei Ito 7042982145 .
Tom Joad 209/963/2764 2099-66-8474
;
```

The following items correspond to the lines that are numbered in the DATA step that is shown above.

❶ Create a DATA step.

❷ Build a Perl regular expression to identify a phone number that matches (XXX)XXX-XXXX, and assign the variable PAREN to hold the result. Use the following syntax elements to build the Perl regular expression:

\(	matches the open parenthesis in the area code.
[2–9]	matches the digits 2–9. This is the first number in the area code.
\d	matches a digit. This is the second number in the area code.
\d	matches a digit. This is the third number in the area code.
\)	matches the closed parenthesis in the area code.
?	matches the space (which is the preceding subexpression) zero or one time. Spaces are significant in Perl regular expressions. They match a space in the text that you are searching. If a space precedes the question mark metacharacter (as it does in this case), the pattern matches either zero spaces or one space in this position in the phone number.

❸ Build a Perl regular expression to identify a phone number that matches XXX-XXX-XXXX, and assign the variable DASH to hold the result.

❹ Build a Perl regular expression that concatenates the regular expressions for (XXX)XXX-XXXX and XXX—XXX—XXXX. The concatenation enables you to search for both phone number formats from one regular expression.

   The PAREN and DASH regular expressions are placed within parentheses. The bar metacharacter (|) that is located between PAREN and DASH instructs the compiler to match either pattern. The slashes around the entire pattern tell the compiler where the start and end of the regular expression is located.

❺ Pass the Perl regular expression to PRXPARSE and compile the expression. PRXPARSE returns a value to the compiled pattern. Using the value with other Perl regular expression functions and CALL routines enables SAS to perform operations with the compiled Perl regular expression.

❻ Use the MISSING function to check whether the regular expression was successfully compiled.

❼ Use the PUTLOG statement to write an error message to the SAS log if the regular expression did not compile.

❽ Search for a valid home phone number. PRXMATCH uses the value from PRXPARSE along with the search text and returns the position where the regular expression was found in the search text. If there is no match for the home phone number, the PUTLOG statement writes a note to the SAS log.

❾ Search for a valid business phone number. PRXMATCH uses the value from PRXPARSE along with the search text and returns the position where the regular expression was found in the search text. If there is no match for the business phone number, the PUTLOG statement writes a note to the SAS log.

The following lines are written to the SAS log:

```
NOTE: Invalid home phone number for Palinor Kent
NOTE: Invalid home phone number for Ruby Archuleta
NOTE: Invalid business phone number for Ruby Archuleta
NOTE: Invalid home phone number for Takei Ito 7042982145
NOTE: Invalid business phone number for Takei Ito
NOTE: Invalid home phone number for Tom Joad 209/963/2764
NOTE: Invalid business phone number for Tom Joad 2099-66-8474
```

Example 2: Replacing Text

You can use Perl regular expressions to find specific characters within a string. You can then remove the characters or replace them with other characters. In this example, the two occurrences of the less-than character (<) are replaced by < and the two occurrences of the greater-than character (>) are replaced by >.

```
data _null_;  ❶
   if _N_ = 1 then
      do;
         retain lt_re gt_re;
         lt_re = prxparse('s/</&lt;/');  ❷
         gt_re = prxparse('s/>/&gt;/');  ❸
         if missing(lt_re) or missing(gt_re) then  ❹
            do;
               putlog "ERROR: Invalid regexp.";  ❺
               stop;
            end;
      end;
   input;
   call prxchange(lt_re, -1, _infile_);  ❻
   call prxchange(gt_re, -1, _infile_);  ❼
   put _infile_;
   datalines4;
The bracketing construct ( ... ) creates capture buffers. To refer to
the digit'th buffer use \<digit> within the match. Outside the match
use "$" instead of "\". (The \<digit> notation works in certain
circumstances outside the match. See the warning below about \1 vs $1
for details.) Referring back to another part of the match is called
backreference.
;;;;
```

The following items correspond to the numbered lines in the DATA step that is shown above.

❶ Create a DATA step.

❷ Use metacharacters to create a substitution syntax for a Perl regular expression, and compile the expression. The substitution syntax specifies that a less-than character (<) in the input is replaced by the value **<** in the output.

❸ Use metacharacters to create a substitution syntax for a Perl regular expression, and compile the expression. The substitution syntax specifies that a greater-than character (>) in the input is replaced by the value **>** in the output.

❹ Use the MISSING function to check whether the Perl regular expression compiled without error.

❺ Use the PUTLOG statement to write an error message to the SAS log if neither of the regular expressions was found.

❻ Call the PRXCHANGE routine. Pass the LT_RE *pattern-id*, and search for and replace all matching patterns. Put the results in _INFILE_ and write the observation to the SAS log.

❼ Call the PRXCHANGE routine. Pass the GT_RE *pattern-id*, and search for and replace all matching patterns. Put the results in _INFILE_ and write the observation to the SAS log.

The following lines are written to the SAS log:

```
The bracketing construct ( ... ) creates capture buffers. To refer to
the digit'th buffer use \&lt;digit&gt; within the match. Outside the match
use "$" instead of "\". (The \&lt;digit&gt; notation works in certain
circumstances outside the match. See the warning below about \1 vs $1
for details.) Referring back to another part of the match is called a
backreference.
```

Example 3: Extracting a Substring from a String

You can use Perl regular expressions to find and easily extract text from a string. In this example, the DATA step creates a subset of North Carolina business phone numbers. The program extracts the area code and checks it against a list of area codes for North Carolina.

```
data _null_;  ❶
   if _N_ = 1 then
      do;
         paren = "\(([2-9]\d\d)\) ?[2-9]\d\d-\d\d\d\d";  ❷
         dash = "([2-9]\d\d)-[2-9]\d\d-\d\d\d\d";  ❸
         regexp = "/(" || paren || ")|(" || dash || ")/";  ❹
         retain re;
         re = prxparse(regexp);  ❺
         if missing(re) then  ❻
            do;
               putlog "ERROR: Invalid regexp " regexp;  ❼
               stop;
            end;

         retain areacode_re;
         areacode_re = prxparse("/828|336|704|910|919|252/");  ❽
         if missing(areacode_re) then
```

```
              do;
                   putlog "ERROR: Invalid area code regexp";
                   stop;
              end;
          end;

      length first last home business $ 16;
      length areacode $ 3;
      input first last home business;

      if ^prxmatch(re, home) then
          putlog "NOTE: Invalid home phone number for " first last home;

      if prxmatch(re, business) then      ❾
          do;
              which_format = prxparen(re);      ❿
              call prxposn(re, which_format, pos, len);      ⓫
              areacode = substr(business, pos, len);
              if prxmatch(areacode_re, areacode) then      ⓬
                  put "In North Carolina: " first last business;
          end;
          else
              putlog "NOTE: Invalid business phone number for " first last business;
      datalines;
Jerome Johnson (919)319-1677 (919)846-2198
Romeo Montague 800-899-2164 360-973-6201
Imani Rashid (508)852-2146 (508)366-9821
Palinor Kent 704-782-4673 704-782-3199
Ruby Archuleta 905-384-2839 905-328-3892
Takei Ito 704-298-2145 704-298-4738
Tom Joad 515-372-4829 515-389-2838
;
```

The following items correspond to the numbered lines in the DATA step that is shown above.

❶ Create a DATA step.

❷ Build a Perl regular expression to identify a phone number that matches (XXX)XXX-XXXX, and assign the variable PAREN to hold the result. Use the following syntax elements to build the Perl regular expression:

\\(	matches the open parenthesis in the area code. The open parenthesis marks the start of the submatch.
[2–9]	matches the digits 2–9. This is the first number in the area code.
\\d	matches a digit. This is the second number in the area code.
\\d	matches a digit. This is the third number in the area code.
\\)	matches the closed parenthesis in the area code. The closed parenthesis marks the end of the submatch.
?	matches the space (which is the preceding subexpression) zero or one time. Spaces are significant in Perl regular expressions. They match a space in the text that you are searching. If a

space precedes the question mark metacharacter (as it does in this case), the pattern matches either zero spaces or one space in this position in the phone number.

❸ Build a Perl regular expression to identify a phone number that matches XXX-XXX-XXXX, and assign the variable DASH to hold the result.

❹ Build a Perl regular expression that concatenates the regular expressions for (XXX)XXX-XXXX and XXX—XXX—XXXX. The concatenation enables you to search for both phone number formats from one regular expression.

The PAREN and DASH regular expressions are placed within parentheses. The bar metacharacter (|) that is located between PAREN and DASH instructs the compiler to match either pattern. The slashes around the entire pattern tell the compiler where the start and end of the regular expression is located.

❺ Pass the Perl regular expression to PRXPARSE and compile the expression. PRXPARSE returns a value to the compiled pattern. Using the value with other Perl regular expression functions and CALL routines enables SAS to perform operations with the compiled Perl regular expression.

❻ Use the MISSING function to check whether the Perl regular expression compiled without error.

❼ Use the PUTLOG statement to write an error message to the SAS log if the regular expression did not compile.

❽ Compile a Perl regular expression that searches a string for a valid North Carolina area code.

❾ Search for a valid business phone number.

❿ Use the PRXPAREN function to determine which submatch to use. PRXPAREN returns the last submatch that was matched. If an area code matches the form (XXX), PRXPAREN returns the value 2. If an area code matches the form XXX, PRXPAREN returns the value 4.

⓫ Call the PRXPOSN routine to retrieve the position and length of the submatch.

⓬ Use the PRXMATCH function to determine whether the area code is a valid North Carolina area code, and write the observation to the log.

The following lines are written to the SAS log:

```
In North Carolina: Jerome Johnson (919)846-2198
In North Carolina: Palinor Kent 704-782-3199
In North Carolina: Takei Ito 704-298-4738
```

Writing Perl Debug Output to the SAS Log

The DATA step provides debugging support with the CALL PRXDEBUG routine. CALL PRXDEBUG enables you to turn on and off Perl debug output messages that are sent to the SAS log.

The following example writes Perl debug output to the SAS log.

```
data _null_;

    /* CALL PRXDEBUG(1) turns on Perl debug output. */
call prxdebug(1);
putlog 'PRXPARSE: ';
re = prxparse('/[bc]d(ef*g)+h[ij]k$/');
putlog 'PRXMATCH: ';
pos = prxmatch(re, 'abcdefg_gh_');
```

```
        /* CALL PRXDEBUG(0) turns off Perl debug output. */
    call prxdebug(0);
run;
```

SAS writes the following output to the log.

Output 4.3 SAS Debugging Output

```
PRXPARSE:
Compiling REx '[bc]d(ef*g)+h[ij]k$'
size 41 first at 1
rarest char g at 0
rarest char d at 0
   1: ANYOF[bc](10)
  10: EXACT <d>(12)
  12: CURLYX[0] {1,32767}(26)
  14:   OPEN1(16)
  16:     EXACT <e>(18)
  18:     STAR(21)
  19:       EXACT <f>(0)
  21:     EXACT <g>(23)
  23:   CLOSE1(25)
  25:   WHILEM[1/1](0)
  26: NOTHING(27)
  27: EXACT <h>(29)
  29: ANYOF[ij](38)
  38: EXACT <k>(40)
  40: EOL(41)
  41: END(0)
anchored 'de' at 1 floating 'gh' at 3..2147483647 (checking floating) stclass
'ANYOF[bc]' minlen 7

PRXMATCH:
Guessing start of match, REx '[bc]d(ef*g)+h[ij]k$' against 'abcdefg_gh_'...
Did not find floating substr 'gh'...
Match rejected by optimizer
```

For a detailed explanation of Perl debug output, see the "CALL PRXDEBUG Routine" in *SAS Language Reference: Dictionary*.

Base SAS Functions for Web Applications

Four functions that manipulate Web-related content are available in Base SAS software. HTMLENCODE and URLENCODE return encoded strings. HTMLDECODE and URLDECODE return decoded strings. For information about Web-based SAS tools, follow the Communities link on the SAS customer support home page, at support.sas.com.

ARM Macros

Definition of ARM Macros

The ARM macros provide a way to measure the performance of applications as they are executing. The macros write transaction records to the ARM log. The ARM log is an external output text file that contains the logged ARM transaction records. You insert the ARM macros into your SAS program at strategic points in order to generate calls to the ARM API function calls. The ARM API function calls typically log the time of the call and other related data to the log file. Measuring the time between these ARM API function calls yields an approximate response-time measurement.

An ARM macro is self-contained and does not affect any code surrounding it, provided that the variable name passed as an option to the ARM macro is unique. The ARM macros are used in open code (code that is not in PROC or DATA steps) and in DATA step or SCL environments.

There are two categories of ARM macros:

□ ARM macros to instrument applications

□ ARM post-processing macros to use with the ARM log.

Note: The ARM macros are not part of SAS Macro Facility. They are part of the SAS ARM interface. See Chapter 15, "Monitoring Performance Using Application Response Measurement (ARM)," on page 225 for information about the SAS ARM interface that consists of the implementation of the ARM API as an ARM agent, ARM macros, and ARM system options. △

Using ARM Macros

Overview of ARM Macros

The ARM macros invoke the ARM API function calls. The ARM macros automatically manage the returned IDs from the ARM API function calls.

The ARM API function calls are implemented in SAS software with SAS ARM macros and these function calls provide a way to measure the performance of SAS applications as they are running. For each ARM API function call, there is a corresponding macro. The following table shows the relationship among the SAS ARM macros and the ARM API function calls:

Table 4.4 Relationship among SAS ARM Macros and ARM API Function Calls

SAS ARM Macro	ARM API Function Call
%ARMINIT	ARM_INIT
%ARMGTID	ARM_GETID
%ARMSTRT	ARM_START
%ARMUPDT	ARM_UPDATE
%ARMSTOP	ARM_STOP
%ARMEND	ARM_END

The SAS ARM macro invokes the ARM API function call.

The following ARM macros are available:

%ARMINIT Macro — generates a call to the ARM_INIT function call, which names the application and optionally the users of the application and initializes the ARM environment for the application. Typically, you would insert this macro in your code once.

%ARMGTID Macro — generates a call to the ARM_GETID function call, which names a transaction. Use %ARMGTID for each unique transaction in order to describe the type of transactions to be logged. A %ARMGTID is typically coded for each transaction class in an application.

%ARMSTRT Macro
generates a call to the ARM_START function call, which signals the start of a transaction instance. Insert %ARMSTRT before each transaction that you want to log. Whereas %ARMGTID defines a transaction class, %ARMSTRT indicates that a transaction is executing.

%ARMUPDT Macro
is an optional macro that generates a call to the ARM_UPDATE function call, which provides additional information about the progress of a transaction. Insert %ARMUPDT between %ARMSTRT and %ARMSTOP in order to supply information about the transaction that is in progress.

%ARMSTOP Macro
generates a call to the ARM_STOP function call, which signals the end of a transaction instance. Insert %ARMSTOP where the transaction is known to be complete.

%ARMEND Macro
generates a call to the ARM_END function call, which terminates the ARM environment and signals that the application will not make any more ARM calls.

The ARM macros permit conditional execution by setting the appropriate macro options and variables.

Some general points about the ARM macros follow:

□ A general recommendation with all ARM macros is to avoid, in the program, the use of either macro variables or SAS variables beginning with the letters "_ARM."

□ All macro options are keyword parameters. There are no positional parameters. Values for the macro options should be valid SAS values—that is, a SAS variable, quoted character string, numeric constant, and so on.

□ ARM macros can function either inside a DATA step or in open code. Use the _ARMACRO global variable or the MACONLY=YES|NO macro option to tell the macro execution which mode is being used. For more information, see "Setting the Macro Environment" on page 67.

Using Variables with ARM Macros

The ARM macros use variables to pass IDs and other information from one macro to another. Because the ARM macros function within the same DATA step, across DATA steps, and in open code, variables that are used by the macros can take the form of DATA step variables or macro variables as determined by the macro environment.

SAS DATA step variables are used to pass ID information between two or more ARM macros in the same DATA step. In the DATA step environment, but not in the SCL environment, DROP statements are generated for these variables so that they are not inadvertently included in any output data sets.

If ID information must be passed between two or more ARM macros across separate DATA steps, then macro global variables are used.

The following SAS DATA step variables and macro variables are considered global:

Table 4.5 Global ARM Macro Variables

Variable	Description	Set By	Used as Input by
_ARMAPID	application ID	%ARMINIT	%ARMEND
_ARMTXID	transaction class ID	%ARMGTID	%ARMSTRT

Variable	Description	Set By	Used as Input by
_ARMSHDL	start handle	%ARMSTRT	%ARMUPDT, %ARMSTOP
_ARMRC	error status	%ARMUPDT %ARMSTOP %ARMEND	none
_ARMGLVL	global level indicator	calling program	all
_ARMTLVL	target level indicator	calling program	all
_ARMEXEC	global enablement	calling program	all
_ARMACRO	open code enablement	calling program	all
_ARMSCL	SCL code enablement	calling program	all

ARM API Objects

The following three classes of objects are specified in the ARM API:

□ *applications* represent the systems that you are creating, such as an inventory or order entry application. Because the SAS interface to the ARM API provides totals on a per application basis, you might want to consider this when you define the scope of your application.

□ *transaction classes* specify a unit of work. You should create a transaction class for each major type of work that you want to create within an application. In concept, the transaction class is a template for the started transaction.

□ *transaction instances* specify the actual start time for a unit of work. Transaction instances have response time information that is associated with them.

The ARM API uses numeric identifiers or IDs to uniquely identify the ARM objects that are input and output from the ARM macro. The three different classes of IDs that correspond to the three ARM classes are

□ application IDs

□ transaction class IDs

□ start handles (start time) for transaction instances.

ID Management Using ARM Macros

These examples demonstrate how the ARM macros work. The ARM macros automatically manage application IDs, transaction IDs, and start handles. The default ID management works best in simple ARM call schemes. See "Complex ARM Macro Call Schemes" on page 61 for more information. By default, the ARM macros use IDs that were generated from the most recent macro call. The following example demonstrates how to use all of the ARM macros:

```
    /*global macro variable to indicate ARM macros are outside the data step*/
%let _armacro=1;

    /* start of the application */
%arminit(appname='Sales App', appuser='userxyz');

    /* define the transaction classes */
%armgtid(txnname='Sales Order', txndet='Sales Order Transaction');
```

```
    /* more arm_getid calls go here for different transaction classes */

    /* start of a transaction */
%armstrt;

data _null_;
    /* place the actual transaction code here */
    /* update the status of the transaction as it is running */
%armupdt(data='Sales transaction still running...',maconly=no);
run;

    /* place the actual transaction stop here */
    /* the transaction has stopped */
%armstop(status=0);

    /* end of the application */
%armend;
```

All ID management is performed by the macros without requiring the calling program to track IDs. Each macro in the previous example uses the most recently generated ID values from previous macros. The following example is identical, but the comments explain the passing of IDs in more detail:

```
%let _armacro=1;

    /*
     *  This %arminit macro will generate both a SAS
     *  variable and global macro variable by the name
     *  of _armapid and set it in the ID that is returned
     *  from the arm_init() function call that is
     *  wrapped by the macro.
     */
%arminit(appname='Sales App', appuser='userxyz');

    /*
     *  This %armgtid macro uses the _armapid SAS variable
     *  as input to the arm_getid() function call that it wraps.
     *  It also generates both a SAS variable and global macro
     *  variable by the name of _armtxid and sets them to the
     *  ID that is returned from the arm_getid function call that
     *  it wraps.
     */
%armgtid(txnname='Sales Order', txndet='Sales Order Transaction');

    /*
     * Because we are still in the same DATA step, the %armstrt
     * macro below will use the _armtxid SAS variable that is
     * generated from the previous %armgtid macro as input
     * to the arm_start() function call that it wraps. It
     * also generates an _armshdl variable.
     */
%armstrt;

    /*
```

```
      * The %armupdt call below uses the _armshdl SAS variable
      * that is generated from the previous %armstrt macro.
      */
    %armupdt(data='Sales transaction still running...');

      /*
      * The armstop call also uses the same _armshdl SAS
      * variable from the %armstrt.
      */
    %armstop(status=0);

      /*
      * The %armend call uses the _armapid SAS variable
      * generated by the %arminit macro earlier to end
      * the application.
      */
    %armend;

  run;
```

You can code the ARM macros across different DATA steps as follows and achieve the same results:

```
data _null_;
    /* note the end of the application */
  %arminit(appname='Sales App', appuser=''userxyz');
run;

data _null_;
  %armgtid(txnname='Sales Order', txndet='Sales Order Transaction');
    /* more arm_getid function calls go here for different transaction classes */
run;

data _null_;
    /* note the start of the transaction */
  %armstrt;

    /* place the actual transaction here */
run;

data _null_;
    /* update the status of the transaction as it is running */
  %armupdt(data='Sales transaction still running...');
run;

data _null_;
    /* place the actual transaction stop here */

    /* note that the transaction has stopped */
  %armstop(status=0);
run;

data _null_;
    /* note the end of the application */
  %armend;
```

```
run;
```

The end result is the same as in the first example, except that the macros are using the generated macro variables rather than the SAS variables for passing IDs.

Complex ARM Macro Call Schemes

Allowing the macros to automatically use the global variables in basic scenarios simplifies coding. However, macros that use global variables can lead to misleading results in more complicated scenarios when you attempt to monitor concurrent applications or transactions as follows:

```
data _null_;
  %arminit(appname='App 1',getid=yes,txnname='txn 1');
run;


    /* start transaction instance 1*/
data _null_;
  %armstrt;
run;


    /*  start transaction instance 2 */
data _null_;
  %armstrt;
run;


    /* WRONG!  This assumes that the %armupdt is updating
     *  the first transaction. However, it is actually updating the
     *  second transaction instance because _armshdl contains the value
     *  from the last macro call that was executed, which is the second
     *  transaction.
     */
data _null_;
  %armupdt(data='txn instance 1 still running...');
run;
```

To save the IDs use the *var options (APPIDVAR=, TXNIDVAR=, and SHDLVAR=) to pass or return the IDs in your own named variables. Here is an example that uses the SHDLVAR= option to save the start handles:

```
data _null_;
  %arminit(appname='xyz',getid=YES,txname='txn 1');
run;


    /*  start transaction instance 1 and save the ID using shdlvar= */
data _null_;
  %armstrt(shdlvar=savhdl1 );
run;


    /*  start transaction instance 2 and save the ID using shdlvar= */
data _null_;
  /*armstrt( shdlvar=savhdl2 );
run;


    /*  Now use the shandle= parameter after retrieving the first id. */
data _null_;
  %armupdt(data='updating txn 1', shdlvar=savhdl1);
```

```
run;

    /*  Use the same technique to stop the transactions */
    /*  in the order they were started. */
data _null_;
  %armstop(shdlvar=savhdl1);
  %armstop(shdlvar=savhdl2);
  %armend();
run;
```

As the previous example shows, using the *var option simplifies the code. The previous technique is recommended for use on all ARM macro calls.

The following example demonstrates how to use all of the *var options to automatically manage IDs for concurrent applications, transaction classes, transaction instances, and correlated transaction instances:

```
data _null_;
  %arminit(appname='Appl 1', appuser='userid', appidvar=app1);
  %arminit(appname='Appl 2', appuser='userid', appidvar=app2);
  %arminit(appname='Appl 3', appuser='userid', appidvar=app3);
run;

data _null_;
  %armgtid(txnname='Txn 1A', txndet='Txn Class 1A',
           appidvar=app1,txnidvar=txnidvar=txn1a);
  %armgtid(txnname='Txn 1B', txndet='Txn Class 1B',
           appidvar=app1,txnidvar=txnidvar=txn1b);
  %armgtid(txnname='Txn 2A', txndet='Txn Class 2A',
           appidvar=app2,txnidvar=txnidvar=txn2a);
  %armgtid(txnname='Txn 2B', txndet='Txn Class 2B',
           appidvar=app2,txnidvar=txnidvar=txn2b);
  %armgtid(txnname='Txn 3A', txndet='Txn Class 3A',
           appidvar=app3,txnidvar=txnidvar=txn3a);
  %armgtid(txnname='Txn 3B', txndet='Txn Class 3B',
           appidvar=app3,txnidvar=txnidvar=txn3b);
run;

data _null_;
  %armstrt(txnidvar=txn1a,shdlvar=sh1a);
  %armstrt(txnidvar=txn1b,shdlvar=sh1b);
  %armstrt(txnidvar=txn2a,shdlvar=sh2a);
  %armstrt(txnidvar=txn2b,shdlvar=sh2b);
  %armstrt(txnidvar=txn3a,shdlvar=sh3a);
  %armstrt(txnidvar=txn3b,shdlvar=sh3b);
run;

data _null_;
  %armupdt(data='Updating txn instance 1a...', shdlvar=sh1a);
  %armupdt(data='Updating txn instance 1b...', shdlvar=sh1b);
  %armupdt(data='Updating txn instance 2a...', shdlvar=sh2a);
  %armupdt(data='Updating txn instance 2b...', shdlvar=sh2b);
  %armupdt(data='Updating txn instance 3a...', shdlvar=sh3a);
  %armupdt(data='Updating txn instance 3b...', shdlvar=sh3b);
run;
```

```
data _null_;
  %armstop(status=0, shdlvar=sh1a);   %armstop(status=1, shdlvar=sh1b);
  %armstop(status=0, shdlvar=sh2a);   %armstop(status=1, shdlvar=sh2b);
  %armstop(status=0, shdlvar=sh3a);   %armstop(status=1, shdlvar=sh3b);
run;

data _null_;
  %armend(appidvar=app1);
  %armend(appidvar=app2);
  %armend(appidvar=app3); run;
```

As the previous example demonstrates, you can establish your own naming conventions to uniquely identify applications, transaction classes, and transaction instances across different DATA steps, in open code, or in SCL programs.

The macros support explicit passing of the IDs using the APPID=, TXNID=, and SHANDLE= options. These options are similar to the *var options, except that they do not retrieve values across DATA steps using macro variables. The primary use of the options is to supply numeric constants as ID values to the macros, because the *var options do not accept numeric constants.

Note: The use of APPID=, TXNID=, and SHANDLE= is not recommended for new applications. These options are maintained for compatibility with earlier ARM macro releases only. Use APPIDVAR=, TXNIDVAR=, and SHDLVAR= instead of APPID=, TXNID=, and SHANDLE=, respectively. △

Because IDs are generated by the ARM agent, to pass a numeric literal requires that you start a new SAS session. If any SAS subsystems are also functioning, you will not know what the ID will be at execution time.

The use of APPIDVAR=, TXNIDVAR=, and SHDLVAR= options is recommended when coding new applications.

Defining User Metrics in ARM Macros

A metric is a counter, gauge, numeric ID, or string that you define. You specify one or more metrics for each ARM transaction class. When a start handle (instance of the transaction class) is started, updated, or stopped, the application indicates a value for the metric and writes it to the ARM log by the ARM agent.

The user metric name and user metric definition must be specified together in the %ARMGTID. METRNAM1–7= names the user metric and must be a SAS character variable or quoted literal value up to eight characters in length. METRDEF1–7= defines the output of the user-defined metric. The value of METRDEF1–6= must be one of the following:

COUNT32, COUNT64, COUNTDIV	use the counter to sum up the values over an interval. A counter can also calculate average values, maximums, and minimums per transaction, and other statistical calculations.
GAUGE32, GAUGE64, GAUGEDIV	use the gauge when a sum of values is not needed. A gauge can calculate average values, maximums, and minimums per transaction, and other statistical calculations.
ID32, ID64	use the numeric ID simply as an identifier but not as a measurement value, such as an error code or an employee ID. No calculations can be performed on the numeric ID.
SHORTSTR, LONGSTR	use the string ID as an identifier. No calculations can be performed on the string ID.

Restriction: METRDEF7= can only equal LONGSTR and can be a long string of 32 bytes. METRDEF1–6 cannot equal LONGSTR.

Note: 32 and 64 signify the number of bits in the counter, gauge, divisor, or ID. △

The METRVAL1–7= sends the value of the user-defined metric to the ARM agent for logging when used in the %ARMSTRT, %ARMUPDT, and %ARMSTOP. The value of the user-defined metric must conform to the corresponding user metrics defined in the %ARMGTID. The following example shows the user metrics:

```
%let _armacro=1;

 %arminit(appname='Sales App', appuser='userxyz');

    /* name and define the user defined metrics */
%armgtid(txnname='Sales Order', txndet='Sales Order Transaction',
        metrnam1=aname, metrdef1=count32);
    /* aname is the NAME of the metric and can be anything up to 8 characters */

    /* start of user defined metric */
    /* initial value of the metric */
%armstrt(metrval1=0);

data myfile;
.
.    /*some SAS statements*/
.
end=EOF;
run;

    /* value of the metric is the automatic observation */
%armupdt(data='Sales transaction still running...',maconly=no,
        metrval1=_N_);

data myfile;
.
.    /*more SAS statements*/
.
if EOF then

    /* value of the metric is at the highest observation count */
%armstop(status=0, metrval1=_N_,maconly=no);
run;

%armend;
```

Defining Correlators in ARM Macros

A primary or parent transaction can contain several component or child transactions nested within them. Child transactions can also contain other child transactions. It can be very useful to know how much each child transaction contributes to the total response time of the parent transaction. If a failure occurs within a parent transaction, knowing which child transaction contains the failure is also useful information. Correlators are used to track these parent and child transactions.

The use of correlators requires that multiple transaction start handles be active simultaneously. This requires the use of the CORR= and SHDLVAR= options in the

%ARMSTRT macro. You define each parent and child transaction in the %ARMSTRT macro using the SHDLVAR= option. For each child transaction, you must also define the parent transaction using the PARNTVAR= option.

Each child transaction is started after the parent transaction starts. Parent or child transactions can be of the same or different transaction classes. You define the transaction classes in the %ARMGTID macro using the TXNIDVAR= option.

Both parent and child transactions can have updates specified in the %ARMUPDT macro. User metrics can be specified for both transaction types in the %ARMSTRT macro if the user metrics were defined in the corresponding transaction class in the %ARMGTID macro.

All child transactions must stop in the %ARMSTOP macro before the parent transaction stops. The sibling (multiple child) transactions can be stopped in any order.

For example, the parent transaction 100 consists of child transactions 110, 120, and 130, each performing a different part of the unit of work represented by the parent transaction 100. The child transaction 120 contains child transactions 121 and 122. Transaction 200 has no child transactions. Here is a code fragment used to create these relationships:

```
%arminit(appname='Application",appidvar=appid);
%armgtid(appidvar=appid,txnname='TranCls',txndet='Transaction Class Def',
         txnidvar=txnid);
%armstrt(txnidvar=txnid,corr=1,shdlvar=HDL100);
%armstrt(txnidvar=txnid,corr=0,shdlvar=HDL200<,...user metrics>);
%armstrt(txnidvar=txnid,corr=2,shldvar=HDL110,parntvar=HDL100);
%armstrt(txnidvar=txnid,corr=3,shldvar=HDL120,parntvar=HDL100);
%armstrt(txnidvar=txnid,corr=2,shldvar=HDL130,parntvar=HDL100);
%armstrt(txnidvar=txnid,corr=2,shldvar=HDL121,parntvar=HDL120);
%armstrt(txnidvar=txnid,corr=2,shldvar=HDL122,parntvar=HDL120);

...

%armstop(shdlvar=HDL200);
%armstop(shdlvar=HDL121);
%armstop(shdlvar=HDL122);
%armstop(shdlvar=HDL120);
%armstop(shdlvar=HDL130);
%armstop(shdlvar=HDL110);
%armstop(shdlvar=HDL100);
```

Enabling ARM Macro Execution

Setting the _ARMEXEC Macro Variable

All ARM macros are disabled by default so that insertion of ARM macros within created code will not result in inadvertent, unwanted logging. To globally activate execution of the ARM macros, you must set the _ARMEXEC global macro variable to a value of 1. Any other value for _ARMEXEC disables the ARM macros.

There are two methods of setting the _ARMEXEC macro variable. The first method sets the variable during DATA step or SCL program compilation using %LET:

```
%let _armexec = 1;
```

If the _ARMEXEC value is not set to 1, then no code is generated and a message is written in the log:

```
NOTE: ARMSTRT macro bypassed by _armexec.
```

The second method of setting _ARMEXEC variables is to use SYMPUT during execution. To set the _ARMEXEC variable during DATA step or SCL program execution:

```
call symput('_armexec', '1');
```

With this technique, the macro checks the _ARMEXEC variable during program execution and the ARM function call is executed or bypassed as appropriate.

Enabling ARM Macro Execution with SCL

There are two methods of setting the _ARMEXEC macro variable—during compilation or execution. Both methods are explained in "Setting the _ARMEXEC Macro Variable" on page 65, or you can use a combination of these methods. For example, set _ARMEXEC to 1 using the compilation technique (perhaps in an autoexec at SAS initialization), and then code a drop-down menu option or other means within the application to turn _ARMEXEC on and off dynamically using CALL SYMPUT.

In SCL, if _ARMEXEC is not 1, when the program compiles, all macros will be set to null and the ARM interface will be unavailable until it is recompiled with _ARMEXEC set to 1.

Additionally, to enable proper compilation of the ARM macros within SCL, you must set the _ARMSCL global macro variable to 1 prior to issuing any ARM macros. This variable suppresses the generation of DROP statements, which are invalid in SCL.

Conditional ARM Macro Execution

It is useful to code the ARM macros in your program but to execute them only when needed. All ARM macros support a LEVEL= option that specifies the execution level of that particular macro.

If it is coded, then the execution level of the macro is compared to two global macro variables, _ARMGLVL and _ARMTLVL. _ARMGLVL is the global level macro variable. If the LEVEL= value on the ARM macro is less than or equal to the _ARMGLVL value, then the macro is executed. If the LEVEL= value on the ARM macro is greater than the _ARMGLVL value, then macro execution is bypassed:

```
    /*  Set the global level to 10 */
  %let _armglvl = 10;

data _null_;
  %arminit(appname='Appl 1', appuser='userid' );
  %armgtid(txnname='Txn 1', txndet='Transaction #1 detail' );

    /*  These macros are executed */
  %armstrt( level=9 );
  %armstop( level=9 );

    /*  These macros are executed */
  %armstrt( level=10 );
  %armstop( level=10 );

    /*  These macros are NOT executed */
  %armstrt( level=11 );
  %armstop( level=11 );

  %armend
run;
```

_ARMTLVL is the target level macro variable and works similarly to the ARMGLVL, except the LEVEL= value on the ARM macro must be exactly equal to the _ARMTLVL value for the macro to execute:

```
    /*  Set the target level to 10 */
  %let _armtlvl = 10;

data _null_;
  %arminit(appname='Appl 1', appuser='userid' );
  %armgtid(txnname='Txn 1', txndet='Transaction #1 detail' );

  /*  These macros are NOT executed */
  %armstrt( level=9 );
  %armstop( level=9 );

  /*  These macros are executed */
  %armstrt( level=10 );
  %armstop( level=10 );

  /*  These macros are NOT executed */
  %armstrt( level=11 );
  %armstop( level=11 );

  %armend
run;
```

The LEVEL= option can be placed on any ARM macro and this is highly recommended. It allows you to design more granular levels of logging that can serve as an effective filtering device by logging only as much data as you want. If you set both _ARMGLVL and _ARMTLVL at the same time, then both values are compared to determine whether the macro should be executed or not.

Setting the Macro Environment

You set the global ARM macro environment by using the _ARMACRO variable with the value of 1 or 0. The value of 1 specifies that all ARM macros occur in open code and the value of 0 specifies that the ARM macros occur only in DATA steps. You use the MACONLY= option if an individual ARM macro is not placed outside of the global environment that is defined by the _ARMACRO setting. For SCL programs, you specify _ARMSCL with a value of 1.

The following table shows the global value, the temporary option needed, and the results.

Table 4.6 Using _ARMACRO and _ARMSCL to Set the ARM Macro Environment

Global Value	Temporary Option	Result
%let _ARMACRO=0;	MACONLY=NO	macro is in DATA step
%let _ARMACRO=1;	MACONLY=YES	macro is in open code
%let _ARMSCL=1;	none	macro is in SCL
%let _ARMSCL=0;	none	macro is not in SCL

The following example shows how to set the macro environment in a DATA step:

```
      /* set global environment */
   %let _armacro = 1;
data _null_;
   %arminit(appname='Appl 1', appuser='user1',
          appidvar=appl, maconly=no);
     /* exception to global value */
run;

      /* using global setting */
      /* maconly= parameter not needed */
   %armgtid(txnname='Txn 1A', txndet='Txn Class 1A',
          appidvar=appl, txnidvar=txn1a);
```

The following example shows how to set the macro environment in SCL using autoexec:

```
      /* set global environment */
   %let _armscl = 1;
   %let _armexec = 1;
```

The following example shows how to set the macro environment in SCL:

```
init:
   %arminit(appname='Appl 1', appuser='user1',
          appidvar=appl);
   %armgtid(txnname='Txn 1A', txndet='Txn Class 1A',
          appidvar=appl, txnidvar=txn1a);
return;
main:
   %armstrt(txnidvar=txn1a,shdlvar=strt1);
return;
term:
   %armstop(shdlvar=strt1);
   %armend(appidvar=appl);
return;
```

Using ARM Post-Processing Macros

Post-processing ARM macros are also available. These ARM macros are specific to the SAS ARM implementation; they are not part of the ARM API standard.

After logging performance data to the ARM log, you can then use the ARM macros to read the log and create SAS data sets for reporting and analysis. The default name of the file is ARMLOG.LOG. To specify a different output file, use the ARMLOC= system option. There are three ARM post-processing macros:

%ARMCONV Macro — converts an ARM log created in SAS 9 or later, which uses a simple format, into the label=item ARM format used in SAS 8.2.

%ARMPROC Macro — processes the ARM log and outputs six SAS data sets that contain the information from the log. It processes ARM logs that include user metadata definitions on class transactions and user data values on start handles, update, and stop transactions.

%ARMJOIN Macro	processes the six SAS data sets that are created by %ARMPROC and creates data sets and SQL views that contain common information about applications and transactions.

For SAS 9 or later, the *simple* format of the ARM log records is comma delimited, which consists of columns of data separated by commas. The datetime stamp and the call identifier always appear in the same column location.

The format used in SAS 8.2. is a *label=item* format and is easier to read. Unfortunately, SAS spends a lot of time formatting the string, and this affects performance. In SAS 9 or later, ARM logs can be compared with SAS 8.2 ARM logs by using the following methods:

1 You can generate the SAS 9 or later ARM log and process it using the SAS 9 or later %ARMPROC and %ARMJOIN. The resulting data sets contain the complete statistics for the end of the start handle and the end of the application.

2 To convert SAS 9 or later ARM log format to the SAS 8.2 format you use the SAS ARM macro %ARMCONV.

Statements

Definition of Statements

A *SAS statement* is a series of items that may include keywords, SAS names, special characters, and operators. All SAS statements end with a semicolon. A SAS statement either requests SAS to perform an operation or gives information to the system.

This section covers two kinds of SAS statements:

□ those that are used in DATA step programming

□ those that are global in scope and can be used anywhere in a SAS program.

Base SAS Procedures Guide gives detailed descriptions of the SAS statements that are specific to each SAS procedure. *SAS Output Delivery System: User's Guide* gives detailed descriptions of the Output Delivery System (ODS) statements.

Executable and Declarative DATA Step Statements

DATA step statements are executable or declarative statements that can appear in the DATA step. *Executable statements* result in some action during individual iterations of the DATA step; *declarative statements* supply information to SAS and take effect when the system compiles program statements.

The following tables show the SAS executable and declarative statements that you can use in the DATA step.

Table 4.7 Executable Statements in the DATA Step

Executable Statements

ABORT	IF, Subsetting	PUT
assignment	IF-THEN/ELSE	PUT, Column
CALL	INFILE	PUT, Formatted
CONTINUE	INPUT	PUT, List

Executable Statements

DECLARE	INPUT, Column	PUT, Named
DELETE	INPUT, Formatted	PUT, _ODS_
DESCRIBE	INPUT, List	PUTLOG
DISPLAY	INPUT, Named	REDIRECT
DO	LEAVE	REMOVE
DO, Iterative	LINK	REPLACE
DO Until	LIST	RETURN
DO While	LOSTCARD	SELECT
ERROR	MERGE	SET
EXECUTE	MODIFY	STOP
FILE	_NEW_	Sum
FILE, ODS	Null	UPDATE
GO TO	OUTPUT	

Table 4.8   Declarative Statements in the DATA Step

Declarative Statements

ARRAY	DATALINES	LABEL
Array Reference	DATALINES4	Labels, Statement
ATTRIB	DROP	LENGTH
BY	END	RENAME
CARDS	FORMAT	RETAIN
CARDS4	INFORMAT	WHERE
DATA	KEEP	WINDOW

Global Statements

Global statements generally provide information to SAS, request information or data, move between different modes of execution, or set values for system options. Other global statements (ODS statements) deliver output in a variety of formats, such as in Hypertext Markup Language (HTML). You can use global statements anywhere in a SAS program. Global statements are not executable; they take effect as soon as SAS compiles program statements.

Other SAS software products have additional global statements that are used with those products. For information, see the SAS documentation for those products.

SAS System Options

Definition of SAS System Options

System options are instructions that affect your SAS session. They control the way that SAS performs operations such as SAS System initialization, hardware and software interfacing, and the input, processing, and output of jobs and SAS files.

Syntax of SAS System Options

The syntax for specifying system options in an OPTIONS statement is

OPTIONS *option(s)*;

Here is an explanation of the syntax:

option
    specifies one or more SAS system options that you want to change.

The following example shows how to use the system options NODATE and LINESIZE= in an OPTIONS statement:

```
options nodate linesize=72;
```

Operating Environment Information: On the command line or in a configuration file, the syntax is specific to your operating environment. For details, see the SAS documentation for your operating environment. △

Using SAS System Options

Default Settings

Operating Environment Information: SAS system options are initialized with default settings when SAS is invoked. However, the default settings for some SAS system options vary both by operating environment and by site. For details, see the SAS documentation for your operating environment. △

Determining Which Settings Are in Effect

To determine which settings are in effect for SAS system options, use one of the following:

OPLIST system option
    writes to the SAS log the settings that were specified on the SAS invocation command line. (See the SAS documentation for your operating environment for more information.)

VERBOSE
    writes to the SAS log the system options that were specified in the configuration file and on the SAS invocation command line.

SAS System Options window
    lists all system option settings.

OPTIONS procedure
: writes system option settings to the SAS log. To display the settings of system options with a specific functionality, such as error handling, use the GROUP= option:

```
proc options GROUP=errorhandling;
run;
```

(See *Base SAS Procedures Guide* for more information.)

GETOPTION function
: returns the value of a specified system option.

VOPTION DICTIONARY table
: lists in the SASHELP library, all current system option settings. You can view this table with SAS Explorer, or you can extract information from the VOPTION table using PROC SQL.

dictionary.options SQL table
: accessed with the SQL procedure, lists the system options that are in effect.

Determining Which SAS System Options Are Restricted

To determine which system options are restricted by your system administrator, use the RESTRICT option of the OPTIONS procedure. The RESTRICT option display the option's value, scope, and how it was set. In the following example, the SAS log shows that only one option, CMPOPT, is restricted:

```
proc options restrict;
run;
```

Output 4.4   Restricted Option Information

```
1    proc options restrict;
2    run;
     SAS (r) Proprietary Software Release 9.1   TS1B0

Option Value Information For SAS Option CMPOPT
     Option Value: (NOEXTRAMATH NOMISSCHECK NOPRECISE NOGUARDCHECK)
     Option Scope: SAS Session
     How option value set:  Site Administrator Restricted
```

The OPTIONS procedure will display this information for all options that are restricted. If your site administrator has not restricted any options, then the following message will appear in the SAS log:

```
Your site administrator has not restricted any options.
```

Determining How a SAS System Option Value Was Set

To determine how a system option value was set, use the OPTIONS procedure with the VALUE option specified in the OPTIONS statement. The VALUE option displays the specified option's value and scope. For example, the following statements write a message to the SAS log that tells you how the option value for the system option CENTER was set:

```
proc options option=center value;
run;
```

The following partial SAS log shows that the option value for CENTER is the default that was shipped with the product..

Output 4.5   Option Value Information for the System Option CENTER

```
2     proc options option=center value;
3     run;


Option Value Information for SAS Option CENTER
    Option Value: CENTER
    Option Scope: NoReb
    How option value set:  Shipped Default
```

Obtaining Descriptive Information about a System Option

You can quickly obtain basic descriptive information about a system option by specifying the DEFINE option in the PROC OPTIONS statement.
The DEFINE option writes the following descriptive information about a system option to the SAS log:

- □ description
- □ type
- □ when in the SAS session it can be set

For example, the following statements write a message to the SAS log that contains descriptive information about the system option CENTER:

```
proc options option=center define;
run;
```

This partial SAS log tells you specific information about the system option CENTER.

Output 4.6   Descriptive Information for the System Option CENTER

```
1     proc options option=center define;
      2    run;
  CENTER
  Option Definition Information for SAS Option CENTER
     Group= LISTCONTROL
     Group Description: Procedure output and display settings
     Description: Center SAS procedure output
     Type: The option value is of type BOOLEAN
     When Can Set: Startup or anytime during the SAS Session
     Restricted: Your Site Administrator can restrict modification of this option
     Optsave: Proc Optsave or command Dmoptsave will save this option.
```

Changing SAS System Option Settings

SAS provides default settings for SAS system options. You can override the default settings of any unrestricted system option. Depending on the function of the system option, you can specify a setting in any of the following ways:

- □ *on the command line:* You can specify any unrestricted SAS system option setting either on the SAS command line or in a configuration file. If you use the same option settings frequently, it is usually more convenient to specify the options in a configuration file, rather than on the command line. Either method sets your SAS system options during SAS invocation. Many SAS system option settings can be specified only during SAS invocation. Descriptions of the individual options provide details.

□ *in a configuration file:* If you use the same option settings frequently, it is usually more convenient to specify the options in a configuration file, rather than on the command line.

□ *in an OPTIONS statement:* You can specify an OPTIONS statement at any time during a session except within data lines or parmcard lines. Settings remain in effect throughout the current program or process unless you reset them with another OPTIONS statement or change them in the SAS System Options window. You can also place an OPTIONS statement in an autoexec file.

□ *in a SAS System Options window:* If you are in a windowing environment, type **options** in the toolbox or on the command line to open the SAS System Options window. The SAS System Options window lists the names of the SAS system options groups. You can then expand the groups to see the option names and to change their current settings. Alternatively, you can use the Find Option command in the Options pop-up menu to go directly to an option. Changes take effect immediately and remain in effect throughout the session unless you reset them with an OPTIONS statement or change them in the SAS System Options window.

Operating Environment Information: On UNIX, Open VMS, and z/OS hosts, SAS system options can be restricted by a site administrator so that they cannot be changed by a user. Depending upon your operating environment, system options can be restricted globally, by group, or by user. You can use the OPTIONS procedure to determine which options are restricted. For more information about how to restrict options, see the SAS configuration guide for your operating environment. For more information about the OPTIONS procedure, see the SAS documentation for your operating environment. △

How Long System Option Settings Are in Effect

When you specify a SAS system option setting, the setting applies to all subsequent steps for the duration of the SAS session or until you reset, as shown:

```
data one;
   set items;
run;

   /* option applies to all subsequent steps */
options obs=5;

  /* printing ends with the fifth observation */
proc print data=one;
run;

   /* the SET statement stops reading
      after the fifth observation */
data two;
   set items;
run;
```

To read more than five observations, you must reset the OBS= system option. For more information about the "OBS= System Option" , see *SAS Language Reference: Dictionary*.

Order of Precedence

If a system option appears in more than one place, the order of precedence from highest to lowest is as follows:

1 OPTIONS statement and SAS System Options window
2 autoexec file (that contains an OPTIONS statement)
3 command-line specification
4 configuration file specification
5 SAS system default settings.

Operating Environment Information: In some operating environments, you can specify system options in other places. See the SAS documentation for your operating environment. △

Table 4.9 on page 75 shows the order of precedence that SAS uses for execution mode options. These options are a subset of the SAS invocation options and are specified on the command line during SAS invocation.

Table 4.9   Order of Precedence for SAS Execution Mode Options

Execution Mode Option	Precedence
OBJECTSERVER	Highest
DMR	2nd
INITCMD	3rd
DMS	3rd
DMSEXP	3rd
EXPLORER	3rd

The order of precedence of SAS execution mode options consists of the following rules:

□ SAS uses the execution mode option with the highest precedence.
□ If you specify more than one execution mode option of equal precedence, SAS uses only the last option listed.

See the descriptions of the individual options for more details.

Interaction with Data Set Options

Some system options share the same name as a data set option that has the same function. System options remain in effect for all DATA step and PROC steps in a SAS session until their settings are changed. The data set option, however, overrides a system option only for the particular data set in the step in which it appears.

In this example, the OBS= system option in the OPTIONS statement specifies that only the first 100 observations will be read from any data set within the SAS job. The OBS= data set option in the SET statement, however, overrides the system option and specifies that only the first five observations will be read from data set TWO. The PROC PRINT step uses the system option setting and reads and prints the first 100 observations from data set THREE:

```
options obs=100;

data one;
   set two(obs=5);
run;
```

```
proc print data=three;
run;
```

Comparisons

Note the differences between system options, data set options, and statement options.

system options

remain in effect for all DATA and PROC steps in a SAS job or current process unless they are respecified.

data set options

apply to the processing of the SAS data set with which they appear. Some data set options have corresponding system options or LIBNAME statement options. For an individual data set, you can use the data set option to override the setting of these other options.

statement options

control the action of the statement in which they appear. Options in global statements, such as in the LIBNAME statement, can have a broader impact.

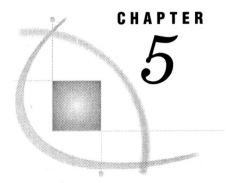

CHAPTER
5

SAS Variables

Definition of SAS Variables   **78**
SAS Variable Attributes   **78**
Ways to Create Variables   **80**
   Overview   **80**
   Using an Assignment Statement   **81**
   Reading Data with the INPUT Statement in a DATA Step   **82**
   Specifying a New Variable in a FORMAT or an INFORMAT Statement   **82**
   Specifying a New Variable in a LENGTH Statement   **82**
   Specifying a New Variable in an ATTRIB Statement   **83**
   Using the IN= Data Set Option   **83**
Variable Type Conversions   **84**
Aligning Variable Values   **85**
Automatic Variables   **85**
SAS Variable Lists   **86**
   Definition   **86**
   Numbered Range Lists   **86**
   Name Range Lists   **87**
   Name Prefix Lists   **87**
   Special SAS Name Lists   **88**
Dropping, Keeping, and Renaming Variables   **88**
   Using Statements or Data Set Options   **88**
   Using the Input or Output Data Set   **88**
   Order of Application   **89**
   Examples of Dropping, Keeping, and Renaming Variables   **90**
Numeric Precision in SAS Software   **90**
   How SAS Stores Numeric Values   **90**
   Troubleshooting Problems Regarding Floating-Point Representation   **91**
      Overview   **91**
      Floating-Point Representation on IBM Mainframes   **91**
      Floating-Point Representation on OpenVMS   **93**
      Floating-Point Representation Using the IEEE Standard   **94**
      Precision Versus Magnitude   **94**
      Computational Considerations of Fractions   **94**
      Numeric Comparison Considerations   **95**
      Storing Numbers with Less Precision   **95**
      Truncating Numbers and Making Comparisons   **97**
      Determining How Many Bytes Are Needed to Store a Number Accurately   **97**
      Double-Precision Versus Single-Precision Floating-Point Numbers   **98**
      Transferring Data between Operating Systems   **98**

Definition of SAS Variables

variables
> are containers that you create within a program to store and use character and numeric values. Variables have attributes, such as name and type, that enable you to identify them and that define how they can be used.

character variables
> are variables of type *character* that contain alphabetic characters, numeric digits 0 through 9, and other special characters.

numeric variables
> are variables of type *numeric* that are stored as floating-point numbers, including dates and times.

numeric precision
> refers to the degree of accuracy with which numeric variables are stored in your operating environment.

SAS Variable Attributes

A SAS variable has the attributes that are listed in the following table:

Table 5.1 Variable Attributes

Variable Attribute	Possible Values	Default Value
Name	Any valid SAS name. See Chapter 3, "Rules for Words and Names in the SAS Language," on page 15.	None
Type [1]	Numeric and character	Numeric
Length [1]	2 to 8 bytes [2] 1 to 32,767 bytes for character	8 bytes for numeric and character
Format	See "Formats and Informats" on page 27.	BEST12. for numeric, $w. for character
Informat	See "Formats and Informats" on page 27.	$w.d$ for numeric, $w. for character
Label	Up to 256 characters	None
Position in observation	1- n	None
Index type	NONE, SIMPLE, COMPOSITE, or BOTH	None

1   If they are not explicitly defined, a variable's type and length are implicitly defined by its first occurrence in a DATA step.
2   The minimum length is 2 bytes in some operating environments, 3 bytes in others. See the SAS documentation for your operating environment.

Note: Starting with SAS 9.1, the maximum number of variables can be greater than 32,767. The maximum number is dependent on your environment and the file's attributes. △

You can use the CONTENTS procedure, or the functions that are named in the following definitions, to obtain information about a variable's attributes:

name
> identifies a variable. A variable name must conform to SAS naming rules. A SAS name can be up to 32 characters long. The first character must be a letter (A, B, C, . . . , Z) or underscore (_). Subsequent characters can be letters, digits (0 to 9), or underscores. Note that blanks are not allowed. Mixed case variables are allowed. See Chapter 3, "Rules for Words and Names in the SAS Language," on page 15 for more details on mixed case variables.
>
> The names _N_, _ERROR_, _FILE_, _INFILE_, _MSG_, _IORC_, and _CMD_ are reserved for the variables that are generated automatically for a DATA step. Note that SAS products use variable names that start and end with an underscore; it is recommended that you do not use names that start and end with an underscore in your own applications. See "Automatic Variables" on page 85 for more information.
>
> To determine the value of this attribute, use the VNAME or VARNAME function.
>
> *Note:* The rules for variable names that are described in this section apply when the VALIDVARNAME= system option is set to VALIDVARNAME=V7, which is the default setting. Other rules apply when this option is set differently. See Chapter 3, "Rules for Words and Names in the SAS Language," on page 15 for more information. △

type
> identifies a variable as numeric or character. Within a DATA step, a variable is assumed to be numeric unless character is indicated. Numeric values represent numbers, can be read in a variety of ways, and are stored in floating-point format. Character values can contain letters, numbers, and special characters and can be from 1 to 32,767 characters long.
>
> To determine the value of this attribute, use the VTYPE or VARTYPE function.

length
> refers to the number of bytes used to store each of the variable's values in a SAS data set. You can use a LENGTH statement to set the length of both numeric and character variables. Variable lengths specified in a LENGTH statement affect the length of numeric variables only in the output data set; during processing, all numeric variables have a length of 8. Lengths of character variables specified in a LENGTH statement affect both the length during processing and the length in the output data set.
>
> In an INPUT statement, you can assign a length other than the default length to character variables. You can also assign a length to a variable in the ATTRIB statement. A variable that appears for the first time on the left side of an assignment statement has the same length as the expression on the right side of the assignment statement.
>
> To determine the value of this attribute, use the VLENGTH or VARLEN function.

format
> refers to the instructions that SAS uses when printing variable values. If no format is specified, the default format is BEST12. for a numeric variable, and $w. for a character variable. You can assign SAS formats to a variable in the FORMAT or ATTRIB statement. You can use the FORMAT procedure to create your own format for a variable.
>
> To determine the value of this attribute, use the VFORMAT or VARFMT function.

informat

> refers to the instructions that SAS uses when reading data values. If no informat is specified, the default informat is *w.d* for a numeric variable, and $w. for a character variable. You can assign SAS informats to a variable in the INFORMAT or ATTRIB statement. You can use the FORMAT procedure to create your own informat for a variable.
>
> To determine the value of this attribute, use the VINFORMAT or VARINFMT function.

label

> refers to a descriptive label up to 256 characters long. A variable label, which can be printed by some SAS procedures, is useful in report writing. You can assign a label to a variable with a LABEL or ATTRIB statement.
>
> To determine the value of this attribute, use the VLABEL or VARLABEL function.

position in observation

> is determined by the order in which the variables are defined in the DATA step. You can find the position of a variable in the observations of a SAS data set by using the CONTENTS procedure. This attribute is generally not important within the DATA step except in variable lists, such as the following:

```
var rent-phone;
```

> See "SAS Variable Lists" on page 86 for more information.
>
> The positions of variables in a SAS data set affect the order in which they appear in the output of SAS procedures, unless you control the order within your program, for example, with a VAR statement.
>
> To determine the value of this attribute, use the VARNUM function.

index type

> indicates whether the variable is part of an index for the data set. See "Understanding SAS Indexes" on page 518 for more information.
>
> To determine the value of this attribute, use the OUT= option with the CONTENTS procedure to create an output data set. The IDXUSAGE variable in the output data set contains one of the following values for each variable:

Table 5.2 Index Type Attribute Values

Value	Definition
NONE	The variable is not indexed.
SIMPLE	The variable is part of a simple index.
COMPOSITE	The variable is part of one or more composite indexes.
BOTH	The variable is part of both simple and composite indexes.

Ways to Create Variables

Overview

You can create variables in a DATA step in the following ways:

□ using an assignment statement

□ reading data with the INPUT statement in a DATA step

  □ specifying a new variable in a FORMAT or INFORMAT statement
  □ specifying a new variable in a LENGTH statement
  □ specifying a new variable in an ATTRIB statement.

Note: You can also create variables with the FGET function. See *SAS Language Reference: Dictionary* for more information. △

Using an Assignment Statement

In a DATA step, you can create a new variable and assign it a value by using it for the first time on the left side of an assignment statement. SAS determines the length of a variable from its first occurrence in the DATA step. The new variable gets the same type and length as the expression on the right side of the assignment statement.

When the type and length of a variable are not explicitly set, SAS gives the variable a default type and length as shown in the examples in the following table.

Table 5.3 Resulting Variable Types and Lengths Produced When They Are Not Explicitly Set

Expression	Example	Resulting Type of X	Resulting Length of X	Explanation
Numeric variable	`length a 4;` `x=a;`	Numeric variable	8	Default numeric length (8 bytes unless otherwise specified)
Character variable	`length a $ 4;` `x=a;`	Character variable	4	Length of source variable
Character literal	`x='ABC';` `x='ABCDE';`	Character variable	3	Length of first literal encountered

Concatenation of variables	`length a $ 4`
	 `b $ 6`
	 `c $ 2;`
	 `x=a||b||c;`
		Character variable	12	Sum of the lengths of all variables

Concatenation of variables and literal	`length a $ 4;`
	 `x=a||'CAT';`
	 `x=a||'CATNIP';`
		Character variable	7	Sum of the lengths of variables and literals encountered in first assignment statement

If a variable appears for the first time on the right side of an assignment statement, SAS assumes that it is a numeric variable and that its value is missing. If no later statement gives it a value, SAS prints a note in the log that the variable is uninitialized.

Note: A RETAIN statement initializes a variable and can assign it an initial value, even if the RETAIN statement appears after the assignment statement. △

Reading Data with the INPUT Statement in a DATA Step

When you read raw data in SAS by using an INPUT statement, you define variables based on positions in the raw data. You can use one of the following methods with the INPUT statement to provide information to SAS about how the raw data is organized:

☐ column input

☐ list input (simple or modified)

☐ formatted input

☐ named input.

See *SAS Language Reference: Dictionary* for more information about using each method.

The following example uses simple list input to create a SAS data set named GEMS and defines four variables based on the data provided:

```
data gems;
   input Name $ Color $ Carats Owner $;
   datalines;
emerald green 1 smith
sapphire blue 2 johnson
ruby red 1 clark
;
```

Specifying a New Variable in a FORMAT or an INFORMAT Statement

You can create a variable and specify its format or informat with a FORMAT or an INFORMAT statement. For example, the following FORMAT statement creates a variable named Sale_Price with a format of 6.2 in a new data set named SALES:

```
data sales;
   Sale_Price=49.99;
   format Sale_Price 6.2;
run;
```

SAS creates a numeric variable with the name Sale_Price and a length of 8.

See *SAS Language Reference: Dictionary* for more information about using the FORMAT and INFORMAT statements.

Specifying a New Variable in a LENGTH Statement

You can use the LENGTH statement to create a variable and set the length of the variable, as in the following example:

```
data sales;
   length Salesperson $20;
run;
```

For character variables, you must allow for the longest possible value in the first statement that uses the variable, because you cannot change the length with a subsequent LENGTH statement within the same DATA step. The maximum length of any character variable in SAS is 32,767 bytes. For numeric variables, you can change the length of the variable by using a subsequent LENGTH statement.

When SAS assigns a value to a character variable, it pads the value with blanks or truncates the value on the right side, if necessary, to make it match the length of the target variable. Consider the following statements:

```
length address1 address2 address3 $ 200;
address3=address1||address2;
```

Because the length of ADDRESS3 is 200 bytes, only the first 200 bytes of the concatenation (the value of ADDRESS1) are assigned to ADDRESS3. You might be able to avoid this problem by using the TRIM function to remove trailing blanks from ADDRESS1 before performing the concatenation, as follows:

```
address3=trim(address1)||address2;
```

See *SAS Language Reference: Dictionary* for more information about using the LENGTH statement.

Specifying a New Variable in an ATTRIB Statement

The ATTRIB statement enables you to specify one or more of the following variable attributes for an existing variable:

- □ FORMAT=
- □ INFORMAT=
- □ LABEL=
- □ LENGTH=.

If the variable does not already exist, one or more of the FORMAT=, INFORMAT=, and LENGTH= attributes can be used to create a new variable. For example, the following DATA step creates a variable named Flavor in a data set named LOLLIPOPS:

```
data lollipops;
   Flavor="Cherry";
   attrib Flavor format=$10.;
run;
```

Note: You cannot create a new variable by using a LABEL statement or the ATTRIB statement's LABEL= attribute by itself; labels can only be applied to existing variables. △

See *SAS Language Reference: Dictionary* for more information about using the ATTRIB statement.

Using the IN= Data Set Option

The IN= data set option creates a special boolean variable that indicates whether the data set contributed data to the current observation. The variable has a value of 1 when true, and a value of 0 when false. You can use IN= on the SET, MERGE, and UPDATE statements in a DATA step.

The following example shows a merge of the OLD and NEW data sets where the IN= option is used to create a variable named X that indicates whether the NEW data set contributed data to the observation:

```
data master missing;
   merge old new(in=x);
   by id;
   if x=0 then output missing;
   else output master;
run;
```

Variable Type Conversions

If you define a numeric variable and assign the result of a character expression to it, SAS tries to convert the character result of the expression to a numeric value and to execute the statement. If the conversion is not possible, SAS prints a note to the log, assigns the numeric variable a value of missing, and sets the automatic variable _ERROR_ to 1. For a listing of the rules by which SAS automatically converts character variables to numeric variables and vice-versa, see "Automatic Numeric-Character Conversion" on page 116.

If you define a character variable and assign the result of a numeric expression to it, SAS tries to convert the numeric result of the expression to a character value using the BEST*w.* format, where *w* is the width of the character variable and has a maximum value of 32. SAS then tries to execute the statement. If the character variable you use is not long enough to contain a character representation of the number, SAS prints a note to the log and assigns the character variable asterisks. If the value is too small, SAS provides no error message and assigns the character variable the character zero (0).

Output 5.1   Automatic Variable Type Conversions (partial SAS log)

```
4
5              data _null_;
6                 x= 3626885;
7                 length y $ 4;
8                 y=x;
9                 put y;

36E5
NOTE: Numeric values have been converted to character
      values at the places given by:
      (Number of times) at (Line):(Column).
      1 at 8:5

10             data _null_;
11                x1= 3626885;
12                length y1 $ 1;
13                y1=x1;
14                xs=0.000005;
15                length ys $ 1;
16                ys=xs;
17                put y1= ys=;
18             run;

NOTE: Invalid character data, XL=3626885.00 ,
      at line 13 column 6.
YL=* YS=0
XL=3626885 YL=* XS=5E-6 YS=0 _ERROR_=1 _N_=1
NOTE: Numeric values have been converted
      to character values at the places
      given by: (Number of times) at
      (Line):(Column).
      1 at 13:6
      1 at 16:6
```

In the first DATA step of the example, SAS is able to fit the value of Y into a 4-byte field by representing its value in scientific notation. In the second DATA step, SAS cannot fit the value of YL into a 1-byte field and displays an asterisk (*) instead.

Aligning Variable Values

In SAS, numeric variables are automatically aligned. You can further control their alignment by using a format.

However, when you assign a character value in an assignment statement, SAS stores the value as it appears in the statement and does not perform any alignment. Output 5.2 illustrates the character value alignment produced by the following program:

```
data aircode;
   input city $1-13;
   length airport $ 10;
   if city='San Francisco' then airport='SFO';
      else if city='Honolulu' then airport='HNL';
      else if city='New York' then airport='JFK or EWR';
      else if city='Miami' then airport='   MIA   ';
   datalines;
San Francisco
Honolulu
New York
Miami
;

proc print data=aircode;
run;
```

This example produces the following output:

Output 5.2   Output from the PRINT Procedure

```
                      The SAS System

          OBS     CITY               AIRPORT

           1      San Francisco      SFO
           2      Honolulu           HNL
           3      New York           JFK or EWR
           4      Miami                 MIA
```

Automatic Variables

Automatic variables are created automatically by the DATA step or by DATA step statements. These variables are added to the program data vector but are not output to the data set being created. The values of automatic variables are retained from one iteration of the DATA step to the next, rather than set to missing.

Automatic variables that are created by specific statements are documented with those statements. For examples, see the BY statement, the MODIFY statement, and the WINDOW statement in *SAS Language Reference: Dictionary*.

Two automatic variables are created by every DATA step: _N_ and _ERROR_.

_N_
> is initially set to 1. Each time the DATA step loops past the DATA statement, the variable _N_ increments by 1. The value of _N_ represents the number of times the DATA step has iterated.

ERROR
> is 0 by default but is set to 1 whenever an error is encountered, such as an input data error, a conversion error, or a math error, as in division by 0 or a floating point overflow. You can use the value of this variable to help locate errors in data records and to print an error message to the SAS log.
>
> For example, either of the two following statements writes to the SAS log, during each iteration of the DATA step, the contents of an input record in which an input error is encountered:

```
if _error_=1 then put _infile_;
```

```
if _error_ then put _infile_;
```

SAS Variable Lists

Definition

A SAS *variable list* is an abbreviated method of referring to a list of variable names. SAS allows you to use the following variable lists:

☐ numbered range lists

☐ name range lists

☐ name prefix lists

☐ special SAS name lists.

With the exception of the numbered range list, you refer to the variables in a variable list in the same order that SAS uses to keep track of the variables. SAS keeps track of active variables in the order that the compiler encounters them within a DATA step, whether they are read from existing data sets, an external file, or created in the step. In a numbered range list, you can refer to variables that were created in any order, provided that their names have the same prefix.

You can use variable lists in many SAS statements and data set options, including those that define variables. However, they are especially useful *after* you define all of the variables in your SAS program because they provide a quick way to reference existing groups of data.

Note: Only the numbered range list is allowed in the RENAME= option. △

Numbered Range Lists

Numbered range lists require you to have a series of variables with the same name, except for the last character or characters, which are consecutive numbers. For example, the following two lists refer to the same variables:

```
x1,x2,x3,...,xn
```

```
x1-xn
```

In a numbered range list, you can begin with any number and end with any number as long as you do not violate the rules for user-supplied variable names and the numbers are consecutive.

For example, suppose you decide to give some of your numeric variables sequential names, as in VAR1, VAR2, and so on. Then, you can write an INPUT statement as follows:

```
input idnum name $ var1-var3;
```

Note that the character variable NAME is not included in the abbreviated list.

Name Range Lists

Name range lists rely on the order of variable definition, as shown in the following table:

Table 5.4 Name Range Lists

Variable list	Included variables
x-a	all variables in order of variable definition, from X to A inclusive.
x-numeric-a	all numeric variables from X to A inclusive.
x-character-a	all character variables from X to A inclusive.

You can use the VARNUM option in PROC CONTENTS to print the variables in the order of definition.

For example, consider the following INPUT statement:

```
input idnum name $ weight pulse chins;
```

In later statements you can use these variable lists:

```
/* keeps only the numeric variables idnum, weight, and pulse */

keep idnum-numeric-pulse;
```

```
/* keeps the consecutive variables name, weight, and pulse */

keep name-pulse;
```

Name Prefix Lists

Some SAS functions and statements allow you to use a name prefix list to refer to all variables that begin with a specified character string:

```
sum(of SALES:)
```

tells SAS to calculate the sum of all the variables that begin with "SALES," such as SALES_JAN, SALES_FEB, and SALES_MAR.

Special SAS Name Lists

Special SAS name lists include

NUMERIC
     specifies all numeric variables that are already defined in the current DATA step.

CHARACTER
     specifies all character variables that are currently defined in the current DATA step.

ALL
     specifies all variables that are currently defined in the current DATA step.

Dropping, Keeping, and Renaming Variables

Using Statements or Data Set Options

The DROP, KEEP, and RENAME statements or the DROP=, KEEP=, and RENAME= data set options control which variables are processed or output during the DATA step. You can use one or a combination of these statements and data set options to achieve the results you want. The action taken by SAS depends largely on whether you

□ use a statement or data set option or both

□ specify the data set options on an input or an output data set.

The following table summarizes the general differences between the DROP, KEEP, and RENAME statements and the DROP=, KEEP=, and RENAME= data set options.

Table 5.5   Statements versus Data Set Options for Dropping, Keeping, and Renaming Variables

Statements	Data Set Options
apply to output data sets only.	apply to output or input data sets.
affect all output data sets.	affect individual data sets.
can be used in DATA steps only.	can be used in DATA steps and PROC steps.
can appear anywhere in DATA steps.	must immediately follow the name of each data set to which they apply.

Using the Input or Output Data Set

You must also consider whether you want to drop, keep, or rename the variable before it is read into the program data vector or as it is written to the new SAS data set. If you use the DROP, KEEP, or RENAME statement, the action always occurs as the variables are written to the output data set. With SAS data set options, where you use the option determines when the action occurs. If the option is used on an input data set, the variable is dropped, kept, or renamed before it is read into the program data vector. If used on an output data set, the data set option is applied as the variable is written to the new SAS data set. (In the DATA step, an input data set is one that is specified in a SET, MERGE, or UPDATE statement. An output data set is one that is specified in the DATA statement.) Consider the following facts when you make your decision:

□ If variables are not written to the output data set and they do not require any processing, using an input data set option to exclude them from the DATA step is more efficient.

□ If you want to rename a variable before processing it in a DATA step, you must use the RENAME= data set option in the input data set.

□ If the action applies to output data sets, you can use either a statement or a data set option in the output data set.

The following table summarizes the action of data set options and statements when they are specified for input and output data sets. The last column of the table tells whether the variable is available for processing in the DATA step. If you want to rename the variable, use the information in the last column.

Table 5.6 Status of Variables and Variable Names When Dropping, Keeping, and Renaming Variables

Where Specified	Data Set Option or Statement	Purpose	Status of Variable or Variable Name
Input data set	DROP= KEEP=	includes or excludes variables from processing	if excluded, variables are not available for use in DATA step
	RENAME=	changes name of variable before processing	use new name in program statements and output data set options; use old name in other input data set options
Output data set	DROP, KEEP	specifies which variables are written to all output data sets	all variables available for processing
	RENAME	changes name of variables in all output data sets	use old name in program statements; use new name in output data set options
	DROP= KEEP=	specifies which variables are written to individual output data sets	all variables are available for processing
	RENAME=	changes name of variables in individual output data sets	use old name in program statements and other output data set options

Order of Application

If your program requires that you use more than one data set option or a combination of data set options and statements, it is helpful to know that SAS drops, keeps, and renames variables in the following order:

□ First, options on input data sets are evaluated left to right within SET, MERGE, and UPDATE statements. DROP= and KEEP= options are applied before the RENAME= option.

□ Next, DROP and KEEP statements are applied, followed by the RENAME statement.

□ Finally, options on output data sets are evaluated left to right within the DATA statement. DROP= and KEEP= options are applied before the RENAME= option.

Examples of Dropping, Keeping, and Renaming Variables

The following examples show specific ways to handle dropping, keeping, and renaming variables:

□ This example uses the DROP= and RENAME= data set options and the INPUT function to convert the variable POPRANK from character to numeric. The name POPRANK is changed to TEMPVAR before processing so that a new variable POPRANK can be written to the output data set. Note that the variable TEMPVAR is dropped from the output data set and that the new name TEMPVAR is used in the program statements.

```
data newstate(drop=tempvar);
   length poprank 8;
   set state(rename=(poprank=tempvar));
   poprank=input(tempvar,8.);
run;
```

□ This example uses the DROP statement and the DROP= data set option to control the output of variables to two new SAS data sets. The DROP statement applies to both data sets, CORN and BEAN. You must use the RENAME= data set option to rename the output variables BEANWT and CORNWT in each data set.

```
data corn(rename=(cornwt=yield) drop=beanwt)
     bean(rename=(beanwt=yield) drop=cornwt);
   set harvest;
   if crop='corn' then output corn;
   else if crop='bean' then output bean;
   drop crop;
run;
```

□ This example shows how to use data set options in the DATA statement and the RENAME statement together. Note that the new name QTRTOT is used in the DROP= data set option.

```
data qtr1 qtr2 ytd(drop=qtrtot);
   set ytdsales;
   if qtr=1 then output qtr1;
   else if qtr=2 then output qtr2;
   else output ytd;
   rename total=qtrtot;
run;
```

Numeric Precision in SAS Software

How SAS Stores Numeric Values

To store numbers of large magnitude and to perform computations that require many digits of precision to the right of the decimal point, SAS stores all numeric values using *floating-point*, or real binary, representation. Floating-point representation is an implementation of what is generally known as scientific notation, in which values are represented as numbers between 0 and 1 times a power of 10. The following is an example of a number in scientific notation:

$$.1234 \times 10^4$$

Numbers in scientific notation are comprised of the following parts:

☐ The *base* is the number raised to a power; in this example, the base is 10.

☐ The *mantissa* is the number multiplied by the base; in this example, the mantissa is .1234.

☐ The *exponent* is the power to which the base is raised; in this example, the exponent is 4.

Floating-point representation is a form of scientific notation, except that on most operating systems the base is not 10, but is either 2 or 16. The following table summarizes various representations of floating-point numbers that are stored in 8 bytes.

Table 5.7 Summary of Floating-Point Numbers Stored in 8 Bytes

Representation	Base	Exponent Bits	Maximum Mantissa Bits
IBM mainframe	16	7	56
IEEE	2	11	52

SAS allows for truncated floating-point numbers via the LENGTH statement, which reduces the number of mantissa bits. For more information on the effects of truncated lengths, see "Storing Numbers with Less Precision" on page 95.

Troubleshooting Problems Regarding Floating-Point Representation

Overview

In most situations, the way that SAS stores numeric values does not affect you as a user. However, floating-point representation can account for anomalies you might notice in SAS program behavior. The following sections identify the types of problems that can occur in various operating environments and how you can anticipate and avoid them.

Floating-Point Representation on IBM Mainframes

SAS for z/OS uses the traditional IBM mainframe floating-point representation as follows:

```
SEEEEEEE MMMMMMMM MMMMMMMM MMMMMMMM
byte 1   byte 2   byte 3   byte 4


MMMMMMMM MMMMMMMM MMMMMMMM MMMMMMMM
byte 5   byte 6   byte 7   byte 8
```

This representation corresponds to bytes of data with each character being 1 bit, as follows:

□ The S in byte 1 is the *sign bit* of the number. A value of 0 in the sign bit is used to represent positive numbers.

□ The seven E characters in byte 1 represent a binary integer known as the *characteristic*. The characteristic represents a signed exponent and is obtained by adding the bias to the actual exponent. The *bias* is an offset used to allow for both negative and positive exponents with the bias representing 0. If a bias is not used, an additional sign bit for the exponent must be allocated. For example, if a system employs a bias of 64, a characteristic with the value 66 represents an exponent of +2, while a characteristic of 61 represents an exponent of -3.

□ The remaining M characters in bytes 2 through 8 represent the bits of the mantissa. There is an implied *radix point* before the leftmost bit of the mantissa; therefore, the mantissa is always less than 1. The term radix point is used instead of decimal point because decimal point implies that you are working with decimal (base 10) numbers, which might not be the case. The radix point can be thought of as the generic form of decimal point.

The exponent has a base associated with it. Do not confuse this with the base in which the exponent is represented; the exponent is always represented in binary, but the exponent is used to determine how many times the base should be multiplied by the mantissa. In the case of the IBM mainframes, the exponent's base is 16. For other machines, it is commonly either 2 or 16.

Each bit in the mantissa represents a fraction whose numerator is 1 and whose denominator is a power of 2. For example, the leftmost bit in byte 2 represents $\left(\frac{1}{2}\right)^1$, the next bit represents $\left(\frac{1}{2}\right)^2$, and so on. In other words, the mantissa is the sum of a series of fractions such as $\frac{1}{2}, \frac{1}{4}, \frac{1}{8}$, and so on. Therefore, for any floating-point number to be represented exactly, you must be able to express it as the previously mentioned sum. For example, 100 is represented as the following expression:

$$\left(\frac{1}{4} + \frac{1}{8} + \frac{1}{64}\right) \times 16^2$$

To illustrate how the above expression is obtained, two examples follow. The first example is in base 10. The value 100 is represented as follows:

```
100.
```

The period in this number is the radix point. The mantissa must be less than 1; therefore, you normalize this value by shifting the radix point three places to the right, which produces the following value:

$$.100$$

Because the radix point is shifted three places to the right, 3 is the exponent:

$$.100 \times 10^3 = 100$$

The second example is in base 16. In hexadecimal notation, 100 (base 10) is written as follows:

64.

Shifting the radix point two places to the left produces the following value:

.64

Shifting the radix point also produces an exponent of 2, as in:

$$.64 \times 16^{2}$$

The binary value of this number is **.01100100**, which can be represented in the following expression:

$$\left(\frac{1}{2}\right)^{2} + \left(\frac{1}{2}\right)^{3} + \left(\frac{1}{2}\right)^{6} = \frac{1}{4} + \frac{1}{8} + \frac{1}{64}$$

In this example, the exponent is 2. To represent the exponent, you add the bias of 64 to the exponent. The hexadecimal representation of the resulting value, 66, is 42. The binary representation is as follows:

```
01000010 01100100 00000000 00000000
00000000 00000000 00000000 00000000
```

Floating-Point Representation on OpenVMS

On OpenVMS, SAS stores numeric values in the D-floating format, which has the following scheme:

```
MMMMMMMM MMMMMMMM MMMMMMMM MMMMMMMM
byte 8   byte 7   byte 6   byte 5

MMMMMMMM MMMMMMMM SEEEEEEE EMMMMMMM
byte 4   byte 3   byte 2   byte 1
```

In D-floating format, the exponent is 8 bits instead of 7, but uses base 2 instead of base 16 and a bias of 128, which means the magnitude of the D-floating format is not as great as the magnitude of the IBM representation. The mantissa of the D-floating format is, physically, 55 bits. However, all floating-point values under OpenVMS are normalized, which means it is guaranteed that the high-order bit will always be 1. Because of this guarantee, there is no need to physically represent the high-order bit in the mantissa; therefore, the high-order bit is hidden.

For example, the decimal value 100 represented in binary is as follows:

```
01100100.
```

This value can be normalized by shifting the radix point as follows:

```
0.1100100
```

Because the radix was shifted to the left seven places, the exponent, 7 plus the bias of 128, is 135. Represented in binary, the number is as follows:

```
10000111
```

To represent the mantissa, subtract the hidden bit from the fraction field:

```
.100100
```

You can combine the sign (0), the exponent, and the mantissa to produce the D-floating format:

```
MMMMMMMM MMMMMMMM MMMMMMMM MMMMMMMM
00000000 00000000 00000000 00000000

MMMMMMMM MMMMMMMM SEEEEEEE EMMMMMMM
00000000 00000000 01000011 11001000
```

Floating-Point Representation Using the IEEE Standard

The Institute of Electrical and Electronic Engineers (IEEE) representation is used by many operating systems, including Windows and UNIX. The IEEE representation uses an 11-bit exponent with a base of 2 and bias of 1023, which means that it has much greater magnitude than the IBM mainframe representation, but sometimes at the expense of 3 bits less in the mantissa. The value of 1 represented by the IEEE standard is as follows:

```
3F F0 00 00 00 00 00 00
```

Precision Versus Magnitude

As discussed in previous sections, floating-point representation allows for numbers of very large magnitude (numbers such as 2 to the 30th power) and high degrees of precision (many digits to the right of the decimal place). However, operating systems differ on how much precision and how much magnitude they allow.

In "How SAS Stores Numeric Values" on page 90, you can see that the number of exponent bits and mantissa bits varies. The more bits that are reserved for the mantissa, the more precise the number; the more bits that are reserved for the exponent, the greater the magnitude the number can have.

Whether precision or magnitude is more important depends on the characteristics of your data. For example, if you are working with physics applications, very large numbers may be needed, and magnitude is probably more important. However, if you are working with banking applications, where every digit is important but the number of digits is not great, then precision is more important. Most often, SAS applications need a moderate amount of both precision and magnitude, which is sufficiently provided by floating-point representation.

Computational Considerations of Fractions

Regardless of how much precision is available, there is still the problem that some numbers cannot be represented exactly. In the decimal number system, the fraction 1/3 cannot be represented exactly in decimal notation. Likewise, most decimal fractions (for example, .1) cannot be represented exactly in base 2 or base 16 numbering systems. This is the principle reason for difficulty in storing fractional numbers in floating-point representation.

Consider the IBM mainframe representation of .1:

```
40 19 99 99 99 99 99 99
```

Notice the trailing 9 digit, similar to the trailing 3 digit in the attempted decimal representation of 1/3 (.3333 ...). This lack of precision is aggravated by arithmetic operations. Consider what would happen if you added the decimal representation of 1/3 several times. When you add .33333 ... to .99999 ... , the theoretical answer is 1.33333 ... 2, but in practice, this answer is not possible. The sums become imprecise as the values continue.

Likewise, the same process happens when the following DATA step is executed:

```
data _null_;
   do i=-1 to 1 by .1;
      if i=0 then put 'AT ZERO';
   end;
run;
```

The AT ZERO message in the DATA step is never printed because the accumulation of the imprecise number introduces enough error that the exact value of 0 is never encountered. The number is close, but never exactly 0. This problem is easily resolved by explicitly rounding with each iteration, as the following statements illustrate:

```
data _null_;
   i=-1;
   do while(i<=1);
      i=round(i+.1,.001);
      if i=0 then put 'AT ZERO';
   end;
run;
```

Numeric Comparison Considerations

As discussed in "Computational Considerations of Fractions" on page 94, imprecision can cause problems with computations. Imprecision can also cause problems with comparisons. Consider the following example in which the PUT statement is not executed:

```
data _null_;
   x=1/3;
   if x=.33333 then put 'MATCH';
run;
```

However, if you add the ROUND function, as in the following example, the PUT statement is executed:

```
data _null_;
   x=1/3;
   if round(x,.00001)=.33333 then put 'MATCH';
run;
```

In general, if you are doing comparisons with fractional values, it is good practice to use the ROUND function.

Storing Numbers with Less Precision

As discussed in "How SAS Stores Numeric Values" on page 90, SAS allows for numeric values to be stored on disk with less than full precision. Use the LENGTH statement to dictate the number of bytes that are used to store the floating-point number. Use the LENGTH statement carefully to avoid significant data loss.

For example, the IBM mainframe representation uses 8 bytes for full precision, but you can store as few as 2 bytes on disk. The value 1 is represented as 41 10 00 00 00 00 00 00 in 8 bytes. In 2 bytes, it would be truncated to 41 10. You still have the full range of magnitude because the exponent remains intact; there are simply fewer digits involved. A decrease in the number of digits means either fewer digits to the right of the decimal place or fewer digits to the left of the decimal place before trailing zeroes must be used.

For example, consider the number 1234567890, which would be .1234567890 to the 10th power of 10 (in base 10). If you have only five digits of precision, the number becomes 123460000 (rounding up). Note that this is the case regardless of the power of 10 that is used (.12346, 12.346, .0000012346, and so on).

The only reason to truncate length by using the LENGTH statement is to save disk space. All values are expanded to full size to perform computations in DATA and PROC steps. In addition, you must be careful in your choice of lengths, as the previous discussion shows.

Consider a length of 2 bytes on an IBM mainframe system. This value allows for 1 byte to store the exponent and sign, and 1 byte for the mantissa. The largest value that can be stored in 1 byte is 255. Therefore, if the exponent is 0 (meaning 16 to the 0th power, or 1 multiplied by the mantissa), then the largest integer that can be stored with complete certainty is 255. However, some larger integers can be stored because they are multiples of 16. For example, consider the 8-byte representation of the numbers 256 to 272 in the following table:

Table 5.8   Representation of the Numbers 256 to 272 in Eight Bytes

Value	Sign/Exp	Mantissa 1	Mantissa 2-7	Considerations
256	43	10	000000000000	trailing zeros; multiple of 16
257	43	10	100000000000	extra byte needed
258	43	10	200000000000	
259	43	10	300000000000	
.				
.				
.				
271	43	10	F00000000000	
272	43	11	000000000000	trailing zeros; multiple of 16

The numbers from 257 to 271 cannot be stored exactly in the first 2 bytes; a third byte is needed to store the number precisely. As a result, the following code produces misleading results:

```
data temp;
    length x 2;
    x=257;
    y1=x+1;
run;

data _null_;
    set temp;
    if x=257 then put 'FOUND';
    y2=x+1;
run;
```

The PUT statement is never executed because the value of X is actually 256 (the value 257 truncated to 2 bytes). Recall that 256 is stored in 2 bytes as 4310, but 257 is also stored in 2 bytes as 4310, with the third byte of 10 truncated.

You receive no warning that the value of 257 is truncated in the first DATA step. Note, however, that Y1 has the value 258 because the values of X are kept in full, 8-byte floating-point representation in the program data vector. The value is only truncated when stored in a SAS data set. Y2 has the value 257, because X is truncated before the number is read into the program data vector.

CAUTION:
Do not use the LENGTH statement if your variable values are not integers. Fractional numbers lose precision if truncated. Also, use the LENGTH statement to truncate values only when disk space is limited. Refer to the length table in the SAS documentation for your operating environment for maximum values. △

Truncating Numbers and Making Comparisons

The TRUNC function truncates a number to a requested length and then expands the number back to full length. The truncation and subsequent expansion duplicate the effect of storing numbers in less than full length and then reading them. For example, if the variable

```
x=1/3;
```

is stored with a length of 3, then the following comparison is not true:

```
if x=1/3 then ...;
```

However, adding the TRUNC function makes the comparison true, as in the following:

```
if x=trunc(1/3,3) then ...;
```

Determining How Many Bytes Are Needed to Store a Number Accurately

To determine the minimum number of bytes needed to store a value accurately, you can use the TRUNC function. For example, the following program finds the minimum length of bytes (MINLEN) needed for numbers stored in a native SAS data set named NUMBERS. The data set NUMBERS contains the variable VALUE. VALUE contains a range of numbers, in this example, from 269 to 272:

```
data numbers;
   input value;
   datalines;
269
270
271
272
;

data temp;
   set numbers;
   x=value;
   do L=8 to 1 by -1;
      if x NE trunc(x,L) then
      do;
         minlen=L+1;
         output;
         return;
```

```
        end;
    end;
run;

proc print noobs;
    var value minlen;
run;
```

The following output shows the results from this code.

Output 5.3   Using the TRUNC Function

```
                    The SAS System

                 VALUE      MINLEN

                  269          3
                  270          3
                  271          3
                  272          2
```

Note that the minimum length required for the value 271 is greater than the minimum required for the value 272. This fact illustrates that it is possible for the largest number in a range of numbers to require fewer bytes of storage than a smaller number. If precision is needed for all numbers in a range, you should obtain the minimum length for all the numbers, not just the largest one.

Double-Precision Versus Single-Precision Floating-Point Numbers

You might have data created by an external program that you want to read into a SAS data set. If the data is in floating-point representation, you can use the RB*w.d* informat to read in the data. However, there are exceptions.

The RB*w.d* informat might truncate double-precision floating-point numbers if the *w* value is less than the size of the double-precision floating-point number (8 on all the operating systems discussed in this section). Therefore, the RB8. informat corresponds to a full 8-byte floating point. The RB4. informat corresponds to an 8-byte floating point truncated to 4 bytes, exactly the same as a LENGTH 4 in the DATA step.

An 8-byte floating point that is truncated to 4 bytes might not be the same as *float* in a C program. In the C language, an 8-byte floating-point number is called a *double*. In FORTRAN, it is a REAL*8. In IBM's PL/I, it is a FLOAT BINARY(53). A 4-byte floating-point number is called a *float* in the C language, REAL*4 in FORTRAN, and FLOAT BINARY(21) in IBM's PL/I.

On the IBM mainframes, a single-precision floating-point number is exactly the same as a double-precision number truncated to 4 bytes. On operating systems that use the IEEE standard, this is not the case; a single-precision floating-point number uses a different number of bits for its exponent and uses a different bias, so that reading in values using the RB4. informat does not produce the expected results.

Transferring Data between Operating Systems

The problems of precision and magnitude when you use floating-point numbers are not confined to a single operating system. Additional problems can arise when you move from one operating system to another, unless you use caution. This section discusses factors to consider when you are transporting data sets with very large or very small numeric values by using the UPLOAD and DOWNLOAD procedures, the CPORT and CIMPORT procedures, or transport engines.

Table 5.7 on page 91 shows the maximum number of digits of the base, exponent, and mantissa. Because there are differences in the maximum values that can be stored in different operating environments, there might be problems in transferring your floating-point data from one machine to another.

Consider, for example, transporting data between an IBM mainframe and a PC. The IBM mainframe has a range limit of approximately .54E–78 to .72E76 (and their negative equivalents and 0) for its floating-point numbers. Other machines, such as the PC, have wider limits (the PC has an upper limit of approximately 1E308). Therefore, if you are transferring numbers in the magnitude of 1E100 from a PC to a mainframe, you lose that magnitude. During data transfer, the number is set to the minimum or maximum allowable on that operating system, so 1E100 on a PC is converted to a value that is approximately .72E76 on an IBM mainframe.

CAUTION:

Transfer of data between machines can affect numeric precision. If you are transferring data from an IBM mainframe to a PC, notice that the number of bits for the mantissa is 4 less than that for an IBM mainframe, which means you lose 4 bits when moving to a PC. This precision and magnitude difference is a factor when moving from one operating environment to any other where the floating-point representation is different. △

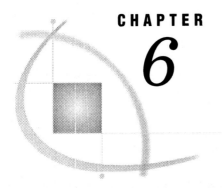

CHAPTER

6

Missing Values

Definition of Missing Values   **101**
Special Missing Values   **102**
    Definition   **102**
    Tips   **102**
    Example   **102**
Order of Missing Values   **103**
    Numeric Variables   **103**
    Character Variables   **104**
When Variable Values Are Automatically Set to Missing by SAS   **104**
    When Reading Raw Data   **104**
    When Reading a SAS Data Set   **105**
When Missing Values Are Generated by SAS   **105**
    Propagation of Missing Values in Calculations   **105**
    Illegal Operations   **105**
    Illegal Character-to-Numeric Conversions   **105**
    Special Missing Values   **106**
    Preventing Propagation of Missing Values   **106**
Working with Missing Values   **107**
    How to Represent Missing Values in Raw Data   **107**
    How to Set Variable Values to Missing in a DATA Step   **107**
    How to Check for Missing Values in a DATA Step   **108**

Definition of Missing Values

missing value
    is a value that indicates that no data value is stored for the variable in the current observation. There are three kinds of missing values:

      □ numeric

      □ character

      □ special numeric.

By default, SAS prints a missing numeric value as a single period (.) and a missing character value as a blank space. See "Special Missing Values" on page 102 for more information about special numeric missing values.

Special Missing Values

Definition

special missing value
   is a type of numeric missing value that enables you to represent different
   categories of missing data by using the letters A-Z or an underscore.

Tips

□ SAS accepts either uppercase or lowercase letters. Values are displayed and
   printed as uppercase.

□ If you do not begin a special numeric missing value with a period, SAS identifies it
   as a variable name. Therefore, to use a special numeric missing value in a SAS
   expression or assignment statement, you must begin the value with a period,
   followed by the letter or underscore, as in the following example:

```
x=.d;
```

□ When SAS prints a special missing value, it prints only the letter or underscore.

□ When data values contain characters in numeric fields that you want SAS to
   interpret as special missing values, use the MISSING statement to specify those
   characters. For further information, see the MISSING statement in *SAS
   Language Reference: Dictionary*.

Example

The following example uses data from a marketing research company. Five testers
were hired to test five different products for ease of use and effectiveness. If a tester
was absent, there is no rating to report, and the value is recorded with an X for
"absent." If the tester was unable to test the product adequately, there is no rating, and
the value is recorded with an I for "incomplete test." The following program reads the
data and displays the resulting SAS data set. Note the special missing values in the
first and third data lines:

```
data period_a;
  missing X I;
    input Id $4. Foodpr1 Foodpr2 Foodpr3 Coffeem1 Coffeem2;
    datalines;
1001 115 45 65 I 78
1002 86 27 55 72 86
1004 93 52 X 76 88
1015 73 35 43 112 108
1027 101 127 39 76 79
  ;

proc print data=period_a;
  title 'Results of Test Period A';
  footnote1 'X indicates TESTER ABSENT';
  footnote2 'I indicates TEST WAS INCOMPLETE';
run;
```

The following output is produced:

Output 6.1   Output with Multiple Missing Values

```
                       Results of Test Period A
     Obs    Id    Foodpr1    Foodpr2    Foodpr3    Coffeem1    Coffeem2

      1    1001      115         45         65          I          78
      2    1002       86         27         55         72          86
      3    1004       93         52          X         76          88
      4    1015       73         35         43        112         108
      5    1027      101        127         39         76          79

                   X indicates TESTER ABSENT
                 I indicates TEST WAS INCOMPLETE
```

Order of Missing Values

Numeric Variables

Within SAS, a missing value for a numeric variable is smaller than all numbers; if you sort your data set by a numeric variable, observations with missing values for that variable appear first in the sorted data set. For numeric variables, you can compare special missing values with numbers and with each other. Table 6.1 on page 103 shows the sorting order of numeric values.

Table 6.1   Numeric Value Sort Order

Sort Order	Symbol	Description
smallest	._	underscore
	.	period
	.A-.Z	special missing values A (smallest) through Z (largest)
	-*n*	negative numbers
	0	zero
largest	+*n*	positive numbers

For example, the numeric missing value (.) is sorted before the special numeric missing value .A, and both are sorted before the special missing value .Z. SAS does not distinguish between lowercase and uppercase letters when sorting special numeric missing values.

Note: The numeric missing value sort order is the same regardless of whether your system uses the ASCII or EBCDIC collating sequence. △

Character Variables

Missing values of character variables are smaller than any printable character value. Therefore, when you sort a data set by a character variable, observations with missing (blank) values of the BY variable always appear before observations in which values of the BY variable contain only printable characters. However, some usually unprintable characters (for example, machine carriage-control characters and real or binary numeric data that have been read in error as character data) have values less than the blank. Therefore, when your data includes unprintable characters, missing values may not appear first in a sorted data set.

When Variable Values Are Automatically Set to Missing by SAS

When Reading Raw Data

At the beginning of each iteration of the DATA step, SAS sets the value of each variable you create in the DATA step to missing, with the following exceptions:

- □ variables named in a RETAIN statement
- □ variables created in a SUM statement
- □ data elements in a _TEMPORARY_ array
- □ variables created with options in the FILE or INFILE statements
- □ variables created by the FGET function
- □ data elements which are initialized in an ARRAY statement
- □ automatic variables.

SAS replaces the missing values as it encounters values that you assign to the variables. Thus, if you use program statements to create new variables, their values in each observation are missing until you assign the values in an assignment statement, as shown in the following DATA step:

```
data new;
   input x;
   if x=1 then y=2;
   datalines;
4
1
3
1
;
```

This DATA step produces a SAS data set with the following variable values:

```
OBS   X   Y
 1    4   .
 2    1   2
 3    3   .
 4    1   2
```

When X equals 1, the value of Y is set to 2. Since no other statements set Y's value when X is not equal to 1, Y remains missing (.) for those observations.

When Reading a SAS Data Set

When variables are read with a SET, MERGE, or UPDATE statement, SAS sets the values to missing only before the first iteration of the DATA step. (If you use a BY statement, the variable values are also set to missing when the BY group changes.) The variables retain their values until new values become available; for example, through an assignment statement or through the next execution of the SET, MERGE, or UPDATE statement. Variables created with options in the SET, MERGE, and UPDATE statements also retain their values from one iteration to the next.

When all of the rows in a data set in a match-merge operation (with a BY statement) have been processed, the variables in the output data set retain their values as described earlier. That is, as long as there is no change in the BY value in effect when all of the rows in the data set have been processed, the variables in the output data set retain their values from the final observation. FIRST.*variable* and LAST.*variable*, the automatic variables that are generated by the BY statement, both retain their values. Their initial value is 1.

When the BY value changes, the variables are set to missing and remain missing because the data set contains no additional observations to provide replacement values. When all of the rows in a data set in a one-to-one merge operation (without a BY statement) have been processed, the variables in the output data set are set to missing and remain missing.

When Missing Values Are Generated by SAS

Propagation of Missing Values in Calculations

SAS assigns missing values to prevent problems from arising. If you use a missing value in an arithmetic calculation, SAS sets the result of that calculation to missing. Then, if you use that result in another calculation, the next result is also missing. This action is called *propagation of missing values*. SAS prints notes in the log to notify you which arithmetic expressions have missing values and when they were created; however, processing continues.

Illegal Operations

SAS prints a note in the log and assigns a missing value to the result if you try to perform an illegal operation, such as the following:

- □ dividing by zero
- □ taking the logarithm of zero
- □ using an expression to produce a number too large to be represented as a floating-point number (known as overflow).

Illegal Character-to-Numeric Conversions

SAS automatically converts character values to numeric values if a character variable is used in an arithmetic expression. If a character value contains nonnumerical information and SAS tries to convert it to a numeric value, a note is printed in the log, the result of the conversion is set to missing, and the _ERROR_ automatic variable is set to 1.

Special Missing Values

The result of any numeric missing value in a SAS expression is a period. Thus, both special missing values and ordinary numeric missing values propagate as a period.

```
data a;
     x=.d;
     y=x+1;
     put y=;
  run;
```

This DATA step results in the following log:

Output 6.2   SAS Log Results for a Missing Value

```
1      data a;
2        x= .d;
3        y=x+1;
4        put y=;
5      run;

y=.
NOTE: Missing values were generated as a result of performing an
      operation on missing values.
      Each place is given by:
      (Number of times) at (Line):(Column).
      1 at 3:6
NOTE: The data set WORK.A has 1 observations and 2 variables.
NOTE: DATA statement used:
      real time           0.58 seconds
      cpu time            0.05 seconds
```

Preventing Propagation of Missing Values

If you do not want missing values to propagate in your arithmetic expressions, you can omit missing values from computations by using the sample statistic functions. For a list of these functions, see the descriptive statistics category in "Functions and CALL Routines by Category" in the *SAS Language Reference: Dictionary*. For example, consider the following DATA step:

```
data test;
  x=.;
  y=5;
  a=x+y;
  b=sum(x,y);
  c=5;
  c+x;
  put a= b= c=;
run;
```

Output 6.3 SAS Log Results for a Missing Value in a Statistic Function

```
1    data test;
2      x=.;
3      y=5;
4      a=x+y;
5      b=sum(x,y);
6      c=5;
7      c+x;
8      put a= b= c=;
9    run;

a=. b=5 c=5
NOTE: Missing values were generated as a result of performing
      an operation on missing values.
      Each place is given by:
      (Number of times) at (Line):(Column).
      1 at 4:6
NOTE: The data set WORK.TEST has 1 observations and 5 variables.
NOTE: DATA statement used:
      real time              0.11 seconds
      cpu time               0.03 seconds
```

Adding X and Y together in an expression produces a missing result because the value of X is missing. The value of A, therefore, is missing. However, since the SUM function ignores missing values, adding X to Y produces the value 5, not a missing value.

Note: The SUM statement also ignores missing values, so the value of C is also 5. △

Working with Missing Values

How to Represent Missing Values in Raw Data

Table 6.2 on page 107 shows how to represent each type of missing value in raw data so that SAS will read and store the value appropriately.

Table 6.2 Representing Missing Values

These missing values ...	Are represented by ...	Explanation
Numeric	.	a single decimal point
Character	' '	a blank enclosed in quotes
Special	*.letter*	a decimal point followed by a letter, for example, .B
Special	._	a decimal point followed by an underscore

How to Set Variable Values to Missing in a DATA Step

You can set values to missing within your DATA step by using program statements such as this one:

```
if age<0 then age=.;
```

This statement sets the stored value of AGE to a numeric missing value if AGE has a value less than 0.

Note: You can display a missing numeric value with a character other than a period by using the DATA step's MISSING statement or the MISSING= system option. △

The following example sets the stored value of NAME to a missing character value if NAME has a value of "none":

```
if name="none" then name=' ';
```

Alternatively, if you want to set to a missing value for one or more variable values, you can use the CALL MISSING routine. For example,

```
call missing(sales, name);
```

sets both variable values to a missing value.

Note: You can mix character and numeric variables in the CALL MISSING routine argument list. △

How to Check for Missing Values in a DATA Step

You can use the N and NMISS functions to return the number of nonmissing and missing values, respectively, from a list of numeric arguments.

When you check for ordinary missing numeric values, you can use code that is similar to the following:

```
if numvar=. then do;
```

If your data contains special missing values, you can check for either an ordinary or special missing value with a statement that is similar to the following:

```
if numvar<=.z then do;
```

To check for a missing character value, you can use a statement that is similar to the following:

```
if charvar=' ' then do;
```

The MISSING function enables you to check for either a character or numeric missing value, as in:

```
if missing(var) then do;
```

In each case, SAS checks whether the value of the variable in the current observation satisfies the condition specified. If it does, SAS executes the DO group.

Note: Missing values have a value of **false** when you use them with logical operators such as AND or OR. △

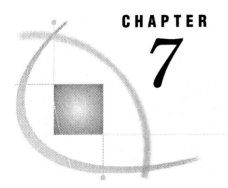

7

Expressions

Definitions for SAS Expressions   **110**
Examples of SAS Expressions   **110**
SAS Constants in Expressions   **110**
 Definition   **110**
 Character Constants   **111**
 Using Quotation Marks With Character Constants   **111**
 Comparing Character Constants and Character Variables   **111**
 Character Constants Expressed in Hexadecimal Notation   **112**
 Numeric Constants   **112**
 Numeric Constants Expressed in Standard Notation   **112**
 Numeric Constants Expressed in Scientific Notation   **113**
 Numeric Constants Expressed in Hexadecimal Notation   **113**
 Date, Time, and Datetime Constants   **113**
 Bit Testing Constants   **114**
 Avoiding a Common Error With Constants   **115**
SAS Variables in Expressions   **116**
 Definition   **116**
 Automatic Numeric-Character Conversion   **116**
SAS Functions in Expressions   **117**
SAS Operators in Expressions   **117**
 Definitions   **117**
 Arithmetic Operators   **118**
 Comparison Operators   **118**
 Numeric Comparisons   **119**
 The IN Operator in Numeric Comparisons   **120**
 Character Comparisons   **120**
 The IN Operator in Character Comparisons   **121**
 Logical (Boolean) Operators and Expressions   **121**
 The AND Operator   **121**
 The OR Operator   **122**
 The NOT Operator   **122**
 Boolean Numeric Expressions   **122**
 The MIN and MAX Operators   **123**
 The Concatenation Operator   **123**
 Order of Evaluation in Compound Expressions   **124**

Definitions for SAS Expressions

expression

is generally a sequence of operands and operators that form a set of instructions that are performed to produce a resulting value. You use expressions in SAS program statements to create variables, assign values, calculate new values, transform variables, and perform conditional processing. SAS expressions can resolve to numeric values, character values, or Boolean values.

operands

are constants or variables that can be numeric or character.

operators

are symbols that represent a comparison, arithmetic calculation, or logical operation; a SAS function; or grouping parentheses.

simple expression

is an expression with no more than one operator. A simple expression can consist of a single

□ constant

□ variable

□ function.

compound expression

is an expression that includes several operators. When SAS encounters a compound expression, it follows rules to determine the order in which to evaluate each part of the expression.

WHERE *expressions*

is a type of SAS expression that is used within a WHERE statement or WHERE= data set option to specify a condition for selecting observations for processing in a DATA or PROC step. For syntax and further information on WHERE expressions, see Chapter 12, "WHERE-Expression Processing," on page 197 and *SAS Language Reference: Dictionary*

Examples of SAS Expressions

The following are examples of SAS expressions:

□ **3**

□ **x**

□ **x+1**

□ **age<100**

□ **trim(last)||', '||first**

SAS Constants in Expressions

Definition

A SAS *constant* is a number or a character string that indicates a fixed value. Constants can be used as expressions in many SAS statements, including variable assignment and IF-THEN statements. They can also be used as values for certain options. Constants are also called *literals*.

The following are types of SAS constants:

□ character

□ numeric

□ date, time, and datetime

□ bit testing.

Character Constants

A *character constant* consists of 1 to 32,767 characters and must be enclosed in quotation marks. Character constants can also be represented in hexadecimal form.

Using Quotation Marks With Character Constants

In the following SAS statement, **Tom** is a character constant:

```
if name='Tom' then do;
```

If a character constant includes a single quotation mark, surround it with double quotation marks. For example, to specify the character value **Tom's** as a constant, enter

```
name="Tom's"
```

Another way to write the same string is to enclose the string in single quotation marks and to express the apostrophe as two consecutive quotation marks. SAS treats the two consecutive quotation marks as one quotation mark:

```
name='Tom''s'
```

The same principle holds true for double quotation marks:

```
name="Tom""s"
```

CAUTION:
> **Matching quotation marks correctly is important.** Missing or extraneous quotation marks cause SAS to misread both the erroneous statement and the statements that follow it. For example, in **name='O'Brien';**, **O** is the character value of NAME, **Brien** is extraneous, and **';** begins another quoted string. △

Comparing Character Constants and Character Variables

It is important to remember that character constants are enclosed in quotation marks, but names of character variables are not. This distinction applies wherever you can use a character constant, such as in titles, footnotes, labels, and other descriptive strings; in option values; and in operating environment-specific strings, such as file specifications and commands.

The following statements use character constants:

□ **x='abc';**

□ **if name='Smith' then do;**

The following statements use character variables:

□ **x=abc;**

□ **if name=Smith then do;**

In the second set of examples, SAS searches for variables named ABC and SMITH, instead of constants.

Note: SAS distinguishes between uppercase and lowercase when comparing quoted values. For example, the character values `'Smith'` and `'SMITH'` are not equivalent. △

Character Constants Expressed in Hexadecimal Notation

SAS character constants can be expressed in hexadecimal notation. A character hex constant is a string of an even number of hex characters enclosed in single or double quotation marks, followed immediately by an X, as in this example:

```
'534153'x
```

A comma can be used to make the string more readable, but it is not part of and does not alter the hex value. If the string contains a comma, the comma must separate an even number of hex characters within the string, as in this example:

```
if value='3132,3334'x then do;
```

CAUTION:
   Trailing blanks or leading blanks cause an error. Any trailing blanks or leading blanks within the quotation marks cause an error message to be written to the log. △

Numeric Constants

A *numeric constant* is a number that appears in a SAS statement. Numeric constants can be presented in many forms, including

   □ standard notation

   □ scientific (E) notation

   □ hexadecimal notation.

Numeric Constants Expressed in Standard Notation

Most numeric constants are written just as numeric data values are. The numeric constant in the following expression is 100:

```
part/all*100
```

Numeric constants can be expressed in standard notation in the following ways:

Table 7.1   Standard Notation for Numeric Constants

Numeric Constant	Description
1	is an unsigned integer
−5	contains a minus sign
+49	contains a plus sign

Numeric Constant	Description
1.23	contains decimal places
01	contains a leading zero which is not significant

Numeric Constants Expressed in Scientific Notation

In scientific notation, the number before the E is multiplied by the power of ten that is indicated by the number after the E. For example, 2E4 is the same as 2×10^4 or 20,000. For numeric constants larger than $(10^{32})-1$, you must use scientific notation. Additional examples follow:

- □ **1.2e23**
- □ **0.5e-10**

Numeric Constants Expressed in Hexadecimal Notation

A numeric constant that is expressed as a hexadecimal value starts with a numeric digit (usually 0), can be followed by more hexadecimal digits, and ends with the letter X. The constant can contain up to 16 valid hexadecimal digits (0 to 9, A to F). The following are numeric hex constants:

- □ **0c1x**
- □ **9x**

You can use numeric hex constants in a DATA step, as follows:

```
data test;
   input abend pib2.;
   if abend=0c1x or abend=0b0ax then do;
   … more SAS statements …
 run;
```

Date, Time, and Datetime Constants

You can create a *date constant*, *time constant*, or *datetime constant* by specifying the date or time in single or double quotation marks, followed by a D (date), T (time), or DT (datetime) to indicate the type of value.

Any trailing blanks or leading blanks included within the quotation marks will not affect the processing of the *date constant*, *time constant*, or *datetime constant*.

Use the following patterns to create date and time constants:

'*ddmmm<yy>yy*'D or "*ddmmm<yy>yy*"D represents a SAS date value:

- □ **date='1jan2006'd;**
- □ **date='01jan04'd;**

'*hh:mm<:ss.s>*'T or "*hh:mm<:ss.s>*"T represents a SAS time value:

- □ **time='9:25't;**
- □ **time='9:25:19pm't;**

'*ddmmm<yy>yy:hh:mm<:ss.s>*'DT or "*ddmmm<yy>yy:hh:mm<:ss.s>*"DT represents a SAS datetime value:

- □ **if begin='01may04:9:30:00'dt then end='31dec90:5:00:00'dt;**
- □ **dtime='18jan2003:9:27:05am'dt;**

For more information on SAS dates, refer to Chapter 8, "Dates, Times, and Intervals," on page 127.

Bit Testing Constants

Bit masks are used in bit testing to compare internal bits in a value's representation. You can perform bit testing on both character and numeric variables. The general form of the operation is:

expression comparison-operator bit-mask

The following are the components of the bit-testing operation:

expression

> can be any valid SAS expression. Both character and numeric variables can be bit tested. When SAS tests a character value, it aligns the left-most bit of the mask with the left-most bit of the string; the test proceeds through the corresponding bits, moving to the right. When SAS tests a numeric value, the value is truncated from a floating-point number to a 32-bit integer. The right-most bit of the mask is aligned with the right-most bit of the number, and the test proceeds through the corresponding bits, moving to the left.

comparison-operator

> compares an expression with the bit mask. Refer to "Comparison Operators" on page 118 for a discussion of these operators.

bit-mask

> is a string of 0s, 1s, and periods in quotation marks that is immediately followed by a B. Zeros test whether the bit is off; ones test whether the bit is on; and periods ignore the bit. Commas and blanks can be inserted in the bit mask for readability without affecting its meaning.

CAUTION:

> **Truncation can occur when SAS uses a bit mask.** If the expression is longer than the bit mask, SAS truncates the expression before it compares it with the bit mask. A false comparison may result. An expression's length (in bits) must be less than or equal to the length of the bit mask. If the bit mask is longer than a character expression, SAS prints a warning in the log, stating that the bit mask is truncated on the left, and continues processing. △

The following example tests a character variable:

```
if a='..1.0000'b then do;
```

If the third bit of A (counting from the left) is on, and the fifth through eighth bits are off, the comparison is true and the expression result is 1. Otherwise, the comparison is false and the expression result is 0. The following is a more detailed example:

```
data test;
   input @88 bits $char1.;
   if bits='10000000'b
     then category='a';
   else if bits='01000000'b
     then category='b';
   else if bits='00100000'b
     then category='c';
   run;
```

Note: Bit masks cannot be used as bit literals in assignment statements. For example, the following statement is not valid:

```
x='0101'b;     /* incorrect */
```

△

The $BINARY*w*. and BINARY*w*. formats and the $BINARY*w*., BINARY*w*.*d*, and BITS*w*.*d* informats can be useful for bit testing. You can use them to convert character and numeric values to their binary values, and vice versa, and to extract specified bits from input data. See *SAS Language Reference: Dictionary* for complete descriptions of these formats and informats.

Avoiding a Common Error With Constants

When you use a string in quotation marks followed by a variable name, always put a blank space between the closing quotation mark and the variable name. Otherwise, SAS might interpret a character constant followed by a variable name as a special SAS constant as illustrated in this table.

Table 7.2 Characters That Cause Misinterpretation When Following a Character Constant

Characters that follow a character constant	Possible interpretation	Examples
b	bit testing constant	'00100000'b
d	date constant	'01jan04'd
dt	datetime constant	'18jan2005:9:27:05am'dt
n	name literal	'My Table'n
t	time constant	'9:25:19pm't
x	hexadecimal notation	'534153'x

In the following example, '821't is evaluated as a time constant. For more information about SAS time constants, see "Date, Time, and Datetime Constants" on page 113.

```
data work.europe;
   set ia.europe;
   if flight='821'then
      flight='230';
run;
```

The program writes the following lines to the SAS log:

Output 7.1 Log Results from an Error Caused by a Time Literal Misinterpretation

```
ERROR: Invalid date/time/datetime constant '821't.
ERROR 77--185: Invalid number conversion on '821't.

ERROR 388--185: Expecting an arithmetic operator.
```

Inserting a blank space between the ending quotation mark and the succeeding character in the IF statement eliminates this misinterpretation. No error message is generated and all observations with a FLIGHT value of 821 are replaced with a value of 230.

```
if flight='821' then
   flight='230';
```

SAS Variables in Expressions

Definition

variable
> is a set of data values that describe a given characteristic. A variable can be used in an expression.

Automatic Numeric-Character Conversion

If you specify a variable in an expression, but the variable value does not match the type called for, SAS attempts to convert the value to the expected type. SAS automatically converts character variables to numeric variables and numeric variables to character variables, according to the following rules:

- ☐ If you use a character variable with an operator that requires numeric operands, such as the plus sign, SAS converts the character variable to numeric.

- ☐ If you use a comparison operator, such as the equal sign, to compare a character variable and a numeric variable, the character variable is converted to numeric.

- ☐ If you use a numeric variable with an operator that requires a character value, such as the concatenation operator, the numeric value is converted to character using the BEST12. format. Because SAS stores the results of the conversion beginning with the right-most byte, you must store the converted values in a variable of sufficient length to accommodate the BEST12. format. You can use the LEFT function to left-justify a result.

- ☐ If you use a numeric variable on the left side of an assignment statement and a character variable on the right, the character variable is converted to numeric. In the opposite situation, where the character variable is on the left and the numeric is on the right, SAS converts the numeric variable to character using the BEST*n*. format, where *n* is the length of the variable on the left.

When SAS performs an automatic conversion, it prints a note in the SAS log informing you that the conversion took place. If converting a character variable to numeric produces invalid numeric values, SAS assigns a missing value to the result, prints an error message in the log, and sets the value of the automatic variable _ERROR_ to 1.

Note: You can also use the PUT and INPUT functions to convert data values. These functions can be more efficient than automatic conversion. See "The Concatenation Operator" on page 123 for an example of the PUT function. See *SAS Language Reference: Dictionary* for more details on these functions. △

For more information on SAS variables, see Chapter 5, "SAS Variables," on page 77 or the *SAS Language Reference: Dictionary*.

SAS Functions in Expressions

A SAS *function* is a keyword that you use to perform a specific computation or system manipulation. Functions return a value, might require one or more arguments, and can be used in expressions. For further information on SAS functions, see *SAS Language Reference: Dictionary*.

SAS Operators in Expressions

Definitions

A SAS *operator* is a symbol that represents a comparison, arithmetic calculation, or logical operation; a SAS function; or grouping parentheses. SAS uses two major kinds of operators:

- □ prefix operators
- □ infix operators.

A *prefix operator* is an operator that is applied to the variable, constant, function, or parenthetic expression that immediately follows it. The plus sign (+) and minus sign (−) can be used as prefix operators. The word NOT and its equivalent symbols are also prefix operators. The following are examples of prefix operators used with variables, constants, functions, and parenthetic expressions:

- □ `+y`
- □ `-25`
- □ `-cos(angle1)`
- □ `+(x*y)`

An *infix operator* applies to the operands on each side of it, for example, 6<8. Infix operators include the following:

- □ arithmetic
- □ comparison
- □ logical, or Boolean
- □ minimum
- □ maximum
- □ concatenation.

When used to perform arithmetic operations, the plus and minus signs are infix operators.

SAS also provides several other operators that are used only with certain SAS statements. The WHERE statement uses a special group of SAS operators, valid only when used with WHERE expressions. For a discussion of these operators, see Chapter 12, "WHERE-Expression Processing," on page 197.

Arithmetic Operators

Arithmetic operators indicate that an arithmetic calculation is performed, as shown in the following table:

Table 7.3 Arithmetic Operators

Symbol	Definition	Example	Result
**	exponentiation	`a**3`	raise A to the third power
*	multiplication[1]	`2*y`	multiply 2 by the value of Y
/	division	`var/5`	divide the value of VAR by 5
+	addition	`num+3`	add 3 to the value of NUM
-	subtraction	`sale-discount`	subtract the value of DISCOUNT from the value of SALE

1 The asterisk (*) is always necessary to indicate multiplication; **2Y** and **2(Y)** are not valid expressions.

If a missing value is an operand for an arithmetic operator, the result is a missing value. See Chapter 6, "Missing Values," on page 101 for a discussion of how to prevent the propagation of missing values.

See "Order of Evaluation in Compound Expressions" on page 124 for the order in which SAS evaluates these operators.

Comparison Operators

Comparison operators set up a comparison, operation, or calculation with two variables, constants, or expressions. If the comparison is true, the result is 1. If the comparison is false, the result is 0.

Comparison operators can be expressed as symbols or with their mnemonic equivalents, which are shown in the following table:

Table 7.4 Comparison Operators

Symbol	Mnemonic Equivalent	Definition	Example
=	EQ	equal to	`a=3`
^=	NE	not equal to[1]	`a ne 3`
¬=	NE	not equal to	
~=	NE	not equal to	
>	GT	greater than	`num>5`
<	LT	less than	`num<8`
>=	GE	greater than or equal to[2]	`sales>=300`

Symbol	Mnemonic Equivalent	Definition	Example
<=	LE	less than or equal to[3]	`sales<=100`
	IN	equal to one of a list	`num in (3, 4, 5)`

1 The symbol you use for NE depends on your terminal.
2 The symbol => is also accepted for compatibility with previous releases of SAS. It is not supported in WHERE clauses or in PROC SQL.
3 The symbol =< is also accepted for compatibility with previous releases of SAS. It is not supported in WHERE clauses or in PROC SQL.

See "Order of Evaluation in Compound Expressions" on page 124 for the order in which SAS evaluates these operators.

Note: You can add a colon (:) modifier to any of the operators to compare only a specified prefix of a character string. See "Character Comparisons" on page 120 for details. △

Note: You can use the IN operator to compare a value that is produced by an expression on the left of the operator to a list of values that are given on the right. The form of the comparison is:

```
expression IN (value-1<...,value-n>)
```

The components of the comparison are as follows:

expression   can be any valid SAS expression, but is usually a variable name when it is used with the IN operator.

value   must be a constant.

For examples of using the IN operator, see "The IN Operator in Numeric Comparisons" on page 120. △

Numeric Comparisons

SAS makes numeric comparisons that are based on values. In the expression A<=B, if A has the value 4 and B has the value 3, then A<=B has the value 0, or false. If A is 5 and B is 9, then the expression has the value 1, or true. If A and B each have the value 47, then the expression is true and has the value 1.

Comparison operators appear frequently in IF-THEN statements, as in this example:

```
if x<y then c=5;
    else c=12;
```

You can also use comparisons in expressions in assignment statements. For example, the preceding statements can be recoded as follows:

```
c=5*(x<y)+12*(x>=y);
```

Since SAS evaluates quantities inside parentheses before performing any operations, the expressions `(x<y)` and `(x>=y)` are evaluated first and the result (1 or 0) is substituted for the expressions in parentheses. Therefore, if X=6 and Y=8, the expression evaluates as follows:

```
c=5*(1)+12*(0)
```

The result of this statement is C=5.

You might get an incorrect result when you compare numeric values of different lengths because values less than 8 bytes have less precision than those longer than 8 bytes. Rounding also affects the outcome of numeric comparisons. See Chapter 5, "SAS Variables," on page 77 for a complete discussion of numeric precision.

A missing numeric value is smaller than any other numeric value, and missing numeric values have their own sort order (see Chapter 6, "Missing Values," on page 101 for more information).

The IN Operator in Numeric Comparisons

You can use the IN operator for specifying sequential integers in an IN list. The increment value is always +1. The following statements produce the same results:

☐ `y = x in (1, 2, 3, 4, 5, 6, 7, 8, 9, 10);`

☐ `y = x in (1:10);`

In a DATA step, you can also use a shorthand notation to specify a range of sequential integers with other values within an IN list, as the following example shows:

```
if x in (0,9,1:5);
```

Note: PROC SQL or WHERE clauses do not support this syntax.   △

Character Comparisons

You can perform comparisons on character operands, but the comparison always yields a numeric result (1 or 0). Character operands are compared character by character from left to right. Character order depends on the *collating sequence*, usually ASCII or EBCDIC, used by your computer.

For example, in the EBCDIC and ASCII collating sequences, **G** is greater than **A**; therefore, this expression is true:

```
'Gray'>'Adams'
```

Two character values of unequal length are compared as if blanks were attached to the end of the shorter value before the comparison is made. A blank, or missing character value, is smaller than any other printable character value. For example, because . is less than **h**, this expression is true:

```
'C. Jones'<'Charles Jones'
```

Since trailing blanks are ignored in a comparison, `'fox '` is equivalent to `'fox'`. However, because blanks at the beginning and in the middle of a character value are significant to SAS, `' fox'` is not equivalent to `'fox'`.

You can compare only a specified prefix of a character string by using a colon (:) after the comparison operator. In the following example, the colon modifier after the equal sign tells SAS to look at only the first character of values of the variable LASTNAME and to select the observations with names beginning with the letter **s**:

```
if lastname=:'S';
```

Because printable characters are greater than blanks, both of the following statements select observations with values of LASTNAME that are greater than or equal to the letter **s**:

☐ `if lastname>='S';`

☐ `if lastname>=:'S';`

The operations that are discussed in this section show you how to compare entire character strings and the beginnings of character strings. Several SAS character functions enable you to search for and extract values from within character strings. See *SAS Language Reference: Dictionary* for complete descriptions of all SAS functions.

The IN Operator in Character Comparisons

You can use the IN operator with character strings to determine whether a variable's value is among a list of character values. The following statements produce the same results:

□ `if state in ('NY','NJ','PA') then region+1;`

□ `if state='NY' or state='NJ' or state='PA' then region+1;`

Logical (Boolean) Operators and Expressions

Logical operators, also called *Boolean operators*, are usually used in expressions to link sequences of comparisons. The logical operators are shown in the following table:

Table 7.5 Logical Operators

Symbol	Mnemonic Equivalent	Example
&	AND	`(a>b & c>d)`
|	OR[1]	`(a>b or c>d)`
!	OR	
¦	OR	
¬	NOT[2]	`not(a>b)`
^	NOT	
~	NOT	

1 The symbol you use for OR depends on your operating environment.
2 The symbol you use for NOT depends on your operating environment.

See "Order of Evaluation in Compound Expressions" on page 124 for the order in which SAS evaluates these operators.

In addition, a numeric expression without any logical operators can serve as a Boolean expression. For an example of Boolean numeric expressions, see "Boolean Numeric Expressions" on page 122.

The AND Operator

If *both* of the quantities linked by AND are 1 (true), then the result of the AND operation is 1; otherwise, the result is 0. For example, in the following comparison:

`a<b & c>0`

the result is true (has a value of 1) only when both A<B *and* C>0 are 1 (true): that is, when A is less than B *and* C is positive.

Two comparisons with a common variable linked by AND can be condensed with an implied AND. For example, the following two subsetting IF statements produce the same result:

☐ `if 16<=age and age<=65;`

☐ `if 16<=age<=65;`

The OR Operator

If *either* of the quantities linked by an OR is 1 (true), then the result of the OR operation is 1 (true); otherwise, the OR operation produces a 0. For example, consider the following comparison:

`a<b|c>0`

The result is true (with a value of 1) when A<B is 1 (true) regardless of the value of C. It is also true when the value of C>0 is 1 (true), regardless of the values of A and B. Therefore, it is true when either or both of those relationships hold.

Be careful when using the OR operator with a series of comparisons (in an IF, SELECT, or WHERE statement, for instance). Remember that only one comparison in a series of OR comparisons must be true to make a condition true, and any nonzero, nonmissing constant is always evaluated as true (see "Boolean Numeric Expressions" on page 122). Therefore, the following subsetting IF statement is always true:

`if x=1 or 2;`

SAS first evaluates X=1, and the result can be either true or false; however, since the 2 is evaluated as nonzero and nonmissing (true), the entire expression is true. In this statement, however, the condition is not necessarily true because either comparison can evaluate as true or false:

`if x=1 or x=2;`

The NOT Operator

The prefix operator NOT is also a logical operator. The result of putting NOT in front of a quantity whose value is 0 (false) is 1 (true). That is, the result of negating a false statement is 1 (true). For example, if X=Y is 0 (false) then NOT(X=Y) is 1 (true). The result of NOT in front of a quantity whose value is missing is also 1 (true). The result of NOT in front of a quantity with a nonzero, nonmissing value is 0 (false). That is, the result of negating a true statement is 0 (false).

For example, the following two expressions are equivalent:

☐ `not(name='SMITH')`

☐ `name ne 'SMITH'`

Furthermore, NOT(A&B) is equivalent to NOT A|NOT B, and NOT(A|B) is the same as NOT A & NOT B. For example, the following two expressions are equivalent:

☐ `not(a=b & c>d)`

☐ `a ne b | c le d`

Boolean Numeric Expressions

In computing terms, a value of true is a 1 and a value of false is a 0. In SAS, any numeric value other than 0 or missing is true, and a value of 0 or missing is false. Therefore, a numeric variable or expression can stand alone in a condition. If its value is a number other than 0 or missing, the condition is true; if its value is 0 or missing, the condition is false.

```
0 | . = False
1 = True
```

For example, suppose that you want to fill in variable REMARKS depending on whether the value of COST is present for a given observation. You can write the IF-THEN statement as follows:

```
if cost then remarks='Ready to budget';
```

This statement is equivalent to:

```
if cost ne . and cost ne 0
   then remarks='Ready to budget';
```

A numeric expression can be simply a numeric constant, as follows:

```
if 5 then do;
```

The numeric value that is returned by a function is also a valid numeric expression:

```
if index(address,'Avenue') then do;
```

The MIN and MAX Operators

The MIN and MAX operators are used to find the minimum or maximum value of two quantities. Surround the operators with the two quantities whose minimum or maximum value you want to know. The MIN (><) operator returns the lower of the two values. The MAX (<>) operator returns the higher of the two values. For example, if A<B, then A><B returns the value of A.

If missing values are part of the comparison, SAS uses the sorting order for missing values that is described in "Order of Missing Values" on page 103. For example, the maximum value that is returned by .A<>.Z is the value .Z.

Note: In a WHERE statement or clause, the <> operator is equivalent to NE. △

The Concatenation Operator

The concatenation operator (| |) concatenates character values. The results of a concatenation operation are usually stored in a variable with an assignment statement, as in **level='grade '||'A'**. The length of the resulting variable is the sum of the lengths of each variable or constant in the concatenation operation, unless you use a LENGTH or ATTRIB statement to specify a different length for the new variable.

The concatenation operator does not trim leading or trailing blanks. If variables are padded with trailing blanks, check the lengths of the variables and use the TRIM function to trim trailing blanks from values before concatenating them. See *SAS Language Reference: Dictionary* for descriptions and examples of additional character functions.

For example, in this DATA step, the value that results from the concatenation contains blanks because the length of the COLOR variable is eight:

```
data namegame;
     length color name $8 game $12;
     color='black';
     name='jack';
     game=color||name;
     put game=;
  run;
```

The value of GAME is `'black      jack'`. To correct this problem, use the TRIM function in the concatenation operation as follows:

```
game=trim(color)||name;
```

This statement produces a value of `'blackjack'` for the variable GAME. The following additional examples demonstrate uses of the concatenation operator:

- □ If A has the value `'fortune'`, B has the value `'five'`, and C has the value `'hundred'`, then the following statement produces the value `'fortunefivehundred'` for the variable D:

  ```
  d=a||b||c;
  ```

- □ This example concatenates the value of a variable with a character constant.

  ```
  newname='Mr. or Ms. ' ||oldname;
  ```

  If the value of OLDNAME is `'Jones'`, then NEWNAME will have the value `'Mr. or Ms. Jones'`.

- □ Because the concatenation operation does not trim blanks, the following expression produces the value `'JOHN    SMITH'`:

  ```
  name='JOHN    '||'SMITH';
  ```

- □ This example uses the PUT function to convert a numeric value to a character value. The TRIM function is used to trim blanks.

  ```
  month='sep';
  year=99;
  date=trim(month) || left(put(year,8.));
  ```

  The value of DATE is the character value `'sep99'`.

Order of Evaluation in Compound Expressions

Table 7.6 on page 125 shows the order of evaluation in compound expressions. The table contains the following columns:

Priority
> lists the priority of evaluation. In compound expressions, SAS evaluates the part of the expression containing operators in Group I first, then each group in order.

Order of Evaluation
> lists the rules governing which part of the expression SAS evaluates first. Parentheses are often used in compound expressions to group operands; expressions within parentheses are evaluated before those outside of them. The rules also list how a compound expression that contains more than one operator from the same group is evaluated.

Symbols
> lists the symbols that you use to request the comparisons, operations, and calculations.

Mnemonic Equivalent
> lists alternate forms of the symbol. In some cases, such as when your keyboard does not support special symbols, you should use the alternate form.

Definition
> defines the symbol.

Example
provides an example of how to use the symbol or mnemonic equivalent in a SAS expression.

Table 7.6 Order of Evaluation in Compound Expressions

Priority	Order of Evaluation	Symbols	Mnemonic Equivalent	Definition	Example
Group I	right to left	**		exponentiation[1]	`y=a**2;`
		+		positive prefix[2]	`y=+(a*b);`
		-		negative prefix[3]	`z=-(a+b);`
		^ ¬ ~	NOT	logical not[4]	`if not z` `then put x;`
		><	MIN	minimum[5]	`x=(a><b);`
		<>	MAX	maximum	`x=(a<>b);`
Group II	left to right	*		multiplication	`c=a*b;`
		/		division	`f=g/h;`
Group III	left to right	+		addition	`c=a+b;`
		-		subtraction	`f=g-h;`
Group IV	left to right	|| ¦¦ !!		concatenate character values[6]	`name=` `'J'||'SMITH';`
Group V[7]	left to right[8]	<	LT	less than	`if x<y then` `c=5;`
		<=	LE	less than or equal to	`if x le` `y then a=0;`
		=	EQ	equal to	`if y eq (x+a)` `then output;`
		¬=	NE	not equal to	`if x ne z` `then output;`
		>=	GE	greater than or equal to	`if y>=a` `then output;`
		>	GT	greater than	`if z>a` `then output;`

			IN	equal to one of a list	`if state in`
					`('NY','NJ','PA')`
					`then region='NE';`
					
					`y = x in (1:10);`

| Group VI | left to right | & | AND | logical and | `if a=b & c=d`
`then x=1;` |
| Group VII | left to right | \| ¦ ! | OR | logical or[9] | `if y=2 or x=3`
`then a=d;` |

1 Because Group I operators are evaluated from right to left, the expression **x=2**3**4** is evaluated as **x=(2**(3**4))**.

2 The plus (+) sign can be either a prefix or arithmetic operator. A plus sign is a prefix operator only when it appears at the beginning of an expression or when it is immediately preceded by a left parenthesis or another operator.

3 The minus (−) sign can be either a prefix or arithmetic operator. A minus sign is a prefix operator only when it appears at the beginning of an expression or when it is immediately preceded by a left parenthesis or another operator.

4 Depending on the characters available on your keyboard, the symbol can be the not sign (¬), tilde (~), or caret (^). The SAS system option CHARCODE allows various other substitutions for unavailable special characters.

5 For example, the SAS System evaluates **−3><−3** as **−(3><−3)**, which is equal to **−(−3)**, which equals **+3**. This is because Group I operators are evaluated from right to left.

6 Depending on the characters available on your keyboard, the symbol you use as the concatenation operator can be a double vertical bar (\|\|), broken vertical bar (¦¦), or exclamation mark (!!).

7 Group V operators are comparison operators. The result of a comparison operation is 1 if the comparison is true and 0 if it is false. Missing values are the lowest in any comparison operation.The symbols =< (less than or equal to) are also allowed for compatibility with previous versions of the SAS System.When making character comparisons, you can use a colon (:) after any of the comparison operators to compare only the first character(s) of the value. SAS truncates the longer value to the length of the shorter value during the comparison. For example, if **name=:'P'** compares the value of the first character of NAME to the letter P.

8 An exception to this rule occurs when two comparison operators surround a quantity. For example, the expression **x<y<z** is evaluated as **(x<y)** and **(y<z)**.

9 Depending on the characters available on your keyboard, the symbol you use for the logical or can be a single vertical bar (\|), broken vertical bar (¦), or exclamation mark (!). You can also use the mnemonic equivalent OR.

CHAPTER

8

Dates, Times, and Intervals

About SAS Date, Time, and Datetime Values **127**
   Definitions **127**
   Two-Digit and Four-Digit Years **128**
   The Year 2000 **128**
      Using the YEARCUTOFF= System Option **128**
      Example: How YEARCUTOFF= Affects Two and Four-Digit Years **129**
      Practices That Help Ensure Date Integrity **130**
   Working with SAS Dates and Times **131**
      Informats and Formats **131**
      Date and Time Tools by Task **131**
   Examples **136**
      Example 1: Displaying Date, Time, and Datetime Values as Recognizable Dates and Times **136**
      Example 2: Reading, Writing, and Calculating Date Values **137**
About Date and Time Intervals **137**
   Definitions **137**
   Syntax **138**
   Intervals By Category **138**
   Example: Calculating a Duration **140**
   Boundaries of Intervals **141**
   Single-Unit Intervals **142**
   Multiunit Intervals **142**
      Multiunit Intervals Other Than Multiweek Intervals **142**
      Multiweek Intervals **143**
   Shifted Intervals **144**
      How to Use Shifted Intervals **144**
      How the SAS System Creates Shifted Intervals **144**

About SAS Date, Time, and Datetime Values

Definitions

SAS date value
   is a value that represents the number of days between January 1, 1960, and a specified date. SAS can perform calculations on dates ranging from A.D. 1582 to A.D. 19,900. Dates before January 1, 1960, are negative numbers; dates after are positive numbers.

   □ SAS date values account for all leap year days, including the leap year day in the year 2000.

□ SAS date values can reliably tell you what day of the week a particular day fell on as far back as September 1752, when the calendar was adjusted by dropping several days. SAS day-of-the-week and length-of-time calculations are accurate in the future to A.D. 19,900.

□ Various SAS language elements handle SAS date values: functions, formats and informats.

SAS time value
is a value representing the number of seconds since midnight of the current day. SAS time values are between 0 and 86400.

SAS datetime value
is a value representing the number of seconds between January 1, 1960 and an hour/minute/second within a specified date.

The following figure shows some dates written in calendar form and as SAS date values.

Figure 8.1   How SAS Converts Calendar Dates to SAS Date Values

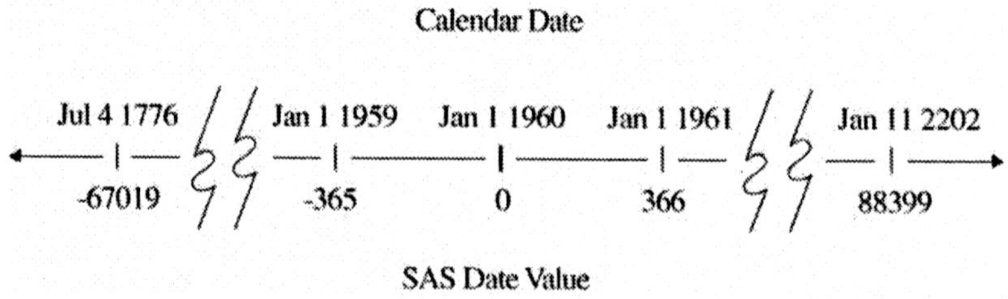

Two-Digit and Four-Digit Years

SAS software can read two-digit or four-digit year values. If SAS encounters a two-digit year, the YEARCUTOFF= option can be used to specify which century within a 100 year span the two-digit year should be attributed to. For example, YEARCUTOFF=1950 means that two-digit years 50 through 99 correspond to 1950 through 1999, while two-digit years 00 through 49 correspond to 2000 through 2049. Note that while the default value of the YEARCUTOFF= option in Version 8 of the SAS System is 1920, you can adjust the YEARCUTOFF= value in a DATA step to accommodate the range of date values you are working with at the moment. To correctly handle 2-digit years representing dates between 2000 and 2099, you should specify an appropriate YEARCUTOFF= value between 1901 and 2000. For more information, see the "YEARCUTOFF= System Option" in *SAS Language Reference: Dictionary*.

The Year 2000

Using the YEARCUTOFF= System Option

SAS software treats the year 2000 like any other leap year. If you use two-digit year numbers for dates, you'll probably need to adjust the default setting for the

YEARCUTOFF= option to work with date ranges for your data, or switch to four-digit years. The following program changes the YEARCUTOFF= value to 1950. This change means that all two digit dates are now assumed to fall in the 100-year span from 1950 to 2049.

```
options yearcutoff=1950;
data _null_;
   a='26oct02'd;
   put 'SAS date='a;
   put 'formatted date='a date9.;
run;
```

The PUT statement writes the following lines to the SAS log:

```
SAS date=15639
formated date=26OCT2002
```

Note: Whenever possible, specify a year using all four digits. Most SAS date and time language elements support four digit year values. △

Example: How YEARCUTOFF= Affects Two and Four-Digit Years

The following example shows what happens with data that contains both two and four-digit years. Note how the YEARCUTOFF= option is set to 1920.

```
options yearcutoff=1920 nodate pageno=1 linesize=80 pagesize=60;

data schedule;
   input @1 jobid $ @6 projdate mmddyy10.;
   datalines;
A100 01/15/25
A110 03/15/2025
A200 01/30/96
B100 02/05/00
B200 06/15/2000
;

proc print data=schedule;
   format projdate mmddyy10.;
run;
```

The resulting output from the PROC PRINT statement looks like this:

Output 8.1 Output from The Previous DATA Step Showing 4–Digit Years That Result from Setting YEARCUTOFF= to 1920

```
                        The SAS System              1

                  Obs     jobid     projdate

                   1      A100     01/15/1925
                   2      A110     03/15/2025
                   3      A200     01/30/1996
                   4      B100     02/05/2000
                   5      B200     06/15/2000
```

Here are some facts to note in this example:

☐ In the datalines in the DATA step, the first record contains a two-digit year of 25, and the second record contains a four-digit year of 2025. Because the YEARCUTOFF= system option is set to 1920, the two-digit year defaults to a year in the 1900s in observation number 1. The four-digit year in observation number 2 is unaffected by the YEARCUTOFF= option.

☐ The third record is similar to the first and defaults to a year in the 1900s based on the value of YEARCUTOFF=.

☐ The output from records 4 and 5 shows results that are similar to records 1 and 2. The fourth record specifies a two-digit year of 00, and the fifth one specifies a four-digit year of 2000. Because of the value of the YEARCUTOFF= option, the years in the two resulting observations are the same.

As you can see, specifying a two-digit year may or may not result in the intended century prefix. The optimal value of the YEARCUTOFF= option depends on the range of the dates that you are processing.

In Releases 6.06 through 6.12 of SAS, the default value for the YEARCUTOFF= system option is 1900; in Version 7 and Version 8, the default value is 1920.

For more information on how SAS handles dates, see the section on dates, times and datetime values.

Practices That Help Ensure Date Integrity

The following practices help ensure that your date values are correct during all the conversions that occur during processing:

☐ Store dates as SAS date values, not as simple numeric or character values.

☐ Use the YEARCUTOFF= system option when converting two-digit dates to SAS date values.

☐ Examine sets of raw data coming into your SAS process to make sure that any dates containing two-digit years will be correctly interpreted by the YEARCUTOFF= system option. Look out for

  ☐ two-digit years that are distributed over more than a 100-year period. For dates covering more than a 100-year span, you must either use four digit years in the data, or use conditional logic in a DATA step to interpret them correctly.

  ☐ two-digit years that need an adjustment to the default YEARCUTOFF= range. For example, if the default value for YEARCUTOFF= in your operating environment is 1920 and you have a two-digit date in your data that represents 1919, you will have to adjust your YEARCUTOFF= value downward by a year in the SAS program that processes this value.

☐ Make sure that output SAS data sets represent dates as SAS date values.

☐ Check your SAS programs to make sure that formats and informats that use two-digit years, such as DATE7., MMDDYY6., or MMDDYY8., are reading and writing data correctly.

Note: The YEARCUTOFF= option has no effect on dates that are already stored as SAS date values. △

Working with SAS Dates and Times

Informats and Formats

The SAS System converts date, time and datetime values back and forth between calendar dates and clock times with SAS language elements called *formats* and *informats*.

- ☐ Formats present a value, recognized by SAS, such as a time or date value, as a calendar date or clock time in a variety of lengths and notations.
- ☐ Informats read notations or a value, such as a clock time or a calendar date, which may be in a variety of lengths, and then convert the data to a SAS date, time, or datetime value.

Date and Time Tools by Task

The following table correlates tasks with various SAS System language elements that are available for working with time and date data.

Table 8.1 Tasks with Dates and Times, Part 1

To do this	Use this	List	Input	Result
Write SAS date values in recognizable forms	Date formats	DATE*w*.	14686	17MAR00
		DATE9.	14686	17MAR2000a
		DAY*w*.	14686	17
		DDMMYY*w*.	14686	17/03/00
		DDMMYY10.	14686	17/03/2000
		DDMMYYB*w*.	14686	17 03 00
		DDMMYYB10.	14686	17 03 2000
		DDMMYYC*w*.	14686	17:03:20
		DDMMYYC10.	14686	17:03:2000
		DDMMYYD*w*.	14686	17-03-00
		DDMMYYD10.	14686	17-03-2000
		DDMMYYN*w*.	14686	17MAR00
		DDMMYYN10	14686	17MAR2000
		DDMMYYP*w*.	14686	17.03.00
		DDMMYYP10.	14686	17.03.2000
		DDMMYYS*w*.	14686	17/03/00
		DDMMYYS10.	14686	17/03/2000
		DOWNAME.	14686	Friday
		JULDAY*w*.	14686	77
		JULIAN*w*.	14686	00077
		MMDDYY*w*.	14686	03/17/00

To do this	Use this	List	Input	Result
		MMDDYY10.	14686	03/17/2000
		MMDDYYB*w*.	14686	03 17 00
		MMDDYYB10.*w*.	14686	03 17 2000
		MMDDYYC*w*.	14686	03:17:00
		MMDDYYC10	14686	03:17:2000
		MMDDYYD*w*.	14686	03-17-00
		MMDDYYD10.	14686	03-17-2000
		MMDDYYN*w*.	14686	031700
		MMDDYYN10.	14686	03172000
		MMDDYYP	14686	03.17.00
		MMDDYYP10.	14686	03.17.2000
		MMDDYYS	14686	03/17/00
		MMDDYYS10.	14686	03/17/2000
		MMYY.*xw*.	14686	03M2000
		MMYYC*w*.	14686	03:2000
		MMYYD.	14686	03-2000
		MMYYN.	14686	032000
		MMYYP.	14686	03.2000
		MMYYS.	14686	03/2000
		MONNAME.	14686	March
		MONTH.	14686	3
		MONYY.	14686	MAR2000
		PDJULG*w*.	14686	2000077F
		PDJULI*w*.	14686	0100077F
		QTR*w*.	14686	1
		QTRR*w*.	14686	I
		TIME*w.d*	14686	4:04:46
		TIMEAMPM*w.d*	14686	4:04:46 AM
		TOD	14686	4:04:46
		WEEKDATE*w*.	14686	Friday, March 17, 2000
		WEEKDAY*w*.	14686	6
		WORDDATE.*w*.	14686	March 17, 2000
		WORDDATX*w*.	14686	17 MARCH 2000
		YEAR*w*.	14686	2000
		YYMM*w*.	14686	2000M03

To do this	Use this	List	Input	Result
		YYMMC*w*.	14686	2000:03
		YYMMDD*w*.	14686	2000-03
		YYMMP*w*.	14686	2000.03
		YYMMS.	14686	2000/03
		YYMMN.	14686	200003
		YYMMDD*w*.	14686	00-03-17
		YYMON.	14686	2000MAR
		YYQ*xw*.	14686	2000Q1
		YYQC*w*.	14686	2000:1
		YYQD*w*.	14686	2000-1
		YYQP*w*.	14686	2000.1
		YYQS*w*.	14686	2000/1
		YYQN*w*.	14686	20001
		YYQR*w*.	14686	2000QI
		YYQRC*w*.	14686	2000:I
		YYQRD*w*.	14686	2000-I
		YYQRP*w.w*.	14686	2000.I
		YYQRS*w*.	14686	2000/I
		YYQRN*w*.	14686	III

Table 8.2 Tasks with Dates and Times, Part 2

To do this	Use this	List	Input	Result
Date Tasks				
Read calendar dates as SAS date Note: YEARCUTOFF=1920	Date informats	DATE*w*.	17MAR2000	14686
		DATE9.	17MAR2000	14686
		DDMMYY*w*.	170300	14686
		DDMMYY8.	17032000	14686
		JULIAN*w*.	0077	14686
		JULIAN7.	2000077	14686
		MMDDYY*w*.	031700	14686
		MMDDYY10.	03172000	14686
		MONYY*w*.	MAR00	14670
		YYMMDD*w*.	000317	14686
		YYMMDD10.	20000317	14686
		YYQ*w*.	00Q1	14610

To do this	Use this	List	Input	Result
Create date values from pieces	Date functions	DATEJUL	2000077	14686
		DATETIME	'17MAR2000'D, 00,00,00	1268870400
		TIME	14,45,32	53132
		MDY	03,17,00	14686
		MDY	03,17,2000	14686
		YYQ	00,1	14610
Extract a date from a datetime value	Date functions	DATEPART	'17MAR00:00:00'DT	14686
Return today's date as a SAS date	Date functions	DATE() or TODAY() (equivalent)	( )	SAS date for today
Extract calendar dates from SAS	Date functions	DAY	14686	17
		HOUR	14686	4
		JULDATE	14686	77
		JULDATE7	14686	2000077
		MINUTE	14686	4
		MONTH	14686	3
		QTR	14686	3
		SECOND	14686	46
		WEEKDAY	14686	6
		YEAR	14686	2000
Write a date as a constant in an expression	SAS date constant	'ddmmmyy'd or 'ddmmmyyyy'	`'17mar00'd` `'17mar2000'd`	14686
Write today's date as a string	SYSDATE automatic macro variable	SYSDATE	&SYSDATE	Date at time of SAS initialization in DDMMMYY
	SYSDATE9	SYSDATE9	&SYSDATE9	Date at time of SAS initialization in DDMMMYYYY

Time Tasks

Write SAS time values as time values	time formats	HHMM.	53132	14:46
		HOUR.	53132	15

To do this	Use this	List	Input	Result
		MMSS.	53132	885
		TIME.	53132	14:45:32
		TOD.	53132	14:45:32
Read time values as SAS time values	Time informats	TIME	14:45:32	53132
Write the current time as a string	SYSTIME automatic macro variable	SYSTIME	&SYSTIME	Time at moment of execution in HH:MM
Return the current time of day as a SAS time value	Time functions	TIME( )	( )	SAS time value at moment of execution in NNNNN.NN
Return the time part of a SAS datetime value	Time functions	TIMEPART	SAS datetime value in NNNNNNNNNN.N	SAS time value part of date value in NNNNN.NN

Datetime Tasks

To do this	Use this	List	Input	Result
Write SAS datetime values as datetime values	Datetime formats	DATEAMPM	1217083532	26JUL98:02:45 PM
		DATETIME	1268870400	17MAR00:00:00:00
Read datetime values as SAS datetime values	Datetime informats	DATETIME	17MAR00:00:00:00	1268870400
Return the current date and time of day as a SAS datetime value	Datetime functions	DATETIME()	()	SAS datetime value at moment of execution in NNNNNNNNNN.N

Interval Tasks

To do this	Use this	List	Input	Result
Return the number of specified time intervals that lie between the two date or datetime values	Interval functions	INTCK	week 2 01aug60 01jan01	1055
Advances a date, time, or datetime value by a given interval, and returns a date, time, or datetime value	Interval functions	INTNX	day 14086 01jan60	14086

The SAS System also supports international formats and informats that are equivalent to some of the most commonly used English-language date formats and informats. For details, see the SAS formats and informats in *SAS Language Reference: Dictionary*.

Examples

Example 1: Displaying Date, Time, and Datetime Values as Recognizable Dates and Times

The following example demonstrates how a value may be displayed as a date, a time, or a datetime. Remember to select the SAS language element that converts a SAS date, time, or datetime value to the intended date, time or datetime format. See the previous tables for examples.

Note:

□ Time formats count the number of seconds within a day, so the values will be between 0 and 86400.

□ DATETIME formats count the number of seconds since January 1, 1960, so for datetimes that are greater than 02JAN1960:00:00:01, (integer of 86401) the datetime value will always be greater than the time value.

□ When in doubt, look at the contents of your data set for clues as to which type of value you are dealing with.

△

This program uses the DATETIME, DATE and TIMEAMPM formats to display the value 86399 to a date and time, a calendar date, and a time.

```
data test;
options nodate pageno=1 linesize=80 pagesize=60;
Time1=86399;
format Time1 datetime.;
Date1=86399;
format Date1 date.;
Time2=86399;
format Time2 timeampm.;
run;
proc print data=test;
title   'Same Number, Different SAS Values';
footnote1 'Time1 is a SAS DATETIME value';
footnote2 'Date1 is a SAS DATE value';
footnote3 'Time2 is a SAS TIME value'.;
run;
```

Output 8.2   Datetime, Date and Time Values for 86399

```
                Same Number, Different SAS Values                  1

        Obs          Time1             Date1          Time2

         1      01JAN60:23:59:59      20JUL96     11:59:59 PM




                 Time1 is a SAS DATETIME value
                  Date1 is a SAS DATE value
                  Time2 is a SAS TIME value.
```

Example 2: Reading, Writing, and Calculating Date Values

This program reads four regional meeting dates and calculates the dates on which announcements should be mailed.

```
data meeting;
options nodate pageno=1 linesize=80 pagesize=60;
   input region $ mtg : mmddyy8.;
   sendmail=mtg-45;
   datalines;
N   11-24-99
S   12-28-99
E   12-03-99
W   10-04-99
;

proc print data=meeting;
   format mtg sendmail date9.;
   title 'When To Send Announcements';
run;
```

Output 8.3 Calculated Date Values: When to Send Mail

```
                    When To Send Announcements

        Obs    region        mtg       sendmail

         1       N        24NOV1999    10OCT1999
         2       S        28DEC1999    13NOV1999
         3       E        03DEC1999    19OCT1999
         4       W        04OCT1999    20AUG1999
```

About Date and Time Intervals

Definitions

duration
> is an integer representing the difference between any two dates or times or datetimes. Date durations are integer values representing the difference, in the number of days, between two SAS dates. Time durations are decimal values representing the number of seconds between two times or datetimes.

> **Tip:** Date and datetimes durations can be easily calculated by subtracting the smaller date or datetime from the larger. When dealing with SAS times, special care must be taken if the beginning and the end of a duration are on different calendar days. Whenever possible, the simplest solution is to use datetimes rather than times.

interval
> is a unit of measurement that SAS can count within an elapsed period of time, such as DAYS, MONTHS, or HOURS. The SAS System determines date and time

intervals based on fixed points on the calendar and/or the clock. The starting point of an interval calculation defaults to the beginning of the period in which the beginning value falls, which may not be the actual beginning value specified. For instance, if you are using the INTCK function to count the months between two dates, regardless of the actual day of the month specified by the date in the beginning value, SAS treats it as the first of that month.

Syntax

SAS provides date, time, and datetime intervals for counting different periods of elapsed time. You can create multiples of the intervals and shift their starting point. Use them with the INTCK and INTNX functions and with procedures that support numbered lists (such as the PLOT procedure). The form of an interval is

name<multiple><.starting-point>

The terms in an interval have the following definitions:

name
> is the name of the interval. See the following table for a list of intervals and their definitions.

multiple
> creates a multiple of the interval. *Multiple* can be any positive number. The default is 1. For example, YEAR2 indicates a two-year interval.

.starting-point
> is the starting point of the interval. By default, the starting point is 1. A value greater than 1 shifts the start to a later point within the interval. The unit for shifting depends on the interval, as shown in the following table. For example, YEAR.3 specifies a yearly period from the first of March through the end of February of the following year.

Intervals By Category

Table 8.3   Intervals Used with Date and Time Functions

Category	Interval	Definition	Default Starting Point	Shift Period	Example	Description
Date	DAY	Daily intervals	Each day	Days	DAY3	Three-day intervals starting on Sunday
	WEEK	Weekly intervals of seven days	Each Sunday	Days (1=Sunday ... 7=Saturday)	WEEK.7	Weekly with Saturday as the first day of the week
	WEEKDAY <*days*W>	Daily intervals with Friday-Saturday-Sunday	Each day	Days	WEEKDAY1W	Six-day week with Sunday as a weekend day

Category	Interval	Definition	Default Starting Point	Shift Period	Example	Description
		counted as the same day (five-day work week with a Saturday-Sunday weekend). *Days* identifies the weekend days by number (1=Sunday ... 7=Saturday). By default, *days*=17.			WEEKDAY35W	Five-day week with Tuesday and Thursday as weekend days (W indicates that day 3 and day 5 are weekend days)
	TENDAY	Ten-day intervals (a U.S. automobile industry convention)	First, eleventh, and twenty-first of each month	Ten-day periods	TENDAY4.2	Four ten-day periods starting at the second TENDAY period
	SEMIMONTH	Half-month intervals	First and sixteenth of each month	Semi-monthly periods	SEMIMONTH2.2	Intervals from the sixteenth of one month through the fifteenth of the next month
	MONTH	Monthly intervals	First of each month	Months	MONTH2.2	February-March, April-May, June-July, August-September, October-November, and December-January of the following year
	QTR	Quarterly (three-month) intervals	January 1 April 1 July 1 October 1	Months	QTR3.2	Three-month intervals starting on April 1, July 1, October 1, and January 1

Category	Interval	Definition	Default Starting Point	Shift Period	Example	Description
	SEMIYEAR	Semiannual (six-month) intervals	January 1 July 1	Months	SEMIYEAR.3	Six-month intervals, March-August and September-February
	YEAR	Yearly intervals	January 1	Months		
Datetime	Add DT	To any date interval	Midnight of January 1, 1960		DTMONTH DTWEEKDAY	
Time	SECOND	Second intervals	Start of the day (midnight)	Seconds		
	MINUTE	Minute intervals	Start of the day (midnight)	Minutes		
	HOUR	Hourly intervals	Start of the day (midnight)	Hours		

Example: Calculating a Duration

This program reads the project start and end dates and calculates the duration between them.

```
data projects;
options nodate pageno=1 linesize=80 pagesize=60;
   input Projid startdate date9. enddate date9.;
   Duration=enddate-startdate;
   datalines;
398 17oct1997 02nov1997
942 22jan1998 10mar1998
167 15dec1999 15feb2000
250 04jan2001 11jan2001
;

proc print data=projects;
   format startdate enddate date9.;
      title 'Days Between Project Start and Project End';
run;
```

Output 8.4 Output from the PRINT Procedure

```
        Days Between Project Start and Project End run                8

        Obs     Projid     Startdate     Enddate     Duration

         1       398       17OCT1997    02NOV1997       16
         2       942       22JAN1998    10MAR1998       47
         3       167       15DEC1999    15FEB2000       62
         4       250       04JAN2001    11JAN2001        7
```

Boundaries of Intervals

The SAS System associates date and time intervals with fixed points on the calendar. For example, the MONTH interval represents the time from the beginning of one calendar month to the next, not a period of 30 or 31 days. When you use date and time intervals (for example, with the INTCK or INTNX functions), the SAS System bases its calculations on the calendar divisions that are present. Consider the following examples:

Table 8.4 Using INTCK And INTNX

Example	Results	Explanation
mnthnum1= intck('month', '25aug2000'd, '05sep2000'd);	mnthnum1=1	The number of MONTH intervals the INTCK function counts depends on whether the first day of a month falls within the period.
mnthnum2= intck('month', '01aug2000'd, '31aug2000'd);	mnthnum2=0	
next=intnx('month', '25aug2000'd,1);	next represents 01sep2000	The INTNX function produces the SAS date value that corresponds to the beginning of the next interval.

Note: The only intervals that do not begin on the same date in each year are WEEK and WEEKDAY. A Sunday can occur on any date because the year is not divided evenly into weeks. △

Single-Unit Intervals

Single-unit intervals begin at the following points on the calendar:

Table 8.5   Single-Unit Intervals

These single-unit intervals	Begin at this point on the calendar
DAY and WEEKDAY	each day
WEEK	each Sunday
TENDAY	the first, eleventh, and twenty-first of each month
SEMIMONTH	the first and sixteenth of each month
MONTH	the first of each month
QTR	the first of January, April, July and October
SEMIYEAR	the first of January and July
YEAR	the first of January

Single-unit time intervals begin as follows:

Table 8.6   Single-Unit Time Intervals

These single-unit time intervals	Begin at this point
SECOND	each second
MINUTE	each minute
HOUR	each hour

Multiunit Intervals

Multiunit Intervals Other Than Multiweek Intervals

Multiunit intervals, such as MONTH2 or DAY50, also depend on calendar measures, but they introduce a new problem: the SAS System can find the beginning of a unit (for example, the first of a month), but where does that unit fall in the interval? For example, does the first of October mark the first or the second month in a two-month interval?

For all multiunit intervals except multiweek intervals, the SAS System creates an interval beginning on January 1, 1960, and counts forward from that date to determine where individual intervals begin on the calendar. As a practical matter, when a year can be divided evenly by an interval, think of the intervals as beginning with the current year. Thus, MONTH2 intervals begin with January, March, May, July, September, and November. Consider this example:

Table 8.7 Month2 Intervals

SAS statements	Results
howmany1=intck ('month2','15feb2000'd,'15mar2000'd);	howmany1=1
count=intck ('day50','01oct2000'd,'01jan2000'd);	count=1

In the above example, the SAS System counts 50 days beginning with January 1, 1960; then another 50 days; and so on. As part of this count, the SAS System counts one DAY50 interval between October 1, 1998 and January 1, 1999. As an example, to determine the date on which the next DAY50 interval begins, use the INTNX function, as follows:

Table 8.8 Using the INTNX Function

SAS statements	Results
start=intnx ('day50','01oct98'd,1);	SAS date value 14200, or Nov 17, 1998

The next interval begins on November 17, 1998.

Time intervals (those that represent divisions of a day) are aligned with the start of the day, that is, midnight. For example, HOUR8 intervals divide the day into the periods 00:00 to 08:00, 8:00 to 16:00, and 16:00 to 24:00 (the next midnight).

Multiweek Intervals

Multiweek intervals, such as WEEK2, present a special case. In general, weekly intervals begin on Sunday, and the SAS System counts a week whenever it passes a Sunday. However, the SAS System cannot calculate multiweek intervals based on January 1, 1960, because that date fell on a Friday, as shown:

Figure 8.2 Calculating Multi Week Intervals

Dec	Su	Mo	Tu	We	Th	Fr	Sa	Jan
1959	27	28	29	30	31	1	2	1960

Therefore, the SAS System begins the first interval on Sunday of the week containing January 1, 1960—that is, on Sunday, December 27, 1959. The SAS System counts multiweek intervals from that point. The following example counts the number of two-week intervals in the month of August, 1998:

Table 8.9 Counting Two-Week Intervals

SAS statements	Results
count=intck ('week2','01aug98'D, '31aug98'D);	count=3

To see the beginning date of the next interval, use the INTNX function, as shown here:

Table 8.10   Using INTNX to See The Beginning Date of an Interval

SAS statements	Results
`begin=intnx('week2','01aug1998'd,1);`	"Begin" represents SAS date 14093 or August 02, 1998

The next interval begins on August 16.

Shifted Intervals

Shifting the beginning point of an interval is useful when you want to make the interval represent a period in your data. For example, if your company's fiscal year begins on July 1, you can create a year beginning in July by specifying the YEAR.7 interval. Similarly, you can create a period matching U.S. presidential elections by specifying the YEAR4.11 interval. This section discusses how to use shifted intervals and how the SAS System creates them.

How to Use Shifted Intervals

When you shift a time interval by a subperiod, the shift value must be less than or equal to the number of subperiods in the interval. For example, YEAR.12 is valid (yearly periods beginning in December), but YEAR.13 is not. Similarly, YEAR2.25 is not valid because there is no twenty-fifth month in the two-year period.

In addition, you cannot shift an interval by itself. For example, you cannot shift the interval MONTH because the shifting subperiod for MONTH is one month and MONTH contains only one monthly subperiod. However, you can shift multi-unit intervals by the subperiod. For example, MONTH2.2 specifies bimonthly periods starting on the first day of the second month.

How the SAS System Creates Shifted Intervals

For all intervals except those based on weeks, the SAS System creates shifted intervals by creating the interval based on January 1, 1960, by moving forward the required number of subperiods, and by counting shifted intervals from that point. For example, suppose you create a shifted interval called DAY50.5. The SAS System creates a 50-day interval in which January 1, 1960 is day 1. The SAS System then moves forward to day 5. (Note that the *difference*, or amount of movement, is 4 days.) The SAS System begins counting shifted intervals from that point. The INTNX function demonstrates that the next interval begins on January 5, 1960:

Table 8.11   Using INTNX to Determine When an Interval Begins

SAS statements	Results
`start=intnx('day50.5','01jan1960'd,1);`	SAS date value 4, or Jan 5, 1960

For shifted intervals based on weeks, the SAS System first creates an interval based on Sunday of the week containing January 1, 1960 (that is, December 27, 1959), then moves forward the required number of days. For example, suppose you want to create the interval WEEK2.8 (biweekly periods beginning on the second Sunday of the period). The SAS System measures a two-week interval based on Sunday of the week containing January 1, 1960, and begins counting shifted intervals on the eighth day of that. The INTNX function shows the beginning of the next interval:

Table 8.12   Using the INTNX Function to Show the Beginning of the Next Interval

SAS statements	Results
`start=intnx` `('week2.8','01jan1960'd,1);`	SAS date value 2, or Jan 3, 1960

You can also shift time intervals. For example, HOUR8.7 intervals divide the day into the periods 06:00 to 14:00, 14:00 to 22:00, and 22:00 to 06:00.

Error Processing and Debugging

Types of Errors in SAS   **147**
   Summary of Types of Errors That SAS Recognizes   **147**
   Syntax Errors   **148**
   Semantic Errors   **150**
   Execution-Time Errors   **151**
      Definition   **151**
      Out-of-Resources Condition   **152**
      Examples   **152**
   Data Errors   **154**
      Format Modifiers for Error Reporting   **156**
   Macro-related Errors   **156**
Error Processing in SAS   **156**
   Syntax Check Mode   **156**
   Enabling Syntax Check Mode   **157**
   Processing Multiple Errors   **157**
   Using System Options to Control Error Handling   **158**
   Using Return Codes   **159**
   Other Error-Checking Options   **159**
Debugging Logic Errors in the DATA Step   **159**

Types of Errors in SAS

Summary of Types of Errors That SAS Recognizes

SAS performs *error processing* during both the compilation and the execution phases of SAS processing. You can *debug* SAS programs by understanding processing messages in the SAS log and then fixing your code. You can use the DATA Step Debugger to detect logic errors in a DATA step during execution.

SAS recognizes five types of errors.

Type of error	When this error occurs	When the error is detected
syntax	when programming statements do not conform to the rules of the SAS language	compile time
semantic	when the language element is correct, but the element may not be valid for a particular usage	compile time

Type of error	When this error occurs	When the error is detected
execution-time	when SAS attempts to execute a program and execution fails	execution time
data	when data values are invalid	execution time
macro-related	when you use the macro facility incorrectly	macro compile time or execution time, DATA or PROC step compile time or execution time

Syntax Errors

Syntax errors occur when program statements do not conform to the rules of the SAS language. Here are some examples of syntax errors:

- □ misspelled SAS keyword
- □ unmatched quotation marks
- □ missing a semicolon
- □ invalid statement option
- □ invalid data set option.

When SAS encounters a syntax error, it first attempts to correct the error by attempting to interpret what you mean, then continues processing your program based on its assumptions. If SAS cannot correct the error, it prints an error message to the log.

In the following example, the DATA statement is misspelled, and SAS prints a warning message to the log. Because SAS could interpret the misspelled word, the program runs and produces output.

```
date temp;
    x=1;
run;

proc print data=temp;
run;
```

Output 9.1 SAS Log: Syntax Error (misspelled key word)

```
1    date temp;
     ----
     14
WARNING 14-169: Assuming the symbol DATA was misspelled as date.

2       x=1;
3    run;

NOTE: The data set WORK.TEMP has 1 observations and 1 variables.
NOTE: DATA statement used:
      real time          0.17 seconds
      cpu time           0.04 seconds


4
5    proc print data=temp;
6    run;

NOTE: PROCEDURE PRINT used:
      real time          0.14 seconds
      cpu time           0.03 seconds
```

Some errors are explained fully by the message that SAS prints in the log; other error messages are not as easy to interpret because SAS is not always able to detect exactly where the error occurred. For example, when you fail to end a SAS statement with a semicolon, SAS does not always detect the error at the point where it occurs because SAS statements are free-format (they can begin and end anywhere). In the following example, the semicolon at the end of the DATA statement is missing. SAS prints the word ERROR in the log, identifies the possible location of the error, prints an explanation of the error, and stops processing the DATA step.

```
data temp
   x=1;
run;

proc print data=temp;
run;
```

Output 9.2   SAS Log: Syntax Error (missing semicolon)

```
1    data temp
2       x=1;
        -
        76
ERROR 76-322: Syntax error, statement will be ignored.

3    run;

NOTE: The SAS System stopped processing this step because of errors.
NOTE: DATA statement used:
      real time          0.11 seconds
      cpu time           0.02 seconds


4
5    proc print data=temp;
ERROR: File WORK.TEMP.DATA does not exist.
6    run;

NOTE: The SAS System stopped processing this step because of errors.
NOTE: PROCEDURE PRINT used:
      real time          0.06 seconds
      cpu time           0.01 seconds
```

Whether subsequent steps are executed depends on which method of running SAS you use, as well as on your operating environment.

Semantic Errors

Semantic errors occur when the form of the elements in a SAS statement is correct, but the elements are not valid for that usage. Semantic errors are detected at compile time and can cause SAS to enter syntax check mode. (For a description of syntax check mode, see "Syntax Check Mode" on page 156.)

Examples of semantic errors include the following:

☐ specifying the wrong number of arguments for a function

☐ using a numeric variable name where only a character variable is valid

☐ using illegal references to an array.

In the following example, SAS detects an illegal reference to the array ALL.

```
data _null_;
   array all{*} x1-x5;
   all=3;
   datalines;
1 1.5
. 3
2 4.5
3 2 7
3 . .
;

run;
```

Output 9.3 SAS Log: Semantic Error (illegal reference to an array)

```
        cpu time               0.02 seconds

1    data _null_;
2        array all{*} x1-x5;
ERROR: Illegal reference to the array all.
3        all=3;
4        datalines;
NOTE: The SAS System stopped processing this step because of errors.
NOTE: DATA statement used:
        real time              2.28 seconds
        cpu time               0.06 seconds


10    ;
11
```

The following is another example of a semantic error. In this DATA step, the libref SOMELIB has not been previously assigned in a LIBNAME statement.

```
data test;
    set somelib.old;
run;
```

Output 9.4 SAS Log: Semantic Error (libref not previously assigned)

```
        cpu time               0.00 seconds

1    data test;
ERROR: Libname SOMELIB is not assigned.
2        set somelib.old;
3    run;
NOTE: The SAS System stopped processing this step because of errors.
WARNING: The data set WORK.TEST may be incomplete.  When this step was stopped
         there were 0 observations and 0 variables.
NOTE: DATA statement used:
        real time              0.17 seconds
```

Execution-Time Errors

Definition

Execution-time errors are errors that occur when SAS executes a program that processes data values. Most execution-time errors produce warning messages or notes in the SAS log but allow the program to continue executing. *The location of an execution-time error is usually given as line and column numbers in a note or error message.

Common execution-time errors include the following:

□ illegal arguments to functions

□ illegal mathematical operations (for example, division by 0)

□ observations in the wrong order for BY-group processing

---

* When you run SAS in noninteractive mode, more serious errors can cause SAS to enter syntax check mode and stop processing the program.

- □ reference to a nonexistent member of an array (occurs when the array's subscript is out of range)
- □ open and close errors on SAS data sets and other files in INFILE and FILE statements
- □ INPUT statements that do not match the data lines (for example, an INPUT statement in which you list the wrong columns for a variable or fail to indicate that the variable is a character variable).

Out-of-Resources Condition

An execution-time error can also occur when you encounter an out-of-resources condition, such as a full disk, or insufficient memory for a SAS procedure to complete. When these conditions occur, SAS attempts to find resources for current use. For example, SAS may ask the user for permission to delete temporary data sets that might no longer be needed, or to free the memory in which macro variables are stored.

When an out-of-resources condition occurs in a windowing environment, you can use the SAS CLEANUP system option to display a requestor panel that enables you to choose how to resolve the error. When you run SAS in batch, noninteractive, or interactive line mode, the operation of CLEANUP depends on your operating environment. For more information, see the CLEANUP system option in *SAS Language Reference: Dictionary*, and in the SAS documentation for your operating environment.

Examples

In the following example, an execution-time error occurs when SAS uses data values from the second observation to perform the division operation in the assignment statement. Division by 0 is an illegal mathematical operation and causes an execution-time error.

```
options linesize=64 nodate pageno=1 pagesize=25;

data inventory;
   input Item $ 1-14 TotalCost 15-20
         UnitsOnHand 21-23;
   UnitCost=TotalCost/UnitsOnHand;
   datalines;
Hammers        440    55
Nylon cord     35     0
Ceiling fans   1155   30
;

proc print data=inventory;
   format TotalCost dollar8.2 UnitCost dollar8.2;
run;
```

Output 9.5 SAS Log: Execution-Time Error (division by 0)

```
        cpu time                 0.02 seconds

 1
 2      options linesize=64 nodate pageno=1 pagesize=25;
 3
 4      data inventory;
 5         input Item $ 1-14 TotalCost 15-20
 6              UnitsOnHand 21-23;
 7         UnitCost=TotalCost/UnitsOnHand;
 8         datalines;
NOTE: Division by zero detected at line 12 column 22.
RULE:----+----1----+----2----+----3----+----4----+----5----+----
10   Nylon cord    35    0
Item=Nylon cord TotalCost=35 UnitsOnHand=0 UnitCost=. _ERROR_=1
_N_=2
NOTE: Mathematical operations could not be performed at the
      following places. The results of the operations have been
      set to missing values.
      Each place is given by:
      (Number of times) at (Line):(Column).
      1 at 12:22
NOTE: The data set WORK.INVENTORY has 3 observations and 4
      variables.
NOTE: DATA statement used:
      real time                 2.78 seconds
      cpu time                  0.08 seconds

12   ;
13
14   proc print data=inventory;
15      format TotalCost dollar8.2 UnitCost dollar8.2;
16   run;
NOTE: There were 3 observations read from the dataset
      WORK.INVENTORY.
NOTE: PROCEDURE PRINT used:
      real time                 2.62 seconds
```

Output 9.6 SAS Listing Output: Execution-Time Error (division by 0)

```
                        The SAS System                        1

                        Total      Units
     Obs    Item         Cost      OnHand     UnitCost

      1     Hammers      $440.00     55        $8.00
      2     Nylon cord    $35.00      0          .
      3     Ceiling fans $1155.00    30        $38.50
```

SAS executes the entire step, assigns a missing value for the variable UnitCost in the output, and writes the following to the SAS log:

☐ a note that describes the error

☐ the values that are stored in the input buffer

☐ the contents of the program data vector at the time the error occurred

☐ a note explaining the error.

Note that the values that are listed in the program data vector include the _N_ and _ERROR_ automatic variables. These automatic variables are assigned temporarily to each observation and are not stored with the data set.

In the following example of an execution-time error, the program processes an array and SAS encounters a value of the array's subscript that is out of range. SAS prints an error message to the log and stops processing.

```
options linesize=64 nodate pageno=1 pagesize=25;

data test;
   array all{*} x1-x3;
   input I measure;
   if measure > 0 then
      all{I} = measure;
   datalines;
1 1.5
. 3
2 4.5
;

proc print data=test;
run;
```

Output 9.7 SAS Log: Execution-Time Error (subscript out of range)

```
      cpu time             0.02 seconds

1     options linesize=64 nodate pageno=1 pagesize=25;
2
3     data test;
4        array all{*} x1-x3;
5        input I measure;
6        if measure > 0 then
7           all{I} = measure;
8        datalines;
ERROR: Array subscript out of range at line 12 column 7.
RULE:----+----1----+----2----+----3----+----4----+----5----+----
10    . 3
x1=. x2=. x3=. I=. measure=3 _ERROR_=1 _N_=2
NOTE: The SAS System stopped processing this step because of
      errors.
WARNING: The data set WORK.TEST may be incomplete.  When this
         step was stopped there were 1 observations and 5
         variables.
NOTE: DATA statement used:
      real time            0.90 seconds
      cpu time             0.09 seconds

12    ;
13
14    proc print data=test;
15    run;
NOTE: There were 1 observations read from the dataset WORK.TEST.
NOTE: PROCEDURE PRINT used:
      real time            0.81 seconds
```

Data Errors

Data errors occur when some data values are not appropriate for the SAS statements that you have specified in the program. For example, if you define a variable as numeric, but the data value is actually character, SAS generates a data error. SAS detects data errors during program execution and continues to execute the program, and does the following:

- □ writes an invalid data note to the SAS log.
- □ prints the input line and column numbers that contain the invalid value in the SAS log. Unprintable characters appear in hexadecimal. To help determine column numbers, SAS prints a rule line above the input line.
- □ prints the observation under the rule line.
- □ sets the automatic variable _ERROR_ to 1 for the current observation.

In this example, a character value in the Number variable results in a data error during program execution:

```
options linesize=64 nodate pageno=1 pagesize=25;

data age;
   input Name $ Number;
   datalines;
Sue 35
Joe xx
Steve 22
;

proc print data=age;
run;
```

The SAS log shows that there is an error in line 8, position 5–6 of the program.

Output 9.8 SAS Log: Data Error

```
        cpu time             0.01 seconds

1
2     options linesize=64 nodate pageno=1 pagesize=25;
3
4     data age;
5        input Name $ Number;
6        datalines;
NOTE: Invalid data for Number in line 8 5-6.
RULE:----+----1----+----2----+----3----+----4----+----5----+----6
8   Joe xx
Name=Joe Number=. _ERROR_=1 _N_=2
NOTE: The data set WORK.AGE has 3 observations and 2 variables.
NOTE: DATA statement used:
        real time            0.06 seconds
        cpu time             0.02 seconds

10   ;
11
12    proc print data=age;
13    run;
NOTE: There were 3 observations read from the dataset WORK.AGE.
NOTE: PROCEDURE PRINT used:
        real time            0.01 seconds
```

Output 9.9   SAS Listing Output: Data Error

```
                         The SAS System                          1

                  Obs     Name     Number

                   1      Sue        35
                   2      Joe         .
                   3      Steve      22
```

You can also use the INVALIDDATA= system option to assign a value to a variable when your program encounters invalid data. For more information, see the INVALIDDATA= system option in *SAS Language Reference: Dictionary*.

Format Modifiers for Error Reporting

The INPUT statement uses the ? and the ?? format modifiers for error reporting. The format modifiers control the amount of information that is written to the SAS log. Both the ? and the ?? modifiers suppress the invalid data message. However, the ?? modifier also sets the automatic variable _ERROR_ to 0. For example, these two sets of statements are equivalent:

☐   input x ?? 10-12;

☐   input x ? 10-12;
    error=0;

In either case, SAS sets the invalid values of X to missing values.

Macro-related Errors

Several types of macro-related errors exist:

☐   macro compile time and macro execution-time errors, generated when you use the macro facility itself

☐   errors in the SAS code produced by the macro facility.

For more information about macros, see *SAS Macro Language: Reference*.

Error Processing in SAS

Syntax Check Mode

If you want processing to stop when a statement in a DATA step has a syntax error, you can enable SAS to enter syntax check mode. SAS internally sets the OBS= option to 0 and the REPLACE/NOREPLACE option to NOREPLACE. When these options are in effect, SAS acts as follows:

☐   reads the remaining statements in the DATA step or PROC step

☐   checks that statements are valid SAS statements

☐   executes global statements

- □ writes errors to the SAS log
- □ creates the descriptor portion of any output data sets that are specified in program statements
- □ does not write any observations to new data sets that SAS creates
- □ does not execute most of the subsequent DATA steps or procedures in the program (exceptions include PROC DATASETS and PROC CONTENTS).

Note: Any data sets that are created after SAS has entered syntax check mode do not replace existing data sets with the same name. △

When syntax checking is enabled, if SAS encounters a syntax or semantic error in a DATA step, SAS underlines the point where it detects the error and identifies the error by number. SAS then enters syntax check mode and remains in this mode until the program finishes executing. When SAS enters syntax check mode, all DATA step statements and PROC step statements are validated.

Enabling Syntax Check Mode

You use the SYNTAXCHECK system option to enable syntax check mode when you run SAS in non-interactive or batch mode. You use the DMSSYNCHK system option to enable syntax check mode when you run SAS in the windowing environment. To disable syntax check mode, use the NOSYNTAXCHECK and NODMSSYNCHK system options.

In an OPTIONS statement, place the OPTIONS statement that enables SYNTAXCHECK or DMSSYNCHK before the step for which you want it to apply. If you place the OPTIONS statement inside a step, then SYNTAXCHECK or DMSSYNCHK will not take effect until the beginning of the next step.

For more information about the DMSSYNCHK system option and the SYNTAXCHECK system option in *SAS Language Reference: Dictionary*.

Processing Multiple Errors

Depending on the type and severity of the error, the method you use to run SAS, and your operating environment, SAS either stops program processing or flags errors and continues processing. SAS continues to check individual statements in procedures after it finds certain kinds of errors. Thus, in some cases SAS can detect multiple errors in a single statement and may issue more error messages for a given situation, particularly if the statement containing the error creates an output SAS data set.

The following example illustrates a statement with two errors:

```
data temporary;
   Item1=4;
run;

proc print data=temporary;
   var Item1 Item2 Item3;
run;
```

Output 9.10 SAS Log: Multiple Program Errors

```
      cpu time              0.00 seconds

1  data temporary;
2     Item1=4;
3  run;
NOTE: The data set WORK.TEMPORARY has 1 observations and 1
      variables.
NOTE: DATA statement used:
      real time             0.10 seconds
      cpu time              0.01 seconds

4
5  proc print data=temporary;
ERROR: Variable ITEM2 not found.
ERROR: Variable ITEM3 not found.
6     var Item1 Item2 Item3;
7  run;
NOTE: The SAS System stopped processing this step because of
      errors.
NOTE: PROCEDURE PRINT used:
      real time             0.53 seconds
      cpu time              0.01 seconds
```

SAS displays two error messages, one for the variable Item2 and one for the variable Item3.

When you are running debugged production programs that are unlikely to encounter errors, you might want to force SAS to abend after a single error occurs. You can use the ERRORABEND system option to do this.

Using System Options to Control Error Handling

You can use the following system options to control error handling (resolve errors) in your program:

BYERR	controls whether SAS generates an error message and sets the error flag when a _NULL_ data set is used in the SORT procedure.
DKRICOND=	controls the level of error detection for input data sets during the processing of DROP=, KEEP=, and RENAME= data set options.
DKROCOND=	controls the level of error detection for output data sets during the processing of DROP=, KEEP=, and RENAME= data set options and the corresponding DATA step statements.
DSNFERR	controls how SAS responds when a SAS data set is not found.
ERRORABEND	specifies how SAS responds to errors.
ERRORCHECK=	controls error handling in batch processing.
ERRORS=	controls the maximum number of observations for which complete error messages are printed.
FMTERR	determines whether SAS generates an error message when a format of a variable cannot be found.
INVALIDDATA=	specifies the value that SAS assigns to a variable when invalid numeric data is encountered.
MERROR	controls whether SAS issues a warning message when a macro-like name does not match a macro keyword.

SERROR   controls whether SAS issues a warning message when a defined
                    macro variable reference does not match a macro variable.

VNFERR   controls how SAS responds when a _NULL_ data set is used.

For more information about SAS system options, see *SAS Language Reference: Dictionary*.

Using Return Codes

In some operating environments, SAS passes a return code to the system, but the way in which return codes are accessed is specific to your operating environment.

Operating Environment Information: For more information about return codes, see the SAS documentation for your operating environment. △

Other Error-Checking Options

To help determine your programming errors, you can use the following methods:

□ the _IORC_ automatic variable that SAS creates (and the associated IORCMSG function) when you use the MODIFY statement or the KEY= data set option in the SET statement

□ the ERROR= system option to limit the number of identical errors that SAS writes to the log

□ the SYSRC and SYSMSG functions to return information when a data set or external-files access function encounters an error condition

□ the SYSRC and SYSERR macro variables

□ log control options:

MSGLEVEL=   controls the level of detail in messages that are written to the SAS log.

PRINTMSGLIST   controls the printing of extended lists of messages to the SAS log.

SOURCE   controls whether SAS writes source statements to the SAS log.

SOURCE2   controls whether SAS writes source statements included by %INCLUDE to the SAS log.

Debugging Logic Errors in the DATA Step

To debug logic errors in a DATA step, you can use the DATA step debugger. This tool enables you to issue commands to execute DATA step statements one by one and then pause to display the resulting variables' values in a window. By observing the results that are displayed, you can determine where the logic error lies. Because the debugger is interactive, you can repeat the process of issuing commands and observing results as many times as needed in a single debugging session. To invoke the debugger, add the DEBUG option to the DATA statement and execute the program. For detailed information about how to use the DATA step debugger, see *SAS Language Reference: Dictionary*.

160

CHAPTER

10

SAS Output

Definitions for SAS Output   **162**
Routing SAS Output   **163**
The SAS Log   **163**
   Structure of the Log   **163**
   Writing to the Log   **165**
   Customizing the Log   **165**
      Altering the Contents of the Log   **165**
      Customizing the Appearance of the Log   **166**
Traditional SAS Listing Output   **167**
   Example of Traditional Listing Output   **167**
   Making Output Descriptive   **168**
   Reformatting Values   **169**
   Printing Missing Values   **169**
Changing the Destination of the Log and the Output   **170**
Output Delivery System   **170**
   What Is the Output Delivery System?   **170**
   Gallery of ODS Samples   **171**
      Introduction to the ODS Samples   **171**
      Listing Output   **171**
      PostScript Output   **173**
      HTML Output   **173**
      RTF Output   **174**
      PDF Output   **175**
      XML Output   **176**
   Commonly Used ODS Terminology   **178**
   How Does ODS Work?   **179**
      Components of SAS Output   **179**
      Features of ODS   **180**
   What Are the ODS Destinations?   **181**
      Overview of ODS Destination Categories   **181**
      Definition of Destination-Independent Input   **181**
      The SAS Formatted Destinations   **182**
      The Third-Party Formatted Destinations   **183**
      What Controls the Formatting Features of Third-Party Formats?   **184**
      ODS Destinations and System Resources   **185**
   What Are Table Definitions, Table Elements, and Table Attributes?   **185**
   What Are Style Definitions, Style Elements, and Style Attributes?   **185**
      What Style Definitions Are Shipped with SAS Software?   **186**
      How Do I Use Style Definitions with Base SAS Procedures?   **187**
   Changing SAS Registry Settings for ODS   **187**
      Overview of ODS and the SAS Registry   **187**

Changing Your Default HTML Version Setting   **188**
Changing ODS Destination Default Settings   **189**
Customized ODS Output   **189**
SAS Output   **189**
Selection and Exclusion Lists   **190**
How Does ODS Determine the Destinations for an Output Object?   **190**
Customized Output for an Output Object   **191**
Summary of ODS   **192**

Definitions for SAS Output

SAS output is the result of executing SAS programs. Most SAS procedures and some DATA step applications produce output.

There are three types of SAS output:

SAS log
> contains a description of the SAS session and lists the lines of source code that were executed. Depending on the setting of SAS system options, the method of running SAS, and the program statements that you specify, the log can include the following types of information:
>
> □ program statements
>
> □ names of data sets created by the program
>
> □ notes, warnings, or error messages encountered during program execution
>
> □ the number of variables and observations each data set contains
>
> □ processing time required for each step.
>
> You can write specific information to the SAS log (such as variable values or text strings) by using the SAS statements that are described in "Writing to the Log" on page 165.
>
> The log is also used by some of the SAS procedures that perform utility functions, for example the DATASETS and OPTIONS procedures. See *Base SAS Procedures Guide* for more information.
>
> Because the SAS log provides a journal of program processing, it is an essential debugging tool. However, certain system options must be in effect to make the log effective for debugging your SAS programs. "Customizing the Log" on page 165 describes several SAS system options that you can use.

program results
> contain the results of most SAS procedures and some DATA step applications. Results can be routed to a file, and printed as a listing. If you use the Output Delivery System (ODS), you can produce results for a high resolution printer or create HTML output for use with a web browser. You can customize your output by modifying or creating your own table definitions, which are descriptions of how you want to format your output. For more information about the flexibility of ODS, see *SAS Output Delivery System: User's Guide*.

SAS console log
> When the SAS log is not active, it contains information, warning, and error messages. When the SAS log is active, the SAS console log is used only for fatal system initialization errors or late termination messages.
>
> *Operating Environment Information:*   See the SAS documentation for your operating environment for specific information on the destination of the SAS console log. △

Routing SAS Output

The destination of your output depends on

□ the operating environment

□ the setting of SAS system options

□ whether you use ODS

□ the method of running SAS.

There are several ways to route SAS output to a destination other than the default destination. You can route the output to your terminal, to an external file, or directly to a printer. If you use ODS, you can route output to a data set for most procedures.

Operating Environment Information: See the SAS documentation for your operating environment for specific information. △

The following table shows the default destination of SAS output for each method of operation.

Table 10.1 Default Destinations of SAS Output

Method of Running SAS	Destination of SAS Output
windowing mode (Explorer window)	the Log window or the output window
interactive line mode	the terminal display (as statements are entered)
noninteractive mode	depends on the operating environment
batch mode	depends on the operating environment

Operating Environment Information: The default destination for SAS output is specific to your operating environment. For specific information, see the SAS documentation for your operating environment. △

The SAS Log

Structure of the Log

The SAS log is a record of everything you do in your SAS session or with your SAS program. Original program statements are identified by line numbers. Interspersed with SAS statements are messages from SAS. These messages may begin with the words NOTE, INFO, WARNING, ERROR, or an error number, and they may refer to a SAS statement by its line number in the log.

For example, in the following output, the number 1 prints to the left of the OPTIONS statement. This means that it is the first line in the program. In interactive mode, SAS continues with the sequence of line numbering until you end your session. If you submit the program again (or submit other programs in your current SAS session), the first program line number will be the next consecutive number.

Operating Environment Information: The SAS log appears differently depending on your operating environment. See the SAS documentation for your operating environment. △

Output 10.1 Sample SAS Log

```
NOTE: Copyright (c) 2002--2003 by SAS Institute Inc., Cary, NC, USA.  ❶
NOTE: SAS (r) 9.1 (TS1B0) ❷
      Licensed to SAS Institute Inc., Site 0000000001.  ❸
NOTE: This session is executing on the HP-UX B.10.20 platform.  ❹


NOTE: SAS initialization used:
      real time            4.20 seconds
      cpu time             1.18 seconds

1     options pagesize=24 linesize=64 nodate;  ❺
2
3     data logsample;  ❻
4        infile '/u/abcdef/testdir/sampledata.dat';
5        input LastName $ 1-12 ID $ Gender $ Birth : date7.  ❼
5   ! score1 score2 score3
6                                                            score
6   ! 4 score5 score6;
7        format Birth mmddyy8.;
8     run;

NOTE: The infile '/u/abcdef/testdir/sampledata.dat' is:  ❽
      File Name=/u/abcdef/testdir/sampledata.dat,
      Owner Name=abcdef,Group Name=pubs,
      Access Permission=rw-r--r--,
      File Size (bytes)=296

NOTE: 5 records were read from the infile  ❾
      '/u/abcdef/testdir/sampledata.dat'.
      The minimum record length was 58.
      The maximum record length was 59.
NOTE: The data set WORK.LOGSAMPLE has 5 observations and 10
      variables.  ❿
NOTE: DATA statement used:
      real time            0.44 seconds
      cpu time             0.13 seconds

9
10    proc sort data=logsample;  ⓫
11       by LastName;
12

NOTE: There were 5 observations read from the dataset
      WORK.LOGSAMPLE.
NOTE: The data set WORK.LOGSAMPLE has 5 observations and 10
      variables.  ⓬
NOTE: PROCEDURE SORT used:
      real time            0.16 seconds
      cpu time             0.03 seconds


13    proc print data=logsample;  ⓭
14       by LastName;
15    run;

NOTE: There were 5 observations read from the dataset
      WORK.LOGSAMPLE.
NOTE: PROCEDURE PRINT used:
      real time            0.31 seconds
      cpu time             0.05 seconds
```

The following list corresponds to the circled numbers in the SAS log shown above:

❶ copyright information.

❷ SAS system release used to run this program.

❸ name and site number of the computer installation where the program ran.

❹ platform used to run the program.

❺ OPTIONS statement. This statement uses SAS system options to set a page size of 24 and a line size of 64, and to suppress the date in the output.

❻ SAS statements that make up the program (if the SAS system option SOURCE is enabled).

❼ long statement continued to the next line. Note that the continuation line is preceded by an exclamation point (!), and that the line number does not change.

❽ input file information-notes or warning messages about the raw data and where they were obtained (if the SAS system option NOTES is enabled).

❾ the number and record length of records read from the input file (if the SAS system option NOTES is enabled).

❿ SAS data set that your program created; notes that contain the number of observations and variables for each data set created (if the SAS system option NOTES is enabled).

⓫ procedure that sorts your data set

⓬ note about the sorted SAS data set

⓭ procedure that prints your data set.

Writing to the Log

You can instruct SAS to write additional information to the log by using the following statements:

PUT statement
  writes selected lines (including text strings and DATA step variable values) to the SAS log. This behavior of the PUT statement requires that your program does not execute a FILE statement before the PUT statement in the current iteration of a DATA step, and that it does not execute a `FILE LOG;` statement.

%PUT statement
  enables you to write a text string or macro variable values to the SAS log. %PUT is a SAS macro program statement that is independent of the DATA step and can be used anywhere.

LIST statement
  writes to the SAS log the input data records for the data line that is being processed. The LIST statement operates only on data that are read with an INPUT statement. It has no effect on data that are read with a SET, MERGE, MODIFY, or UPDATE statement. Use the LIST statement in a DATA step.

ERROR statement
  sets the automatic _ERROR_ variable to 1 and optionally writes to the log a message that you specify. Use the ERROR statement in a DATA step.

Use the PUT, LIST, and ERROR statements in combination with conditional processing to debug DATA steps by writing selected information to the log.

Customizing the Log

Altering the Contents of the Log

When you have large SAS production programs or an application that you run on a regular basis without changes, you might want to suppress part of the log. SAS system options enable you to suppress SAS statements and system messages, as well as to limit the number of error messages. Note that all SAS system options remain in effect for the duration of your session or until you change the options. You should not suppress log messages until you have successfully executed the program without errors.

The following list describes some of the SAS system options that you can use to alter the contents of the log:

CPUID | NOCPUID
>   controls whether hardware information is written to the SAS log.

ECHOAUTO | NOECHOAUTO
>   controls whether autoexec code in an input file is written to the log.

ERRORS=*n*
>   specifies the maximum number of observations for which data error messages are printed.

MPRINT | NOMPRINT
>   controls whether SAS statements that are generated by macro execution are written to the SAS log.

MSGLEVEL=N | I
>   controls the level of detail in messages that are written to the SAS log. If the MSGLEVEL system option is set to N, the log displays notes, warnings, and error messages only. If MSGLEVEL is set to I, the log displays additional notes pertaining to index usage, merge processing, and sort utilities, along with standard notes, warnings, and error messages.

NEWS=*external-file*
>   controls whether news information that is maintained at your site is written to the SAS log.

NOTES | NONOTES
>   controls whether notes (messages beginning with NOTE) are written to the SAS log. NONOTES does not suppress error or warning messages.

OVP | NOOVP
>   controls whether output lines that are printed by SAS are overprinted.

PRINTMSGLIST | NOPRINTMSGLIST
>   controls whether extended lists of messages are written to the SAS log.

SOURCE | NOSOURCE
>   controls whether SAS writes source statements to the SAS log.

SOURCE2 | NOSOURCE2
>   controls whether SAS writes secondary source statements from files included by %INCLUDE statements to the SAS log.

SYMBOLGEN | NOSYMBOLGEN
>   controls whether the results of resolving macro variable references are written to the SAS log.

See *SAS Language Reference: Dictionary* for more information about how to use these and other SAS system options.

Operating Environment Information: See the documentation for your operating environment for other options that affect log output. △

Customizing the Appearance of the Log

The following SAS statements and SAS system options enable you to customize the log. Customizing the log is helpful when you use the log for report writing or for creating a permanent record.

| DATE system option | controls whether the date and time that the SAS job began are printed at the top of each page of the SAS log and any output created by SAS. |
| FILE statement | enables you to write the results of PUT statements to an external file. You can use the following two options in the FILE statement to customize the log for that report. |

| | LINESIZE=*value* | specifies the maximum number of columns per line for reports and the maximum record length for data files. |
| | PAGESIZE=*value* | specifies the maximum number of lines to print on each page of output. |

Note: FILE statement options apply only to the output specified in the FILE statement, whereas the LINESIZE= and PAGESIZE= SAS system options apply to all subsequent listings. △

LINESIZE= system option	specifies the line size (printer line width) for the SAS log and SAS output that are used by the DATA step and procedures.
MISSING= system option	specifies the character to be printed for missing numeric variable values.
NUMBER system option	controls whether the page number prints on the first title line of each page of printed output.
PAGE statement	skips to a new page in the SAS log and continues printing from there.
PAGESIZE= system option	specifies the number of lines that you can print per page of SAS output.
SKIP statement	skips a specified number of lines in the SAS log.

Operating Environment Information: The range of values for the FILE statement and for SAS system options depends on your operating environment. See the SAS documentation for your operating environment for more information. △

For more information about how to use these and other SAS system options and statements, see *SAS Language Reference: Dictionary*.

Traditional SAS Listing Output

Example of Traditional Listing Output

Many SAS procedures process or analyze data and can produce output as one result. You can also generate a listing by the DATA step, using a combination of the FILE and PUT statements.

See the procedure descriptions in *Base SAS Procedures Guide* for examples of output from SAS procedures. For a discussion and examples of DATA step output, see the FILE and PUT statements in *SAS Language Reference: Dictionary*.

This example produces a listing that is generated by the PUT and FILE statements in a DATA step. The input file is the SAS data set GRAIN_PRODUCERS.

```
options pagesize=60 linesize=64 nodate pageno=1;

title 'Leading Grain Producers';
title2 'for 1996';

data _null_;
    set grain_producers;
    file print header=newpage;
    if year=1996;
    format country $cntry.;
    label type='Grain';
    put country @25 type @50 kilotons;
    return;
    newpage:
        put 'Country' @25 'Grain' @50 'Kilotons';
        put 60*'=';
        return;
  run;
```

```
                     Leading Grain Producers                    1
                            for 1996
Country                  Grain                    Kilotons
================================================================
Brazil                   Wheat                    3302
Brazil                   Rice                     10035
Brazil                   Corn                     31975
China                    Wheat                    109000
China                    Rice                     190100
China                    Corn                     119350
India                    Wheat                    62620
India                    Rice                     120012
India                    Corn                     8660
Indonesia                Wheat                    .
Indonesia                Rice                     51165
Indonesia                Corn                     8925
United States            Wheat                    62099
United States            Rice                     7771
United States            Corn                     236064
```

Making Output Descriptive

There are several ways to customize SAS procedure output and DATA step output. You can change the look of output by adding informative titles, footnotes, and labels, and by changing the way the information is formatted on the page. The following list describes some of the statements and SAS system options that you can use.

CENTER | NOCENTER system option
> controls whether output is centered. By default, SAS centers titles and procedure output on the page and on the terminal display.

DATE | NODATE system option
> controls printing of date and time values. When this option is enabled, SAS prints on the top of each page of output the date and time the SAS job started. When you run SAS in interactive mode, the date and time the job started is the date and time you started your SAS session.

FOOTNOTE statements
> print footnotes at the bottom of each output page. You can also use the FOOTNOTES window for this purpose.

FORMCHAR=
> specifies the default output formatting characters for some procedures such as CALENDAR, FREQ, REPORT, and TABULATE.

FORMDLIM=
> specifies a character that is used to delimit page breaks in SAS output.

LABEL statement
> associates descriptive labels with variables. With most procedure output, SAS writes the label rather than the variable name.
>
> The LABEL statement also provides descriptive labels when it is used with certain SAS procedures. See *Base SAS Procedures Guide* for information on using the LABEL statement with a specific procedure (for example, the PRINT procedure).

LINESIZE= and PAGESIZE= system options
> can change the default number of lines per page (page size) and characters per line (line size) for printed output. The default depends on the method of running SAS and the settings of certain SAS system options. Specify new page and line sizes in the OPTIONS statement or OPTIONS window. You can also specify line and page size for DATA step output in the FILE statement.
>
> The values you use for the LINESIZE= and PAGESIZE= system options can significantly affect the appearance of the output that is produced by some SAS procedures.

NUMBER | NONUMBER and PAGENO= system options
> control page numbering. The NUMBER system option controls whether the page number prints on the first title line of each page of printed output. You can also specify a beginning page number for the next page of output produced by SAS by using the PAGENO= system option.

TITLE statements
> print titles at the top of each output page. By default, SAS prints the following title:
>
>  ```
>  The SAS System
>  ```
>
> You can use the TITLE statement or TITLES window to replace the default title or specify other descriptive titles for SAS programs. You can use the null title statement (`title;`) to suppress a TITLE statement.

See *SAS Language Reference: Dictionary* for more information about how to use these and other SAS system options and statements.

Reformatting Values

Certain SAS statements, procedures, and options enable you to print values using specified formats. You can apply or change formats with the FORMAT and ATTRIB statements, or with the VAR window in a windowing environment.

The FORMAT procedure enables you to design your own formats and informats, giving you added flexibility in displaying values. See the FORMAT procedure in *Base SAS Procedures Guide* for more information.

Printing Missing Values

SAS represents ordinary missing numeric values in a SAS listing as a single period, and missing character values as a blank space. If you specified special missing values for numeric variables, SAS writes the letter or the underscore. For character variables, SAS writes a series of blanks equal to the length of the variable.

The MISSING= system option enables you to specify a character to print in place of the period for ordinary missing numeric values.

Changing the Destination of the Log and the Output

You can redirect both the SAS log and procedure output to your terminal display, to a printer, or to an external file. You can redirect output using the following methods:

PRINTTO procedure
   routes DATA step, log, or procedure output from the system default destinations to the destination you choose.

FILENAME statement
   associates a fileref with an external file or output device and enables you to specify file and device attributes.

FILE command
   stores the contents of the LOG or OUTPUT windows in files you specify, when the command is issued from within the windowing environment.

SAS system options
   redefine the destination of log and output for an entire SAS program. These system options are specified when you invoke SAS. The system options used to route output are the ALTLOG=, ALTPRINT=, LOG=, and PRINT= options.

Operating Environment Information: The way you specify output destinations when you use SAS system options is dependent on your operating environment. See the SAS documentation for your operating environment for details. △

Output Delivery System

What Is the Output Delivery System?

The Output Delivery System (ODS) gives you greater flexibility in generating, storing, and reproducing SAS procedure and DATA step output, with a wide range of formatting options. ODS provides formatting functionality that is not available from individual procedures or from the DATA step alone. ODS overcomes these limitations and enables you to format your output more easily.

Prior to Version 7, most SAS procedures generated output that was designed for a traditional line-printer. This type of output has limitations that prevents you from getting the most value from your results:

□ Traditional SAS output is limited to monospace fonts. With today's desktop document editors and publishing systems, you need more versatility in printed output.

□ Some commonly used procedures do not produce output data sets. Prior to ODS, if you wanted to use output from one of these procedures as input to another procedure, then you relied on PROC PRINTTO and the DATA step to retrieve results.

Gallery of ODS Samples

Introduction to the ODS Samples

This section shows you samples of the different kinds of formatted output that you can produce with ODS. The input file contains sales records for TruBlend Coffee Makers, a company that distributes coffee machines.

Listing Output

Traditional SAS output is Listing output. You do not need to change your SAS programs to create listing output. By default, you continue to create this kind of output even if you also create a type of output that contains more formatting.

Output 10.2 Listing Output

```
          Average Quarterly Sales Amount by Each Sales Representative      1

------------------------------ Quarter=1 ------------------------------

                           The MEANS Procedure

                         Analysis Variable : AmountSold

                    N
SalesRep          Obs      N      Mean     Std Dev    Minimum    Maximum
Garcia              8      8    14752.5    22806.1      495.0    63333.7

Hollingsworth       5      5    11926.9    12165.2      774.3    31899.1

Jensen              5      5    10015.7     8009.5     3406.7    20904.8


          Average Quarterly Sales Amount by Each Sales Representative      2

------------------------------ Quarter=2 ------------------------------

                           The MEANS Procedure

                         Analysis Variable : AmountSold

                    N
SalesRep          Obs      N      Mean     Std Dev    Minimum    Maximum
Garcia              6      6    18143.3    20439.6     1238.8    53113.6

Hollingsworth       6      6    16026.8    14355.0     1237.5    34686.4

Jensen              6      6    12455.1    12713.7     1393.7    34376.7


          Average Quarterly Sales Amount by Each Sales Representative      3

------------------------------ Quarter=3 ------------------------------

                           The MEANS Procedure

                         Analysis Variable : AmountSold

                    N
SalesRep          Obs      N      Mean     Std Dev    Minimum    Maximum
Garcia             21     21    10729.8    11457.0     2787.3    38712.5

Hollingsworth      15     15     7313.6     7280.4     1485.0    30970.0

Jensen             21     21    10585.3     7361.7     2227.5    27129.7


          Average Quarterly Sales Amount by Each Sales Representative      4

------------------------------ Quarter=4 ------------------------------

                           The MEANS Procedure

                         Analysis Variable : AmountSold

                    N
SalesRep          Obs      N      Mean     Std Dev    Minimum    Maximum
Garcia              5      5    11973.0    10971.8     3716.4    30970.0

Hollingsworth       6      6    13624.4    12624.6     5419.8    38093.1

Jensen              6      6    19010.4    15441.0     1703.4    38836.4
```

PostScript Output

With ODS, you can produce output in PostScript format.

Display 10.1 PostScript Output Viewed with Ghostview

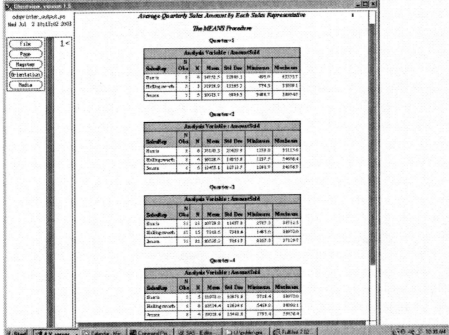

HTML Output

With ODS, you can produce output in HTML (Hypertext Markup Language.) You can browse these files with Internet Explorer, Netscape, or any other browser that fully supports the HTML 3.2 tagset.

Note: To create HTML 4.0 tagsets, use the ODS HTML4 statement. In SAS 9, the ODS HTML statement generates HTML 3.2 tagsets. In future releases of SAS, the ODS HTML statement will support the most current HTML tagsets available. △

Display 10.2   HTML Output Viewed with Microsoft Internet Explorer

RTF Output

With ODS, you can produce RTF (Rich Text Format) output which is used with Microsoft Word.

Display 10.3 RTF Output Viewed with Microsoft Word

Average Quarterly Sales Amount by Each Sales Representative

The MEANS Procedure

Quarter=1

Analysis Variable : AmountSold						
SalesRep	N Obs	N	Mean	Std Dev	Minimum	Maximum
Garcia	8	8	14752.49	22806.09	495.0000000	63333.65
Hollingsworth	5	5	11926.94	12165.18	774.2500000	31899.10
Jensen	5	5	10015.70	8009.46	3406.70	20904.75

Quarter=2

Analysis Variable : AmountSold						
SalesRep	N Obs	N	Mean	Std Dev	Minimum	Maximum
Garcia	6	6	18143.26	20439.58	1238.80	53113.55
Hollingsworth	6	6	16026.76	14355.04	1237.50	34686.40
Jensen	6	6	12455.10	12713.73	1398.65	34376.70

Quarter=3

Analysis Variable : AmountSold						
SalesRep	N Obs	N	Mean	Std Dev	Minimum	Maximum
Garcia	21	21	10729.82	11457.05	2787.30	38712.50
Hollingsworth	15	15	7313.62	7280.44	1485.00	30970.00
Jensen	21	21	10585.29	7361.68	2227.50	27129.72

Quarter=4

Analysis Variable : AmountSold						
SalesRep	N Obs	N	Mean	Std Dev	Minimum	Maximum
Garcia	5	5	11973.00	10971.73	3716.40	30970.00
Hollingsworth	6	6	13624.42	12624.61	5419.75	38093.10
Jensen	6	6	19010.42	13440.98	1703.35	38836.38

PDF Output

With ODS, you can produce output in PDF (Portable Document Format), which can be viewed with the Adobe Acrobat Reader.

Display 10.4   PDF Output Viewed with Adobe Acrobat Reader

Average Quarterly Sales Amount by Each Sales Representative   1

The MEANS Procedure

Quarter=1

SalesRep	N Obs	N	Mean	Std Dev	Minimum	Maximum
			Analysis Variable : AmountSold			
Garcia	8	8	14752.49	22806.09	495.0000000	63333.65
Hollingsworth	5	5	11926.94	12165.18	774.2500000	31899.10
Jensen	5	5	10015.70	8009.46	3486.70	20904.75

Quarter=2

SalesRep	N Obs	N	Mean	Std Dev	Minimum	Maximum
			Analysis Variable : AmountSold			
Garcia	6	6	18143.26	20439.58	1238.80	53113.55
Hollingsworth	6	6	16026.76	14355.04	1237.50	34686.40
Jensen	6	6	12455.10	12713.73	1393.65	34376.70

Quarter=3

SalesRep	N Obs	N	Mean	Std Dev	Minimum	Maximum
			Analysis Variable : AmountSold			
Garcia	21	21	10729.82	11457.05	2787.30	38712.50
Hollingsworth	15	15	7313.62	7280.44	1485.00	30970.00
Jensen	21	21	10585.29	7361.68	2227.50	27129.72

Quarter=4

SalesRep	N Obs	N	Mean	Std Dev	Minimum	Maximum
			Analysis Variable : AmountSold			
Garcia	5	5	11973.00	10971.77	3716.40	30970.00
Hollingsworth	6	6	13624.42	12624.61	5419.75	38093.10
Jensen	6	6	19010.42	15440.98	1703.35	38836.38

XML Output

With ODS, you can produce output that is tagged with XML (Extensible Markup Language) tags.

Output 10.3 XML Output file

```
<?xml version="1.0" encoding="windows-1252"?>

<odsxml>
<head>
<meta operator="user"/>
</head>
<body>
<proc name="Print">
<label name="IDX"/>
<title class="SystemTitle" toc-level="1">US Census of Population and Housing</title>
<branch name="Print" label="The Print Procedure" class="ContentProcName" toc-level="1">
<leaf name="Print" label="Data Set SASHELP.CLASS" class="ContentItem" toc-level="2">
<output name="Print" label="Data Set SASHELP.CLASS" clabel="Data Set SASHELP.CLASS">
<output-object type="table" class="Table">

  <style>
    <border spacing="1" padding="7" rules="groups" frame="box"/>
  </style>
<colspecs columns="6">
<colgroup>
<colspec name="1" width="2" align="right" type="int"/>
</colgroup>
<colgroup>
<colspec name="2" width="7" type="string"/>
<colspec name="3" width="1" type="string"/>
<colspec name="4" width="2" align="decimal" type="double"/>
<colspec name="5" width="4" align="decimal" type="double"/>
<colspec name="6" width="5" align="decimal" type="double"/>
</colgroup>
</colspecs>
<output-head>
<row>
<header type="string" class="Header" row="1" column="1">
<value>Obs</value>
</header>
<header type="string" class="Header" row="1" column="2">
<value>Name</value>
</header>
<header type="string" class="Header" row="1" column="3">
<value>Sex</value>
</header>
<header type="string" class="Header" row="1" column="4">
<value>Age</value>
</header>
<header type="string" class="Header" row="1" column="5">
<value>Height</value>
</header>
<header type="string" class="Header" row="1" column="6">
<value>Weight</value>
</header>
</row>
</output-head>
<output-body>
<row>
<header type="double" class="RowHeader" row="2" column="1">
<value> 1</value>
</header>
<data type="string" class="Data" row="2" column="2">
<value>Alfred</value>
</data>
... more xml tagged output...
<
/odsxml>
```

Commonly Used ODS Terminology

data component
> is a form, similar to a SAS data set, that contains the results (numbers and characters) of a DATA step or PROC step that supports ODS.

table definition
> is a set of instructions that describes how to format the data. This description includes but is not limited to

> □ the order of the columns

> □ text and order of column headings

> □ formats for data

> □ font sizes and font faces.

output object
> is an object that contains both the results of a DATA step or PROC step and information about how to format the results. An output object has a name, label, and path. For example, the Basic Statistical Measurement table generated from the UNIVARIATE procedure is an output object. It contains the data component and formatted presentation of the mean, median, mode, standard deviation, variance, range, and interquartile range.

> *Note:* Although many output objects include formatting instructions, not all of them do. In some cases the output object consists of only the data component. △

ODS destinations
> are designations that produce specific types of output. ODS supports a number of destinations, including the following:

> LISTING
>> produces traditional SAS output (monospace format).

> Markup Languages
>> produce SAS output that is formatted using one of many different markup languages such as HTML (Hypertext Markup Language), XML (Extensible Markup Language), and LaTeX that you can access with a web browser. SAS supplies many markup languages for you to use ranging from DOCBOOK to TROFF. You can specify a markup language that SAS supplies or create one of your own and store it as a user-defined markup language.

> DOCUMENT
>> produces a hierarchy of output objects that enables you to produce multiple ODS output formats without rerunning a PROC or DATA step and gives you more control over the structure of the output.

> OUTPUT
>> produces a SAS data set.

> Printer Family
>> produces output that is formatted for a high-resolution printer such as a PostScript (PS), PDF, or PCL file.

> RTF
>> produces output that is formatted for use with Microsoft Word.

ODS output
ODS output consists of formatted output from any of the ODS destinations. For example, the OUTPUT destination produces SAS data sets; the LISTING destination produces listing output; the HTML destination produces output that is formatted in Hypertext Markup Language.

How Does ODS Work?

Components of SAS Output

The PROC or DATA step supplies raw data and the name of the table definition that contains the formatting instructions, and ODS formats the output. You can use the Output Delivery System to format output from individual procedures and from the DATA step in many different forms other than the default SAS listing output.
The following figure shows how SAS produces ODS output.

Figure 10.1 ODS Processing: What Goes in and What Comes Out

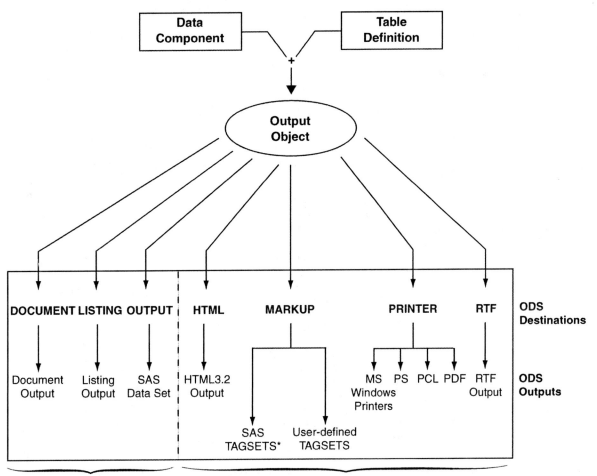

* List of Tagsets that SAS Supplies and Supports

Table 10.2 * List of Tagsets that SAS Supplies and Supports

CHTML	HTML4	SASIOXML	SASXMOH
CSVALL	HTMLCSS	SASREPORT	SASXMOIM
DEFAULT	IMODE	SASXML	SASXMOR
DOCBOOK	PHTML	SASXMOG	WML
EVENT_MAP			

* List of Tagsets that SAS Supplies but Does Not Support

Table 10.3 Additional Tagsets that SAS Supplies but Does Not Support

COLORLATEX	LATEX	SHORT_MAP	TPL_STYLE_MAP
CSV	LATEX2	STYLE_DISPLAY	TROFF
CSVBYLINE	NAMEDHTML	STYLE_POPUP	WMLOLIST
GRAPH	ODSSTYLE	TEXT_MAP	
GTABLEAPPLET	PYX	TPL_STYLE_LIST	

CAUTION:
These tagsets are experimental tagsets. Do not use these tagsets in production jobs. △

Features of ODS

ODS is designed to overcome the limitations of traditional SAS output and to make it easy to access and create the new formatting options. ODS provides a method of delivering output in a variety of formats, and makes the formatted output easy to access.
Important features of ODS include the following:

□ ODS combines raw data with one or more table definitions to produce one or more output objects. These objects can be sent to any or all ODS destinations. You control the specific type of output from ODS by selecting an ODS destination. The currently available ODS destinations can produce

   □ traditional monospace output

   □ an output data set

   □ an ODS document that contains a hierarchy file of the output objects

   □ output that is formatted for a high-resolution printer such as PostScript and PDF

   □ output that is formatted in various markup languages such as HTML

   □ RTF output that is formatted for use with Microsoft Word.

□ ODS provides table definitions that define the structure of the output from SAS procedures and from the DATA step. You can customize the output by modifying these definitions, or by creating your own.

□ ODS provides a way for you to choose individual output objects to send to ODS destinations. For example, PROC UNIVARIATE produces five output objects. You can easily create HTML output, an output data set, traditional listing output, or printer output from any or all of these output objects. You can send different output objects to different destinations.

    ☐ In the SAS windowing environment, ODS stores a link to each output object in the Results folder in the Results window.

    ☐ Because formatting is now centralized in ODS, the addition of a new ODS destination does not affect any procedures or the DATA step. As future destinations are added to ODS, they will automatically become available to the DATA step and all procedures that support ODS.

    ☐ With ODS, you can produce output for numerous destinations from a single source, but you do not need to maintain separate sources for each destination. This feature saves you time and system resources by enabling you to produce multiple kinds of output with a single run of your procedure or data query.

What Are the ODS Destinations?

Overview of ODS Destination Categories

ODS enables you to produce SAS procedure and DATA step output to many different destinations. ODS destinations are organized into two categories.

SAS Formatted destinations
    produce output that is controlled and interpreted by SAS, such as a SAS data set, SAS output listing, or an ODS document.

Third-Party Formatted destinations
    produce output which enables you to apply styles, markup languages, or enables you to print to physical printers using page description languages. For example, you can produce output in PostScript, HTML, XML, or a style or markup language that you created.

The following table lists the ODS destination categories, the destination that each category includes, and the formatted output that results from each destination.

Table 10.4 Destination Category Table

Category	Destinations	Results
SAS Formatted	DOCUMENT	ODS document
	LISTING	SAS output listing
	OUTPUT	SAS data set
Third-Party Formatted	HTML	HTML file for online viewing
	MARKUP	markup language tagsets
	PRINTER	printable output in one of three different formats: PCL, PDF, or PS (PostScript)
	RTF	output written in Rich Text Format for use with Microsoft Word 2000

As future destinations are added to ODS, they automatically will become available to the DATA step and to all procedures that support ODS.

Definition of Destination-Independent Input

Destination-independent input means that one destination can support a feature even though another destination does not support it. In this case, the request is ignored by the destination that does not support it. Otherwise, ODS would support a small subset of features that are only common to all destinations. If this was true, then it would be difficult to move your reports from one output format to another output format. ODS provides many output formatting options, so that you can use the appropriate format for the output that you want. It is best to use the appropriate destination suited for your purpose.

The SAS Formatted Destinations

The SAS formatted destinations create SAS entities such as a SAS data set, a SAS output listing, or an ODS document. The statements in the ODS SAS Formatted category create the SAS entities.

The three SAS formatted destinations are:

DOCUMENT Destination
> The DOCUMENT destination enables you to restructure, navigate, and replay your data in different ways and to different destinations as you like without needing to rerun your analysis or repeat your database query. The DOCUMENT destination makes your entire output stream available in "raw" form and accessible to you to customize. The output is kept in the original internal representation as a data component plus a table definition. When the output is in a DOCUMENT form, it is possible to rearrange, restructure, and reformat without rerunning your analysis. Unlike other ODS destinations, the DOCUMENT destination has a GUI interface. However, everything that you can do through the GUI, you can also do with batch commands using the ODS DOCUMENT statement and the DOCUMENT procedure.
>
> Prior to SAS 9, each procedure or DATA step produced output that was sent to each destination that you specified. While you could always send your output to as many destinations as you wanted, you needed to rerun your procedure or data query if you decided to use a destination that you had not originally designated. The DOCUMENT destination eliminates the need to rerun procedures or repeat data queries by enabling you to store your output objects and replay them to different destinations.

LISTING Destination
> The LISTING destination produces output that looks the same as the traditional SAS output. The LISTING destination is the default destination that opens when you start your SAS session. Thus ODS is always being used, even when you do not explicitly invoke ODS.
>
> The LISTING destination enables you to produce traditional SAS output with the same look and presentation as it had in previous versions of SAS.
>
> Because most procedures share some of the same table definitions, the output is more consistent. For example, if you have two different procedures producing an ANOVA table, they will both produce it in the same way because each procedure uses the same template to describe the table. However, there are four procedures that do not use a default table definition to produce their output: PRINT procedure, REPORT procedure, TABULATE procedure, and FREQ procedure's n-way tables. These procedures use the structure that you specified in your program code to define their tables.

OUTPUT Destination
> The OUTPUT destination produces SAS output data sets. Because ODS already knows the logical structure of the data and its native form, ODS can output a SAS data set that represents exactly the same resulting data set that the procedure worked with internally. The output data sets can be used for further analysis, or for sophisticated reports in which you want to combine similar statistics across

different data sets into a single table. You can easily access and process your output data sets using all of the SAS data set features. For example, you can access your output data using variable names and perform WHERE-expression processing just as you would process data from any other SAS data set.

The Third-Party Formatted Destinations

The third-party formatted destinations enable you to apply styles to the output objects that are used by applications other than SAS. For example, these destinations support attributes such as "font" and "color."

Note: For a list of style elements and valid values, see the style elements table in the *SAS Output Delivery System: User's Guide.* △

The four categories of third-party formatted destinations are:

□ *HTML (Hypertext Markup Language)*

The HTML destination produces HTML 3.2-compatible output. You can, however, produce (HTML 4 stylesheet) output using the HTML4 tagsets.

The HTML destination can create some or all of the following:

□ an HTML file (called the *body file*) that contains the results from the procedure

□ a table of contents that links to the body file

□ a table of pages that links to the body file

□ a frame that displays the table of contents, the table of pages, and the body file.

The body file is required with all ODS HTML output. If you do not want to link to your output, then you do not have to create a table of contents, a table of pages, or a frame file. However, if your output is very large, you might want to create a table of contents and a table of pages for easier reading and transversing through your file.

The HTML destination is intended only for on-line use, not for printing. To print hard-copies of the output objects, use the PRINTER destination.

□ *Markup Languages (MARKUP) Family*

Just as table definitions describe how to lay out a table, and style attributes describe the style of the output, *tagsets* describe how to produce a markup language output. You can use a tagset that SAS supplies or you can create your own using the TEMPLATE procedure. Like table definitions and style attributes, tagsets enable you to modify your markup language output. For example, each variety of XML can be specified as a new tagset. SAS supplies you with a collection of XML tagsets and enables you to produce a customized variety of XML. The important point is that you can implement a tagset that SAS supplies or a customized tagset that you created without having to wait for the next release of SAS. With the addition of modifying and creating your own tagsets by using PROC TEMPLATE, now you have greater flexibility in customizing your output.

Because the MARKUP destination is so flexible, you can use either the SAS tagsets or a tagset that you created. For a complete listing of the markup language tagsets that SAS supplies, see the section on listing tagset names in the *SAS Output Delivery System: User's Guide*. To learn how to define your own tagsets, see the section on methods to create your own tagsets in the *SAS Output Delivery System: User's Guide*.

The MARKUP destination cannot replace ODS PRINTER or ODS RTF destinations because it cannot do text measurement. Therefore, it cannot produce output for a page description language or a hybrid language like RTF which requires all of the text to be measured and placed at a specific position on the page.

☐ *PRINTER Family*

The PRINTER destination produces output for

☐ printing to physical printers such as Windows printers under Windows, PCL, and PostScript printers on other operating systems

☐ producing portable PostScript, PCL, and PDF files.

The PRINTER destinations produce ODS output that contain page description languages: they describe precise positions where each line of text, each rule, and each graphical element are to be placed on the page. In general, you cannot edit or alter these formats. Therefore, the output from ODS PRINTER is intended to be the final form of the report.

☐ *Rich Text Format (RTF)*

RTF produces output for Microsoft Word. While there are other applications that can read RTF files, the RTF output might not work successfully with them.

The RTF destination enables you to view and edit the RTF output. ODS does not define the "vertical measurement," meaning that SAS does not determine the optimal place to position each item on the page. For example, page breaks are not always fixed, so when you edit your text, you do not want your RTF output tables to split at inappropriate places. Your tables can remain whole and intact on one page or can have logical breaks where you specified.

However, because Microsoft Word needs to know the widths of table columns and it cannot adjust tables if they are too wide for the page, ODS measures the width of the text and tables (horizontal measurement). Therefore, all the column widths can be set properly by SAS and the table can be divided into panels if it is too wide to fit on a single page.

In short, when producing RTF output for input to Microsoft Word, SAS determines the horizontal measurement and Microsoft Word controls the vertical measurement. Because Microsoft Word can determine how much room there is on the page, your tables will display consistently as you specified even after you modified your RTF file.

What Controls the Formatting Features of Third-Party Formats?

All of the formatting features that control the appearance of the third-party formatted destinations beyond what the LISTING destination can do are controlled by two mechanisms:

☐ ODS statement options

☐ ODS style attributes

The ODS statement options control three features:

1 Features that are specific to a given destination, such as stylesheets for HTML.

2 Features that are global to the document, such as AUTHOR and table of contents generation.

3 Features that we expect users to change on each document, such as the output file name.

The ODS style attributes control the way that individual elements are created. Attributes are aspects of a given style, such as type face, weight, font size, and color. The values of the attributes collectively determine the appearance of each part of the document to which the style is applied. With style attributes, it is unnecessary to insert destination-specific code (such as raw HTML) into the document. Each output destination will interpret the attributes that are necessary to generate the presentation of the document. Because not all destinations are the same, not all attributes can be interpreted by all destinations. Style attributes that are incompatible with a selected destination are ignored. For example, PostScript does not support active links, so the URL= attribute is ignored when producing PostScript output.

ODS Destinations and System Resources

ODS destinations can be open or closed. You open and close a destination with the appropriate ODS statement. When a destination is open, ODS sends the output objects to it. An open destination uses system resources even if you use the selection and exclusion features of ODS to select or exclude all objects from the destination. Therefore, to conserve resources, close unnecessary destinations. For more information about using each destination, see the topic on ODS statements in the *SAS Output Delivery System: User's Guide*.

By default, the LISTING destination is open and all other destinations are closed. Consequently, if you do nothing, your SAS programs run and produce listing output looking just as they did in previous releases of SAS before ODS was available.

What Are Table Definitions, Table Elements, and Table Attributes?

A *table definition* describes how to generate the output for a tabular output object. (Most ODS output is tabular.) A table definition determines the order of column headers and the order of variables, as well the overall look of the output object that uses it. For information about customizing the table definition, see the topic on the TEMPLATE procedure in the *SAS Output Delivery System: User's Guide*.

In addition to the parts of the table definition that order the headers and columns, each table definition contains or references *table elements*. A table element is a collection of table attributes that apply to a particular header, footer, or column. Typically, a *table attribute* specifies something about the data rather than about its presentation. For example, FORMAT specifies the SAS format, such as the number of decimal places. However, some table attributes describe presentation aspects of the data, such as how many blank characters to place between columns.

Note: The attributes of table definitions that control the presentation of the data have no effect on output objects that go to the LISTING or OUTPUT destination. However, the attributes that control the structure of the table and the data values do affect listing output. △

For information on table attributes, see the section on table attributes in the *SAS Output Delivery System: User's Guide*.

What Are Style Definitions, Style Elements, and Style Attributes?

To customize the output at the level of your entire output stream in a SAS session, you specify a style definition. A *style definition* describes how to generate the presentation aspects (color, font face, font size, and so on) of the entire SAS output. A style definition determines the overall look of the documents that use it.

Each style definition is composed of *style elements*. A style element is a collection of style attributes that apply to a particular part of the output. For example, a style element may contain instructions for the presentation of column headers, or for the presentation of the data inside the cells. Style elements may also specify default colors and fonts for output that uses the style definition.

Each *style attribute* specifies a value for one aspect of the presentation. For example, the BACKGROUND= attribute specifies the color for the background of an HTML table or for a colored table in printed output. The FONT_STYLE= attribute specifies whether to use a Roman or an italic font. For information on style attributes, see the section on style attributes in the *SAS Output Delivery System: User's Guide*.

Note: Because style definitions control the presentation of the data, they have no effect on output objects that go to the LISTING or OUTPUT destination. △

What Style Definitions Are Shipped with SAS Software?

Base SAS software is shipped with many style definitions. To see a list of these styles, you can view them in the SAS Explorer Window, use the TEMPLATE procedure, or use the SQL procedure.

□ *SAS Explorer Window:*

To display a list of the available styles using the SAS Explorer Window, follow these steps:

1   From any window in an interactive SAS session, select

2   In the Results window, select

View ▶ Templates

3   In the Templates window, select and open **Sashelp.tmplmst**.

4   Select and open the **Styles** folder, which contains a list of available style definitions. If you want to view the underlying SAS code for a style definition, then select the style and open it.

Operating Environment Information: For information on navigating in the Explorer window without a mouse, see the section on "Window Controls and General Navigation" in the SAS documentation for your operating environment. △

□ *TEMPLATE Procedure:*

You can also display a list of the available styles by submitting the following PROC TEMPLATE statements:

```
proc template;
   list styles;
run;
```

□ *SQL Procedure:*

You can also display a list of the available styles by submitting the following PROC SQL statements:

```
proc sql;
select * from styles.style-name;
```

The *style–name* is the name of any style from the template store (for example, **styles.default** or **styles.beige**).

For more information on how ODS destinations use styles and how you can customize styles, see the section on the DEFINE STYLE statement in the *SAS Output Delivery System: User's Guide*.

How Do I Use Style Definitions with Base SAS Procedures?

☐ Most Base SAS Procedures

Most Base SAS procedures that support ODS use one or more table definitions to produce output objects. These table definitions include definitions for table elements: columns, headers, and footers. Each table element can specify the use of one or more style elements for various parts of the output. These style elements cannot be specified within the syntax of the procedure, but you can use customized styles for the ODS destinations that you use. For more information about customizing tables and styles, see the TEMPLATE procedure in the *SAS Output Delivery System: User's Guide*.

☐ The PRINT, REPORT and TABULATE Procedures

The PRINT, REPORT and TABULATE procedures provide a way for you to access table elements from the procedure step itself. Accessing the table elements enables you to do such things as specify background colors for specific cells, change the font face for column headers, and more. The PRINT, REPORT, and TABULATE procedures provide a way for you to customize the markup language and printed output directly from the procedure statements that create the report. For more information about customizing the styles for these procedures, see the *Base SAS Procedures Guide*.

Changing SAS Registry Settings for ODS

Overview of ODS and the SAS Registry

The SAS registry is the central storage area for configuration data that ODS uses. This configuration data is stored in a hierarchical form, which works in a similar manner to the way directory-based file structures work under UNIX, Windows, VMS, and the z/OS UNIX system. However, the SAS registry uses keys and subkeys as the basis for its structure, instead of using directories and subdirectories, like similar file systems in DOS or UNIX. A key is a word or a text string that refers to a particular aspect of SAS. Each key may be a place holder without values or subkeys associated with it, or it may have many subkeys with associated values. For example, the ODS key has DESTINATIONS, GUI, ICONS, and PREFERENCES subkeys. A subkey is a key inside another key. For example, PRINTER is a subkey of the DESTINATIONS subkey.

Display 10.5   SAS Registry of ODS Subkeys

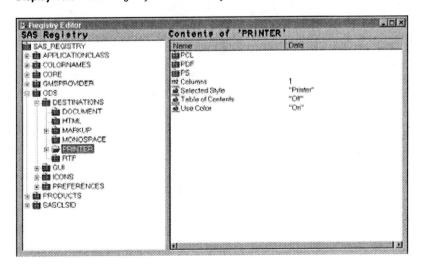

Changing Your Default HTML Version Setting

By default, the SAS registry is configured to generate HTML4 output when you specify the ODS HTML statement. To permanently change the default HTML version, you can change the setting of the HTML version in the SAS registry.

CAUTION:

If you make a mistake when you modify the SAS registry, then your system might become unstable or unusable. You will not be warned if an entry is incorrect. Incorrect entries can cause errors, and can even prevent you from bringing up a SAS session. For more information about how to configure the SAS registry, see the SAS registry section in *SAS Language Reference: Concepts.* △

To change the default setting of the HTML version in the SAS registry:

1 Select

 Solutions ▶ Accessories ▶ Registry Editor

or
Issue the command **REGEDIT**.

2 Select

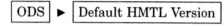 ODS ▶ Default HMTL Version

3 Select

 Edit ▶ Modify

or
Click the right mouse button and select **MODIFY**. The Edit String Value window appears.

4 Type the HTML version in the **Value Data** text box and select **OK**.

Display 10.6   SAS Registry Showing HTML Version Setting

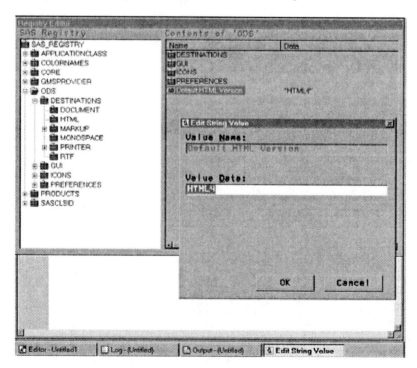

Changing ODS Destination Default Settings

ODS destination subkeys are stored in the SAS registry. To change the values for these destinations subkeys:

1 Select

$\boxed{\text{ODS}}$ ▶ $\boxed{\text{Destinations}}$

2 Select a destination subkey

3 Select a subkey in the Contents of window

4 Select

$\boxed{\text{Edit}}$ ▶ $\boxed{\text{Modify}}$

or
Click the right mouse button and select **MODIFY**.

5 Type in the Value Data entry into the Edit Value String or Edit Signed Integer Value window and select **OK**.

Display 10.7 Registry Editor Window

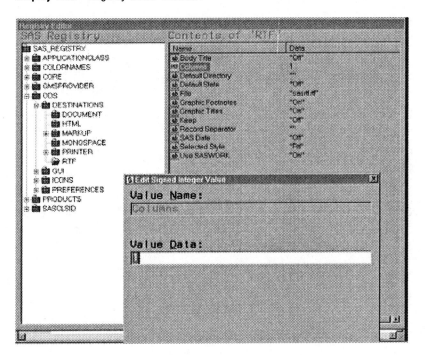

Customized ODS Output

SAS Output

By default, ODS output is formatted according to instructions that a PROC step or DATA step defines. However, ODS provides ways for you to customize the output. You can customize the output for an entire SAS job, or you can customize the output for a single output object.

Selection and Exclusion Lists

You can specify which output objects that you want to produce by selecting or excluding them in a list. For each ODS destination, ODS maintains either a selection list or an exclusion list. A selection list is a list of output objects that are sent to the destination. An exclusion list is a list of output objects that are excluded from the destination. ODS also maintains an overall selection list or an overall exclusion list. You can use these lists to control which output objects go to the specified ODS destinations.

To see the contents of the lists use the ODS SHOW statement. The lists are written to the SAS log. The following table shows the default lists:

Table 10.5   Default List for Each ODS Destination

ODS Destination	Default List
OUTPUT	EXCLUDE ALL
All others	SELECT ALL

How Does ODS Determine the Destinations for an Output Object?

To specify an output object, you need to know which output objects your SAS program produces. The ODS TRACE statement writes to the SAS log a trace record that includes the path, the label, and other information about each output object that is produced. For more information, about the ODS TRACE statement see *SAS Output Delivery System: User's Guide*. You can specify an output object as any of the following:

□ a full path. For example,

    Univariate.City_Pop_90.TestsForLocation

is the full path of the output object.

□ a partial path. A partial path consists of any part of the full path that begins immediately after a period (.) and continues to the end of the full path. For example, if the full path is

    Univariate.City_Pop_90.TestsForLocation

then the partial paths are:

    City_Pop_90.TestsForLocation
    TestsForLocation

□ a label that is surrounded by quotation marks.

For example,

    "Tests For Location"

□ a label path. For example, the label path for the output object is

"The UNIVARIATE Procedure"."CityPop_90"."Tests For Location"

Note: The trace record shows the label path only if you specify the LABEL option in the ODS TRACE statement. △

□ a partial label path. A partial label path consists of any part of the label that begins immediately after a period (.) and continues to the end of the label. For example, if the label path is

    "The UNIVARIATE Procedure"."CityPop_90"."Tests For Location" then the partial label paths are:

```
"CityPop_90"."Tests For Location"
"Tests For Location"
```

☐ a mixture of labels and paths.

☐ any of the partial path specifications, followed by a pound sign (#) and a number. For example, TestsForLocation#3 refers to the third output object that is named TestsForLocation.

As each output object is produced, ODS uses the selection and exclusion lists to determine which destination or destinations the output object will be sent to. The following figure illustrates this process:

Figure 10.2 Directing an Output Object to a Destination

For each destination, ODS first asks if the list for that destination includes the object. If it does not, ODS does not send the output object to that destination. If the list for that destination does include the object, ODS reads the overall list. If the overall list includes the object, ODS sends it to the destination. If the overall list does not include the object, ODS does not send it to the destination.

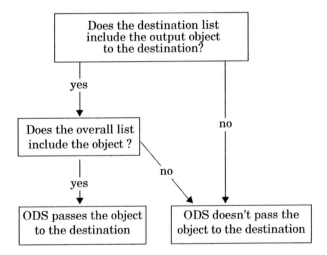

Note: Although you can maintain a selection list for one destination and an exclusion list for another, it is easier to understand the results if you maintain the same types of lists for all the destinations where you route output. △

Customized Output for an Output Object

For a procedure, the name of the table definition that is used for an output object comes from the procedure code. The DATA step uses a default table definition unless you specify an alternative with the TEMPLATE= suboption in the ODS option in the FILE statement. For more information, see the section on the TEMPLATE= suboption in the *SAS Output Delivery System: User's Guide*.

To find out which table definitions a procedure or the DATA step uses for the output objects, you must look at a trace record. To produce a trace record in your SAS log, submit the following SAS statements:

```
ods trace on;
your-proc-or-DATA-step
ods trace off;
```

Remember that not all procedures use table definitions. If you produce a trace record for one of these procedures, no definition appears in the trace record. Conversely, some procedures use multiple table definitions to produce their output. If you produce a trace record for one of these procedures, more than one definition appears in the trace record.

The trace record refers to the table definition as a template. For a detailed explanation of the trace record, see the section on the ODS TRACE statement in the *SAS Output Delivery System: User's Guide*.

You can use PROC TEMPLATE to modify an entire table definition. When a procedure or DATA step uses a table definition, it uses the elements that are defined or referenced in its table definition. In general, you cannot directly specify a table element for your procedure or DATA step to use without modifying the definition itself.

Note: Three Base SAS procedures, PROC PRINT, PROC REPORT and PROC TABULATE, do provide a way for you to access table elements from the procedure step itself. Accessing the table elements enables you to customize your report. For more information about these procedures, see the *Base SAS Procedures Guide* △

Summary of ODS

In the past, the term "output" has generally referred to the outcome of a SAS procedure and DATA step. With the advent of the Output Delivery System, "output" takes on a much broader meaning. ODS is designed to optimize output from SAS procedures and the DATA step. It provides a wide range of formatting options and greater flexibility in generating, storing, and reproducing SAS output.

Important features of ODS include the following:

- ODS combines raw data with one or more table definitions to produce one or more *output objects*. An output object tells ODS how to format the results of a procedure or DATA step.

- ODS provides table definitions that define the structure of the output from SAS procedures and from the DATA step. You can customize the output by modifying these definitions, or by creating your own definitions.

- ODS provides a way for you to choose individual output objects to send to ODS destinations.

- ODS stores a link to each output object in the Results folder for easy retrieval and access.

- As future destinations are added to ODS, they will automatically become available to the DATA step and all procedures that support ODS.

One of the main goals of ODS is to enable you to produce output for numerous destinations from a single source, without requiring separate sources for each destination. ODS supports many destinations:

DOCUMENT
: enables you to capture output objects from single run of the analysis and produce multiple reports in various formats whenever you want without re-running your SAS programs.

LISTING
> produces output that looks the same as the traditional SAS output.

HTML
> produces output for online viewing.

MARKUP
> produces output for markup language tagsets.

OUTPUT
> produces SAS output data sets, thereby eliminating the need to parse PROC PRINTTO output.

PRINTER
> produces presentation-ready printed reports.

RTF
> produces output suitable for Microsoft Word reports.

By default, ODS output is formatted according to instructions that the procedure or DATA step defines. However, ODS provides ways for you to customize the presentation of your output. You can customize the presentation of your SAS output, or you can customize the look of a single output object. ODS gives you greater flexibility in generating, storing, and reproducing SAS procedure and DATA step output with a wide range of formatting options.

CHAPTER

11

BY-Group Processing in SAS Programs

Definition of BY-Group Processing   **195**
References for BY-Group Processing   **195**

Definition of BY-Group Processing

BY-group processing is a method of processing observations from one or more SAS data sets that are grouped or ordered by values of one or more common variables. You can use BY-group processing in both DATA and PROC steps.

The most common use of BY-group processing in the DATA step is to combine two or more SAS data sets by using the BY statement with a SET, MERGE, MODIFY, or UPDATE statement. When you create reports or summaries with SAS procedures, BY-group processing allows you to group information in the output according to values of one or more variables.

References for BY-Group Processing

□ For more information about BY-Group processing, see Chapter 22, "BY-Group Processing in the DATA Step," on page 375.

□ For information about how to use BY-group processing with SAS procedures, see "Fundamental Concepts for Using Base SAS Procedures" and individual procedures in *Base SAS Procedures Guide*.

□ For information about using BY-group processing to combine information from multiple SAS data sets, see Chapter 23, "Reading, Combining, and Modifying SAS Data Sets," on page 387. For even more extensive examples of BY-group processing, see *Combining and Modifying SAS Data Sets: Examples*.

□ For information about the BY statement, see Statements in *SAS Language Reference: Dictionary*.

□ For information about how to use BY-group processing with other software products, see the SAS documentation for those products.

CHAPTER
12

WHERE-Expression Processing

Definition of WHERE-Expression Processing   **197**
Where to Use a WHERE Expression   **198**
Syntax of WHERE Expression   **199**
   Specifying an Operand   **199**
      Variable   **199**
      SAS Function   **200**
      Constant   **200**
   Specifying an Operator   **201**
      Arithmetic Operators   **201**
      Comparison Operators   **201**
      IN Operator   **202**
      Fully-Bounded Range Condition   **202**
      BETWEEN-AND Operator   **203**
      CONTAINS Operator   **203**
      IS NULL or IS MISSING Operator   **204**
      LIKE Operator   **204**
      Sounds-like Operator   **205**
      SAME-AND Operator   **205**
      MIN and MAX Operators   **206**
      Concatenation Operator   **206**
      Prefix Operators   **206**
Combining Expressions by Using Logical Operators   **207**
   Syntax   **207**
   Processing Compound Expressions   **207**
   Using Parentheses to Control Order of Evaluation   **208**
Constructing Efficient WHERE Expressions   **208**
Processing a Segment of Data That Is Conditionally Selected   **208**
   Applying FIRSTOBS= and OBS= to a Subset of Data   **209**
   Processing a SAS View   **209**
Deciding Whether to Use a WHERE Expression or a Subsetting IF Statement   **211**

Definition of WHERE-Expression Processing

WHERE-expression processing
    enables you to conditionally select a subset of observations, so that SAS processes
    only the observations that meet a set of specified conditions. For example, if you
    have a SAS data set containing sales records, you may want to print just the
    subset of observations for which the sales are greater than $300,000 but less than
    $600,000. In addition, WHERE-expression processing may improve efficiency of a
    request. For example, if a WHERE expression can be optimized with an index, it

is not necessary for SAS to read all observations in the data set in order to perform the request.

WHERE expression
defines a condition that selected observations must satisfy in order to be processed. You can have a single WHERE expression, referred to as a *simple expression*, such as the following:

```
where sales gt 600000;
```

Or you can have multiple WHERE expressions, referred to as a *compound expression*, such as the following:

```
where sales gt 600000 and salary lt 100000;
```

Where to Use a WHERE Expression

In SAS, you can use a WHERE expression in the following situations:

☐ WHERE statement in both DATA and PROC steps. For example, the following PRINT procedure includes a WHERE statement so that only the observations where the year is greater than 2001 are printed:

```
proc print data=employees;
   where startdate > '01jan2001'd;
run;
```

☐ WHERE= data set option. The following PRINT procedure includes the WHERE= data set option:

```
proc print data=employees (where=(startdate > '01jan2001'd));
run;
```

☐ WHERE clause in the SQL procedure, SCL, and SAS/IML software. For example, the following SQL procedure includes a WHERE clause to select only the states where the murder count is greater than seven:

```
proc sql;
   select state from crime
   where murder > 7;
```

☐ WHERE command in windowing environments like SAS/FSP software:

```
where age > 15
```

☐ SAS view (DATA step view, SAS/ACCESS view, PROC SQL view), stored with the definition. For example, the following SQL procedure creates an SQL view named STAT from the data file CRIME and defines a WHERE expression for the SQL view definition:

```
proc sql;
   create view stat as
   select * from crime
   where murder > 7;
```

In some cases, you can combine the methods that you use to specify a WHERE expression. That is, you can use a WHERE statement as follows:

☐ in conjunction with a WHERE= data set option

☐ along with the WHERE= data set option in windowing procedures, and in conjunction with the WHERE command

□ on a SAS view that has a stored WHERE expression.

For example, it might be useful to combine methods when you merge data sets. That is, you might want different criteria to apply to each data set when you create a subset of data. However, when you combine methods to create a subset of data, there are some restrictions. For example, in the DATA step, if a WHERE statement and a WHERE= data set option apply to the same data set, the data set option takes precedence. For details, see the documentation for the method you are using to specify a WHERE expression.

Note: By default, a WHERE expression does not evaluate added and modified observations. To specify whether a WHERE expression should evaluate updates, you can specify the WHEREUP= data set option. See the WHEREUP= data set option in *SAS Language Reference: Dictionary.* △

Syntax of WHERE Expression

A WHERE expression is a type of SAS expression that defines a condition for selecting observations. A WHERE expression can be as simple as a single variable name or a constant (which is a fixed value). A WHERE expression can be a SAS function, or it can be a sequence of operands and operators that define a condition for selecting observations. In general, the syntax of a WHERE expression is as follows:

WHERE *operand* <*operator*> <*operand*>

operand
something to be operated on. An operand can be a variable, a SAS function, or a constant. See "Specifying an Operand" on page 199.

operator
a symbol that requests a comparison, logical operation, or arithmetic calculation. All SAS expression operators are valid for a WHERE expression, which include arithmetic, comparison, logical, minimum and maximum, concatenation, parentheses to control order of evaluation, and prefix operators. In addition, you can use special WHERE expression operators, which include BETWEEN-AND, CONTAINS, IS NULL or IS MISSING, LIKE, sounds-like, and SAME-AND. See "Specifying an Operator" on page 201.

For more information on SAS expressions, see Chapter 7, "Expressions," on page 109.

Specifying an Operand

Variable

A variable is a column in a SAS data set. Each SAS variable has attributes like name and type (character or numeric). The variable type determines how you specify the value for which you are searching. For example:

```
where score > 50;
where date >= '01jan2001'd and time >= '9:00't;
where state = 'Texas';
```

In a WHERE expression, you cannot use automatic variables created by the DATA step (for example, FIRST.*variable*, LAST.*variable*, _N_, or variables created in assignment statements).

As in other SAS expressions, the names of numeric variables can stand alone. SAS treats numeric values of 0 or missing as false; other values are true. For example, the following WHERE expression returns all values for EMPNUM and ID that are not missing or that have a value of 0:

```
where empnum and id;
```

The names of character variables can also stand alone. SAS selects observations where the value of the character variable is not blank. For example, the following WHERE expression returns all values not equal to blank:

```
where lastname;
```

SAS Function

A SAS function returns a value from a computation or system manipulation. Most functions use arguments that you supply, but a few obtain their arguments from the operating environment. To use a SAS function in a WHERE expression, type its name and argument(s) enclosed in parentheses. Some functions you may want to specify include:

- □ SUBSTR extracts a substring
- □ TODAY returns the current date
- □ PUT returns a given value using a given format.

The following DATA step produces a SAS data set that contains only observations from data set CUSTOMER in which the value of NAME begins with **Mac** and the value of variable CITY is **Charleston** or **Atlanta**:

```
data testmacs;
   set customer;
   where substr (name,1,3) = 'Mac' and
   (city='Charleston' or city='Atlanta');
run;
```

Note: SAS functions used in a WHERE expression that can be optimized by an index are the SUBSTR function and the TRIM function. △

For more information on SAS functions, see "Functions and CALL Routines" on page 38.

Constant

A constant is a fixed value such as a number or quoted character string, that is, the value for which you are searching. A constant is a value of a variable obtained from the SAS data set, or values created within the WHERE expression itself. Constants are also called literals. For example, a constant could be a flight number or the name of a city. A constant can also be a time, date, or datetime value.

The value will be either numeric or character. Note the following rules regarding whether to use quotation marks:

- □ If the value is numeric, do not use quotation marks.

  ```
  where price > 200;
  ```

- □ If the value is character, use quotation marks.

  ```
  where lastname eq 'Martin';
  ```

▫ You can use either single or double quotation marks, but do not mix them. Quoted values must be exact matches, including case.

▫ It might be necessary to use single quotation marks when double quotation marks appear in the value, or use double quotation marks when single quotation marks appear in the value.

```
where item = '6" decorative pot';
where name ? "D'Amico";
```

▫ A SAS date constant must be enclosed in quotation marks. When you specify date values, case is not important. You can use single or double quotation marks. The following expressions are equivalent:

```
where birthday = '24sep1975'd;
where birthday = "24sep1975"d;
```

Specifying an Operator

Arithmetic Operators

Arithmetic operators allow you to perform a mathematical operation. The arithmetic operators include the following:

Table 12.1 Arithmetic Operators

Symbol	Definition	Example
*	multiplication	where bonus = salary * .10;
/	division	where f = g/h;
+	addition	where c = a+b;
-	subtraction	where f = g-h;
**	exponentiation	where y = a**2;

Comparison Operators

Comparison operators (also called binary operators) compare a variable with a value or with another variable. Comparison operators propose a relationship and ask SAS to determine whether that relationship holds. For example, the following WHERE expression accesses only those observations that have the value 78753 for the numeric variable ZIPCODE:

```
where zipcode eq 78753;
```

The following table lists the comparison operators:

Table 12.2 Comparison Operators

Symbol	Mnemonic Equivalent	Definition	Example
=	EQ	equal to	where empnum eq 3374;
^= or ~= or ¬= or <>	NE	not equal to	where status ne fulltime;

Symbol	Mnemonic Equivalent	Definition	Example
>	GT	greater than	where hiredate gt '01jun1982'd;
<	LT	less than	where empnum < 2000;
>=	GE	greater than or equal to	where empnum >= 3374;
<=	LE	less than or equal to	where empnum <= 3374;
	IN	equal to one from a list of values	where state in ('NC','TX');

When you do character comparisons, you can use the colon (:) modifier to compare only a specified prefix of a character string. For example, in the following WHERE expression, the colon modifier, used after the equal sign, tells SAS to look at only the first character in the values for variable LASTNAME and to select the observations with names beginning with the letter **s**:

```
where lastname=: 'S';
```

Note that in the SQL procedure, the colon modifier that is used in conjunction with an operator is not supported; you can use the LIKE operator instead.

IN Operator

The IN operator, which is a comparison operator, searches for character and numeric values that are equal to one from a list of values. The list of values must be in parentheses, with each character value in quotation marks and separated by either a comma or blank.

For example, suppose you want all sites that are in North Carolina or Texas. You could specify:

```
where state = 'NC' or state = 'TX';
```

However, it is easier to use the IN operator, which selects any state in the list:

```
where state in ('NC','TX');
```

In addition, you can use the NOT logical operator to exclude a list.

```
where state not in ('CA', 'TN', 'MA');
```

Fully-Bounded Range Condition

A fully-bounded range condition consists of a variable between two comparison operators, specifying both an upper and lower limit. For example, the following expression returns the employee numbers that fall within the range of 500 to 1000 (inclusive):

```
where 500 <= empnum <= 1000;
```

Note that the previous range condition expression is equivalent to the following:

```
where empnum >= 500 and empnum <= 1000;
```

You can combine the NOT logical operator with a fully-bounded range condition to select observations that fall outside the range. Note that parentheses are required:

```
where not (500 <= empnum <= 1000);
```

BETWEEN-AND Operator

The BETWEEN-AND operator is also considered a fully-bounded range condition that selects observations in which the value of a variable falls within an inclusive range of values.

You can specify the limits of the range as constants or expressions. Any range you specify is an inclusive range, so that a value equal to one of the limits of the range is within the range. The general syntax for using BETWEEN-AND is as follows:

WHERE *variable* BETWEEN *value* AND *value*;

For example:

```
where empnum between 500 and 1000;
where taxes between salary*0.30 and salary*0.50;
```

You can combine the NOT logical operator with the BETWEEN-AND operator to select observations that fall outside the range:

```
where empnum not between 500 and 1000;
```

Note: The BETWEEN-AND operator and a fully-bounded range condition produce the same results. That is, the following WHERE expressions are equivalent:

```
where 500 <= empnum <= 1000;
where empnum between 500 and 1000;
```

△

CONTAINS Operator

The most common usage of the CONTAINS (?) operator is to select observations by searching for a specified set of characters within the values of a character variable. The position of the string within the variable's values does not matter; however, the operator is case sensitive when making comparisons.

The following examples select observations having the values **Mobay** and **Brisbayne** for the variable COMPANY, but they do not select observations containing **Bayview**:

```
where company contains 'bay';
where company ? 'bay';
```

You can combine the NOT logical operator with the CONTAINS operator to select observations that are not included in a specified string:

```
where company not contains 'bay';
```

You can also use the CONTAINS operator with two variables, that is, to determine if one variable is contained in another. When you specify two variables, keep in mind the possibility of trailing spaces, which can be resolved using the TRIM function.

```
proc sql;
   select *
   from table1 as a, table2 as b
   where a.fullname contains trim(b.lastname) and
      a.fullname contains trim(b.firstname);
```

In addition, the TRIM function is helpful when you search on a macro variable.

```
proc print;
   where fullname contains trim("&lname");
run;
```

IS NULL or IS MISSING Operator

The IS NULL or IS MISSING operator selects observations in which the value of a variable is missing. The operator selects observations with both regular or special missing value characters and can be used for both character and numeric variables.

```
where idnum is missing;
where name is null;
```

The following are equivalent for character data:

```
where name is null;
where name = ' ';
```

And the following is equivalent for numeric data. This statement differentiates missing values with special missing value characters:

```
where idnum <= .z;
```

You can combine the NOT logical operator with IS NULL or IS MISSING to select nonmissing values, as follows:

```
where salary is not missing;
```

LIKE Operator

The LIKE operator selects observations by comparing the values of a character variable to a specified pattern, which is referred to as pattern matching. The LIKE operator is case sensitive. There are two special characters available for specifying a pattern:

percent sign (%)   specifies that any number of characters can occupy that position. The following WHERE expression selects all employees with a name that starts with the letter **N**. The names can be of any length.

```
where lastname like 'N%';
```

underscore (_)   matches just one character in the value for each underscore character. You can specify more than one consecutive underscore character in a pattern, and you can specify a percent sign and an underscore in the same pattern. For example, you can use different forms of the LIKE operator to select character values from this list of first names:

Diana

Diane

Dianna

Dianthus

Dyan

The following table shows which of these names is selected by using various forms of the LIKE operator:

Pattern	Name Selected
like 'D_an'	Dyan
like 'D_an_'	Diana, Diane
like 'D_an__'	Dianna
like 'D_an%'	all names from list

You can use a SAS character expression to specify a pattern, but you cannot use a SAS character expression that uses a SAS function.

You can combine the NOT logical operator with LIKE to select values that do not have the specified pattern, such as the following:

```
where frstname not like 'D_an%';
```

Sounds-like Operator

The sounds-like (=*) operator selects observations that contain a spelling variation of a specified word or words. The operator uses the Soundex algorithm to compare the variable value and the operand. For more information, see the SOUNDEX function in *SAS Language Reference: Dictionary*.

Note: Note that the SOUNDEX algorithm is English-biased, and is less useful for languages other than English. △

Although the sounds-like operator is useful, it does not always select all possible values. For example, consider that you want to select observations from the following list of names that sound like Smith:

Schmitt

Smith

Smithson

Smitt

Smythe

The following WHERE expression selects all the names from this list except **Schmitt** and **Smithson**:

```
where lastname=* 'Smith';
```

You can combine the NOT logical operator with the sounds-like operator to select values that do not contain a spelling variation of a specified word or words, such as:

```
where lastname not =* 'Smith';
```

Note: The sounds-like operator cannot be optimized with an index. △

SAME-AND Operator

Use the SAME-AND operator to add more conditions to an existing WHERE expression later in the program without retyping the original conditions. This is useful with the following:

□ interactive SAS procedures

□ full-screen SAS procedures that allow you to type a WHERE expression on the command line

□ any kind of RUN-group processing.

Use the SAME-AND operator when you already have a WHERE expression defined and you want to insert additional conditions. The SAME-AND operator has the following form:

where-expression-1;

... SAS statements...

WHERE SAME AND *where-expression-2*;

... SAS statements...

WHERE SAME AND *where-expression-n*;

SAS selects observations that satisfy the conditions after the SAME-AND operator in addition to any previously defined conditions. SAS treats all of the existing conditions as though they were conditions separated by AND operators in a single WHERE expression.

The following example shows how to use the SAME-AND operator within RUN groups in the GPLOT procedure. The SAS data set YEARS has three variables and contains quarterly data for the 1990–1997 period:

```
proc gplot data=years;
   plot unit*quar=year;
run;

   where year > '01jan1991'd;
run;

   where same and year < '01jan1996'd;
run;
```

The following WHERE expression is equivalent to the preceding code:

```
where year > '01jan1991'd and year < '01jan1996'd;
```

MIN and MAX Operators

Use the MIN or MAX operators to find the minimum or maximum value of two quantities. Surround the operators with the two quantities whose minimum or maximum value you want to know.

- □ The MIN operator returns the lower of the two values.
- □ The MAX operator returns the higher of two values.

For example, if A is less than B, then the following would return the value of A:

```
where x = (a min b);
```

Note: The symbol representation >< is not supported, and <> is interpreted as "not equal to." △

Concatenation Operator

The concatenation operator concatenates character values. You indicate the concatenation operator as follows:

- □ || (two OR symbols)
- □ !! (two explanation marks)
- □ ¦¦ (two broken vertical bars).

For example,

```
where name = 'John'||'Smith';
```

Prefix Operators

The plus sign (+) and minus sign (–) can be either prefix operators or arithmetic operators. They are prefix operators when they appear at the beginning of an expression or immediately preceding a left parentheses. A prefix operator is applied to the variable, constant, SAS function, or parenthetic expression.

```
where z = -(x + y);
```

Note: The NOT operator is also considered a prefix operator. △

Combining Expressions by Using Logical Operators

Syntax

You can combine or modify WHERE expressions by using the logical operators (also called Boolean operators) AND, OR, and NOT. The basic syntax of a compound WHERE expression is as follows:

WHERE *where-expression-1 logical-operator where-expression-n* ;

AND   combines two conditions by finding observations that satisfy both conditions. For example:

```
where skill eq 'java' and years eq 4;
```

OR   combines two conditions by finding observations that satisfy either condition or both. For example:

```
where skill eq 'java' or years eq 4;
```

NOT   modifies a condition by finding the complement of the specified criteria. You can use the NOT logical operator in combination with any SAS and WHERE expression operator. And you can combine the NOT operator with AND and OR. For example:

```
where skill not eq 'java' or years not eq 4;
```

The logical operators and their equivalent symbols are shown in the following table:

Table 12.3 Logical (Boolean) Operators

Symbol	Mnemonic Equivalent
&	AND
! or | or ¦	OR
^ or ~ or ¬	NOT

Processing Compound Expressions

When SAS encounters a compound WHERE expression (multiple conditions), the software follows rules to determine the order in which to evaluate each expression. When WHERE expressions are combined, SAS processes the conditions in a specific order:

1 The NOT expression is processed first.

2 Then the expressions joined by AND are processed.

3 Finally, the expressions joined by OR are processed.

For a complete discussion of the rules for evaluating compound expressions, see "Order of Evaluation in Compound Expressions" on page 124.

Using Parentheses to Control Order of Evaluation

Even though SAS evaluates logical operators in a specific order, you can control the order of evaluation by nesting expressions in parentheses. That is, an expression enclosed in parentheses is processed before one not enclosed. The expression within the innermost set of parentheses is processed first, followed by the next deepest, moving outward until all parentheses have been processed.

For example, suppose you want a list of all the Canadian sites that have both SAS/GRAPH and SAS/STAT software, so you issue the following expression:

```
where product='GRAPH' or product='STAT' and country='Canada';
```

The result, however, includes all sites that license SAS/GRAPH software along with the Canadian sites that license SAS/STAT software. To obtain the correct results, you can use parentheses, which causes SAS to evaluate the comparisons within the parentheses first, providing a list of sites with either product licenses, then the result is used for the remaining condition:

```
where (product='GRAPH' or product='STAT') and country='Canada';
```

Constructing Efficient WHERE Expressions

Indexing a SAS data set can significantly improve the performance of WHERE processing. An index is an optional file that you can create for SAS data files in order to provide direct access to specific observations. Processing a WHERE expression without an index requires SAS to sequentially read every observation to find the ones that match the selection criteria. Having an index allows the software to determine which observations satisfy the criteria without having to read all the observations, which is referred to as optimizing the WHERE expression. However, by default, SAS decides whether to use the index or read the entire data set sequentially. For details on how SAS uses an index to process a WHERE expression, see "Using an Index for WHERE Processing" on page 527.

In addition to creating indexes for the data set, here are some guidelines for writing efficient WHERE expressions:

Table 12.4 Constructing Efficient WHERE Expressions

Guideline	Efficient	Inefficient
Avoid using the LIKE operator that begins with % or _.	where country like 'A%INA';	where country like '%INA';
Avoid using arithmetic expressions.	where salary > 48000;	where salary > 12*4000;
Use the IN operator instead of a compound expression.	where state in ('NC' , 'PA' , 'VA');	where state ='NC' or state = 'PA' or state = 'VA';

Processing a Segment of Data That Is Conditionally Selected

When you conditionally select a subset of observations with a WHERE expression, you can also segment that subset by applying FIRSTOBS= and/or OBS= processing (both as data set options and system options). When used with a WHERE expression,

□ FIRSTOBS= specifies the observation number within the subset of data selected by the WHERE expression to begin processing.

□ OBS= specifies when to stop processing observations from the subset of data selected by the WHERE expression.

When used with a WHERE expression, the values specified for OBS= and FIRSTOBS= are not the physical observation number in the data set, but a logical number in the subset. For example, **obs=3** does not mean the third observation number in the data set; instead, it means the third observation in the subset of data selected by the WHERE expression.

Applying OBS= and FIRSTOBS= processing to a subset of data is supported for the WHERE statement, WHERE= data set option, and WHERE clause in the SQL procedure.

If you are processing a SAS view that is a view of another view (nested views), applying OBS= and FIRSTOBS= to a subset of data could produce unexpected results. For nested views, OBS= and FIRSTOBS= processing is applied to each view, starting with the root (lowest-level) view, and then filtering observations for each view. The result could be that no observations meet the subset and segment criteria. See "Processing a SAS View" on page 209.

Applying FIRSTOBS= and OBS= to a Subset of Data

The following SAS program illustrates how to specify a condition to subset data, and how to specify a segment of the subset of data to process.

```
data A; ❶
   do I=1 to 100;
   X=I + 1;
   output;
   end;
run;

proc print data=work.a (firstobs=2 ❸ obs=4 ❹ ;
   where I > 90; ❷
run;
```

❶ The DATA step creates a data set named WORK.A containing 100 observations and two variables: I and X.

❷ The WHERE expression **I > 90** tells SAS to process only the observations that meet the specified condition, which results in the subset of observations 91 through 100.

❸ The FIRSTOBS= data set option tells SAS to begin processing with the 2nd observation in the subset of data, which is observation 92.

❹ The OBS= data set option tells SAS to stop processing when it reaches the 4th observation in the subset of data, which is observation 94.

The result of PROC PRINT is observations 92, 93, and 94.

Processing a SAS View

The following SAS program creates a data set, a view for the data set, then a second view that subsets data from the first view. Both a WHERE statement and the OBS= system option are used.

```
data a;  ❶
   do I=1 to 100;
   X=I + 1;
   output;
   end;
run;

data viewa/view=viewa;  ❷
   set a;
      Z = X+1;
run;

data viewb/view=viewb;  ❸
   set viewa;
      where I > 90;
run;

options obs=3;  ❹

proc print data=work.viewb;  ❺
run;
```

❶ The first DATA step creates a data set named WORK.A, which contains 100 observations and two variables: I and X.

❷ The second DATA step creates a view named WORK.VIEWA containing 100 observations and three variables: I, X (from data set WORK.A), and Z (assigned in this DATA step).

❸ The third DATA step creates a view named WORK.VIEWB and subsets the data with a WHERE statement, which results in the view accessing ten observations.

❹ The OBS= system option applies to the previous SET VIEWA statement, which tells SAS to stop processing when it reaches the 3rd observation in the subset of data being processed.

❺ When SAS processes the PRINT procedure, the following occurs:

  1 First, SAS applies **obs=3** to WORK.VIEWA, which stops processing at the 3rd observation.

  2 Next, SAS applies the condition **I > 90** to the three observations being processed. None of the observations meet the criteria.

  3 PROC PRINT results in no observations.

To prevent the potential of unexpected results, you can specify **obs=max** when creating WORK.VIEWA to force SAS to read all the observations in the root (lowest-level) view:

```
data viewa/view=viewa;
   set a (obs=max);
      Z = X+1;
run;
```

The PRINT procedure processes observations 91, 92, and 93.

Deciding Whether to Use a WHERE Expression or a Subsetting IF Statement

To conditionally select observations from a SAS data set, you can use either a WHERE expression or a subsetting IF statement. While they both test a condition to determine if SAS should process an observation, they differ as follows:

□ The subsetting IF statement can be used only in a DATA step. A subsetting IF statement tests the condition after an observation is read into the Program Data Vector (PDV). If the condition is true, SAS continues processing the current observation. Otherwise, the observation is discarded, and processing continues with the next observation.

□ You can use a WHERE expression in both a DATA step and SAS procedures, as well as in a windowing environment, SCL programs, and as a data set option. A WHERE expression tests the condition before an observation is read into the PDV. If the condition is true, the observation is read into the PDV and processed. If the condition is false, the observation is not read into the PDV, and processing continues with the next observation, which can yield substantial savings when observations contain many variables or very long character variables (up to 32K bytes). Additionally, a WHERE expression can be optimized with an index, and the WHERE expression allows more operators, such as LIKE and CONTAINS.

Note: Although it is generally more efficient to use a WHERE expression and avoid the move to the PDV prior to processing, if the data set contains observations with very few variables, the move to the PDV could be cheap. However, one variable containing 32K bytes of character data is not cheap, even though it is only one variable. △

In most cases, you can use either method. However, the following table provides a list of tasks that require you to use a specific method:

Table 12.5 Tasks Requiring Either WHERE Expression or Subsetting IF Statement

Task	Method
Make the selection in a procedure without using a preceding DATA step	WHERE expression
Take advantage of the efficiency available with an indexed data set	WHERE expression
Use one of a group of special operators, such as BETWEEN-AND, CONTAINS, IS MISSING or IS NULL, LIKE, SAME-AND, and Sounds-Like	WHERE expression
Base the selection on anything other than a variable value that already exists in a SAS data set. For example, you can select a value that is read from raw data, or a value that is calculated or assigned during the course of the DATA step	subsetting IF
Make the selection at some point during a DATA step rather than at the beginning	subsetting IF
Execute the selection conditionally	subsetting IF

CHAPTER

13

Optimizing System Performance

Definitions for Optimizing System Performance **213**
Collecting and Interpreting Performance Statistics **214**
    Using the FULLSTIMER and STIMER System Options **214**
    Interpreting FULLSTIMER and STIMER Statistics **214**
    Using Application Response Measurement to Monitor Performance **215**
Techniques for Optimizing I/O **215**
    Overview of Techniques for Optimizing I/O **215**
    Using WHERE Processing **216**
    Using DROP and KEEP Statements **216**
    Using LENGTH Statements **216**
    Using the OBS= and FIRSTOBS= Data Set Options **217**
    Creating SAS Data Sets **217**
    Using Indexes **217**
    Accessing Data Through Views **217**
    Using Engines Efficiently **218**
    Setting the BUFNO=, BUFSIZE=, CATCACHE=, and COMPRESS= System Options **218**
    Using the SASFILE Statement **219**
Techniques for Optimizing Memory Usage **220**
Techniques for Optimizing CPU Performance **220**
    Reducing CPU Time by Using More Memory or Reducing I/O **220**
    Storing a Compiled Program for Computation-Intensive DATA Steps **220**
    Reducing Search Time for SAS Executable Files **220**
    Specifying Variable Lengths **221**
    Using Parallel Processing **221**
Calculating Data Set Size **221**

Definitions for Optimizing System Performance

performance statistics
    are measurements of the total input and output operations (I/O), memory, and CPU time used to process individual DATA or PROC steps. You can obtain these statistics by using SAS system options that can help you measure your job's initial performance and to determine how to improve performance.

system performance
    is measured by the overall amount of I/O, memory, and CPU time that your system uses to process SAS programs. By using the techniques discussed in the following sections, you can reduce or reallocate your usage of these three critical resources to improve system performance. While you may not be able to take

advantage of every technique for every situation, you can choose the ones that are best suited for a particular situation.

Collecting and Interpreting Performance Statistics

Using the FULLSTIMER and STIMER System Options

The FULLSTIMER and STIMER system options control the printing of performance statistics in the SAS log. These options produce different results, depending on your operating environment. See the SAS documentation for your operating environment for details about the output that SAS generates for these options.

The following output shows an example of the FULLSTIMER output in the SAS log, as produced in a UNIX operating environment.

Output 13.1 Sample Results of Using the FULLSTIMER Option in a UNIX Operating Environment

```
NOTE: DATA statement used:
      real time             0.19 seconds
      user cpu time         0.06 seconds
      system cpu time       0.01 seconds
      Memory                            460k
      Semaphores     exclusive 194 shared 9 contended 0
      SAS Task context switches        1     splits 0
```

The STIMER option reports a subset of the FULLSTIMER statistics. The following output shows an example of the STIMER output in the SAS log in a UNIX operating environment.

Output 13.2 Sample Results of Using the STIMER Option in a UNIX Operating Environment

```
NOTE: DATA statement used:
      real time             1.16 seconds
      cpu time              0.09 seconds
```

Operating Environment Information: See the documentation for your operating environment for information about how STIMER differs from FULLSTIMER in your operating environment. The information that these options display varies depending on your operating environment, so statistics that you see might differ from the ones shown. △

Interpreting FULLSTIMER and STIMER Statistics

Several types of resource usage statistics are reported by the STIMER and FULLSTIMER options, including real time (elapsed time) and CPU time. *Real time* represents the clock time it took to execute a job or step; it is heavily dependent on the capacity of the system and the current load. As more users share a particular resource, less of that resource is available to you. *CPU time* represents the actual processing time required by the CPU to execute the job, exclusive of capacity and load factors. If you must wait longer for a resource, your CPU time will not increase, but your real time will increase. It is not advisable to use real time as the only criterion for the efficiency of your program because you cannot always control the capacity and load demands on your system. A more accurate assessment of system performance is CPU time, which decreases more predictably as you modify your program to become more efficient.

The statistics reported by FULLSTIMER relate to the three critical computer resources: I/O, memory, and CPU time. Under many circumstances, reducing the use of any of these three resources usually results in better throughput of a particular job and a reduction of real time used. However, there are exceptions, as described in the following sections.

Using Application Response Measurement to Monitor Performance

SAS provides the ability to monitor the performance of your applications using Application Response Measurement (ARM). ARM enables you to monitor the availability and performance of transactions within and across diverse applications. The SAS ARM interface consists of the implementation of the ARM API as ARM functions and an ARM agent. In addition, SAS supplies ARM macros, which generate calls to the ARM functions, and new ARM system options, which enable you to manage the ARM environment and to log internal SAS processing transactions. For information, see Chapter 15, "Monitoring Performance Using Application Response Measurement (ARM)," on page 225.

Techniques for Optimizing I/O

Overview of Techniques for Optimizing I/O

I/O is one of the most important factors for optimizing performance. Most SAS jobs consist of repeated cycles of reading a particular set of data to perform various data analysis and data manipulation tasks. To improve the performance of a SAS job, you must reduce the number of times SAS accesses disk or tape devices.

To do this, you can modify your SAS programs to process only the necessary variables and observations by:

☐ using WHERE processing
☐ using DROP and KEEP statements
☐ using LENGTH statements
☐ using the OBS= and FIRSTOBS= data set options.

You can also modify your programs to reduce the number of times it processes the data internally by:

☐ creating SAS data sets
☐ using indexes
☐ accessing data through views
☐ using engines efficiently.

You can reduce the number of data accesses by processing more data each time a device is accessed by

☐ setting the BUFNO=, BUFSIZE=, CATCACHE=, and COMPRESS= system options

   □ using the SASFILE global statement to open a SAS data set and allocate enough buffers to hold the entire data set in memory.

Note: Sometimes you may be able to use more than one method, making your SAS job even more efficient. △

Using WHERE Processing

You might be able to use a WHERE statement in a procedure in order to perform the same task as a DATA step with a subsetting IF statement. The WHERE statement can eliminate extra DATA step processing when performing certain analyses because unneeded observations are not processed.

For example, the following DATA step creates a data set SEATBELT, which contains only those observations from the AUTO.SURVEY data set for which the value of SEATBELT is YES. The new data set is then printed.

```
libname auto '/users/autodata';
data seatbelt;
   set auto.survey;
   if seatbelt='yes';
run;


proc print data=seatbelt;
run;
```

However, you can get the same output from the PROC PRINT step without creating a data set if you use a WHERE statement in the PRINT procedure, as in the following example:

```
proc print data=auto.survey;
   where seatbelt='yes';
run;
```

The WHERE statement can save resources by eliminating the number of times you process the data. In this example, you might be able to use less time and memory by eliminating the DATA step. Also, you use less I/O because there is no intermediate data set. Note that you cannot use a WHERE statement in a DATA step that reads raw data.

The extent of savings that you can achieve depends on many factors, including the size of the data set. It is recommended that you test your programs to determine which is the most efficient solution. See "Deciding Whether to Use a WHERE Expression or a Subsetting IF Statement" on page 211 for more information.

Using DROP and KEEP Statements

Another way to improve efficiency is to use DROP and KEEP statements to reduce the size of your observations. When you create a temporary data set and include only the variables that you need, you can reduce the number of I/O operations that are required to process the data. See *SAS Language Reference: Dictionary* for more information on the DROP and KEEP statements.

Using LENGTH Statements

You can also use LENGTH statements to reduce the size of your observations. When you include only the necessary storage space for each variable, you can reduce the number of I/O operations that are required to process the data. Before you change the length of a numeric variable, however, see "Specifying Variable Lengths" on page 221. See *SAS Language Reference: Dictionary* for more information on the LENGTH statement.

Using the OBS= and FIRSTOBS= Data Set Options

You can also use the OBS= and FIRSTOBS= data set options to reduce the number of observations processed. When you create a temporary data set and include only the necessary observations, you can reduce the number of I/O operations that are required to process the data. See *SAS Language Reference: Dictionary* for more information on the OBS= and FIRSTOBS= data set options.

Creating SAS Data Sets

If you process the same raw data repeatedly, it is usually more efficient to create a SAS data set. SAS can process SAS data sets more efficiently than it can process raw data files.

Another consideration involves whether you are using data sets created with previous releases of SAS. If you frequently process data sets created with previous releases, it is sometimes more efficient to convert that data set to a new one by creating it in the most recent version of SAS. See Chapter 35, "SAS 9.1 Compatibility with SAS Files From Earlier Releases," on page 583 for more information.

Using Indexes

An index is an optional file that you can create for a SAS data file to provide direct access to specific observations. The index stores values in ascending value order for a specific variable or variables and includes information as to the location of those values within observations in the data file. In other words, an index allows you to locate an observation by the value of the indexed variable.

Without an index, SAS accesses observations sequentially in the order in which they are stored in the data file. With an index, SAS accesses the observation directly. Therefore, by creating and using an index, you can access an observation faster.

In general, SAS can use an index to improve performance in these situations:

- ☐ For WHERE processing, an index can provide faster and more efficient access to a subset of data.

- ☐ For BY processing, an index returns observations in the index order, which is in ascending value order, without using the SORT procedure.

- ☐ For the SET and MODIFY statements, the KEY= option allows you to specify an index in a DATA step to retrieve particular observations in a data file.

Note: An index exists to improve performance. However, an index conserves some resources at the expense of others. Therefore, you must consider costs associated with creating, using, and maintaining an index. See "Understanding SAS Indexes" on page 518 for more information about indexes and deciding whether to create one. △

Accessing Data Through Views

You can use the SQL procedure or a DATA step to create views of your data. A view is a stored set of instructions that subsets your data with fewer statements. Also, you can use a view to group data from several data sets without creating a new one, saving both processing time and disk space. See Chapter 29, "SAS Data Views," on page 539 and the *Base SAS Procedures Guide* for more details.

Using Engines Efficiently

If you do not specify an engine on a LIBNAME statement, SAS must perform extra processing steps in order to determine which engine to associate with the data library. SAS must look at all of the files in the directory until it has enough information to determine which engine to use. For example, the following statement is efficient because it explicitly tells SAS to use a specific engine for the libref FRUITS:

```
/* Engine specified. */


libname fruits v9 '/users/myid/mydir';
```

The following statement does not explicitly specify an engine. In the output, notice the NOTE about mixed engine types that is generated:

```
/* Engine not specified. */


libname fruits '/users/myid/mydir';
```

Output 13.3   Output From the LIBNAME Statement

```
NOTE: Directory for library FRUITS contains files of mixed engine types.
NOTE: Libref FRUITS was successfully assigned as follows:
      Engine:        V9
      Physical Name: /users/myid/mydir
```

Operating Environment Information: In the z/OS operating environment, you do not need to specify an engine for certain types of libraries. △

See Chapter 37, "SAS Engines," on page 597 for more information about SAS engines.

Setting the BUFNO=, BUFSIZE=, CATCACHE=, and COMPRESS= System Options

The following SAS system options can help you reduce the number of disk accesses that are needed for SAS files, though they might increase memory usage.

BUFNO=

SAS uses the BUFNO= option to adjust the number of open page buffers when it processes a SAS data set. Increasing this option's value can improve your application's performance by allowing SAS to read more data with fewer passes; however, your memory usage increases. Experiment with different values for this option to determine the optimal value for your needs.

Note: You can also use the CBUFNO= system option to control the number of extra page buffers to allocate for each open SAS catalog. △

See system options in *SAS Language Reference: Dictionary* and the SAS documentation for your operating environment for more details on this option.

BUFSIZE=

When the Base SAS engine creates a data set, it uses the BUFSIZE= option to set the permanent page size for the data set. The page size is the amount of data that can be transferred for an I/O operation to one buffer. The default value for BUFSIZE= is determined by your operating environment. Note that the default is set to optimize the sequential access method. To improve performance for direct (random) access, you should change the value for BUFSIZE=.

Whether you use your operating environment's default value or specify a value, the engine always writes complete pages regardless of how full or empty those pages are.

If you know that the total amount of data is going to be small, you can set a small page size with the BUFSIZE= option, so that the total data set size remains small and you minimize the amount of wasted space on a page. In contrast, if you know that you are going to have many observations in a data set, you should optimize BUFSIZE= so that as little overhead as possible is needed. Note that each page requires some additional overhead.

Large data sets that are accessed sequentially benefit from larger page sizes because sequential access reduces the number of system calls that are required to read the data set. Note that because observations cannot span pages, typically there is unused space on a page.

"Calculating Data Set Size" on page 221 discusses how to estimate data set size.

See system options in *SAS Language Reference: Dictionary* and the SAS documentation for your operating environment for more details on this option.

CATCACHE=
SAS uses this option to determine the number of SAS catalogs to keep open at one time. Increasing its value can use more memory, although this may be warranted if your application uses catalogs that will be needed relatively soon by other applications. (The catalogs closed by the first application are cached and can be accessed more efficiently by subsequent applications.)

See system options in *SAS Language Reference: Dictionary* and the SAS documentation for your operating environment for more details on this option.

COMPRESS=
One further technique that can reduce I/O processing is to store your data as compressed data sets by using the COMPRESS= data set option. However, storing your data this way means that more CPU time is needed to decompress the observations as they are made available to SAS. But if your concern is I/O, and not CPU usage, compressing your data may improve the I/O performance of your application.

See *SAS Language Reference: Dictionary* for more details on this option.

Using the SASFILE Statement

The SASFILE global statement opens a SAS data set and allocates enough buffers to hold the entire data set in memory. Once it is read, data is held in memory, available to subsequent DATA and PROC steps, until either a second SASFILE statement closes the file and frees the buffers or the program ends, which automatically closes the file and frees the buffers.

Using the SASFILE statement can improve performance by

- □ reducing multiple open/close operations (including allocation and freeing of memory for buffers) to process a SAS data set to one open/close operation

- □ reducing I/O processing by holding the data in memory.

If your SAS program consists of steps that read a SAS data set multiple times and you have an adequate amount of memory so that the entire file can be held in real memory, the program should benefit from using the SASFILE statement. Also, SASFILE is especially useful as part of a program that starts a SAS server such as a

SAS/SHARE server. See *SAS Language Reference: Dictionary* for more information on the SASFILE global statement.

Techniques for Optimizing Memory Usage

If memory is a critical resource, several techniques can reduce your dependence on increased memory. However, most of them also increase I/O processing or CPU usage.

However, by *increasing* memory available to SAS by increasing the value of the MEMSIZE= system option (or by using the MEMLEAVE= option, in some operating environments), you can decrease processing time because the amount of time that is spent on paging, or reading pages of data into memory, is reduced. The SORTSIZE= and SUMSIZE= system options enable you to limit the amount of memory that is available to sorting and summarization procedures.

You can also make tradeoffs between memory and other resources, as discussed in "Reducing CPU Time by Using More Memory or Reducing I/O" on page 220. To make the most of the I/O subsystem, you must use more and larger buffers. However, these buffers share space with the other memory demands of your SAS session.

Operating Environment Information: The MEMSIZE= system option is not available in some operating environments. If MEMSIZE= is available in your operating environment, it might not increase memory. See the documentation for your operating environment for more information. △

Techniques for Optimizing CPU Performance

Reducing CPU Time by Using More Memory or Reducing I/O

Executing a single stream of code takes approximately the same amount of CPU time each time that code is executed. Optimizing CPU performance in these instances is usually a tradeoff. For example, you might be able to reduce CPU time by using more memory, because more information can be read and stored in one operation, but less memory is available to other processes.

Also, because the CPU performs all the processing that is needed to perform an I/O operation, an option or technique that reduces the number of I/O operations can also have a positive effect on CPU usage.

Storing a Compiled Program for Computation-Intensive DATA Steps

Another technique that can improve CPU performance is to store a DATA step that is executed repeatedly as a compiled program rather than as SAS statements. This is especially true for large DATA step jobs that are not I/O-intensive. For more information on storing compiled DATA steps, see Chapter 30, "Stored Compiled DATA Step Programs," on page 547.

Reducing Search Time for SAS Executable Files

The PATH= system option specifies the list of directories (or libraries, in some operating environments) that contain SAS executable files. Your default configuration file specifies a certain order for these directories. You can rearrange the directory specifications in the PATH= option so that the most commonly accessed directories are listed first. Place the least commonly accessed directories last.

Operating Environment Information: The PATH= system option is not available in some operating environments. See the documentation for your operating environment for more information. △

Specifying Variable Lengths

When SAS processes the program data vector, it typically moves the data in one large operation rather than by individual variables. When data is properly aligned (in 8-byte boundaries), data movement can occur in as little as 2 clock cycles (a single load followed by a single store). SAS moves unaligned data by more complex means, at worst, a single byte at a time. This would be at least eight times slower for an 8-byte variable.

Many high performance RISC (Reduced Instruction Set Computer) processors pay a very large performance penalty for movement of unaligned data. When possible, leave numeric data at full width (eight bytes). Note that SAS must widen short numeric data for any arithmetic operation. On the other hand, short numeric data can save both memory and I/O. You must determine which method is most advantageous for your operating environment and situation.

Note: Alignment can be especially important when you process a data set by selecting only specific variables or when you use WHERE processing. △

Using Parallel Processing

SAS System 9 supports a new wave of SAS functionality related to parallel processing. Parallel processing means that processing is handled by multiple CPUs simultaneously. This technology takes advantage of SMP machines and provides performance gains for two types of SAS processes: threaded I/O and threaded application processing.

For information, see Chapter 14, "Support for Parallel Processing," on page 223.

Calculating Data Set Size

If you have already applied optimization techniques but still experience lengthy processing times or excessive memory usage, the size of your data sets might be very large, in which case, further improvement might not be possible.

You can estimate the size of a data set by creating a dummy data set that contains the same variables as your data set. Run the CONTENTS procedure, which shows the size of each observation. Multiply the size by the number of observations in your data set to obtain the total number of bytes that must be processed. You can compare processing statistics with smaller data sets to determine if the performance of the large data sets is in proportion to their size. If not, further optimization might still be possible.

Note: When you use this technique to calculate the size of a data set, you obtain only an estimate. Internal requirements, such as the storage of variable names, might cause the actual data set size to be slightly different. △

CHAPTER

14

Support for Parallel Processing

Definition of Parallel Processing **223**
Threaded I/O **223**
Threaded Application Processing **224**

Definition of Parallel Processing

SAS 9 supports a new wave of SAS functionality related to parallel processing. *Parallel processing* refers to processing that is handled by multiple CPUs simultaneously. This technology takes advantage of hardware that has multiple CPUs, called *SMP machines*, and provides performance gains for two types of SAS processes:

□ threaded I/O

□ threaded application processing.

SMP machines have multiple CPUs and an operating environment that can spawn and manage multiple pieces of executable code called *threads*. A thread is a single, independent flow of control through a program or within a process. Threading takes advantage of multiple CPUs by dividing processing among the available CPUs. A thread-enabled operating environment provides support for threads; for example, each thread needs a context (like a register set and a program counter), a segment of code to execute, and a piece of memory to use in the process.

Even if your site does not use an SMP machine, SAS 9 can still provide increased performance. Some types of threading can be performed using a single CPU.

Threaded I/O

Some applications can process data faster than the data can be delivered to the application. When an application cannot keep the available CPUs busy, the application is said to be *I/O-bound*.

SAS supports threaded I/O for SAS applications by providing the SAS Scalable Performance Data (SPD) engine. The SPD engine boosts the performance of SAS applications that are I/O bound through parallel processing of partitioned data sets. Partitioned data sets can span disk drives but still be referenced as a single data set. In this way, the SPD engine can read many millions of observations into SAS applications very rapidly by spawning a thread for each data partition and evaluating WHERE expressions in multiple CPUs. SAS 9.1 support for multiple CPUs, for example on a Symmetric Multiprocessor (SMP) machine, and support for multiple disks per CPU make SPD engine's parallel I/O possible. See *SAS Scalable Performance Data Engine: Reference* for full details on this engine's capabilities.

The benefits of support for multiple disks in SAS 9.1 is not limited to use by the SPD engine. Multiple disks can be on an SMP machine, but they can also be a bank of disks on a single-CPU machine. Increasing the number of disks that can be accessed simultaneously increases the amount of data that can be delivered to an application. This is because reading or writing data to and from disk takes much more time than the associated CPU processing that directs the I/O. Even a single-CPU machine can support multiple disk drives, which boosts performance. When an SMP machine is used, the performance gain can be quite significant because each CPU can support multiple disk drives. However, multiple CPUs cannot speed up I/O from a single disk drive. The minimum configuration for I/O performance gain is at least one controller per CPU and at least two disk drives for each controller. For example, a site with four CPUs should have at least four controllers and eight disk drives.

Threaded Application Processing

Some applications receive data faster than they can perform the necessary processing on that data. These applications are sometimes referred to as *CPU-bound*. For CPU-bound applications, the solution is to increase processing power. Support for SMP machines provides access to threaded processing for CPU-bound applications. Even if your application is not currently CPU-bound, if you increase the amount of data that can be delivered to an application, you will naturally increase the need for faster processing of that data. Modifying your application to process data in threads solves this problem.

For SAS 9, certain procedures such as SORT and SUMMARY have been modified so that they can thread the processing through multiple CPUs, if they are available. In addition, threaded processing is being integrated into a variety of other SAS features in order to improve performance. For example, when you create an index, if sorting is required, SAS attempts to sort the data using the thread-enabled sort.

Some types of processing are not suited to threading, while other types of processing can benefit greatly. For example, sorting can be performed in multiple threads by dividing the sorting process into separately executable sorting processes. One or more of these threads can process data in each CPU. The sorted data from each thread is then joined together and written to the output data set. Sorting can be performed in threads, but the join process and the output process are nonthreadable processes. Even with applications that are highly-threadable processes, simply providing additional disks and CPUs might not improve performance. That is, a particular algorithm can benefit by using four CPUs but cannot benefit an equal amount by adding four more CPUs.

For SAS procedures that are thread-enabled, new SAS system options are introduced with SAS 9:

CPUCOUNT=
    specifies how many CPUs can be used.

THREAD|NOTHREADS
    controls whether to use threads.

For documentation on the SAS system options, see *SAS Language Reference: Dictionary*. In addition, the documentation for each thread-enabled procedure provides more information. See *Base SAS Procedures Guide*.

CHAPTER

15

Monitoring Performance Using Application Response Measurement (ARM)

Introduction to ARM   **225**
   What Is ARM?   **225**
   Why Is ARM Needed?   **225**
   Definitions for ARM   **226**
How Does ARM Work?   **227**
Will ARM Affect an Application's Performance?   **227**
Using the ARM Interface   **228**
   Overview   **228**
   ARM System Options   **228**
   ARM API Function Calls   **228**
   ARM Macros   **229**
   Logging the Transaction Records: the ARM Log   **230**
Examples of Gathering Performance Data   **231**
   Logging Internal SAS Processing Transactions   **231**
   Using ARM System Options and ARM Macros to Log Performance Statistics   **233**
   Post Processing an ARM Log   **234**

Introduction to ARM

What Is ARM?

Application Response Measurement (ARM) enables you to monitor the availability and performance of transactions within and across diverse applications.

Why Is ARM Needed?

There are many techniques for measuring response times, but only ARM measures them accurately. Other approaches, although useful in other ways, can only measure business service levels by making assumptions or guesses about what is a business transaction, and when it begins and ends. Also, other approaches cannot provide important information that ARM can, such as whether a transaction completed successfully.

Using ARM, you can log transaction records from an application in order to

☐ determine the application response times

☐ determine the workload/throughput of your applications

☐ verify that service level objectives are being met

☐ determine why the application is not available

- □ verify who is using an application
- □ determine why a user is having poor response time
- □ determine what queries are being issued by an application
- □ determine the subcomponents of an application's response time
- □ determine which servers are being used
- □ calculate the load time for data warehouses.

Definitions for ARM

application
> a computer program that processes data for a specific use such as for payroll, inventory, and billing. It is the program for which you want to monitor performance.

Application Response Measurement (ARM) API
> an application programming interface that is used to implement software in order to monitor the availability and performance of transactions within and across diverse applications. The API is an open, vendor-neutral approach to monitor the performance of distributed and client/server applications. The ARM API consists of definitions for a standard set of function calls that are callable from an application. The ARM API was jointly developed by the industry partnership Computer Measurement Group, Inc. (CMG).

ARM agent
> a software vendor's implementation of the ARM API. Each ARM agent is a set of executable routines that can be called by applications. The ARM agent runs concurrently with SAS. The SAS application passes transaction information to the agent, which collects the ARM transaction records and writes them to the ARM log.

ARM log
> an external file that contains records of ARM transactions.

ARM macros
> a group of SAS macros that provide user control for identifying transactions that you want to log. You insert the macro calls into your SAS program at strategic points; the macros generate calls to the ARM API function calls.

ARM system options
> a group of SAS system options that control various aspects of the SAS ARM interface.

ARM subsystem
> a group of internal SAS processing transactions such as PROC and DATA step processing and file input/output processing. You use the ARM system option ARMSUBSYS= to turn on a subsystem or all subsystems.

SAS ARM interface
> an interface that can be used to monitor the performance of SAS applications. In the SAS ARM interface, the ARM API is implemented as an ARM agent. In addition, SAS supplies ARM macros, which generate calls to the ARM API function calls, and ARM system options, which enable you to manage the ARM environment and to log internal SAS processing transactions.

transaction
> a unit of work that is meaningful for monitoring an application's performance. A transaction can be started and stopped one or more times within a single

execution of an application. For example, in a SAS application, a transaction could be a step that updates a customer database. In SAS/MDDB Server software, a transaction might be a query on a subcube. Another type of transaction might be internal SAS processing that you want to monitor.

How Does ARM Work?

The ARM API is an application programming interface that a vendor, such as SAS, can implement in order to monitor the availability and performance of transactions in distributed or client/server applications. The ARM API consists of definitions for a standard set of function calls that are callable from an application.

SAS implemented the ARM API as an ARM agent. In addition, SAS supplies ARM macros, which generate calls to the ARM API function calls, and ARM SAS system options, which manage the ARM environment and enable you to log internal SAS processing transactions.

You must determine the transactions within your application that you want to measure.

☐ To log internal SAS processing transactions, simply use the ARM system option ARMSUBSYS= in order to turn on the transactions that you want to log.

☐ To log transactions that you want to identify, insert ARM macros into the application's code.

You insert ARM macros at strategic points in the application's code so that the desired transaction response time and other statistics that you want are collected. The ARM macros generate calls to the ARM API function calls that are contained on the executable module that contains the ARM agent. The module accepts the function call parameters, performs error checking, and passes the ARM data to the agent to calculate the statistics and to log the records to an ARM log.

Typically, an ARM API function call occurs just before a transaction is initiated in order to signify the beginning of the transaction. Then, an associated ARM API function call occurs in the application where the transaction is known to be complete. Basically, the application calls the ARM agent before a transaction starts and then again after it ends, allowing those transactions to be measured and monitored.

The transaction's response time and additional statistics are then routed to the ARM agent, which then logs the information to the ARM log. The ARM API function calls typically log the data to a file. The time between these ARM API function calls provides an approximate response time measurement.

Will ARM Affect an Application's Performance?

ARM is designed to be a high-speed interface that has minimal impact on applications. An ARM agent is designed to quickly extract the information that is needed and return control to the application immediately. Processing of the information is done in a different process that can run when the system is otherwise idle.

Using the ARM Interface

Overview

The SAS ARM interface provides the ability to monitor the performance of SAS applications. The interface consists of the implementation of the ARM API as an ARM agent. In addition, SAS supplies ARM macros, which generate calls to the ARM API function calls; and ARM system options, which manage the ARM environment and also enable you to log internal SAS processing transactions.

ARM System Options

SAS provides ARM system options, which are SAS system options that manage the ARM environment and provide the ability to log internal SAS processing transactions, such as file opening and closing and DATA step and PROC step response time.

The following ARM SAS system options are available:

ARMAGENT=
   specifies another vendor's ARM agent, which is an executable module that contains a vendor's implementation of the ARM API. By default, SAS uses the SAS ARM agent.

ARMLOC=
   specifies the location of the ARM log.

ARMSUBSYS=
   initializes the SAS ARM subsystems, which determine the internal SAS processing transactions to be monitored. Each subsystem is a group of internal SAS processing transactions.

You can specify the ARM SAS system options

   □ in a configuration file so that they are set automatically when you invoke SAS

   □ on the command line when you invoke SAS

   □ using the global OPTIONS statement either in the SAS program or in an autoexec file

   □ from the System Options window.

See SAS system options in *SAS Language Reference: Dictionary* for details on each ARM system option.

See "Logging Internal SAS Processing Transactions" on page 231 for an example that sets the ARM system options.

ARM API Function Calls

The ARM API function calls are contained in the SAS ARM agent. Note that for the SAS implementation, you do not explicitly insert ARM API function calls in a SAS application; you insert ARM macros, which generate calls to the ARM API function calls.

These are the six ARM API function calls:

ARM_INIT
   names the application and optionally the users of the application and initializes the ARM environment for the application.

ARM_GETID
> names a transaction.

ARM_START
> signals the start of a unique transaction.

ARM_UPDATE
> provides information (optional) about the progress of a transaction.

ARM_STOP
> signals the end of a transaction.

ARM_END
> terminates the ARM environment and signals the end of an application.

ARM calls use numeric identifiers (IDs) to uniquely identify the ARM objects that are input and output from the ARM API function calls. The three classes of IDs are

□ application IDs

□ transaction class IDs

□ start handles (start time) for each instance of a transaction.

IDs are numeric, assigned integers. The agent usually assigns IDs. The scheme for assigning IDs varies from one vendor's agent to another, but, at a minimum, a unique ID within a single session is guaranteed. Some agents allow you to preassign IDs.

ARM Macros

The ARM macros provide an efficient method for you to identify which transactions in a SAS application you want to log. You insert the ARM macro calls in the SAS program code, which in turn generate calls to the ARM API function calls in order to log transaction information. The ARM macros automatically manage the returned IDs from the ARM API function calls.

The following table shows the relationship between the ARM API function calls and the ARM macros:

Table 15.1 Relationship Between ARM API Function Calls and ARM Macros

ARM API Function Calls	ARM Macro
ARM_INIT	%ARMINIT
ARM_GETID	%ARMGTID
ARM_START	%ARMSTRT
ARM_UPDATE	%ARMUPDT
ARM_STOP	%ARMSTOP
ARM_END	%ARMEND

The following ARM macros are available:

%ARMINIT
> generates a call to ARM_INIT, which names the application and optionally the users of the application and initializes the ARM environment for the application. Typically, you would insert this macro in your code once.

%ARMGTID

generates a call to ARM_GETID, which names a transaction. Use %ARMGTID for each unique transaction in order to describe the type of transactions to be logged. A %ARMGTID is typically coded for each transaction class in an application.

%ARMSTRT

generates a call to ARM_START, which signals the start of an instance of a transaction. Insert %ARMSTRT before each transaction that you want to log. Whereas %ARMGTID defines a transaction class, %ARMSTRT indicates that a transaction is executing.

%ARMUPDT

is an optional macro that generates a call to ARM_UPDATE, which provides additional information about the progress of a transaction. Insert %ARMUPDT between %ARMSTRT and %ARMSTOP in order to supply information about the transaction that is in progress.

%ARMSTOP

generates a call to ARM_STOP, which signals the end of a transaction instance. Insert %ARMSTOP where the transaction is known to be complete.

%ARMEND

generates a call to ARM_END, which terminates the ARM environment and signals that the application will not make any more ARM calls.

The following post-processing ARM macros are also available. These macros are specific to the SAS ARM implementation; they are not part of the ARM API standard.

%ARMCONV

converts an ARM log created in SAS 9 or later, which uses a comma delimited format, into the ARM log format used in Release 8.2.

%ARMPROC

processes the ARM log and writes six SAS data sets that contain the information from the log.

%ARMJOIN

processes the six SAS data sets that are created by %ARMPROC and creates data sets that contain common information about applications and transactions.

For more information, see SAS ARM macros in *SAS Language Reference: Dictionary*. See "Using ARM System Options and ARM Macros to Log Performance Statistics" on page 233 for an example of inserting ARM macros in SAS code.

Logging the Transaction Records: the ARM Log

The SAS ARM agent supplies a basic logger that captures response time and CPU time statistics and handles logging the information. By default, the logger runs in the same session as your application and logs all ARM data synchronously to the external file that is specified with the ARMLOC= SAS system option.

All information that is passed by the application during ARM calls is written to the log, as well as other calculated statistics.

All ARM records are routed to the file to which the fileref points. Note that in Release 8.2, the ARM records were either written to the SAS log or to a specified external file. For SAS 9 or later, all ARM records are written to an external file. To specify the external output file, use the ARMLOC= SAS system option.

For SAS 9 or later, the format of the log records is comma delimited, which consists of columns of data separated by commas. The format of the ARM log that is written to by the logger was designed to be easily readable. The date/time stamp and the call identifier always appear in the same column location. Subsequent information appears as a name=value pair.

Here is a sample of an ARM log:

Output 15.1 ARM Log (SAS 9 or Later Format)

```
I,1320332339.838000,1,2.814046,5.988611,SAS,xxxxxx
G,1320332339.858000,1,1,MVA_DSIO.OPEN_CLOSE,DATA SET OPEN/CLOSE,LIBNAME,
    ShortStr,MEMTYPE,ShortStr,MEMNAME,LongStr
S,1320332347.549000,1,1,1,2.914190,6.669590,WORK    ,DATA    ,ONE
S,1320332348.390000,1,1,2,2.934219,6.729676,WORK    ,DATA    ,TWO
P,1320332348.410000,1,1,1,2.954248,6.729676,0,WORK    ,DATA    ,ONE
P,1320332348.420000,1,1,2,2.964262,6.729676,0,WORK    ,DATA    ,TWO
S,1320332348.490000,1,1,3,2.994305,6.739691,WORK    ,DATA    ,THREE
P,1320332348.530000,1,1,3,3.14334,6.749705,0,WORK    ,DATA    ,THREE
S,1320332359.216000,1,1,4,3.224636,7.661016,WORK    ,DATA    ,THREE
P,1320332360.948000,1,1,4,3.254680,7.851289,0,WORK    ,DATA    ,THREE
S,1320332362.170000,1,1,5,3.304752,7.951433,WORK    ,DATA    ,THREE
P,1320332367.358000,1,1,5,3.334795,8.51577,0,WORK    ,DATA    ,THREE
S,1320332367.388000,1,1,6,3.354824,8.61592,WORK    ,DATA    ,THREE
P,1320332367.398000,1,1,6,3.364838,8.61592,0,WORK    ,DATA    ,THREE
S,1320332367.428000,1,1,7,3.384867,8.71606,WORK    ,DATA    ,ONE
S,1320332367.438000,1,1,8,3.394881,8.71606,WORK    ,DATA    ,TWO
P,1320332372.655000,1,1,8,3.424924,8.131692,0,WORK    ,DATA    ,TWO
P,1320332372.665000,1,1,7,3.424924,8.141707,0,WORK    ,DATA    ,ONE
S,1320332375.970000,1,1,9,3.454968,8.392067,WORK    ,DATA    ,THREE
P,1320332377.282000,1,1,9,3.515054,8.562312,0,WORK    ,DATA    ,THREE
S,1320332377.302000,1,1,10,3.525068,8.572326,WORK    ,DATA    ,THREE
P,1320332377.923000,1,1,10,3.575140,8.632412,0,WORK    ,DATA    ,THREE
S,1320332377.953000,1,1,11,3.585155,8.652441,WORK    ,DATA    ,THREE
P,1320332383.521000,1,1,11,3.655256,8.832700,0,WORK    ,DATA    ,THREE
S,1320332389.89000,1,1,12,3.715342,8.912816,WORK    ,DATA    ,THREE
S,1320332389.159000,1,1,13,3.725356,8.922830,SASUSER ,DATA    ,THREE
P,1320332391.182000,1,1,12,3.765414,9.32988,0,WORK    ,DATA    ,THREE
P,1320332391.192000,1,1,13,3.775428,9.32988,0,SASUSER ,DATA    ,THREE
E,1320336057.253000,1,4.105904,10.194659
```

To convert the SAS 9 or later log format into the Release 8.2 format, use the SAS macro %ARMCONV. For example, you might want to convert SAS 9 or later format to the Release 8.2 format if you have an application that analyzes the output in Release 8.2 format.

Note: The record layout is described in the ARMSUBSYS= SAS system option in *SAS Language Reference: Dictionary.* △

Examples of Gathering Performance Data

Logging Internal SAS Processing Transactions

This example illustrates how to collect transaction statistics on internal SAS processing. For this example, only file input/output information is logged.

The only additional code that is added to the SAS program is the OPTIONS statement, which specifies the name of the ARM log output file and the ARMSUBSYS= system option, which specifies the specific SAS subsystem ARM_DSIO.

The following SAS program does the following:

1 Creates three SAS data sets: WORK.ONE, WORK.TWO, and WORK.THREE.

2 Builds an index for the variable A in WORK.THREE.

3 Prints two reports that are subsets of WORK.THREE.

4 Appends WORK.ONE to WORK.TWO.

5 Uses PROC SQL to modify WORK.THREE.

6 Prints the contents of WORK.THREE.

7 Copies all three WORK data sets to the permanent library SASUSER.

```
options armloc='myarmlog.txt' armsubsys=(ARM_DSIO OPENCLOSE);

data work.one work.two;
   input a $ b;
datalines;
1 1
2 2
3 3
;

data work.three;
   do a = 1 to 200;
      b = a;
      c = a;
      output;
   end;
run;

proc datasets library=work;
   modify three;
   index create a;
run;
quit;

proc print data=work.three;
   where a <= 101;
run;

proc print data=work.three;
   where a <= 10;
run;

proc append data=work.one base=work.two;
run;

proc sql;
   delete from work.three where a > 100;
   run;

   update work.three set a = 75 where a > 75;
   run;
quit;

proc contents data=work.three;
run;
```

```
proc copy in=work out=sasuser;
   select three;
run;
```

Here is the resulting ARM log:

Output 15.2 ARM Log

```
I,1320332339.838000,1,2.814046,5.988611,SAS,xxxxxx
G,1320332339.858000,1,1,MVA_DSIO.OPEN_CLOSE,DATA SET OPEN/CLOSE,LIBNAME,
   ShortStr,MEMTYPE,ShortStr,MEMNAME,LongStr
S,1320332347.549000,1,1,1,2.914190,6.669590,WORK    ,DATA    ,ONE
S,1320332348.390000,1,1,2,2.934219,6.729676,WORK    ,DATA    ,TWO
P,1320332348.410000,1,1,1,2.954248,6.729676,0,WORK    ,DATA    ,ONE
P,1320332348.420000,1,1,2,2.964262,6.729676,0,WORK    ,DATA    ,TWO
S,1320332348.490000,1,1,3,2.994305,6.739691,WORK    ,DATA    ,THREE
P,1320332348.530000,1,1,3,3.14334,6.749705,0,WORK    ,DATA    ,THREE
S,1320332359.216000,1,1,4,3.224636,7.661016,WORK    ,DATA    ,THREE
P,1320332360.948000,1,1,4,3.254680,7.851289,0,WORK    ,DATA    ,THREE
S,1320332362.170000,1,1,5,3.304752,7.951433,WORK    ,DATA    ,THREE
P,1320332367.358000,1,1,5,3.334795,8.51577,0,WORK    ,DATA    ,THREE
S,1320332367.388000,1,1,6,3.354824,8.61592,WORK    ,DATA    ,THREE
P,1320332367.398000,1,1,6,3.364838,8.61592,0,WORK    ,DATA    ,THREE
S,1320332367.428000,1,1,7,3.384867,8.71606,WORK    ,DATA    ,ONE
S,1320332367.438000,1,1,8,3.394881,8.71606,WORK    ,DATA    ,TWO
P,1320332372.655000,1,1,8,3.424924,8.131692,0,WORK    ,DATA    ,TWO
P,1320332372.665000,1,1,7,3.424924,8.141707,0,WORK    ,DATA    ,ONE
S,1320332375.970000,1,1,9,3.454968,8.392067,WORK    ,DATA    ,THREE
P,1320332377.282000,1,1,9,3.515054,8.562312,0,WORK    ,DATA    ,THREE
S,1320332377.302000,1,1,10,3.525068,8.572326,WORK    ,DATA    ,THREE
P,1320332377.923000,1,1,10,3.575140,8.632412,0,WORK    ,DATA    ,THREE
S,1320332377.953000,1,1,11,3.585155,8.652441,WORK    ,DATA    ,THREE
P,1320332383.521000,1,1,11,3.655256,8.832700,0,WORK    ,DATA    ,THREE
S,1320332389.89000,1,1,12,3.715342,8.912816,WORK    ,DATA    ,THREE
S,1320332389.159000,1,1,13,3.725356,8.922830,SASUSER ,DATA    ,THREE
P,1320332391.182000,1,1,12,3.765414,9.32988,0,WORK    ,DATA    ,THREE
P,1320332391.192000,1,1,13,3.775428,9.32988,0,SASUSER ,DATA    ,THREE
E,1320336057.253000,1,4.105904,10.194659
```

Using ARM System Options and ARM Macros to Log Performance Statistics

This example uses the ARM system options as well as the ARM macros.

```
/* set up ARM environment with ARM system options */
options
   armagent=sasarmmg
   armsubsys=arm_all
   armloc=mylog;

filename mylog 'C:\MyDocuments\myfiles\ARMlog.txt';

/* enable ARM macros */
%let _armexec=1;

/* initialize work datasets */
data work1 work2 work3;
do _I_ = 1 to 100;
  output;
end;
```

```
run;

%arminit(APPNAME='Sample ARM',APPUSER='Arm UserID',MACONLY=YES);
%armgtid(TXNNAME='Sample 1',MACONLY=YES);
    /* armgtid and armstrt can be combined */
%armstrt(LEVEL=1,MACONLY=YES);
    /* Step 1 */
data one;
    set work1;
run;
%armstop(MACONLY=YES);
%armgtid(TXNNAME='Sample 2',MACONLY=YES);
%armstrt(LEVEL=1,MACONLY=YES);
    /* Step 2 */
data two;
    set work2;
run;
%armstop(MACONLY=YES);
%armgtid(TXNNAME='Sample 3',MACONLY=YES);
%armstrt(LEVEL=1,MACONLY=YES);
    /* Step 3 */
data three;
    set work3;
run;
%armstop(MACONLY=YES);
%armend(MACONLY=YES);
run;
```

Post Processing an ARM Log

The following code uses the post-processing ARM macros in order to convert the ARM log into SAS data sets.

```
%armproc;
%armjoin;
run;

    /* redirect output to text file */
proc printto print='F:\arm\armlogs\USWest2ARM.log';
run;

proc print data=updtview;
    title "Results of ARM calls";
    sum deltelap deltcpu noncpu;
    by txname;
    sumby txname;
run;

    /* redirect proc output to normal queue */
proc printto print=print;
run;
```

CHAPTER

16

The SAS Registry

Introduction to the SAS Registry   **236**
    What Is the SAS Registry?   **236**
    Who Should Use the SAS Registry?   **236**
    Where the SAS Registry Is Stored   **236**
        Registry Files in the SASUSER and the SASHELP Libraries   **236**
        How to Restore the Site Defaults   **237**
    How Do I Display the SAS Registry?   **237**
    Definitions for the SAS Registry   **237**
Managing the SAS Registry   **238**
    Primary Concerns about Managing the SAS Registry   **238**
    Backing Up the SASUSER Registry   **239**
        Why Back Up the SASUSER Registry?   **239**
        When SAS Resets to the Default Settings   **239**
        Ways to Back Up the Registry   **239**
        Using the Explorer to Back Up the SAS Registry   **240**
        Using the Registry Editor to Back Up the SAS Registry   **240**
    Recovering from Registry Failure   **241**
    Using the SAS Registry to Control Color   **242**
    Using the Registry Editor   **242**
        When to Use the Registry Editor   **242**
        Starting the Registry Editor   **242**
        Finding Specific Data in the Registry   **243**
        Changing a Value in the SAS Registry   **243**
        Adding a New Value or Key to the SAS Registry   **244**
        Deleting an Item from the SAS Registry   **245**
        Renaming an Item in the SAS Registry   **245**
        Displaying the SASUSER and SASHELP Registry Items Separately   **245**
        Importing a Registry File   **245**
        Exporting or Save a Registry File   **246**
    When to Use PROC REGISTRY   **246**
Configuring Your Registry   **246**
    Configuring Universal Printing   **246**
    Configuring SAS Explorer   **246**
    Configuring Libraries and File Shortcuts with the SAS Registry   **247**
    Fixing Library Reference (Libref) Problems with the SAS Registry   **249**

Introduction to the SAS Registry

What Is the SAS Registry?

The SAS registry is the central storage area for configuration data for SAS. For example, the registry stores

- the libraries and file shortcuts that SAS assigns at startup
- the menu definitions for Explorer pop-up menus
- the printers that are defined for use
- configuration data for various SAS products.

This configuration data is stored in a hierarchical form, which works in a similar manner to the way directory-based file structures work under the operating environments in UNIX, Windows, VMS and under the z/OS UNIX System Services (USS).

Who Should Use the SAS Registry?

The SAS registry is designed for use by system administrators and experienced SAS users. This section provides an overview of registry tools, and describes how to import and export portions of the registry.

CAUTION:
   If you make a mistake when you edit the registry, your system might become unstable or unusable. △

Wherever possible, use the administrative tools, such as the New Library window, the PRTDEF procedure, Universal Print windows, and the Explorer Options window, to make configuration changes, rather than editing the registry directly. Using the administrative tools ensures that values are stored properly in the registry when you change the configuration.

CAUTION:
   If you use the Registry Editor to change values, you will not be warned if any entry is incorrect. Incorrect entries can cause errors, and can even prevent you from starting a SAS session. △

Where the SAS Registry Is Stored

Registry Files in the SASUSER and the SASHELP Libraries

Although the SAS registry is logically one data store, physically it consists of two different files located in both the SASUSER and SASHELP libraries. The physical filename for the registry is regstry.sas7bitm. By default, these registry files are hidden in the SAS Explorer views of the SASHELP and SASUSER libraries.

- The SASHELP library registry file contains the site defaults. The system administrator usually configures the printers that a site uses, the global file shortcuts or libraries that will be assigned at startup, and any other configuration defaults for your site.

□ The SASUSER library registry file contains the user defaults. When you change your configuration information through a specialized window such as the Print Setup window or the Explorer Options window, the settings are stored in the SASUSER library.

How to Restore the Site Defaults

If you want to restore the original site defaults to your SAS session, delete the regstry.sas7bitm file from your SASUSER library and restart your SAS session.

How Do I Display the SAS Registry?

You can use one of the following three methods to view the SAS registry:

□ Issue the REGEDIT command. This opens the SAS Registry Editor

□ Select

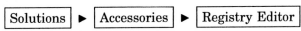

□ Submit the following line of code:

```
proc registry list;
run;
```

This method prints the registry to the SAS log, and it produces a large list that contains all registry entries, including subkeys. Because of the large size, it might take a few minutes to display the registry using this method.

For more information about how to view the SAS registry, see "The REGISTRY Procedure" in *Base SAS Procedures Guide*.

Definitions for the SAS Registry

The SAS registry uses *keys* and *subkeys* as the basis for its structure, instead of using directories and subdirectories like the file systems in DOS or UNIX. These terms and several others described here are frequently used when discussing the SAS Registry:

key
An entry in the registry file that refers to a particular aspect of SAS. Each entry in the registry file consists of a key name, followed on the next line by one or more values. Key names are entered on a single line between square brackets ([and]).

The key can be a place holder without values or subkeys associated with it, or it can have many subkeys with associated values. Subkeys are delimited with a backslash (\). The length of a single key name or a sequence of key names cannot exceed 255 characters (including the square brackets and the backslash). Key names can contain any character except the backslash and are not case-sensitive.

The SAS Registry contains only one top-level key, called SAS_REGISTRY. All the keys under SAS_REGISTRY are subkeys.

subkey
A key inside another key. Subkeys are delimited with a backslash (\). Subkey names are not case-sensitive. The following key contains one root key and two subkeys:

[SAS_REGISTRY\HKEY_USER_ROOT\CORE]

SAS_REGISTRY
is the root key.

HKEY_USER_ROOT
is a subkey of SAS_REGISTRY. In the SAS registry, there is
one other subkey at this level it is HKEY_SYSTEM_ROOT.

CORE
is a subkey of HKEY_USER_ROOT, containing many default
attributes for printers, windowing and so on.

link   a value whose contents reference a key. Links are designed for
internal SAS use only. These values always begin with the word
"link:".

value   the names and content associated with a key or subkey. There are
two components to a value, the value name and the value content,
also known as a value datum.

Display 16.1   Section of the Registry Editor Showing Value Names and Value Data for
the Subkey 'HTML'

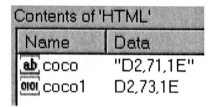

.SASXREG file   a text file with the file extension .SASXREG that contains the text
representation of the actual binary SAS Registry file.

Managing the SAS Registry

Primary Concerns about Managing the SAS Registry

CAUTION:
**If you make a mistake when you edit the registry, your system might become unstable or
unusable.** Whenever possible, use the administrative tools, such as the New Library
window, the PRTDEF procedure, Universal Print windows, and the Explorer Options
window, to make configuration changes, rather than editing the registry. This is to
insure values are stored properly in the registry when changing the configuration. △

CAUTION:
**If you use the Registry Editor to change values, you will not be warned if any entry is
incorrect.** Incorrect entries can cause errors, and can even prevent you from starting
a SAS session. △

Backing Up the SASUSER Registry

Why Back Up the SASUSER Registry?

The SASUSER* part of the registry contains personal settings. It is a good idea to back up the SASUSER part of the registry if you have made substantial customizations to your SAS session. Substantial customizations include the following:

☐ installing new printers

☐ modifying printer settings from the default printer settings that your system administrator provides for you

☐ changing localization settings

☐ altering translation tables with TRANTAB.

When SAS Resets to the Default Settings

When SAS starts up, it automatically scans the registry file. SAS restores the registry to its original settings under two conditions:

☐ If SAS detects that the registry is corrupt, then SAS rebuilds the file.

☐ If you delete the registry file called regstry.sas7bitm, which is located in the SASUSER library, then SAS will restore the SASUSER registry to its default settings.

> *CAUTION:*
> **Do not delete the registry file that is located in SASHELP; this will prevent SAS from starting.** △

Ways to Back Up the Registry

There are two methods for backing up the registry and each achieves different results:

Method 1: Save a copy of the SASUSER registry file called regstry.sas7bitm.
The result is an exact copy of the registry at the moment you copied it. If you need to use that copy of the registry to restore a broken copy of the registry, then any changes to the registry after the copy date are lost. However, it is probably better to have this backup file than to revert to the original default registry.

Method 2: Use the Registry Editor or PROC REGISTRY to back up the parts of the SASUSER registry that have changed.
The result is a concatenated copy of the registry, which can be restored from the backup file. When you create the backup file using the EXPORT= statement in PROC REGISTRY, or by using the **Export Registry File** utility in the Registry Editor, SAS saves any portions of the registry that have been changed. When SAS restores this backup file to the registry, the backup file is concatenated with the current registry in the following way:

☐ Any completely new keys, subkeys or values that were added to the SASUSER registry after the back up date are retained in the new registry.

---

* The SASHELP part of the registry contains settings that are common to all users at your site. SASHELP is write protected, and can only be updated by a system administrator.

□ Any existing keys, subkeys or values that were changed after SAS was initially installed, then changed again after the back up, are overwritten and revert to the back up file values after the restore.

□ Any existing keys, subkeys or values that retain the original default values, will have the default values after the restore.

Using the Explorer to Back Up the SAS Registry

To use the Explorer to back up the SAS Registry:

1 Start SAS Explorer with the **EXPLORER** command, or select

2 Select

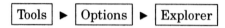

The Explorer Options window appears.

3 Select the **Members** tab

4 Select **ITEMSTOR** in the **Type** list.

5 Click Unhide .

If **ITEMSTOR** does not have an icon associated with it in the **Type** list, you will be prompted to select an icon.

6 Open the Sasuser library in the Explorer window.

7 Right-click the **Regstry.Itemstor** file.

8 Select **Copy** from the pop-up menu and copy the **Regstry** file. SAS will name the file **Regstry_copy**.

Note: You can also use a copy command from your operating environment to make a copy of your registry file for back up purposes. When viewed from outside SAS Explorer, the file name is **regstry.sas7bitm**. Under z/OS, you cannot use the environment copy command to copy your registry file unless your SASUSER library is assigned to an HFS directory. △

Using the Registry Editor to Back Up the SAS Registry

Using the Registry Editor to back up the SAS registry is generally the preferred backup method, because it retains any new keys or values in case you must restore the registry from the backup.

To use the Registry Editor to back up the SAS Registry:

1 Open the Registry Editor with the **regedit** command.

2 Select the top-level key in the left pane of the registry window.

3 From the Registry Editor, select

File ► Export Registry File

A Save As window appears.

4 Type a name for your registry backup file in the filename field. (SAS will apply the proper file extension name for your operating system.)

5 Click Save .

This saves the registry backup file in SASUSER. You can control the location of your registry backup file by specifying a different location in the Save As window.

Recovering from Registry Failure

This section gives instructions for restoring the registry with a back up file, and shows you how to repair a corrupt registry file.

To install the registry backup file that was created using SAS Explorer or an operating system copy command:

1 Change the name of your corrupt registry file to something else.

2 Rename your backup file to *regstry.sas7bitm*, which is the name of your registry file.

3 Copy your renamed registry file to the SASUSER location where your previous registry file was located.

4 Restart your SAS session.

To restore a registry backup file created with the Registry Editor:

1 Open the Registry Editor with the **regedit** command.

2 Select

$\boxed{\text{File}}$ ▶ $\boxed{\text{Import Registry File}}$

3 Select the registry file that you previously exported.

4 Click $\boxed{\text{Open}}$.

5 Restart SAS.

To restore a registry backup file created with PROC REGISTRY:

1 Open the Program editor and submit the following program to import the registry file that you created previously.

```
proc registry import=<registry file specification>;
run;
```

This imports the registry file to the SASUSER library.

2 If the file is not already properly named, then use Explorer to rename the registry file to regstry.sas7bitm:

3 Restart SAS.

To attempt to repair a damaged registry

1 Rename the damaged registry file to something other than "regstry"; for example, *temp*.

2 Start your SAS session.

3 Define a library pointing to where the *temp* registry is

```
libname here '.'
```

4 Run the REGISTRY procedure and redefine the SASUSER registry:

```
proc registry setsasuser="here.temp";
run;
```

5 Start the Registry Editor with the **regedit** command. Select

$\boxed{\text{Solutions}}$ ▶ $\boxed{\text{Accessories}}$ ▶ $\boxed{\text{Registry Editor}}$ ▶ $\boxed{\text{View All}}$

6 Edit any damaged fields under the HKEY_USER_ROOT key.

7 Close your SAS session and rename the modified registry back to the original name.

8 Open a new SAS session to see if the changes fixed the problem.

Using the SAS Registry to Control Color

The SAS registry contains the RGB values for color names that are common to most web browsers. These colors can be used for ODS and GRAPH output. The RGB value is a triplet (Red, Green, Blue) with each component having a range of 00 to FF (0 to 255).

The registry values for color are located in the COLORNAMES\HTML subkey. You can create your own new color values by adding them to the registry in the COLORNAMES\HTML subkey, using the Registry Editor:

1 Open the SAS Registry Editor using the REGEDIT command.

2 Select the COLORNAMES\HTML subkey.

3 Select

Edit ▶ New Binary Value

A pop-up menu appears.

4 Type the color name in the **Value Name** field and the RGB value in the **Value Data** field.

5 Click OK.

Using the Registry Editor

When to Use the Registry Editor

The best way to view the contents of the registry is using the Registry Editor. The Registry Editor is a graphical alternative to PROC REGISTRY, an experienced SAS user might use the Registry Editor to do the following:

- View the contents of the registry, which shows keys and values stored in keys.
- Add, modify, and delete keys and values stored in the registry.
- Import registry files into the registry, starting at any key.
- Export the contents of the registry to a file, starting at any key.
- Uninstall a registry file.
- Compare a registry file to the SAS registry.

Many of the windows in the SAS windowing environment update the registry for you when you make changes to such items as your printer setting or your color preferences. Because these windows update the registry using the correct syntax and semantics, it is often best to use these alternatives when making adjustments to SAS.

Starting the Registry Editor

To run the Registry Editor, issue the **regedit** command on a SAS command line. You can also open the registry window by selecting

Solutions ▶ Accessories ▶ Registry Editor

Finding Specific Data in the Registry

In the Registry Editor window, double-click a folder icon that contains a registry key. This displays the contents of that key.

Another way to find things is to use the Find utility.

1 From the Registry Editor, select

 Edit ▶ Find

2 Type all or part of the text string that you want to find, and click **Options** to specify whether you want to find a **key name**, a **value name**, or **data**.

3 Click Find .

Display 16.2   The Registry Editor Find Utility

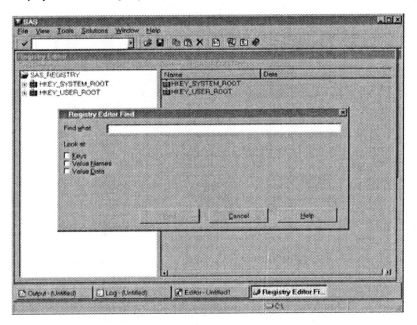

Changing a Value in the SAS Registry

CAUTION:

Before modifying registry values, always back up the regstry.sas7bitm file from SASUSER.

△

1 In the left pane of the Registry Editor window, click the key that you want to change. The values contained in the key appear in the right pane.

2 Double-click the value. The Registry Editor displays several types of windows, depending on the type of value you are changing.

Display 16.3 Example Window for Changing a Value in the SAS Registry

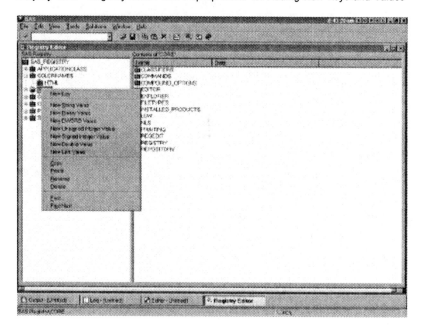

Adding a New Value or Key to the SAS Registry

1 In the SAS Registry Editor, right-click the key that you want to add the value to.

2 From the pop-up menu, select the **New** menu item with the type that you want to create.

3 Enter the values for the new key or value in the window that is displayed.

Display 16.4 Registry Editor with Pop-up Menu for Adding New Keys and Values

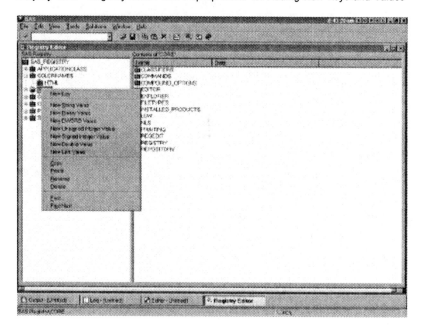

Deleting an Item from the SAS Registry

From the SAS Registry Editor:

1 Right-click the item that you want to delete.

2 Select **Delete** from the pop-up menu and confirm the deletion.

Renaming an Item in the SAS Registry

From the SAS Registry Editor:

1 Right-click the item you want to rename.

2 Select **Rename** from the context menu and enter the new name.

Displaying the SASUSER and SASHELP Registry Items Separately

After you open the Registry Editor, you can change your view from the default, which shows the registry contents without regard to the storage location. The other registry view displays both SASUSER and SASHELP items in separate trees in the Registry Editor's left pane.

1 Select

| TOOLS | ► | Options | ► | Registry Editor |

This opens the **Select Registry View** group box.

2 Select **View All** to display the SASUSER and SASHELP items separately in the Registry Editor's left pane.

  ☐ The SASHELP portion of the registry will be listed under the HKEY_SYSTEM_ROOT folder in the left pane.

  ☐ The SASUSER portion of the registry will be listed under the HKEY_USER_ROOT folder in the left pane.

Display 16.5   The Registry Editor in View Overlay Mode

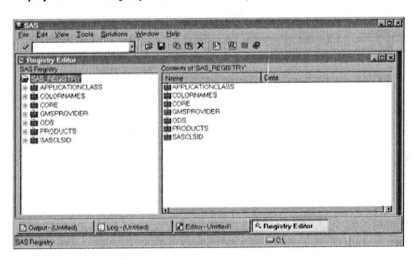

Importing a Registry File

You usually import a registry file, or SASXREG file when you are restoring a back-up registry file. A registry file can contain a complete registry or just part of a registry.

To import a registry file using the SAS Registry Editor:

1 Select

| File | ► | Import Registry File |

2 In the Open window, select the SASXREG file to import.

Note: In order to first create the back-up registry file, you can use the REGISTRY Procedure or the `Export Registry File` menu choice in the Registry Editor. △

Exporting or Save a Registry File

You usually export a registry file or SASXREG file, when you are preparing a back-up registry file. You can export a complete registry or just part of a registry.
To export a registry file using the SAS Registry Editor:

1 In the left hand pane of the Registry Editor, select the key you want to export to a SASXREG file. To export the entire registry, select the top key.

2 Select

| File | ► | Export Registry File |

3 In the Save As window, give the export file a name.

4 Click | Save |.

When to Use PROC REGISTRY

Use PROC REGISTRY to modify the registry using a SAS program. PROC REGISTRY has basically the same functionality as the Registry Editor in a noninteractive mode. For detailed information about PROC REGISTRY, see *Base SAS Procedures Guide*.

Configuring Your Registry

Configuring Universal Printing

Universal Printers should be configured by using either the PRTDEF procedure or the Print Setup window. The REGISTRY procedure can to used to back up a printer definition and to restore a printer definition from a SASXREG file. Any other direct modification of the registry values should only be done under the guidance of SAS Technical Support.

Configuring SAS Explorer

While it is best to use the Explorer Options window to configure your Explorer settings, you can use the Registry Editor to view the current Explorer settings in the SAS registry. The Explorer Options Window is available from the

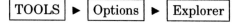

| TOOLS | ► | Options | ► | Explorer |

drop-down menu from within the Explorer. All the Explorer configuration data is stored in the registry under CORE\Explorer. The following table outlines the location of the most commonly used Explorer configuration data.

Registry Key	What portion of the Explorer it configures
CORE\EXPLORER\CONFIGURATION	the portions of the Explorer get initialized at startup.
CORE\EXPLORER\MENUS	the context menus that get displayed in the Explorer.
CORE\EXPLORER\KEYEVENTS	the valid key events for the 3270 interface. This key is only used on the mainframe platforms.
CORE\EXPLORER\ICONS	Which icons to display in the Explorer. If the icon value is ¼-1, this causes the icon to be hidden in the Explorer.
CORE\EXPLORER\NEWS	This subkey controls what types of objects are available from the ⟨File ► New⟩ menu in the Explorer.

Configuring Libraries and File Shortcuts with the SAS Registry

When you use the New Library window or the File Shortcut Assignment window to create a library reference (libref) or a file reference (fileref), these references are stored for future use when you click the **Enable at Startup** check box in either of these two windows.

Library references (librefs) and file references (filerefs) are saved when you check "Enable at startup" and they are stored in the SAS registry, where it is possible to modify or delete them, as follows:

Deleting an "Enable at Startup" library reference
You can use the Registry Editor to delete an "Enable at Startup" library reference by deleting the corresponding key under CORE\OPTIONS\LIBNAMES\"*your libref*". However, it is best to delete your library reference by using the SAS Explorer, which removes this key from the registry when you delete the library reference.

Deleting an "Enable at Startup" file shortcut
You can use the Registry Editor to delete an "Enable at Startup" file shortcut by deleting the corresponding key under CORE\OPTIONS\FILEREFS\"*your fileref*". However, it is best to delete your library reference by using the SAS Explorer, which removes this key automatically when you delete the file shortcut.

Creating an "Enable at Startup" File Shortcut as a site default
A site administrator might want to create a file shortcut which is available to all users at a site. To do this, you first create a version of the file shortcut definition in the SASUSER registry, then modify it so that it can be used in the SASHELP registry.

Note: You need special permission to write to the SASHELP part of the SAS registry. △

1 Type the **DMFILEASSIGN** command. This opens the File Shortcut Assignment window.

2 Create the file shortcut that you want to use.

3 Check **Enable at Startup**.

4 Click OK.

5 Type the command **REGEDIT** after verifying that the file shortcut was created successfully.

6 Find and select the key CORE\OPTIONS\FILEREFS*<your fileref>*.

7 Select

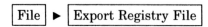 File ▶ Export Registry File

and export the file.

8 Edit the exported file and replace all instances of HKEY_USER_ROOT with HKEY_SYSTEM_ROOT.

9 To apply your changes to the site's SASHELP, use PROC REGISTRY. The following code will import the file:

```
proc registry import="yourfile.sasxreg" usesashelp;
run;
```

Creating an "Enable at Startup" Library as a site default

A site administrator might want to create a library which is available to all users at a site. To do this, the SASUSER version of the library definition needs to be migrated to SASHELP.

Note: You need special permission to write to the SASHELP part of the SAS registry. △

1 Type the **dmlibassign** command. This opens the New Library window.

2 Create the library reference that you want to use.

3 Select **Enable at Startup**.

4 Click OK.

5 Issue the **regedit** command after verifying that the library was created successfully.

6 Find and select the registry key CORE\OPTIONS\LIBNAMES*<your libref>*.

7 Select

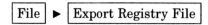 File ▶ Export Registry File

The Save As window appears.

8 Select a location to store your registry file.

9 Enter a file name for your registry file in the **File name** field.

10 Click Save to export the file.

11 Right-click the file and select **Edit in Notepad** to edit the file.

12 Edit the exported file and replace all instances of "HKEY_USER_ROOT" with "HKEY_SYSTEM_ROOT".

13 To apply your changes to the site's SASHELP use PROC REGISTRY. The following code will import the file:

```
proc registry import="yourfile.sasxreg" usesashelp;
run;
```

Fixing Library Reference (Libref) Problems with the SAS Registry

Library references (librefs) are stored in the SAS Registry. You may encounter a situation where a libref that previously worked, fails. In some situations, editing the registry is the fastest way to fix the problem. The following section describes what is involved in repairing a missing or failed libref.

If any permanent libref that is stored in the SAS Registry fails at startup, then the following note appears in the SAS Log:

NOTE: One or more library startup assignments were not restored.

The following errors are common causes of library assignment problems:

- □ Required field values for libref assignment in the SAS Registry are missing
- □ Required field values for libref assignment in the SAS Registry are invalid. For example, library names are limited to eight characters, and engine values must match actual engine names.
- □ encrypted password data for a libref has changed in the SAS Registry.

Note: You can also use the New Library window to add and delete librefs. You can open this window by typing LIBASSIGN in the toolbar, or selecting

 File ▶ New

from the Explorer window. △

CAUTION:

You can correct many libref assignment errors in the SAS Registry Editor. If you are unfamiliar with librefs or the SAS Registry Editor, then ask for technical support. Errors can be made easily in the SAS Registry Editor, and can prevent your libraries from being assigned at startup. △

To correct a libref assignment error using the SAS Registry Editor:

1 Select

 Solutions ▶ Accessories ▶ Registry Editor

or issue the **regedit** command to open the Registry Editor.

2 Select one of the following paths, depending on your operating environment, and then make modifications to keys and key values as needed:

    CORE\OPTIONS\LIBNAMES

or

    CORE\OPTIONS\LIBNAMES\CONCATENATED

For example, if you determine that a key for a permanent, concatenated library has been renamed to something other than a positive whole number, then you can rename that key again so that it is in compliance. Select the key, and then select **Rename** from the pop-up menu to begin the process.

251

CHAPTER
17

Printing with SAS

Introduction to Universal Printing **252**
   What Is Universal Printing? **252**
   Turning Universal Printing On and Off **252**
   What Type of Print Output Formats Are Available from Universal Printing? **252**
   Universal Printing and ODS **253**
Managing Printing Tasks with the Universal Printing User Interface **254**
   Overview of the Universal Printing Menu **254**
   Setting Up Printers **255**
      Print Setup Window **255**
      Changing the Default Printer **255**
      Removing a Printer from the Selection List **255**
      Defining a New Printer **256**
      Setting Printer Properties for Your Default Printer **259**
      How to Specify a Printer for Your Session **264**
   Printing with Universal Printing **264**
      Printing a Test Page **264**
      Printing the Contents of an Active SAS Window **264**
   Working with Previewers **266**
      Defining a New Previewer **266**
      Seeding the Print Previewer Command Box **269**
      Previewing Print Jobs **270**
   Setting Page Properties **270**
Configuring Universal Printing with Programming Statements **273**
   Introduction **273**
   System Options That Control Universal Printing **273**
   Defining Printers for Batch-Mode **274**
   Defining New Printers and Previewers with PROC PRTDEF **274**
      Introduction **274**
      Creating a Data Set that Defines Multiple Printers **274**
      Installing a Printer Definition for Multiple Users **275**
      Adding, Modifying, and Deleting Printer Definitions **275**
      Creating a Ghostview Previewer Definition for Previewing Postscript Output **276**
      Exporting and Backing Up Printer Definitions **277**
      Sample Values for the Device Type, Destination and Host Options Fields **277**
Forms Printing **279**
   Overview of Forms Printing **279**
   Creating or Editing a Form **279**

Introduction to Universal Printing

What Is Universal Printing?

Universal Printing is a printing system that provides both interactive and batch printing capabilities to SAS applications and procedures on all the operating environments that are supported by SAS.

When Universal Printing is ON, SAS routes all printing through Universal Printing services. All Universal Printing features are controlled by system options, thereby enabling you to control many print features even in batch mode.

Note: Prior to the introduction of Universal Printing, SAS supported a utility for print jobs known as Forms. Forms printing is still available if you select

 File ► Print

from the menu, then check the **Use Forms** check box. This turns off Universal Printing menus and functionality. For more information, see "Forms Printing" on page 279. △

Turning Universal Printing On and Off

Universal Printing is available on all operating environments that SAS supports. By default, Universal Printing is turned ON on all operating environments except Windows.

The UNIVERSALPRINT system option (alias UPRINT) must be set for Universal Printing to be ON and used by SAS. This option can be set only in the SAS configuration file or at startup. You cannot turn Universal Printing menus on or off after startup.

Note: When you use the PRINTERPATH option to specify a printer, the print job is controlled by Universal Printing. △

Operating Environment Information: In the Windows operating environment, you must set an additional system option, UPRINTMENUSWITCH, in order to access the Universal Printing user interface. You must also set UPRINTMENUSWITCH, in order to configure all menus in SAS to use the Universal Printing windows. To do this, include

```
-uprint -uprintmenuswitch
```

in the string that you use to invoke SAS under Windows. △

What Type of Print Output Formats Are Available from Universal Printing?

In addition to sending print jobs to a printer, you can also direct output to external files that are widely recognized by different types of printers and print viewing software programs. You can use Universal Printing to produce the following commonly recognized file types:

Table 17.1 Available Print Output Formats

Type	Full Name	Description
PCL	Printer Control Language	Developed by Hewlett-Packard as a language that applications use to control a wide range of printer features across a number of printing devices. Universal Printing currently supports PCL5, PCL5e and PCL5c levels of the language.
PDF	Portable Document Format	A file format developed by Adobe Systems for viewing and printing a formatted document. To view a file in PDF format, you need Adobe Acrobat Reader, a free application distributed by Adobe Systems.
Optimized PDF	Optimized Portable Document Format	A compressed PDF file format developed by Adobe Systems.
PS	Postscript	A page description language also developed by Adobe Systems. PostScript is primarily a language for printing documents on laser printers, but it can be adapted to produce images on other types of devices.

Universal Printing and ODS

The ODS PRINTER destination uses Universal Printing whether the UNIVERSALPRINT option is on or off. The PRINTER destinations used by the ODS PRINTER statement are described in *SAS Output Delivery System: User's Guide*.

The Output Delivery System (ODS) uses Universal Printing for the following ODS statements:

Table 17.2 ODS Destinations that make use of the Universal Printing interface

ODS PRINTER Destination	Description
PRINTER= option	uses the selected printer
ODS PDF statement	uses Universal Printing's PDF printer
ODS PS statement	uses Universal Printing's Postscript Level 1 printer
ODS PCL statement	uses Universal Printing's PCL5 printer

Operating Environment Information: In the Windows operating environment, the ODS PRINTER destination will use the Windows system printers unless SAS was started with the UNIVERSALPRINT option, or when you specify a printer with the PRINTERPATH option. If Universal Printing is enabled in Windows, SAS will override the use of the Windows system printer and cause ODS to use Universal Printing. △

For more information on ODS, see *SAS Output Delivery System: User's Guide*.

Managing Printing Tasks with the Universal Printing User Interface

Overview of the Universal Printing Menu

You can open most Universal Printing windows by entering commands at the command line or into the command box in the menu bar. The following table lists the commands that you use to do the most common tasks.

Table 17.3 Commands to Open Universal Printing Windows

To do this...	Use this command
Print the current window	DMPRINT
Change the default printer	DMPRINT, or DMPRINTSETUP
Create a new printer or previewer definition	DMPRTCREATE PRINTER, or DMPRTCREATE PREVIEWER
Modify, add, remove or test printer definitions	DMPRINTSETUP
Show default printer properties sheet	DMPRINTPROPS
Show page properties sheet	DMPAGESETUP
Print preview the current window	DMPRTPREVIEW

The SAS Universal Printing windows are also accessible from the **File** menu.

The following display shows the File menu containing the Universal Printing choices of Page Setup, Print Setup, Print Preview and Print.

Display 17.1 File Menu Displaying Universal Printing Options

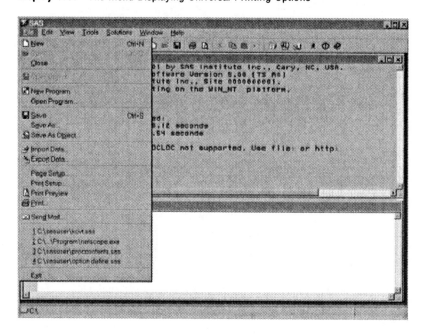

Table 17.4 Menu choices or commands open Universal Printing windows

Menu Choice	Equivalent command
Page Setup	DMPAGESETUP
Print Setup	DMPRINTSETUP
Print Preview	DMPRTPREVIEW
Print	DMPRINT

Operating Environment Information: In the Windows operating environment, SAS uses the Windows print windows as the default. To access the Universal Printing user interface, UPRINTMENUSWITCH must also be set along with the UNIVERSALPRINT option to configure all menus in SAS to use the Universal Printing windows. To do this, include

```
-uprint -uprintmenuswitch
```

in the string that you use to invoke SAS in Windows. △

Setting Up Printers

Print Setup Window

The DMPRTSETUP command opens the Print Setup window, where you can

□ change the default printer

□ remove a printer from the selection list

□ print a test page

□ open the Printer Properties window

□ launch the New Printer wizard.

Changing the Default Printer

To change the default printer device for this SAS session and future SAS sessions,

1 Issue the DMPRTSETUP command. The Print Setup window appears.

2 Select the new default device from the list of printers in the **Printer** field.

3 Click OK .

Removing a Printer from the Selection List

To remove a printer from the selection list, follow these steps.

1 Issue the DMPRTSETUP command. The Print Setup window appears.

2 Select the printer you want to delete from the list of printers in the **Printer** field

3 Click Remove

Note: Only your system administrator can remove printers that the administrator has defined for your site. If you select a printer that was defined by your system administrator, the Remove button will be unavailable. △

Defining a New Printer

While Universal Printing provides you with predefined printers, you can also add your own printers with the Define a New Printer wizard, which guides you step-by-step through the process of installing a printer.

To start the New Printer wizard and define a new printer:

1 Issue the command DMPRTCREATE PRINTER. The following window appears.

Display 17.2   Printer Definition Window to Enter Name and Description

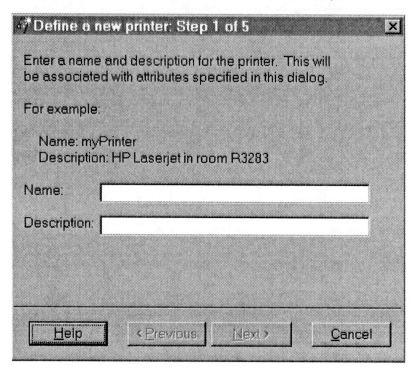

Alternatively, you can issue the DMPRTSETUP command and click [New].

2 Enter the name and a description for the new printer (127 character maximum, no backslashes).

3 Click [Next] to proceed to Step 2. Select a printer model. If your exact printer model is not available, select a more general model that is compatible with your printer. For example, for the HP LaserJet printer series, select PCL5.

Note: More general models might provide fewer options than the more specific models. △

Display 17.3   Printer Definition Window to Select Printer Model

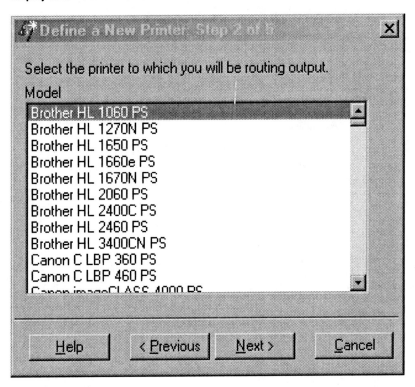

4 Click Next to proceed to Step 3. The following window appears:

Display 17.4   Printer Definition Window to Select Ouput Device

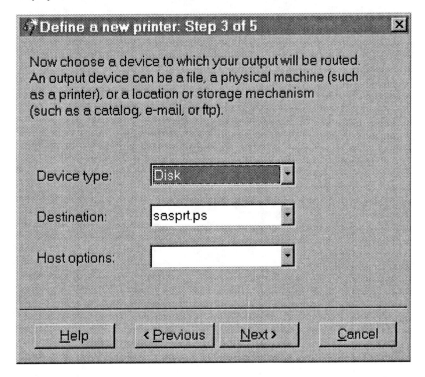

5 Select the **Device type** for your print output. The device type selections are host-dependent.

If you select **Catalog, Disk, Ftp, Socket,** or **Pipe** as the device type, then you must specify a destination.

If you select a device type of **Printer**, then a destination might not be required, because some operating environments use the Host options box to route output.

Note: Examples for your operating system of Device Type, Destination and Host options are also provided in "Sample Values for the Device Type, Destination and Host Options Fields" on page 277 △

6 Enter the **Destination** for your file. The destination is the target location for your device type. For example, if your device type is **disk**, then your destination would be an operating environment-specific file name. With some system device types, the destination might be blank and you can specify the target location using the **Host options** box.

7 Select or enter any host-specific options for the device that you chose. This field might be optional for your operating environment. For a list of host options, refer to the FILENAME statement information for your operating environment.

Note: The **Destination** and **Host Options** lists can also be populated using PROC REGISTRY. Click the Help button in step 3 to refer to the "Populating Destination and Host Option Lists" topic, which contains more details. △

8 Click Next to proceed to Step 4, in which you select from a list of installed print previewers. If no previewers are defined, proceed to the next step.

Display 17.5 Printer Definition Window to Select Previewer

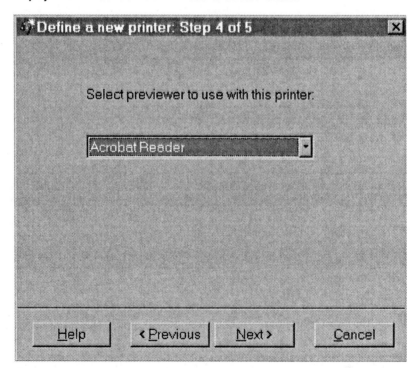

If the previewer selection box appears, select the previewer for this printer. If you do not need a previewer, choose **None** or leave the field blank.

Note: You can add a previewer to any printer through the DMPRTPROPS, **Advanced Tab, Previewer** box. See "Defining a New Previewer" on page 266. △

Note: It is not required that printers and print previewers share a common language. △

9 Click Next to proceed to Step 5. The following window appears:

Display 17.6   Printer Definition Window to Complete Process

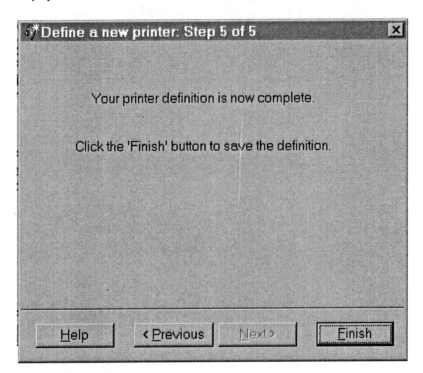

10 Click Previous to change any information. Click Finish when you have completed your printer definition.

You have now finished setting your default printer.

After you have returned to the Print Setup window, you can test your default printer by clicking Print Test Page .

Setting Printer Properties for Your Default Printer

Printer properties that you can change include

☐ the printer name and description

☐ the printer destination device and its properties

☐ the default font for the printer

☐ advanced features such as translation tables, printer resolution and the print previewer associated with the printer.

To change printer properties for your default printer:

1 Issue the DMPRTPROPS command. The Printer Properties window appears.

2 From the Printer Properties window, select the tab that contains the information that you need to modify.

☐ In the **Name** tab, you can modify the printer name and the printer description.

Display 17.7 Printer Properties Window Displaying Name Tab

□ The **Destination** tab enables you to designate the device type, destination, and host options for the printer. See "Sample Values for the Device Type, Destination and Host Options Fields" on page 277 for examples.

Display 17.8   Printer Properties Window Displaying Destination Tab

□ The **Font** tab controls the available font options. The selections available in the drop-down boxes are printer specific. The font size is in points.

Display 17.9   Printer Properties Window Displaying Font Tab

☐ The **Advanced** tab lists the Resolution, Protocol, Translate table, Buffer size, Previewer, and Preview command options for the printer. The information in the drop-down fields is printer specific.

Display 17.10   Printer Properties Window Displaying Advanced Tab

Resolution
> specifies the resolution for the printed output in dots per inch (dpi).

Protocol
> provides the mechanism for converting the output to a format that can be
> processed by a protocol converter that connects the EBCDIC host
> mainframe to an ASCII device. Protocol is required in the z/OS operating
> environment, and if you must use one of the protocol converters that are
> listed.

Translate table
> manages the transfer of data between an EBCDIC host and an ASCII
> device. Normally, the driver selects the correct table for your locale; the
> translate table needs to be specified only when you require nonstandard
> translation.

Buffer size
> controls the size of the output buffer or record length. If the buffer size is
> left blank, a default size will be used.

Previewer
> specifies the Previewer definition to use when Print Preview is requested.
> The Previewer box contains the previewer application that you have
> defined. See "Defining a New Previewer" on page 266.

Preview command
> is the command that will be used to open an external printer language
> viewer. For example, if you want Ghostview as your previewer, type
> **ghostview %s**. When a Preview Command is entered into a Printer
> definition, the printer definition becomes a previewer definition.

Note: The `Previewer` and `Preview Command` fields are mutually exclusive. When you enter a command path into the `Preview Command` field, the `Previewer` box will dim. △

How to Specify a Printer for Your Session

The PRINTERPATH option enables you to specify a printer to use for the current SAS session. This printer specification is not retained across SAS sessions. PRINTERPATH is primarily used in batch mode, when there is no windowing environment in which to set the default printer. This option accepts a character string as its value, for example:

```
options printerpath="myprinter";
options printerpath="Print PostScript to disk";
```

You can get a list of valid character strings from two places:

□ the list of printers in the `Printer` field of the Print Setup window.

□ the list of defined printers in the registry under
SAS_REGISTRY\\CORE\\PRINTING\\PRINTERS

You can also override the printer destination by specifying a fileref with the PRINTERPATH= option:

```
options printerpath= (myprinter printout);
filename printout ...;
```

Printing with Universal Printing

Printing a Test Page

To print a test page:

1 Issue the DMPRTSETUP command to open the Print Setup window.

2 Select the printer for which you would like a test page from `Printer` listview.

3 Click $\boxed{\text{Print Test Page}}$.

Printing the Contents of an Active SAS Window

To print the contents of a window in SAS:

1 Click inside the window to make it active.

2 Select

$\boxed{\text{File}}$ ► $\boxed{\text{Print}}$

A print window appears. Your print window might differ from the window that follows.

Display 17.11 Print Window

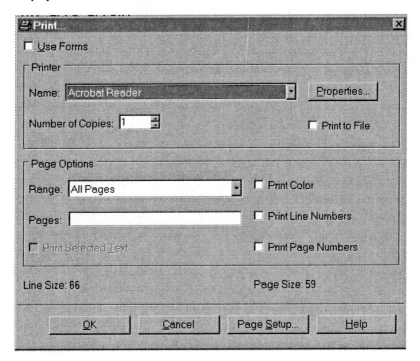

3 If the **Use Forms** check box is visible, clear it in order to use Universal Printing.

4 From the Printer group box, select the name of the printer definition.

5 Enter the number of copies that you want.

6 If you want to save your print job to a file,

    a Select **Print to File**.
    b Select OK; the **File Selection** window appears.
    c Select an existing file or enter a new filename.

Note: If you print to an already existing file, the contents of the file may be overwritten or appended, depending on whether you choose **replace** or **append** from the print window that is open. △

7 Set additional printing options.

    The fields in the Page Options area provide choices according to the content in the SAS window that you are trying to print. By default, SAS prints the entire contents of the selected window.

To print	Do this
selected lines of text in a window *Note:* not available on OS/390	Select the text that you want to print, and then open the **Print** window. In the **Page Options** box, check the **Print Selected Text** box.
the page that is currently displayed in the window	Select **Current page**.

To print	Do this
a range of pages or other individual pages	Select **Range** and enter the page numbers in the **Pages** field. Separate individual page numbers and page ranges with either a comma (,) or a blank. You can enter page ranges in any of these formats: ☐ n–m prints all pages from n to m, inclusive. ☐ –n prints all pages from page 1 to page n. ☐ n– prints all pages from page n to the last page.
in color	Check the **Print Color** box.
line numbers	Check the **Print Line Numbers** box.
page numbers	Check the **Print Page Numbers** box.
a graph	Use the DMPRINT command, or select File ▶ Print Verify that the **Use SAS/GRAPH Drivers** check box is deselected in order to use Universal Printing.

8 Click OK to print.

Working with Previewers

Defining a New Previewer

Previewers enable you to preview a print job. SAS does not set a default previewer application. To use the Print Preview feature in SAS, you or your system administrator must first define a previewer for your system.

Operating Environment Information: Print Previewers are not supported on z/OS △

Previewers can be defined using the New Previewer wizard. To use the New Previewer wizard to define a new print previewer:

1 Issue the DMPRTCREATE PREVIEWER command. The following window appears:

Display 17.12 Previewer Definition Window to Enter Name and Description

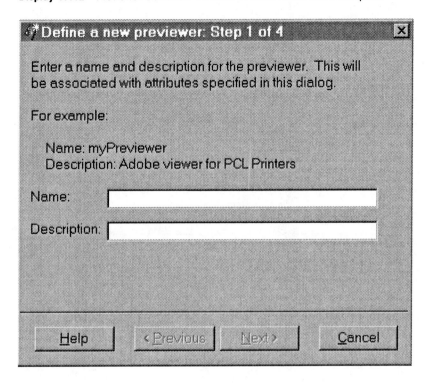

2 Enter the name and a description for the new previewer (127 character maximum, no backslashes).

3 Click [Next] to proceed to Step 2.

Display 17.13 Previewer Definition Window to Enter Previewer Language

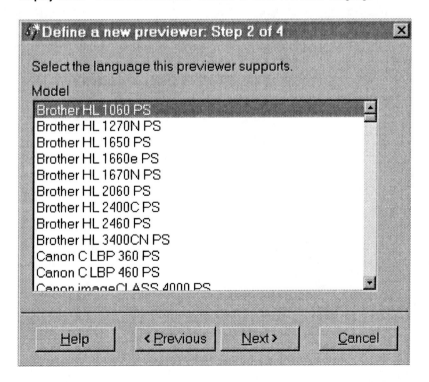

4 Select the printer model that you want to associate with your previewer definition. The Postscript, PCL or PDF language generated for the model must be a language that your external viewer package supports. For best results, select the generic models such as PostScript Level 1 (Color) or PCL 5.

5 Click ⬚Next⬚ to proceed to Step 3.

Display 17.14 Previewer Definition Window to Enter Command to Open Previewer Application

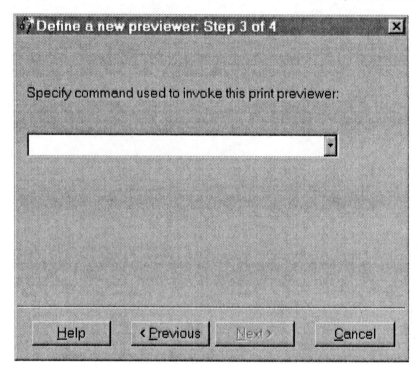

6 Enter the command or commands used to open the previewer application, followed by %s where you would normally put a file name. For example, if the command for starting your previewer is "ghostview," then you would type **ghostview %s** in the text field.

   Note: The %s can be used as many times as needed in the commands for starting the viewer. △

7 Click ⬚Next⬚ to proceed to Step 4.

Display 17.15 Previewer Definition Window to Complete Process

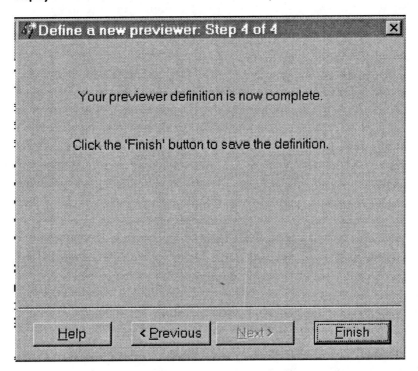

8 Click Previous to correct any information. Click Finish when you have finished defining your default previewer.

The newly defined previewer will display a previewer icon in the Print Setup window.

Display 17.16 Print Setup Window Displaying New Previewer

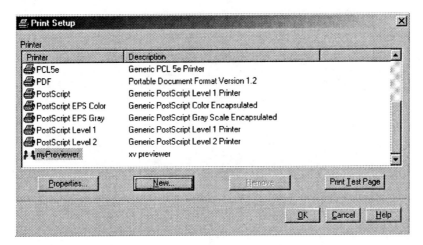

This previewer application can be tested with the Print Test Page button on the Print Setup window.

Seeding the Print Previewer Command Box

Print Preview is supported by print previewer applications such as Ghostview, gv, and Adobe Acrobat. The Preview command box that appears in the Previewer

Definition wizard and on the **Advanced** tab of the Printer Properties window can be prepopulated or "seeded" with a list of commands used to invoke print previewer applications that are available at your site. Users and administrators can manually update the registry, or define and import a registry file that contains a list of previewer commands. An example of a registry file is:

```
[CORE\PRINTING\PREVIEW COMMANDS]
 "1"="/usr/local/gv %s"
 "2"="/usr/local/ghostview %s"
```

Previewing Print Jobs

You can use the print preview feature if a print viewer is installed for the designated printer. Print Preview is always available from the File menu in SAS. You can also issue the DMPRTPREVIEW command.

Setting Page Properties

For your current SAS session, you can customize how your printed output appears in the Page Setup window. Depending on which printer you have currently set, some of the Page Setup options that are described in the following steps may be unavailable.

To customize your printed output:

1 Issue the DMPAGESETUP command. The Page Setup window appears.

2 Select a tab to open windows that control various aspects of your printed output. Descriptions of the tabbed windows follow.

The Page Setup window consists of four tabs: **General**, **Orientation**, **Margins**, and **Paper**.

☐ The **General** tab enables you to change the options for Binding, Collate, Duplex, and Color Printing.

Display 17.17   Page Setup Window Displaying General Tab

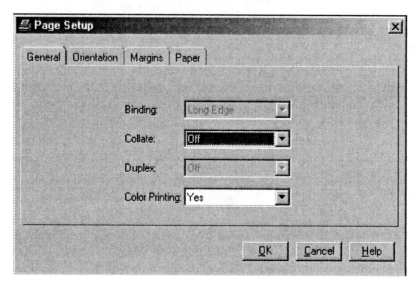

Binding
  specifies the binding edge (Long Edge or Short Edge) to use with duplexed output. This sets the BINDING option.

Collate
specifies whether the printed output should be collated. This sets the COLLATE option.

Duplex
specifies whether the printed output should be single-sided or double-sided. This sets the DUPLEX option.

Color Printing
specifies whether output should be printed in color. This sets the COLORPRINTING option.

□ The **Orientation** tab enables you to change the output's orientation on the page. The default is Portrait. This tab sets the ORIENTATION option.

Display 17.18   Page Setup Window Displaying Orientation Tab

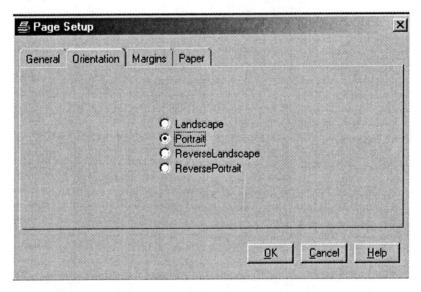

□ The **Margin** tab enables you to change the top, bottom, left and right margins for your pages. The value range depends upon the type of printer that you are using. The values that are specified on this tab set the TOPMARGIN, BOTTOMMARGIN, LEFTMARGIN, and RIGHTMARGIN options.

Display 17.19 Page Setup Window Displaying Margins Tab

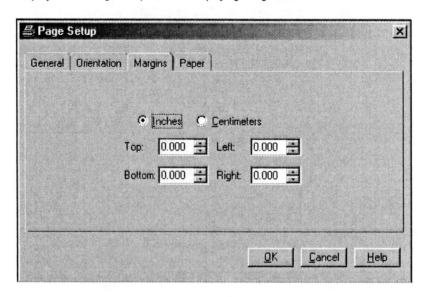

□ The **Paper** tab specifies the Size, Type, Source, and Destination of the paper used for the printed output.

Display 17.20 Page Setup Window Displaying Paper Tab

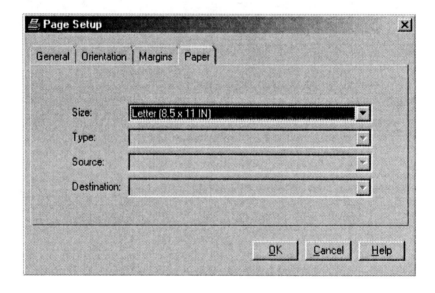

Size

> specifies the size of paper to use by setting the PAPERSIZE option. Paper sizes include Letter, Legal, A4, and so on.

Type

> specifies the type of paper to use. Examples of choices include Standard, Glossy, and Transparency. This sets the PAPERTYPE option.

Source

> designates which input paper tray is to be used. This sets the PAPERSOURCE option.

Destination

specifies the bin or output paper tray that is to be used for the resulting output. This sets the PAPERDEST option.

Note: Although your Page Settings should remain in effect for your current working session, changing default printers could cause some of the settings to have no effect. If you change printers during a SAS session, check the Page Setup window to see if any of your settings are not valid for your new default printer. △

Configuring Universal Printing with Programming Statements

Introduction

Universal Printing windows give you control over most printing functions through a graphical user interface. (You can also write a program that uses various SAS language elements to configure your printing environment and to control print jobs.)

System Options That Control Universal Printing

Universal Printing can configured in batch mode and interactive mode by setting option values within an OPTIONS statement. The following options control Universal Printing.

Table 17.5 System options that control Universal Printing

System Option	Description
BINDING	Specifies the binding edge for the printer
BOTTOMMARGIN	Specifies the size of the margin at the bottom of the page for printing
COLLATE	Specifies the collation of multiple copies for output for the printer
COLORPRINTING	Specifies color printing, if it is supported
COPIES	Specifies the number of copies to make when printing
DUPLEX	Specifies duplexing controls for printing
LEFTMARGIN	Specifies the size of the margin on the left side of the page
ORIENTATION	Specifies the paper orientation to use (either portrait or landscape)
PAPERDEST	Specifies the bin or output paper tray to receive printed output
PAPERSIZE	Specifies the paper size to use when printing.
PAPERSOURCE	Specifies the input paper tray to use for printing
PAPERTYPE	Specifies the type of paper to use for printing.
PRINTERPATH	Specifies a printer for Universal Printing print jobs (see Note on page 274)

System Option	Description
RIGHTMARGIN	Specifies the size of the margin on the right side of the page
SYSPRINTFONT	Specifies the font to use when printing
TOPMARGIN	Specifies the size of the margin at the top of the page

Note: The PRINTERPATH option specifies which printer will be used.

□ If PRINTERPATH is blank, the default printer will be used.

□ If PRINTERPATH is not blank, Universal Printing will be used.

In the Windows environment, the default printer is the current Windows system printer or the printer specified by the SYSPRINT option; therefore, Universal Printing is not used. In all other operating environments, Universal Printing is used and the default printer is Postscript Level 1. To change this printer, use the DMPRINTSETUP command to open the Print Setup window. △

Defining Printers for Batch-Mode

Printer definitions can be created for an individual, or for all SAS users at a site, by using the PRTDEF procedure. PROC PRTDEF can be used to do many of the same printer management activities that you can also do with the Universal Printing windows. PROC PRTDEF is especially useful if you use SAS in batch mode, where the Universal Printing windows are unavailable.

Only system administrators or others who have write permission to the SASHELP library can use PROC PRTDEF to create printer definitions for all SAS users at a site.

To define one or more printers with PROC PRTDEF, you first create a SAS data set that contains variables corresponding to printer attributes. PROC PRTDEF reads the data set and converts the variable attributes into one or more printer definitions in the SAS registry.

See *Base SAS Procedures Guide* for more information about PROC PRTDEF.

Defining New Printers and Previewers with PROC PRTDEF

Introduction

These examples show you how to use PROC PRTDEF to define new printers and to manage your installed printers and previewers.

After a program statement containing PROC PRINTDEF runs successfully, the printers or previewers that have been defined will be displayed in the Print Setup window. A complete set of all available printers and previewers will be displayed in the Printer name list. Printer definitions can also be seen in the Registry Editor window under CORE\\PRINTING\\PRINTERS.

Creating a Data Set that Defines Multiple Printers

When you create a data set to use with PROC PRTDEF to define a printer, you must specify the name, model, device and destination variables.

See the PRTDEF procedure in *Base SAS Procedures Guide* for the names of the optional variables that you can also use.

```
data printers;
   input name $& model $& device $& dest $&;
   datalines;
Myprinter              PostScript Level 1    PRINTER    printer1
Laserjet               PCL 5 Printer         PIPE       lp -dprinter5
Color LaserJet         PostScript Level 2    PIPE       lp -dprinter2
;
run;
```

After you create the data set containing the variables, you run a SAS program that contains PROC PRTDEF. PROC PRTDEF defines the printers that are named in the data set by creating the appropriate entries in the SAS registry.

```
proc prtdef data=printers usesashelp;
run;
```

Installing a Printer Definition for Multiple Users

This example creates a Tektronix Phaser 780 printer definition with a Ghostview print previewer in the SASUSER registry. The bottom margin is set to two centimeters, the font size to 14 point, and the paper size to A4.

```
data tek780;
   name = "Tek780";
   desc = "Test Lab Phaser 780P";
   model = "Tek Phaser 780 Plus";
   device = "PRINTER";
   dest = "testlab3";
   preview = "Ghostview";
   units = "cm";
   bottom = 2;
   fontsize = 14;
   papersiz = "ISO A4";
run;

proc prtdef data=tek780;
run;
```

Adding, Modifying, and Deleting Printer Definitions

This example uses the PRINTERS data set to add, modify, and delete printer definitions. See the PRTDEF procedure in *Base SAS Procedures Guide* for more variables that you can use to define a printer. The following list describes the variables used in the example:

- ☐ The MODEL variable specifies the printer prototype to use when defining this printer.
- ☐ The DEVICE variable specifies the type of I/O device to use when sending output to the printer.
- ☐ The DEST variable specifies the output destination for the printer.
- ☐ The OPCODE variable specifies what action (Add, Delete, or Modify) to perform on the printer definition.
- ☐ The first Add operation creates a new printer definition for Color Postscript in the registry and the second Add operation creates a new printer definition for ColorPS in the registry.
- ☐ The Mod operation modifies the existing printer definition for LaserJet 5 in the registry.

□ The Del operation deletes the printer definitions for printers named "Gray Postscript" and "test" from the registry.

The following example creates a printer definition in the SASHELP library. Because the definition is in SASHELP, the definition becomes available to all users. Special system administration privileges are required to write to the SASHELP library. An individual user can create a personal printer definition by specifying the SASUSER library instead.

```
data printers;
length name   $ 80
       model  $ 80
       device $ 8
       dest   $ 80
       opcode $ 3;

input opcode $ & name $ & model $ & device $ & dest $ &;
datalines;
add  Color Postscript   PostScript Level 2 (Color)        DISK      sasprt.ps
mod  LaserJet 5         PCL 5                              DISK      sasprt.pcl
del  Gray Postscript    PostScript Level 2 (Gray Scale)   DISK      sasprt.ps
del  test               PostScript Level 2 (Color)        DISK      sasprt.ps
add  ColorPS            PostScript Level 2 (Color)        DISK      sasprt.ps
;

proc prtdef data=printers list
library=sashelp;
run;
```

Note: If the end user modifies and saves new attributes for an administrator-defined printer in the SASHELP library, the printer will become a user-defined printer in the SASUSER library. Values that are specified by the user will override the values that were set by the administrator. If the user-defined printer definition is deleted, the administrator-defined printer will reappear. △

Creating a Ghostview Previewer Definition for Previewing Postscript Output

This example creates the GSVIEW data set. The variables in the GSVIEW data set have values that PROC PRTDEF uses to produce the print previewer definition in the SAS registry.

□ The NAME variable specifies the printer name that will be associated with the rest of the attributes in the printer definition data record.

□ The DESC variable specifies the description of the printer.

□ The MODEL variable specifies the printer prototype to use when defining this printer.

□ The VIEWER variable specifies the host system commands for print preview.

□ The DEVICE variable should always be DUMMY.

□ DEST should be blank to specify that output is not returned.

```
data gsview;
   name = "Ghostview";
   desc = "Print Preview with Ghostview";
```

```
       model= "PostScript Level 2 (Color)";
       viewer = 'ghostview %s';
       device = "dummy";
       dest = " ";
run;
proc prtdef data=gsview list replace;
run;
```

Exporting and Backing Up Printer Definitions

PROC PRTEXP enables you to backup your printer definitions as a SAS data set that can be restored with PROC PRTDEF.

PROC PRTEXP has the following syntax:

```
    PROC PRTEXP [USESASHELP] [OUT=dataset]
  [SELECT | EXCLUDE] printer_1 printer_2 ... printer_n;
```

The following example shows how to back up four printer definitions (named PDF, postscript, PCL5 and PCL5c) using PROC PRTEXP.

```
proc prtexp out=printers;
select PDF postscript PCL5 PCL5c;
run;
```

For more information, see the PRTEXP procedure in *Base SAS Procedures Guide*.

Sample Values for the Device Type, Destination and Host Options Fields

The following list provides examples of the printer values for device type, destination and host options. Because these values can be dependent on each other, and the values can vary by operating environment, several different examples are shown. You might want to refer to this list when you are installing or modifying a printer or when you change the destination of your output.

□ Device Type: Printer
   □ z/OS
      □ Device type: Printer
      □ Destination: (leave blank)
      □ Host options: sysout=*class-value* dest=*printer-name*

   □ UNIX and Windows
      □ Device type: Printer
      □ Destination: *printer name*
      □ Host options: (leave blank)

   □ VMS
      □ Device type: Printer
      □ Destination: *printer name*
      □ Host options: passall=yes queue=*printer-name*

□ Device Type: Pipe

   Note: A sample command to send output to an lp-defined printer queue on a UNIX host is *lp -ddest* △
      □ UNIX
         □ Device Type: Pipe

☐ Destination: *command*

☐ Host options: (leave blank)

☐ Device type: Email

☐ Windows, UNIX and VMS

☐ Device Type: Email

☐ Destination: *name@isp.com*

☐ Host options: (leave blank)

☐ z/OS

☐ Device Type: Email

☐ Destination: *name@isp.com*

☐ Host options: recfm=vb

☐ Device Type: FTP

Note: An example of a nodename is *pepper.unx* △

☐ z/OS

☐ Device type: FTP

☐ Destination: ftp.out

☐ Host options: host='*nodename*' recfm=vb prompt

☐ Device type: Printer

☐ Destination: *printer name*

☐ Host options: (leave blank)

☐ Windows

☐ Device type: FTP

☐ Destination: ftp.out

☐ Host options: host='*nodename*' prompt

☐ UNIX and VMS

☐ Device type: FTP

☐ Destination: host='*nodename*' prompt

☐ Host options: (leave blank)

☐ Device Type: Socket

Note: An example of an lp destination queue is *lp286nc0.prt:9100* △

☐ UNIX and VMS

☐ Device type: Socket

☐ Destination: *destination-queue*

☐ Host options: (leave blank)

Forms Printing

Overview of Forms Printing

Before Universal Printing was introduced, SAS provided a utility for print jobs called a form. A *form* was a standard template that let you control such things as line size and margin information for pages in a print job. While Universal Printing is easier to use and has more features than the simple controls offered in forms printing, SAS still supports forms.

Printing with forms is still available through the Print window. You can switch to forms print mode by selecting

 File ▶ Print

and selecting **Use Forms**.

Note: Forms printing is not available in batch mode. △

Creating or Editing a Form

If your organization has legacy reports that need to be printed using forms, you might have to use the FORM window to create or edit a form. SAS still supports the ability to create or edit forms, though Universal Printing provides more features, and is the recommended method of printing.

You can create or edit a form by entering the FSFORM command:

FSFORM<*catalog-name.>form-name*

If you do not specify a catalog-name, SAS uses the SASUSER.PROFILE catalog. If the form name that you specify does not exist, SAS creates a new form.

If you are creating a new form, SAS displays the Printer Selection frame. If you are editing an existing form, SAS displays the Text Body and Margin Information frame.

To move between the FORMS frames, you can

☐ use the NEXTSCR command to scroll to the next frame and the PREVSCR command to scroll to the previous frame.

☐ enter an equals sign (=) and the number of the frame that you want to go to. For example, **=1** displays the Text Body and Margin Information frame, and **=2** displays the Carriage Control Information frame.

☐ select the name of the frame from the **Tools** menu.

☐ select **Next Screen** or **Previous Screen** from the **Tools** menu.

You can move between fields on a frame with the TAB key.

After you have finished defining or editing your form, issue the END command to save your changes and exit the FORM window.

Note: Turning on Forms by checking the **Use Forms** checkbox in the print window turns Universal Printing off for printing non-graphic windows. △

Operating Environment Information: For more information on printing with Forms, see the documentation for your operating environment. △

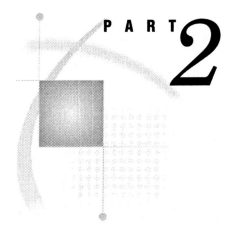

PART 2

Windowing Environment Concepts

Chapter *18*........Introduction to the SAS Windowing Environment *283*

Chapter *19*........Managing Your Data in the SAS Windowing Environment *307*

CHAPTER

18

Introduction to the SAS Windowing Environment

Basic Features of the SAS Windowing Environment   **283**
    What Is the SAS Windowing Environment?   **283**
    Using SAS Window Features   **284**
        Overview of SAS Windowing Environment Features   **284**
        Keyboard Equivalents for z/OS   **284**
        Drop-Down Menus in SAS   **285**
        Pop-Up Menus in SAS   **286**
        Toolbars in SAS   **287**
        Getting Help from the Help Menu in SAS   **287**
        Getting Help from the Toolbar in SAS   **288**
Main Windows of the SAS Windowing Environment   **288**
    List of SAS Windows and Window Commands   **288**
    The Five Main Windows in the Windowing Environment   **290**
        Overview   **290**
    SAS Explorer Window   **291**
        Exploring Files with the SAS Explorer   **291**
        Using SAS Explorer to Assign File Shortcuts (filerefs)   **292**
        Using SAS Explorer to Copy a SAS Data Set   **293**
        Using SAS Explorer to Rename a File   **295**
        Using SAS Explorer to View Details about Files   **295**
        Using SAS Explorer to Sort Files   **296**
        Using SAS Explorer to Open a File   **296**
        Using SAS Explorer and NOTEPAD to Create and Save a Program   **297**
    Program Editor Window   **298**
    Log Window   **299**
    Output Window   **300**
    Results Window   **301**
    New Library Window   **302**
        Using the New Library Window to Assign a New Library   **303**
    Properties Window   **303**
    Keys Window   **304**
        Valid Commands in the Keys Window   **304**

Basic Features of the SAS Windowing Environment

What Is the SAS Windowing Environment?

SAS provides a graphical user interface that makes SAS easier to use. Collectively, all the windows in SAS are called the SAS windowing environment.

The SAS windowing environment contains the windows that you use to create SAS programs, but you will also find other windows that enable you to manipulate data or change your SAS settings without writing a single line of code.

You might find the SAS windowing environment a convenient alternative to writing a SAS program when you want to work with a SAS data set, or control some aspect of your SAS session.

Using SAS Window Features

Overview of SAS Windowing Environment Features

SAS windows have several features that operate in a similar manner across all operating environments: drop-down menus, pop-up menus, toolbars, and online help. You can customize many features of the SAS windowing environment, including toolbars, menus, icons, and so on. Select **Tools** to explore some of the customization options that are available. The examples in this section are from the Microsoft Windows operating environment; menus and toolbars in other operating environments have a similar appearance and behavior.

Operating Environment Information: If you are using Microsoft Windows, the active window determines what items are available on the main menu bar. If you can not find an option on the menu where you expect to find it, be sure you have opened the correct window. △

Keyboard Equivalents for z/OS

Operating Environment Information: The following table shows you how to select items if you use SAS in the z/OS operating environment. △

Table 18.1   Mouse Actions and Keyboard Equivalents for z/OS

Mouse Action	Keyboard Equivalent
double-click the item	type an **s** or an **x** in the space next to the item, then press ENTER or RETURN
right-click the item	type **?** in the space next to the item, then press ENTER or RETURN.

Operating Environment Information: Other features that are specific to z/OS and other operating environments are found later in this section. △

Display 18.1   SAS z/OS Display

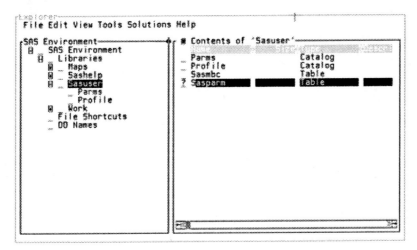

Drop-Down Menus in SAS

A drop-down menu is a list of commands that appears when you click on a menu name in the menu bar.

Display 18.2   A Typical SAS Menu Bar with a Drop-Down Menu for Help

Drop-down menu choices change as you change the windows you are using.

The following steps demonstrate that selecting **View** from a menu bar results in a different drop-down menu, depending on which window you are using when you make the selection.

1 Select

| View | ► | Explorer |

from the menu. The Explorer window appears.

2 Select

| View |

from the menu bar again. The drop-down menu lists the View commands that are available for the Explorer window.

Display 18.3 View Commands for Explorer Window

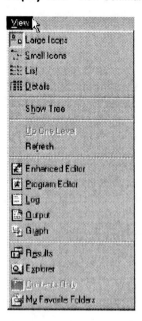

3 Click

Program Editor

The Program Editor window appears.

4 Select **view** from the menu again and notice that it offers different selections.

Display 18.4 View Commands for Program Editor Window

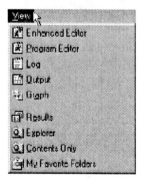

Pop-Up Menus in SAS

A pop-up menu is a menu that appears when you select an item or an option. In SAS windows, a pop-up menu displays when you right-click an item. A pop-up menu remains visible until you make a selection from the menu or until you click something outside of the pop-up menu area.

Display 18.5 A Typical Pop-Up Menu

To see a typical pop-up menu in SAS, perform the following steps:

1 In the Explorer window, right-click the Libraries icon. Notice that **Open** and **New** are available in the pop-up menu. Select **Open**.

2 Right-click the **Sasuser** icon. The pop-up menu contains additional selections. Click anywhere outside the pop-up menu to close it without selecting an action.

Operating Environment Information: To open a pop-up menu using SAS on z/OS, you select the item by placing a question mark (?) in the space next to the item, and then press ENTER. See Table 18.1 on page 284 for more information. △

Toolbars in SAS

A toolbar is a block of window buttons or icons. When you click on items in the toolbar, a function or an action is started. For example, clicking on a picture of a printer in a toolbar starts a print process. The toolbar displays icons for many of the actions that you perform most often in a particular window.

Operating Environment Information: SAS on z/OS is not equipped with a toolbar. △

Display 18.6 Typical SAS Toolbar from Microsoft Windows Operating System

To see a typical toolbar menu in SAS, perform the following steps:

1 Click the **Explorer** window and look at the toolbar. Notice that currently unavailable tools are grayed.

2 Move your mouse pointer to a tool and hold it there for a moment. A Tool Tip displays the name of the tool.

3 Click the Editor (or Program Editor) window and view the tools available.

Getting Help from the Help Menu in SAS

There are several ways to access the Help system that comes with SAS. You can either type *help* in the menubar, or select different choices from the Help menu. The following list describes the Help menu choices.

Using This Window
  Opens a Help system window that describes the current active window.

SAS Help and Documentation
  Opens the SAS Help and documentation system. Help is available for Base SAS and other SAS products that are installed on your system.

Getting Started with SAS Software
  Opens Getting Started with SAS Tutorial. This is a good way to learn the basics of how to use SAS.

Learning SAS Programming
  Opens *SAS OnlineTutor* sample data sets. *SAS OnlineTutor* is a separately licensed product that provides 50–60 hours of instruction for beginning as well as experienced SAS programmers.

SAS on the Web
  If you have web access, then this selection provides links to the SAS web site, where you can
    □ contact Technical Support
    □ read Frequently Asked Questions (FAQs)
    □ find information about Training Services
    □ send feedback
    □ browse the SAS home page.

About SAS System
  Provides version and release information about SAS.

Getting Help from the Toolbar in SAS

You can get help when you type *help <language element name>* in the toolbar or at the command line. This opens the Help system and displays the documentation for the language element name that you typed.

Main Windows of the SAS Windowing Environment

List of SAS Windows and Window Commands

The basic SAS windows are the Explorer, Results, Program Editor, Log, and Output windows, but there are more than thirty other windows to help you with such things as printing and fine-tuning your SAS session.

The following table lists all portable SAS windows and the commands that open them.

Note: Additional information about how many of these windows work can be found by clicking the help button inside each window. △

Table 18.2 List of Portable SAS Windows and Window Opening Commands

Window Name	Window Command(s)
Define a new previewer"Defining a New Previewer" on page 266	DMPRTCREATE PREVIEWER
Define a new printer"Defining a New Printer" on page 256	DMPRTCREATE PRINTER
Distributed Multidimensional Metadata	MDMDDB*

Window Name	Window Command(s)
Documents	ODSDOCUMENTS
Explorer	ACCESS, BUILD, CATALOG, DIR, EXPLORER, FILENAME, LIBNAME, V6CAT, V6DIR, V6FILENAME, V6LIBNAME
Explorer Options	DMEXPOPTS
EFI (External File Interface)	EFI*
File Shortcut Assignment	DMFILEASSIGN
Find	EXPFIND
Font (host-specific)	DLGFONT*
Footnotes	FOOTNOTES
FSBrowse	FSBROWSE
FSEdit	FSEDIT
FSForm	FSFORM *formname*
FSLetter	FSLETTER
FSList	FSLIST
FSView	FSVIEW
Help	HELP
Keys	KEYS
Log	LOG
Metadata Browser	METABROWSE*
Metafind	METAFIND
Metadata Server Connections	METACON
My Favorite Folders	EXPROOT FILES*
New Library	DMLIBASSIGN
Notepad	NOTEPAD, NOTE, FILEPAD *filename*
Options (SAS system options)	OPTIONS
Output	OUTPUT, OUT, LISTING, LIST, LST
Page Setup	DMPAGESETUP
Password	SETPASSWORD (followed by a two-level data set name)
Preferences (host-specific)	DLGPREF*
Print	DMPRINT
Print Setup	DMPRTSETUP
Printer Properties	DMPRTPROPS
Program Editor	PROGRAM, PGM
Properties	VAR *libref.SAS-data-set*, V6VAR *libref.SAS-data-set*
Query	QUERY

Window Name	Window Command(s)
Registry Editor	REGEDIT
Results	ODSRESULTS
SAS/AF	AF, AFA
SAS/ASSIST	ASSIST
SASCOLOR	SASCOLOR
SAS/EIS*	EIS
System Options	OPTIONS
Templates	ODSTEMPLATES
Titles	TITLES
Tool Editor (host-specific)	TOOLEDIT*
Viewtable	VIEWTABLE, VT

Window commands marked with * are not supported under z/OS.

Note: Some additional SAS windows that are specific to your operating environment may also be available. Refer to the SAS documentation for your operating environment for more information. △

The Five Main Windows in the Windowing Environment

Overview

The five main windows in SAS are: Explorer, Results, Program Editor, Log, and Output windows.

Display 18.7   Default View of SAS Windowing Environment (Microsoft Windows)

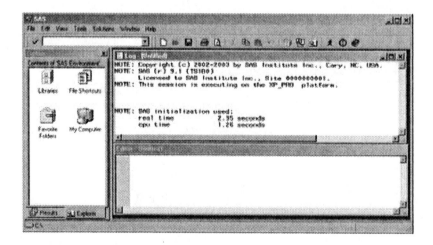

Operating Environment Information: The arrangement of your SAS windows depends on your operating environment. For example, in the Microsoft Windows operating environment, the Editor window appears instead of the Program Editor.   △

SAS Explorer Window

Use to   View, add or delete files, libraries, shortcuts.

Open by   Typing **EXPLORER** in the command line, or select

                   View ▶ Explorer

Description   The Explorer window enables you to manage your files in the windowing environment. You can use the SAS Explorer to do the following tasks:

         □ view lists of your SAS files

         □ create shortcuts to external files

         □ create new SAS files

         □ open any SAS file and view its contents

         □ move, copy, and delete files

         □ open related windows, such as the new library window.

You can display the Explorer window with or without a tree view of its contents.

Display 18.8 SAS Explorer, with Tree View, Microsoft Windows Operating Environment

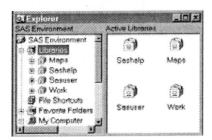

Display 18.9 SAS Explorer, Without Tree View, Microsoft Windows Operating Environment

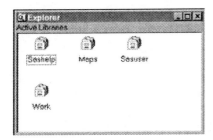

Note: You can resize the Explorer window by dragging an edge or a corner of the window. You can resize the left and right panes of the Explorer window by clicking the split bar between the two panes and dragging it to the right or left. △

Exploring Files with the SAS Explorer

You can use the SAS Explorer to explore and manage SAS files and other files. In the Explorer window, you can view and manage your SAS files, which are stored in libraries. A library is a storage location for SAS files and catalogs. By default, SAS defines several libraries for you.

This example uses the SAS Explorer to display the contents of a library:

1 In the Explorer window, double-click **Libraries**. The active libraries are listed.

Display 18.10 Typical Explorer Window, Without Tree View, Showing Active Libraries

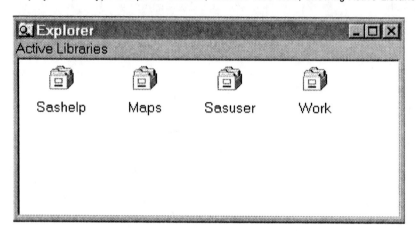

2 Double-click the **Sashelp** library. All members of the Sashelp library are listed.

Display 18.11 Explorer Window, Without Tree View, Showing the Contents of a Sashelp Library

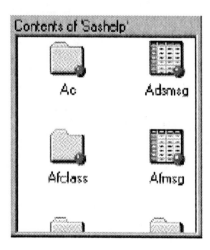

3 Move back up to the top level of the Explorer window by clicking twice on the **Up One Level** selection under **View** on the toolbar.

Using SAS Explorer to Assign File Shortcuts (filerefs)

A file shortcut is also known as a file reference or fileref. Filerefs save you programming time by enabling you to assign a nickname to a commonly used file. You can use the FILENAME statement to create a fileref or you can use the file shortcut assignment window from SAS Explorer.

The following example shows you how to create a file shortcut with SAS Explorer.

1 In the top level of the Explorer window, select **File Shortcuts**.

2 Select

The File Shortcut Assignment window appears.

Display 18.12 File Shortcut Assignment Window

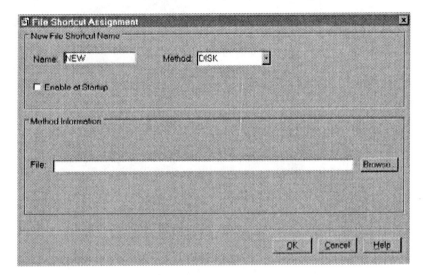

3 Type a name in the **Name** field (up to eight alphanumeric characters). This name is the file shortcut reference (fileref), and you can use it to point to an external file.

4 Select the **Method** that you want to use for the file shortcut. The devices that are available from the Method drop-down list depend on your operating environment. DISK is the default (if available for your operating environment). See your operating environment documentation for more information.

5 Select **Enable at Startup** if you want SAS to automatically assign the file shortcut each time that SAS starts. This option is not available for all file shortcut methods. If it is not available, the Enable at Startup check box is disabled. If you want to stop a file shortcut from being enabled at startup, select the file shortcut in the SAS Explorer window, and then select Delete from the pop-up menu.

6 Fill in the fields of the **Method Information** area. The fields available in this area depend on the method that you selected.

   Note: Selecting a new method type erases any entries that you may have made in the Method information field. △

7 Select OK to create the new file shortcut. The file shortcut appears in the File Shortcut folder of the SAS Explorer window.

Using SAS Explorer to Copy a SAS Data Set

This example shows you how to copy a data set called Prdsale, which is a sample data file included when you install SAS software.

1 Open the Explorer window by selecting

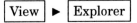

Display 18.13 SAS Explorer in Tree View Mode, Showing Some Members of a Sashelp Library

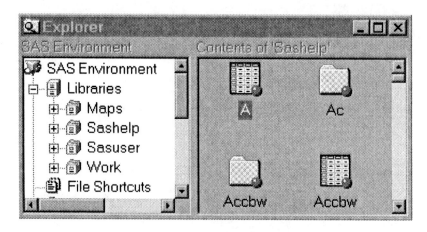

2 In the left pane, single-click the **Sashelp** library to show the library contents in the right pane. Scroll to the icon for the Prdsale data set.

3 Right-click the **Prdsale** data set.

4 Select **Copy** from the menu.

5 Right-click the **Work** Library.

6 Select **Paste** from the menu.

7 The Prdsale data set appears in the contents of the Work Library.

Display 18.14 SAS Explorer In Tree View Mode, Showing a File in a Work Library

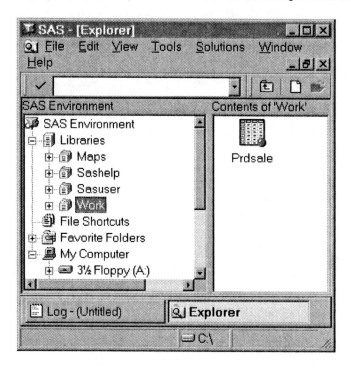

Because the contents of the Work library are temporary, this copy of the Prdsale data set will be deleted when you end your SAS session.

Using SAS Explorer to Rename a File

You can use SAS Explorer to rename anything in a SAS library that is not write protected. This set of instructions outlines how to use SAS Explorer to rename a data set:

1 Open SAS Explorer and click on a library. A list of files in the library appears.

2 Select the file you want to rename and right-click it. A pop-up menu appears.

3 Select **Rename** from the pop-up menu. A Rename window appears, containing the name of the file you selected, and a blank space for typing in the new name.

4 Type in the new name and click OK.

Note: Changing a file name may cause a SAS program that uses the old file name to stop working. △

Using SAS Explorer to View Details about Files

You can use the **View** menu to view the contents of a library with large icons or small icons, as a list, and with details displayed. This example shows you how use Explorer to view the details for the Sashelp.Prdsale data set.

1 Open the Sashelp library.

2 Select

View ▶ Details

from the menu. Information about the files is displayed.

Note: The DETAILS system option controls how many details you can see about a data set. If you enable the DETAILS system option, you can see additional row and column information in the Explorer window. △

3 Resize the Details columns by moving the pointer over the separator bar between the detail fields. When the pointer changes to a resizing tool, click and drag the separator bar to get the desired size.

Display 18.15 Explorer Window with Pointer in Position (between Name and Engine) to Resize Columns. DETAILS Option Set to NODETAILS

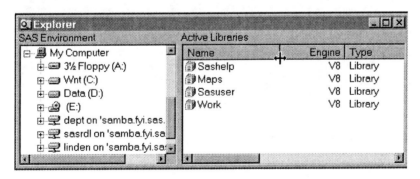

Display 18.16 Explorer Window with DETAILS Option Enabled

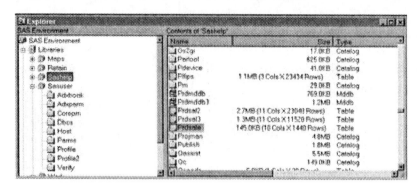

For more information about the DETAILS system option, see the *SAS Language Reference: Dictionary*.

Using SAS Explorer to Sort Files

Files in the Explorer window are sorted alphabetically by file name. You can sort by any column in ascending or descending order:

1 Open the Sashelp library.

2 Click the Type column to sort the files by file type.

3 Click the Type column again to reverse the sort order.

4 To return the files to their original order, select

Using SAS Explorer to Open a File

You can view the contents of SAS files directly from the Explorer window:

1 Double-click the **Sashelp** library.

2 Find the **Prdsale** data set in the list and double-click it to open it. The table opens in the VIEWTABLE window in browse mode.

3 When you are finished looking at the data in the data set, select

from the VIEWTABLE window.

4 Return to the top level of the Explorer window.

Display 18.17 Viewtable Window Displaying a Data Set

	Actual Sales	Predicted Sales	Country	Region
1	$925.00	$850.00	CANADA	EAST
2	$999.00	$297.00	CANADA	EAST
3	$608.00	$846.00	CANADA	EAST
4	$642.00	$533.00	CANADA	EAST
5	$656.00	$646.00	CANADA	EAST
6	$948.00	$486.00	CANADA	EAST
7	$612.00	$717.00	CANADA	EAST
8	$114.00	$564.00	CANADA	EAST
9	$685.00	$230.00	CANADA	EAST
10	$657.00	$494.00	CANADA	EAST
11	$608.00	$903.00	CANADA	EAST
12	$353.00	$266.00	CANADA	EAST
13	$107.00	$190.00	CANADA	EAST

Using SAS Explorer and NOTEPAD to Create and Save a Program

In addition to the NOTEPAD, which is described here, you can also use the Program Editor (or Editor in some operating systems) to create and save programs. You can also use NOTEPAD and the Program Editor to work on two programs in the same session.

The following set of instructions shows you how to create and save a SAS program:

1 In the top level of the Explorer window, select

   File ► New

2 Select **Source Program**, and click OK. The NOTEPAD window appears.

3 Type the following program into the NOTEPAD window:

```
proc options;
run;
```

4 Select

   Run ► Submit

As a result, the Log window lists the settings for your system options.

5 Select

   File ► Save As

6 With the default directory selected, type *sysopt.sas* in the **File name** box.

7 Click OK or Save.

Display 18.18   SAS Notepad, with a Program

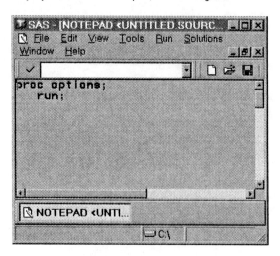

To recall and run the program that you just saved, follow this set of instructions:

1 Select

2 From the menu, select the library where you saved your program, if that library is not already available.

3 Select **sysopt.sas** (the program you just saved) from the menu. The program appears in NOTEPAD.

4 Select

Program Editor Window

Purpose   Compose, edit, and submit SAS programs.

To open   Type **PROGRAM** in a command line, or select

                        View ▶ Program Editor

Details   In the Program Editor window, you can enter, edit, and submit SAS
                        programs. To open your SAS programs in the SAS windowing
                        environment, you can drag and drop them onto the Program Editor
                        window.

Display 18.19 Program Editor Window, with a Sample Program

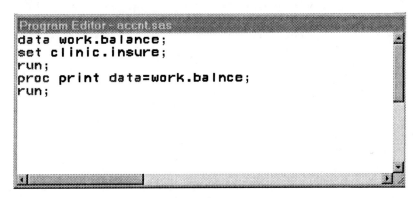

This set of instructions shows you how to use the Program Editor to create and save a SAS program, submit the program, and view and save your results.

Create and Save a Program

1 In the top level of the Explorer window, select

2 Select **Source Program** and click $\boxed{\text{OK}}$.

3 Type the following program into the Editor or Program Editor window:

```
proc datasets lib=sasuser;
run;
quit;
```

4 This program prints a listing of the contents of the SASUSER library (or to the log on z/OS).

5 Click

to run the program.

6 Click

to save the program.

7 Type a name and select a location for the file in the **Save as** window.

Operating Environment Information: In the Microsoft Windows operating environment, the Results window is docked along with the Explorer window. When a program produces output, the Results window comes to the front and overlays the Explorer window. △

Log Window

Purpose   View messages about your SAS session and SAS programs.

To open   Type **LOG** in a command line, or select

$\boxed{\text{View}}$ ► $\boxed{\text{Log}}$

Details

The Log window displays messages about your SAS session and any SAS programs you submit. If the program you submit has unexpected results, the SAS log is usually the first place you look to gather clues about what changes you need to make in order to get the intended results.

Note: To keep the lines of your log from wrapping when your window is maximized, use the LINESIZE= system option. △

Display 18.20   Log Window

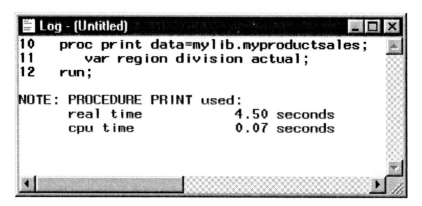

Output Window

Purpose

View the output of SAS programs

To open

Type **OUTPUT** in a command line, or type **LISTING** in a command line, or select

View ► Output

Details

In the Output window, you can browse output from SAS programs that you submit. By default, the Output window is positioned behind the other windows. When you create output, the Output window automatically moves to the front of your display.

Note: To keep the lines of your output from wrapping when your window is maximized, use the LINESIZE= system option. △

Display 18.21 Output Window

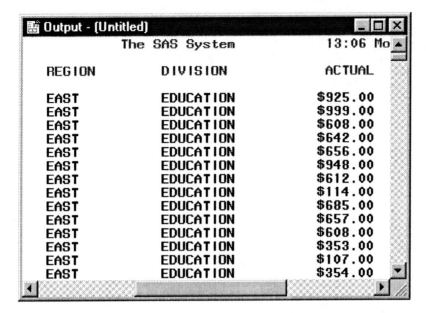

Results Window

Purpose
: View the output from running a SAS program.

To open
: Type **ODSRESULTS** in a command line, or select

| View | ► | Results |

Details
: The Results window uses a tree structure to display various types of output that you may have while you are running SAS. You can view, save, and print individual items of output. By default, the Results window is positioned behind the Explorer window and it is empty until you submit a SAS program that creates output. Then the Results window moves to the front of your display.

To use the Results window, you first run a SAS program that generates output. You can run any SAS program that creates output, such as the following program, which creates a graph with PROC PLOT.

```
options linesize=80;
   data generate;
      do x=0 to 100 by 2;
         y=2.54+3.83*x;
         output;
      end;
   run;
   proc plot data=generate;
      plot y*x;
   run;
```

After running a program that produces output, the results window adds a line indicating that the output was successfully generated. You can then select this output from the Results Window and view it.

Display 18.22   Results Window, Showing an Output List

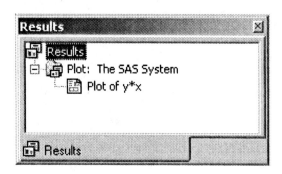

New Library Window

Purpose   Assign a new library.

To open   Type **DMLIBASSIGN** in a command line, or from the Explorer window,
                   select

                   | File | ▶ | New |

Details   The New Library Window makes it easy to create libraries. After
                   you create a new library, you can use SAS Explorer to associate SAS
                   files, such as data sets, catalogs, and programs, with the library. By
                   default, SAS software defines several libraries for you (including
                   Sashelp, Sasuser, and Work).

When you define a library, you specify a location for your SAS files. When you
undefine a SAS library, SAS no longer has access to the contents of the library.
However, the contents of the library still exist in your operating environment. After you
create a library, you can manage SAS files within it.

Display 18.23   New Library Window

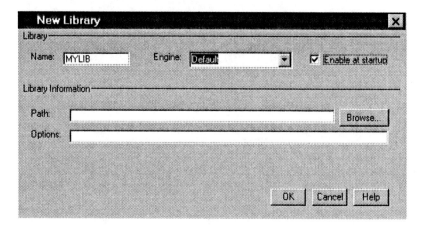

Operating Environment Information: Depending on your operating environment, you
can create libraries using engines that allow you to read different file formats, including
file formats from other vendors. △

Using the New Library Window to Assign a New Library

1 In the Explorer window, double-click **Libraries**.

2 From the Explorer menu, select

 File ▶ New

3 In the New Library window, type *Mylib* for the name, and leave the **Default** engine selected.

4 Select **Enable at startup** so that the library is created each time you start SAS.

5 Click Browse and select a directory to use for this library. In the Select dialog you must open the directory you want to use so that the full path into that directory is assigned. Click OK.

6 Click OK to assign the library. **Mylib** appears in the **Active Libraries** list.

Properties Window

Purpose
    View and change the properties of a data set.

To open
    Type **VAR** in the command line, followed by the name of the data set that you want to open, in the form of *libref.SAS-data-set*, or right-click on a data set from the SAS Explorer window and select **Properties**.

Details
    When you open the Properties window, you can select tabs that give you additional information about the data set.

Display 18.24 Properties Window Displaying the Details for Sashelp.Prdsale. Select Other Tabs for More Information.

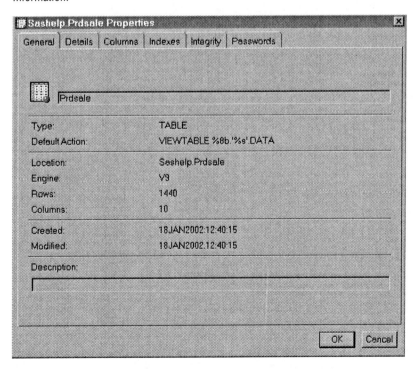

Keys Window

Purpose   Change or create new keyboard commands.

To open   Type **KEYS** in a command line, or select

Details   The Keys window displays function key definitions for the current
                   window. Default function key settings are provided with the SAS
                   System, but you can easily add, edit, or delete them.

To add new function key definitions:

1 After opening the Keys window, place your cursor next to the key you want to
assign to a command. Make sure your cursor is under the **Definition** column.

2 Type the name of the command you want to assign.

3 Click

| File | ▶ | Save |

to save your changes.

To change existing key functions:

1 Type over the command that is already assigned to a particular key with the name
of a new function.

2 Click

| File | ▶ | Save |

to save your changes.

To delete key functions:

1 Type over the command that is already assigned to a particular key.

2 Save the Keys window.

Valid Commands in the Keys Window

In the Keys window you can use these commands:

□ SAS windows commands

□ the Color, Search, Scrolling, Text Store, Window Management, and Window Size
and Position commands.

In addition, you can use the following commands:

Table 18.3 Other Commands That You Can Use in the Keys Window

Command	Result
CANCEL	Cancels any changes made to the current key settings and closes the Keys window.
COPY <*name*>	Copies another stored set of key definitions into the window. If <*name*> is omitted, any changes that are made are cancelled and the definitions from your user profile catalog are copied.
	Note: If you change a key definition in the current Keys window and then save the Keys window, you must close and reopen the Keys window before issuing the COPY command. △
END	Saves the definitions and closes the Keys window.
PURGE	Removes key definitions that are not shared among devices.
SAVE <*name*>	Stores the current function key settings and lets you continue editing the keys definitions. If <*name*> is omitted, the keys are, by default, stored in the catalog SASUSER.PROFILE.

See SAS Help and Documentation for more information about commands.

Managing Your Data in the SAS Windowing Environment

Introduction to Managing Your Data in the SAS Windowing Environment **307**
Copying and Viewing Files in a Data Library **307**
    Copying a Practice File to the WORK Data Library **307**
    Viewing the Contents of a Data Set with the VIEWTABLE Window **310**
    Saving a Data Set as HTML **312**
    Copying a Data Set to Excel **312**
Using the Workspace to Manipulate Data in a Data Set **313**
    Moving and Labeling Columns with the VIEWTABLE Window **313**
    Sorting Values of a Column with the VIEWTABLE Window **315**
    Creating a WHERE Expression with the VIEWTABLE Window **317**
    Editing Values in a Cell with the VIEWTABLE Window **320**
    Clearing Subsetted Data from the VIEWTABLE Window **321**
Importing and Exporting Data **321**
    Importing Data into a Data Set **321**
    Exporting Your Data with the Export Wizard **324**

Introduction to Managing Your Data in the SAS Windowing Environment

The SAS windowing environment contains windows that enable you to do common data manipulation and changes without writing code.

If you are new to SAS and are unfamiliar with writing code in the SAS language, then you might find the windowing environment helpful. With the windowing environment, you can open a data set in a window, point to rows and columns in your data, and then click on menu items to reorganize and perform analyses on the information.

This section shows the main features of the SAS windowing environment, and demonstrates many of the tools that enable you to view, modify, import and export data.

Operating Environment Information: If you use SAS on z/OS, refer to "Keyboard Equivalents for z/OS" on page 284 to see the keyboard alternatives to using a mouse. △

Copying and Viewing Files in a Data Library

Copying a Practice File to the WORK Data Library

The following examples use a copy of the SASHELP.PRDSALE data set, which is a read-only data set in the SASHELP library. In this section, you will learn how to copy

SASHELP.PRDSALE to the WORK library, so that you can use it with the other examples in this section.

Note: By default, files located in the WORK directory are deleted at the close of a SAS session. △

To copy the PRDSALE file in the SASHELP library to the WORK library, follow these steps:

1 Open the Explorer window by selecting

from the menu.

2 Make sure you are in Tree view mode by enabling

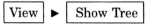

The Explorer window now contains two panels.

Display 19.1 Explorer Window Displaying Tree View

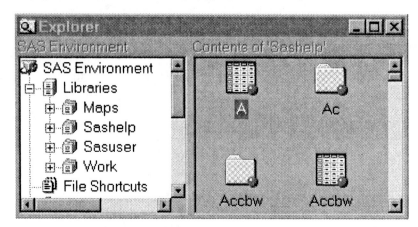

3 In the left panel, click the SASHELP library to show the library contents in the right panel. Scroll to the PRDSALE data set.

4 Right-click the PRDSALE data set and select **Copy** from the menu.

Display 19.2 Explorer Window Displaying Copy Menu Option

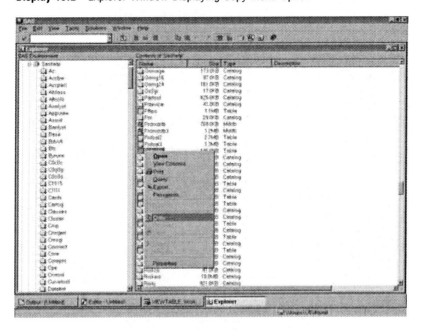

5 In the left panel, right-click **WORK** and select **Paste**.

Display 19.3 Explorer Window Displaying Paste Menu Option

6 Double-click **Work** and confirm that the data set was copied.

Display 19.4   Explorer Window Displaying Copied PRDSALE Data Set (Icon View)

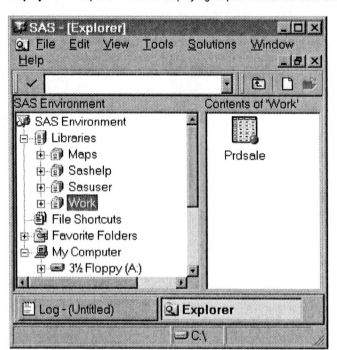

Viewing the Contents of a Data Set with the VIEWTABLE Window

To quickly view the contents of your SAS data set, you can either

☐ double-click a file in the SAS Explorer, or

☐ open the VIEWTABLE window with the **VT** command, select

| File | ▶ | Open |

then select the data set.

For this example, use the SAS data set WORK.PRDSALE, which contains sample data for product sales. The WORK.PRDSALE data set was created by copying PRDSALE from the SASUSER library in the previous example. See "Copying a Practice File to the WORK Data Library" on page 307.

1 Select

| Tools | ▶ | Table Editor |

to open the **VIEWTABLE** window.

2 Select

| File | ▶ | Open |

The Open dialog box displays the current SAS libraries.

3 Under **Libraries**, select **WORK**. The data sets and views in the WORK library are displayed on the right.

4 Double-click PRDSALE. The VIEWTABLE window opens.

Display 19.5 Explorer Window Displaying Copied PRDSALE Data Set (Details View)

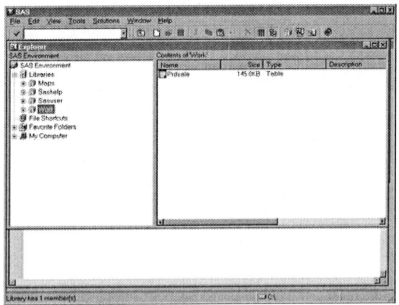

5 Scroll the VIEWTABLE window to view the WORK.PRDSALE data.

Display 19.6 VIEWTABLE Window Displaying PRDSALE Data

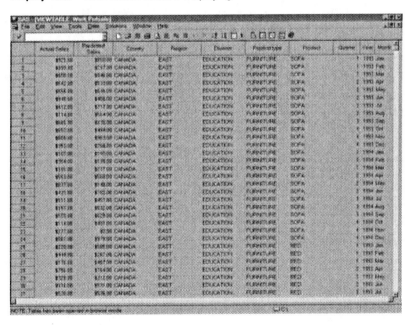

6 To save a copy of this file to use for practice in the next example, click

File ▶ Save as

The **Save As** dialog box opens.

Display 19.7 Data Table Save As Dialog Box

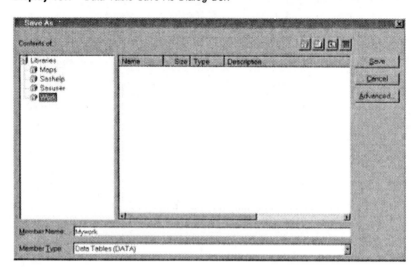

7 Select the WORK library as your storage location and type **Mywork** in the **Member Name** field.

8 Click ⎡Save⎤.

Saving a Data Set as HTML

To save a SAS data set as HTML, follow these steps:

1 Right-click the file in the SAS Explorer.

2 Select **Save as HTML** from the pop-up menu.

3 Select a location in the **Save in** box or leave it in the default location.

4 If you want to save the file with the default name of *table-name.html*, select **Save**. If you do not want the default name, you can enter a file name and then select **Save**.

Copying a Data Set to Excel

To copy a SAS data set to Microsoft Excel, you can right-click a file in the SAS Explorer and either

☐ select **Copy Contents to Clipboard** and then click

 ⎡File⎤ ► ⎡Paste⎤

in Microsoft Excel, or

☐ select **View in Excel**.

Display 19.8 Explorer Window Displaying Copy to Clipboard Menu Option

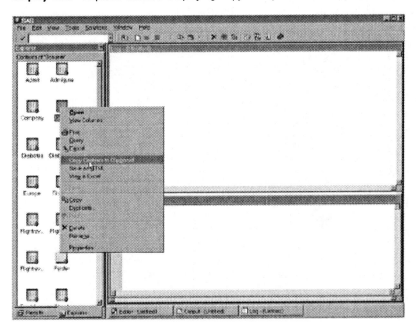

Using the Workspace to Manipulate Data in a Data Set

Moving and Labeling Columns with the VIEWTABLE Window

With the **VIEWTABLE** window, you can rearrange columns and temporarily change column headings. This example uses the WORK.MYWORK data set that was previously created in the WORK library (see " Viewing the Contents of a Data Set with the VIEWTABLE Window" on page 310):

1 Click the heading for the **Country** Column.

Display 19.9 VIEWTABLE Window Displaying MYWORK Data Set With Country Column Selected

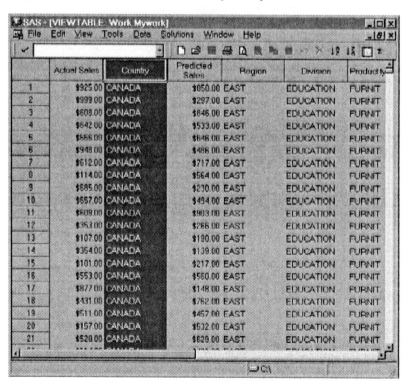

2 Drag and drop **Country** onto **Actual Sales**. The Country column moves to the right of the Actual Sales column.

Display 19.10 VIEWTABLE Window Showing Country Column Has Moved

3 Right-click the heading for **Region** and select **Column Attributes** from the menu.

Display 19.11   VIEWTABLE Window Displaying Column Attributes Menu Option

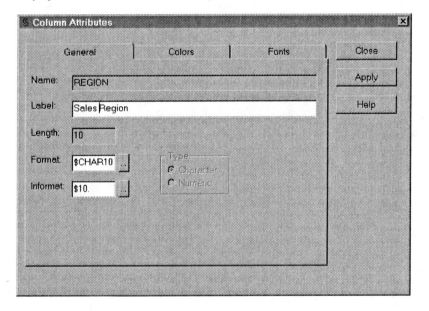

4 In the **Label** box, type **Sales Region** and then click Apply .

Display 19.12   Column Attributes Dialog Box

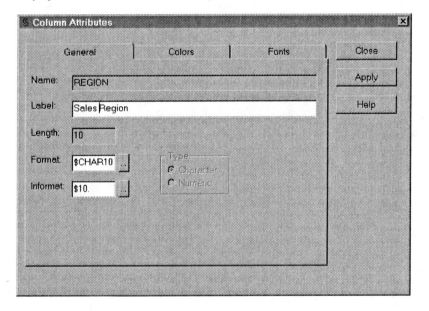

5 Click Close when you are finished.

Sorting Values of a Column with the VIEWTABLE Window

You can sort a data set in ascending or descending order, based on the values of a column. You can sort data permanently or create a sorted copy of a data set. This example creates a sorted copy.

This example continues to use the data set WORK.MYWORK that was created previously in " Viewing the Contents of a Data Set with the VIEWTABLE Window" on page 310.

To sort the values of a column in WORK.MYWORK with the **VIEWTABLE** window:

1 Make sure that the WORK.MYWORK data set is still available.

 □ If it is available, open it from SAS Explorer or VIEWTABLE.

□ If it is not available, recreate it from " Viewing the Contents of a Data Set with the VIEWTABLE Window" on page 310.

2 Right-click the heading for `Product`.

3 Select `Sort`.

Display 19.13 VIEWTABLE Window Displaying Sort Menu Option

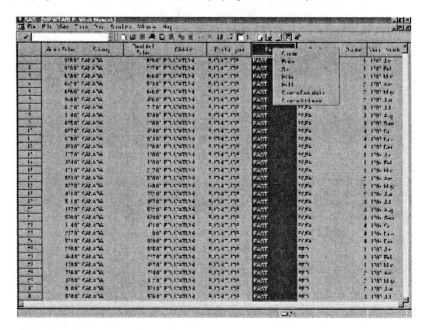

4 Select `Descending` from the window.

5 When a warning message asks you if you want to create a new table, click Yes to create a sorted copy of the data set.

6 In the `Sort` dialog box, `Table Name` field, type `WORK.Mysorted` as the name for the sorted data set.

Display 19.14 Sort Dialog Box

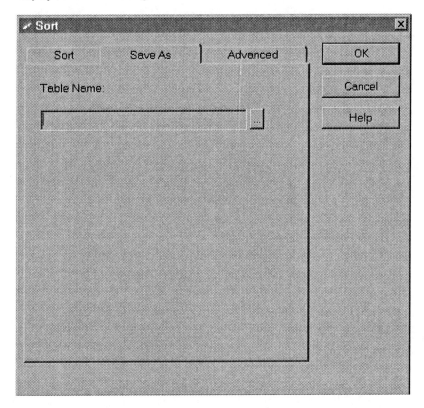

7 Click OK . Rows in the new data set are sorted in descending order by values of
`Product`.

Creating a WHERE Expression with the VIEWTABLE Window

You can create a WHERE expression with the **VIEWTABLE** window. SAS generates the
WHERE expression code automatically, and you can modify or edit the code.

A WHERE expression helps you subset a data set. A WHERE expression in SAS is
modeled after the WHERE clause in SQL.

This example uses the PRDSALE data set that was created at the beginning of this
topic, and shows you how to create a WHERE expression.

To create a WHERE Expression using the SAS workspace:

1 Double-click the WORK.PRDSALE data set created in the previous example. This
opens the PRDSALE data set in the **VIEWTABLE** window.

2 Right-click any table cell (not a heading) and select **Where**. The **WHERE
EXPRESSION** dialog box opens.

Display 19.15 VIEWTABLE Window Displaying Where Menu Option

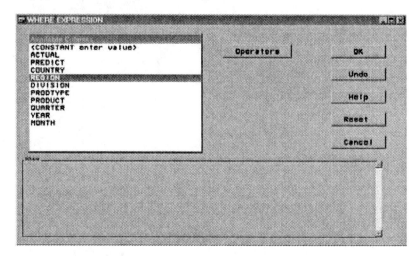

3 In the **Available Columns** list, click **REGION**.

Display 19.16 Where Expression Dialog Box

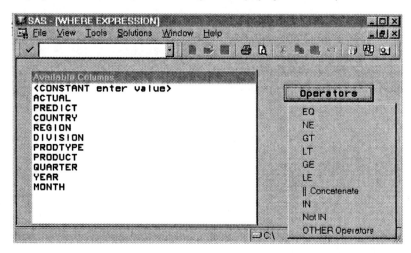

4 Select **EQ** (equal to) from the pop-up list.

Display 19.17 Where Expression Dialog Box Displaying EQ Menu Option

5 Click **<Lookup Distinct Values>**. This opens a window containing values. You can select values from the list.

Display 19.18 Where Expression Dialog Box Displaying LOOKUP Option

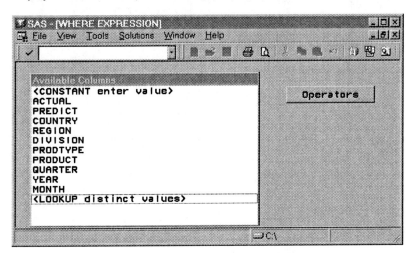

6 In the **Lookup Distinct Values** window, select **WEST**.

Display 19.19 Lookup Distinct Values Dialog Box

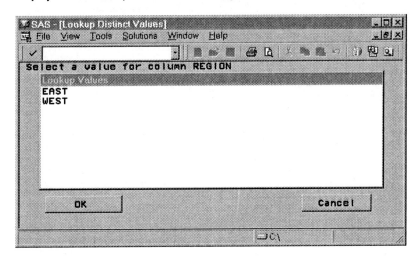

7 Notice that the complete **Where** expression appears in the **Where** box near the bottom of the display.

Figure 19.1 Where Expression Dialog Box Displaying the Complete Where Expression

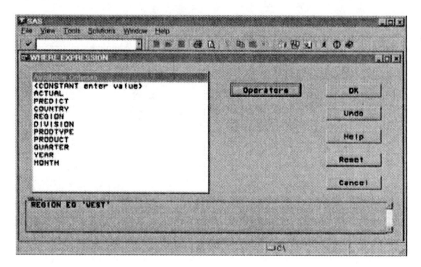

8 Click OK. The VIEWTABLE window now displays only the rows where the value of Region is **WEST**.

Editing Values in a Cell with the VIEWTABLE Window

You can edit a cell in a data set by opening the data set in the VIEWTABLE window and switching to edit mode. These are general instructions for editing cells in a SAS data set.

1 Open the Explorer window by selecting

 View ▶ Explorer

from the menu, or alternatively, by entering the **explorer** command in the command line.

2 Select a file that contains the cell that you want to edit.

3 Double-click the selected file to open it in the **VIEWTABLE** window.

4 Select

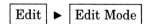 Edit ▶ Edit Mode

from the **VIEWTABLE** menu.

Display 19.20 Where Expression Dialog Box Displaying Edit Mode Menu Option

5 Click the cell that you want to edit.

6 Highlight the existing value and type a new value.

7 Press ENTER.

8 Select

| File | ► | Close |

When prompted about saving changes to the data set, click Yes, if you want to save the change.

Clearing Subsetted Data from the VIEWTABLE Window

If you have subset rows in the **VIEWTABLE** window, as in the previous example, you can clear subsets and then redisplay all data in the data set.

1 Right-click anywhere in the data set except a column heading.

2 Select **Where Clear**. The VIEWTABLE window removes any existing subset(s) and displays all rows in the data set.

3 Select

| File | ► | Close |

Importing and Exporting Data

Importing Data into a Data Set

The Import wizard guides you through the steps of importing data from many different file types into a SAS data set.

Note: The types of files that can be imported depend on your operating system. △

If your data is not in a standard file format, you can use the External File Interface (EFI) facility to import data. This tool enables you to define your file format, and offers you a range of format options. To use the EFI, select **User-defined formats** in the

Import wizard and follow the instructions for describing your data file. This example shows you how to import a standard file and view the results.

To import a standard file:

1 Select

File ► Import Data

to open the Import wizard. Notice that **Standard data source** is selected by default.

Display 19.21   Import Wizard Window Displaying Default Values

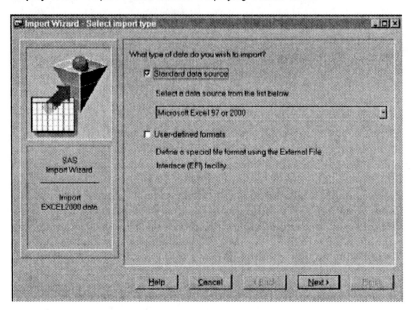

2 Click the drop-down arrow to see the list of data sources. If you exported data to Excel, select Excel 97 Spreadsheet (*.xls). Otherwise, select the file format in which your data are stored.

Display 19.22   Import Wizard Window Displaying List of Data Sources

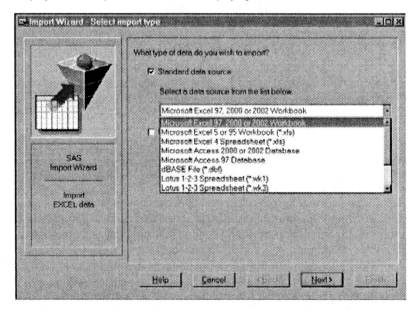

3 Click ⌈Next⌉ to continue.

4 In the **Select File** dialog box, type the full path for your file, or click ⌈Browse⌉ to find it.

Display 19.23 Import Wizard File Selection Window

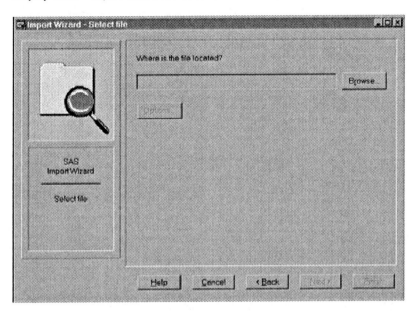

5 Click ⌈Next⌉ to continue. The **Select library and member** dialog box appears.

Display 19.24 Import Wizard Library Selection Window

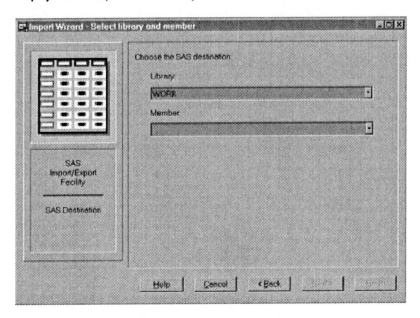

6 Type **WORK** for the library name and **MyImport** for the member name.

7 Click ⌈Next⌉ to continue. If you are importing data from the Excel 97 Spreadsheet format, you are asked about saving PROC IMPORT statements. Skip this option and click ⌈Finish⌉. Your data are imported into the SAS data set WORK.MyImport.

Exporting Your Data with the Export Wizard

You can easily export SAS data to a variety of file formats, using the Export Wizard. The formats that are available depend on your operating environment and on the SAS software products that you have installed. The example uses the PRDSALE data set that was created in a previous example (see "Copying a Practice File to the WORK Data Library" on page 307).

To export SAS data, do the following:

1 If it is not already open, double-click the WORK.PRDSALE data set to open it in the VIEWTABLE window.

2 Select

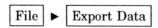

The Export Wizard window opens. Note that the **LIBRARY** and **MEMBER** lists contain the name of the data set (WORK.PRDSALE) that is currently displayed in the **VIEWTABLE** window.

Display 19.25   Export Wizard Window Displaying Default Values

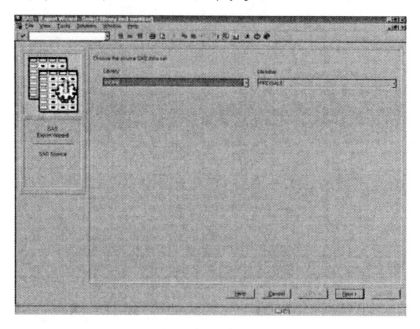

3 Click [Next] to proceed to selecting an export type. Notice that **Standard data source** is selected by default. In the data source list, select **Tab Delimited File (*.txt)**, or another format that is available on your operating environment.

Display 19.26 Export Wizard Window Displaying List of Data Sources

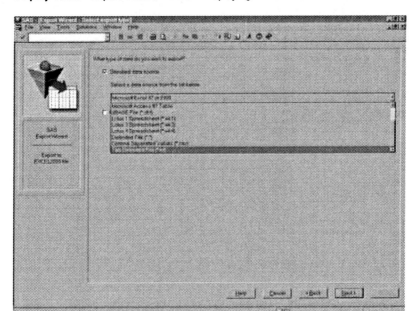

4 Click Browse and select a directory.

5 Click Next to proceed to selecting a destination file.

6 Type the file name **MYEXPORT** and click OK.

7 Click Finish.

The SAS data set is exported to MYEXPORT in the directory that you selected.

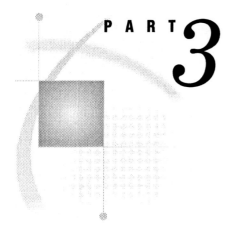

P A R T 3

DATA Step Concepts

Chapter **20**........DATA Step Processing   *329*

Chapter **21**........Reading Raw Data   *357*

Chapter **22**........BY-Group Processing in the DATA Step   *375*

Chapter **23**........Reading, Combining, and Modifying SAS Data Sets   *387*

Chapter **24**........Using DATA Step Component Objects   *437*

Chapter **25**........Array Processing   *449*

CHAPTER

20

DATA Step Processing

Why Use a DATA Step? **329**
Overview of DATA Step Processing **330**
    Flow of Action **330**
    The Compilation Phase **332**
    The Execution Phase **332**
Processing a DATA Step: A Walkthrough **333**
    Sample DATA Step **333**
    Creating the Input Buffer and the Program Data Vector **333**
    Reading a Record **334**
    Writing an Observation to the SAS Data Set **335**
    Reading the Next Record **336**
    When the DATA Step Finishes Executing **337**
About DATA Step Execution **337**
    The Default Sequence of Execution in the DATA Step **337**
    Changing the Default Sequence of Execution **338**
        Using Statements to Change the Default Sequence of Execution **338**
        Using Functions to Change the Default Sequence of Execution **339**
        Altering the Flow for a Given Observation **339**
    Step Boundary — How To Know When Statements Take Effect **340**
    What Causes a DATA Step to Stop Executing **341**
About Creating a SAS Data Set with a DATA Step **342**
    Creating a SAS Data File or a SAS Data View **342**
    Sources of Input Data **343**
    Reading Raw Data **343**
        Example 1: Reading External File Data **343**
        Example 2: Reading Instream Data Lines **343**
        Example 3: Reading Instream Data Lines with Missing Values **344**
        Example 4: Using Multiple Input Files in Instream Data **345**
    Reading Data from SAS Data Sets **346**
    Generating Data from Programming Statements **346**
Writing a Report with a DATA Step **347**
    Example 1: Creating a Report without Creating a Data Set **347**
    Example 2: Creating a Customized Report **348**
    Example 3: Creating a HTML Report Using ODS and the DATA Step **352**
The DATA Step and ODS **354**

Why Use a DATA Step?

Using the DATA step is the primary method for creating a SAS data set with base
SAS software. A *DATA step* is a group of SAS language statements that begin with a

DATA statement and contains other programming statements that manipulate existing SAS data sets or create SAS data sets from raw data files.

You can use the DATA step for

- □ creating SAS data sets (SAS data files or SAS data views)
- □ creating SAS data sets from input files that contain raw data (external files)
- □ creating new SAS data sets from existing ones by subsetting, merging, modifying, and updating existing SAS data sets
- □ analyzing, manipulating, or presenting your data
- □ computing the values for new variables
- □ report writing, or writing files to disk or tape
- □ retrieving information
- □ file management.

Note: A DATA step creates a *SAS data set*. This data set can be a SAS data file or a SAS data view. A SAS data file stores data values while a SAS data view stores instructions for retrieving and processing data. When you can use a SAS data view as a SAS data file, as is true in most cases, this documentation uses the broader term SAS data set.   △

Overview of DATA Step Processing

Flow of Action

When you submit a DATA step for execution, it is first compiled and then executed. The following figure shows the flow of action for a typical SAS DATA step.

Figure 20.1 Flow of Action in the DATA Step

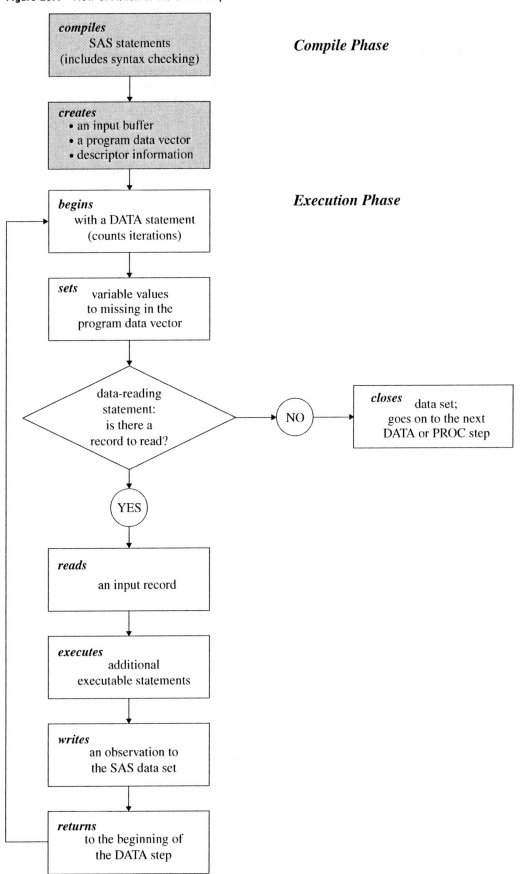

The Compilation Phase

When you submit a DATA step for execution, SAS checks the syntax of the SAS statements and compiles them, that is, automatically translates the statements into machine code. In this phase, SAS identifies the type and length of each new variable, and determines whether a type conversion is necessary for each subsequent reference to a variable. During the compile phase, SAS creates the following three items:

input buffer
: is a logical area in memory into which SAS reads each record of raw data when SAS executes an INPUT statement. Note that this buffer is created only when the DATA step reads raw data. (When the DATA step reads a SAS data set, SAS reads the data directly into the program data vector.)

program data vector (PDV)
: is a logical area in memory where SAS builds a data set, one observation at a time. When a program executes, SAS reads data values from the input buffer or creates them by executing SAS language statements. The data values are assigned to the appropriate variables in the program data vector. From here, SAS writes the values to a SAS data set as a single observation.

Along with data set variables and computed variables, the PDV contains two automatic variables, _N_ and _ERROR_. The _N_ variable counts the number of times the DATA step begins to iterate. The _ERROR_ variable signals the occurrence of an error caused by the data during execution. The value of _ERROR_ is either 0 (indicating no errors exist), or 1 (indicating that one or more errors have occurred). SAS does not write these variables to the output data set.

descriptor information
: is information that SAS creates and maintains about each SAS data set, including data set attributes and variable attributes. It contains, for example, the name of the data set and its member type, the date and time that the data set was created, and the number, names and data types (character or numeric) of the variables.

The Execution Phase

By default, a simple DATA step iterates once for each observation that is being created. The flow of action in the Execution Phase of a simple DATA step is described as follows:

1 The DATA step begins with a DATA statement. Each time the DATA statement executes, a new iteration of the DATA step begins, and the _N_ automatic variable is incremented by 1.

2 SAS sets the newly created program variables to missing in the program data vector (PDV).

3 SAS reads a data record from a raw data file into the input buffer, or it reads an observation from a SAS data set directly into the program data vector. You can use an INPUT, MERGE, SET, MODIFY, or UPDATE statement to read a record.

4 SAS executes any subsequent programming statements for the current record.

5 At the end of the statements, an output, return, and reset occur automatically. SAS writes an observation to the SAS data set, the system automatically returns to the top of the DATA step, and the values of variables created by INPUT and assignment statements are reset to missing in the program data vector. Note that

variables that you read with a SET, MERGE, MODIFY, or UPDATE statement are not reset to missing here.

6 SAS counts another iteration, reads the next record or observation, and executes the subsequent programming statements for the current observation.

7 The DATA step terminates when SAS encounters the end-of-file in a SAS data set or a raw data file.

Note: The figure shows the default processing of the DATA step. You can place data-reading statements (such as INPUT or SET), or data-writing statements (such as OUTPUT), in any order in your program. △

Processing a DATA Step: A Walkthrough

Sample DATA Step

The following statements provide an example of a DATA step that reads raw data, calculates totals, and creates a data set:

```
data total_points (drop=TeamName);   ❶
    input TeamName $ ParticipantName $ Event1 Event2 Event3;   ❷
    TeamTotal + (Event1 + Event2 + Event3);   ❸
    datalines;
Knights Sue     6  8  8
Cardinals Jane  9  7  8
Knights John    7  7  7
Knights Lisa    8  9  9
Knights Fran    7  6  6
Knights Walter  9  8 10
;
```

❶ The DROP= data set option prevents the variable TeamName from being written to the output SAS data set called TOTAL_POINTS.

❷ The INPUT statement describes the data by giving a name to each variable, identifying its data type (character or numeric), and identifying its relative location in the data record.

❸ The Sum statement accumulates the scores for three events in the variable TeamTotal.

Creating the Input Buffer and the Program Data Vector

When DATA step statements are compiled, SAS determines whether to create an input buffer. If the input file contains raw data (as in the example above), SAS creates an input buffer to hold the data before moving the data to the program data vector (PDV). (If the input file is a SAS data set, however, SAS does not create an input buffer. SAS writes the input data directly to the PDV.)

The PDV contains all the variables in the input data set, the variables created in DATA step statements, and the two variables, _N_ and _ERROR_, that are automatically generated for every DATA step. The _N_ variable represents the number of times the DATA step has iterated. The _ERROR_ variable acts like a binary switch whose value is 0 if no errors exist in the DATA step, or 1 if one or more errors exist.

The following figure shows the Input Buffer and the program data vector after DATA step compilation.

Figure 20.2   Input Buffer and Program Data Vector

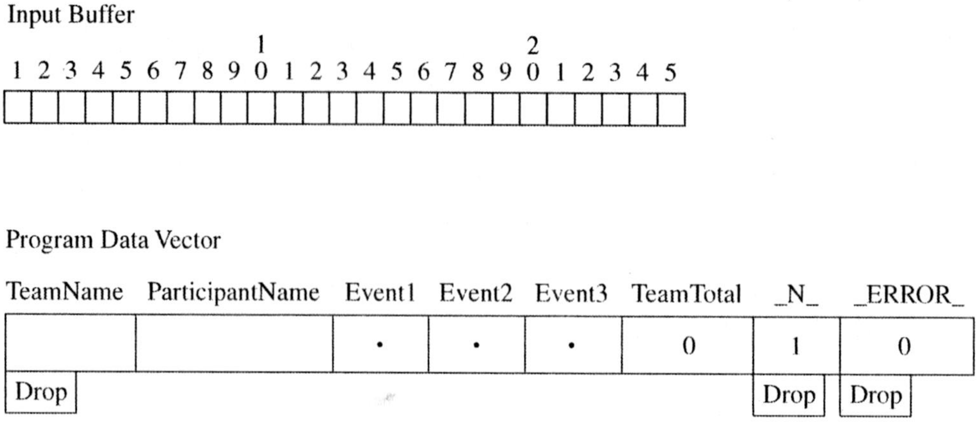

Input Buffer

Program Data Vector

Variables that are created by the INPUT and the Sum statements (TeamName, ParticipantName, Event1, Event2, Event3, and TeamTotal) are set to missing initially. Note that in this representation, numeric variables are initialized with a period and character variables are initialized with blanks. The automatic variable _N_ is set to 1; the automatic variable _ERROR_ is set to 0.

The variable TeamName is marked Drop in the PDV because of the DROP= data set option in the DATA statement. Dropped variables are not written to the SAS data set. The _N_ and _ERROR_ variables are dropped because automatic variables created by the DATA step are not written to a SAS data set. See Chapter 5, "SAS Variables," on page 77 for details about automatic variables.

Reading a Record

SAS reads the first data line into the input buffer. The input *pointer*, which SAS uses to keep its place as it reads data from the input buffer, is positioned at the beginning of the buffer, ready to read the data record. The following figure shows the position of the input pointer in the input buffer before SAS reads the data.

Figure 20.3   Position of the Pointer in the Input Buffer Before SAS Reads Data

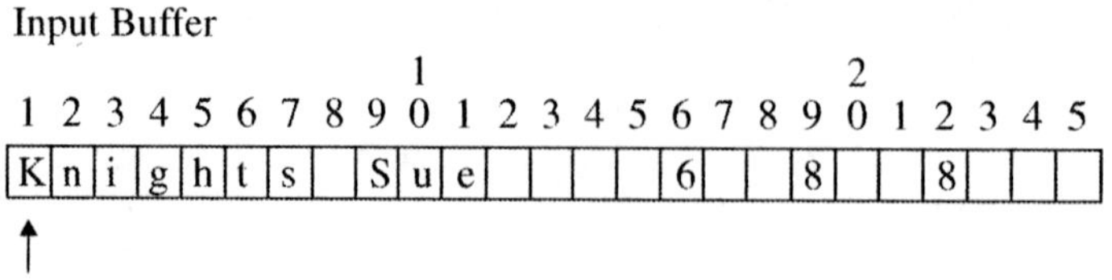

Input Buffer

The INPUT statement then reads *data values* from the record in the input buffer and writes them to the PDV where they become *variable values*. The following figure shows both the position of the pointer in the input buffer, and the values in the PDV after SAS reads the first record.

Figure 20.4 Values from the First Record are Read into the Program Data Vector

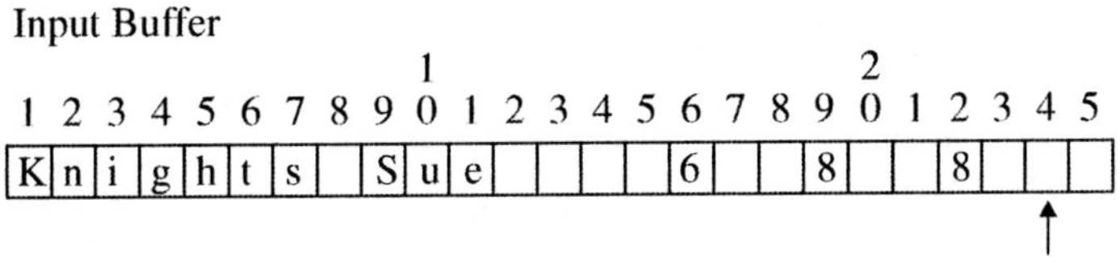

Input Buffer

```
                    1                   2
1 2 3 4 5 6 7 8 9 0 1 2 3 4 5 6 7 8 9 0 1 2 3 4 5
K n i g h t s   S u e         6     8     8
```

Program Data Vector

TeamName	ParticipantName	Event1	Event2	Event3	TeamTotal	_N_	_ERROR_
Knights	Sue	6	8	8	0	1	0
Drop						Drop	Drop

After the INPUT statement reads a value for each variable, SAS executes the Sum statement. SAS computes a value for the variable TeamTotal and writes it to the PDV. The following figure shows the PDV with all of its values before SAS writes the observation to the data set.

Figure 20.5 Program Data Vector with Computed Value of the Sum Statement

Program Data Vector

TeamName	ParticipantName	Event1	Event2	Event3	TeamTotal	_N_	_ERROR_
Knights	Sue	6	8	8	22	1	0
Drop						Drop	Drop

Writing an Observation to the SAS Data Set

When SAS executes the last statement in the DATA step, all values in the PDV, except those marked to be dropped, are written as a single observation to the data set TOTAL_POINTS. The following figure shows the first observation in the TOTAL_POINTS data set.

Figure 20.6 The First Observation in Data Set TOTAL_POINTS

Output SAS Data Set TOTAL_POINTS: 1st observation

ParticipantName	Event1	Event2	Event3	TeamTotal
Sue	6	8	8	22

SAS then returns to the DATA statement to begin the next iteration. SAS resets the values in the PDV in the following way:

☐ The values of variables created by the INPUT statement are set to missing.

□ The value created by the Sum statement is automatically retained.

□ The value of the automatic variable _N_ is incremented by 1, and the value of _ERROR_ is reset to 0.

The following figure shows the current values in the PDV.

Figure 20.7 Current Values in the Program Data Vector

Program Data Vector

TeamName	ParticipantName	Event1	Event2	Event3	TeamTotal	_N_	_ERROR_
		•	•	•	22	2	0
Drop						Drop	Drop

Reading the Next Record

SAS reads the next record into the input buffer. The INPUT statement reads the data values from the input buffer and writes them to the PDV. The Sum statement adds the values of Event1, Event2, and Event3 to TeamTotal. The value of 2 for variable _N_ indicates that SAS is beginning the second iteration of the DATA step. The following figure shows the input buffer, the PDV for the second record, and the SAS data set with the first two observations.

Figure 20.8 Input Buffer, Program Data Vector, and First Two Observations

Input Buffer

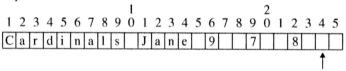

Program Data Vector

TeamName	ParticipantName	Event1	Event2	Event3	TeamTotal	_N_	_ERROR_
Cardinals	Jane	9	7	8	46	2	0
Drop						Drop	Drop

Output SAS Data Set TOTAL_POINTS: 1st and 2nd observations

ParticipantName	Event1	Event2	Event3	TeamTotal
Sue	6	8	8	22
Jane	9	7	8	46

As SAS continues to read records, the value in TeamTotal grows larger as more participant scores are added to the variable. _N_ is incremented at the beginning of each iteration of the DATA step. This process continues until SAS reaches the end of the input file.

When the DATA Step Finishes Executing

The DATA step stops executing after it processes the last input record. You can use PROC PRINT to print the output in the TOTAL_POINTS data set:

Output 20.1   Output from the Walkthrough DATA Step

```
                          Total Team Scores                              1

                 Participant                                Team
        Obs        Name        Event1    Event2    Event3   Total

         1         Sue           6         8         8       22
         2         Jane          9         7         8       46
         3         John          7         7         7       67
         4         Lisa          8         9         9       93
         5         Fran          7         6         6      112
         6         Walter        9         8        10      139
```

About DATA Step Execution

The Default Sequence of Execution in the DATA Step

The following table outlines the default sequence of execution for statements in a DATA step. The DATA statement begins the step and identifies usually one or more SAS data sets that the step will create. (You can use the keyword _NULL_ as the data set name if you do not want to create an output data set.) Optional programming statements process your data. SAS then performs the default actions at the end of processing an observation.

Table 20.1   Default Execution for Statements in a DATA Step

Structure of a DATA Step	Action Taken
DATA statement	begins the step
	counts iterations
Data-reading statements: *	
INPUT	describes the arrangement of values in the input data record from a raw data source
SET	reads an observation from one or more SAS data sets
MERGE	joins observations from two or more SAS data sets into a single observation
MODIFY	replaces, deletes, or appends observations in an existing SAS data set in place

Structure of a DATA Step	Action Taken
UPDATE	updates a master file by applying transactions
Optional SAS programming statements, for example:	further processes the data for the current observation.
FirstQuarter=Jan+Feb+Mar;	computes the value for FirstQuarter for the current observation.
if RetailPrice < 500;	subsets by value of variable RetailPrice for the current observation
Default actions at the end of processing an observation	
At end of DATA step:	writes an observation to a SAS data set
Automatic write, automatic return	returns to the DATA statement
At top of DATA step:	resets values to missing in program data vector
Automatic reset	

* The table shows the default processing of the DATA step. You can alter the sequence of statements in the DATA step. You can code optional programming statements, such as creating or reinitializing a constant, before you code a data-reading statement.

Note: You can also use functions to read and process data. For information about how statements and functions process data differently, see "Using Functions to Manipulate Files" on page 42. For specific information about SAS functions, see the SAS I/O Files and External Files categories in "Functions and CALL Routines by Category" in *SAS Language Reference: Dictionary*. △

Changing the Default Sequence of Execution

Using Statements to Change the Default Sequence of Execution

You can change the default sequence of execution to control how your program executes. SAS language statements offer you a lot of flexibility to do this in a DATA step. The following list shows the most common ways to control the flow of execution in a DATA step program.

Table 20.2 Common Methods that Alter the Sequence of Execution

Task	Possible Methods
Read a record	merge, modify, join data sets
	read multiple records to create a single observation
	randomly select records for processing
	read from multiple external files
	read selected fields from a record by using statement or data set options
Process data	use conditional logic
	retain variable values
Write an observation	write to a SAS data set or to an external file
	control when output is written to a data set
	write to multiple files

For more information, see the individual statements in *SAS Language Reference: Dictionary*.

Using Functions to Change the Default Sequence of Execution

You can also use functions to read and process data. For information about how statements and functions process data differently, see "Using Functions to Manipulate Files" on page 42. For specific information about SAS functions, see the SAS I/O Files and External Files categories in "Functions and CALL Routines by Category" in *SAS Language Reference: Dictionary*.

Altering the Flow for a Given Observation

You can use statements, statement options, and data set options to alter the way SAS processes specific observations. The following table lists SAS language elements and their effects on processing.

Table 20.3 Language Elements that Alter Programming Flow

SAS Language Element	Function
subsetting IF statement	stops the current iteration when a condition is false, does not write the current observation to the data set, and returns control to the top of the DATA step.
IF-THEN/ELSE statement	stops the current iteration when a conditon is true, writes the current observation to the data set, and returns control to the top of the DATA step.
DO loops	cause parts of the DATA step to be executed multiple times.
LINK and RETURN statements	alter the flow of control, execute statements following the label specified, and return control of the program to the next statement following the LINK statement.

SAS Language Element	Function
HEADER= option in the FILE statement	alters the flow of control whenever a PUT statement causes a new page of output to begin; statements following the label specified in the HEADER= option are executed until a RETURN statement is encountered, at which time control returns to the point from which the HEADER= option was activated.
GO TO statement	alters the flow of execution by branching to the label that is specified in the GO TO statement. SAS executes subsequent statements then returns control to the beginning of the DATA step.
EOF= option in an INFILE statement	alters the flow of execution when the end of the input file is reached; statements following the label that is specified in the EOF= option are executed at that time.
_N_ automatic variable in an IF-THEN construct	causes parts of the DATA step to execute only for particular iterations.
SELECT statement	conditionally executes one of a group of SAS statements.
OUTPUT statement in an IF-THEN construct	outputs an observation before the end of the DATA step, based on a condition; prevents automatic output at the bottom of the DATA step.
DELETE statement in an IF-THEN construct	deletes an observation based on a condition and causes a return to the top of the DATA step.
ABORT statement in an IF-THEN construct	stops execution of the DATA step and instruct SAS to resume execution with the next DATA or PROC step. It can also stop executing a SAS program altogether, depending on the options specified in the ABORT statement and on the method of operation.
WHERE statement or WHERE= data set option	causes SAS to read certain observations based on one or more specified criteria.

Step Boundary — How To Know When Statements Take Effect

Understanding step boundaries is an important concept in SAS programming because step boundaries determine when SAS statements take effect. SAS executes program statements only when SAS crosses a default or an explicit step boundary. Consider the following DATA steps:

```
data _null_;  ❶
   set allscores(drop=score5-score7);
   title 'Student Test Scores';  ❷

data employees;  ❸
   set employee_list;
run;
```

❶ The DATA statement begins a DATA step and is a step boundary.

❷ The TITLE statement is in effect for both DATA steps because it appears before the boundary of the first DATA step. (Because the TITLE statement is a global statement,

❸ The DATA statement is the default boundary for the first DATA step.

The TITLE statement in this example is in effect for the first DATA step as well as for the second because the TITLE statement appears before the boundary of the first DATA step. This example uses the default step boundary `data employees;`.

The following example shows an OPTIONS statement inserted after a RUN statement.

```
data scores; ❶
   set allscores(drop=score5-score7);
run; ❷

options firstobs=5 obs=55; ❸

data test;
   set alltests;
run;
```

The OPTIONS statement specifies that the first observation that is read from the input data set should be the 5th, and the last observation that is read should be the 55th. Inserting a RUN statement immediately before the OPTIONS statement causes the first DATA step to reach its boundary (`run;`)before SAS encounters the OPTIONS statement. In this case, the step boundary is explicit. The OPTIONS statement settings, therefore, are put into effect for the second DATA step only.

❶ The DATA statement is a step boundary.

❷ The RUN statement is the explicit boundary for the first DATA step.

❸ The OPTIONS statement affects the second DATA step only.

Following the statements in a DATA step with a RUN statement is the simplest way to make the step begin to execute, but a RUN statement is not always necessary. SAS recognizes several step boundaries for a SAS step:

□ another DATA statement

□ a PROC statement

□ a RUN statement.

    Note: For SAS programs executed in interactive mode, a RUN statement is required to signal the step boundary for the last step you submit. △

□ the semicolon (with a DATALINES or CARDS statement) or four semicolons (with a DATALINES4 or CARDS4 statement) after data lines

□ an ENDSAS statement

□ in noninteractive or batch mode, the end of a program file containing SAS programming statements

□ a QUIT statement (for some procedures).

When you submit a DATA step during interactive processing, it does not begin running until SAS encounters a step boundary. This fact enables you to submit statements as you write them while preventing a step from executing until you have entered all the statements.

What Causes a DATA Step to Stop Executing

DATA steps stop executing under different circumstances, depending on the type and number of sources of input.

Table 20.4   Causes that Stop DATA Step Execution

Data Read	Data Source	SAS Statements	DATA Step Stops
no data			after only one iteration
any data			when it executes STOP or ABORT
			when the data is exhausted
raw data	instream data lines	INPUT statement	after the last data line is read
	one external file	INPUT and INFILE statements	when end-of-file is reached
	multiple external files	INPUT and INFILE statements	when end-of-file is first reached on any of the files
observations sequentially	one SAS data set	SET and MODIFY statements	after the last observation is read
	multiple SAS data sets	one SET, MERGE, MODIFY, or UPDATE statement	when all input data sets are exhausted
	multiple SAS data sets	multiple SET, MERGE, MODIFY, or UPDATE statements	when end-of-file is reached by any of the data-reading statements

A DATA step that reads observations from a SAS data set with a SET statement that uses the POINT= option has no way to detect the end of the input SAS data set. (This method is called direct or random access.) Such a DATA step usually requires a STOP statement.

A DATA step also stops when it executes a STOP or an ABORT statement. Some system options and data set options, such as OBS=, can cause a DATA step to stop earlier than it would otherwise.

About Creating a SAS Data Set with a DATA Step

Creating a SAS Data File or a SAS Data View

You can create either a SAS data file, a data set that holds actual data, or a SAS data view, a data set that references data that is stored elsewhere. By default, you create a SAS data file. To create a SAS data view instead, use the VIEW= option on the DATA statement. With a data view you can, for example, process monthly sales figures without having to edit your DATA step. Whenever you need to create output, the output from a data view reflects the current input data values.

The following DATA statement creates a data view called MONTHLY_SALES.

```
data monthly_sales / view=monthly_sales;
```

The following DATA statement creates a data file called TEST_RESULTS.

```
data test_results;
```

Sources of Input Data

You select data-reading statements based on the source of your input data. There are at least six sources of input data:

- □ raw data in an external file
- □ raw data in the jobstream (instream data)
- □ data in SAS data sets
- □ data that is created by programming statements
- □ data that you can remotely access through an FTP protocol, TCP/IP socket, a SAS catalog entry, or through a URL
- □ data that is stored in a Database Management System (DBMS) or other vendor's data files.

Usually DATA steps read input data records from only one of the first three sources of input. However, DATA steps can use a combination of some or all of the sources.

Reading Raw Data

Example 1: Reading External File Data

The components of a DATA step that produce a SAS data set from raw data stored in an external file are outlined here.

```
data weight; ❶
   infile 'your-input-file'; ❷
   input IDnumber $ Week1 Week16; ❸
   WeightLoss=Week1-Week16; ❹
run; ❺

proc print data=weight; ❻
run; ❼
```

❶ Begin the DATA step and create a SAS data set called WEIGHT.

❷ Specify the external file that contains your data.

❸ Read a record and assign values to three variables.

❹ Calculate a value for variable WeightLoss.

❺ Execute the DATA step.

❻ Print data set WEIGHT using the PRINT procedure.

❼ Execute the PRINT procedure.

Example 2: Reading Instream Data Lines

This example reads raw data from instream data lines.

```
data weight2; ❶
   input IDnumber $ Week1 Week16; ❷
   WeightLoss2=Week1-Week16; ❸
   datalines; ❹
2477 195   163
2431 220   198
2456 173   155
2412 135   116
;                        ❺

proc print data=weight2;   ❻
run;   ❼
```

❶ Begin the DATA step and create SAS data set WEIGHT2.

❷ Read a data line and assign values to three variables.

❸ Calculate a value for variable WeightLoss2.

❹ Begin the data lines.

❺ Signal end of data lines with a semicolon and execute the DATA step.

❻ Print data set WEIGHT2 using the PRINT procedure.

❼ Execute the PRINT procedure.

Example 3: Reading Instream Data Lines with Missing Values

You can also take advantage of options on the INFILE statement when you read instream data lines. This example shows the use of the MISSOVER statement option, which assigns missing values to variables for records that contain no data for those variables.

```
data weight2;
   infile datalines missover;   ❶
   input IDnumber $ Week1 Week16;
   WeightLoss2=Week1-Week16;
   datalines;   ❷
2477 195   163
2431
2456 173   155
2412 135   116
;                        ❸

proc print data=weight2; ❹
run;   ❺
```

❶ Use the MISSOVER option to assign missing values to variables that do not contain values.

❷ Begin data lines.

❸ Signal end of data lines and execute the DATA step.

❹ Print data set WEIGHT2 using the PRINT procedure.

❺ Execute the PRINT procedure.

Example 4: Using Multiple Input Files in Instream Data

This example shows how to use multiple input files as instream data to your program. This example reads the records in each file and creates the ALL_ERRORS SAS data set. The program then sorts the observations by Station, and creates a sorted data set called SORTED_ERRORS. The print procedure prints the results.

```
options pageno=1 nodate linesize=60 pagesize=80;

data all_errors;
   length filelocation $ 60;
   input filelocation;  /* reads instream data */
   infile daily filevar=filelocation
               filename=daily end=done;
   do while (not done);
      input Station $ Shift $ Employee $ NumberOfFlaws;
      output;
   end;
   put 'Finished reading ' daily=;
   datalines;
. . .myfile_A. . .
. . .myfile_B. . .
. . .myfile_C. . .
;

proc sort data=all_errors out=sorted_errors;
   by Station;
run;

proc print data = sorted_errors;
   title 'Flaws Report sorted by Station';
run;
```

Output 20.2 Multiple Input Files in Instream Data

```
               Flaws Report sorted by Station                1

                                          Number
         Obs    Station    Shift   Employee   OfFlaws

          1     Amherst      2     Lynne        0
          2     Goshen       2     Seth         4
          3     Hadley       2     Jon          3
          4     Holyoke      1     Walter       0
          5     Holyoke      1     Barb         3
          6     Orange       2     Carol        5
          7     Otis         1     Kay          0
          8     Pelham       2     Mike         4
          9     Stanford     1     Sam          1
         10     Suffield     2     Lisa         1
```

Reading Data from SAS Data Sets

This example reads data from one SAS data set, generates a value for a new variable, and creates a new data set.

```
data average_loss;   ❶
   set weight;       ❷
   Percent=round((AverageLoss * 100) / Week1);   ❸
run;                                              ❹
```

❶ Begin the DATA step and create a SAS data set called AVERAGE_LOSS.

❷ Read an observation from SAS data set WEIGHT.

❸ Calculate a value for variable Percent.

❹ Execute the DATA step.

Generating Data from Programming Statements

You can create data for a SAS data set by generating observations with programming statements rather than by reading data. A DATA step that reads no input goes through only one iteration.

```
data investment;   ❶
   begin='01JAN1990'd;
   end='31DEC2009'd;
   do year=year(begin) to year(end);   ❷
      Capital+2000 + .07*(Capital+2000);
      output;        ❸
   end;
   put 'The number of DATA step iterations is '_n_;   ❹
run;      ❺

proc print data=investment;   ❻
   format Capital dollar12.2;   ❼
run;   ❽
```

❶ Begin the DATA step and create a SAS data set called INVESTMENT.

❷ Calculate a value based on a $2,000 capital investment and 7% interest each year from 1990 to 2009. Calculate variable values for one observation per iteration of the DO loop.

❸ Write each observation to data set INVESTMENT.

❹ Write a note to the SAS log proving that the DATA step iterates only once.

❺ Execute the DATA step.

❻ To see your output, print the INVESTMENT data set with the PRINT procedure.

❼ Use the FORMAT statement to write numeric values with dollar signs, commas, and decimal points.

❽ Execute the PRINT procedure.

Writing a Report with a DATA Step

Example 1: Creating a Report without Creating a Data Set

You can use a DATA step to generate a report without creating a data set by using _NULL_ in the DATA statement. This approach saves system resources because SAS does not create a data set. The report can contain both TITLE statements and FOOTNOTE statements. If you use a FOOTNOTE statement, be sure to include FOOTNOTE as an option on the FILE statement in the DATA step.

```
title1 'Budget Report';            ❶
title2 'Mid-Year Totals by Department';
footnote 'compiled by Manager,
Documentation Development Department';    ❷

data _null_;        ❸
   set budget;      ❹
   file print footnote;    ❺
   MidYearTotal=Jan+Feb+Mar+Apr+May+Jun;    ❻
   if _n_=1 then      ❼
      do;
         put @5 'Department' @30 'Mid-Year Total';
      end;
   put @7 Department @35 MidYearTotal;     ❽
run;    ❾
```

❶ Define titles.

❷ Define the footnote.

❸ Begin the DATA step. _NULL_ specifies that no data set will be created.

❹ Read one observation per iteration from data set BUDGET.

❺ Name the output file for the PUT statements and use the PRINT fileref. By default, the PRINT fileref specifies that the file will contain carriage control characters and titles. The FOOTNOTE option specifies that each page of output will contain a footnote.

❻ Calculate a value for the variable MidYearTotal on each iteration.

❼ Write variable name headings for the report on the first iteration only.

❽ Write the current values of variables Department and MidYearTotal for each iteration.

❾ Execute the DATA step.

The example above uses the FILE statement with the PRINT fileref to produce listing output. If you want to print to a file, specify a fileref or a complete file name. Use the PRINT option if you want the file to contain carriage control characters and titles. The following example shows how to use the FILE statement in this way.

```
file 'external-file' footnote print;
```

You can also use the **data _null_;** statement to write to an external file. For more information about writing to external files, see the FILE statement in *SAS Language Reference: Dictionary*, and the SAS documentation for your operating environment.

Example 2: Creating a Customized Report

You can create very detailed, fully customized reports by using a DATA step with PUT statements. The following example shows a customized report that contains three distinct sections: a header, a table, and a footer. It contains existing SAS variable values, constant text, and values that are calculated as the report is written.

Output 20.3 Sample of a Customized Report

```
                                          Expense Report                                                        1


Around The World Retailers

EMPLOYEE BUSINESS, TRAVEL, AND TRAINING EXPENSE REPORT


Employee Name: ALEJANDRO MARTINEZ        Destination: CARY, NC                      Departure Date: 11JUL1999
   Department: SALES & MARKETING          Purpose of Trip/Activity: MARKETING TRAINING    Return Date: 16JUL1999
      Trip ID#: 93-0002519                                                            Activity from: 11JUL1999
                                                                                                 to: 16JUL1999


+----------------------------------+--------+--------+--------+--------+--------+--------+--------+--------+
|                                  |  SUN   |  MON   |  TUE   |  WED   |  THU   |  FRI   |  SAT   |        |  PAID BY  PAID BY
| EXPENSE DETAIL                   | 07/11  | 07/12  | 07/13  | 07/14  | 07/15  | 07/16  | 07/17  | TOTALS |  COMPANY EMPLOYEE
|----------------------------------|--------|--------|--------|--------|--------|--------|--------|--------|
|Lodging, Hotel                    | 92.96  | 92.96  | 92.96  | 92.96  | 92.96  |        |        | 464.80 | 464.80
|Telephone                         |  4.57  |  4.73  |        |        |        |        |        |   9.30 |              9.30
|Personal Auto   36 miles @.28/mile|  5.04  |        |        |        |        |  5.04  |        |  10.08 |             10.08
|Car Rental, Taxi, Parking, Tolls  |        | 35.32  | 35.32  | 35.32  | 35.32  | 35.32  |        | 176.60 | 176.60
|Airlines, Bus, Train (Attach Stub)| 485.00 |        |        |        |        | 485.00 |        | 970.00 | 970.00
|Dues                              |        |        |        |        |        |        |        |        |
|Registration Fees                 | 75.00  |        |        |        |        |        |        |  75.00 |             75.00
|Other (explain below)             |        |        |        |        |        |  5.00  |        |   5.00 |              5.00
|Tips (excluding meal tips)        |  3.00  |        |        |        |        |  3.00  |        |   6.00 |              6.00
|----------------------------------|--------|--------|--------|--------|--------|--------|--------|--------|
|Meals                             |        |        |        |        |        |        |        |        |
|Breakfast                         |        |        |        |        |        |  7.79  |        |   7.79 |              7.79
|Lunch                             |        |        |        |        |        |        |        |        |
|Dinner                            | 36.00  | 28.63  | 36.00  | 36.00  | 30.00  |        |        | 166.63 |            166.63
|Business Entertainment            |        |        |        |        |        |        |        |        |
|----------------------------------|--------|--------|--------|--------|--------|--------|--------|--------|
|TOTAL EXPENSES                    | 641.57 | 176.64 | 179.28 | 179.28 | 173.28 | 541.15 |        |1891.20 |1611.40   279.80
+----------------------------------+--------+--------+--------+--------+--------+--------+--------+--------+


Travel Advance to Employee ...........................................................................    $0.00


Reimbursement due Employee (or ATWR) ................................................................  $279.80


Other: (i.e. miscellaneous expenses and/or names of employees sharing receipt.)

16JUL1999 CAR RENTAL INCLUDE $5.00 FOR GAS








APPROVED FOR PAYMENT BY: Authorizing Manager: _____    Emp. # _____



                Employee Signature: _____    Emp. #  1118


   Charge to Division: ATW        Region:  TX        Dept:  MKT        Acct:    6003    Date:  27JUL1999
```

The code shown below generates the report example (you must create your own input data). It is beyond the scope of this discussion to fully explain the code that generated the report example. For a complete explanation of this example, see *SAS Guide to Report Writing: Examples*.

```
        options ls=132 ps=66 pageno=1 nodate;

    data travel;

      /* infile 'SAS-data-set' missover; */
      infile '/u/lirezn/input_for_concepts.dat' missover;
     input acct div $ region $ deptchg $ rptdate : date9.
        other1-other10 /
          empid empname & $char35. / dept & $char35. /
          purpose & $char35. / dest & $char35. / tripid & $char35. /
          actdate2 date9. /
          misc1 & $char75. / misc2 & $char75. / misc3 & $char75. /
          misc4 & $char75. /
          misc5 & $char75. / misc6 & $char75. / misc7 & $char75. /
          misc8 & $char75. /
          dptdate : date9. rtrndate : date9. automile permile /
          hotel1-hotel10 /
          phone1-phone10 / peraut1-peraut10 / carrnt1-carrnt10 /
          airlin1-airlin10 / dues1-dues10 / regfee1-regfee10 /
          tips1-tips10 / meals1-meals10 / bkfst1-bkfst10 /
          lunch1-lunch10 / dinner1-dinner10 / busent1-busent10 /
          total1-total10 / empadv reimburs actdate1 : date9.;
    run;


    proc format;
       value category  1='Lodging, Hotel'
                       2='Telephone'
                       3='Personal Auto'
                       4='Car Rental, Taxi, Parking, Tolls'
                       5='Airlines, Bus, Train (Attach Stub)'
                       6='Dues'
                       7='Registration Fees'
                       8='Other (explain below)'
                       9='Tips (excluding meal tips)'
                      10='Meals'
                      11='Breakfast'
                      12='Lunch'
                      13='Dinner'
                      14='Business Entertainment'
                      15='TOTAL EXPENSES';
       value blanks  0=' '
                   other=(|8.2|);
       value $cuscore ' '='_____';
       value nuscore   . ='_____';
    run;


    data _null_;
       file print;
       title 'Expense Report';
       format rptdate actdate1 actdate2 dptdate rtrndate date9.;
       set travel;

       array expenses{15,10} hotel1-hotel10  phone1-phone10
                             peraut1-peraut10 carrnt1-carrnt10
```

```
                        airlin1-airlin10 dues1-dues10
                        regfee1-regfee10 other1-other10
                        tips1-tips10 meals1-meals10
                        bkfst1-bkfst10 lunch1-lunch10
                        dinner1-dinner10 busent1-busent10
                        total1-total10;
      array misc{8} $ misc1-misc8;
      array mday{7} mday1-mday7;
      dptday=weekday(dptdate);
      mday{dptday}=dptdate;
      if dptday>1 then
         do dayofwk=1 to (dptday-1);
           mday{dayofwk}=dptdate-(dptday-dayofwk);
         end;
      if dptday<7 then
         do dayofwk=(dptday+1) to 7;
            mday{dayofwk}=dptdate+(dayofwk-dptday);
         end;
      if rptdate=. then rptdate="&sysdate9"d;

      tripnum=substr(tripid,4,2)||'-'||substr(scan(tripid,1),6);

      put // @1 'Around The World Retailers' //

          @1 'EMPLOYEE BUSINESS, TRAVEL, AND TRAINING EXPENSE REPORT' ///

          @1 'Employee Name: ' @16 empname
          @44 'Destination: ' @57 dest
          @106 'Departure Date:' @122 dptdate /

          @4 'Department: ' @16 dept
          @44 'Purpose of Trip/Activity: ' @70 purpose
          @109 'Return Date:' @122 rtrndate /

          @6  'Trip ID#: ' @16 tripnum
          @107 'Activity from:' @122 actdate1 /

          @118 'to:' @122 actdate2 //
          @1 '+---------------------------------+--------+--------+'
             '--------+--------+--------+--------+--------+--------+' /

          @1 '|                                 |  SUN  |  MON  |'
             '  TUE  |  WED  |  THU  |  FRI  |  SAT  |       |'
             '  PAID BY  PAID BY' /

          @1 '| EXPENSE DETAIL                       '
             '|  ' mday1 mmddyy5. '  |  ' mday2 mmddyy5.
             '|  ' mday3 mmddyy5. '  |  ' mday4 mmddyy5.
             '|  ' mday5 mmddyy5. '  |  ' mday6 mmddyy5.
             '|  ' mday7 mmddyy5.
          @100 '| TOTALS |  COMPANY EMPLOYEE' ;
      do i=1 to 15;

         if i=1 or i=10 or i=15 then
```

```
          put @1 '|-----------------------------------|--------|--------|'
                 '--------|--------|--------|--------|--------|--------|';
      if i=3 then
          put @1 '|' i category. @16 automile 4.0 @21 'miles @'
            @28 permile 3.2 @31 '/mile'  @37 '|' @;
          else put @1 '|' i category.  @37 '|' @;
      col=38;
      do j=1 to 10;
        if j<9 then put @col expenses{i,j} blanks8. '|' @;
            else if j=9 then put @col expenses{i,j} blanks8. @;
            else put @col expenses{i,j} blanks8.;
        col+9;
        if j=8 then col+2;
      end;
    end;
    Put @1 '+-----------------------------------+--------+--------+'
           '--------+--------+--------+--------+--------+--------+' //

        @1 'Travel Advance to Employee .............................'
           '..................................................'
        @121 empadv dollar8.2 //

        @1 'Reimbursement due Employee (or ATWR) ...................'
           '..................................................'
        @121 reimburs dollar8.2 //

        @1 'Other: (i.e. miscellaneous expenses and/or names of '
           'employees sharing receipt.)' /;
    do j=1 to 8;
      put @1 misc{j} ;
    end;
    put / @1   'APPROVED FOR PAYMENT BY: Authorizing Manager:'
        @48 '_____'
        @100 'Emp. #  _____' ///

        @27 'Employee Signature:'
        @48 '_____'
        @100 'Emp. #  ' empid ///

        @6 'Charge to Division:' @26 div $cuscore.
        @39 'Region:'           @48 region $cuscore.
        @59 'Dept:'             @66 deptchg $cuscore.
        @79 'Acct:'             @86 acct nuscore.
        @100 'Date:'            @107 rptdate /
        _page_;
run;
```

Example 3: Creating a HTML Report Using ODS and the DATA Step

```
options nodate pageno=1 linesize=64 pagesize=60;

ods html body='your_file.html';
```

```
title 'Leading Grain Producers';
title2 'for 1996';

proc format;
   value $cntry 'BRZ'='Brazil'
                'CHN'='China'
                'IND'='India'
                'INS'='Indonesia'
                'USA'='United States';
run;

data _null_;
   length Country $ 3 Type $ 5;
   input Year country $ type $ Kilotons;
   format country $cntry.;
   label type='Grain';

file print ods=(variables=(country
                           type
                           kilotons));

put _ods_;

   datalines;
1996 BRZ   Wheat    3302
1996 BRZ   Rice     10035
1996 BRZ   Corn     31975
1996 CHN   Wheat    109000
1996 CHN   Rice     190100
1996 CHN   Corn     119350
1996 IND   Wheat    62620
1996 IND   Rice     120012
1996 IND   Corn     8660
1996 INS   Wheat    .
1996 INS   Rice     51165
1996 INS   Corn     8925
1996 USA   Wheat    62099
1996 USA   Rice     7771
1996 USA   Corn     236064
;
run;


ods html close;
```

Display 20.1   HTML File Produced by ODS

Leading Grain Producers for 1996

Country	Grain	Kilotons
Brazil	Wheat	3302
Brazil	Rice	10035
Brazil	Corn	31975
China	Wheat	109000
China	Rice	190100
China	Corn	119350
India	Wheat	62620
India	Rice	120012
India	Corn	8660
Indonesia	Wheat	
Indonesia	Rice	51165
Indonesia	Corn	8925
United States	Wheat	62099
United States	Rice	7771
United States	Corn	236064

The DATA Step and ODS

The Output Delivery System (ODS) is a method of delivering output in a variety of formats and making these formats easy to access. ODS provides templates that define the structure of the output from DATA steps and from PROC steps. The DATA step allows you to use the ODS option in a FILE statement and in a PUT statement.

ODS combines raw data with one or more templates to produce several types of output called output objects. Output objects are sent to "destinations" such as the output destination, the listing destination, the printer destination, or Hypertext Markup Language (HTML). For more information, see "Output Delivery System" on page 170. For complete information about ODS, see *SAS Output Delivery System: User's Guide*.

CHAPTER
21

Reading Raw Data

Definition of Reading Raw Data   **357**
Ways to Read Raw Data   **358**
Kinds of Data   **358**
   Definitions   **358**
   Numeric Data   **359**
   Character Data   **360**
Sources of Raw Data   **361**
   Instream Data   **361**
   Instream Data Containing Semicolons   **362**
   External Files   **362**
Reading Raw Data with the INPUT Statement   **362**
   Choosing an Input Style   **362**
   List Input   **363**
   Modified List Input   **363**
   Column Input   **364**
   Formatted Input   **365**
   Named Input   **365**
   Additional Data-Reading Features   **366**
How SAS Handles Invalid Data   **367**
Reading Missing Values in Raw Data   **368**
   Representing Missing Values in Input Data   **368**
   Special Missing Values in Numeric Input Data   **368**
Reading Binary Data   **369**
   Definitions   **369**
   Using Binary Informats   **370**
Reading Column-Binary Data   **371**
   Definition   **371**
   How to Read Column-Binary Data   **371**
   Description of Column-Binary Data Storage   **372**

Definition of Reading Raw Data

raw data
> is unprocessed data that has not been read into a SAS data set. You can use a DATA step to read raw data into a SAS data set from two sources:
> - instream data
> - an external file.

CAUTION:
Raw data does not include Database Management System (DBMS) files. You must license SAS/ACCESS software to access data stored in DBMS files. See Chapter 33, "About SAS/ACCESS Software," on page 569 for more information about SAS/ACCESS features. △

Ways to Read Raw Data

You can read raw data by using:

☐ SAS statements

☐ SAS functions

☐ External File Interface (EFI)

☐ Import Wizard.

When you read raw data with a DATA step, you can use a combination of the INPUT, DATALINES, and INFILE statements. SAS automatically reads your data when you use these statements. For more information on these statements, see "Reading Raw Data with the INPUT Statement" on page 362.

You can also use SAS functions to manipulate external files and to read records of raw data. These functions provide more flexibility in handling raw data. For a description of available functions, see the External File and SAS File I/O categories in "Functions and CALL Routines by Category" in *SAS Language Reference: Dictionary*. For further information about how statements and functions manipulate files differently, see "Functions and CALL Routines" on page 38.

If your operating environment supports a graphical user interface, you can use the EFI or the Import Wizard to read raw data. The EFI is a point-and-click graphical interface that you can use to read and write data that is not in SAS software's internal format. By using EFI, you can read data from an external file and write it to a SAS data set, and you can read data from a SAS data set and write it to an external file. See *SAS/ACCESS for PC Files: Reference* for more information about EFI.

The Import Wizard guides you through the steps to read data from an external data source and write it to a SAS data set. As a wizard, it is a series of windows that present simple choices to guide you through a process. See *SAS/ACCESS for PC Files: Reference* for more information on the wizard.

Operating Environment Information: Using external files with your SAS jobs requires that you specify file names with syntax that is appropriate to your operating environment. See the SAS documentation for your operating environment for more information. △

Kinds of Data

Definitions

data values
are character or numeric values.

numeric value

contains only numbers, and sometimes a decimal point, a minus sign, or both. When they are read into a SAS data set, numeric values are stored in the floating-point format native to the operating environment. Nonstandard numeric values can contain other characters as numbers; you can use formatted input to enable SAS to read them.

character value
is a sequence of characters.

standard data
are character or numeric values that can be read with list, column, formatted, or named input. Examples of standard data include:

□ **ARKANSAS**

□ **1166.42**

nonstandard data
is data that can be read only with the aid of informats. Examples of nonstandard data include numeric values that contain commas, dollar signs, or blanks; date and time values; and hexadecimal and binary values.

Numeric Data

Numeric data can be represented in several ways. SAS can read standard numeric values without any special instructions. To read nonstandard values, SAS requires special instructions in the form of informats. Table 21.1 on page 359 shows standard, nonstandard, and invalid numeric data values and the special tools, if any, that are required to read them. For complete descriptions of all SAS informats, see *SAS Language Reference: Dictionary*.

Table 21.1 Reading Different Types of Numeric Data

Example of Numeric Data			Description	Solution Required to Read
			Standard Numeric Data	
		23	input right aligned	None needed
	23		input not aligned	None needed
23			input left aligned	None needed
00023			input with leading zeroes	None needed
23.0			input with decimal point	None needed
2.3E1			in E-notation, 2.30 (ss1)	None needed
230E−1			in E-notation, 230x10 (ss-1)	None needed
−23			minus sign for negative numbers	None needed
			Nonstandard Numeric Data	
2 3			embedded blank	COMMA. or BZ. informat
− 23			embedded blank	COMMA. or BZ. informat
2,341			comma	COMMA. informat
(23)			parentheses	COMMA. informat

Example of Numeric Data	Description	Solution Required to Read
C4A2	hexadecimal value	HEX. informat
1MAR90	date value	DATE. informat
Invalid Numeric Data		
23 –	minus sign follows number	Put minus sign before number or solve programmatically.[1]
..	double instead of single periods	Code missing values as a single period or use the ?? modifier in the INPUT statement to code any invalid input value as a missing value.
J23	not a number	Read as a character value, or edit the raw data to change it to a valid number.

1   It might be possible to use the S370FZDT*w.d* informat, but positive values require the trailing plus sign (+).

Remember the following rules for reading numeric data:

□ Parentheses or a minus sign preceding the number (without an intervening blank) indicates a negative value.

□ Leading zeros and the placement of a value in the input field do not affect the value assigned to the variable. Leading zeros and leading and trailing blanks are not stored with the value. Unlike some languages, SAS does not read trailing blanks as zeros by default. To cause trailing blanks to be read as zeros, use the BZ. informat described in *SAS Language Reference: Dictionary*.

□ Numeric data can have leading and trailing blanks but cannot have embedded blanks (unless they are read with a COMMA. or BZ. informat).

□ To read decimal values from input lines that do not contain explicit decimal points, indicate where the decimal point belongs by using a decimal parameter with column input or an informat with formatted input. See the full description of the INPUT statement in *SAS Language Reference: Dictionary* for more information. An explicit decimal point in the input data overrides any decimal specification in the INPUT statement.

Character Data

A value that is read with an INPUT statement is assumed to be a character value if one of the following is true:

□ A dollar sign ($) follows the variable name in the INPUT statement.

□ A character informat is used.

□ The variable has been previously defined as character: for example, in a LENGTH statement, in the RETAIN statement, by an assignment statement, or in an expression.

Input data that you want to store in a character variable can include any character. Use the guidelines in the following table when your raw data includes leading blanks and semicolons.

Table 21.2 Reading Instream Data and External Files Containing Leading Blanks and Semicolons

Characters in the Data	What to Use	Reason
leading or trailing blanks that you want to preserve	formatted input and the $CHARw. informat	list input trims leading and trailing blanks from a character value before the value is assigned to a variable.
semicolons in instream data	DATALINES4 or CARDS4 statements and four semicolons (;;;;) to mark the end of the data	with the normal DATALINES and CARDS statements, a semicolon in the data prematurely signals the end of the data.
delimiters, blank characters, or quoted strings	DSD option, with DELIMITER= option on the INFILE statement	it enables SAS to read a character value that contains a delimiter within a quoted string; it can also treat two consecutive delimiters as a missing value and remove quotation marks from character values.

Remember the following when reading character data:

□ In a DATA step, when you place a dollar sign ($) after a variable name in the INPUT statement, character data that is read from data lines remains in its original case. If you want SAS to read data from data lines as uppercase, use the CAPS system option or the $UPCASE informat.

□ If the value is shorter than the length of the variable, SAS adds blanks to the end of the value to give the value the specified length. This process is known as padding the value with blanks.

Sources of Raw Data

Instream Data

The following example uses the INPUT statement to read in instream data:

```
data weight;
   input PatientID $ Week1 Week8 Week16;
   loss=Week1-Week16;
   datalines;
2477 195 177 163
2431 220 213 198
2456 173 166 155
2412 135 125 116
;
```

Note: A semicolon appearing alone on the line immediately following the last data line is the convention that is used in this example. However, a PROC statement, DATA statement, or global statement ending in a semicolon on the line immediately following the last data line also submits the previous DATA step. △

Instream Data Containing Semicolons

The following example reads in instream data containing semicolons:

```
data weight;
   input PatientID $ Week1 Week8 Week16;
   loss=Week1-Week16;
   datalines4;
24;77 195 177 163
24;31 220 213 198
24;56 173 166 155
24;12 135 125 116
;;;;
```

External Files

The following example shows how to read in raw data from an external file using the INFILE and INPUT statements:

```
data weight;
   infile file-specification or path-name;
   input PatientID $ Week1 Week8 Week16;
   loss=Week1-Week16;
run;
```

Note: See the SAS documentation for your operating environment for information on how to specify a file with the INFILE statement. △

Reading Raw Data with the INPUT Statement

Choosing an Input Style

The INPUT statement reads raw data from instream data lines or external files into a SAS data set. You can use the following different input styles, depending on the layout of data values in the records:

□ list input

□ column input

□ formatted input

□ named input.

You can also combine styles of input in a single INPUT statement. For details about the styles of input, see the INPUT statement in *SAS Language Reference: Dictionary*.

List Input

List input uses a scanning method for locating data values. Data values are not required to be aligned in columns but must be separated by at least one blank (or other defined delimiter). List input requires only that you specify the variable names and a dollar sign ($), if defining a character variable. You do not have to specify the location of the data fields.

An example of list input follows:

```
data scores;
    length name $ 12;
    input name $ score1 score2;
    datalines;
Riley 1132 1187
Henderson 1015 1102
;
```

List input has several restrictions on the type of data that it can read:

☐ Input values must be separated by at least one blank (the default delimiter) or by the delimiter specified with the DELIMITER= option in the INFILE statement. If you want SAS to read consecutive delimiters as though there is a missing value between them, specify the DSD option in the INFILE statement.

☐ Blanks cannot represent missing values. A real value, such as a period, must be used instead.

☐ To read and store a character input value longer than 8 bytes, define a variable's length by using a LENGTH, INFORMAT, or ATTRIB statement prior to the INPUT statement, or by using modified list input, which consists of an informat and the colon modifier on the INPUT statement. See "Modified List Input" on page 363 for more information.

☐ Character values cannot contain embedded blanks when the file is delimited by blanks.

☐ Fields must be read in order.

☐ Data must be in standard numeric or character format.

Note: Nonstandard numeric values, such as packed decimal data, must use the formatted style of input. See "Formatted Input" on page 365 for more information. △

Modified List Input

A more flexible version of list input, called modified list input, includes format modifiers. The following format modifiers enable you to use list input to read nonstandard data by using SAS informats:

☐ The & (ampersand) format modifier enables you to read character values that contain embedded blanks with list input and to specify a character informat. SAS reads until it encounters multiple blanks.

☐ The : (colon) format modifier enables you to use list input but also to specify an informat after a variable name, whether character or numeric. SAS reads until it encounters a blank column.

☐ The ~ (tilde) format modifier enables you to read and retain single quotation marks, double quotation marks, and delimiters within character values.

The following is an example of the : and ~ format modifiers:

```
data scores;
   infile datalines dsd;
   input Name : $9. Score1-Score3 Team ~ $25. Div $;
   datalines;
Smith,12,22,46,"Green Hornets, Atlanta",AAA
Mitchel,23,19,25,"High Volts, Portland",AAA
Jones,09,17,54,"Vulcans, Las Vegas",AA
;

proc print data=scores noobs;
run;
```

Output 21.1 Output from Example with Format Modifiers

Name	Score1	Score2	Score3	Team	Div
Smith	12	22	46	"Green Hornets, Atlanta"	AAA
Mitchel	23	19	25	"High Volts, Portland"	AAA
Jones	9	17	54	"Vulcans, Las Vegas"	AA

Column Input

Column input enables you to read standard data values that are aligned in columns in the data records. Specify the variable name, followed by a dollar sign ($) if it is a character variable, and specify the columns in which the data values are located in each record:

```
data scores;
   infile datalines truncover;
   input name $ 1-12 score2 17-20 score1 27-30;
   datalines;
Riley          1132      987
Henderson      1015     1102
;
```

Note: Use the TRUNCOVER option on the INFILE statement to ensure that SAS handles data values of varying lengths appropriately. △

To use column input, data values must be:

□ in the same field on all the input lines

□ in standard numeric or character form.

Note: You cannot use an informat with column input. △

Features of column input include the following:

□ Character values can contain embedded blanks.

□ Character values can be from 1 to 32,767 characters long.

□ Placeholders, such as a single period (.), are not required for missing data.

☐ Input values can be read in any order, regardless of their position in the record.

☐ Values or parts of values can be reread.

☐ Both leading and trailing blanks within the field are ignored.

☐ Values do not need to be separated by blanks or other delimiters.

Formatted Input

Formatted input combines the flexibility of using informats with many of the features of column input. By using formatted input, you can read nonstandard data for which SAS requires additional instructions. Formatted input is typically used with pointer controls that enable you to control the position of the input pointer in the input buffer when you read data.

The INPUT statement in the following DATA step uses formatted input and pointer controls. Note that $12. and COMMA5. are informats and +4 and +6 are column pointer controls.

```
data scores;
    input name $12. +4 score1 comma5. +6 score2 comma5.;
    datalines;
Riley          1,132      1,187
Henderson      1,015      1,102
;
```

Note: You also can use informats to read data that is not aligned in columns. See "Modified List Input" on page 363 for more information. △

Important points about formatted input are:

☐ Characters values can contain embedded blanks.

☐ Character values can be from 1 to 32,767 characters long.

☐ Placeholders, such as a single period (.), are not required for missing data.

☐ With the use of pointer controls to position the pointer, input values can be read in any order, regardless of their positions in the record.

☐ Values or parts of values can be reread.

☐ Formatted input enables you to read data stored in nonstandard form, such as packed decimal or numbers with commas.

Named Input

You can use named input to read records in which data values are preceded by the name of the variable and an equal sign (=). The following INPUT statement reads the data lines containing equal signs.

```
data games;
    input name=$ score1= score2=;
    datalines;
name=riley score1=1132 score2=1187
;

proc print data=games;
run;
```

Note: When an equal sign follows a variable in an INPUT statement, SAS expects that data remaining on the input line contains only named input values. You cannot switch to another form of input in the same INPUT statement after using named input.

Also, note that any variable that exists in the input data but is not defined in the INPUT statement generates a note in the SAS log indicating a missing field. △

Additional Data-Reading Features

In addition to different styles of input, there are many tools to meet the needs of different data-reading situations. You can use options in the INFILE statement in combination with the INPUT statement to give you additional control over the reading of data records. Table 21.3 on page 366 lists common data-reading tasks and the appropriate features available in the INPUT and INFILE statements.

Table 21.3   Additional Data-Reading Features

Input Data Feature	Goal	Use
multiple records	create a single observation	#n or / line pointer control in the INPUT statement with a DO loop.
a single record	create multiple observations	trailing @@ in the INPUT statement.
		trailing @ with multiple INPUT and OUTPUT statements.
variable-length data fields and records	read delimited data	list input with or without a format modifier in the INPUT statement and the TRUNCOVER, DELIMITER= and/or DSD options in the INFILE statement.
	read non-delimited data	$VARYINGw.$ informat in the INPUT statement and the LENGTH= and TRUNCOVER options in the INFILE statement.
a file with varying record layouts		IF-THEN statements with multiple INPUT statements, using trailing @ or @@ as necessary.
hierarchical files		IF-THEN statements with multiple INPUT statements, using trailing @ as necessary.
more than one input file or to control the program flow at EOF		EOF= or END= option in an INFILE statement.
		multiple INFILE and INPUT statements.

Input Data Feature	Goal	Use
		FILEVAR=option in an INFILE statement.
		FILENAME statement with concatenation, wildcard, or piping.
only part of each record		LINESIZE=option in an INFILE statement.
some but not all records in the file		FIRSTOBS=and OBS= options in an INFILE statement; FIRSTOBS= and OBS= system options; #n line pointer control.
instream datalines	control the reading with special options	INFILE statement with DATALINES and appropriate options.
starting at a particular column		@ column pointer controls.
leading blanks	maintain them	$CHARw. informat in an INPUT statement.
a delimiter other than blanks (with list input or modified list input with the colon modifier)		DELIMITER= option and/or DSD option in an INFILE statement.
the standard tab character		DELIMITER= option in an INFILE statement; or the EXPANDTABS option in an INFILE statement.
missing values (with list input or modified list input with the colon modifier)	create observations without compromising data integrity; protect data integrity by overriding the default behavior	TRUNCOVER option in an INFILE statement; DSD and/or DELIMITER= options might also be needed.

For further information on data-reading features, see the INPUT and INFILE statements in *SAS Language Reference: Dictionary*.

How SAS Handles Invalid Data

An input value is invalid if it has any of the following characteristics:

☐ It requires an informat that is not specified.

☐ It does not conform to the informat specified.

☐ It does not match the input style used; for example, if it is read as standard numeric data (no dollar sign or informat) but does not conform to the rules for standard SAS numbers.

☐ It is out of range (too large or too small).

Operating Environment Information: The range for numeric values is operating environment-specific. See the SAS documentation for your operating environment for more information. △

If SAS reads a data value that is incompatible with the type specified for that variable, SAS tries to convert the value to the specified type, as described in "How SAS Handles Invalid Data" on page 367. If conversion is not possible, an error occurs, and SAS performs the following actions:

□ sets the value of the variable being read to missing or to the value specified with the INVALIDDATA= system option

□ prints an invalid data note in the SAS log

□ sets the automatic variable _ERROR_ to 1 for the current observation.

□ prints the input line and column number containing the invalid value in the SAS log. If a line contains unprintable characters, it is printed in hexadecimal form. A scale is printed above the input line to help determine column numbers

Reading Missing Values in Raw Data

Representing Missing Values in Input Data

Many collections of data contain some missing values. SAS can recognize these values as missing when it reads them. You use the following characters to represent missing values when reading raw data:

numeric missing values
are represented by a single decimal point (.). All input styles except list input also allow a blank to represent a missing numeric value.

character missing values
are represented by a blank, with one exception: list input requires that you use a period (.) to represent a missing value.

special numeric missing values
are represented by two characters: a decimal point (.) followed by either a letter or an underscore (_).

For more information about missing values, see Chapter 6, "Missing Values," on page 101.

Special Missing Values in Numeric Input Data

SAS enables you to differentiate among classes of missing values in numeric data. For numeric variables, you can designate up to 27 special missing values by using the letters A through Z, in either upper- or lowercase, and the underscore character (_).

The following example shows how to code missing values by using a MISSING statement in a DATA step:

```
data test_results;
   missing a b c;
   input name $8. Answer1 Answer2 Answer3;
   datalines;
Smith    2 5 9
Jones    4 b 8
Carter   a 4 7
Reed     3 5 c
;
```

```
proc print;
run;
```

Note that you must use a period when you specify a special missing numeric value in an expression or assignment statement, as in the following:

```
x=.d;
```

However, you do not need to specify each special missing numeric data value with a period in your input data. For example, the following DATA step, which uses periods in the input data for special missing values, produces the same result as the input data without periods:

```
data test_results;
   missing a b c;
   input name $8. Answer1 Answer2 Answer3;
   datalines;
Smith    2 5 9
Jones    4 .b 8
Carter   .a 4 7
Reed     3 5 .c
;

proc print;
run;
```

Output for both examples is shown here:

Output 21.2 Output of Data with Special Missing Numeric Values

```
                       The SAS System

        Obs      name      Answer1     Answer2     Answer3

         1      Smith        2           5           9
         2      Jones        4           B           8
         3      Carter       A           4           7
         4      Reed         3           5           C
```

Note: SAS displays and prints special missing values that use letters in uppercase. △

Reading Binary Data

Definitions

binary data
>   is numeric data that is stored in binary form. Binary numbers have a base of two and are represented with the digits 0 and 1.

packed decimal data
>   are binary decimal numbers that are encoded by using each byte to represent two decimal digits. Packed decimal representation stores decimal data with exact

precision; the fractional part of the number must be determined by using an informat or format because there is no separate mantissa and exponent.

zoned decimal data
> are binary decimal numbers that are encoded so that each digit requires one byte of storage. The last byte contains the number's sign as well as the last digit. Zoned decimal data produces a printable representation.

Using Binary Informats

SAS can read binary data with the special instructions supplied by SAS informats. You can use formatted input and specify the informat in the INPUT statement. The informat you choose is determined by the following factors:

☐ the type of number being read: binary, packed decimal, zoned decimal, or a variation of one of these

☐ the type of system on which the data was created

☐ the type of system that you use to read the data.

Different computer platforms store numeric binary data in different forms. The ordering of bytes differs by platforms that are referred to as either "big endian" or "little endian." For more information, see "Byte Ordering for Integer Binary Data on Big Endian and Little Endian Platforms" on page 32.

SAS provides a number of informats for reading binary data and corresponding formats for writing binary data. Some of these informats read data in native mode, that is, by using the byte-ordering system that is standard for the system on which SAS is running. Other informats force the data to be read by the IBM 370 standard, regardless of the native mode of the system on which SAS is running. The informats that read in native or IBM 370 mode are listed in the following table.

Table 21.4   Informats for Native or IBM 370 Mode

Description	Native Mode Informats	IBM 370 Mode Informats
ASCII Character	$w.	$ASCII$w$.
ASCII Numeric	$w.d$	$ASCII$w$.
EBCDIC Character	$w.	$EBCDIC$w$.
EBCDIC Numeric (Standard)	$w.d$	S370FF$w.d$
Integer Binary	IB$w.d$	S370FIB$w.d$
Positive Integer Binary	PIB$w.d$	S370FPIB$w.d$
Real Binary	RB$w.d$	S370FRB$w.d$
Unsigned Integer Binary	PIB$w.d$	S370FIBU$w.d$, S370FPIB$w.d$
Packed Decimal	PD$w.d$	S370FPD$w.d$
Unsigned Packed Decimal	PK$w.d$	S370FPDU$w.d$ or PK$w.d$
Zoned Decimal	ZD$w.d$	S370FZD$w.d$
Zoned Decimal Leading Sign	S370FZDL$w.d$	S370FZDL$w.d$
Zoned Decimal Separate Leading Sign	S370FZDS$w.d$	S370FZDS$w.d$

Description	Native Mode Informats	IBM 370 Mode Informats
Zoned Decimal Separate Trailing Sign	S370FZDT*w.d*	S370FZDT*w.d*
Unsigned Zoned Decimal	ZD*w.d*	S370FZDU*w.d*

If you write a SAS program that reads binary data and that will be run on only one type of system, you can use the native mode informats and formats. However, if you want to write SAS programs that can be run on multiple systems that use different byte-storage systems, use the IBM 370 informats. The IBM 370 informats enable you to write SAS programs that can read data in this format and that can be run in any SAS environment, regardless of the standard for storing numeric data.* The IBM 370 informats can also be used to read data originally written with the corresponding native mode formats on an IBM mainframe.

For complete descriptions of all SAS formats and informats, including how numeric binary data is written, see *SAS Language Reference: Dictionary.*

Reading Column-Binary Data

Definition

column-binary data storage
is an older form of data storage that is no longer widely used and is not needed by most SAS users. Column-binary data storage compresses data so that more than 80 items of data can be stored on a single punched card. The advantage is that this method enables you to store more data in the same amount of space. There are disadvantages, however; special card readers are required and difficulties are frequently encountered when this type of data is read. Because multi-punched decks and card-image data sets remain in existence, SAS provides informats for reading column-binary data. See "Description of Column-Binary Data Storage" on page 372 for a more detailed explanation of column-binary data storage.

How to Read Column-Binary Data

To read column-binary data with SAS, you need to know:
□ how to select the appropriate SAS column-binary informat
□ how to set the RECFM= and LRECL= options in the INFILE statement
□ how to use pointer controls.

The following table lists and describes SAS column-binary informats.

---

* For example, using the IBM 370 informats, you could download data that contain binary integers from a mainframe to a PC and then use the S370FIB informats to read the data.

Table 21.5   SAS Informats for Reading Column-Binary Data

Informat Name	Description
$CB*w*.	reads standard character data from column-binary files
CB*w*.	reads standard numeric data from column-binary files
PUNCH.*d*	reads whether a row is punched
ROW*w.d*	reads a column-binary field down a card column

To read column-binary data, you must set two options in the INFILE statement:

☐ Set RECFM= to F for fixed.

☐ Set the LRECL= to 160, because each card column of column-binary data is expanded to two bytes before the fields are read.

For example, to read column-binary data from a file, use an INFILE statement in the following form before the INPUT statement that reads the data:

```
infile file-specification or path-name
  recfm=f lrecl=160;
```

Note: The expansion of each column of column-binary data into two bytes does *not* affect the position of the column pointer. You use the absolute column pointer control @, as usual, because the informats automatically compute the true location on the doubled record. If a value is in column 23, use the pointer control @23 to move the pointer there. △

Description of Column-Binary Data Storage

The arrangement and numbering of rows in a column on punched cards originated with the Hollerith system of encoding characters and numbers. It is based on using a pair of values to represent either a character or a numeric digit. In the Hollerith system, each column on a card has a maximum of two punches, one punch in the zone portion, and one in the digit portion. These punches correspond to a pair of values, and each pair of values corresponds to a specific alphabetic character or sign and numeric digit.

In the zone portion of the punched card, which is the first three rows, the zone component of the pair can have the values 12, 11, 0 (or 10), or not punched. In the digit portion of the card, which is the fourth through the twelfth rows, the digit component of the pair can have the values 1 through 9, or not punched.

The following figure shows the multi-punch combinations corresponding to letters of the alphabet.

Figure 21.1 Columns and Rows in a Punched Card

```
              row    punch

              12     X X X X X X X X - - - - - - - - - - - - - - - -
zone          11     - - - - - - - - - X X X X X X X X X - - - - - - -
portion       10     - - - - - - - - - - - - - - - - - - X X X X X X X X


               1     X - - - - - - - X - - - - - - - - - - - - - - -
               2     - X - - - - - - - X - - - - - - - X - - - - - -
               3     - - X - - - - - - - X - - - - - - - X - - - - -
               4     - - - X - - - - - - - X - - - - - - - X - - - -
digit          5     - - - - X - - - - - - - X - - - - - - - X - - -
portion        6     - - - - - X - - - - - - - X - - - - - - - X - - -
               7     - - - - - - X - - - - - - - X - - - - - - - X - -
               8     - - - - - - - X - - - - - - - X - - - - - - - X -
               9     - - - - - - - - X - - - - - - - X - - - - - - X

alphabetic
character             A B C D E F G H I J K L M N O P Q R S T U V W X Y Z
```

SAS stores each column of column-binary data in two bytes. Since each column has only 12 positions and since 2 bytes contain 16 positions, the 4 extra positions within the bytes are located at the beginning of each byte. The following figure shows the correspondence between the rows of a punched card and the positions within 2 bytes that SAS uses to store them. SAS stores a punched position as a binary 1 bit and an unpunched position as a binary 0 bit.

Figure 21.2   Column-Binary Representation on a Punched Card

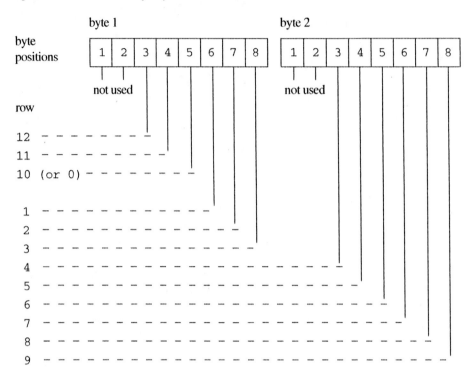

BY-Group Processing in the DATA Step

Definitions for BY-Group Processing **375**
Syntax for BY-Group Processing **376**
Understanding BY Groups **377**
    BY Groups with a Single BY Variable **377**
    BY Groups with Multiple BY Variables **378**
Invoking BY-Group Processing **378**
Determining Whether the Data Requires Preprocessing for BY-Group Processing **379**
Preprocessing Input Data for BY-Group Processing **379**
    Sorting Observations for BY-Group Processing **379**
    Indexing for BY-Group Processing **379**
How the DATA Step Identifies BY Groups **380**
    Processing Observations in a BY Group **380**
    How SAS Determines FIRST.VARIABLE and LAST.VARIABLE **380**
        Grouping Observations by State, City, Zip Code, and Street **380**
        Grouping Observations by City, State, Zip Code, and Street **381**
        Grouping Observations: Another Example **382**
Processing BY-Groups in the DATA Step **383**
    Overview **383**
    Processing BY-Groups Conditionally **383**
    Data Not in Alphabetic or Numeric Order **384**
    Data Grouped by Formatted Values **385**

Definitions for BY-Group Processing

BY-group processing
    is a method of processing observations from one or more SAS data sets that are grouped or ordered by values of one or more common variables. The most common use of BY-group processing in the DATA step is to combine two or more SAS data sets by using the BY statement with a SET, MERGE, MODIFY, or UPDATE statement.

BY variable
    names a variable or variables by which the data set is sorted or indexed. All data sets must be ordered or indexed on the values of the BY variable if you use the SET, MERGE, or UPDATE statements. If you use MODIFY, data does not need to be ordered. However, your program might run more efficiently with ordered data. All data sets that are being combined must include one or more BY variables. The position of the BY variable in the observations does not matter.

BY value
is the value or formatted value of the BY variable.

BY group
includes all observations with the same BY value. If you use more than one variable in a BY statement, a BY group is a group of observations with the same combination of values for these variables. Each BY group has a unique combination of values for the variables.

FIRST.variable and *LAST.variable*
are variables that SAS creates for each BY variable. SAS sets FIRST.*variable* when it is processing the first observation in a BY group, and sets LAST.*variable* when it is processing the last observation in a BY group. These assignments enable you to take different actions, based on whether processing is starting for a new BY group or ending for a BY group. For more information, see "How the DATA Step Identifies BY Groups" on page 380.

For more information about BY-Group processing, see Chapter 23, "Reading, Combining, and Modifying SAS Data Sets," on page 387. See also *Combining and Modifying SAS Data Sets: Examples*.

Syntax for BY-Group Processing

Use one of the following forms for BY-group processing:

BY *variable(s)*;

BY <DESCENDING> *variable(s)* <NOTSORTED> <GROUPFORMAT>;

where

variable
names each variable by which the data set is sorted or indexed.

Note: All data sets must be ordered or indexed on the values of the BY variable if you process them using the SET, MERGE, or UPDATE statements. If you use the MODIFY statement, your data does not need to be ordered. However, your program might run more efficiently with ordered data. All data sets that are being combined must include the BY variable or variables. The position of the BY variable in the observations does not matter.   △

GROUPFORMAT
uses the formatted values, instead of the internal values, of the BY variables to determine where BY-groups begin and end, and therefore how FIRST.*variable* and LAST.*variable* are assigned. Although the GROUPFORMAT option can appear anywhere in the BY statement, the option applies to *all* variables in the BY statement.

DESCENDING
indicates that the data sets are sorted in descending order (largest to smallest) by the variable that is specified. If you have more that one variable in the BY group, DESCENDING applies only to the variable that immediately follows it.

NOTSORTED
specifies that observations with the same BY value are grouped together but are not necessarily stored in alphabetical or numeric order.

For complete information about the BY statement, see *SAS Language Reference: Dictionary*.

Understanding BY Groups

BY Groups with a Single BY Variable

The following figure represents the results of processing your data with the single BY variable ZipCode. The input SAS data set contains street names, cities, states, and ZIP codes that are arranged in an order that you can use with the following BY statement:

```
by ZipCode;
```

The figure shows five BY groups each containing the BY variable ZipCode. The data set is shown with the BY variable ZipCode printed on the left for easy reading, but the position of the BY variable in the observations does not matter.

Figure 22.1 BY Groups for the Single BY Variable ZipCode

BY variable

ZipCode	State	City	Street	
33133	FL	Miami	Rice St	
33133	FL	Miami	Thomas Ave	BY group
33133	FL	Miami	Surrey Dr	
33133	FL	Miami	Trade Ave	
33146	FL	Miami	Nervia St	BY group
33146	FL	Miami	Corsica St	
33801	FL	Lakeland	French Ave	BY group
33809	FL	Lakeland	Egret Dr	BY Group
85730	AZ	Tucson	Domenic Ln	BY group
85730	AZ	Tucson	Gleeson Pl	

The first BY group contains all observations with the smallest BY value, which is 33133; the second BY group contains all observations with the next smallest BY value, which is 33146, and so on.

BY Groups with Multiple BY Variables

The following figure represents the results of processing your data with two BY variables, State and City. This example uses the same data set as in "BY Groups with a Single BY Variable" on page 377, and is arranged in an order that you can use with the following BY statement:

```
by State City;
```

The figure shows three BY groups. The data set is shown with the BY variables State and City printed on the left for easy reading, but the position of the BY variables in the observations does not matter.

Figure 22.2 BY Groups for the BY Variables State and City

BY variables

State	City	Street	ZipCode	
AZ	Tucson	Domenic Ln	85730	BY group
AZ	Tucson	Gleeson Pl	85730	
FL	Lakeland	French Ave	33801	BY group
FL	Lakeland	Egret Dr	33809	
FL	Miami	Nervia St	33146	BY group
FL	Miami	Rice St	33133	
FL	Miami	Corsica St	33146	
FL	Miami	Thomas Ave	33133	
FL	Miami	Surrey Dr	33133	
FL	Miami	Trade Ave	33133	

The observations are arranged so that the observations for Arizona occur first. The observations within each value of State are arranged in order of the value of City. Each BY group has a unique combination of values for the variables State and City. For example, the BY value of the first BY group is **`AZ Tucson`**, and the BY value of the second BY group is **`FL Lakeland`**.

Invoking BY-Group Processing

You can invoke BY-group processing in both DATA steps and PROC steps by using a BY statement. For example, the following DATA step program uses the SET statement to combine observations from three SAS data sets by interleaving the files. The BY statement shows how the data is ordered.

```
data all_sales;
   set region1 region2 region3;
   by State City Zip;
   ... more SAS statements ...
run;
```

This section describes BY-group processing for the DATA step. For information about BY-group processing with procedures, see *Base SAS Procedures Guide*.

Determining Whether the Data Requires Preprocessing for BY-Group Processing

Before you process one or more SAS data sets using grouped or ordered data with the SET, MERGE, or UPDATE statements, you must check the data to determine if they require preprocessing. They require no preprocessing if the observations in all of the data sets occur in one of the following patterns:

□ ascending or descending numeric order

□ ascending or descending character order

□ not alphabetically or numerically ordered, but grouped in some way, such as by calendar month or by a formatted value.

If the observations are not in the order that you want, you must either sort the data set or create an index for it before using BY-group processing.

If you use the MODIFY statement in BY-group processing, you do not need to presort the input data. Presorting, however, can make processing more efficient and less costly.

You can use PROC SQL views in BY-group processing. For complete information, see *SAS SQL Procedure User's Guide*.

SAS/ACCESS Users: If you use views or librefs, refer to the SAS/ACCESS documentation for your operating environment for information about using BY groups in your SAS programs.

Preprocessing Input Data for BY-Group Processing

Sorting Observations for BY-Group Processing

You can use the SORT procedure to change the physical order of the observations in the data set. You can either replace the original data set, or create a new, sorted data set by using the OUT= option of the SORT procedure. In this example, PROC SORT rearranges the observations in the data set INFORMATION based on ascending values of the variables State and ZipCode, and replaces the original data set.

```
proc sort data=information;
   by State ZipCode;
run;
```

As a general rule, when you use PROC SORT, specify the variables in the BY statement in the same order that you plan to specify them in the BY statement in the DATA step. For a detailed description of the default sorting orders for numeric and character variables, see the SORT procedure in *Base SAS Procedures Guide*.

Indexing for BY-Group Processing

You can also ensure that observations are processed in ascending numeric or character order by creating an index based on one or more variables in the SAS data set.

If you specify a BY statement in a DATA step, SAS looks for an appropriate index. If one exists, SAS automatically retrieves the observations from the data set in indexed order.

Note: Because indexes require additional resources to create and maintain, you should determine if their use significantly improves performance. Depending on the nature of the data in your SAS data set, using PROC SORT to order data values can be more advantageous than indexing. For an overview of indexes, see "Understanding SAS Indexes" on page 518. △

How the DATA Step Identifies BY Groups

Processing Observations in a BY Group

In the DATA step, SAS identifies the beginning and end of each BY group by creating two temporary variables for each BY variable: FIRST.*variable* and LAST.*variable*. These temporary variables are available for DATA step programming but are not added to the output data set. Their values indicate whether an observation is

- □ the first one in a BY group
- □ the last one in a BY group
- □ neither the first nor the last one in a BY group
- □ both first and last, as is the case when there is only one observation in a BY group.

You can take actions conditionally, based on whether you are processing the first or the last observation in a BY group.

How SAS Determines FIRST.VARIABLE and LAST.VARIABLE

When an observation is the first in a BY group, SAS sets the value of FIRST.*variable* to 1 for the variable whose value changed, as well as for all of the variables that follow in the BY statement. For all other observations in the BY group, the value of FIRST.*variable* is 0. Likewise, if the observation is the last in a BY group, SAS sets the value of LAST.*variable* to 1 for the variable whose value changes on the next observation, as well as for all of the variables that follow in the BY statement. For all other observations in the BY group, the value of LAST.*variable* is 0. For the last observation in a data set, the value of all LAST.*variable* variables are set to 1.

Grouping Observations by State, City, Zip Code, and Street

This example shows how SAS uses the FIRST.*variable* and LAST.*variable* to flag the beginning and end of four BY groups: State, City, ZipCode, and Street. Six temporary variables are created within the program data vector. These variables can be used during the DATA step, but they do not become variables in the new data set.

In the figure that follows, observations in the SAS data set are arranged in an order that can be used with this BY statement:

```
by State City ZipCode;
```

SAS creates the following temporary variables: FIRST.State, LAST.State, FIRST.City, LAST.City, FIRST.ZipCode, and LAST.ZipCode.

Observations in Four BY Groups				Corresponding FIRST. and LAST. Values					
State	City	ZipCode	Street	FIRST. State	LAST. State	FIRST. City	LAST. City	FIRST. ZipCode	LAST. ZipCode
AZ	Tucson	85730	Glen Pl	1	1	1	1	1	1
FL	Miami	33133	Rice St	1	0	1	0	1	0
FL	Miami	33133	Tom Ave	0	0	0	0	0	0
FL	Miami	33133	Surrey Dr	0	0	0	0	0	1
FL	Miami	33146	Nervia St	0	0	0	0	1	0
FL	Miami	33146	Corsica St	0	1	0	1	0	1
OH	Miami	45056	Myrtle St	1	1	1	1	1	1

Grouping Observations by City, State, Zip Code, and Street

This example shows how SAS uses the FIRST.*variable* and LAST.*variable* to flag the beginning and end of four BY groups: City, State, ZipCode, and Street. Six temporary variables are created within the program data vector. These variables can be used during the DATA step, but they do not become variables in the new data set.

In the figure that follows, observations in the SAS data set are arranged in an order that can be used with this BY statement:

```
by City State ZipCode;
```

SAS creates the following temporary variables: FIRST.City, LAST.City, FIRST.State, LAST.State, FIRST.ZipCode, and LAST.ZipCode.

Observations in Four BY Groups				Corresponding FIRST. and LAST. Values					
City	State	ZipCode	Street	FIRST. City	LAST. City	FIRST. State	LAST. State	FIRST. ZipCode	LAST. ZipCode
Miami	FL	33133	Rice St	1	0	1	0	1	0
Miami	FL	33133	Tom Ave	0	0	0	0	0	0
Miami	FL	33133	Surrey Dr	0	0	0	0	0	1
Miami	FL	33146	Nervia St	0	0	0	0	1	0
Miami	FL	33146	Corsica St	0	0	0	1	0	1
Miami	OH	45056	Myrtle St	0	1	1	1	1	1
Tucson	AZ	85730	Glen Pl	1	1	1	1	1	1

Grouping Observations: Another Example

The value of FIRST.*variable* can be affected by a change in a previous value, even if the current value of the variable remains the same.

In this example, the value of FIRST.*variable* and LAST.*variable* are dependent on sort order, and not just by the value of the BY variable. For observation 3, the value of FIRST.Y is set to 1 because BLUEBERRY is a new value for **Y**. This change in **Y** causes FIRST.Z to be set to 1 as well, even though the value of Z did not change.

```
options pageno=1 nodate linesize=80 pagesize=60;

data testfile;
   input x $ y $ 9-17 z $ 19-26;
   datalines;
apple   banana     coconut
apple   banana     coconut
apricot blueberry  citron
;

data _null_;
   set testfile;
   by x y z;
   if _N_=1 then put 'Grouped by X Y Z';
   put _N_= x= first.x= last.x= first.y= last.y= first.z= last.z= ;
run;

data _null_;
   set testfile;
   by y x z;
   if _N_=1 then put 'Grouped by Y X Z';
   put _N_= x= first.x= last.x= first.y= last.y= first.z= last.z= ;
run;
```

Output 22.1   Partial SAS Log Showing the Results of Processing with BY Variables

```
Grouped by X Y Z
_N_=1 x=Apple FIRST.x=1 LAST.x=0 FIRST.y=1 LAST.y=0 FIRST.z=1 LAST.z=0
_N_=2 x=Apple FIRST.x=0 LAST.x=0 FIRST.y=0 LAST.y=1 FIRST.z=0 LAST.z=1
_N_=3 x=Apple FIRST.x=0 LAST.x=1 FIRST.y=1 LAST.y=1 FIRST.z=1 LAST.z=1
_N_=4 x=Apricot FIRST.x=1 LAST.x=1 FIRST.y=1 LAST.y=1 FIRST.z=1 LAST.z=1

Grouped by Y X Z
_N_=1 x=Apple FIRST.x=1 LAST.x=0 FIRST.y=1 LAST.y=0 FIRST.z=1 LAST.z=0
_N_=2 x=Apple FIRST.x=0 LAST.x=1 FIRST.y=0 LAST.y=1 FIRST.z=0 LAST.z=1
_N_=3 x=Apple FIRST.x=1 LAST.x=1 FIRST.y=1 LAST.y=0 FIRST.z=1 LAST.z=1
_N_=4 x=Apricot FIRST.x=1 LAST.x=1 FIRST.y=0 LAST.y=1 FIRST.z=1 LAST.z=1
```

Processing BY-Groups in the DATA Step

Overview

The most common use of BY-group processing in the DATA step is to combine two or more SAS data sets using a BY statement with a SET, MERGE, MODIFY, or UPDATE statement. (If you use a SET, MERGE, or UPDATE statement with the BY statement, your observations must be grouped or ordered.) When processing these statements, SAS reads one observation at a time into the program data vector. With BY-group processing, SAS selects the observations from the data sets according to the values of the BY variable or variables. After processing all the observations from one BY group, SAS expects the next observation to be from the next BY group.

The BY statement modifies the action of the SET, MERGE, MODIFY, or UPDATE statement by controlling when the values in the program data vector are set to missing. During BY-group processing, SAS retains the values of variables until it has copied the last observation it finds for that BY group in any of the data sets. Without the BY statement, the SET statement sets variables to missing when it reads the last observation from any data set, and the MERGE statement does not set variables to missing after the DATA step starts reading observations into the program data vector.

Processing BY-Groups Conditionally

You can process observations conditionally by using the subsetting IF or IF-THEN statements, or the SELECT statement, with the temporary variables FIRST.*variable* and LAST.*variable* (set up during BY-group processing). For example, you can use them to perform calculations for each BY group and to write an observation when the first or the last observation of a BY group has been read into the program data vector.

The following example computes annual payroll by department. It uses IF-THEN statements and the values of FIRST.*variable* and LAST.*variable* automatic variables to reset the value of PAYROLL to 0 at the beginning of each BY group and to write an observation after the last observation in a BY group is processed.

```
options pageno=1 nodate linesize=80 pagesize=60;

data salaries;
   input Department $ Name $ WageCategory $ WageRate;
   datalines;
BAD Carol Salaried 20000
BAD Elizabeth Salaried 5000
BAD Linda Salaried 7000
BAD Thomas Salaried 9000
BAD Lynne Hourly 230
DDG Jason Hourly 200
DDG Paul Salaried 4000
PPD Kevin Salaried 5500
PPD Amber Hourly 150
PPD Tina Salaried 13000
STD Helen Hourly 200
STD Jim Salaried 8000
;
```

```
proc print data=salaries;
run;


proc sort data=salaries out=temp;
   by Department;
run;

data budget (keep=Department Payroll);
   set temp;
   by Department;
   if WageCategory='Salaried' then YearlyWage=WageRate*12;
   else if WageCategory='Hourly' then YearlyWage=WageRate*2000;

      /* SAS sets FIRST.variable to 1 if this is a new      */
      /* department in the BY group.                        */
   if first.Department then Payroll=0;
   Payroll+YearlyWage;

      /* SAS sets LAST.variable to 1 if this is the last    */
      /* department in the current BY group.                */
   if last.Department;
run;

proc print data=budget;
   format Payroll dollar10.;
   title 'Annual Payroll by Department';
run;
```

Output 22.2   Output from Conditional BY-Group Processing

```
                     Annual Payroll by Department                         1

            Obs      Department        Payroll

             1          BAD           $952,000
             2          DDG           $448,000
             3          PPD           $522,000
             4          STD           $496,000
```

Data Not in Alphabetic or Numeric Order

In BY-group processing, you can use data that is arranged in an order other than
alphabetic or numeric, such as by calendar month or by category. To do this, use the
NOTSORTED option in a BY statement when you use a SET statement. The
NOTSORTED option in the BY statement tells SAS that the data is not in alphabetic or
numeric order, but that it is arranged in groups by the values of the BY variable. You
cannot use the NOTSORTED option with the MERGE statement, the UPDATE
statement, or when the SET statement lists more than one data set.

This example assumes that the data is grouped by the character variable MONTH. The subsetting IF statement conditionally writes an observation, based on the value of LAST.month. This DATA step writes an observation only after processing the last observation in each BY group.

```
data total_sale(drop=sales);
   set region.sales
   by month notsorted;
   total+sales;
   if last.month;
run;
```

Data Grouped by Formatted Values

Use the GROUPFORMAT option in the BY statement to ensure that

□ formatted values are used to group observations when a FORMAT statement and a BY statement are used together in a DATA step

□ the FIRST.*variable* and LAST.*variable* are assigned by the formatted values of the variable.

The GROUPFORMAT option is valid only in the DATA step that creates the SAS data set. It is particularly useful with user-defined formats. The following example illustrates the use of the GROUPFORMAT option.

```
proc format;
   value range
      low -55 = 'Under 55'
      55-60   = '55 to 60'
      60-65   = '60 to 65'
      65-70   = '65 to 70'
      other   = 'Over 70';
run;

proc sort data=class out=sorted_class;
   by height;
run;

data _null_;
   format height range.;
   set sorted_class;
      by height groupformat;
   if first.height then
      put 'Shortest in ' height 'measures ' height:best12.;
run;
```

SAS writes the following output to the log:

```
Shortest in Under 55 measures 51.3
Shortest in 55 to 60 measures 56.3
Shortest in 60 to 65 measures 62.5
Shortest in 65 to 70 measures 65.3
Shortest in Over 70 measures 72
```

CHAPTER

23

Reading, Combining, and Modifying SAS Data Sets

Definitions for Reading, Combining, and Modifying SAS Data Sets **389**
Overview of Tools **389**
Reading SAS Data Sets **390**
    Reading a Single SAS Data Set **390**
    Reading from Multiple SAS Data Sets **390**
    Controlling the Reading and Writing of Variables and Observations **390**
Combining SAS Data Sets: Basic Concepts **391**
    What You Need to Know before Combining Information Stored In Multiple SAS Data Sets **391**
    The Four Ways That Data Can Be Related **391**
        One-to-One **392**
        One-to-Many and Many-to-One **392**
        Many-to-Many **393**
    Access Methods: Sequential versus Direct **394**
        Overview **394**
        Sequential Access **394**
        Direct Access **394**
    Overview of Methods for Combining SAS Data Sets **395**
        Concatenating **395**
        Interleaving **395**
        One-to-One Reading and One-to-One Merging **396**
        Match-Merging **397**
        Updating **397**
    Overview of Tools for Combining SAS Data Sets **398**
        Using Statements and Procedures **398**
        Using Error Checking **400**
    How to Prepare Your Data Sets **400**
        Knowing the Structure and Contents of the Data Sets **400**
        Looking at Sources of Common Problems **400**
        Ensuring Correct Order **401**
        Testing Your Program **401**
Combining SAS Data Sets: Methods **402**
    Concatenating **402**
        Definition **402**
        Syntax **402**
        DATA Step Processing During Concatenation **402**
        Example 1: Concatenation Using the DATA Step **403**
        Example 2: Concatenation Using SQL **404**
        Appending Files **404**
        Efficiency **405**
    Interleaving **405**
        Definition **405**

Syntax   **405**

Sort Requirements   **406**

DATA Step Processing During Interleaving   **406**

Example 1: Interleaving in the Simplest Case   **406**

Example 2: Interleaving with Duplicate Values of the BY variable   **407**

Example 3: Interleaving with Different BY Values in Each Data Set   **408**

Comments and Comparisons   **409**

One-to-One Reading   **409**

Definition   **409**

Syntax   **409**

DATA Step Processing During a One-to-One Reading   **410**

Example 1: One-to-One Reading: Processing an Equal Number of Observations   **410**

Comments and Comparisons   **411**

One-to-One Merging   **411**

Definition   **411**

Syntax   **412**

DATA Step Processing During One-to-One Merging   **412**

Example 1: One-to-One Merging with an Equal Number of Observations   **413**

Example 2: One-to-One Merging with an Unequal Number of Observations   **413**

Example 3: One-to-One Merging with Duplicate Values of Common Variables   **414**

Example 4: One-to-One Merging with Different Values of Common Variables   **415**

Comments and Comparisons   **416**

Match-Merging   **416**

Definition   **416**

Syntax   **416**

DATA Step Processing During Match-Merging   **417**

Example 1: Combining Observations Based on a Criterion   **417**

Example 2: Match-Merge with Duplicate Values of the BY Variable   **418**

Example 3: Match-Merge with Nonmatched Observations   **419**

Updating with the UPDATE and the MODIFY Statements   **420**

Definitions   **420**

Syntax of the UPDATE Statement   **420**

Syntax of the MODIFY Statement   **421**

DATA Step Processing with the UPDATE Statement   **421**

Updating with Nonmatched Observations, Missing Values, and New Variables   **422**

Sort Requirements for the UPDATE Statement   **422**

Using an Index with the MODIFY Statement   **422**

Choosing between UPDATE or MODIFY with BY   **422**

Primary Uses of the MODIFY Statement   **423**

Example 1: Using UPDATE for Basic Updating   **424**

Example 2: Using UPDATE with Duplicate Values of the BY Variable   **424**

Example 3: Using UPDATE for Processing Nonmatched Observations, Missing Values, and New Variables   **425**

Example 4: Updating a MASTER Data Set by Adding an Observation   **427**

Error Checking When Using Indexes to Randomly Access or Update Data   **428**

The Importance of Error Checking   **428**

Error-Checking Tools   **428**

Example 1: Routing Execution When an Unexpected Condition Occurs   **429**

Overview   **429**

Input Data Sets   **429**

Original Program   **430**

Resulting Log   **430**

Resulting Data Set   **430**

Revised Program   **431**

Resulting Log **431**
Correctly Updated MASTER Data Set **432**
Example 2: Using Error Checking on All Statements That Use KEY= **432**
Overview **432**
Input Data Sets **432**
Original Program with Logic Error **432**
Resulting Log **433**
Resulting Data Set **434**
Revised Program **434**
Resulting Log **435**
Correctly Created COMBINE Data Set **436**

Definitions for Reading, Combining, and Modifying SAS Data Sets

In the context of DATA step processing, the terms reading, combining and modifying have these meanings:

Reading a SAS data set
refers to opening a SAS data set and bringing an observation into the program data vector for processing.

Combining SAS data sets
refers to reading data from two or more SAS data sets and processing them by

- concatenating
- interleaving
- one-to-one reading
- one-to-one merging
- match-merging
- updating a master data set with a transaction data set.

The methods for combining SAS data sets are defined in "Combining SAS Data Sets: Methods" on page 402.

Modifying SAS data sets
refers to using the MODIFY statement to update information in a SAS data set in place. The MODIFY statement can save disk space because it modifies data in place, without creating a copy of the data set. You can modify a SAS data set with programming statements or with information that is stored in another data set.

Overview of Tools

The primary tools that are used for reading, combining, and modifying SAS data sets are four statements: SET, MERGE, MODIFY, and UPDATE. This section describes these tools and shows examples. For complete information about these statements see the *SAS Language Reference: Dictionary*.

Reading SAS Data Sets

Reading a Single SAS Data Set

To read data from an existing SAS data set, use a SET statement. In this example, the DATA step creates data set PERM.TOUR155_PEAKCOST by reading data from data set PERM.TOUR155_BASIC_COST and by calculating values for the three new variables Total_Cost, Peak_Cost, and Average_Night_Cost.

```
data perm.tour155_peakcost;
   set perm.tour155_basic_cost;
   Total_Cost=AirCost+LandCost;
   Peak_Cost=(AirCost*1.15);
   Average_Night_Cost=LandCost/Nights;
run;
```

Reading from Multiple SAS Data Sets

You can read from multiple SAS data sets and combine and modify data in different ways. You can, for example, combine two or more input data sets to create one output data set, merge data from two or more input data sets that share a common variable, and update a master file based on transaction records.

For details about reading from multiple SAS data sets, see "Combining SAS Data Sets: Methods" on page 402.

Controlling the Reading and Writing of Variables and Observations

If you do not instruct it to do otherwise, SAS writes all variables and all observations from input data sets to output data sets. You can, however, control which variables and observations you want to read and write by using SAS statements, data set options, and functions. The statements and data set options that you can use are listed in the following table.

Table 23.1 Statements and Options That Control Reading and Writing

Task	Statements	Data set options	System options
Control variables	DROP	DROP=	
	KEEP	KEEP=	
	RENAME	RENAME=	
Control observations	WHERE	WHERE=	FIRSTOBS=
	subsetting IF	FIRSTOBS=	OBS=
	DELETE	OBS=	
	REMOVE		

Task	Statements	Data set options	System options
	OUTPUT		

Use statements or data set options (such as KEEP= and DROP=) to control the variables and observations you want to write to the output data set. The WHERE statement is an exception: it controls which observations are read into the program data vector based on the value of a variable. You can use data set options (including WHERE=) on input or output data sets, depending on their function and what you want to control. You can also use SAS system options to control your data.

Combining SAS Data Sets: Basic Concepts

What You Need to Know before Combining Information Stored In Multiple SAS Data Sets

Many applications require input data to be in a specific format before the data can be processed to produce meaningful results. The data typically comes from multiple sources and may be in different formats. Therefore, you often, if not always, have to take intermediate steps to logically relate and process data before you can analyze it or create reports from it.

Application requirements vary, but there are common factors for all applications that access, combine, and process data. Once you have determined what you want the output to look like, you must

□ determine how the input data is related

□ ensure that the data is properly sorted or indexed, if necessary

□ select the appropriate access method to process the input data

□ select the appropriate SAS tools to complete the task.

The Four Ways That Data Can Be Related

Relationships among multiple sources of input data exist when each of the sources contains common data, either at the physical or logical level. For example, employee data and department data could be related through an employee ID variable that shares common values. Another data set could contain numeric sequence numbers whose partial values logically relate it to a separate data set by observation number.

You must be able to identify the existing relationships in your data. This knowledge is crucial for understanding how to process input data in order to produce desired results. All related data fall into one of these four categories, characterized by how observations relate among the data sets:

□ one-to-one

□ one-to-many

□ many-to-one

□ many-to-many.

To obtain the results you want, you should understand how each of these methods combines observations, how each method treats duplicate values of common variables, and how each method treats missing values or nonmatched values of common variables. Some of the methods also require that you preprocess your data sets by sorting them or by creating indexes. See the description of each method in "Combining SAS Data Sets: Methods" on page 402.

One-to-One

In a one-to-one relationship, typically a single observation in one data set is related to a single observation from another based on the values of one or more selected variables. A one-to-one relationship implies that each value of the selected variable occurs no more than once in each data set. When you work with multiple selected variables, this relationship implies that each combination of values occurs no more than once in each data set.

In the following example, observations in data sets SALARY and TAXES are related by common values for EmployeeNumber.

Figure 23.1   One-to-One Relationship

SALARY			TAXES	
EmployeeNumber	Salary		EmployeeNumber	TaxBracket
1234	55000		1111	0.18
3333	72000		1234	0.28
4876	32000		3333	0.32
5489	17000		4222	0.18
			4876	0.24

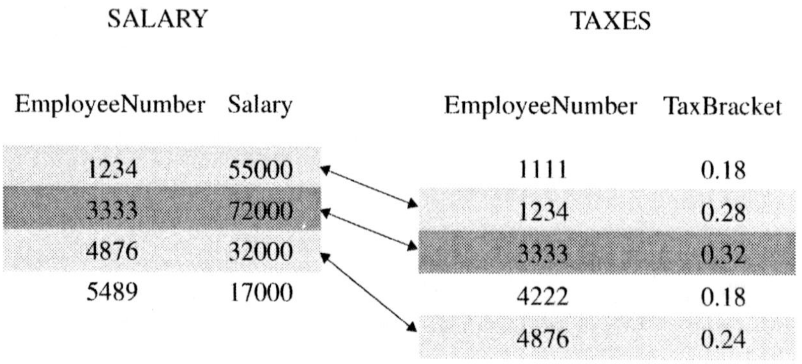

One-to-Many and Many-to-One

A one-to-many or many-to-one relationship between input data sets implies that one data set has at most one observation with a specific value of the selected variable, but the other input data set may have more than one occurrence of each value. When you work with multiple selected variables, this relationship implies that each combination of values occurs no more than once in one data set, but may occur more than once in the other data set. The order in which the input data sets are processed determines whether the relationship is one-to-many or many-to-one.

In the following example, observations in data sets ONE and TWO are related by common values for variable A. Values of A are unique in data set ONE but not in data set TWO.

Figure 23.2 One-to-Many Relationship

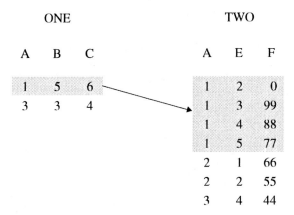

ONE
TWO
A B C
A E F
1 5 6
3 3 4
1 2 0
1 3 99
1 4 88
1 5 77
2 1 66
2 2 55
3 4 44

In the following example, observations in data sets ONE, TWO, and THREE are related by common values for variable ID. Values of ID are unique in data sets ONE and THREE but not in TWO. For values 2 and 3 of ID, a one-to-many relationship exists between observations in data sets ONE and TWO, and a many-to-one relationship exists between observations in data sets TWO and THREE.

Figure 23.3 One-to-Many and Many-to-One Relationships

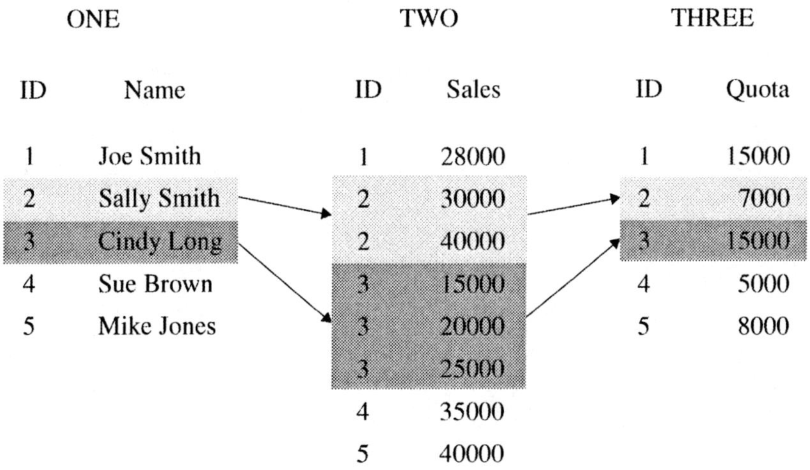

ONE
TWO
THREE
ID Name
ID Sales
ID Quota
1 Joe Smith
2 Sally Smith
3 Cindy Long
4 Sue Brown
5 Mike Jones
1 28000
2 30000
2 40000
3 15000
3 20000
3 25000
4 35000
5 40000
1 15000
2 7000
3 15000
4 5000
5 8000

Many-to-Many

The many-to-many category implies that multiple observations from each input data set may be related based on values of one or more common variables.

In the following example, observations in data sets BREAKDOWN and MAINTENANCE are related by common values for variable Vehicle. Values of Vehicle are not unique in either data set. A many-to-many relationship exists between observations in these data sets for values AAA and CCC of Vehicle.

Figure 23.4 Many-to-Many Relationship

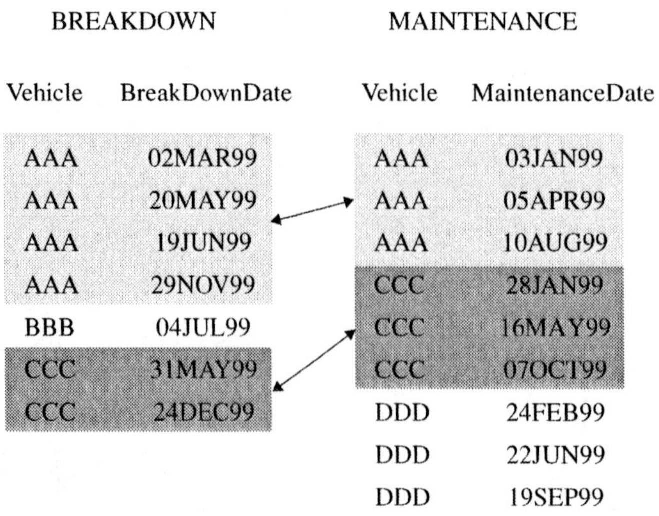

BREAKDOWN   MAINTENANCE

Vehicle	BreakDownDate		Vehicle	MaintenanceDate
AAA	02MAR99		AAA	03JAN99
AAA	20MAY99		AAA	05APR99
AAA	19JUN99		AAA	10AUG99
AAA	29NOV99		CCC	28JAN99
BBB	04JUL99		CCC	16MAY99
CCC	31MAY99		CCC	07OCT99
CCC	24DEC99		DDD	24FEB99
			DDD	22JUN99
			DDD	19SEP99

Access Methods: Sequential versus Direct

Overview

Once you have established data relationships, the next step is to determine the best mode of data access to relate the data. You can access observations sequentially in the order in which they appear in the physical file. Or you can access them directly, that is, you can go straight to an observation in a SAS data set without having to process each observation that precedes it.

Sequential Access

The simplest and perhaps most common way to process data with a DATA step is to read observations in a data set sequentially. You can read observations sequentially using the SET, MERGE, UPDATE, or MODIFY statements. You can also use the SAS File I/O functions, such as OPEN, FETCH, and FETCHOBS.

Direct Access

Direct access allows a program to access specific observations based on one of two methods:

- □ by an observation number
- □ by the value of one or more variables through a simple or composite index.

To access observations directly by their observation number, use the POINT= option with the SET or MODIFY statement. The POINT= option names a variable whose current value determines which observation a SET or MODIFY statement reads.

To access observations directly based on the values of one or more specified variables, you must first create an index for the variables and then read the data set using the KEY= statement option with the SET or MODIFY statement. An *index* is a separate structure that contains the data values of the key variable or variables, paired with a location identifier for the observations containing the value.

Note: You can also use the SAS File I/O functions such as CUROBS, NOTE, POINT and FETCHOBS to access observations by observation number. △

Overview of Methods for Combining SAS Data Sets

You can use these methods to combine SAS data sets:

- □ concatenating
- □ interleaving
- □ one-to-one reading
- □ one-to-one merging
- □ match merging
- □ updating.

Concatenating

The following figure shows the results of concatenating two SAS data sets. Concatenating the data sets appends the observations from one data set to another data set. The DATA step reads DATA1 sequentially until all observations have been processed, and then reads DATA2. Data set COMBINED contains the results of the concatenation. Note that the data sets are processed in the order in which they are listed in the SET statement.

Figure 23.5 Concatenating Two Data Sets

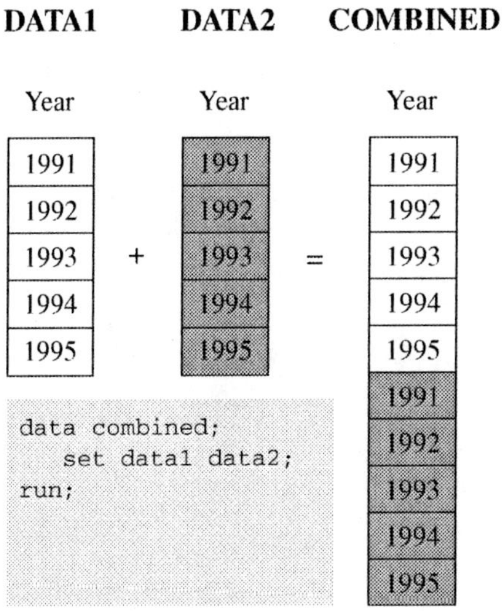

Interleaving

The following figure shows the results of interleaving two SAS data sets. Interleaving intersperses observations from two or more data sets, based on one or more common variables. Data set COMBINED shows the result.

Figure 23.6   Interleaving Two Data Sets

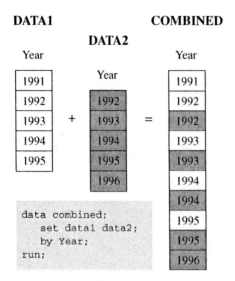

```
data combined;
   set data1 data2;
   by Year;
run;
```

One-to-One Reading and One-to-One Merging

The following figure shows the results of one-to-one reading and one-to-one merging. One-to-one reading combines observations from two or more SAS data sets by creating observations that contain all of the variables from each contributing data set. Observations are combined based on their relative position in each data set, that is, the first observation in one data set with the first in the other, and so on. The DATA step stops after it has read the last observation from the smallest data set. One-to-one merging is similar to a one-to-one reading, with two exceptions: you use the MERGE statement instead of multiple SET statements, and the DATA step reads all observations from all data sets. Data set COMBINED shows the result.

Figure 23.7   One-to-One Reading and One-to-One Merging

DATA1	DATA2	COMBINED
VarX	VarY	VarX VarY

DATA1	DATA2	COMBINED
X1	Y1	X1 Y1
X2	Y2	X2 Y2
X3	Y3	X3 Y3
X4	Y4	X4 Y4
X5	Y5	X5 Y5

```
data combined;
   set data1;
   set data2;
run;

data combined;
   merge data1 data2;
run;
```

Match-Merging

The following figure shows the results of match-merging. Match-merging combines observations from two or more SAS data sets into a single observation in a new data set based on the values of one or more common variables. Data set COMBINED shows the results.

Figure 23.8 Match-Merging Two Data Sets

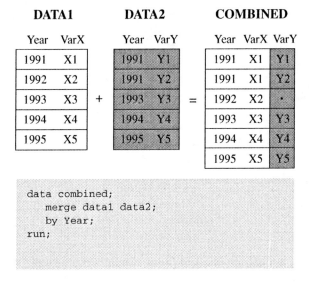

```
data combined;
   merge data1 data2;
      by Year;
run;
```

Updating

The following figure shows the results of updating a master data set. Updating uses information from observations in a transaction data set to delete, add, or alter information in observations in a master data set. You can update a master data set by using the UPDATE statement or the MODIFY statement. If you use the UPDATE statement, your input data sets must be sorted by the values of the variables listed in the BY statement. (In this example, MASTER and TRANSACTION are both sorted by Year.) If you use the MODIFY statement, your input data does not need to be sorted.

UPDATE replaces an existing file with a new file, allowing you to add, delete, or rename columns. MODIFY performs an update in place by rewriting only those records that have changed, or by appending new records to the end of the file.

Note that by default, UPDATE and MODIFY do not replace nonmissing values in a master data set with missing values from a transaction data set.

Figure 23.9 Updating a Master Data Set

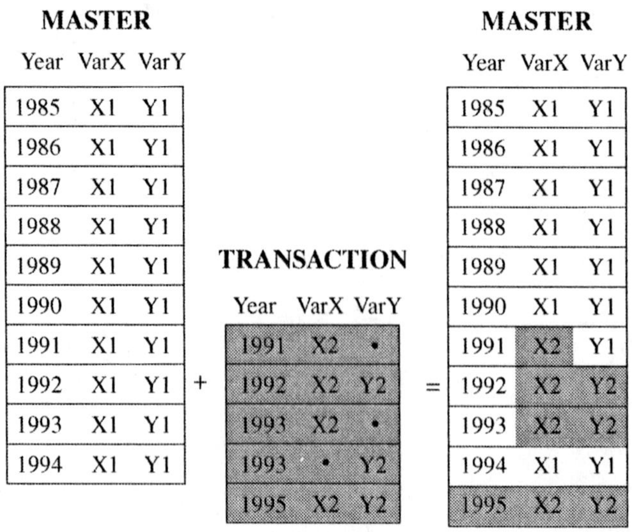

MASTER		
Year	VarX	VarY
1985	X1	Y1
1986	X1	Y1
1987	X1	Y1
1988	X1	Y1
1989	X1	Y1
1990	X1	Y1
1991	X1	Y1
1992	X1	Y1
1993	X1	Y1
1994	X1	Y1

TRANSACTION		
Year	VarX	VarY
1991	X2	•
1992	X2	Y2
1993	X2	•
1993	•	Y2
1995	X2	Y2

MASTER		
Year	VarX	VarY
1985	X1	Y1
1986	X1	Y1
1987	X1	Y1
1988	X1	Y1
1989	X1	Y1
1990	X1	Y1
1991	X2	Y1
1992	X2	Y2
1993	X2	Y2
1994	X1	Y1
1995	X2	Y2

```
data master;
   update master transaction;
   by Year;
run;
```

Overview of Tools for Combining SAS Data Sets

Using Statements and Procedures

Once you understand the basics of establishing relationships among data, the ways to access data, and the ways that you can combine SAS data sets, you can choose from a variety of SAS tools for accessing, combining, and processing your data. The following table lists and briefly describes the DATA step statements and the procedures that you can use for combining SAS data sets.

Table 23.2 Statements or Procedures for Combining SAS Data Sets

Statement or Procedure	Action Performed	Access Method			Comments
		Sequential	Direct	Can Use with BY statement	
BY	controls the operation of a SET, MERGE, UPDATE, or MODIFY statement in the DATA step and sets up special grouping variables.	NA	NA	NA	BY-group processing is a means of processing observations that have the same values of one or more variables.
MERGE	reads observations from two or more SAS data sets and joins them into a single observation.	X		X	When using MERGE with BY, the data must be sorted or indexed on the BY variable.
MODIFY	processes observations in a SAS data set in place. (Contrast with UPDATE.)	X	X	X	Sorted or indexed data are not required for use with BY, but are recommended for performance.
SET	reads an observation from one or more SAS data sets.	X	X	X	Use KEY= or POINT= statement options for directly accessing data.
UPDATE	applies transactions to observations in a master SAS data set. UPDATE does not update observations in place; it produces an updated copy of the current data set.	X		X	Both the master and transaction data sets must be sorted by or indexed on the BY variable.
PROC APPEND	adds the observations from one SAS data set to the end of another SAS data set.	X			
PROC SQL[1]	reads an observation from one or more SAS data sets; reads observations from up to 32 SAS data sets and joins them into single observations; manipulates observations in a SAS data set in place; easily produces a Cartesian product.	X	X	X	All three access methods are available in PROC SQL, but the access method is chosen by the internal optimizer.

1 PROC SQL is the SAS implementation of Structured Query Language. In addition to expected SQL capabilities, PROC SQL includes additional capabilities specific to SAS, such as the use of formats and SAS macro language.

Using Error Checking

You can use the _IORC_ automatic variable and the SYSRC autocall macro to perform error checking in a DATA step. Use these tools with the MODIFY statement or with the SET statement and the KEY= option. For more information about these tools, see "Error Checking When Using Indexes to Randomly Access or Update Data" on page 428.

How to Prepare Your Data Sets

Before combining SAS data sets, follow these guidelines to produce the results you want:

- ☐ Know the structure and the contents of the data sets.
- ☐ Look at sources of common problems.
- ☐ Ensure that observations are in the correct order, or that they can be retrieved in the correct order (for example, by using an index).
- ☐ Test your program.

Knowing the Structure and Contents of the Data Sets

To help determine how your data are related, look at the structure of the data sets. To see the data set structure, execute the DATASETS procedure, the CONTENTS procedure, or access the SAS Explorer window in your windowing environment to display the descriptor information. Descriptor information includes the number of observations in each data set, the name and attributes of each variable, and which variables are included in indexes. To print a sample of the observations, use the PRINT procedure or the REPORT procedure.

You can also use functions such as VTYPE, VLENGTH, and VLENGTHX to show specific descriptor information. For complete information about these functions, see *SAS Language Reference: Dictionary*.

Looking at Sources of Common Problems

If your program does not execute correctly, review your input data for the following errors:

- ☐ *variables that have the same name but that represent different data*

    SAS includes only one variable of a given name in the new data set. If you are merging two data sets that have variables with the same names but different data, the values from the last data set that was read are written over the values from other data sets.

    To correct the error, you can rename variables before you combine the data sets by using the RENAME= data set option in the SET, UPDATE, or MERGE statement, or you can use the DATASETS procedure.

- ☐ *common variables with the same data but different attributes*

    The way SAS handles these differences depends on which attributes are different:

    - ☐ *type attribute*

        If the type attribute is different, SAS stops processing the DATA step and issues an error message stating that the variables are incompatible.

        To correct this error, you must use a DATA step to re-create the variables. The SAS statements you use depend on the nature of the variable.

□ *length attribute*

If the length attribute is different, SAS takes the length from the first data set that contains the variable. In the following example, all data sets that are listed in the MERGE statement contain the variable Mileage. In QUARTER1, the length of the variable Mileage is four bytes; in QUARTER2, it is eight bytes and in QUARTER3 and QUARTER4, it is six bytes. In the output data set YEARLY, the length of the variable Mileage is four bytes, which is the length derived from QUARTER1.

```
data yearly;
    merge quarter1 quarter2 quarter3 quarter4;
    by Account;
run;
```

To override the default and set the length yourself, specify the appropriate length in a LENGTH statement that *precedes* the SET, MERGE, or UPDATE statement.

□ *label, format, and informat attributes*

If any of these attributes are different, SAS takes the attribute from the first data set that contains the variable with that attribute. However, any label, format, or informat that you explicitly specify overrides a default. If all data sets contain explicitly specified attributes, the one specified in the first data set overrides the others. To ensure that the new output data set has the attributes you prefer, use an ATTRIB statement.

You can also use the SAS File I/O functions such as VLABEL, VLABELX, and other Variable Information functions to access this information. For complete information about these functions, see *SAS Language Reference: Dictionary*.

Ensuring Correct Order

If you use BY-group processing with the UPDATE, SET, and MERGE statements to combine data sets, ensure that the observations in the data sets are sorted in the order of the variables that are listed in the BY statement, or that the data sets have an appropriate index. If you use BY-group processing in a MODIFY statement, your data does not need to be sorted, but sorting the data improves efficiency. The BY variable or variables must be common to both data sets, and they must have the same attributes. For more information, see Chapter 22, "BY-Group Processing in the DATA Step," on page 375.

Testing Your Program

As a final step in preparing your data sets, you should test your program. Create small temporary SAS data sets that contain a sample of observations that test all of your program's logic. If your logic is faulty and you get unexpected output, you can use the DATA step debugger to debug your program. For complete information about the DATA Step Debugger, see *SAS Language Reference: Dictionary*.

Combining SAS Data Sets: Methods

Concatenating

Definition

Concatenating data sets is the combining of two or more data sets, one after the other, into a single data set. The number of observations in the new data set is the sum of the number of observations in the original data sets. The order of observations is sequential. All observations from the first data set are followed by all observations from the second data set, and so on.

In the simplest case, all input data sets contain the same variables. If the input data sets contain different variables, observations from one data set have missing values for variables defined only in other data sets. In either case, the variables in the new data set are the same as the variables in the old data sets.

Syntax

Use this form of the SET statement to concatenate data sets:

SET *data-set(s)*;

where

data-set
    specifies any valid SAS data set name.

For a complete description of the SET statement, see *SAS Language Reference: Dictionary*.

DATA Step Processing During Concatenation

Compilation phase
    SAS reads the descriptor information of each data set that is named in the SET statement and then creates a program data vector that contains all the variables from all data sets as well as variables created by the DATA step.

Execution — Step 1
    SAS reads the first observation from the first data set into the program data vector. It processes the first observation and executes other statements in the DATA step. It then writes the contents of the program data vector to the new data set.

    The SET statement does not reset the values in the program data vector to missing, except for variables whose value is calculated or assigned during the DATA step. Variables that are created by the DATA step are set to missing at the beginning of each iteration of the DATA step. Variables that are read from a data set are not.

Execution — Step 2
    SAS continues to read one observation at a time from the first data set until it finds an end-of-file indicator. The values of the variables in the program data

vector are then set to missing, and SAS begins reading observations from the
second data set and so forth until it reads all observations from all data sets.

Example 1: Concatenation Using the DATA Step

In this example, each data set contains the variables Common and Number, and the
observations are arranged in the order of the values of Common. Generally, you
concatenate SAS data sets that have the same variables. In this case, each data set also
contains a unique variable to show the effects of combining data sets more clearly. The
following shows the ANIMAL and the PLANT input data sets in the library that is
referenced by the libref EXAMPLE:

```
        ANIMAL                                   PLANT

OBS   Common  Animal  Number     OBS   Common  Plant     Number

 1      a      Ant       5        1      g     Grape       69
 2      b      Bird               2      h     Hazelnut    55
 3      c      Cat      17        3      i     Indigo
 4      d      Dog       9        4      j     Jicama      14
 5      e      Eagle             5      k     Kale         5
 6      f      Frog     76        6      l     Lentil      77
```

The following program uses a SET statement to concatenate the data sets and then
prints the results:

```
libname example 'SAS-data-library';

data example.concatenation;
   set example.animal example.plant;
run;

proc print data=example.concatenation;
   var Common Animal Plant Number;
   title 'Data Set CONCATENATION';
run;
```

Output 23.1 Concatenated Data Sets (DATA Step)

```
                    Data Set CONCATENATION                          1

        Obs      Common     Animal     Plant      Number

         1         a        Ant                      5
         2         b        Bird                      .
         3         c        Cat                      17
         4         d        Dog                       9
         5         e        Eagle                     .
         6         f        Frog                     76
         7         g                   Grape         69
         8         h                   Hazelnut      55
         9         i                   Indigo         .
        10         j                   Jicama        14
        11         k                   Kale           5
        12         l                   Lentil        77
```

The resulting data set CONCATENATION has 12 observations, which is the sum of the observations from the combined data sets. The program data vector contains all variables from all data sets. The values of variables found in one data set but not in another are set to missing.

Example 2: Concatenation Using SQL

You can also use the SQL language to concatenate tables. In this example, SQL reads each row in both tables and creates a new table named COMBINED. The following shows the YEAR1 and YEAR2 input tables:

```
YEAR1              YEAR2

Date1              Date2

1996
1997               1997
1998               1998
1999               1999
                   2000
                   2001
```

The following SQL code creates and prints the table COMBINED.

```
proc sql;
   title 'SQL Table COMBINED';
   create table combined as
      select * from year1
      outer union corr
      select * from year2;
      select * from combined;
quit;
```

Output 23.2   Concatenated Tables (SQL)

```
                          SQL Table COMBINED                        1

                                Year
                              --------
                                1996
                                1997
                                1998
                                1999
                                1997
                                1998
                                1999
                                2000
                                2001
```

Appending Files

Instead of concatenating data sets or tables, you can append them and produce the same results as concatenation. SAS concatenates data sets (DATA step) and tables (SQL) by reading each row of data to create a new file. To avoid reading all the records, you can append the second file to the first file by using the APPEND procedure:

```
proc append base=year1 data=year2;
run;
```

The YEAR1 file will contain all rows from both tables.

Note: You cannot use PROC APPEND to add observations to a SAS data set in a sequential library. △

Efficiency

If no additional processing is necessary, using PROC APPEND or the APPEND statement in PROC DATASETS is more efficient than using a DATA step to concatenate data sets.

Interleaving

Definition

Interleaving uses a SET statement and a BY statement to combine multiple data sets into one new data set. The number of observations in the new data set is the sum of the number of observations from the original data sets. However, the observations in the new data set are arranged by the values of the BY variable or variables and, within each BY group, by the order of the data sets in which they occur. You can interleave data sets either by using a BY variable or by using an index.

Syntax

Use this form of the SET statement to interleave data sets when you use a BY variable:

SET *data-set(s)*;

BY *variable(s)*;

where

data-set
   specifies a one-level name, a two-level name, or one of the special SAS data set names.

variable
   specifies each variable by which the data set is sorted. These variables are referred to as BY variables for the current DATA or PROC step.

Use this form of the SET statement to interleave data sets when you use an index:

SET *data-set-1* . . . *data-set-n* KEY= *index*;

where

data-set
   specifies a one-level name, a two-level name, or one of the special SAS data set names.

index
   provides nonsequential access to observations in a SAS data set, which are based on the value of an index variable or key.

For a complete description of the SET statement, including SET with the KEY= option, see *SAS Language Reference: Dictionary*.

Sort Requirements

Before you can interleave data sets, the observations must be sorted or grouped by the same variable or variables that you use in the BY statement, or you must have an appropriate index for the data sets.

DATA Step Processing During Interleaving

Compilation phase

□ SAS reads the descriptor information of each data set that is named in the SET statement and then creates a program data vector that contains all the variables from all data sets as well as variables created by the DATA step.

□ SAS creates the FIRST.*variable* and LAST.*variable* for each variable listed in the BY statement.

Execution — Step 1

SAS compares the first observation from each data set that is named in the SET statement to determine which BY group should appear first in the new data set. It reads all observations from the first BY group from the selected data set. If this BY group appears in more than one data set, it reads from the data sets in the order in which they appear in the SET statement. The values of the variables in the program data vector are set to missing each time SAS starts to read a new data set and when the BY group changes.

Execution — Step 2

SAS compares the next observations from each data set to determine the next BY group and then starts reading observations from the selected data set in the SET statement that contains observations for this BY group. SAS continues until it has read all observations from all data sets.

Example 1: Interleaving in the Simplest Case

In this example, each data set contains the BY variable Common, and the observations are arranged in order of the values of the BY variable. The following shows the ANIMAL and the PLANT input data sets in the library that is referenced by the libref EXAMPLE:

ANIMAL				PLANT		
OBS	Common	Animal		OBS	Common	Plant
1	a	Ant		1	a	Apple
2	b	Bird		2	b	Banana
3	c	Cat		3	c	Coconut
4	d	Dog		4	d	Dewberry
5	e	Eagle		5	e	Eggplant
6	f	Frog		6	f	Fig

The following program uses SET and BY statements to interleave the data sets, and prints the results:

```
data example.interleaving;
   set example.animal example.plant;
   by Common;
run;


proc print data=example.interleaving;
```

```
        title 'Data Set INTERLEAVING';
run;
```

Output 23.3   Interleaved Data Sets

```
                        Data Set INTERLEAVING                           1

                Obs    common    animal    plant

                 1       a       Ant
                 2       a                 Apple
                 3       b       Bird
                 4       b                 Banana
                 5       c       Cat
                 6       c                 Coconut
                 7       d       Dog
                 8       d                 Dewberry
                 9       e       Eagle
                10       e                 Eggplant
                11       f       Frog
                12       f                 Fig
```

The resulting data set INTERLEAVING has 12 observations, which is the sum of the observations from the combined data sets. The new data set contains all variables from both data sets. The value of variables found in one data set but not in the other are set to missing, and the observations are arranged by the values of the BY variable.

Example 2: Interleaving with Duplicate Values of the BY variable

If the data sets contain duplicate values of the BY variables, the observations are written to the new data set in the order in which they occur in the original data sets. This example contains duplicate values of the BY variable Common. The following shows the ANIMAL1 and PLANT1 input data sets:

ANIMAL1				PLANT1		
OBS	Common	Animal1		OBS	Common	Plant1
1	a	Ant		1	a	Apple
2	a	Ape		2	b	Banana
3	b	Bird		3	c	Coconut
4	c	Cat		4	c	Celery
5	d	Dog		5	d	Dewberry
6	e	Eagle		6	e	Eggplant

The following program uses SET and BY statements to interleave the data sets, and prints the results:

```
data example.interleaving2;
   set example.animal1 example.plant1;
   by Common;
run;


proc print data=example.interleaving2;
   title 'Data Set INTERLEAVING2: Duplicate BY Values';
run;
```

Output 23.4   Interleaved Data Sets with Duplicate Values of the BY Variable

```
              Data Set INTERLEAVING2: Duplicate BY Values                1

                   Obs     Common     Animal1    Plant1

                    1        a        Ant
                    2        a        Ape
                    3        a                   Apple
                    4        b        Bird
                    5        b                   Banana
                    6        c        Cat
                    7        c                   Coconut
                    8        c                   Celery
                    9        d        Dog
                   10        d                   Dewberry
                   11        e        Eagle
                   12        e                   Eggplant
```

The number of observations in the new data set is the sum of the observations in all the data sets. The observations are written to the new data set in the order in which they occur in the original data sets.

Example 3: Interleaving with Different BY Values in Each Data Set

The data sets ANIMAL2 and PLANT2 both contain BY values that are present in one data set but not in the other. The following shows the ANIMAL2 and the PLANT2 input data sets:

```
    ANIMAL2                          PLANT2

OBS   Common   Animal2        OBS   Common   Plant2

 1      a      Ant             1      a      Apple
 2      c      Cat             2      b      Banana
 3      d      Dog             3      c      Coconut
 4      e      Eagle           4      e      Eggplant
                               5      f      Fig
```

This program uses SET and BY statements to interleave these data sets, and prints the results:

```
data example.interleaving3;
   set example.animal2 example.plant2;
   by Common;
run;

proc print data=example.interleaving3;
   title 'Data Set INTERLEAVING3: Different BY Values';
run;
```

Output 23.5 Interleaving Data Sets with Different BY Values

```
                Data Set INTERLEAVING3: Different BY Values              1

              Obs     Common     Animal2     Plant2

               1        a        Ant
               2        a                    Apple
               3        b                    Banana
               4        c        Cat
               5        c                    Coconut
               6        d        Dog
               7        e        Eagle
               8        e                    Eggplant
               9        f                    Fig
```

The resulting data set has nine observations arranged by the values of the BY variable.

Comments and Comparisons

□ In other languages, the term *merge* is often used to mean *interleave*. SAS reserves the term *merge* for the operation in which observations from two or more data sets are combined into one observation. The observations in interleaved data sets are not combined; they are copied from the original data sets in the order of the values of the BY variable.

□ If one table has multiple rows with the same BY value, the DATA step preserves the order of those rows in the result.

□ To use the DATA step, the input tables must be appropriately sorted or indexed. SQL does not require the input tables to be in order.

One-to-One Reading

Definition

One-to-one reading combines observations from two or more data sets into one observation by using two or more SET statements to read observations independently from each data set. This process is also called *one-to-one matching*. The new data set contains all the variables from all the input data sets. The number of observations in the new data set is the number of observations in the smallest original data set. If the data sets contain common variables, the values that are read in from the last data set replace the values that were read in from earlier data sets.

Syntax

Use this form of the SET statement for one-to-one reading:

SET *data-set-1*;

SET *data-set-2*;

where

data-set-1

specifies a one-level name, a two-level name, or one of the special SAS data set names. *data-set-1* is the first file that the DATA step reads.

data-set-2

specifies a one-level name, a two-level name, or one of the special SAS data set names. *data-set-2* is the second file that the DATA step reads.

CAUTION:

Use care when you combine data sets with multiple SET statements. Using multiple SET statements to combine observations can produce undesirable results. Test your program on representative samples of the data sets before using this method to combine them. △

For a complete description of the SET statement, see *SAS Language Reference: Dictionary*.

DATA Step Processing During a One-to-One Reading

Compilation phase

SAS reads the descriptor information of each data set named in the SET statement and then creates a program data vector that contains all the variables from all data sets as well as variables created by the DATA step.

Execution — Step 1

When SAS executes the first SET statement, SAS reads the first observation from the first data set into the program data vector. The second SET statement reads the first observation from the second data set into the program data vector. If both data sets contain the same variables, the values from the second data set replace the values from the first data set, even if the value is missing. After reading the first observation from the last data set and executing any other statements in the DATA step, SAS writes the contents of the program data vector to the new data set. The SET statement does not reset the values in the program data vector to missing, except for those variables that were created or assigned values during the DATA step.

Execution — Step 2

SAS continues reading from one data set and then the other until it detects an end-of-file indicator in one of the data sets. SAS stops processing with the last observation of the shortest data set and does not read the remaining observations from the longer data set.

Example 1: One-to-One Reading: Processing an Equal Number of Observations

The SAS data sets ANIMAL and PLANT both contain the variable Common, and are arranged by the values of that variable. The following shows the ANIMAL and the PLANT input data sets:

```
        ANIMAL                      PLANT


OBS   Common   Animal        OBS   Common   Plant


 1       a      Ant           1       a      Apple
 2       b      Bird          2       b      Banana
 3       c      Cat           3       c      Coconut
 4       d      Dog           4       d      Dewberry
```

```
5      e      Eagle      5      e      Eggplant
6      f      Frog       6      g      Fig
```

The following program uses two SET statements to combine observations from ANIMAL and PLANT, and prints the results:

```
data twosets;
   set animal;
   set plant;
run;

proc print data=twosets;
   title 'Data Set TWOSETS - Equal Number of Observations';
run;
```

Output 23.6 Data Set Created from Two Data Sets That Have Equal Observations

```
            Data Set TWOSETS - Equal Number of Observations            1

                 Obs     Common     Animal     Plant

                  1        a        Ant        Apple
                  2        b        Bird       Banana
                  3        c        Cat        Coconut
                  4        d        Dog        Dewberry
                  5        e        Eagle      Eggplant
                  6        g        Frog       Fig
```

Each observation in the new data set contains all the variables from all the data sets. Note, however, that the Common variable value in observation 6 contains a "g." The value of Common in observation 6 of the ANIMAL data set was overwritten by the value in PLANT, which was the data set that SAS read last.

Comments and Comparisons

□ The results that are obtained by reading observations using two or more SET statements are similar to those that are obtained by using the MERGE statement with no BY statement. However, with one-to-one reading, SAS stops processing before all observations are read from all data sets if the number of observations in the data sets is not equal.

□ Using multiple SET statements with other DATA step statements makes the following applications possible:

    □ merging one observation with many
    □ conditionally merging observations
    □ reading from the same data set twice.

One-to-One Merging

Definition

One-to-one merging combines observations from two or more SAS data sets into a single observation in a new data set. To perform a one-to-one merge, use the MERGE statement without a BY statement. SAS combines the first observation from all data sets in the MERGE statement into the first observation in the new data set, the second observation from all data sets into the second observation in the new data set, and so on. In a one-to-one merge, the number of observations in the new data set equals the number of observations in the largest data set that was named in the MERGE statement.

If you use the MERGENOBY= SAS system option, you can control whether SAS issues a message when MERGE processing occurs without an associated BY statement.

Syntax

Use this form of the MERGE statement to merge SAS data sets:

MERGE *data-set(s)*;

where

data-set
    names at least two existing SAS data sets.

CAUTION:
Avoid using duplicate values or different values of common variables. One-to-one merging with data sets that contain duplicate values of common variables can produce undesirable results. If a variable exists in more than one data set, the value from the last data set that is read is the one that is written to the new data set. The variables are combined exactly as they are read from each data set. Using a one-to-one merge to combine data sets with different values of common variables can also produce undesirable results. If a variable exists in more than one data set, the value from the last data set read is the one that is written to the new data set even if the value is missing. Once SAS has processed all observations in a data set, all subsequent observations in the new data set have missing values for the variables that are unique to that data set. △

For a complete description of the MERGE statement, see *SAS Language Reference: Dictionary*.

DATA Step Processing During One-to-One Merging

Compilation phase
    SAS reads the descriptor information of each data set that is named in the MERGE statement and then creates a program data vector that contains all the variables from all data sets as well as variables created by the DATA step.

Execution — Step 1
    SAS reads the first observation from each data set into the program data vector, reading the data sets in the order in which they appear in the MERGE statement. If two data sets contain the same variables, the values from the second data set replace the values from the first data set. After reading the first observation from the last data set and executing any other statements in the DATA step, SAS writes the contents of the program data vector to the new data set. Only those variables that are created or assigned values during the DATA step are set to missing.

Execution — Step 2
    SAS continues until it has read all observations from all data sets.

Example 1: One-to-One Merging with an Equal Number of Observations

The SAS data sets ANIMAL and PLANT both contain the variable Common, and the observations are arranged by the values of Common. The following shows the ANIMAL and the PLANT input data sets:

```
        ANIMAL                          PLANT

OBS   Common   Animal      OBS    Common   Plant

 1      a      Ant          1       a      Apple
 2      b      Bird         2       b      Banana
 3      c      Cat          3       c      Coconut
 4      d      Dog          4       d      Dewberry
 5      e      Eagle        5       e      Eggplant
 6      f      Frog         6       g      Fig
```

The following program merges these data sets and prints the results:

```
data combined;
    merge animal plant;
run;

proc print data=combined;
    title 'Data Set COMBINED';
run;
```

Output 23.7 Merged Data Sets That Have an Equal Number of Observations

```
                    Data Set COMBINED                          1

            Obs     Common    Animal    Plant

             1        a       Ant       Apple
             2        b       Bird      Banana
             3        c       Cat       Coconut
             4        d       Dog       Dewberry
             5        e       Eagle     Eggplant
             6        g       Frog      Fig
```

Each observation in the new data set contains all variables from all data sets. If two data sets contain the same variables, the values from the second data set replace the values from the first data set, as shown in observation 6.

Example 2: One-to-One Merging with an Unequal Number of Observations

The SAS data sets ANIMAL1 and PLANT1 both contain the variable Common, and the observations are arranged by the values of Common. The PLANT1 data set has fewer observations than the ANIMAL1 data set. The following shows the ANIMAL1 and the PLANT1 input data sets:

```
        ANIMAL1                         PLANT1

OBS   Common   Animal      OBS    Common   Plant

 1      a      Ant          1       a      Apple
 2      b      Bird         2       b      Banana
```

```
3       c       Cat              3       c       Coconut
4       d       Dog
5       e       Eagle
6       f       Frog
```

The following program merges these unequal data sets and prints the results:

```
data combined1;
    merge animal1 plant1;
run;

proc print data=combined1;
    title 'Data Set COMBINED1';
run;
```

Output 23.8   Merged Data Sets That Have an Unequal Number of Observations

```
                        Data Set COMBINED1                              1

              Obs     Common      Animal      Plant

               1        a         Ant         Apple
               2        b         Bird        Banana
               3        c         Cat         Coconut
               4        d         Dog
               5        e         Eagle
               6        f         Frog
```

Note that observations 4 through 6 contain missing values for the variable Plant.

Example 3: One-to-One Merging with Duplicate Values of Common Variables

The following example shows the undesirable results that you can obtain by using one-to-one merging with data sets that contain duplicate values of common variables. The value from the last data set that is read is the one that is written to the new data set. The variables are combined exactly as they are read from each data set. In the following example, the data sets ANIMAL1 and PLANT1 contain the variable Common, and each data set contains observations with duplicate values of Common. The following shows the ANIMAL1 and the PLANT1 input data sets:

```
        ANIMAL1                          PLANT1

OBS   Common   Animal          OBS   Common   Plant

 1       a      Ant             1       a      Apple
 2       a      Ape             2       b      Banana
 3       b      Bird            3       c      Coconut
 4       c      Cat             4       c      Celery
 5       d      Dog             5       d      Dewberry
 6       e      Eagle           6       e      Eggplant
```

The following program produces the data set MERGE1 data set and prints the results:

```
    /* This program illustrates undesirable results. */
data merge1;
    merge animal1 plant1;
run;

proc print data=merge1;
    title 'Data Set MERGE1';
run;
```

Output 23.9 Undesirable Results with Duplicate Values of Common Variables

```
                        Data Set MERGE1                          1

            Obs     Common     Animal1     Plant1

             1        a         Ant        Apple
             2        b         Ape        Banana
             3        c         Bird       Coconut
             4        c         Cat        Celery
             5        d         Dog        Dewberry
             6        e         Eagle      Eggplant
```

The number of observations in the new data set is six. Note that observations 2 and 3 contain undesirable values. SAS reads the second observation from data set ANIMAL1. It then reads the second observation from data set PLANT1 and replaces the values for the variables Common and Plant1. The third observation is created in the same way.

Example 4: One-to-One Merging with Different Values of Common Variables

The following example shows the undesirable results obtained from using the one-to-one merge to combine data sets with different values of common variables. If a variable exists in more than one data set, the value from the last data set that is read is the one that is written to the new data set even if the value is missing. Once SAS processes all observations in a data set, all subsequent observations in the new data set have missing values for the variables that are unique to that data set. In this example, the data sets ANIMAL2 and PLANT2 have different values of the Common variable. The following shows the ANIMAL2 and the PLANT2 input data sets:

```
        ANIMAL2                        PLANT2

OBS   Common   Animal        OBS   Common   Plant

 1      a      Ant            1      a      Apple
 2      c      Cat            2      b      Banana
 3      d      Dog            3      c      Coconut
 4      e      Eagle          4      e      Eggplant
                              5      f      Fig
```

The following program produces the data set MERGE2 and prints the results:

```
    /* This program illustrates undesirable results. */
data merge2;
    merge animal2 plant2;
run;
```

```
proc print data=merge2;
   title 'Data Set MERGE2';
run;
```

Output 23.10   Undesirable Results with Different Values of Common Variables

```
                        Data Set MERGE2                            1

             Obs      Common     Animal2     Plant2

              1         a         Ant        Apple
              2         b         Cat        Banana
              3         c         Dog        Coconut
              4         e         Eagle      Eggplant
              5         f                    Fig
```

Comments and Comparisons

The results from a one-to-one merge are similar to the results obtained from using two or more SET statements to combine observations. However, with the one-to-one merge, SAS continues processing all observations in all data sets that were named in the MERGE statement.

Match-Merging

Definition

Match-merging combines observations from two or more SAS data sets into a single observation in a new data set according to the values of a common variable. The number of observations in the new data set is the sum of the largest number of observations in each BY group in all data sets. To perform a match-merge, use the MERGE statement with a BY statement. Before you can perform a match-merge, all data sets must be sorted by the variables that you specify in the BY statement or they must have an index.

Syntax

Use this form of the MERGE statement to match-merge data sets:

MERGE *data-set(s)*;

BY *variable(s)*;

where

data-set
    names at least two existing SAS data sets from which observations are read.

variable
    names each variable by which the data set is sorted or indexed. These variables are referred to as BY variables.

For a complete description of the MERGE and the BY statements, see *SAS Language Reference: Dictionary*.

DATA Step Processing During Match-Merging

Compilation phase
   SAS reads the descriptor information of each data set that is named in the
   MERGE statement and then creates a program data vector that contains all the
   variables from all data sets as well as variables created by the DATA step. SAS
   creates the FIRST.*variable* and LAST.*variable* for each variable that is listed in
   the BY statement.

Execution – Step 1
   SAS looks at the first BY group in each data set that is named in the MERGE
   statement to determine which BY group should appear first in the new data set.
   The DATA step reads into the program data vector the first observation in that BY
   group from each data set, reading the data sets in the order in which they appear
   in the MERGE statement. If a data set does not have observations in that BY
   group, the program data vector contains missing values for the variables unique to
   that data set.

Execution – Step 2
   After processing the first observation from the last data set and executing other
   statements, SAS writes the contents of the program data vector to the new data
   set. SAS retains the values of all variables in the program data vector except
   those variables that were created by the DATA step; SAS sets those values to
   missing. SAS continues to merge observations until it writes all observations from
   the first BY group to the new data set. When SAS has read all observations in a
   BY group from all data sets, it sets all variables in the program data vector to
   missing. SAS looks at the next BY group in each data set to determine which BY
   group should appear next in the new data set.

Execution – Step 3
   SAS repeats these steps until it reads all observations from all BY groups in all
   data sets.

Example 1: Combining Observations Based on a Criterion

The SAS data sets ANIMAL and PLANT each contain the BY variable Common, and
the observations are arranged in order of the values of the BY variable. The following
shows the ANIMAL and the PLANT input data sets:

```
        ANIMAL                    PLANT

OBS   Common  Animal      OBS   Common  Plant

 1      a     Ant          1      a     Apple
 2      b     Bird         2      b     Banana
 3      c     Cat          3      c     Coconut
 4      d     Dog          4      d     Dewberry
 5      e     Eagle        5      e     Eggplant
 6      f     Frog         6      f     Fig
```

The following program merges the data sets according to the values of the BY
variable Common, and prints the results:

```
data combined;
    merge animal plant;
    by Common;
run;
```

```
proc print data=combined;
   title 'Data Set COMBINED';
run;
```

Output 23.11   Data Sets Combined by Match-Merging

```
                     Data Set COMBINED                        1

                Obs    Common    Animal    Plant

                 1       a       Ant       Apple
                 2       b       Bird      Banana
                 3       c       Cat       Coconut
                 4       d       Dog       Dewberry
                 5       e       Eagle     Eggplant
                 6       f       Frog      Fig
```

Each observation in the new data set contains all the variables from all the data sets.

Example 2: Match-Merge with Duplicate Values of the BY Variable

When SAS reads the last observation from a BY group in one data set, SAS retains its values in the program data vector for all variables that are unique to that data set until all observations for that BY group have been read from all data sets. In the following example, the data sets ANIMAL1 and PLANT1 contain duplicate values of the BY variable Common. The following shows the ANIMAL1 and the PLANT1 input data sets:

```
     ANIMAL1                        PLANT1

OBS   Common   Animal1        OBS   Common   Plant1

 1      a      Ant             1      a      Apple
 2      a      Ape             2      b      Banana
 3      b      Bird            3      c      Coconut
 4      c      Cat             4      c      Celery
 5      d      Dog             5      d      Dewberry
 6      e      Eagle           6      e      Eggplant
```

The following program produces the merged data set MATCH1, and prints the results:

```
data match1;
   merge animal1 plant1;
   by Common;
run;

proc print data=match1;
   title 'Data Set MATCH1';
run;
```

Output 23.12 Match-Merged Data Set with Duplicate BY Values

```
                        Data Set MATCH1                          1

              Obs    Common    Animal1    Plant1

               1       a        Ant        Apple
               2       a        Ape        Apple
               3       b        Bird       Banana
               4       c        Cat        Coconut
               5       c        Cat        Celery
               6       d        Dog        Dewberry
               7       e        Eagle      Eggplant
```

In observation 2 of the output, the value of the variable Plant1 is retained until all observations in the BY group are written to the new data set. Match-merging also produced duplicate values in ANIMAL1 for observations 4 and 5.

Example 3: Match-Merge with Nonmatched Observations

When SAS performs a match-merge with nonmatched observations in the input data sets, SAS retains the values of all variables in the program data vector even if the value is missing. The data sets ANIMAL2 and PLANT2 do not contain all values of the BY variable Common. The following shows the ANIMAL2 and the PLANT2 input data sets:

```
      ANIMAL2                        PLANT2

OBS   Common   Animal2        OBS   Common   Plant2

 1      a       Ant            1      a       Apple
 2      c       Cat            2      b       Banana
 3      d       Dog            3      c       Coconut
 4      e       Eagle          4      e       Eggplant
                               5      f       Fig
```

The following program produces the merged data set MATCH2, and prints the results:

```
data match2;
   merge animal2 plant2;
   by Common;
run;

proc print data=match2;
   title 'Data Set MATCH2';
run;
```

Output 23.13   Match-Merged Data Set with Nonmatched Observations

```
                        Data Set MATCH2                                 1

             Obs     Common     Animal2     Plant2

              1        a          Ant        Apple
              2        b                     Banana
              3        c          Cat        Coconut
              4        d          Dog
              5        e          Eagle      Eggplant
              6        f                     Fig
```

As the output shows, all values of the variable Common are represented in the new data set, including missing values for the variables that are in one data set but not in the other.

Updating with the UPDATE and the MODIFY Statements

Definitions

Updating a data set refers to the process of applying changes to a master data set. To update data sets, you work with two input data sets. The data set containing the original information is the *master data set*, and the data set containing the new information is the *transaction data set*.

You can update data sets by using the UPDATE statement or the MODIFY statement:

UPDATE   uses observations from the transaction data set to change the values of corresponding observations from the master data set. You must use a BY statement with the UPDATE statement because all observations in the transaction data set are keyed to observations in the master data set according to the values of the BY variable.

MODIFY   can replace, delete, and append observations in an existing data set. Using the MODIFY statement can save disk space because it modifies data in place, without creating a copy of the data set.

The number of observations in the new data set is the sum of the number of observations in the master data set and the number of unmatched observations in the transaction data set.

For complete information about the UPDATE and the MODIFY statements, see *SAS Language Reference: Dictionary*.

Syntax of the UPDATE Statement

Use this form of the UPDATE statement to update a master data set:

UPDATE *master-data-set transaction-data-set*;

BY *variable-list*;

where

master-data-set
      names the SAS data set that is used as the master file.

transaction-data-set
  names the SAS data set that contains the changes to be applied to the master data set.

variable-list
  specifies the variables by which observations are matched.

If the transaction data set contains duplicate values of the BY variable, SAS applies both transactions to the observation. The last values that are copied into the program data vector are written to the new data set. If your data is in this form, use the MODIFY statement instead of the UPDATE statement to process your data.

CAUTION:
  Values of the BY variable must be unique for each observation in the master data set. If the master data set contains two observations with the same value of the BY variable, the first observation is updated and the second observation is ignored. SAS writes a warning message to the log when the DATA step executes. △

For complete information about the UPDATE statement, see *SAS Language Reference: Dictionary*.

Syntax of the MODIFY Statement

This form of the MODIFY statement is used in the examples that follow:

MODIFY *master-data–set*;

BY *variable-list*;

where

master-data–set
  specifies the SAS data set that you want to modify.

variable-list
  names each variable by which the data set is ordered.

Note: The MODIFY statement does not support changing the descriptor portion of a SAS data set, such as adding a variable. △

For complete information about the MODIFY statement, see *SAS Language Reference: Dictionary*.

DATA Step Processing with the UPDATE Statement

Compilation phase
  □ SAS reads the descriptor information of each data set that is named in the UPDATE statement and creates a program data vector that contains all the variables from all data sets as well as variables created by the DATA step.
  □ SAS creates the FIRST.*variable* and LAST.*variable* for each variable that is listed in the BY statement.

Execution – Step 1
  SAS looks at the first observation in each data set that is named in the UPDATE statement to determine which BY group should appear first. If the transaction BY value precedes the master BY value, SAS reads from the transaction data set only and sets the variables from the master data set to missing. If the master BY value precedes the transaction BY value, SAS reads from the master data set only and sets the unique variables from the transaction data set to missing. If the BY

values in the master and transaction data sets are equal, it applies the first transaction by copying the nonmissing values into the program data vector.

Execution – Step 2

After completing the first transaction, SAS looks at the next observation in the transaction data set. If SAS finds one with the same BY value, it applies that transaction too. The first observation then contains the new values from both transactions. If no other transactions exist for that observation, SAS writes the observation to the new data set and sets the values in the program data vector to missing. SAS repeats these steps until it has read all observations from all BY groups in both data sets.

Updating with Nonmatched Observations, Missing Values, and New Variables

In the UPDATE statement, if an observation in the master data set does not have a corresponding observation in the transaction data set, SAS writes the observation to the new data set without modifying it. Any observation from the transaction data set that does not correspond to an observation in the master data set is written to the program data vector and becomes the basis for an observation in the new data set. The data in the program data vector can be modified by other transactions before it is written to the new data set. If a master data set observation does not need updating, the corresponding observation can be omitted from the transaction data set.

SAS does not replace existing values in the master data set with missing values if those values are coded as periods (for numeric variables) or blanks (for character variables) in the transaction data set. To replace existing values with missing values, you must either create a transaction data set in which missing values are coded with the special missing value characters, or use the UPDATEMODE=NOMISSINGCHECK statement option.

With UPDATE, the transaction data set can contain new variables to be added to all observations in the master data set.

To view a sample program, see "Example 3: Using UPDATE for Processing Nonmatched Observations, Missing Values, and New Variables" on page 425.

Sort Requirements for the UPDATE Statement

If you do not use an index, both the master data set and the transaction data set must be sorted by the same variable or variables that you specify in the BY statement that accompanies the UPDATE statement. The values of the BY variable should be unique for each observation in the master data set. If you use more than one BY variable, the combination of values of all BY variables should be unique for each observation in the master data set. The BY variable or variables should be ones that you never need to update.

Note: The MODIFY statement does not require sorted files. However, sorting the data improves efficiency. △

Using an Index with the MODIFY Statement

The MODIFY statement maintains the index. You do not have to rebuild the index like you do for the UPDATE statement.

Choosing between UPDATE or MODIFY with BY

Using the UPDATE statement is comparable to using MODIFY with BY to apply transactions to a data set. While MODIFY is a more powerful tool with several other applications, UPDATE is still the tool of choice in some cases. The following table helps you choose whether to use UPDATE or MODIFY with BY.

Table 23.3 MODIFY with BY versus UPDATE

Issue	MODIFY with BY	UPDATE
Disk space	saves disk space because it updates data in place	requires more disk space because it produces an updated copy of the data set
Sort and index	sorted input data sets are not required, although for good performance, it is strongly recommended that both data sets be sorted and that the master data set be indexed	requires only that both data sets be sorted
When to use	use only when you expect to process a SMALL portion of the data set	use if you expect to need to process most of the data set
Where to specify the modified data set	specify the updated data set in both the DATA and the MODIFY statements	specify the updated data set in the DATA and the UPDATE statements
Duplicate BY-values	allows duplicate BY-values in both the master and the transaction data sets	allows duplicate BY-values in the transaction data set only (If duplicates exist in the master data set, SAS issues a warning.)
Scope of changes	cannot change the data set descriptor information, so changes such as adding or deleting variables, variable labels, and so on, are not valid	can make changes that require a change in the descriptor portion of a data set, such as adding new variables, and so on
Error checking	has error-checking capabilities using the _IORC_ automatic variable and the SYSRC autocall macro	needs no error checking because transactions without a corresponding master record are not applied but are added to the data set
Data set integrity	data may only be partially updated due to an abnormal task termination	no data loss occurs because UPDATE works on a copy of the data

For more information about tools for combining SAS data sets, see Table 23.2 on page 399.

Primary Uses of the MODIFY Statement

The MODIFY statement has three primary uses:

☐ modifying observations in a single SAS data set.

☐ modifying observations in a single SAS data set directly, either by observation number or by values in an index.

☐ modifying observations in a master data set, based on values in a transaction data set. MODIFY with BY is similar to using the UPDATE statement.

Several of the examples that follow demonstrate these uses.

Example 1: Using UPDATE for Basic Updating

In this example, the data set MASTER contains original values of the variables Animal and Plant. The data set NEWPLANT is a transaction data set with new values of the variable Plant. The following shows the MASTER and the NEWPLANT input data sets:

```
         MASTER                              NEWPLANT


OBS  Common  Animal  Plant           OBS  Common  Plant


 1     a      Ant    Apple            1     a      Apricot
 2     b      Bird   Banana           2     b      Barley
 3     c      Cat    Coconut          3     c      Cactus
 4     d      Dog    Dewberry         4     d      Date
 5     e      Eagle  Eggplant         5     e      Escarole
 6     f      Frog   Fig              6     f      Fennel
```

The following program updates MASTER with the transactions in the data set NEWPLANT, writes the results to UPDATE_FILE, and prints the results:

```
data update_file;
   update master newplant;
   by common;
run;


proc print data=update_file;
   title 'Data Set Update_File';
run;
```

Output 23.14   Master Data Set Updated by Transaction Data Set

```
                    Data Set Update_File                        1

            Obs      Common     Animal     Plant

             1         a         Ant       Apricot
             2         b         Bird      Barley
             3         c         Cat       Cactus
             4         d         Dog       Date
             5         e         Eagle     Escarole
             6         f         Frog      Fennel
```

Each observation in the new data set contains a new value for the variable Plant.

Example 2: Using UPDATE with Duplicate Values of the BY Variable

If the master data set contains two observations with the same value of the BY variable, the first observation is updated and the second observation is ignored. SAS writes a warning message to the log. If the transaction data set contains duplicate values of the BY variable, SAS applies both transactions to the observation. The last values copied into the program data vector are written to the new data set. The following shows the MASTER1 and the DUPPLANT input data sets.

```
       MASTER1                              DUPPLANT

OBS Common Animal1 Plant1         OBS Common Plant1

  1    a    Ant    Apple            1    a    Apricot
  2    b    Bird   Banana           2    b    Barley
  3    b    Bird   Banana           3    c    Cactus
  4    c    Cat    Coconut          4    d    Date
  5    d    Dog    Dewberry         5    d    Dill
  6    e    Eagle  Eggplant         6    e    Escarole
  7    f    Frog   Fig              7    f    Fennel
```

The following program applies the transactions in DUPPLANT to MASTER1 and prints the results:

```
data update1;
   update master1 dupplant;
   by Common;
run;


proc print data=update1;
   title 'Data Set Update1';
run;
```

Output 23.15 Updating Data Sets with Duplicate BY Values

```
                    Data Set Update1                           1

              Obs    Common    Animal1    Plant1

               1       a        Ant       Apricot
               2       b        Bird      Barley
               3       b        Bird      Banana
               4       c        Cat       Cactus
               5       d        Dog       Dill
               6       e        Eagle     Escarole
               7       f        Frog      Fennel
```

When this DATA step executes, SAS generates a warning message stating that there is more than one observation for a BY group. However, the DATA step continues to process, and the data set UPDATE1 is created.

The resulting data set has seven observations. Observations 2 and 3 have duplicate values of the BY variable Common. However, the value of the variable PLANT1 was not updated in the second occurrence of the duplicate BY value.

Example 3: Using UPDATE for Processing Nonmatched Observations, Missing Values, and New Variables

In this example, the data set MASTER2 is a master data set. It contains a missing value for the variable Plant2 in the first observation, and not all of the values of the BY variable Common are included. The transaction data set NONPLANT contains a new variable Mineral, a new value of the BY variable Common, and missing values for several observations. The following shows the MASTER2 and the NONPLANT input data sets:

```
              MASTER2                                    NONPLANT

    OBS   Common   Animal2   Plant2      OBS   Common   Plant2    Mineral

     1      a       Ant                   1      a      Apricot   Amethyst
     2      c       Cat      Coconut      2      b      Barley    Beryl
     3      d       Dog      Dewberry     3      c      Cactus
     4      e       Eagle    Eggplant     4      e
     5      f       Frog     Fig          5      f      Fennel
                                          6      g      Grape     Garnet
```

The following program updates the data set MASTER2 and prints the results:

```
data update2_file;
   update master2 nonplant;
   by Common;
run;

proc print data=update2_file;
   title 'Data Set Update2_File';
run;
```

Output 23.16   Results of Updating with New Variables, Nonmatched Observations, and Missing Values

```
                      Data Set Update2_File                            1

        Obs       Common      Animal2     Plant2      Mineral

         1          a          Ant        Apricot     Amethyst
         2          b                     Barley      Beryl
         3          c          Cat        Cactus
         4          d          Dog        Dewberry
         5          e          Eagle      Eggplant
         6          f          Frog       Fennel
         7          g                     Grape       Garnet
```

As shown, all observations now include values for the variable Mineral. The value of Mineral is set to missing for some observations. Observations 2 and 6 in the transaction data set did not have corresponding observations in MASTER2, and they have become new observations. Observation 3 from the master data set was written to the new data set without change, and the value for Plant2 in observation 4 was not changed to missing. Three observations in the new data set have updated values for the variable Plant2.

The following program uses the UPDATEMODE statement option on the UPDATE statement, and prints the results:

```
data update2_file;
   update master2 nonplant updatemode=nomissingcheck;
   by Common;
run;
proc print data=update2_file;
```

```
        title 'Data Set Update2_File - UPDATEMODE Option';
    run;
```

Output 23.17 Results of Updating with the UPDATEMODE Option

```
                    Data Set Update2_File - UPDATEMODE Option                    1

             Obs     Common     Animal2     Plant2       Mineral

              1        a        Ant        Apricot      Amethyst
              2        b                   Barley       Beryl
              3        c        Cat        Cactus
              4        d        Dog        Dewberry
              5        e        Eagle
              6        f        Frog       Fennel
              7        g                   Grape        Garnet
```

The value of Plant2 in observation 5 is set to missing because the UPDATEMODE=NOMISSINGCHECK option is in effect.

For detailed examples for updating data sets, see *Combining and Modifying SAS Data Sets: Examples*.

Example 4: Updating a MASTER Data Set by Adding an Observation

If the transaction data set contains an observation that does not match an observation in the master data set, you must alter the program. The Year value in observation 5 of TRANSACTION has no match in MASTER. The following shows the MASTER and the TRANSACTION input data sets:

```
        MASTER                          TRANSACTION

OBS   Year   VarX   VarY      OBS   Year   VarX   VarY

 1    1985   x1     y1         1    1991   x2
 2    1986   x1     y1         2    1992   x2     y2
 3    1987   x1     y1         3    1993   x2
 4    1988   x1     y1         4    1993          y2
 5    1989   x1     y1         5    1995   x2     y2
 6    1990   x1     y1
 7    1991   x1     y1
 8    1992   x1     y1
 9    1993   x1     y1
10    1994   x1     y1
```

You must use an explicit OUTPUT statement to write a new observation to a master data set. (The default action for a DATA step using a MODIFY statement is REPLACE, not OUTPUT.) Once you specify an explicit OUTPUT statement, you must also specify a REPLACE statement. The following DATA step updates data set MASTER, based on values in TRANSACTION, and adds a new observation. This program also uses the _IORC_ automatic variable for error checking. (For more information about error checking, see "Error Checking When Using Indexes to Randomly Access or Update Data" on page 428.)

Output 23.18 Modified MASTER Data Set

```
                    Updated Master Data Set -- MODIFY                    1
                          One Observation Added

                  Obs    Year    VarX    VarY

                   1     1985     x1      y1
                   2     1986     x1      y1
                   3     1987     x1      y1
                   4     1988     x1      y1
                   5     1989     x1      y1
                   6     1990     x1      y1
                   7     1991     x2      y1
                   8     1992     x2      y2
                   9     1993     x2      y2
                  10     1994     x1      y1
                  11     1995     x2      y2
```

SAS added a new observation, observation 11, to the MASTER data set and updated observations 7, 8, and 9.

Error Checking When Using Indexes to Randomly Access or Update Data

The Importance of Error Checking

When reading observations with the SET statement and KEY= option or with the MODIFY statement, error checking is imperative for several reasons. The most important reason is that these tools use nonsequential access methods, and so there is no guarantee that an observation will be located that satisfies the request. Error checking enables you to direct execution to specific code paths, depending on the outcome of the I/O operation. Your program will continue execution for expected conditions and terminate execution when unexpected results occur.

Error-Checking Tools

Two tools have been created to make error checking easier when you use the MODIFY statement or the SET statement with the KEY= option to process SAS data sets:

☐ _IORC_ automatic variable

☐ SYSRC autocall macro.

IORC is created automatically when you use the MODIFY statement or the SET statement with KEY=. The value of _IORC_ is a numeric return code that indicates the status of the I/O operation from the most recently executed MODIFY or SET statement with KEY=. Checking the value of this variable enables you to detect abnormal I/O conditions and to direct execution down specific code paths instead of having the application terminate abnormally. For example, if the KEY= variable value does match between two observations, you might want to combine them and output an observation. If they don't match, however, you may want only to write a note to the log.

Because the values of the _IORC_ automatic variable are internal and subject to change, the SYSRC macro was created to enable you to test for specific I/O conditions while protecting your code from future changes in _IORC_ values. When you use

SYSRC, you can check the value of _IORC_ by specifying one of the mnemonics listed in the following table.

Table 23.4 Most Common Mnemonic Values of _IORC_ for DATA Step Processing

Mnemonic value	Meaning of return code	When return code occurs
_DSENMR	The TRANSACTION data set observation does not exist in the MASTER data set.	MODIFY with BY is used and no match occurs.
_DSEMTR	Multiple TRANSACTION data set observations with the same BY variable value do not exist in the MASTER data set.	MODIFY with BY is used and consecutive observations with the same BY values do not find a match in the first data set. In this situation, the first observation that fails to find a match returns _DSENMR. The subsequent observations return _DSEMTR.
_DSENOM	No matching observation was found in the MASTER data set.	SET or MODIFY with KEY= finds no match.
_SENOCHN	The output operation was unsuccessful.	the KEY= option in a MODIFY statement contains duplicate values.
_SOK	The I/O operation was successful.	a match is found.

Example 1: Routing Execution When an Unexpected Condition Occurs

Overview

This example shows how to prevent an unexpected condition from terminating the DATA step. The goal is to update a master data set with new information from a transaction data set. This application assumes that there are no duplicate values for the common variable in either data set.

Note: This program works as expected only if the master and transaction data sets contain no consecutive observations with the same value for the common variable. For an explanation of the behavior of MODIFY with KEY= when duplicates exist, see the MODIFY statement in *SAS Language Reference: Dictionary.* △

Input Data Sets

The TRANSACTION data set contains three observations: two updates to information in MASTER and a new observation about PartNumber value 6 that needs to be added. MASTER is indexed on PartNumber. There are no duplicate values of PartNumber in MASTER or TRANSACTION. The following shows the MASTER and the TRANSACTION input data sets:

```
        MASTER                           TRANSACTION

OBS   PartNumber   Quantity      OBS   PartNumber   AddQuantity

 1        1           10          1        4            14
 2        2           20          2        6            16
```

3	3	30	3	2	12
4	4	40			
5	5	50			

Original Program

The objective is to update the MASTER data set with information from the TRANSACTION data set. The program reads TRANSACTION sequentially. MASTER is read directly, not sequentially, using the MODIFY statement and the KEY= option. Only observations with matching values for PartNumber, which is the KEY= variable, are read from MASTER.

```
data master;  ❶
   set transaction;  ❷
   modify master key=PartNumber;  ❸
   Quantity = Quantity + AddQuantity;  ❹
run;
```

❶ Open the MASTER data set for update.

❷ Read an observation from the TRANSACTION data set.

❸ Match observations from the MASTER data set based on the values of PartNumber.

❹ Update the information on Quantity by adding the new values from the TRANSACTION data set.

Resulting Log

This program has correctly updated one observation but it stopped when it could not find a match for PartNumber value 6. The following lines are written to the SAS log:

```
ERROR: No matching observation was found in MASTER data set.
PartNumber=6 AddQuantity=16 Quantity=70 _ERROR_=1
_IORC_=1230015 _N_=2
NOTE: The SAS System stopped processing this step because
      of errors.
NOTE: The data set WORK.MASTER has been updated.  There were
      1 observations rewritten, 0 observations added and 0
      observations deleted.
```

Resulting Data Set

The MASTER file was incorrectly updated. The updated master has five observations. One observation was updated correctly, a new one was not added, and a second update was not made. The following shows the incorrectly updated MASTER data set:

```
MASTER
```

OBS	PartNumber	Quantity
1	1	10
2	2	20
3	3	30
4	4	54
5	5	50

Revised Program

The objective is to apply two updates and one addition to MASTER, preventing the DATA step from stopping when it does not find a match in MASTER for the PartNumber value 6 in TRANSACTION. By adding error checking, this DATA step is allowed to complete normally and produce a correctly revised version of MASTER. This program uses the _IORC_ automatic variable and the SYSRC autocall macro in a SELECT group to check the value of the _IORC_ variable and execute the appropriate code based on whether or not a match is found.

```
data master; ❶
   set transaction;  ❷
   modify master key=PartNumber;  ❸
select(_iorc_);  ❹
      when(%sysrc(_sok)) do;
         Quantity = Quantity + AddQuantity;
         replace;
      end;
      when(%sysrc(_dsenom)) do;
         Quantity = AddQuantity;
         _error_ = 0;
         output;
      end;
      otherwise do;
         put 'ERROR: Unexpected value for _IORC_= ' _iorc_;
         put 'Program terminating. Data step iteration # ' _n_;
         put _all_;
         stop;
      end;
   end;
run;
```

❶ Open the MASTER data set for update.

❷ Read an observation from the TRANSACTION data set.

❸ Match observations from the MASTER data set based on the value of PartNumber.

❹ Take the correct course of action based on whether a matching value for PartNumber is found in MASTER. Update Quantity by adding the new values from TRANSACTION. The SELECT group directs execution to the correct code. When a match occurs (_SOK), update Quantity and replace the original observation in MASTER. When there is no match (_DSENOM), set Quantity equal to the AddQuantity amount from TRANSACTION, and append a new observation. _ERROR_ is reset to 0 to prevent an error condition that would write the contents of the program data vector to the SAS log. When an unexpected condition occurs, write messages and the contents of the program data vector to the log, and stop the DATA step.

Resulting Log

The DATA step executed without error and observations were appropriately updated and added. The following lines are written to the SAS log:

```
NOTE: The data set WORK.MASTER has been updated.  There were
      2 observations rewritten, 1 observations added and 0
      observations deleted.
```

Correctly Updated MASTER Data Set

MASTER contains updated quantities for PartNumber values 2 and 4 and a new observation for PartNumber value 6. The following shows the correctly updated MASTER data set:

```
                MASTER

   OBS    PartNumber     Quantity
    1          1            10
    2          2            32
    3          3            30
    4          4            54
    5          5            50
    6          6            16
```

Example 2: Using Error Checking on All Statements That Use KEY=

Overview

This example shows how important it is to use error checking on all statements that use the KEY= option when reading data.

Input Data Sets

The MASTER and DESCRIPTION data sets are both indexed on PartNumber. The ORDER data set contains values for all parts in a single order. Only ORDER contains the PartNumber value 8. The following shows the MASTER, ORDER, and DESCRIPTION input data sets:

```
            MASTER                               ORDER

 OBS    PartNumber    Quantity         OBS    PartNumber

  1        100           10             1        200
  2        200           20             2        400
  3        300           30             3        100
  4        400           40             4        300
  5        500           50             5        800
                                        6        500
                                        7        600

            DESCRIPTION

 OBS    PartNumber    PartDescription

  1        400           Nuts
  2        300           Bolts
  3        200           Screws
  4        600           Washers
```

Original Program with Logic Error

The objective is to create a data set that contains the description and number in stock for each part in a single order, except for the parts that are not found in either of the two input data sets, MASTER and DESCRIPTION. A transaction data set contains the part numbers of all parts in a single order. One data set is read to retrieve the description of the part and another is read to retrieve the quantity that is in stock.

The program reads the ORDER data set sequentially and then uses SET with the KEY= option to read the MASTER and DESCRIPTION data sets directly, based on the key value of PartNumber. When a match occurs, an observation is written that contains all the necessary information for each value of PartNumber in ORDER. This first attempt at a solution uses error checking for only one of the two SET statements that use KEY= to read a data set.

```
data combine; ❶
   length PartDescription $ 15;
   set order;  ❷
   set description key=PartNumber;  ❷
   set master key=PartNumber;  ❷
   select(_iorc_); ❸
         when(%sysrc(_sok)) do;
            output;
         end;
         when(%sysrc(_dsenom)) do;
            PartDescription = 'No description';
            _error_ = 0;
            output;
         end;
         otherwise do;
            put 'ERROR: Unexpected value for _IORC_ = ' _iorc_;
            put 'Program terminating.';
            put _all_;
            stop;
         end;
   end;
run;
```

❶ Create the COMBINE data set.

❷ Read an observation from the ORDER data set. Read an observation from the DESCRIPTION and the MASTER data sets based on a matching value for PartNumber, the key variable. Note that no error checking occurs after an observation is read from DESCRIPTION.

❸ Take the correct course of action, based on whether a matching value for PartNumber is found in MASTER or DESCRIPTION. (This logic is based on the erroneous assumption that this SELECT group performs error checking for both of the preceding SET statements that contain the KEY= option. It actually performs error checking for only the most recent one.) The SELECT group directs execution to the correct code. When a match occurs (_SOK), the value of PartNumber in the observation that is being read from MASTER matches the current PartNumber value from ORDER. So, output an observation. When there is no match (_DSENOM), no observations in MASTER contain the current value of PartNumber, so set the value of PartDescription appropriately and output an observation. _ERROR_ is reset to 0 to prevent an error condition that would write the contents of the program data vector to the SAS log. When an unexpected condition occurs, write messages and the contents of the program data vector to the log, and stop the DATA step.

Resulting Log

This program creates an output data set but executes with one error. The following lines are written to the SAS log:

```
PartNumber=1 PartDescription=Nuts Quantity=10 _ERROR_=1
_IORC_=0 _N_=3
PartNumber=5 PartDescription=No description Quantity=50
_ERROR_=1 _IORC_=0 _N_=6
NOTE: The data set WORK.COMBINE has 7 observations and 3 variables.
```

Resulting Data Set

The following shows the incorrectly created COMBINE data set. Observation 5 should not be in this data set. PartNumber value 8 does not exist in either MASTER or DESCRIPTION, so no Quantity should be listed for it. Also, observations 3 and 7 contain descriptions from observations 2 and 6, respectively.

```
                      COMBINE

OBS     PartNumber     PartDescription     Quantity
 1          2          Screws                 20
 2          4          Nuts                   40
 3          1          Nuts                   10
 4          3          Bolts                  30
 5          8          No description         30
 6          5          No description         50
 7          6          No description         50
```

Revised Program

To create an accurate output data set, this example performs error checking on both SET statements that use the KEY= option:

```
data combine(drop=Foundes); ❶
   length PartDescription $ 15;
   set order;  ❷
   Foundes = 0;  ❸
   set description key=PartNumber;  ❹
   select(_iorc_);  ❺
      when(%sysrc(_sok)) do;
         Foundes = 1;
      end;
      when(%sysrc(_dsenom)) do;
         PartDescription = 'No description';
         _error_ = 0;
      end;
      otherwise do;
         put 'ERROR: Unexpected value for _IORC_= ' _iorc_;
         put 'Program terminating. Data set accessed is DESCRIPTION';
         put _all_;
         _error_ = 0;
         stop;
      end;
   end;
   set master key=PartNumber;  ❻
   select(_iorc_);  ❼
      when(%sysrc(_sok)) do;
         output;
      end;
      when(%sysrc(_dsenom)) do;
```

```
            if not Foundes then do;
               _error_ = 0;
               put 'WARNING: PartNumber ' PartNumber 'is not in'
                   ' DESCRIPTION or MASTER.';
            end;
            else do;
               Quantity = 0;
               _error_ = 0;
               output;
            end;
         end;
         otherwise do;
            put 'ERROR: Unexpected value for _IORC_= ' _iorc_;
            put 'Program terminating. Data set accessed is MASTER';
            put _all_;
            _error_ = 0;
            stop;
         end;
      end;        /* ends the SELECT group */
```

❶ Create the COMBINE data set.

❷ Read an observation from the ORDER data set.

❸ Create the variable Foundes so that its value can be used later to indicate when a PartNumber value has a match in the DESCRIPTION data set.

❹ Read an observation from the DESCRIPTION data set, using PartNumber as the key variable.

❺ Take the correct course of action based on whether a matching value for PartNumber is found in DESCRIPTION. The SELECT group directs execution to the correct code based on the value of _IORC_. When a match occurs (_SOK), the value of PartNumber in the observation that is being read from DESCRIPTION matches the current value from ORDER. Foundes is set to 1 to indicate that DESCRIPTION contributed to the current observation. When there is no match (_DSENOM), no observations in DESCRIPTION contain the current value of PartNumber, so the description is set appropriately. _ERROR_ is reset to 0 to prevent an error condition that would write the contents of the program data vector to the SAS log. Any other _IORC_ value indicates that an unexpected condition has been met, so messages are written to the log and the DATA step is stopped.

❻ Read an observation from the MASTER data set, using PartNumber as a key variable.

❼ Take the correct course of action based on whether a matching value for PartNumber is found in MASTER. When a match is found (_SOK) between the current PartNumber value from ORDER and from MASTER, write an observation. When a match isn't found (_DSENOM) in MASTER, test the value of Foundes. If Foundes is not true, then a value wasn't found in DESCRIPTION either, so write a message to the log but do not write an observation. If Foundes is true, however, the value is in DESCRIPTION but not MASTER. So write an observation but set Quantity to 0. Again, if an unexpected condition occurs, write a message and stop the DATA step.

Resulting Log

The DATA step executed without error. Six observations were correctly created and the following message was written to the log:

```
          WARNING: PartNumber 8 is not in DESCRIPTION or MASTER.
          NOTE: The data set WORK.COMBINE has 6 observations
               and 3 variables.
```

Correctly Created COMBINE Data Set

The following shows the correctly updated COMBINE data set. Note that COMBINE does not contain an observation with the PartNumber value 8. This value does not occur in either MASTER or DESCRIPTION.

```
                    COMBINE

    OBS    PartNumber    PartDescription    Quantity

    1          2         Screws                20
    2          4         Nuts                  40
    3          1         No description        10
    4          3         Bolts                 30
    5          5         No description        50
    6          6         Washers                0
```

CHAPTER

24

Using DATA Step Component Objects

Introduction   **437**
Using the Hash Object   **438**
    Why Use the Hash Object?   **438**
    Declaring and Instantiating a Hash Object   **438**
    Initializing Hash Object Data Using a Constructor   **439**
    Defining Keys and Data   **440**
    Storing and Retrieving Data   **441**
        Example 1: Using the ADD and FIND Methods to Store and Retrieve Data   **441**
        Example 2: Loading a Data Set and Using the FIND Method to Retrieve Data   **442**
    Replacing and Removing Data   **442**
    Saving Hash Object Data in a Data Set   **444**
Using the Hash Iterator Object   **445**
    Introducing the Hash Iterator Object   **445**
    Declaring and Instantiating a Hash Iterator Object   **445**
    Example: Retrieving Hash Object Data by Using the Hash Iterator   **446**

Introduction

SAS provides two predefined component objects for use in a DATA step: the hash object and the hash iterator object. These objects enable you to quickly and efficiently store, search, and retrieve data based on lookup keys. The hash object keys and data are DATA step variables. Key and data values can be directly assigned constant values or values from a SAS data set.

The DATA step Component Interface enables you to create and manipulate these component objects using statements, attributes, and methods. You use the DATA step object dot notation to access the component object's attributes and methods. For detailed information about dot notation and the DATA step objects' statements, attributes, and methods, see "DATA Step Object Attributes and Methods" in *SAS Language Reference: Dictionary*.

Note: The hash and hash iterator object attributes and methods are limited to those defined for these objects. You cannot use the SAS Component Language functionality with these predefined DATA step objects. △

Using the Hash Object

Why Use the Hash Object?

The hash object provides an efficient, convenient mechanism for quick data storage and retrieval. The hash object stores and retrieves data based on lookup keys.

To use the DATA step Component Object Interface, follow these steps:

1 Declare the hash object.

2 Create an instance of (*instantiate*) the hash object.

3 Initialize look-up keys and data.

After you declare and instantiate a hash object, you can perform many tasks, including the following:

□ Store and retrieve data.

□ Replace and remove data.

□ Output a data set that contains the data in the hash object.

For example, suppose that you have a large data set that contains numeric lab results that correspond to patient number and weight and a small data set that contains patient numbers (a subset of those in the large data set). You can load the large data set into a hash object using the patient number as the key and the weight values as the data. You can then iterate over the small data set using the patient number to look up the current patient in the hash object whose weight is over a certain value and output that data to a different data set.

Depending on the number of lookup keys and the size of the data set, the hash object lookup can be significantly faster than a standard format lookup.

Declaring and Instantiating a Hash Object

You declare a hash object using the DECLARE statement. After you declare the new hash object, use the _NEW_ statement to instantiate the object.

```
declare hash myhash;
myhash = _new_ hash();
```

The DECLARE statement tells the compiler that the variable MYHASH is of type hash. At this point, you have only declared the variable MYHASH. It has the potential to hold a component object of type hash. You should declare the hash object only once. The _NEW_ statement creates an instance of the hash object and assigns it to the variable MYHASH.

As an alternative to the two-step process of using the DECLARE and the _NEW_ statement to declare and instantiate a component object, you can use the DECLARE statement to declare and instantiate the component object in one step.

```
declare hash myhash();
```

The above statement is equivalent to the following code:

```
declare hash myhash;
myhash = _new_ hash();
```

For more information about the "DECLARE Statement" and the "_NEW_ Statement", see *SAS Language Reference: Dictionary*.

Initializing Hash Object Data Using a Constructor

When you create a hash object, you might want to provide initialization data. A *constructor* is a method that you can use to instantiate a hash object and initialize the hash object data.

The hash object constructor can have either of the following formats:

☐ declare hash *variable_name*(*argument_tag-1* : *value-1*
    <, ...*argument_tag-n*: *value-n*>);

☐ *variable_name* = _new_ hash(*argument_tag-1*: *value-1*
    <, ...*argument_tag-n*: *value-n*>);

These are the valid hash object argument tags:

hashexp: *n*
    is the hash object's internal table size, where the size of the hash table is 2^n.

    The value of hashexp is used as a power-of-two exponent to create the hash table size. For example, a value of 4 for hashexp equates to a hash table size of 2^4, or 16. The maximum value for hashexp is 16, which equates to a hash table size of 2^{16} or 65536.

    The hash table size is not equal to the number of items that can be stored. Think of the hash table as an array of containers. A hash table size of 16 would have 16 containers. Each container can hold an infinite number of items. The efficiency of the hash tables lies in the ability of the hash function to map items to and retrieve items from the containers.

    In order to maximize the efficiency of the hash object lookup routines, you should set the hash table size according to the amount of data in the hash object. Try different hashexp values until you get the best result. For example, if the hash object contains one million items, a hash table size of 16 (hashexp = 4) would not be very efficient. A hash table size of 512 or 1024 (hashexp = 9 or 10) would result in better performance.

    Default: 8, which equates to a hash table size of 2^8 or 256.

dataset: '*dataset_name*'
    is the name of a SAS data set to load into the hash object.

    The name of the SAS data set can be a literal or a character variable. The data set name must be enclosed in single or double quotation marks. Macro variables must be in double quotation marks.

    Note: If the data set contains duplicate keys, the first instance will be in the hash object; subsequent instances will be ignored. △

ordered: '*option*'
    specifies whether or how the data is returned in key-value order if you use the hash object with a hash iterator object or if you use the hash object OUTPUT method.

    option can be one of the following values:

'ascending' | 'a'   Data is returned in ascending key-value order. Specifying 'ascending' is the same as specifying 'yes'.

'descending' | 'd'   Data is returned in descending key-value order.

'YES' | 'Y'   Data is returned in ascending key-value order. Specifying 'yes' is the same as specifying 'ascending'.

'NO' | 'N'   Data is returned in an undefined order.

Default: NO

    The argument can also be enclosed in double quotation marks.

For more information on the "DECLARE Statement" and the "_NEW_ Statement", see *SAS Language Reference: Dictionary*.

Defining Keys and Data

The hash object uses lookup keys to store and retrieve data. The keys and the data are DATA step variables that you use to initialize the hash object by using dot notation method calls. A key is defined by passing the key variable name to the DEFINEKEY method. Data is defined by passing the data variable name to the DEFINEDATA method. When all key and data variables have been defined, the DEFINEDONE method is called. Keys and data can consist of any number of character or numeric DATA step variables.

For example, the following code initializes a character key and a character data variable.

```
length d $20;
length k $20;

if _N_ = 1 then do;
   declare hash h(hashexp: 4);
   rc = h.defineKey('k');
   rc = h.defineData('d');
   rc = h.defineDone();
end;
```

You can have multiple key and data variables. You can store more than one data item with a particular key. For example, you could modify the previous example to store auxiliary numeric values with the character key and data. In this example, each key and each data item consists of a character value and a numeric value.

```
length d1 8;
length d2 $20;
length k1 $20;
length k2 8;

if _N_ = 1 then do;
   declare hash h(hashexp: 4);
   rc = h.defineKey('k1', 'k2');
   rc = h.defineData('d1', 'd2');
   rc = h.defineDone();
end;
```

For more information about the "DEFINEDATA Method", the "DEFINEDONE Method", and the "DEFINEKEY Method", see *SAS Language Reference: Dictionary*.

Note: The hash object does not assign values to key variables (for example, h.find(key: 'abc')), and the SAS compiler cannot detect the implicit key and data variable assignments done by the hash object and the hash iterator. Therefore, if no explicit assignment to a key or data variable appears in the program, SAS will issue a note stating that the variable is uninitialized. To avoid receiving these notes, you can perform one of the following actions:

☐ Set the NONOTES system option.

☐ Provide an initial assignment statement (typically to a missing value) for each key and data variable.

☐ Use the CALL MISSING routine with all the key and data variables as parameters. Here is an example.

```
length d $20;
length k $20;

if _N_ = 1 then do;
   declare hash h(hashexp: 4);
   rc = h.defineKey('k');
   rc = h.defineData('d');
   rc = h.defineDone();
      call missing(k, d);
end;
```

△

Storing and Retrieving Data

After you initialize the hash object's key and data variables, you can store data in the hash object using the ADD method, or you can use the *dataset* argument tag to quickly load a data set into the hash object.

You can then use the FIND method to search and retrieve data from the hash object.

For more information about the "ADD Method" and the "FIND Method", see *SAS Language Reference: Dictionary*.

Note: You can also use the hash iterator object to retrieve the hash object data, one data element at a time, in forward and reverse order. For more information, see "Using the Hash Iterator Object" on page 445. △

Example 1: Using the ADD and FIND Methods to Store and Retrieve Data

The following example uses the ADD method to store the data in the hash object and associate the data with the key. The FIND method is then used to retrieve the data that is associated with the key value 'Homer'.

```
data _null_;
length d $20;
length k $20;

/* Declare the hash object and key and data variables */
if _N_ = 1 then do;
   declare hash h(hashexp: 4);
   rc = h.defineKey('k');
   rc = h.defineData('d');
   rc = h.defineDone();
end;

/* Define constant value for key and data */
k = 'Homer';
d = 'Odyssey';
/* Use the ADD method to add the key and data to the hash object */
rc = h.add();
if (rc ne 0) then
   put 'Add failed.';

/* Define constant value for key and data */
k = 'Joyce';
d = 'Ulysses';
/* Use the ADD method to add the key and data to the hash object */
```

```
rc = h.add();
if (rc ne 0) then
   put 'Add failed.';


k = 'Homer';
/* Use the FIND method to retrieve the data associated with 'Homer' key */
rc = h.find();
if (rc = 0) then
   put d=;
else
   put 'Key Homer not found.';
run;
```

The FIND method assigns the data value 'Odyssey', which is associated with the key value 'Homer', to the variable D.

Example 2: Loading a Data Set and Using the FIND Method to Retrieve Data

Assume the data set SMALL contains two numeric variables K (key) and S (data) and another data set, LARGE, contains a corresponding key variable K. The following code loads the SMALL data set into the hash object, and then searches the hash object for key matches on the variable K from the LARGE data set.

```
data match;
   length k 8;
   length s 8;
   if _N_ = 1 then do;
      /* load SMALL data set into the hash object */
      declare hash h(dataset: "work.small", hashexp: 6);
      /* define SMALL data set variable K as key and S as value */
      h.defineKey('k');
      h.defineData('s');
      h.defineDone();
      /* avoid uninitialized variable notes */
      call missing(k, s);
   end;

/* use the SET statement to iterate over the LARGE data set using */
/* keys in the LARGE data set to match keys in the hash object */
set large;
rc = h.find();
if (rc = 0) then output;
run;
```

The *dataset* argument tag specifies the SMALL data set whose keys and data will be read and loaded by the hash object during the DEFINEDONE method. The FIND method is then used to retrieve the data.

Replacing and Removing Data

You can remove or replace data in the hash object.

In the following example, the REPLACE method replaces the data 'Odyssey' with 'Iliad' and the REMOVE method deletes the entire data entry associated with the 'Joyce' key from the hash object.

```
data _null_;
length d $20;
length k $20;

/* Declare the hash object and key and data variables */
if _N_ = 1 then do;
   declare hash h(hashexp: 4);
   rc = h.defineKey('k');
   rc = h.defineData('d');
   rc = h.defineDone();
end;

/* Define constant value for key and data */
k = 'Joyce';
d = 'Ulysses';
/* Use the ADD method to add the key and data to the hash object */
rc = h.add();
if (rc ne 0) then
   put 'Add failed.';

/* Define constant value for key and data */
k = 'Homer';
d = 'Odyssey';
/* Use the ADD method to add the key and data to the hash object */
rc = h.add();
if (rc ne 0) then
   put 'Add failed.';

/* Use the REPLACE method to replace 'Odyssey' with 'Iliad' */
k = 'Homer';
d = 'Iliad';
rc = h.replace();
if (rc = 0) then
   put d=;
else
   put 'Replace not successful.';

/* Use the REMOVE method to remove the 'Joyce' key and data */
k = 'Joyce';
rc = h.remove();
if (rc = 0) then
   put k 'removed from hash object';
else
   put 'Deletion not successful.';

run;
```

For more information on the "REMOVE Method" and the "REPLACE Method", see *SAS Language Reference: Dictionary*.

Saving Hash Object Data in a Data Set

You can create a data set that contains the data in a specified hash object by using the OUTPUT method. In the following example, two keys and data are added to the hash object and then output to the Work.out data set.

```
data test;
length d1 8;
length d2 $20;
length k1 $20;
length k2 8;

/* Declare the hash object and two key and data variables */
if _N_ = 1 then do;
   declare hash h(hashexp: 4);
   rc = h.defineKey('k1', 'k2');
   rc = h.defineData('d1', 'd2');
   rc = h.defineDone();
end;

/* Define constant value for key and data */
k1 = 'Joyce';
k2 = 1001;
d1 = 3;
d2 = 'Ulysses';
rc = h.add();

/* Define constant value for key and data */
k1 = 'Homer';
k2 = 1002;
d1 = 5;
d2 = 'Odyssey';
rc = h.add();

/* Use the OUTPUT method to save the hash object data to the OUT data set */
rc = h.output(dataset: "work.out");
run;

proc print data=work.out;
run;
```

The following output shows the report that PROC PRINT generates.

Output 24.1   Data Set Created from the Hash Object

```
                        The SAS System                              1

                   Obs      d1        d2

                    1        5      Odyssey
                    2        3      Ulysses
```

Note that the hash object keys are not stored as part of the output data set. If you want to include the keys in the output data set, you must define the keys as data in the DEFINEDATA method. In the previous example, the DEFINEDATA method would be written this way:

```
rc = h.defineData('k1', 'k2', 'd1', 'd2');
```

For more information on the "OUTPUT Method" , see *SAS Language Reference: Dictionary*.

Using the Hash Iterator Object

Introducing the Hash Iterator Object

Use the hash object to store and search data based on lookup keys. The hash iterator object enables you to retrieve the hash object data in forward or reverse key order.

Declaring and Instantiating a Hash Iterator Object

You declare a hash iterator object by using the DECLARE statement. After you declare the new hash iterator object, use the _NEW_ statement to instantiate the object, using the hash object name as an argument tag. For example:

```
declare hiter myiter
myiter = _new_ hiter('h');
```

the DECLARE statement tells the compiler that the variable MYITER is of type hash iterator. At this point, you have only declared the variable MYITER. It has the potential to hold a component object of type hash iterator. You should declare the hash iterator object only once. The _NEW_ statement creates an instance of the hash iterator object and assigns it to the variable MYITER. The hash object, H, is passed as a constructor argument.

As an alternative to the two-step process of using the DECLARE and the _NEW_ statements to declare and instantiate a component object, you can declare and instantiate a hash iterator object in one step by using the DECLARE statement as a constructor method. The syntax is as follows:

```
declare hiter variable_name(hash_object_name);
```

In the above example, the hash object name must be enclosed in single or double quotation marks.

For example:

```
declare hiter myiter('h');
```

The previous statement is equivalent to these:

```
declare hiter myiter;
myiter = _new_ hiter('h');
```

Note: You must declare and instantiate a hash object before you create a hash iterator object. For more information, see "Declaring and Instantiating a Hash Object" on page 438. △

For example:

```
if _N_ = 1 then do;
    length key $10;
    declare hash myhash(hashexp: 4, dataset:"work.x", ordered: 'yes');
    declare hiter myiter('myhash');
    myhash.defineKey('key');
    myhash.defineDone();
end;
```

This code creates an instance of a hash iterator object with the variable name MYITER. The hash object, MYHASH, is passed as the constructor argument. Because the hash object was created with the *ordered* argument tag set to '**yes**', the data will be returned in ascending key-value order.

For more information about the "DECLARE Statement" and the "_NEW_ Statement", see *SAS Language Reference: Dictionary*.

Example: Retrieving Hash Object Data by Using the Hash Iterator

Using the data set ASTRO that contains astronomical data, the following code creates the data set that contains Messier (OBJ) objects whose right-ascension (RA) values are greater than 12. The FIRST and NEXT methods are used to sort the data in ascending order. The FIRST and NEXT methods are used to sort the data. For more information about the "FIRST Method" and the "NEXT Method", see *SAS Language Reference: Dictionary*.

```
data astro;
    input obj $1-4 ra $6-12 dec $14-19;
    datalines;
 M31 00 42.7 +41 16
 M71 19 53.8 +18 47
 M51 13 29.9 +47 12
 M98 12 13.8 +14 54
 M13 16 41.7 +36 28
 M39 21 32.2 +48 26
 M81 09 55.6 +69 04
M100 12 22.9 +15 49
 M41 06 46.0 -20 44
 M44 08 40.1 +19 59
 M10 16 57.1 -04 06
 M57 18 53.6 +33 02
  M3 13 42.2 +28 23
 M22 18 36.4 -23 54
```

```
   M23 17 56.8 -19 01
   M49 12 29.8 +08 00
   M68 12 39.5 -26 45
   M17 18 20.8 -16 11
   M14 17 37.6 -03 15
   M29 20 23.9 +38 32
   M34 02 42.0 +42 47
   M82 09 55.8 +69 41
   M59 12 42.0 +11 39
   M74 01 36.7 +15 47
   M25 18 31.6 -19 15
;
run;

data out;
   if _N_ = 1 then do;
      length obj $10;
      length ra $10;
      length dec $10;
      /* Read ASTRO data set as ordered */
      declare hash h(hashexp: 4, dataset:"work.astro", ordered: 'yes');
      /* Define variables RA and OBJ as key and data for hash object */
      declare hiter iter('h');
      h.defineKey('ra');
      h.defineData('ra', 'obj');
      h.defineDone();
      /* Avoid uninitialized variable notes */
      call missing(obj, ra, dec);
   end;
/* Sort hash object by right ascension values */
rc = iter.first();
do while (rc = 0);
/* Find hash object keys greater than 12 and output data */
   if ra GE '12' then
      output;
   rc = iter.next();
end;
run;

proc print data=work.out;
   var ra obj;
   title 'Messier Objects Greater than 12 Sorted by Right Ascension Values';
run;
```

The following output shows the report that PROC PRINT generates.

Output 24.2   Messier Objects Greater than 12, Sorted by Right Ascension Values

```
          Messier Objects Greater than 12 Sorted by Right Ascension Values        1

                          Obs       ra        obj

                           1      12 13.8     M98
                           2      12 22.9     M100
                           3      12 29.8     M49
                           4      12 39.5     M68
                           5      12 42.0     M59
                           6      13 29.9     M51
                           7      13 42.2     M3
                           8      16 41.7     M13
                           9      16 57.1     M10
                          10      17 37.6     M14
                          11      17 56.8     M23
                          12      18 20.8     M17
                          13      18 31.6     M25
                          14      18 36.4     M22
                          15      18 53.6     M57
                          16      19 53.8     M71
                          17      20 23.9     M29
                          18      21 32.2     M39
```

CHAPTER

25

Array Processing

Definitions for Array Processing   **449**
A Conceptual View of Arrays   **450**
 One-Dimensional Array   **450**
 Two-Dimensional Array   **451**
Syntax for Defining and Referencing an Array   **451**
Processing Simple Arrays   **452**
 Grouping Variables in a Simple Array   **452**
 Using a DO Loop to Repeat an Action   **453**
 Using a DO Loop to Process Selected Elements in an Array   **453**
 Selecting the Current Variable   **453**
 Defining the Number of Elements in an Array   **455**
 Rules for Referencing Arrays   **455**
Variations on Basic Array Processing   **456**
 Determining the Number of Elements in an Array Efficiently   **456**
 DO WHILE and DO UNTIL Expressions   **456**
 Using Variable Lists to Define an Array Quickly   **456**
Multidimensional Arrays: Creating and Processing   **457**
 Grouping Variables in a Multidimensional Array   **457**
 Using Nested DO Loops   **457**
Specifying Array Bounds   **459**
 Identifying Upper and Lower Bounds   **459**
 Determining Array Bounds: LBOUND and HBOUND Functions   **460**
 When to Use the HBOUND Function instead of the DIM Function   **460**
 Specifying Bounds in a Two-Dimensional Array   **460**
Examples of Array Processing   **461**
 Example 1: Using Character Variables in an Array   **461**
 Example 2: Assigning Initial Values to the Elements of an Array   **462**
 Example 3: Creating an Array for Temporary Use in the Current DATA Step   **463**
 Example 4: Performing an Action on All Numeric Variables   **464**

Definitions for Array Processing

array
 is a temporary grouping of SAS variables that are arranged in a particular order and identified by an *array-name*. The array exists only for the duration of the current DATA step. The array-name distinguishes it from any other arrays in the same DATA step; it is not a variable.

Note: Arrays in SAS are different from those in many other programming languages. In SAS, an array is not a data structure but is just a convenient way of temporarily identifying a group of variables. △

array processing
is a method that enables you to perform the same tasks for a series of related variables.

array reference
is a method to reference the elements of an array.

one-dimensional array
is a simple grouping of variables that, when processed, results in output that can be represented in simple row format.

multidimensional array
is a more complex grouping of variables that, when processed, results in output that could have two or more dimensions, such as columns and rows.

Basic array processing involves the following steps:

☐ grouping variables into arrays

☐ selecting a current variable for an action

☐ repeating an action.

A Conceptual View of Arrays

One-Dimensional Array

The following figure is a conceptual representation of two one-dimensional arrays, MISC and MDAY.

Figure 25.1   One-Dimensional Array

Arrays	Variables							
	1	2	3	4	5	6	7	8
MISC	misc1	misc2	misc3	misc4	misc5	misc6	misc7	misc8
	1	2	3	4	5	6	7	
MDAY	mday1	mday2	mday3	mday4	mday5	mday6	mday7	

MISC contains eight elements, the variables MISC1 through MISC8. To reference the data in these variables, use the form MISC{n}, where n is the element number in the array. For example, MISC{6} is the sixth element in the array.

MDAY contains seven elements, the variables MDAY1 through MDAY7. MDAY{3} is the third element in the array.

Two-Dimensional Array

The following figure is a conceptual representation of the two-dimensional array EXPENSES.

Figure 25.2   Example of a Two-Dimensional Array

First Dimension		Second Dimension							
Expense Categories				Days of the Week					Total
		1	2	3	4	5	6	7	8
Hotel	1	hotel1	hotel2	hotel3	hotel4	hotel5	hotel6	hotel7	hotel8
Phone	2	phone1	phone2	phone3	phone4	phone5	phone6	phone7	phone8
Pers. Auto	3	peraut1	peraut2	peraut3	peraut4	peraut5	peraut6	peraut7	peraut8
Rental Car	4	carrnt1	carrnt2	carrnt3	carrnt4	carrnt5	carrnt6	carrnt7	carrnt8
Airfare	5	airlin1	airlin2	airlin3	airlin4	airlin5	airlin6	airlin7	airlin8
Dues	6	dues1	dues2	dues3	dues4	dues5	dues6	dues7	dues8
Registration Fees	7	regfee1	regfee2	regfee3	regfee4	regfee5	regfee6	regfee7	regfee8
Other	8	other1	other2	other3	other4	other5	other6	other7	other8
Tips (non-meal)	9	tips1	tips2	tips3	tips4	tips5	tips6	tips7	tips8
Meals	10	meals1	meals2	meals3	meals4	meals5	meals6	meals7	meals8

The EXPENSES array contains ten groups of eight variables each. The ten groups (expense categories) comprise the first dimension of the array, and the eight variables (days of the week) comprise the second dimension. To reference the data in the array variables, use the form EXPENSES{m,n}, where m is the element number in the first dimension of the array, and n is the element number in the second dimension of the array. EXPENSES{6,4} references the value of dues for the fourth day (the variable is DUES4).

Syntax for Defining and Referencing an Array

To define a simple or a multidimensional array, use the ARRAY statement. The ARRAY statement has the following form:

ARRAY *array-name* {*number-of-elements*} <*list-of-variables*>;

where

array-name
> is a SAS name that identifies the group of variables.

number-of-elements
> is the number of variables in the group. You must enclose this value in parentheses, braces, or brackets.

list-of-variables
> is a list of the names of the variables in the group. All variables that are defined in a given array must be of the same type-either all character or all numeric.

For complete information about the ARRAY statement, see *SAS Language Reference: Dictionary*.

To reference an array that was previously defined in the same DATA step, use an Array Reference statement. An array reference has the following form:

array-name {subscript}

where

array-name
> is the name of an array that was previously defined with an ARRAY statement in the same DATA step.

subscript
> specifies the subscript, which can be a numeric constant, the name of a variable whose value is the number, a SAS numeric expression, or an asterisk (*).

> *Note:* Subscripts in SAS are 1-based by default, and not 0-based as they are in some other programming languages. △

For complete information about the Array Reference statement, see *SAS Language Reference: Dictionary*.

Processing Simple Arrays

Grouping Variables in a Simple Array

The following ARRAY statement creates an array named BOOKS that contains the three variables Reference, Usage, and Introduction:

```
array books{3} Reference Usage Introduction;
```

When you define an array, SAS assigns each array element an *array reference* with the form *array-name{subscript}*, where *subscript* is the position of the variable in the list. The following table lists the array reference assignments for the previous ARRAY statement:

Variable	Array reference
Reference	books{1}
Usage	books{2}
Introduction	books{3}

Later in the DATA step, when you want to process the variables in the array, you can refer to a variable by either its name or its array reference. For example, the names Reference and books{1} are equivalent.

Using a DO Loop to Repeat an Action

To perform the same action several times, use an iterative DO loop. A simple iterative DO loop that processes an array has the following form:

DO *index-variable*=1 **TO** *number-of-elements-in-array*;
    ... *more SAS statements* ...

END;

The loop is processed repeatedly (iterates) according to the instructions in the iterative DO statement. The iterative DO statement contains an *index-variable* whose name you specify and whose value changes at each iteration of the loop.

To execute the loop as many times as there are variables in the array, specify that the values of *index-variable* are 1 TO *number-of-elements-in-array*. SAS increases the value of *index-variable* by 1 before each new iteration of the loop. When the value exceeds the *number-of-elements-in-array*, SAS stops processing the loop. By default, SAS automatically includes *index-variable* in the output data set. Use a DROP statement or the DROP= data set option to prevent the index variable from being written to your output data set.

An iterative DO loop that executes three times and has an index variable named count has the following form:

```
do count=1 to 3;
    ... more SAS statements ...
end;
```

The first time the loop processes, the value of count is 1; the second time, 2; and the third time, 3. At the beginning of the fourth iteration, the value of count is 4, which exceeds the specified range and causes SAS to stop processing the loop.

Using a DO Loop to Process Selected Elements in an Array

To process particular elements of an array, specify those elements as the range of the iterative DO statement. For example, the following statement creates an array DAYS that contains seven elements:

```
array days{7} D1-D7;
```

The following DO statements process selected elements of the array DAYS:

`do i=2 to 4;`	processes elements 2 through 4
`do i=1 to 7 by 2;`	processes elements 1, 3, 5, and 7
`do i=3,5;`	processes elements 3 and 5

Selecting the Current Variable

You must tell SAS which variable in the array to use in each iteration of the loop. Recall that you identify variables in an array by their array references and that you use a variable name, a number, or an expression as the subscript of the reference. Therefore, you can write programming statements so that the index variable of the DO loop is the subscript of the array reference (for example, *array-name{index-variable}*). When the value of the index variable changes, the subscript of the array reference (and therefore the variable that is referenced) also changes.

The following example uses the index variable count as the subscript of array references inside a DO loop:

```
array books{3} Reference Usage Introduction;
do count=1 to 3;
   if books{count}=. then books{count}=0;
end;
```

When the value of count is 1, SAS reads the array reference as books{1} and processes the IF-THEN statement on books{1}, which is the variable Reference. When count is 2, SAS processes the statement on books{2}, which is the variable Usage. When count is 3, SAS processes the statement on books{3}, which is the variable Introduction.

The statements in the example tell SAS to

- □ perform the actions in the loop three times
- □ replace the array subscript count with the current value of count for each iteration of the IF-THEN statement
- □ locate the variable with that array reference and process the IF-THEN statement on it
- □ replace missing values with zero if the condition is true.

The following DATA step defines the array BOOK and processes it with a DO loop.

```
options nodate pageno=1 linesize=80 pagesize=60;

data changed(drop=count);
   input Reference Usage Introduction;
   array book{3} Reference Usage Introduction;
   do count=1 to 3;
      if book{count}=. then book{count}=0;
   end;
   datalines;
45 63 113
.  75 150
62 .   98
;

proc print data=changed;
   title 'Number of Books Sold';
run;
```

The following output shows the CHANGED data set.

Output 25.1   Using an Array Statement to Process Missing Data Values

```
                       Number of Books Sold                              1

          Obs     Reference     Usage     Introduction

           1         45          63           113
           2          0          75           150
           3         62           0            98
```

Defining the Number of Elements in an Array

When you define the number of elements in an array, you can either use an asterisk enclosed by braces ({*}), brackets ([*]), or parentheses ((*)) to count the number of elements or to specify the number of elements. You must list each array element if you use the asterisk to designate the number of elements. In the following example, the array C1TEMP references five variables with temperature measures.

```
array c1temp{*} c1t1 c1t2 c1t3 c1t4 c1t5;
```

If you specify the number of elements explicitly, you can omit the names of the variables or array elements in the ARRAY statement. SAS then creates variable names by concatenating the array name with the numbers 1, 2, 3, and so on. If a variable name in the series already exists, SAS uses that variable instead of creating a new one. In the following example, the array c1t references five variables: c1t1, c1t2, c1t3, c1t4, and c1t5.

```
array c1t{5};
```

Rules for Referencing Arrays

Before you make any references to an array, an ARRAY statement must appear in the same DATA step that you used to create the array. Once you have created the array, you can

- □ use an array reference anywhere that you can write a SAS expression
- □ use an array reference as the arguments of some SAS functions
- □ use a subscript enclosed in braces, brackets, or parentheses to reference an array
- □ use the special array subscript asterisk (*) to refer to all variables in an array in an INPUT or PUT statement or in the argument of a function.

> *Note:* You cannot use the asterisk with _TEMPORARY_ arrays. △

An array definition is in effect only for the duration of the DATA step. If you want to use the same array in several DATA steps, you must redefine the array in each step. You can, however, redefine the array with the same variables in a later DATA step by using a macro variable. A macro variable is useful for storing the variable names you need, as shown in this example:

```
%let list=NC SC GA VA;

data one;
    array state(*) &list;
    … more SAS statements …
run;

data two;
    array state(*) &list;
    … more SAS statements …
run;
```

Variations on Basic Array Processing

Determining the Number of Elements in an Array Efficiently

The DIM function in the iterative DO statement returns the number of elements in a one-dimensional array or the number of elements in a specified dimension of a multidimensional array, when the lower bound of the dimension is 1. Use the DIM function to avoid changing the upper bound of an iterative DO group each time you change the number of elements in the array.

The form of the DIM function is as follows:

DIMn(*array-name*)

where n is the specified dimension that has a default value of 1.

You can also use the DIM function when you specify the number of elements in the array with an asterisk. Here are some examples of the DIM function:

□ `do i=1 to dim(days);`

□ `do i=1 to dim4(days) by 2;`

DO WHILE and DO UNTIL Expressions

Arrays are often processed in iterative DO loops that use the array reference in a DO WHILE or DO UNTIL expression. In this example, the iterative DO loop processes the elements of the array named TREND.

```
data test;
   array trend{5} x1-x5;
   input x1-x5 y;
   do i=1 to 5 while(trend{i}<y);
   … more SAS statements …
   end;
   datalines;
… data lines …
;
```

Using Variable Lists to Define an Array Quickly

SAS reserves the following three names for use as variable list names:

CHARACTER

NUMERIC

ALL

You can use these variable list names to reference variables that have been previously defined in the same DATA step. The _CHARACTER_ variable lists character values only. The _NUMERIC_ variable lists numeric values only. The _ALL_ variable lists either all character or all numeric values, depending on how you previously defined the variables.

For example, the following INPUT statement reads in variables X1 through X3 as character values using the $8. informat, and variables X4 through X5 as numeric variables. The following ARRAY statement uses the variable list _CHARACTER_ to include only the character variables in the array. The asterisk indicates that SAS will determine the subscript by counting the variables in the array.

```
input (X1-X3) ($8.) X4-X5;
array item {*} _character_;
```

You can use the _NUMERIC_ variable in your program if, for example, you need to convert currency. In this application, you do not need to know the variable names. You need only to convert all values to the new currency.

For more information about variable lists, see the ARRAY statement in *SAS Language Reference: Dictionary*.

Multidimensional Arrays: Creating and Processing

Grouping Variables in a Multidimensional Array

To create a multidimensional array, place the number of elements in each dimension after the array name in the form {*n*, ... } where *n* is required for each dimension of a multidimensional array.

From right to left, the rightmost dimension represents columns; the next dimension represents rows. Each position farther left represents a higher dimension. The following ARRAY statement defines a two-dimensional array with two rows and five columns. The array contains ten variables: five temperature measures (t1 through t5) from two cities (c1 and c2):

```
array temprg{2,5} c1t1-c1t5 c2t1-c2t5;
```

SAS places variables into a multidimensional array by filling all rows in order, beginning at the upper-left corner of the array (known as row-major order). You can think of the variables as having the following arrangement:

```
c1t1 c1t2 c1t3 c1t4 c1t5
c2t1 c2t2 c2t3 c2t4 c2t5
```

To refer to the elements of the array later with an array reference, you can use the array name and subscripts. The following table lists some of the array references for the previous example:

Variable	Array reference
c1t1	temprg{1,1}
c1t2	temprg{1,2}
c2t2	temprg{2,2}
c2t5	temprg{2,5}

Using Nested DO Loops

Multidimensional arrays are usually processed inside nested DO loops. As an example, the following is one form that processes a two-dimensional array:

DO *index-variable-1*=1 **TO** *number-of-rows*;

> **DO** *index-variable-2*=1 **TO** *number-of-columns*;
>   *... more SAS statements ...*
>
> **END**;
>
> **END**;

An array reference can use two or more index variables as the subscript to refer to two or more dimensions of an array. Use the following form:

array-name {*index-variable-1, ...,index-variable-n*}

The following example creates an array that contains ten variables- five temperature measures (t1 through t5) from two cities (c1 and c2). The DATA step contains two DO loops.

□ The outer DO loop (DO I=1 TO 2) processes the inner DO loop twice.

□ The inner DO loop (DO J=1 TO 5) applies the ROUND function to all the variables in one row.

For each iteration of the DO loops, SAS substitutes the value of the array element corresponding to the current values of I and J.

```
options nodate pageno=1 linesize=80 pagesize=60;

data temps;
   array temprg{2,5} c1t1-c1t5 c2t1-c2t5;
   input c1t1-c1t5 /
         c2t1-c2t5;
   do i=1 to 2;
     do j=1 to 5;
        temprg{i,j}=round(temprg{i,j});
     end;
   end;
   datalines;
89.5 65.4 75.3 77.7 89.3
73.7 87.3 89.9 98.2 35.6
75.8 82.1 98.2 93.5 67.7
101.3 86.5 59.2 35.6 75.7
;

proc print data=temps;
   title 'Temperature Measures for Two Cities';
run;
```

The following data set TEMPS contains the values of the variables rounded to the nearest whole number.

Output 25.2   Using a Multidimensional Array

```
                    Temperature Measures for Two Cities                    1

    Obs  c1t1  c1t2  c1t3  c1t4  c1t5  c2t1  c2t2  c2t3  c2t4  c2t5  i  j

     1    90    65    75    78    89    74    87    90    98    36   3  6
     2    76    82    98    94    68   101    87    59    36    76   3  6
```

The previous example can also use the DIM function to produce the same result:

```
do i=1 to dim1(temprg);
   do j=1 to dim2(temprg);
      temprg{i,j}=round(temprg{i,j});
   end;
end;
```

The value of DIM1(TEMPRG) is 2; the value of DIM2(TEMPRG) is 5.

Specifying Array Bounds

Identifying Upper and Lower Bounds

Typically in an ARRAY statement, the subscript in each dimension of the array ranges from 1 to *n*, where *n* is the number of elements in that dimension. Thus, 1 is the lower bound and *n* is the upper bound of that dimension of the array. For example, in the following array, the lower bound is 1 and the upper bound is 4:

```
array new{4} Jackson Poulenc Andrew Parson;
```

In the following ARRAY statement, the bounds of the first dimension are 1 and 2 and those of the second dimension are 1 and 5:

```
array test{2,5} test1-test10;
```

Bounded array dimensions have the following form:

{<*lower-1*:>*upper-1*<,...<*lower-n*:>*upper-n*>}

Therefore, you can also write the previous ARRAY statements as follows:

```
array new{1:4} Jackson Poulenc Andrew Parson;
array test{1:2,1:5} test1-test10;
```

For most arrays, 1 is a convenient lower bound, so you do not need to specify the lower bound. However, specifying both the lower and the upper bounds is useful when the array dimensions have beginning points other than 1.

In the following example, ten variables are named Year76 through Year85. The following ARRAY statements place the variables into two arrays named FIRST and SECOND:

```
array first{10} Year76-Year85;
array second{76:85} Year76-Year85;
```

In the first ARRAY statement, the element first{4} is variable Year79, first{7} is Year82, and so on. In the second ARRAY statement, element second{79} is Year79 and second{82} is Year82.

To process the array names SECOND in a DO group, be sure that the range of the DO loop matches the range of the array as follows:

```
do i=76 to 85;
   if second{i}=9 then second{i}=.;
end;
```

Determining Array Bounds: LBOUND and HBOUND Functions

You can use the LBOUND and HBOUND functions to determine array bounds. The LBOUND function returns the lower bound of a one-dimensional array or the lower bound of a specified dimension of a multidimensional array. The HBOUND function returns the upper bound of a one-dimensional array or the upper bound of a specified dimension of a multidimensional array.

The form of the LBOUND and HBOUND functions is as follows:

LBOUNDn(*array-name*)

HBOUNDn(*array-name*)

where

n

is the specified dimension and has a default value of 1.

You can use the LBOUND and HBOUND functions to specify the starting and ending values of the iterative DO loop to process the elements of the array named SECOND:

```
do i=lbound{second} to hbound{second};
   if second{i}=9 then second{i}=.;
end;
```

In this example, the index variable in the iterative DO statement ranges from 76 to 85.

When to Use the HBOUND Function instead of the DIM Function

The following ARRAY statement defines an array containing a total of five elements, a lower bound of 72, and an upper bound of 76. It represents the calendar years 1972 through 1976:

```
array years{72:76} first second third fourth fifth;
```

To process the array named YEARS in an iterative DO loop, be sure that the range of the DO loop matches the range of the array as follows:

```
do i=lbound(years) to hbound(years);
   if years{i}=99 then years{i}=.;
end;
```

The value of LBOUND(YEARS) is 72; the value of HBOUND(YEARS) is 76.

For this example, the DIM function would return a value of 5, the total count of elements in the array YEARS. Therefore, if you used the DIM function instead of the HBOUND function for the upper bound of the array, the statements inside the DO loop would not have executed.

Specifying Bounds in a Two-Dimensional Array

The following list contains 40 variables named X60 through X99. They represent the years 1960 through 1999.

```
X60   X61   X62   X63   X64   X65   X66   X67   X68   X69
X70   X71   X72   X73   X74   X75   X76   X77   X78   X79
X80   X81   X82   X83   X84   X85   X86   X87   X88   X89
X90   X91   X92   X93   X94   X95   X96   X97   X98   X99
```

The following ARRAY statement arranges the variables in an array by decades. The rows range from 6 through 9, and the columns range from 0 through 9.

```
array X{6:9,0:9} X60-X99;
```

In array X, variable X63 is element X{6,3} and variable X89 is element X{8,9}. To process array X with iterative DO loops, use one of these methods:

Method 1:

```
do i=6 to 9;
   do j=0 to 9;
      if X{i,j}=0 then X{i,j}=.;
   end;
end;
```

Method 2:

```
do i=lbound1(X) to hbound1(X);
   do j=lbound2(X) to hbound2(X);
      if X{i,j}=0 then X{i,j}=.;
   end;
end;
```

Both examples change all values of 0 in variables X60 through X99 to missing. The first example sets the range of the DO groups explicitly, and the second example uses the LBOUND and HBOUND functions to return the bounds of each dimension of the array.

Examples of Array Processing

Example 1: Using Character Variables in an Array

You can specify character variables and their lengths in ARRAY statements. The following example groups variables into two arrays, NAMES and CAPITALS. The dollar sign ($) tells SAS to create the elements as character variables. If the variables have already been declared as character variables, a dollar sign in the array is not necessary. The INPUT statement reads all the variables in array NAMES.

The statement inside the DO loop uses the UPCASE function to change the values of the variables in array NAMES to uppercase and then store the uppercase values in the variables in the CAPITALS array.

```
options nodate pageno=1 linesize=80 pagesize=60;

data text;
   array names{*} $ n1-n10;
   array capitals{*} $ c1-c10;
   input names{*};
      do i=1 to 10;
         capitals{i}=upcase(names{i});
      end;
   datalines;
smithers michaels gonzalez hurth frank bleigh
rounder joseph peters sam
;
```

```
proc print data=text;
   title 'Names Changed from Lowercase to Uppercase';
run;
```

The following output shows the TEXT data set.

Output 25.3   Using Character Variables in an Array

```
                  Names Changed from Lowercase to Uppercase                      1

Obs    n1        n2        n3       n4      n5     n6      n7      n8      n9     n10

 1   smithers michaels gonzalez hurth  frank  bleigh rounder joseph  peters  sam

Obs    c1        c2        c3       c4      c5     c6      c7      c8      c9     c10   i

 1   SMITHERS MICHAELS GONZALEZ HURTH  FRANK  BLEIGH ROUNDER JOSEPH  PETERS  SAM   11
```

Example 2: Assigning Initial Values to the Elements of an Array

This example creates variables in the array TEST and assigns them the initial values 90, 80, and 70. It reads values into another array named SCORE and compares each element of SCORE to the corresponding element of TEST. If the value of the element in SCORE is greater than or equal to the value of the element in TEST, the variable NewScore is assigned the value in the element SCORE, and the OUTPUT statement writes the observation to the SAS data set.

The INPUT statement reads a value for the variable named ID and then reads values for all the variables in the SCORE array.

```
options nodate pageno=1 linesize=80 pagesize=60;

data score1(drop=i);
   array test{3} t1-t3 (90 80 70);
   array score{3} s1-s3;
   input id score{*};
   do i=1 to 3;
      if score{i}>=test{i} then
         do;
            NewScore=score{i};
            output;
         end;
   end;
   datalines;
1234  99 60 82
5678  80 85 75
;

proc print noobs data=score1;
   title 'Data Set SCORE1';
run;
```

The following output shows the SCORE1 data set.

Output 25.4   Assigning Initial Values to the Elements of an Array

```
                              Data Set SCORE1                                1

                                                              New
            t1    t2    t3    s1    s2    s3     id          Score

            90    80    70    99    60    82    1234           99
            90    80    70    99    60    82    1234           82
            90    80    70    80    85    75    5678           85
            90    80    70    80    85    75    5678           75
```

Example 3: Creating an Array for Temporary Use in the Current DATA Step

When elements of an array are constants that are needed only for the duration of the DATA step, you can omit variables from an array group and instead use temporary array elements. You refer to temporary data elements by the array name and dimension. Although they behave like variables, temporary array elements do not have names, and they do not appear in the output data set. Temporary array elements are automatically retained, instead of being reset to missing at the beginning of the next iteration of the DATA step.

To create a temporary array, use the _TEMPORARY_ argument. The following example creates a temporary array named TEST:

```
options nodate pageno=1 linesize=80 pagesize=60;

data score2(drop=i);
     array test{3} _temporary_ (90 80 70);
     array score{3} s1-s3;
     input id score{*};
        do i=1 to 3;
           if score{i}>=test{i} then
              do;
                 NewScore=score{i};
                 output;
              end;
        end;
     datalines;
  1234  99 60 82
  5678  80 85 75
  ;

proc print noobs data=score2;
   title 'Data Set SCORE2';
run;
```

The following output shows the SCORE2 data set.

Output 25.5   Using _TEMPORARY_ Arrays

```
                              Data Set SCORE2                              1

                                              New
                  s1    s2    s3     id      Score

                  99    60    82    1234      99
                  99    60    82    1234      82
                  80    85    75    5678      85
                  80    85    75    5678      75
```

Example 4: Performing an Action on All Numeric Variables

This example multiplies all the numeric variables in array TEST by 3.

```
options nodate pageno=1 linesize=80 pagesize=60;

data sales;
   infile datalines;
   input Value1 Value2 Value3 Value4;
   datalines;
11 56 58 61
22 51 57 61
22 49 53 58
;

data convert(drop=i);
   set sales;
   array test{*} _numeric_;
   do i=1 to dim(test);
      test{i} = (test{i}*3);
   end;
run;

proc print data=convert;
   title 'Data Set CONVERT';
run;
```

The following output shows the CONVERT data set.

Output 25.6   Output From Using a _NUMERIC_ Variable List

```
                              Data Set CONVERT                             1

              Obs     Value1     Value2     Value3     Value4

                1        33        168        174        183
                2        66        153        171        183
                3        66        147        159        174
```

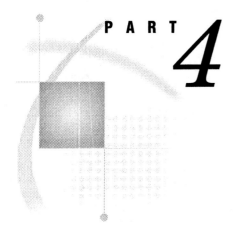

P A R T *4*

SAS Files Concepts

Chapter **26**. . . . .**SAS Data Libraries** *467*

Chapter **27**. . . . .**SAS Data Sets** *481*

Chapter **28**. . . . .**SAS Data Files** *487*

Chapter **29**. . . . .**SAS Data Views** *539*

Chapter **30**. . . . .**Stored Compiled DATA Step Programs** *547*

Chapter **31**. . . . .**DICTIONARY Tables** *557*

Chapter **32**. . . . .**SAS Catalogs** *561*

Chapter **33**. . . . .**About SAS/ACCESS Software** *569*

Chapter **34**. . . . .**Processing Data Using Cross-Environment Data Access
(CEDA)** *575*

Chapter **35**. . . . .**SAS 9.1 Compatibility with SAS Files From Earlier
Releases** *583*

Chapter **36**. . . . .**File Protection** *587*

Chapter **37**. . . . .**SAS Engines** *597*

Chapter **38**. . . . .**SAS File Management** *607*

Chapter **39**. . . . .**External Files** *611*

CHAPTER

26

SAS Data Libraries

Definition of a SAS Data Library   **467**
Library Engines   **469**
Library Names   **469**
    Physical Names and Logical Names (Librefs)   **469**
    Assigning Librefs   **470**
    Associating and Clearing Logical Names (Librefs) With the LIBNAME Statement   **470**
    Reserved Librefs   **471**
Library Concatenation   **471**
    Definition of Library Concatenation   **471**
    How SAS Concatenates Library Members   **472**
    Rules for Library Concatenation   **472**
Permanent and Temporary Libraries   **473**
SAS System Libraries   **474**
    Introduction to SAS System Libraries   **474**
    WORK Library   **474**
        Definition of WORK Library   **474**
        Using the WORK Library   **474**
        Relation to the USER Library   **474**
    USER Library   **475**
        Definition of USER Library   **475**
        Ways to Assign the USER Libref   **475**
        Relation to WORK Library   **476**
    SASHELP Library   **476**
    SASUSER Library   **476**
Sequential Data Libraries   **476**
Tools for Managing Libraries   **477**
    SAS Utilities   **477**
    Library Directories   **478**
    Accessing Permanent SAS Files without a Libref   **478**
    Operating Environment Commands   **479**

Definition of a SAS Data Library

A *SAS data library* is a collection of one or more SAS files that are recognized by SAS and that are referenced and stored as a unit. Each file is a member of the library.

The logical concept of a SAS data library remains constant, regardless of the operating environment. In any operating environment where SAS can be installed, the structure for organizing, locating, and managing SAS files is the same.

At the operating environment level, however, a SAS data library has different physical implementations. Most SAS data libraries implement the storage of files in a manner similar to the way the operating environment stores and accesses files.

For instance, in directory-based operating environments, a SAS data library is a group of SAS files that are stored in the same directory and accessed by the same engine. Other files can be stored in the directory, but only the files with file extensions that are assigned by SAS are recognized as part of the SAS data library. Under OS/390 or z/OS, a SAS data library can be implemented as either a bound library in a traditional OS data set or as a directory under UNIX System Services.

SAS files can be any of the following file types:

☐ SAS data set (SAS data file or SAS data view)

☐ SAS catalog

☐ stored compiled SAS program

☐ SAS utility file

☐ access descriptors

☐ multi-dimensional database files such as MDDB, FDB, and DMDB files

☐ item store files.

Figure 26.1   Types of Files in a SAS Data Library

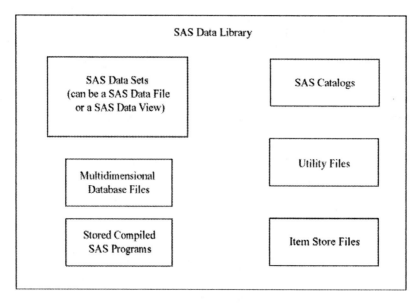

Each SAS file, in turn, stores information in smaller units that are characteristic of the *SAS file type*. For example, SAS data sets store information as variables and observations, while SAS catalogs store information in units called *entries*. SAS determines the type of a file from the context of the SAS program in which the file is created or specified; therefore, a library can contain files with the same name but with different member types.

SAS data libraries can contain files that you create, or they can be one of several special libraries that SAS provides for convenience, support, and customizing capability such as the WORK library. SAS does not limit the number of SAS files you can store in a SAS data library.

Library Engines

Each SAS data library is associated with a library engine. SAS library engines are software components that form the interface between SAS and the SAS data library. It is the SAS library engine that locates files in a SAS data library and renders the file contents to SAS in a form that it can recognize. Library engines perform such tasks as:

- reading and writing data
- listing the files in the library
- deleting and renaming files.

SAS has a *Multiple Engine Architecture* in order to read to and write from files in different formats. Each SAS engine has specific processing characteristics, such as the ability to

- process a SAS file generated by an older version of SAS
- read database files created by other software programs
- store and access files on disk or tape
- determine how variables and observations are placed in a file
- place data into memory from its physical location
- transport SAS files between operating environments.

You generally are not aware of the particular type of engine that is processing data at any given time. If you issue an instruction that is not supported by the engine, an error message is displayed in the log. When needed, you can select a specific engine to perform a task. But usually, you do not have to specify an engine, because SAS automatically selects the appropriate one.

More than one engine may be involved in processing a DATA step; for example, one engine may be used to input data, and another engine may be used to write observations to the output data set.

For more information on library engines, including a list of engines available in Base SAS, see "About Library Engines" on page 602.

Library Names

Physical Names and Logical Names (Librefs)

Before you can use a SAS data library, you must tell SAS where it is. SAS recognizes SAS data libraries based on either operating environment naming conventions or SAS naming conventions. There are two ways to define SAS data libraries.

- a physical location name that the operating environment recognizes
- a logical name (libref) that you assign using the LIBNAME statement, LIBNAME function, or the New Library window.

The physical location name of the SAS data library is a name that identifies your SAS files to the operating environment. The physical location name must conform to the naming conventions of your operating environment. The physical location name fully identifies the directory, or operating environment data set that contains the SAS data library.

The logical name, or *libref*, is the way you identify a group of files to SAS. A libref is a name that you associate with the physical location of the SAS data library.

Assigning Librefs

Librefs can be assigned using the following methods:

□ LIBNAME statement
□ LIBNAME function
□ New Library window that is available in your toolbar
□ operating environment commands.

Once the libref is assigned, you can read, create, or update files in a data library. A libref is valid only for the current SAS session, unless it is assigned using the New Library window with the **Enable at startup** box checked.

A libref can have a maximum length of eight characters. You can use the LIBREF function to verify that a libref has been assigned. Librefs can be referenced repeatedly within a SAS session. SAS does not limit the number of librefs you can assign during a session; however, your operating environment or site may set limitations. If you are running in batch mode, the library must exist before you can allocate or assign it. In interactive mode, you may be allowed to create it if it does not already exist.

Operating Environment Information: Here are examples of the LIBNAME statement for different operating environments. The rules for assigning and using librefs differ across operating environments. See the SAS documentation for your operating environment for specific information. △

Table 26.1 Syntax for Assigning a Libref

Operating Environment	Examples
DOS, Windows	`libname mylibref 'c:\root\mystuff\sasstuff\work';`
UNIX	`libname mylibref '/u/mystuff/sastuff/work';`
UNIX System Services under z/OS	`libname mylibref '/mystuff/sastuff/work';`
z/OS	`libname mylibref 'userid.mystuff.sastuff.work';`
OpenVMS Alpha	`libname mylibref 'filename filetype filemode';`

You can also access files without using a libref. See "Accessing Permanent SAS Files without a Libref" on page 478.

Associating and Clearing Logical Names (Librefs) With the LIBNAME Statement

You can assign or clear a physical name with a libref using the LIBNAME statement or the LIBNAME function, which are described in the *SAS Language Reference: Dictionary*.

Operating Environment Information: For some operating environments, you can use operating environment commands to associate a libref with a SAS data library. When using operating environment commands to assign librefs to a SAS data library, the association may persist beyond the SAS session in which the libref was created. For some operating environments you can use only the LIBNAME statement or function. See the SAS documentation for your operating environment for more information on assigning librefs. △

The most common form of the LIBNAME statement is used in this example to associate the libref ANNUAL with the physical name of the SAS data library.

```
libname annual 'SAS-data-library';
```

If you use the LIBNAME statement to assign the libref, SAS clears (deassigns) the libref automatically at the end of each SAS session. If you want to clear the libref ANNUAL before the end of the session, you can issue the following form of the LIBNAME statement:

```
libname annual clear;
```

SAS also provides a New Library window to assign or clear librefs and SAS Explorer to view, add or delete SAS data libraries. You can select the New Library or the SAS Explorer icon from the Toolbar.

Reserved Librefs

SAS reserves a few names for special uses. You should not use SASHELP, SASUSER or SASWORK as librefs, except as intended. The purpose and content of these libraries are discussed in "Permanent and Temporary Libraries" on page 473.

Operating Environment Information: There are other librefs reserved for SAS under some operating environments. In addition, your operating environment may have reserved certain words that cannot be used as librefs. See the SAS documentation for your operating environment for more information. △

Library Concatenation

Definition of Library Concatenation

Concatenation is the logical combining of two or more libraries. Concatenation allows you to access the SAS data sets in several libraries with one libref.

You can concatenate two or more libraries by specifying their librefs or physical names in the LIBNAME statement or function.

Physical names must be enclosed in single or double quotation marks in a LIBNAME statement. Otherwise SAS looks for a previously assigned libref with the same name.

In the following examples, summer, winter, spring, fall, and annual are previously defined librefs:

```
libname annual (summer winter spring fall);

libname annual ('path1' 'path2' 'path3');

libname annual ('path' winter spring fall);

libname total (annual 'path');
```

How SAS Concatenates Library Members

When there are members of the same name in more than one library, the first occurrence of the member is used for input and update processes. Output will always go to the first library.

This example contains three SAS data libraries, and each library contains two SAS data files:

LIB1   APPLES and PEARS

LIB2   APPLES and ORANGES

LIB3   ORANGES and PLUMS

The LIBNAME statement concatenates LIB1, LIB2, and LIB3:

```
libname fruit (lib1 lib2 lib3);
```

The concatenated library FRUIT has the following members:
APPLES
PEARS
ORANGES
PLUMS

Note: Output will always go to the first library. For example, the following statement writes to the first library in the concatenation, LIB1:

```
data fruit.oranges;
```

△

Note that in this example, if the file APPLES in LIB1 was different from the file APPLES in LIB2, and if an update to APPLES was specified, it will only be updated in LIB1 because that is the first occurrence of the member APPLES.

For complete documentation on library concatenation, see the LIBNAME statement or function in *SAS Language Reference: Dictionary*.

Operating Environment Information: For more information about how specific operating environments handle concatenation, see the SAS documentation for your operating environment. △

Rules for Library Concatenation

After you create a library concatenation, you can specify the libref in any context that accepts a simple (nonconcatenated) libref. These rules determine how SAS files (that is, members of SAS libraries) are located among the concatenated libraries:

- ☐ If you specify any options or an engine, the options apply only to the libraries that you specified with the physical name, not to any library that you specified with a libref.
- ☐ When a SAS file is opened for input or update, the concatenated libraries are searched and the first occurrence of the specified file is used.
- ☐ When a SAS file is opened for output, it is created in the first library that is listed in the concatenation.

    Note: A new SAS file is created in the first library even if there is a file with the same name in another part of the concatenation. △

□ When you delete or rename a SAS file, only the first occurrence of the file is affected.

□ Any time a list of SAS files is displayed, only one occurrence of a filename is shown, even if the name occurs multiple times in the concatenation. For example, if library ONE contains A.DATA and library TWO contains A.DATA, only A.DATA from library ONE is listed because it is the first occurrence of the filename.

In addition, a SAS file that is logically connected to another file (such as an index to a data file) is listed only if the parent file is the first (or only) occurrence of the filename. For example, if library ONE contains A.DATA and library TWO contains A.DATA and A.INDEX, only A.DATA from library ONE is listed. A.DATA and A.INDEX from library TWO are not listed.

□ If any library in the concatenation is sequential, then the concatenated library is considered sequential by applications that require random access. The DATASETS procedure, for example, cannot process sequential libraries, and therefore cannot process a concatenated library that contains one or more sequential libraries.

□ The attributes of the first library that is specified determine the attributes of the concatenation. For example, if the first SAS data library that is listed is "read only," then the entire concatenated library is "read only."

□ Once a libref has been assigned in a concatenation, any changes made to the libref will not affect the concatenation.

Permanent and Temporary Libraries

SAS data libraries are generally stored as permanent data libraries; however, SAS provides a temporary or scratch library where you can store files for the duration of a SAS session or job.

A *permanent SAS data library* is one that resides on the external storage medium of your computer and is not deleted when the SAS session terminates. Permanent SAS data libraries are stored until you delete them. The library is available for processing in subsequent SAS sessions. When working with files in a permanent SAS data library, you generally specify a libref as the first part of a two-level SAS filename. The libref tells SAS where to find or store the file.

Note: You can also skip using a libref and point directly to the file you want to use, using syntax that your operating system understands. An example of this in the Windows environment is

```
data 'C:\root\sasfiles\myfile.ext';
```

Operating Environment Information: Files are specified differently in various operating environments. See the SAS documentation for your operating environment for more information. △

△

A *temporary SAS data library* is one that exists only for the current SAS session or job. SAS files that are created during the session or job are held in a special work space that may or may not be an external storage medium. This work space is generally assigned the default libref WORK. Files in the temporary WORK library can be used in any DATA step or SAS procedure during the SAS session, but they are typically not available for subsequent SAS sessions. Normally, you specify that data sets be stored in or retrieved from this library by specifying a one-level name. Files held in the WORK library are deleted at the end of the SAS session if it ends normally.

There are a number of SAS system options that enable you to customize the way you name and work with your permanent and temporary SAS data libraries. See the

USER=, WORK=, WORKINIT, and WORKTERM system options in *SAS Language Reference: Dictionary* for more information.

SAS System Libraries

Introduction to SAS System Libraries

Four special SAS-supplied libraries provide convenience, support, and customization capability:

☐ WORK

☐ USER

☐ SASHELP

☐ SASUSER

WORK Library

Definition of WORK Library

The WORK library is the temporary (scratch) library that is automatically defined by SAS at the beginning of each SAS session. The WORK library stores two types of temporary files: those that you create and those that are created internally by SAS as part of normal processing. Typically, the WORK library is deleted at the end of each SAS session if the session terminates normally.

Using the WORK Library

To store or retrieve SAS files in the WORK library, specify a one-level name in your SAS program statements. The libref WORK is automatically assigned to these files as a system default unless you have assigned the USER libref. The following examples contain valid names for SAS data sets stored in the WORK library:

☐ `data test2;`

☐ `data work.test2;`

☐ `proc contents data=testdata;`

☐ `proc contents data=work.testdata;`

Operating Environment Information: The WORK library is implemented differently in various operating environments. See the SAS documentation for your operating environment for more information. △

Relation to the USER Library

While the WORK library is designed to hold temporary files used during the current SAS session, the USER library is designed to hold files after the SAS session is over. If you associate the libref USER with a SAS data library, use a one-level name to create and access files that are not deleted at the end of your SAS session. When SAS encounters a one-level filename, it looks first in the USER library, if it has been defined, and then it looks in WORK. If you wish to place a file in the USER library, so that it is not deleted after your SAS session is over, any single-level file goes there by default. At that point, if you want to create a temporary file in WORK, you must use a two-level name, such as WORK.NAME.

USER Library

Definition of USER Library

The USER library allows you to read, create, and write to files in a SAS data library other than WORK without specifying a libref as part of the SAS filename. Once you associate the libref USER with a SAS data library, SAS stores any file with a one-level name in that library. Unlike the WORK library, files stored in this library are not deleted by SAS when the session terminates.

Ways to Assign the USER Libref

You can assign the USER libref using one of the following methods:

□ LIBNAME statement

□ LIBNAME function

□ USER= system option

□ operating environment command.

In this example, the LIBNAME statement is used with a DATA step, which stores the data set REGION in a permanent SAS data library.

```
libname user 'SAS-data-library';
data region;
… more DATA step statements …
run;
```

In this example, the LIBNAME function assigns the USER libref:

```
data _null_;
   x=libname ('user', 'SAS-data-library');
run;
```

When assigning a libref using the USER= system option, you must first assign a libref to a SAS data library, then use the USER= system option to specify that library as the default for one-level names. In this example, the DATA step stores the data set PROCHLOR in the SAS data library TESTLIB.

```
libname testlib 'SAS-data-library';
options user=testlib;
data prochlor;
… more DATA step statements …
run;
```

Operating Environment Information: The methods and results of assigning the USER libref vary slightly from one operating environment to another. See the SAS documentation for your operating environment for more information. △

Relation to WORK Library

The USER libref overrides the default libref WORK for one-level names. When you refer to a file by a one-level name, SAS looks first for the libref USER. If USER is assigned to a SAS data library, files with one-level names are stored there. If you have not assigned the libref USER to a library, the files with one-level names are stored in the temporary library WORK. To refer to SAS files in the WORK library while the USER libref is assigned, you must specify a two-level name with WORK as the libref. Data files that SAS creates internally still go to the WORK library.

SASHELP Library

Each SAS site receives the SASHELP library, which contains a group of catalogs and other files containing information that is used to control various aspects of your SAS session. The defaults stored in this library are for everyone using SAS at your installation. Your personal settings are stored in the SASUSER library, which is discussed later in this section.

If SAS products other than Base SAS are installed at your site, the SASHELP library contains catalogs that are used by those products. In many instances, the defaults in this library are tailored to your site by your SAS Software Representative. You can list the catalogs stored at your site by using one of the file management utilities discussed later in this section.

SASUSER Library

The SASUSER library contains SAS catalogs that enable you to tailor features of SAS for your needs. If the defaults in the SASHELP library are not suitable for your applications, you can modify them and store your personalized defaults in your SASUSER library. For example, in Base SAS, you can store your own defaults for function key settings or window attributes in a personal profile catalog named SASUSER.PROFILE.

SAS assigns the SASUSER library during system initialization, according to the information supplied by the SASUSER system option.

A system option called RSASUSER allows the system administrator to control the mode of access to the SASUSER library at installations that have one SASUSER library for all users and that want to prevent users from modifying it.

Operating Environment Information: In most operating environments, the SASUSER data library is created if it does not already exist. However, the SASUSER library is implemented differently in various operating environments. See the SAS documentation for your operating environment for more information. △

Sequential Data Libraries

SAS provides a number of features and procedures for reading from and writing to files that are stored on sequential format devices, either disk or tape. Before you store SAS data libraries in sequential format, you should consider the following:

□ You cannot use random access methods with sequential SAS data sets.

□ You can access only one of the SAS files in a sequential library, or only one of the SAS files on a tape, at any point in a SAS job.

For example, you cannot read two or more SAS data sets in the same library or on the same tape at the same time in a single DATA step. However, you can access

    ☐ two or more SAS files in different sequential libraries, or on different tapes at the same time, if there are enough tape drives available

    ☐ a SAS file during one DATA or PROC step, then access another SAS file in the same sequential library or on the same tape during a later DATA or PROC step.

Also, when you have more than one SAS data set on a tape or in a sequential library in the same DATA or PROC step, one SAS data set file may be opened during the compilation phase, and the additional SAS data sets are opened during the execution phase. For more information, see the SET statement OPEN= option in *SAS Language Reference: Dictionary*.

☐ For some operating environments, you can only read from or write to SAS data sets during a DATA or PROC step. However, you can always use the COPY procedure to transfer all members of a SAS data library to tape for storage and backup purposes.

☐ Considerations specific to your site can affect your use of tape. For example, it may be necessary to manually mount a tape before the SAS data libraries become available. Consult your operations staff if you are not familiar with using tape storage at your location.

For information on sequential engines, see Chapter 37, "SAS Engines," on page 597.

Operating Environment Information: The details for storing and accessing SAS files in sequential format vary with the operating environment. See the SAS documentation for your operating environment for more information. △

Tools for Managing Libraries

SAS Utilities

The SAS utilities that are available for SAS file management enable you to work with more than one SAS file at a time, as long as the files belong to the same library. The advantage of learning and using SAS Explorer, functions, options, and procedures is that they automatically copy, rename, or delete any index files or integrity constraints, audit trails, backups, and generation data sets that are associated with your SAS data files. Another advantage is that SAS utility procedures work on any operating environment at any level.

There are several SAS window options, functions, and procedures available for performing file management tasks. You can use the following features alone or in combination, depending on what works best for you. See "Choosing the Right Procedure" in *Base SAS Procedures Guide* for detailed information on SAS utility procedures. The SAS windowing environment and how to use it for managing SAS files is discussed in Chapter 18, "Introduction to the SAS Windowing Environment," on page 283 and Chapter 19, "Managing Your Data in the SAS Windowing Environment," on page 307 as well as in the online Help.

CATALOG procedure
    provides catalog management utilities with the COPY, CONTENTS, and APPEND procedures.

DATASETS procedure
>   provides all library management functions for all member types except catalogs. If your site does not use the SAS Explorer, or if SAS executes in batch or interactive line mode, using this procedure can save you time and resources.

SAS Explorer
>   includes windows that enable you to perform most file management tasks without submitting SAS program statements. Type LIBNAME, CATALOG, or DIR in the Toolbar window to use SAS Explorer, or select the Explorer icon from the Toolbar menu.

DETAILS system option
>   Sets the default display for file information when using the CONTENTS, or DATASETS procedure. When enabled, DETAILS provides additional information about files, depending on which procedure or window you use.

Library Directories

SAS Explorer and SAS procedures enable you to obtain a list, or *directory*, of the members in a SAS data library. Each directory contains the name of each member and its member type. For the member type DATA, the directory indicates whether an index, audit trail, backup, or generation data set is associated with the data set. The directory also describes some attributes of the library, but the amount and nature of this information vary with the operating environment.

Note: SAS data libraries can also contain various SAS utility files. These files are not listed in the library directory and are for internal processing. △

Accessing Permanent SAS Files without a Libref

SAS provides another method of accessing files in addition to assigning a libref with the LIBNAME statement or using the New Library window. To use this method, enclose the filename, or the filename and path, in single quotation marks.

For example, in a directory based system, if you want to create a data set named MYDATA in your default directory, that is, in the directory that you are running SAS in, you can write the following line of code:

```
data 'mydata';
```

SAS creates the data set and remembers its location for the duration of the SAS session.

If you omit the single quotation marks, SAS creates the data set MYDATA in the temporary WORK subdirectory, named WORK.MYDATA:

```
data mydata;
```

If you want to create a data set named MYDATA in a library other than the directory in which you are running SAS, enclose the entire path in quotation marks, following the naming conventions of your operating environment. For example, the following DATA step creates a data set named FOO in the directory C:\sasrun\mydata.

```
data 'c:\sasrun\mydata\foo';
```

This method of accessing files works on all operating environments and in most contexts where a *libref.data-set-name* is accepted as a SAS data set. Most data set options can be specified with a quoted name.

You cannot use quoted names for

□ SAS catalogs

□ MDDB and FDB references

□ contexts that do not accept a libref, such as the SELECT statement of PROC COPY and most PROC DATASETS statements

□ PROC SQL

□ DATA step, stored programs, or views

□ SAS Component Language (SCL) open function.

Operating Environment	Examples
DOS, Windows	`data 'c:\root\mystuff\sasstuff\work\myfile';`
UNIX	`data '/u/root/mystuff/sastuff/work/myfile';`

z/OS	`data 'user489.mystuff.saslib(member1)';`
	`    /* bound data library */`
	`data '/mystuff/sasstuff/work/myfile';`
	`    /* UNIX file system library */`

Open VMS Alpha	`data 'filename filetype filemode';`

Operating Environment Commands

You can use operating environment commands to copy, rename, and delete the operating environment file or files that make up a SAS data library. However, to maintain the integrity of your files, you must know how the SAS data library model is implemented in your operating environment. For example, in some operating environments, SAS data sets and their associated indexes can be copied, deleted, or renamed as separate files. If you rename the file containing the SAS data set, but not its index, the data set will be marked as damaged.

CAUTION:
   Using operating environment commands can damage files. You can avoid problems by always using SAS utilities to manage SAS files. △

CHAPTER

27

SAS Data Sets

Definition of a SAS Data Set **481**
Descriptor Information for a SAS Data Set **481**
Data Set Names **482**
  Where to Use Data Set Names **482**
  How and When SAS Data Set Names Are Assigned **483**
  Parts of a Data Set Name **483**
  Two-level SAS Data Set Names **484**
  One-level SAS Data Set Names **484**
Special SAS Data Sets **484**
  Null Data Sets **484**
  Default Data Sets **485**
  Automatic Naming Convention **485**
Sorted Data Sets **485**
Tools for Managing Data Sets **485**
Viewing and Editing SAS Data Sets **486**

Definition of a SAS Data Set

A *SAS data set* is a SAS file stored in a SAS data library that SAS creates and processes. A SAS data set contains data values that are organized as a table of observations (rows) and variables (columns) that can be processed by SAS software. A SAS data set also contains descriptor information such as the data types and lengths of the variables, as well as which engine was used to create the data.

A SAS data set can be one of the following:

SAS data file   contains both the data and the descriptor information. SAS data files have a member type of DATA. For specific information, see Chapter 28, "SAS Data Files," on page 487

SAS data view   is a virtual data set that points to data from other sources. SAS data views have a member type of VIEW. For specific information, see Chapter 29, "SAS Data Views," on page 539.

Note: The term SAS data set is used when a SAS data view and a SAS data file can be used in the same manner. △

Descriptor Information for a SAS Data Set

The descriptor information for a SAS data set makes the file self-documenting; that is, each data set can supply the attributes of the data set and of its variables. Once the data is in the form of a SAS data set, you do not have to specify the attributes of the data set or the variables in your program statements. SAS obtains the information directly from the data set.

Descriptor information includes the number of observations, the observation length, the date that the data set was last modified, and other facts. Descriptor information for individual variables includes attributes such as name, type, length, format, label, and whether the variable is indexed.

The following figure illustrates the logical components of a SAS data set:

Figure 27.1   Logical Components of a SAS Data Set

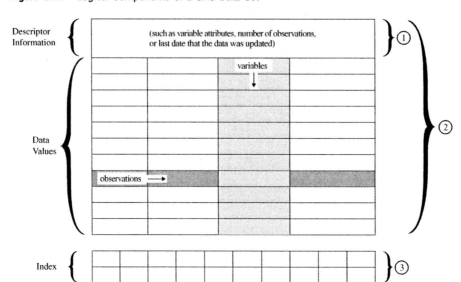

The following items correspond to the numbers in the figure above:

1 A SAS data view (member type VIEW) contains descriptor information and uses data values from one or more data sets.

2 A SAS data file (member type DATA) contains descriptor information and data values. SAS data sets may be of member type DATA (SAS data file) or VIEW (SAS data view).

3 An *index* is a separate file that you can create for a SAS data file in order to provide direct access to specific observations. The index file has the same name as its data file and a member type of INDEX. Indexes can provide faster access to specific observations, particularly when you have a large data set.

Data Set Names

Where to Use Data Set Names

You can use SAS data sets as input for DATA or PROC steps by specifying the name of the data set in

☐ a SET statement

□ a MERGE statement

□ an UPDATE statement

□ a MODIFY statement

□ the DATA= option of a SAS procedure

□ the OPEN function.

How and When SAS Data Set Names Are Assigned

You name SAS data sets when you create them. Output data sets that you create in a DATA step are named in the DATA statement. SAS data sets that you create in a procedure step are usually given a name in the procedure statement or an OUTPUT statement. If you do not specify a name for an output data set, SAS assigns a default name.

If you are creating SAS data views, you assign the data set name using one of the following:

□ the SQL procedure

□ the ACCESS procedure

□ the VIEW= option in the DATA statement.

Note: Because you can specify both SAS data files and SAS data views in the same program statements but cannot specify the member type, SAS cannot determine from the program statement which one you want to process. This is why SAS prevents you from giving the same name to SAS data views and SAS data sets in the same library. △

Parts of a Data Set Name

The complete name of every SAS data set has three elements. You assign the first two; SAS supplies the third. The form for SAS data set names is as follows:

`libref.SAS-data-set.membertype`

The elements of a SAS data set name include the following:

libref
　is the logical name that is associated with the physical location of the SAS data library.

SAS-data-set
　is the data set name, which can be up to 32 bytes long for the Base SAS engine starting in Version 7. Earlier SAS versions are limited to 8-byte names.

membertype
　is assigned by SAS. The member type is DATA for SAS data files and VIEW for SAS data views.

When you refer to SAS data sets in your program statements, use a one- or two-level name. You can use a one-level name when the data set is in the temporary library WORK. In addition, if the reserved libref USER is assigned, you can use a one-level name when the data set is in the permanent library USER. Use a two-level name when the data set is in some other permanent library you have established. A two-level name consists of both the libref and the data set name. A one-level name consists of just the data set name.

Two-level SAS Data Set Names

The form most commonly used to create, read, or write to SAS data sets in permanent SAS data libraries is the two-level name as shown here:

```
libref.SAS-data-set
```

When you create a new SAS data set, the libref indicates where it is to be stored. When you reference an existing data set, the libref tells SAS where to find it. The following examples show the use of two-level names in SAS statements:

```
data revenue.sales;
```

```
proc sort data=revenue.sales;
```

One-level SAS Data Set Names

You can omit the libref, and refer to data sets with a one-level name in the following form:

```
SAS-data-set
```

Data sets with one-level names are automatically assigned to one of two SAS libraries: WORK or USER. Most commonly, they are assigned to the temporary library WORK and are deleted at the end of a SAS job or session. If you have associated the libref USER with a SAS data library or used the USER= system option to set the USER library, data sets with one-level names are stored in that library. See Chapter 26, "SAS Data Libraries," on page 467 for more information on using the USER and WORK libraries. The following examples show how one-level names are used in SAS statements:

```
data 'test3';
```

```
set 'stratifiedsample1';
```

Special SAS Data Sets

Null Data Sets

If you want to execute a DATA step but do not want to create a SAS data set, you can specify the keyword _NULL_ as the data set name. The following statement begins a DATA step that does not create a data set:

```
data _null_;
```

Using _NULL_ causes SAS to execute the DATA step as if it were creating a new data set, but no observations or variables are written to an output data set. This process can be a more efficient use of computer resources if you are using the DATA step for some function, such as report writing, for which the output of the DATA step does not need to be stored as a SAS data set.

Default Data Sets

SAS keeps track of the most recently created SAS data set through the reserved name _LAST_. When you execute a DATA or PROC step without specifying an input data set, by default, SAS uses the _LAST_ data set. Some functions use the _LAST_ default as well.

The _LAST_= system option enables you to designate a data set as the _LAST_ data set. The name you specify is used as the default data set until you create a new data set. You can use the _LAST_= system option when you want to use an existing permanent data set for a SAS job that contains a number of procedure steps. Issuing the _LAST_= system option enables you to avoid specifying the SAS data set name in each procedure statement. The following OPTIONS statement specifies a default SAS data set:

```
options _last_=schedule.january;
```

Automatic Naming Convention

If you do not specify a SAS data set name or the reserved name _NULL_ in a DATA statement, SAS automatically creates data sets with the names DATA1, DATA2, and so on, to successive data sets in the WORK or USER library. This feature is referred to as the DATA*n* naming convention. The following statement produces a SAS data set using the DATA*n* naming convention:

```
data;
```

Sorted Data Sets

A sort indicator is stored with SAS data sets. The sort indicator expresses how the data is sorted. Sort information is used internally for performance improvements, for example, during index creation. For details, see the SORTEDBY data set option in *SAS Language Reference: Dictionary* and the PROC SORT procedure in *Base SAS Procedures Guide*.

Use PROC CONTENTS to view information for a data set.

Tools for Managing Data Sets

To copy, rename, delete, or obtain information about the contents of SAS data sets, use the same windows, procedures, functions and options you do for SAS data libraries. For a list of those windows and procedures, see Chapter 26, "SAS Data Libraries," on page 467.

There are also functions available that allow you to work with your SAS data set. See each individual function for more complete information.

Viewing and Editing SAS Data Sets

The VIEWTABLE window enables you to browse, edit, or create data sets. This window provides two viewing modes:

Table View   uses a tabular format to display multiple observations in the data set.

Form View   displays data one observation at a time in a form layout.

You can customize your view of a data set, for example, by sorting your data, changing the color and fonts of columns, displaying variable labels instead of variable names, or removing or adding variables. You can also load an existing DATAFORM catalog entry in order to apply a previously-defined variable, data set, and viewer attributes.

To view a data set, select the following:

| Tools | ▶ | Table Editor |

This brings up VIEWTABLE or FSVIEW (z/OS). You can also double-click on the data set in the Explorer window.

SAS files supported within the VIEWTABLE window are:

□ SAS data files

□ SAS data views

□ MDDB files.

For more information, see the SAS System Help for VIEWTABLE in Base SAS.

CHAPTER

28

SAS Data Files

Definition of a SAS Data File   **489**
Differences between Data Files and Data Views   **489**
Understanding an Audit Trail   **491**
   Definition of an Audit Trail   **491**
   Audit Trail Description   **491**
      Operation in a Shared Environment   **493**
      Performance Implications   **493**
      Preservation by Other Operations   **493**
      Programming Considerations   **493**
      Other Considerations   **493**
   Initiating an Audit Trail   **494**
   Controlling the Audit Trail   **494**
   Reading and Determining the Status of the Audit Trail   **494**
   Examples of Using Audit Trails   **495**
      Example of Initiating an Audit Trail   **495**
      Example of a Data File Update   **496**
      Example of Using the Audit Trail to Capture Rejected Observations   **497**
Understanding Generation Data Sets   **499**
   Definition of Generation Data Set   **499**
   Terminology for Generation Data Sets   **499**
   Invoking Generation Data Sets   **500**
   Understanding How a Generation Group Is Maintained   **500**
   Processing Specific Versions of a Generation Group   **502**
   Managing Generation Groups   **502**
      Introduction   **502**
      Displaying Data Set Information   **503**
      Copying Generation Groups   **503**
      Appending Generation Groups   **503**
      Modifying the Number of Versions   **503**
      Deleting Versions in a Generation Group   **504**
      Renaming Versions in a Generation Group   **504**
      Using Passwords in a Generation Group   **505**
Understanding Integrity Constraints   **505**
   Definition of Integrity Constraints   **505**
      General Integrity Constraints   **505**
      Referential Integrity Constraints   **505**
      Overlapping Primary Key and Foreign Key Constraints   **506**
   Preservation of Integrity Constraints   **507**
   Indexes and Integrity Constraints   **508**
   Locking Integrity Constraints   **508**
   Passwords and Integrity Constraints   **508**

Specifying Integrity Constraints   **511**
Listing Integrity Constraints   **511**
Rejected Observations   **511**
Examples   **511**
    Creating Integrity Constraints with the DATASETS Procedure   **511**
    Creating Integrity Constraints with the SQL Procedure   **512**
    Creating Integrity Constraints by Using SCL   **513**
    Removing Integrity Constraints   **516**
    Reactivating an Inactive Integrity Constraint   **517**
    Defining Overlapping Primary Key and Foreign Key Constraints   **517**
Understanding SAS Indexes   **518**
Definition of SAS Indexes   **518**
Benefits of an Index   **518**
The Index File   **519**
Types of Indexes   **520**
    Simple Index   **520**
    Composite Index   **520**
    Unique Values   **521**
    Missing Values   **521**
Deciding Whether to Create an Index   **522**
    Costs of an Index   **522**
    CPU Cost   **522**
    I/O Cost   **522**
    Buffer Requirements   **523**
    Disk Space Requirements   **523**
Guidelines for Creating Indexes   **524**
    Data File Considerations   **524**
    Index Use Considerations   **524**
    Key Variable Candidates   **524**
Creating an Index   **525**
    Overview of Creating Indexes   **525**
    Using the DATASETS Procedure   **526**
    Using the INDEX= Data Set Option   **526**
    Using the SQL Procedure   **526**
    Using Other SAS Products   **527**
Using an Index for WHERE Processing   **527**
    Identifying Available Index or Indexes   **527**
    Compound Optimization   **528**
    Estimating the Number of Qualified Observations   **529**
    Comparing Resource Usage   **530**
    Controlling WHERE Processing Index Usage with Data Set Options   **531**
    Displaying Index Usage Information in the SAS Log   **531**
    Using an Index with Views   **532**
Using an Index for BY Processing   **532**
Using an Index for Both WHERE and BY Processing   **533**
Specifying an Index with the KEY= Option for SET and MODIFY Statements   **534**
Taking Advantage of an Index   **534**
Maintaining Indexes   **534**
    Displaying Data File Information   **534**
    Copying an Indexed Data File   **535**
    Updating an Indexed Data File   **536**
    Sorting an Indexed Data File   **536**
    Adding Observations to an Indexed Data File   **536**
    Multiple Occurrences of Values   **536**

Appending Data to an Indexed Data File **537**
Recovering a Damaged Index **537**
Indexes and Integrity Constraints **537**
Compressing Data Files **537**
Definition of Compression **537**
Requesting Compression **538**
Disabling a Compression Request **538**

Definition of a SAS Data File

A *SAS data file* is a type of SAS data set that contains both the data values and the descriptor information. SAS data files have the member type of DATA. There are two general types of SAS data files:

native SAS data file
stores the data values and descriptor information in a file that is formatted by SAS.

interface SAS data file
stores the data in a file that was formatted by software other than SAS. SAS provides engines for reading and writing data from files that were formatted by software such as ORACLE, DB2, SYBASE, ODBC, BMDP, SPSS, and OSIRIS. These files are interface SAS data files, and when their data values are accessed through an engine, SAS recognizes them as SAS data sets.

Note: The availability of engines that can access different types of interface data files is determined by your site licensing agreement. See your system administrator to determine which engines are available. For more information about SAS multiple engine architecture, see Chapter 37, "SAS Engines," on page 597. △

Differences between Data Files and Data Views

While the terms "SAS data files" and "SAS data views" can often be used interchangeably, here are a few differences to consider:

☐ *The main difference is where the values are stored.* A SAS data file is a type of SAS data set that contains both descriptor information about the data and the data values themselves. SAS views contain only descriptor information and instructions for retrieving data that is stored elsewhere. Once the data is retrieved by SAS, it can be manipulated in a DATA step.

☐ *A data file is static; a view is dynamic.* When you reference a data file in a later PROC step, you see the data values as they were when the data file was created or last updated. When you reference a view in a PROC step, the view executes and provides you with an image of the data values as they currently exist, not as they existed when the view was defined.

☐ *SAS data files can be created on tape or on any other storage medium.*

SAS data views cannot be stored on tape. Because of their dynamic nature, SAS data views must derive their information from data files on random-access storage devices, such as disk drives. Views cannot derive their information from files stored on sequentially accessed storage devices, such as tape drives.

☐ *SAS data views are read only.* You cannot write to a view, but some SQL views can be updated.

□ *SAS data files can have an audit trail.* The audit trail is an optional SAS file that logs modifications to a SAS data file. Each time an observation is added, deleted, or updated, information is written to the audit trail about who made the modification, what was modified, and when.

□ *SAS data files can have generations.* Generations provide the ability to keep multiple copies of a SAS data file. The multiple copies represent versions of the same data file, which is archived each time it is replaced.

□ *SAS data files can have integrity constraints.* When you update a SAS data file, you can ensure that the data conforms to certain standards by using integrity constraints. With views, this may only be done indirectly, by assigning integrity constraints to the data files that the views reference.

□ *SAS data files can be indexed.* Indexing might enable SAS to find data in a SAS data file more quickly. SAS data views cannot be indexed.

□ *SAS data files can be encrypted.* Encryption provides an extra layer of security to physical files. SAS data views cannot be encrypted.

□ *SAS data files can be compressed.* Compression makes it possible to store physical files in less space. SAS data views cannot be compressed.

The following figure illustrates native and interface SAS data files and their relationship to SAS views.

Figure 28.1 Types of SAS Data Sets

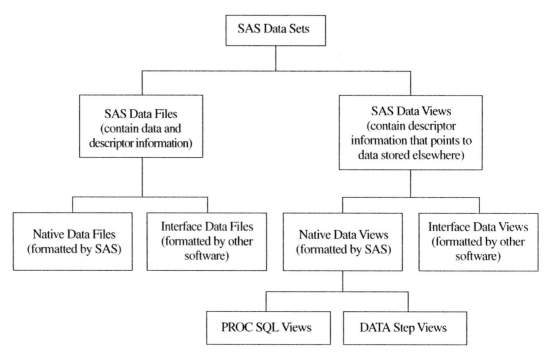

Understanding an Audit Trail

Definition of an Audit Trail

The *audit trail* is an optional SAS file that you can create in order to log modifications to a SAS data file. Each time an observation is added, deleted, or updated, information is written to the audit trail about who made the modification, what was modified, and when.

Many businesses and organizations require an audit trail for security reasons. The audit trail maintains historical information about the data, which gives you the opportunity to develop usage statistics and patterns. The historical information enables you to track individual pieces of data from the moment they enter the data file to the time they leave.

The audit trail is also the only facility in SAS that stores observations from failed append operations and that were rejected by integrity constraints. (The integrity constraints feature is described in "Understanding Integrity Constraints" on page 505.) The audit trail enables you to write a DATA step to extract the failed or rejected observations, use information describing why the observations failed to correct them, and then reapply the observations to the data file.

Audit Trail Description

The audit trail is created by the default Base SAS engine and has the same libref and member name as the data file, but has a data set type of AUDIT. It replicates the variables in the data file and additionally stores two types of audit variables:

□ _AT*_ variables, which automatically store modification data

□ user variables, which are optional variables you can define to collect modification data.

The _AT*_ variables are described in the following table.

Table 28.1   _AT* Variables

_AT*_ Variable	Description
ATDATETIME	Stores the date and time of a modification
ATUSERID	Stores the logon userid that is associated with a modification
ATOBSNO	Stores the observation number that is affected by the modification, except when REUSE=YES (because the observation number is always 0)
ATRETURNCODE	Stores the event return code
ATMESSAGE	Stores the SAS log message at the time of the modification
ATOPCODE	Stores a code that describes the type of modification

The _ATOPCODE_ values are listed in the following table.

Table 28.2 _ATOPCODE_ Values

Code	Modification
AL	Auditing is resumed
AS	Auditing is suspended
DA	Added data record image
DD	Deleted data record image
DR	Before-update record image
DW	After-update record image
EA	Observation add failed
ED	Observation delete failed
EU	Observation update failed

The type of entries stored in the audit trail, along with their corresponding _ATOPCODE_ values, are determined by the options specified in the LOG statement when the audit trail is initiated. Note that if the LOG statement is omitted when the audit trail is initiated, the default behavior is to log all images.

□ The A operation codes are controlled by the ADMIN_IMAGE option.

□ The DR operation code is controlled by the BEFORE_IMAGE option.

□ All other D operation codes are controlled with the DATA_IMAGE option.

□ The E operation codes are controlled by the ERROR_IMAGE option.

The user variable is a variable that associates data values with the data file without making them part of the data file. That is, the data values are stored in the audit file, but you update them in the data file like any other variable. You may want to define a user variable to enable end users to enter a reason for each update.

User variables are defined at audit trail initiation with the USER_VAR statement. For example, the following code initiates an audit trail and creates a user variable REASON_CODE for data file MYLIB.SALES:

```
proc datasets lib=mylib;
  audit sales;
    initiate;
    user_var reason_code $ 20;
run;
```

After the audit trail is initiated, the Base SAS engine retrieves the user variables from the audit trail and displays them when the data file is opened for update. You can enter data values for the user variables as you would for any data variable. The data values are saved to the audit trail as each observation is saved. (In applications like FSEDIT, which save observations as you scroll through them, it may appear that the data values have disappeared.) The user variables are not available when the data file is opened for browsing or printing. However, to rename a user variable or modify its attributes, you modify the data file, not the audit file. The following example uses PROC DATASETS to rename the user variable:

```
proc datasets lib=mylib;
  modify sales;
    rename reason_code =  Reason;
  run;
quit;
```

You must also define attributes such as format and informat in the data file with PROC DATASETS. If you define user variables, you must store values in them for the variables to be meaningful.

A data file can have one audit file, and the audit file must reside in the same SAS library as the data file.

Operation in a Shared Environment

The audit trail operates similarly in local and remote environments. The only difference for applications and users networking with SAS/CONNECT and SAS/SHARE is that the audit trail logs events when the observation is written to permanent storage; that is, when the data is written to the remote SAS session or server. Therefore, the time that the transaction is logged might be different than the user's SAS session.

Performance Implications

Because each update to the data file is also written to the audit file, the audit trail can negatively impact system performance. You might want to consider suspending the audit trail for large, regularly scheduled batch updates. Note that the audit variables are unavailable when the audit trail is suspended.

Preservation by Other Operations

The audit trail is not recommended for data files that are copied, moved, sorted in place, replaced, or transferred to another operating environment, because those operations do not preserve the audit trail. In a copy operation on the same host, you can preserve the data file and audit trail by renaming them using the generation data sets feature; however, logging will stop because neither the auditing process nor the generation data sets feature saves the source program that caused the replacement. For more information about generation data sets, see "Understanding Generation Data Sets" on page 499.

Programming Considerations

For data files whose audit file contains user variables, the variable list is different when browsing and updating the data file. The user variables are selected for update but not for browsing. You should be aware of this difference when you are developing your own full-screen applications.

Other Considerations

Data values that are entered for user variables are not stored in the audit trail for delete operations.

If the audit file becomes damaged, you will not be able to process the data file until you terminate the audit trail. Then you can initiate a new audit trail or process the data file without one. To terminate the audit trail for a generation data set, use the GENNUM= data set option in the AUDIT statement. You cannot initiate an audit trail for a generation data set.

In indexed data sets, the fast-append feature may cause some observations to be written to the audit trail twice, first with a DA operation code and then with an EA operation code. The observations with EA represent those rejected by index restrictions. For more information, see "Appending to an Indexed Data Set" in the PROC DATASETS APPEND statement documentation in *Base SAS Procedures Guide*.

Initiating an Audit Trail

You initiate an audit trail in the DATASETS procedure with the AUDIT statement. Consult the "PROC DATASETS AUDIT Statement" in the *Base SAS Procedures Guide* for syntax information.

The audit file will use the SAS password assigned to its associated data file; therefore, it is recommended that the data file have an ALTER password. An ALTER-level password restricts read and edit access to SAS files. If a password other than ALTER is used, or no password is used, the software will generate a warning message that the files are not protected from accidental update or deletion.

Controlling the Audit Trail

Once active, you can suspend and resume logging, and terminate (delete) the audit trail. The syntax for controlling the audit trail is described in the PROC DATASETS AUDIT statement documentation. Note that replacing the associated data file will also delete the audit trail.

Reading and Determining the Status of the Audit Trail

The audit trail is read-only. You can read the audit trail with any component of SAS that reads a data set. To refer to the audit trail, use the TYPE= data set option. For example, to view the contents of the audit trail, issue the following statement. Note that the parentheses around the TYPE= option are required.

```
proc contents data=mylib.sales (type=audit);
run;
```

The PROC CONTENTS output is shown below. Notice that the listing contains all of the variables from the corresponding data file, the _AT*_ variables, and the user variable.

Output 28.1   PROC CONTENTS Listing for Data File MYLIB.SALES

```
                          The CONTENTS Procedure

Data Set Name        MYLIB.SALES.AUDIT          Observations           0
Member Type          AUDIT                      Variables              10
Engine               V9                         Indexes                0
Created              12:34 Wednesday, January 22, 2003   Observation Length   111
Last Modified        12:34 Wednesday, January 22, 2003   Deleted Observations  0
Protection                                      Compressed             NO
Data Set Type        AUDIT                      Sorted                 NO
Label
Data Representation  WINDOWS
Encoding             Default


                    Engine/Host Dependent Information

        Data Set Page Size         4096
        Number of Data Set Pages   1
        First Data Page            1
        Max Obs per Page           33
        Obs in First Data Page     0
        Number of Data Set Repairs 0
        File Name                  C:\My Documents\myfiles\sales.sas7baud
        Release Created            9.0000A0
        Host Created               WIN_NT


              Alphabetic List of Variables and Attributes

        #     Variable       Type    Len    Format

        5     _ATDATETIME_   Num     8      DATETIME19.
        10    _ATMESSAGE_    Char    8
        6     _ATOBSNO_      Num     8
        9     _ATOPCODE_     Char    2
        7     _ATRETURNCODE_ Num     8
        8     _ATUSERID_     Char    32
        2     invoice        Num     8
        1     product        Char    9
        4     reason_code    Char    20
        3     renewal        Num     8
```

You can also use your favorite reporting tool, such as PROC REPORT or PROC TABULATE, on the audit trail.

Examples of Using Audit Trails

Example of Initiating an Audit Trail

The following example shows the data and code that are used to create and initiate an audit trail for the data file MYLIB.SALES that is used in earlier examples in this section. MYLIB.SALES stores fictional invoice and renewal figures for SAS products. The audit trail will record all events and will store one user variable, REASON_CODE, for users to enter a reason for the update.

Subsequent examples will illustrate the effect of a data file update on the audit trail and how to use audit variables to capture observations that are rejected by integrity constraints. The system option LINESIZE is set in advance for the integrity constraints

example. A large LINESIZE value is recommended to display the content of the
ATMESSAGE variable. The output examples have been modified to fit on the page.

```
options linesize=250;
   /*-------------------------------------*/
   /* Create SALES data set.          */
   /*-------------------------------------*/

data mylib.sales;
   length product  $9;
   input product invoice renewal;
datalines;
FSP         1270.00         570
SAS         1650.00         850
STAT        570.00          0
STAT        970.82          600
OR          239.36          0
SAS         7478.71         1100
SAS         800.00          800
;



   /*-------------------------------------*/
   /* Create an audit trail with a    */
   /* user variable.                  */
   /*-------------------------------------*/

proc datasets lib=mylib nolist;
   audit sales;
      initiate;
      user_var reason_code $ 20;
run;
```

Example of a Data File Update

The following example inserts an observation into MYLIB.SALES.DATA and prints
the update data in the MYLIB.SALES.AUDIT.

```
   /*-------------------------------------*/
   /* Do an update.                   */
   /*-------------------------------------*/
 proc sql;
   insert into mylib.sales
      set product = 'AUDIT',
          invoice = 2000,
          renewal = 970,
      reason_code = "Add new product";
quit;


   /*---------------------------------------*/
   /* Print the audit trail. */
   /*---------------------------------------*/
proc sql;
   select product,
          reason_code,
          _atopcode_,
```

```
            _atuserid_ format=$6.,
            _atdatetime_
            from mylib.sales(type=audit);
    quit;
```

Output 28.2 Updated Data in MYLIB.SALES.AUDIT

```
                              The SAS System

   product     reason_code        _ATOPCODE_  _ATUSERID_      _ATDATETIME_

   AUDIT       Add new product        DA        xxxxxx    31OCT2002:11:24:32
```

Example of Using the Audit Trail to Capture Rejected Observations

The following example adds integrity constraints to MYLIB.SALES.DATA and records observations that are rejected as a result of the integrity constraints in MYLIB.SALES.AUDIT. For more information about integrity constraints, see "Understanding Integrity Constraints" on page 505.

```
    /*--------------------------------*/
    /* Create integrity constraints.  */
    /*--------------------------------*/
proc datasets lib=mylib;
   modify sales;
   ic create null_renewal = not null (invoice)
            message = "Invoice must have a value.";
   ic create invoice_amt = check (where=((invoice > 0) and
               (renewal <= invoice)))
            message = "Invoice and/or renewal are invalid.";
run;

    /*--------------------------------*/
    /* Do some updates.               */
    /*--------------------------------*/
proc sql; /* this update works */
   update mylib.sales
     set invoice = invoice * .9,
         reason_code = "10% price cut"
     where renewal > 800;

proc sql;  /* this update fails */
   insert into mylib.sales
     set product = 'AUDIT',
         renewal = 970,
         reason_code = "Add new product";

proc sql;  /* this update works */
   insert into mylib.sales
     set product = 'AUDIT',
         invoice = 10000,
         renewal = 970,
         reason_code = "Add new product";

proc sql;  /* this update fails */
```

```
          insert into mylib.sales
             set product = 'AUDIT',
                 invoice = 100,
                 renewal = 970,
              reason_code = "Add new product";
       quit;


          /*--------------------------------------*/
          /* Print the audit trail. */
          /*--------------------------------------*/
       proc print data=mylib.sales(type=audit);
          format _atuserid_ $6.;
          var product reason_code _atopcode_ _atuserid_ _atdatetime_;
       title  'Contents of the Audit Trail';
       run;


          /*--------------------------------------*/
          /* Print the rejected records.          */
          /*--------------------------------------*/
       proc print data=mylib.sales(type=audit);
          where _atopcode_ eq "EA";
          format _atmessage_ $250.;
          var product invoice renewal _atmessage_ ;
       title  'Rejected Records';
       run;
```

Output 28.3 shows the contents of MYLIB.SALES.AUDIT after several updates of MYLIB.SALES.DATA were attempted. Integrity constraints were added to the file, then updates were attempted. Output 28.4 prints information about the rejected observations on the audit trail.

Output 28.3   Contents of MYLIB.SALES.AUDIT After an Update with Integrity Constraints

```
                     Contents of the Audit Trail

  Obs     product      reason_code      _ATOPCODE_     _ATUSERID_        _ATDATETIME_

   1      AUDIT      Add new product       DA           xxxxxx       22JAN2003:12:43:27
   2      SAS                              DR           xxxxxx       22JAN2003:13:02:02
   3      SAS        10% price cut         DW           xxxxxx       22JAN2003:13:02:02
   4      SAS                              DR           xxxxxx       22JAN2003:13:02:02
   5      SAS        10% price cut         DW           xxxxxx       22JAN2003:13:02:02
   6      AUDIT                            DR           xxxxxx       22JAN2003:13:02:02
   7      AUDIT      10% price cut         DW           xxxxxx       22JAN2003:13:02:02
   8      AUDIT      Add new product       EA           xxxxxx       22JAN2003:13:02:02
   9      AUDIT      Add new product       DA           xxxxxx       22JAN2003:13:02:02
  10      AUDIT      Add new product       EA           xxxxxx       22JAN2003:13:02:02
```

Output 28.4 Rejected Records on the Audit Trail

```
                      Rejected Records
   Obs    product   invoice   renewal    _ATMESSAGE_
   1      AUDIT        .         970      ERROR: Invoice must have a value. Add/Update
                                         failed for data set MYLIB.SALES because data
                                         value(s) do not comply with integrity constraint
                                         null_renewal.
   2      AUDIT       100        970      ERROR: Invoice and/or renewal are invalid.
                                         Add/update failed for data set MYLIB.SALES
                                         because data value(s) do not comply with
                                         integrity constraint invoice_amt.
```

Understanding Generation Data Sets

Definition of Generation Data Set

A *generation data set* is an archived version of a SAS data set that is stored as part of a generation group. A generation data set is created each time the file is updated. Each generation data set in a generation group has the same root member name, but each has a different version number. The most recent version of the generation data set is called the base version.

You can request generations for a SAS data file only. You cannot request generations for a SAS view.

Note: Generation data sets provide historical versions of a data set; they do not track observation updates for an individual data set. To log each time an observation is added, deleted, or updated, see "Understanding an Audit Trail" on page 491. △

Terminology for Generation Data Sets

The following terms are relevant to generation data sets:

base version
> is the most recently created version of a data set. Its name does not have the four-character suffix for the generation number.

generation group
> is a group of data sets that represent a series of replacements to the original data set. The generation group consists of the base version and a set of historical versions.

generation number
> is a monotonically increasing number that identifies one of the historical versions in a generation group. For example, the data set named AIR#272 has a generation number of 272.

GENMAX=
> is an output data set option that requests generations for a data set and specifies the maximum number of versions (including the base version and all historical versions) to keep for a given data set. The default is GENMAX=0, which means that generations is not in effect.

GENNUM=
> is an input data set option that references a specific version from a generation
> group. Positive numbers are absolute references to a historical version by its
> generation number. Negative numbers are a relative reference to historical
> versions. For example, GENNUM=-1 refers to the youngest version.

historical versions
> are the older copies of the base version of a data set. Names for historical versions
> have a four-character suffix for the generation number, such as #003.

oldest version
> is the oldest version in a generation group.

rolling over
> specifies the process of the version number moving from 999 to 000. When the
> generation number reaches 999, its next value is 000.

youngest version
> is the version that is chronologically closest to the base version.

Invoking Generation Data Sets

To invoke generation data sets and to specify the maximum number of versions to
maintain, include the output data set option GENMAX= when creating or replacing a
data set. For example, the following DATA step creates a new data set and requests
that up to four copies be kept (one base version and three historical versions):

```
data a (genmax=4);
   x=1;
   output;
run;
```

Once the GENMAX= data set option is in effect, the data set member name is limited
to 28 characters (rather than 32), because the last four characters are reserved for a
version number. When the GENMAX= data set option is not in effect, the member
name can be up to 32 characters. See the GENMAX= data set option in *SAS Language
Reference: Dictionary*.

Understanding How a Generation Group Is Maintained

The first time a data set with generations in effect is replaced, SAS keeps the
replaced data set and appends a four-character version number to its member name,
which includes # and a three-digit number. That is, for a data set named A, the
replaced data set becomes A#001. When the data set is replaced for the second time,
the replaced data set becomes A#002; that is, A#002 is the version that is
chronologically closest to the base version. After three replacements, the result is:

A   base (current) version

A#003   most recent (youngest) historical version

A#002   second most recent historical version

A#001   oldest historical version.

With GENMAX=4, a fourth replacement deletes the oldest version, which is A#001.
As replacements occur, SAS will always keep four copies. For example, after ten
replacements, the result is:

A	base (current) version
A#010	most recent (youngest) historical version
A#009	2nd most recent historical version
A#008	oldest historical version

The limit for version numbers that SAS can append is #999. After 999 replacements, the youngest version is #999. After 1,000 replacements, SAS rolls over the youngest version number to #000. After 1,001 replacements, the youngest version number is #001. For example, using data set A with GENNUM=4, the results would be:

999 replacements	A (current)
	A#999 (most recent)
	A#998 (2nd most recent)
	A#997 (oldest)
1,000 replacements	A (current)
	A#000 (most recent)
	A#999 (2nd most recent)
	A#998 (oldest)
1,001 replacements	A (current)
	A#001 (most recent)
	A#000 (2nd most recent)
	A#999 (oldest)

The following table shows how names are assigned to a generation group:

Table 28.3 Naming Generation Group Data Sets

Time	SAS Code	Data Set Name(s)	GENNUM= Absolute Reference	GENNUM= Relative Reference	Explanation
1	data air (genmax=3);	AIR	1	0	The AIR data set is created, and three generations are requested
2	data air;	AIR	2	0	AIR is replaced. AIR from time 1 is renamed AIR#001.
		AIR#001	1	-1	
3	data air;	AIR	3	0	AIR is replaced. AIR from time 2 is renamed AIR#002.
		AIR#002	2	-1	
		AIR#001	1	-2	
4	data air;	AIR	4	0	AIR is replaced. AIR from time 3 is renamed AIR#003. AIR#001 from time 1, which is the oldest, is deleted.
		AIR#003	3	-1	
		AIR#002	2	-2	
5	data air (genmax=2);	AIR	5	0	AIR is replaced, and the number of generations is changed to two. AIR from time 4 is renamed AIR#004. The two oldest versions are deleted.
		AIR#004	4	-1	

Processing Specific Versions of a Generation Group

When a generation group exists, SAS processes the base version by default. For example, the following PRINT procedure prints the base version:

```
proc print data=a;
run;
```

To request a specific version from a generation group, use the GENNUM= input data set option. There are two methods that you can use:

- □ A positive integer (excluding zero) references a specific historical version number. For example, the following statement prints the historical version #003:

  ```
  proc print data=a(gennum=3);
  run;
  ```

  Note: After 1,000 replacements, if you want historical version #000, specify GENNUM=1000. △

- □ A negative integer is a relative reference to a version in relation to the base version, from the youngest predecessor to the oldest. For example, GENNUM=-1 refers to the youngest version. The following statement prints the data set that is three versions previous to the base version:

  ```
  proc print data=a(gennum=-3);
  run;
  ```

Table 28.4   Requesting Specific Generation Data Sets

SAS statement	Result
`proc print data=air (gennum=0);` `proc print data=air;`	Prints the current (base) version of the AIR data set.
`proc print data=air (gennum=-2);`	Prints the version two generations back from the current version.
`proc print data=air (gennum=3);`	Prints the file AIR#003.
`proc print data=air (gennum=1000);`	After 1,000 replacements, prints the file AIR#000, which is the file that is created after AIR#999.

Managing Generation Groups

Introduction

The DATASETS procedure provides a variety of statements for managing generation groups. Note that for the DATASETS procedure, GENNUM= has the following additional functionality:

- □ For the PROC DATASETS and DELETE statements, GENNUM= supports the additional values ALL, HIST, and REVERT.

- □ For the CHANGE statement, GENNUM= supports the additional value ALL.

- □ For the CHANGE statement, specifying GENNUM=0 refers to all versions rather than just the base version.

Displaying Data Set Information

A variety of statements in the DATASETS procedure can process a specific historical version. For example, you can display data set version numbers for historical copies using the CONTENTS statement in PROC DATASETS:

```
proc datasets library=myfiles;
   contents data=test (gennum=2);
run;
```

Copying Generation Groups

You can use the COPY statement in the DATASETS procedure or the COPY procedure to copy a generation group. However, you cannot copy an individual version.

For example, the following DATASETS procedure uses the COPY statement to copy a generation group for data set MYGEN1 from library MYLIB1 to library MYLIB2.

```
libname mylib1 'SAS-data-library-1';
libname mylib2 'SAS-data-library-2';

proc datasets;
  copy in=mylib1 out=mylib2;
  select mygen1;
run;
```

Appending Generation Groups

You can use the GENNUM= data set option to append a specific historical version. For example, the following DATASETS procedure uses the APPEND statement to append a historical version of data set B to data set A. Note that by default, SAS uses the base version for the BASE= data set.

```
proc datasets;
   append base=a data=b(gennum=2);
run;
```

Modifying the Number of Versions

When you modify the attributes of a data set, you can increase or decrease the number of versions for an existing generation group.

For example, the following MODIFY statement in the DATASETS procedure changes the number of generations for data set MYLIB.AIR to 4:

```
libname mylib 'SAS-data-library';

proc datasets library=mylib;
   modify air(genmax=4);
run;
```

CAUTION:
If you decrease the number of versions, SAS will delete the oldest version(s) so as not to exceed the new maximum. For example, the following MODIFY statement decreases the number of versions for MYLIB.AIR from 4 to 0, which causes SAS to automatically delete the three historical versions:

```
proc datasets library=mylib;
    modify air (genmax=0);
run;
```

△

Deleting Versions in a Generation Group

When you delete data sets, you can specify a specific version or an entire generation group to delete. The following table shows the types of delete operations and their effects when you delete versions of a generation group.

The following examples assume that the base version of AIR and two historical versions (AIR#001 and AIR#002) exist for each command.

SAS statement in PROC DATASETS	Results
`delete air;` `delete air(gennum=0);`	Deletes the base version and shifts up historical versions. AIR#002 is renamed to AIR and becomes the new base version.
`delete air(gennum=2);`	Deletes historical version AIR#002.
`delete air(gennum=-2);`	Deletes the second youngest historical version (AIR#001).
`delete air(gennum=all);`	Deletes all data sets in the generation group, including the base version.
`delete air(gennum=hist);`	Deletes all data sets in the generation group, except the base version.

Note: Both an absolute reference and a relative reference refer to a specific version. A relative reference does not skip deleted versions. Therefore, when you are working with a generation group that includes one or more deleted versions, using a relative reference will result in an error if the referenced version has been deleted. For example, if you have the base version AIR and three historical versions (AIR#001, AIR#002, and AIR#003) and you delete AIR#002, the following statements return an error, because AIR#002 does not exist. SAS does not assume that you mean AIR#003:

```
proc print data=air (gennum= -2);
run;
```

△

Renaming Versions in a Generation Group

When you rename a data set, you can rename an entire generation group:

```
proc datasets;
    change a=newa;
run;
```

You can also rename a single version by including GENNUM=:

```
proc datasets;
    change a(gennum=2)=newa;
```

Note: For the CHANGE statement in PROC DATASETS, specifying GENNUM=0 refers to the entire generation group. △

Using Passwords in a Generation Group

Passwords for versions in a generation group are maintained as follows:

□ If you assign a password to the base version, the password is maintained in subsequent historical versions. However, the password is not applied to any existing historical versions.

□ If you assign a password to a historical version, the password applies to that individual data set only.

Understanding Integrity Constraints

Definition of Integrity Constraints

Integrity constraints are a set of data validation rules that you can specify in order to restrict the data values that can be stored for a variable in a SAS data file. Integrity constraints help you preserve the validity and consistency of your data. SAS enforces the integrity constraints when the values associated with an integrity constraint variable are added, updated, or deleted.

There are two categories of integrity constraints: general and referential.

General Integrity Constraints

General integrity constraints enable you to restrict the values of variables within a single file. There are four types of general constraints:

check   limits the data values of variables to a specific set, range, or list of values. Check constraints can also be used to ensure that the data values in one variable within an observation are contingent on the data values of another variable in the same observation.

not null   requires that a variable contain a data value. Null (missing) values are not allowed.

unique   requires that the specified variable(s) contain unique data values. A null data value is allowed but is limited to a single instance, given the unique nature of the constraint.

primary key   requires that the specified variable(s) contain unique data values and that null data values are not allowed. Only one primary key can exist in a data file.

> *Note:* A primary key is a general integrity constraint as long as it does not have any foreign key constraints referencing it. △

Referential Integrity Constraints

A referential integrity constraint is created when a primary key integrity constraint in one data file is referenced by a *foreign key* integrity constraint in another data file.

The foreign key constraint links the data values of one or more variables in the foreign key data file to corresponding variables and values in the primary key data file. Data values in the foreign key data file must have a matching value in the primary key data file, or they must be null. When data is updated or deleted in the primary key data file, the modifications are controlled by a referential action that is defined as part of the foreign key constraint.

Separate referential actions can be defined for the update and delete operations. There are three types of referential actions:

restrict   prevents the data values of the primary key variables from being updated or deleted if there is a matching value in one of the foreign key data file's corresponding foreign key variables. The restrict referential action is the default action if one is not specified.

set null   enables the data values of the primary key variables to be updated or deleted, but matching data values in the foreign key data files are changed to null (missing) values.

cascade   enables the data values in the primary key variables to be updated, and additionally updates matching data values in the foreign key data files to the same value. Cascade is currently supported only for update operations.

The requirements for establishing a referential relationship are as follows:

□ The primary key and foreign key must reference the same number of variables, and the variables must be in the same order.

□ The variables must be of the same type (character or numeric) and length.

□ If the foreign key is being added to a data file that already contains data, the data values in the foreign key data file must match existing values in the primary key data file or be null.

The foreign key data file can exist in the same SAS library as the referenced primary key data file or in a different one. However, if the library that contains the foreign key data file is temporary, then the library containing the primary key data file must be temporary as well. In addition, referential integrity constraints cannot be assigned to data files in concatenated libraries.

There is no limit to the number of foreign keys that can reference a primary key. However, additional foreign keys can adversely impact the performance of update and delete operations.

When a referential constraint exists, a primary key integrity constraint will not be deleted until all of the foreign keys that reference it have been deleted. There are no restrictions on deleting foreign keys.

Overlapping Primary Key and Foreign Key Constraints

Variables in a SAS data file can be part of both a primary key (general integrity constraint) and a foreign key (referential integrity constraint). However, there are restrictions when you define a primary key and a foreign key constraint that use the same variables:

□ The foreign key's update and delete referential actions must both be RESTRICT.

□ When the same variables are used in a primary key and foreign key definition, the variables must be defined in a different order.

For an example, see "Defining Overlapping Primary Key and Foreign Key Constraints" on page 517.

Preservation of Integrity Constraints

These procedures preserve integrity constraints when their operation results in a copy of the original data file:

- □ in Base SAS software, the APPEND, COPY, CPORT, CIMPORT and SORT procedures
- □ in SAS/CONNECT software, the UPLOAD and DOWNLOAD procedures
- □ PROC APPEND
    - □ for an existing BASE= data file, integrity constraints in the BASE= file are preserved, but integrity constraints in the DATA= file that is being appended to the BASE= file are not preserved.
    - □ for a non-existent BASE= data file, general integrity constraints in the DATA= file that is being appended to the new BASE= file are preserved. Referential constraints in the DATA= file are not preserved.
- □ PROC SORT, and PROC UPLOAD, and PROC DOWNLOAD, when an OUT= data file is not specified
- □ the SAS Explorer window.

You can also use the CONSTRAINT option in order to control when integrity constraints are preserved for the COPY, CPORT, CIMPORT, UPLOAD, and DOWNLOAD procedures.

General integrity constraints are preserved in an active state. The state in which referential constraints are preserved depends on whether the procedure causes the primary key and foreign key data files to be written to the same or different SAS libraries (intra-libref versus inter-libref integrity constraints). Intra-libref constraints are preserved in an active state. Inter-libref constraints are preserved in an inactive state; that is, the primary key portion of the integrity constraint is enforced as a general integrity constraint but the foreign key portion is inactive. You must use the DATASETS procedure statement IC REACTIVATE to reactivate the inactive foreign keys.

The following table summarizes the circumstances under which integrity constraints are preserved.

Table 28.5 Circumstances That Cause Integrity Constraints to Be Preserved

Procedure	Condition	Constraints That Are Preserved
APPEND	DATA= data set does not exist	General Referential constraints are not affected
COPY	CONSTRAINT=yes	General Intra-libref are referential in an active state Inter-libref are referential in an inactive state
CPORT/CIMPORT	CONSTRAINT=yes	General Intra-libref are referential in an active state Inter-libref are referential in an inactive state

Procedure	Condition	Constraints That Are Preserved
SORT	OUT= data set is not specified	General
		Referential constraints are not affected
UPLOAD/DOWNLOAD	CONSTRAINT=yes and OUT= data set is not specified	General
		Intra-libref are referential in an active state
		Inter-libref are referential in an inactive state
SAS Explorer window		General

Indexes and Integrity Constraints

The unique, primary key, and foreign key integrity constraints store data values in an index file. If an index file already exists, it is used; otherwise, one is created. Consider the following points when you create or delete an integrity constraint:

□ When a user-defined index exists, the index's attributes must be compatible with the integrity constraint in order for the integrity constraint to be created. For example, when you add a primary key integrity constraint, the existing index must have the UNIQUE attribute. When you add a foreign key integrity constraint, the index must *not* have the UNIQUE attribute.

□ The unique integrity constraint has the same effect as the UNIQUE index attribute; therefore, when one is used, the other is not necessary.

□ The NOMISS index attribute and the not-null integrity constraint have different effects. The integrity constraint prevents missing values from being written to the SAS data file and cannot be added to an existing data file that contains missing values. The index attribute allows missing data values in the data file but excludes them from the index.

□ When any index is created, it is marked as being "owned" by the user and/or by the integrity constraint. A user cannot delete an index that is also owned by an integrity constraint and vice versa. If an index is owned by both, then the index is deleted only after both the integrity constraint and the user have requested the index's deletion. A note in the log indicates when an index cannot be deleted.

Locking Integrity Constraints

Integrity constraints support both member-level and record-level locking. You can override the default locking level with the CNTLLEV= data set option. For more information, see the CNTLLEV= data set option in *SAS Language Reference: Dictionary*.

Passwords and Integrity Constraints

The behavior of a SAS data file that is password protected does not change if the file also has defined integrity constraints. However, for referential integrity constraints, some SAS requests require that both files be open in order to process the request. If both files are password-protected, then both passwords must be provided.

For example, to execute the CONTENTS procedure for a data file with a primary key that is referenced by a foreign key, you must provide both the password for the primary key data file as well as the password for the referential data file, because in order to obtain the information for the CONTENTS output for the primary key data file, SAS must open both files.

For example, the data file SINGERS1 has a primary key that is referenced by a foreign key in data file SINGERS2. Both data sets are read-password protected. In an interactive session, when you submit the following PROC CONTENTS, SAS prompts you to provide the password for the data file with the foreign key that references the primary key in SINGERS1:

```
proc contents data=Singers1 (read=luke);
run;
```

After you submit the above procedure, SAS displays the Missing SAS Password window, with the request:

READ access denied. Enter the password for file WORK.SINGERS2.DATA.

After you enter the password for SINGERS2 and press OK, the output that is displayed contains information from both SINGERS1 (contains the primary key) and SINGERS2 (contains the foreign key):

Output 28.5 PROC CONTENTS Output Showing Primary Key and Referential Integrity Constraints

```
                              The SAS System

                           The CONTENTS Procedure

       Data Set Name        WORK.SINGERS1           Observations          6
       Member Type          DATA                    Variables             3
       Engine               V9                      Indexes               1
       Created              Friday, October 25, 2002 01:29:41  Integrity Constraints  1
       Last Modified        Friday, October 25, 2002 01:29:42  Observation Length     24
       Protection           READ                    Deleted Observations  0
       Data Set Type                                Compressed            NO
       Label                                        Sorted                NO
       Data Representation  WINDOWS_32
       Encoding             wlatin1  Western (Windows)


                        Engine/Host Dependent Information

   Data Set Page Size           4096
   Number of Data Set Pages     2
   First Data Page              1
   Max Obs per Page             168
   Obs in First Data Page       6
   Index File Page Size         4096
   Number of Index File Pages   2
   Number of Data Set Repairs   0
   File Name                    C:\DOCUME~1\xxxxxx\LOCALS~1\Temp\SAS Temporary
                                Files\_TD3500\singers1.sas7bdat
   Release Created              9.0100A0
   Host Created                 XP_PRO


                     Alphabetic List of Variables and Attributes

                      #    Variable     Type    Len

                      3    Age          Num     8
                      1    FirstName    Char    8
                      2    LastName     Char    8


                      Alphabetic List of Integrity Constraints

        Integrity                                              On        On
   #    Constraint    Type          Variables        Reference Delete    Update

   1    _PK0001_      Primary Key   FirstName LastName
        _FK0001_      Referential   FirstName LastName WORK.SINGERS2 Restrict  Restrict


                      Alphabetic List of Indexes and Attributes

                                             # of
                        Unique    Owned    Unique
             #   Index  Option    by IC    Values   Variables

             1   _PK0001_  YES     YES        6      FirstName LastName
```

Note: If you cannot be prompted like in a batch environment, then when the CONTENTS procedure is executed for a data file with a primary key that is referenced by a foreign key, a warning message states that information for the file containing the referencing foreign key cannot be obtained. △

Specifying Integrity Constraints

You create integrity constraints in the SQL procedure, the DATASETS procedure, or in SCL (SAS Component Language). The constraints can be specified when the data file is created or added to an existing data file. When you add integrity constraints to an existing file, SAS first verifies that the data values to which the integrity constraints have been assigned conform to the constraints.

When specifying integrity constraints, you must specify a separate statement for each constraint. In addition, you must specify a separate statement for each variable that you want to have the not null integrity constraint. When multiple variables are included in the specification for a primary key, foreign key, or unique integrity constraint, a composite index is created and the integrity constraint will enforce the combination of variable values. The relationship between SAS indexes and integrity constraints is described in "Indexes and Integrity Constraints" on page 508. For more information, see "Understanding SAS Indexes" on page 518.

When you add an integrity constraint in SCL, open the data set in utility mode. See "Creating Integrity Constraints by Using SCL" on page 513 for an example. Integrity constraints must be deleted in utility open mode. For detailed syntax information, see *SAS Component Language: Reference.*

When generation data sets are used, you must create the integrity constraints in each data set generation that includes protected variables.

Listing Integrity Constraints

PROC CONTENTS and PROC DATASETS report integrity constraint information without special options. In addition, you can print information about integrity constraints and indexes to a data set by using the OUT2= option. In PROC SQL, the DESCRIBE TABLE and DESCRIBE TABLE CONSTRAINTS statements report integrity constraint characteristics as part of the data file definition or alone, respectively. SCL provides the ICTYPE, ICVALUE, and ICDESCRIBE functions for getting information about integrity constraints. Refer to the *Base SAS Procedures Guide* and *SAS Component Language: Reference* for more information.

Rejected Observations

You can customize the error message associated with an integrity constraint when you create the constraint by using the MESSAGE= and MSGTYPE= options. The MESSAGE= option enables you to prepend a user-defined message to the SAS error message associated with an integrity constraint. The MSGTYPE= option enables you to suppress the SAS portion of the message. For more information, see the PROC DATASETS, PROC SQL, and SCL documentation.

Rejected observations can be collected in a special file by using an audit trail.

Examples

Creating Integrity Constraints with the DATASETS Procedure

The following sample code creates integrity constraints by means of the DATASETS procedure. The data file TV_SURVEY checks the percentage of viewing time spent on networks, PBS, and other channels, with the following integrity constraints:

☐ The viewership percentage cannot exceed 100 percent.

□ Only adults can participate in the survey.

□ GENDER can be male or female.

```
data tv_survey(label='Validity checking');
   length idnum age 4 gender $1;
   input idnum gender age network pbs other;
datalines;
1 M 55 80 . 20
2 F 36 50 40 10
3 M 42 20 5 75
4 F 18 30 0 70
5 F 84 0 100 0
;

proc datasets nolist;
  modify tv_survey;
    ic create val_gender = check(where=(gender in ('M','F')))
       message = "Valid values for variable GENDER are
       either 'M' or 'F'.";
    ic create val_age = check(where=(age >= 18 and age <= 120))
       message = "An invalid AGE has been provided.";
    ic create val_new = check(where=(network <= 100));
    ic create val_pbs = check(where=(pbs <= 100));
    ic create val_ot = check(where=(other <= 100));
    ic create val_max = check(where=((network+pbs+other)<= 100));
quit;
```

Creating Integrity Constraints with the SQL Procedure

The following sample program creates integrity constraints by means of the SQL procedure. The data file PEOPLE lists employees and contains employment information. The data file SALARY contains salary and bonus information. The integrity constraints are as follows:

□ The names of employees receiving bonuses must be found in the PEOPLE data file.

□ The names identified in the primary key must be unique.

□ GENDER can be male or female.

□ Job status can be permanent, temporary, or terminated.

```
proc sql;
   create table people
   (
     name       char(14),
     gender     char(6),
     hired      num,
     jobtype    char(1) not null,
     status     char(10),

   constraint prim_key primary key(name),
   constraint gender check(gender in ('male' 'female')),
   constraint status check(status in ('permanent'
                           'temporary' 'terminated'))
   );
```

```
   create table salary
   (
    name      char(14),
    salary    num not null,
    bonus     num,

    constraint for_key foreign key(name) references people
        on delete restrict on update set null
   );
quit;
```

Creating Integrity Constraints by Using SCL

To add integrity constraints to a data file by using SCL, you must create and build an SCL catalog entry. The following sample program creates and compiles catalog entry EXAMPLE.IC_CAT.ALLICS.SCL.

```
INIT:
  put "Test SCL integrity constraint functions start.";
return;


MAIN:
  put "Opening WORK.ONE in utility mode.";
  dsid = open('work.one', 'V');/* Utility mode.*/
  if (dsid = 0) then
    do;
     _msg_=sysmsg();
     put _msg_=;
    end;
    else do;
     if (dsid > 0) then
        put "Successfully opened WORK.ONE in"
            "UTILITY mode.";
    end;

  put "Create a check integrity constraint named teen.";
  rc = iccreate(dsid, 'teen', 'check',
  '(age > 12) && (age < 20)');

  if (rc > 0) then
    do;
     put rc=;
     _msg_=sysmsg();
     put _msg_=;
    end;
    else do;
     put "Successfully created a check"
         "integrity constraint.";
    end;

  put "Create a not-null integrity constraint named nn.";
  rc = iccreate(dsid, 'nn', 'not-null', 'age');

  if (rc > 0) then
```

```
   do;
    put rc=;
    _msg_=sysmsg();
    put _msg_=;
   end;
   else do;
    put "Successfully created a not-null"
        "integrity constraint.";
   end;

put "Create a unique integrity constraint named uq.";
rc = iccreate(dsid, 'uq', 'unique', 'age');

if (rc > 0) then
   do;
    put rc=;
    _msg_=sysmsg();
    put _msg_=;
   end;
   else do;
    put "Successfully created a unique"
        "integrity constraint.";
   end;

put "Create a primary key integrity constraint named pk.";
rc = iccreate(dsid, 'pk', 'Primary', 'name');

 if (rc > 0) then
   do;
    put rc=;
    _msg_=sysmsg();
    put _msg_=;
   end;
   else do;
    put "Successfully created a primary key"
        "integrity constraint.";
   end;

put "Closing WORK.ONE.";
rc = close(dsid);
if (rc > 0) then
   do;
    put rc=;
    _msg_=sysmsg();
    put _msg_=;
   end;

put "Opening WORK.TWO in utility mode.";
dsid2 = open('work.two', 'V');
   /*Utility mode */
if (dsid2 = 0) then
   do;
   _msg_=sysmsg();
    put _msg_=;
```

```
        end;
        else do;
         if (dsid2 > 0) then
            put "Successfully opened WORK.TWO in"
                "UTILITY mode.";
        end;

    put "Create a foreign key integrity constraint named fk.";
    rc = iccreate(dsid2, 'fk', 'foreign', 'name',
    'work.one','null', 'restrict');

    if (rc > 0) then
        do;
         put rc=;
         _msg_=sysmsg();
         put _msg_=;
        end;
        else do;
         put "Successfully created a foreign key"
             "integrity constraint.";
        end;

  put "Closing WORK.TWO.";
    rc = close(dsid2);
    if (rc > 0) then
        do;
         put rc=;
         _msg_=sysmsg();
         put _msg_=;
        end;
return;


TERM:
   put "End of test SCL integrity constraint"
       "functions.";
return;
```

The previous code creates the SCL catalog entry. The following code creates two data files, ONE and TWO, and executes the SCL entry EXAMPLE.IC_CAT.ALLICS.SCL:

```
    /* Submit to create data files. */

data one two;
    input name $ age;
datalines;
Morris 13
Elaine 14
Tina 15
;

    /* after compiling, run the SCL program */

proc display catalog= example.ic_cat.allics.scl;
run;
```

Removing Integrity Constraints

The following sample program segments remove integrity constraints. In those that delete a primary key integrity constraint, note that the foreign key integrity constraint is deleted first.

This program segment deletes integrity constraints using PROC SQL.

```
proc sql;
   alter table salary
     DROP CONSTRAINT for_key;
   alter table people
        DROP CONSTRAINT gender
        DROP CONSTRAINT _nm0001_
        DROP CONSTRAINT status
        DROP CONSTRAINT prim_key
     ;
quit;
```

This program segment removes integrity constraints using PROC DATASETS.

```
proc datasets nolist;
   modify tv_survey;
        ic delete val_max;
        ic delete val_gender;
        ic delete val_age;
run;
quit;
```

This program segment removes integrity constraints using SCL.

```
TERM:
      put "Opening WORK.TWO in utility mode.";
      dsid2 = open( 'work.two' , 'V' );  /* Utility mode.      */
      if (dsid2 = 0) then
        do;
         _msg_=sysmsg();
         put _msg_=;
      end;
      else do;
        if (dsid2 > 0) then
            put "Successfully opened WORK.TWO in Utility mode.";
         end;

rc = icdelete(dsid2, 'fk');
if (rc > 0) then
  do;
   put rc=;
   _msg_=sysmsg();
  end;
else
    do;
    put "Successfully deleted a foreign key integrity constraint.";
    end;
rc = close(dsid2);
return;
```

Reactivating an Inactive Integrity Constraint

The following program segment reactivates a foreign key integrity constraint that has been inactivated as a result of a COPY, CPORT, CIMPORT, UPLOAD, or DOWNLOAD procedure.

```
proc datasets;
   modify SAS-data-set;
      ic reactivate fkname references libref;
   run;
quit;
```

Defining Overlapping Primary Key and Foreign Key Constraints

The following code illustrates defining overlapping primary key and foreign key constraints:

```
data Singers1;
   input FirstName $ LastName $ Age;
   datalines;
Tom Jones 62
Kris Kristofferson 66
Willie Nelson 69
Barbra Streisand 60
Paul McCartney 60
Randy Travis 43
;
data Singers2;
   input FirstName $ LastName $ Style $;
   datalines;
Tom Jones Rock
Kris Kristofferson Country
Willie Nelson Country
Barbra Streisand Contemporary
Paul McCartney Rock
Randy Travis Country
;
proc datasets library=work nolist;
   modify Singers1;
      ic create primary key (FirstName LastName); ❶
   run;
   modify Singers2;
      ic create foreign key (FirstName LastName) references Singers1
         on delete restrict on update restrict; ❷
   run;
   modify Singers2;
      ic create primary key (LastName FirstName); ❸
   run;
   modify Singers1;
      ic create foreign key (LastName FirstName) references Singers2
         on delete restrict on update restrict; ❹
   run;

quit;
```

❶ Defines a primary key constraint for data set Singers1, for variables FirstName and LastName.

❷ Defines a foreign key constraint for data set Singers2 for variables FirstName and LastName that references the primary key defined in Step 1. Because the intention is to define a primary key using the same variables, the foreign key update and delete referential actions must both be RESTRICT.

❸ Defines a primary key constraint for data set Singers2 for variables LastName and FirstName. Because those exact same variables are already defined as a foreign key, the order must be different.

❹ Defines a foreign key constraint for data set Singers1 for variables LastName and FirstName that references the primary key defined in Step 3. Because those exact same variables are already defined as a primary key, the order must be different. Because a primary key is already defined using the same variables, the foreign key's update and delete referential actions must both be RESTRICT.

Understanding SAS Indexes

Definition of SAS Indexes

An *index* is an optional file that you can create for a SAS data file to provide direct access to specific observations. The index stores values in ascending value order for a specific variable or variables and includes information as to the location of those values within observations in the data file. In other words, an index enables you to locate an observation by value.

For example, suppose you want the observation with SSN (social security number) equal to 465-33-8613:

□ Without an index, SAS accesses observations sequentially in the order in which they are stored in the data file. SAS reads each observation, looking for SSN=465-33-8613 until the value is found or all observations are read.

□ With an index on variable SSN, SAS accesses the observation directly. SAS satisfies the condition using the index and goes straight to the observation that contains the value without having to read each observation.

You can either create an index when you create a data file or create an index for an existing data file. The data file can be either compressed or uncompressed. For each data file, you can create one or multiple indexes. Once an index exists, SAS treats it as part of the data file. That is, if you add or delete observations or modify values, the index is automatically updated.

Benefits of an Index

In general, SAS can use an index to improve performance in the following situations:

□ For WHERE processing, an index can provide faster and more efficient access to a subset of data. Note that to process a WHERE expression, SAS decides whether to use an index or to read the data file sequentially.

□ For BY processing, an index returns observations in the index order, which is in ascending value order, without using the SORT procedure even when the data file is not stored in that order.

Note: If you use the SORT procedure, the index is not used. △

□ For the SET and MODIFY statements, the KEY= option enables you to specify an index in a DATA step to retrieve particular observations in a data file.

In addition, an index can benefit other areas of SAS. In SCL (SAS Component Language), an index improves the performance of table lookup operations. For the SQL procedure, an index enables the software to process certain classes of queries more efficiently, for example, join queries. For the SAS/IML software, you can explicitly specify that an index be used for read, delete, list, or append operations.

Even though an index can reduce the time required to locate a set of observations, especially for a large data file, there are costs associated with creating, storing, and maintaining the index. When deciding whether to create an index, you must consider increased resource usage, along with the performance improvement.

Note: An index is never used for the subsetting IF statement in a DATA step, or for the FIND and SEARCH commands in the FSEDIT procedure. △

The Index File

The *index file* is a SAS file that has the same name as its associated data file, and that has a member type of INDEX. There is only one index file per data file; that is, all indexes for a data file are stored in a single file.

The index file might be a separate file, or be part of the data file, depending on the operating environment. In any case, the index file is stored in the same SAS data library as its data file.

The index file consists of entries that are organized hierarchically and connected by pointers, all of which are maintained by SAS. The lowest level in the index file hierarchy consists of entries that represent each distinct value for an indexed variable, in ascending value order. Each entry contains this information:

□ a distinct value

□ one or more unique record identifiers (referred to as a *RID*) that identifies each observation containing the value. (Think of the RID as an internal observation number.)

That is, in an index file, each value is followed by one or more RIDs, which identify the observations in the data file that contains the value. (Multiple RIDs result from multiple occurrences of the same value.) For example, the following represents index file entries for the variable LASTNAME:

```
Value          RID
=======        =====
Avery          10
Brown          6,22,43
Craig          5,50
Dunn           1
```

When an index is used to process a request, such as a WHERE expression, SAS performs a binary search on the index file and positions the index to the first entry that contains a qualified value. SAS then uses the value's RID to read the observation that contains the value. If a value has more than one RID (such as in the value for Brown in the above example), SAS reads the observation that is pointed to by the next RID in the list. The result is that SAS can quickly locate the observations that are associated with a value or range of values.

For example, using an index to process the WHERE expression, SAS positions the index to the index entry for the first value greater than 20 and uses the value's RID(s) to read the observation(s) `where age > 20 and age < 35;`. SAS then moves sequentially through the index entries reading observations until it reaches the index entry for the value that is equal to or greater than 35.

SAS automatically keeps the index file balanced as updates are made, which means that it ensures a uniform cost to access any index entry, and all space that is occupied by deleted values is recovered and reused.

Types of Indexes

When you create an index, you designate which variable(s) to index. An indexed variable is called a *key variable*. You can create two types of indexes:

☐ A *simple index*, which consists of the values of one variable.

☐ A *composite index*, which consists of the values of more than one variable, with the values concatenated to form a single value.

In addition to deciding whether you want a simple index or a composite index, you can also limit an index (and its data file) to *unique values* and exclude from the index *missing values*.

Simple Index

The most common index is a simple index, which is an index of values for one key variable. The variable can be numeric or character. When you create a simple index, SAS assigns to the index the name of the key variable.

The following example shows the DATASETS procedure statements that are used to create two simple indexes for variables CLASS and MAJOR in data file COLLEGE.SURVEY:

```
proc datasets library=college;
   modify survey;
      index create class;
      index create major;
run;
```

To process a WHERE expression using an index, SAS uses only one index. When the WHERE expression has multiple conditions using multiple key variables, SAS determines which condition qualifies the smallest subset. For example, suppose that COLLEGE.SURVEY contains the following data:

☐ 42,000 observations contain CLASS=97.

☐ 6,000 observations contain MAJOR='Biology'.

☐ 350 observations contain both CLASS=97 and MAJOR='Biology'.

With simple indexes on CLASS and MAJOR, SAS would select MAJOR to process the following WHERE expression:

```
where class=97 and major='Biology';
```

Composite Index

A composite index is an index of two or more key variables with their values concatenated to form a single value. The variables can be numeric, character, or a combination. An example is a composite index for the variables LASTNAME and FRSTNAME. A value for this index is composed of the value for LASTNAME immediately followed by the value for FRSTNAME from the same observation. When you create a composite index, you must specify a unique index name.

The following example shows the DATASETS procedure statements that are used to create a composite index for the data file COLLEGE.MAILLIST, specifying two key variables: ZIPCODE and SCHOOLID.

```
proc datasets library=college;
   modify maillist;
      index create zipid=(zipcode schoolid);
run;
```

Often, only the first variable of a composite index is used. For example, for a composite index on ZIPCODE and SCHOOLID, the following WHERE expression can use the composite index for the variable ZIPCODE because it is the first key variable in the composite index:

```
where zipcode = 78753;
```

However, you can take advantage of all key variables in a composite index by the way you construct the WHERE expression, which is referred to as *compound optimization*. Compound optimization is the process of optimizing multiple conditions on multiple variables, which are joined with a logical operator such as AND, using a composite index. If you issue the following WHERE expression, the composite index is used to find all occurrences of ZIPCODE='78753' and SCHOOLID='55'. In this way, all of the conditions are satisfied with a single search of the index:

```
where zipcode = 78753 and schoolid = 55;
```

When you are deciding whether to create a simple index or a composite index, consider how you will access the data. If you often access data for a single variable, a simple index will do. But if you frequently access data for multiple variables, a composite index could be beneficial.

Unique Values

Often it is important to require that values for a variable be unique, like social security number and employee number. You can declare unique values for a variable by creating an index for the variable and including the UNIQUE option. A unique index guarantees that values for one variable or the combination of a composite group of variables remain unique for every observation in the data file. If an update tries to add a duplicate value to that variable, the update is rejected.

The following example creates a simple index for the variable IDNUM and requires that all values for IDNUM be unique:

```
proc datasets library=college;
   modify student;
      index create idnum / unique;
run;
```

Missing Values

If a variable has a large number of missing values, it might be desirable to keep them from using space in the index. Therefore, when you create an index, you can include the NOMISS option to specify that missing values are not maintained by the index.

The following example creates a simple index for the variable RELIGION and specifies that the index does not maintain missing values for the variable:

```
proc datasets library=college;
   modify student;
      index create religion / nomiss;
run;
```

In contrast to the UNIQUE option, observations with missing values for the key variable can be added to the data file, even though the missing values are not added to the index.

SAS will not use an index that was created with the NOMISS option to process a BY statement or to process a WHERE expression that qualifies observations that contain missing values. If no missing values are present, SAS will consider using the index in processing the BY statement or WHERE expression.

In the following example, the index AGE was created with the NOMISS option and observations exist that contain missing values for the variable AGE. In this case, SAS will not use the index:

```
proc print data=mydata.employee;
   where age < 35;
run;
```

Deciding Whether to Create an Index

Costs of an Index

An index exists to improve performance. However, an index conserves some resources at the expense of others. Therefore, you must consider costs associated with creating, using, and maintaining an index. The following topics provide information on resource usage and give you some guidelines for creating indexes.

When you are deciding whether to create an index, you must consider CPU cost, I/O cost, buffer requirements, and disk space requirements.

CPU Cost

Additional CPU time is necessary to create an index as well as to maintain the index when the data file is modified. That is, for an indexed data file, when a value is added, deleted, or modified, it must also be added, deleted, or modified in the appropriate index(es).

When SAS uses an index to read an observation from a data file, there is also increased CPU usage. The increased usage results from SAS using a more complicated process than is used when SAS retrieves data sequentially. Although CPU usage is greater, you benefit from SAS reading only those observations that meet the conditions. Note that this is why using an index is more expensive when there is a larger number of observations that meet the conditions.

Note: To compare CPU usage with and without an index, for some operating environments, you can issue the STIMER or FULLSTIMER system options to write performance statistics to the SAS log. △

I/O Cost

Using an index to read observations from a data file may increase the number of I/O (input/output) requests compared to reading the data file sequentially. For example, processing a BY statement with an index may increase I/O count, but you save in not having to issue the SORT procedure. For WHERE processing, SAS considers I/O count when deciding whether to use an index.

To process a request using an index, the following occurs:

1 SAS does a binary search on the index file and positions the index to the first entry that contains a qualified value.

2 SAS uses the value's RID (identifier) to directly access the observation containing the value. SAS transfers the observation between external storage to a *buffer*, which is the memory into which data is read or from which data is written. The data is transferred in *pages*, which is the amount of data (the number of

observations) that can be transferred for one I/O request; each data file has a specified page size.

3 SAS then continues the process until the WHERE expression is satisfied. Each time SAS accesses an observation, the data file page containing the observation must be read into memory if it is not already there. Therefore, if the observations are on multiple data file pages, an I/O operation is performed for each observation.

The result is that the more random the data, the more I/Os are required to use the index. If the data is ordered more like the index, which is in ascending value order, fewer I/Os are required to access the data.

The number of buffers determines how many pages of data can simultaneously be in memory. Frequently, the larger the number of buffers, the fewer number of I/Os will be required. For example, if the page size is 4096 bytes and one buffer is allocated, then one I/O transfers 4096 bytes of data (or one page). To reduce I/Os, you can increase the page size but you will need a larger buffer. To reduce the buffer size, you can decrease the page size but you will use more I/Os.

For information on data file characteristics like the data file page size and the number of data file pages, issue the CONTENTS procedure (or use the CONTENTS statement in the DATASETS procedure). With this information, you can determine the data file page size and experiment with different sizes. Note that the information that is available from PROC CONTENTS depends on the operating environment.

The BUFSIZE= data set option (or system option) sets the permanent page size for a data file when it is created. The page size is the amount of data that can be transferred for an I/O operation to one buffer. The BUFNO= data set option (or system option) specifies how many buffers to allocate for a data file and for the overall system for a given execution of SAS; that is, BUFNO= is not stored as a data set attribute.

Buffer Requirements

In addition to the resources that are used to create and maintain an index, SAS also requires additional memory for buffers when an index is actually used. Opening the data file opens the index file but none of the indexes. The buffers are not required unless SAS uses the index but they must be allocated in preparation for the index that is being used. The number of buffers that are allocated depends on the number of levels in the index tree and in the data file open mode. If the data file is open for input, the maximum number of buffers is three; for update, the maximum number is four. (Note that these buffers are available for other uses; they are not dedicated to indexes.)

Disk Space Requirements

Additional disk space is required to store the index file, which may show up as a separate file or may appear to be part of the data file, depending on the operating environment.

For information on the index file size, issue the CONTENTS procedure (or the CONTENTS statement in the DATASETS procedure). Note that the available information from PROC CONTENTS depends on the operating environment.

Guidelines for Creating Indexes

Data File Considerations

□ For a small data file, sequential processing is often just as efficient as index processing. *Do not create an index if the data file page count is less than three pages.* It would be faster to access the data sequentially. To see how many pages are in a data file, use the CONTENTS procedure (or use the CONTENTS statement in the DATASETS procedure). Note that the information that is available from PROC CONTENTS depends on the operating environment.

□ Consider the cost of an index for a data file that is frequently changed. If you have a data file that changes often, the overhead associated with updating the index after each change can outweigh the processing advantages you gain from accessing the data with an index.

□ Create an index when you intend to retrieve a small subset of observations from a large data file (for example, less than 25% of all observations). When this occurs, the cost of processing data file pages is lower than the overhead of sequentially reading the entire data file. The smaller the subset, the larger the performance gains.

□ To reduce the number of I/Os performed when you create an index, first sort the data by the key variable. Then to improve performance, maintain the data file in sorted order by the key variable. This technique will reduce the I/Os by grouping like values together. That is, the more ordered the data file is with respect to the key variable, the more efficient the use of the index. If the data file has more than one index, sort the data by the most frequently used key variable.

Index Use Considerations

□ Keep the number of indexes per data file to a minimum to reduce disk storage and to reduce update costs.

□ Consider how often your applications will use an index. An index must be used often in order to make up for the resources that are used in creating and maintaining it. That is, do not rely solely on resource savings from processing a WHERE expression. Take into consideration the resources it takes to actually create the index and to maintain it every time the data file is changed.

□ When you create an index to process a WHERE expression, do not try to create one index that is used to satisfy all queries. If there are several variables that appear in queries, then those queries may be best satisfied with simple indexes on the most discriminating of those variables.

Key Variable Candidates

In most cases, multiple variables are used to query a data file. However, it probably would be a mistake to index all variables in a data file, as certain variables are better candidates than others:

□ The variables to be indexed should be those that are used in queries. That is, your application should require selecting small subsets from a large file, and the most common selection variables should be considered as candidate key variables.

□ A variable is a good candidate for indexing when the variable can be used to precisely identify the observations that satisfy a WHERE expression. That is, the variable should be *discriminating*, which means that the index should select the fewest possible observations. For example, variables such as AGE, FRSTNAME, and GENDER are not discriminating because it is very possible for a large representation of the data to have the same age, first name, and gender. However, a variable such as LASTNAME is a good choice because it is less likely that many employees share the same last name.

For example, consider a data file with variables LASTNAME and GENDER.

□ If many queries against the data file include LASTNAME, then indexing LASTNAME could prove to be beneficial because the values are usually discriminating. However, the same reasoning would not apply if you issued a large number of queries that included GENDER. The GENDER variable is not discriminating (because perhaps half the population are male and half are female).

□ However, if queries against the data file most often include both LASTNAME and GENDER as shown in the following WHERE expression, then creating a composite index on LASTNAME and GENDER could improve performance.

```
where lastname='LeVoux' and gender='F';
```

Note that when you create a composite index, the first key variable should be the most discriminating.

Creating an Index

Overview of Creating Indexes

You can create one index for a data file, which can be either a simple index or a composite index, and you can create multiple indexes, which can be multiple simple indexes, multiple composite indexes, or a combination of both simple and composite.

In general, the process of creating an index is as follows:

1 You request to create an index for one or multiple variables using a method such as the INDEX CREATE statement in the DATASETS procedure.

2 SAS reads the data file one observation at a time, extracts values and RID(s) for each key variable, and places them in the index file. The process to create the index always ensures that the values that are placed in the index are successively the same or increasing. The values cannot decrease, therefore, SAS examines the data file to determine the following:

□ if the data is already sorted by the key variable(s) in ascending order. If the values are in ascending order, SAS does not have to sort the values for the index file and avoids the resource cost.

□ the file's sort assertion, which is set from a previous SORT procedure or from a SORTEDBY= data set option. If the file's sort assertion is set from a SORTEDBY= data set option, SAS validates that the data is sorted as specified by the data set option. If the data is not sorted as asserted, the index will not be created, and a message appears telling you that the index was not created because values are not sorted in asserted order.

If the values are not in ascending order, SAS sorts the data that is included in the index file in ascending value order. To sort the data, SAS follows this procedure:

a SAS first attempts to sort the data using the thread-enabled sort. By dividing the sorting into separately executable processes, the time to sort the data can be reduced. However, in order to use the thread-enabled sort, the size of the index must be sufficiently large (which is determined by SAS), the SAS system option CPUCOUNT= must be set to more than one processor, and the THREADS system option must be enabled.

> *Note:* Adequate memory must be available for the thread-enabled sort. If not enough memory is available, SAS reduces the number of threads to one and begins the sort process again, which will increase the time to create the index. △

b If the thread-enabled sort cannot be done, SAS uses the unthreaded sort.

Note: To display messages regarding what type of sort is used, memory and resource information, and the status of the index being created, set the SAS system option MSGLEVEL=I. △

Using the DATASETS Procedure

The DATASETS procedure provides statements that enable you to create and delete indexes. In the following example, the MODIFY statement identifies the data file, the INDEX DELETE statement deletes two indexes, and the two INDEX CREATE statements specify the variables to index, with the first INDEX CREATE statement specifying the options UNIQUE and NOMISS:

```
proc datasets library=mylib;
modify employee;
    index delete salary age;
    index create empnum / unique nomiss;
    index create names=(lastname frstname);
```

Note: If you delete and create indexes in the same step, place the INDEX DELETE statement before the INDEX CREATE statement so that space occupied by deleted indexes can be reused during index creation. △

Using the INDEX= Data Set Option

To create indexes in a DATA step when you create the data file, use the INDEX= data set option. The INDEX= data set option also enables you to include the NOMISS and UNIQUE options. The following example creates a simple index on the variable STOCK and specifies UNIQUE:

```
data finances(index=(stock /unique));
```

The next example uses the variables SSN, CITY, and STATE to create a simple index named SSN and a composite index named CITYST:

```
data employee(index=(ssn cityst=(city state)));
```

Using the SQL Procedure

The SQL procedure supports index creation and deletion and the UNIQUE option. Note that the variable list requires that variable names be separated by commas (which is an SQL convention) instead of blanks (which is a SAS convention).

The DROP INDEX statement deletes indexes. The CREATE INDEX statement specifies the UNIQUE option, the name of the index, the target data file, and the variable(s) to be indexed. For example:

```
drop index salary from employee;
create unique index empnum on employee (empnum);
create index names on employee (lastname, frstname);
```

Using Other SAS Products

You can also create and delete indexes using other SAS utilities and products, such as SAS/IML software, SAS Component Language, and SAS/Warehouse Administrator software.

Using an Index for WHERE Processing

WHERE processing conditionally selects observations for processing when you issue a WHERE expression. Using an index to process a WHERE expression improves performance and is referred to as *optimizing* the WHERE expression.

To process a WHERE expression, by default SAS decides whether to use an index or read all the observations in the data file sequentially. To make this decision, SAS does the following:

1 Identifies an available index or indexes.

2 Estimates the number of observations that would be qualified. If multiple indexes are available, SAS selects the index that returns the smallest subset of observations.

3 Compares resource usage to decide whether it is more efficient to satisfy the WHERE expression by using the index or by reading all the observations sequentially.

Identifying Available Index or Indexes

The first step for SAS in deciding whether to use an index to process a WHERE expression is to identify if the variable or variables included in the WHERE expression are key variables (that is, have an index). Even though a WHERE expression can consist of multiple conditions specifying different variables, SAS uses only one index to process the WHERE expression. SAS tries to select the index that satisfies the most conditions and selects the smallest subset:

☐ For the most part, SAS selects one condition. The variable specified in the condition will have either a simple index or be the first key variable in a composite index.

☐ However, you can take advantage of multiple key variables in a composite index by constructing an appropriate WHERE expression, referred to as *compound optimization*.

SAS attempts to use an index for the following types of conditions:

Table 28.6 WHERE Conditions That Can Be Optimized

Condition	Examples
comparison operators, which include the EQ operator; directional comparisons like less than or greater than; and the IN operator	where empnum eq 3374; where empnum < 2000; where state in ('NC','TX');
comparison operators with NOT	where empnum ^= 3374; where x not in (5,10);
comparison operators with the colon modifier	where lastname gt: 'Sm';

Condition	Examples
CONTAINS operator	where lastname contains 'Sm';
fully-bounded range conditions specifying both an upper and lower limit, which includes the BETWEEN-AND operator	where 1 < x < 10; where empnum between 500 and 1000;
pattern-matching operators LIKE and NOT LIKE	where frstname like '%Rob_%'
IS NULL or IS MISSING operator	where name is null; where idnum is missing;
TRIM function	where trim(state)="Texas";
SUBSTR function in the form of: WHERE SUBSTR (*variable, position, length*)='string'; when the following conditions are met: *position* is equal to 1, *length* is less than or equal to the length of *variable*, and *length* is equal to the length of *string*	where substr (name,1,3)='Mac' and (city='Charleston' or city='Atlanta');

The following examples illustrate optimizing a single condition:

☐ The following WHERE expressions could use a simple index on the variable MAJOR:

```
where major in ('Biology', 'Chemistry', 'Agriculture');
where class=90 and major in ('Biology', 'Agriculture');
```

☐ With a composite index on variables ZIPCODE and SCHOOLID, SAS could use the composite index to satisfy the following conditions because ZIPCODE is the first key variable in the composite index:

```
where zipcode = 78753;
```

However, the following condition cannot use the composite index because the variable SCHOOLID is not the first key variable in the composite index:

```
where schoolid gt 1000;
```

Note: An index is not supported for arithmetic operators, a variable-to-variable condition, and the sounds-like operator. △

Compound Optimization

Compound optimization is the process of optimizing multiple conditions specifying different variables, which are joined with logical operators such as AND or OR, using a composite index. Using a single index to optimize the conditions can greatly improve performance.

For example, suppose you have a composite index for LASTNAME and FRSTNAME. If you issue the following WHERE expression, SAS uses the concatenated values for the first two variables, then SAS further evaluates each qualified observation for the EMPID value:

```
where lastname eq 'Smith' and frstname eq 'John' and empid=3374;
```

For compound optimization to occur, all of the following must be true.

□ At least the first two key variables in the composite index must be used in the WHERE conditions.

□ The conditions are connected using the AND logical operator:

```
where lastname eq 'Smith' and frstname eq 'John';
```

Any conditions connected using the OR logical operator must specify the same variable:

```
where frstname eq 'John' and (lastname='Smith'
    or lastname = 'Jones');
```

□ At least one condition must be the EQ or IN operator; you cannot have, for example, all fully-bounded range conditions.

Note: The same conditions that are acceptable for optimizing a single condition are acceptable for compound optimization except for the CONTAINS operator, the pattern-matching operators LIKE and NOT LIKE, and the IS NULL and IS MISSING operators. Also, functions are not supported. △

For the following examples, assume there is a composite index named IJK for variables I, J, and K:

1 The following conditions are compound optimized because every condition specifies a variable that is in the composite index, and each condition uses one of the supported operators. SAS will position the composite index to the first entry that meets all three conditions and will retrieve only observations that satisfy all three conditions:

```
where i = 1 and j not in (3,4) and 10 < k < 12;
```

2 This WHERE expression cannot be compound optimized because the range condition for variable I is not fully bounded. In a fully-bounded condition, both an upper and lower bound must be specified. The condition I < 5 only specifies an upper bound. In this case, the composite index can still be used to optimize the single condition I < 5:

```
where i < 5 and j in (3,4) and k =3;
```

3 For the following WHERE expression, only the first two conditions are optimized with index IJK. After retrieving a subset of observations that satisfy the first two conditions, SAS examines the subset and eliminates any observations that fail to match the third condition.

```
where i in (1,4) and j = 5 and k like '%c'1
```

4 The following WHERE expression cannot be optimized with index IJK because J and K are not the first two key variables in the composite index:

```
where j = 1 and k = 2;
```

5 This WHERE expression can be optimized for variables I and J. After retrieving observations that satisfy the second and third conditions, SAS examines the subset and eliminates those observations that do not satisfy the first condition.

```
where x < 5 and i = 1 and j = 2;
```

Estimating the Number of Qualified Observations

Once SAS identifies the index or indexes that can satisfy the WHERE expression, the software estimates the number of observations that will be qualified by an available index. When multiple indexes exist, SAS selects the one that appears to produce the fewest qualified observations.

The software's ability to estimate the number of observations that will be qualified is improved because the software stores additional statistics called cumulative percentiles (or *centiles* for short). Centiles information represents the distribution of values in an index so that SAS does not have to assume a uniform distribution as in prior releases. To print centiles information for an indexed data file, include the CENTILES option in PROC CONTENTS (or in the CONTENTS statement in the DATASETS procedure).

Note that, by default, SAS does not update centiles information after every data file change. When you create an index, you can include the UPDATECENTILES option to specify when centiles information is updated. That is, you can specify that centiles information be updated every time the data file is closed, when a certain percent of values for the key variable have been changed, or never. In addition, you can also request that centiles information is updated immediately, regardless of the value of UPDATECENTILES, by issuing the INDEX CENTILES statement in PROC DATASETS.

As a general rule, SAS uses an index if it estimates that the WHERE expression will select approximately one-third or fewer of the total number of observations in the data file.

Note: If SAS estimates that the number of qualified observations is less than 3% of the data file (or if no observations are qualified), SAS automatically uses the index. In other words, in this case, SAS does not bother comparing resource usage. △

Comparing Resource Usage

Once SAS estimates the number of qualified observations and selects the index that qualifies the fewest observations, SAS must then decide if it is faster (cheaper) to satisfy the WHERE expression by using the index or by reading all of the observations sequentially. SAS makes this determination as follows:

- □ If only a few observations are qualified, it is more efficient to use the index than to do a sequential search of the entire data file.

- □ If most or all of the observations qualify, then it is more efficient to simply sequentially search the data file than to use the index.

This decision is much like a reader deciding whether to use an index at the back of a document. A document's index is designed to enable a reader to locate a topic along with the specific page number(s). Using the index, the reader would go to the specific page number(s) and read only about a specific topic. If the document covers 42 topics and the reader is interested in only a couple of topics, then the index saves time by preventing the reader from reading other topics. However, if the reader is interested in 39 topics, searching the index for each topic would take more time than simply reading the entire document.

To compare resource usage, SAS does the following:

1 First, SAS predicts the number of I/Os it will take to satisfy the WHERE expression using the index. To do so, SAS positions the index to the first entry that contains a qualified value. In a buffer management simulation that takes into account the current number of available buffers, the RIDs (identifiers) on that index page are processed, indicating how many I/Os it will take to read the observations in the data file.

   If the observations are randomly distributed throughout the data file, the observations will be located on multiple data file pages. This means an I/O will be needed for each page. Therefore, the more random the data in the data file, the more I/Os it takes to use the index. If the data in the data file is ordered more like the index, which is in ascending value order, fewer I/Os are needed to use the index.

2 Then SAS calculates the I/O cost of a sequential pass of the entire data file and compares the two resource costs.

Factors that affect the comparison include the size of the subset relative to the size of the data file, data file value order, data file page size, the number of allocated buffers, and the cost to uncompress a compressed data file for a sequential read.

Note: If comparing resource costs results in a tie, SAS chooses the index. △

Controlling WHERE Processing Index Usage with Data Set Options

You can control index usage for WHERE processing with the IDXWHERE= and IDXNAME= data set options.

The IDXWHERE= data set option overrides the software's decision regarding whether to use an index to satisfy the conditions of a WHERE expression as follows:

- □ IDXWHERE=YES tells SAS to decide which index is the best for optimizing a WHERE expression, disregarding the possibility that a sequential search of the data file might be more resource efficient.
- □ IDXWHERE=NO tells SAS to ignore all indexes and satisfy the conditions of a WHERE expression by sequentially searching the data file.
- □ Using an index to process a BY statement cannot be overridden with IDXWHERE=.

The following example tells SAS to decide which index is the best for optimizing the WHERE expression. SAS will disregard the possibility that a sequential search of the data file might be more resource efficient.

```
data mydata.empnew;
   set mydata.employee (idxwhere=yes);
   where empnum < 2000;
```

For details, see the IDXWHERE data set option in *SAS Language Reference: Dictionary*.

The IDXNAME= data set option directs SAS to use a specific index in order to satisfy the conditions of a WHERE expression.

By specifying IDXNAME=*index-name*, you are specifying the name of a simple or composite index for the data file.

The following example uses the IDXNAME= data set option to direct SAS to use a specific index to optimize the WHERE expression. SAS will disregard the possibility that a sequential search of the data file might be more resource efficient and does not attempt to determine if the specified index is the best one. (Note that the EMPNUM index was not created with the NOMISS option.)

```
data mydata.empnew;
   set mydata.employee (idxname=empnum);
   where empnum < 2000;
```

For details, see the IDXNAME data set option in *SAS Language Reference: Dictionary*.

Note: IDXWHERE= and IDXNAME= are mutually exclusive. Using both will result in an error. △

Displaying Index Usage Information in the SAS Log

To display information in the SAS log regarding index usage, change the value of the MSGLEVEL= system option from its default value of N to I. When you issue **options msglevel=i;**, the following occurs:

    ☐ If an index is used, a message displays specifying the name of the index.

    ☐ If an index is not used but one exists that could optimize at least one condition in the WHERE expression, messages provide suggestions as to what you can do to influence SAS to use the index; for example, a message could suggest sorting the data file into index order or specifying more buffers.

    ☐ A message displays the IDXWHERE= or IDXNAME= data set option value if the setting can affect index processing.

Using an Index with Views

You cannot create an index for a data view; it must be a data file. However, if a data view is created from an indexed data file, index usage is available. That is, if the view definition includes a WHERE expression using a key variable, then SAS will attempt to use the index. Additionally, there are other ways to take advantage of a key variable when using a view.

In this example, you create an SQL view named STAT from data file CRIME, which has the key variable STATE. In addition, the view definition includes a WHERE expression:

```
proc sql;
   create view stat as
   select * from crime
   where murder > 7;
quit;
```

If you issue the following PRINT procedure, which refers to the SQL view, along with a WHERE statement that specifies the key variable STATE, SAS cannot optimize the WHERE statement with the index. SQL views cannot join a WHERE expression that was defined in the view to a WHERE expression that was specified in another procedure, DATA step, or SCL:

```
proc print data=stat;
   where state > 42;
run;
```

However, if you issue PROC SQL with an SQL WHERE clause that specifies the key variable STATE, then the SQL view can join the two conditions, which enables SAS to use the index STATE:

```
proc sql;
select * from stat where state > 42;
quit;
```

Using an Index for BY Processing

BY processing enables you to process observations in a specific order according to the values of one or more variables that are specified in a BY statement. Indexing a data file enables you to use a BY statement without sorting the data file. By creating an index based on one or more variables, you can ensure that observations are processed in *ascending numeric or character order*. Simply specify in the BY statement the variable or list of variables that are indexed.

For example, if an index exists for LASTNAME, the following BY statement would use the index to order the values by last names:

```
proc print;
   by lastname;
```

When you specify a BY statement, SAS looks for an appropriate index. If one exists, the software automatically retrieves the observations from the data file in indexed order. A BY statement will use an index in the following situations:

□ The BY statement consists of one variable that is the key variable for a simple index or the first key variable in a composite index.

□ The BY statement consists of two or more variables and the first variable is the key variable for a simple index or the first key variable in a composite index.

For example, if the variable MAJOR has a simple index, the following BY statements use the index to order the values by MAJOR:

```
by major;
by major state;
```

If a composite index named ZIPID exists consisting of the variables ZIPCODE and SCHOOLID, the following BY statements use the index:

```
by zipcode;
by zipcode schoolid;
by zipcode schoolid name;
```

However, the composite index ZIPID is not used for these BY statements:

```
by schoolid;
by schoolid zipcode;
```

In addition, a BY statement will not use an index in these situations:

□ The BY statement includes the DESCENDING or NOTSORTED option.

□ The index was created with the NOMISS option.

□ The data file is physically stored in sorted order based on the variables specified in the BY statement.

Note: Using an index to process a BY statement may not always be more efficient than simply sorting the data file, particularly if the data file has a high blocking factor of observations per page. Therefore, using an index for a BY statement is generally for convenience, not performance. △

Using an Index for Both WHERE and BY Processing

If both a WHERE expression and a BY statement are specified, SAS looks for one index that satisfies requirements for both. If such an index is not found, the BY statement takes precedence.

With a BY statement, SAS cannot use an index to optimize a WHERE expression if the optimization would invalidate the BY order. For example, the following statements could use an index on the variable LASTNAME to optimize the WHERE expression because the order of the observations returned by the index does not conflict with the order required by the BY statement:

```
proc print;
   by lastname;
   where lastname >= 'Smith';
run;
```

However, the following statements cannot use an index on LASTNAME to optimize the WHERE expression because the BY statement requires that the observations be returned in EMPID order:

```
proc print;
   by empid;
```

```
        where lastname = 'Smith';
run;
```

Specifying an Index with the KEY= Option for SET and MODIFY Statements

The SET and MODIFY statements provide the KEY= option, which enables you to specify an index in a DATA step to retrieve particular observations in a data file.

The following MODIFY statement shows how to use the KEY= option to take advantage of the fact that the data file INVTY.STOCK has an index on the variable PARTNO. Using the KEY= option tells SAS to use the index to directly access the correct observations to modify.

```
modify invty.stock key=partno;
```

Note: A BY statement is not allowed in the same DATA step with the KEY= option, and WHERE processing is not allowed for a data file with the KEY= option. △

Taking Advantage of an Index

Applications that typically do not use indexes can be rewritten to take advantage of an index. For example:

☐ Consider replacing a subsetting IF statement (which never uses an index) with a WHERE statement.

CAUTION:

However, be careful because IF and WHERE statements are processed differently and may produce different results in DATA steps that use the SET, MERGE, or UPDATE statements. This is because the WHERE statement selects observations before they are brought into the Program Data Vector (PDV), whereas the subsetting IF statement selects observations after they are read into the PDV. △

☐ Consider using the WHERE command in the FSEDIT procedure in place of the SEARCH and FIND commands.

Maintaining Indexes

SAS provides several procedures that you can issue to maintain indexes, and there are several operations within SAS that automatically maintain indexes for you.

Displaying Data File Information

The CONTENTS procedure (or the CONTENTS statement in PROC DATASETS) reports the following types of information.

☐ number and names of indexes for a data file
☐ the names of key variables
☐ the options in effect for each key variable
☐ data file page size
☐ number of data file pages
☐ centiles information (using the CENTILES option)
☐ amount of disk space used by the index file.

Note: The available information depends on the operating environment. △

Output 28.6 Output of PROC CONTENTS

```
                          The CONTENTS Procedure

Data Set Name      SASUSER.STAFF              Observations          148
Member Type        DATA                       Variables             6
Engine             V9                         Indexes               2
Created            13:23 Wednesday, January 22, 2003  Observation Length    63
Last Modified      13:31 Wednesday, January 22, 2003  Deleted Observations  0
Protection                                    Compressed            NO
Data Set Type                                 Sorted                NO
Label
Data Representation WINDOWS_32
Encoding           wlatin1  Western (Windows)


                    Engine/Host Dependent Information

   Data Set Page Size         8192
   Number of Data Set Pages   3
   First Data Page            1
   Max Obs per Page           129
   Obs in First Data Page     104
   Index File Page Size       4096
   Number of Index File Pages 5
   Number of Data Set Repairs 0
   File Name                  c:\winnt\profiles\sasxxx\sasuser\staff.sas7bdat
   Release Created            9.0000A0
   Host Created               WIN_NT


              Alphabetic List of Variables and Attributes

          #     Variable   Type    Len

          4     city       Char    15
          3     fname      Char    15
          6     hphone     Char    12
          1     idnum      Char     4
          2     lname      Char    15
          5     state      Char     2


              Alphabetic List of Indexes and Attributes

                                 # of
                    Unique     Unique
     #   Index      Option     Values    Variables

     1   idnum      YES          148
     2   name                    148     fname lname
```

Copying an Indexed Data File

When you copy an indexed data file with the COPY procedure (or the COPY statement of the DATASETS procedure), you can specify whether the procedure also recreates the index file for the new data file with the INDEX=YES|NO option; the default is YES, which recreates the index. However, recreating the index does increase the processing time for the PROC COPY step.

If you copy from disk to disk, the index is recreated. If you copy from disk to tape, the index is not recreated on tape. However, after copying from disk to tape, if you then copy back from tape to disk, the index can be recreated. Note that if you move a data file with the MOVE option in PROC COPY, the index file is deleted from IN= library and recreated in OUT= library.

The CPORT procedure also has INDEX=YES|NO to specify whether to export indexes with indexed data files. By default, PROC CPORT exports indexes with indexed data files. The CIMPORT procedure, however, does not handle the index file at all, and the index(es) must be recreated.

Updating an Indexed Data File

Each time that values in an indexed data file are added, modified, or deleted, SAS automatically updates the index. The following activities affect an index as indicated:

Table 28.7   Maintenance Tasks and Index Results

Task	Result
delete a data set	index file is deleted
rename a data set	index file is renamed
rename key variable	simple index is renamed
delete key variable	simple index is deleted
add observation	index entries are added
delete observations	index entries are deleted and space is recovered for reuse
update observations	index entries are deleted and new ones are inserted

Note: Use SAS to perform additions, modifications and deletions to your data sets. Using operating environment commands to perform these operations will make your files unusable. △

Sorting an Indexed Data File

You can sort an indexed data file only if you direct the output of the SORT procedure to a new data file so that the original data file remains unchanged. However, the new data file is not automatically indexed.

Note: If you sort an indexed data file with the FORCE option, the index file is deleted. △

Adding Observations to an Indexed Data File

Adding observations to an indexed data file requires additional processing. SAS automatically keeps the values in the index consistent with the values in the data file.

Multiple Occurrences of Values

An index that is created without the UNIQUE option can result in multiple occurrences of the same value, which results in multiple RIDs for one value. For large data files with many multiple occurrences, the list of RIDs for a given value may require several pages in the index file. Because the RIDs are stored in physical order, any new observation added to the data file with the given value is stored at the end of the list of RIDs. Navigating through the index to find the end of the RID list can cause many I/O operations.

SAS remembers the previous position in the index so that when inserting more occurrences of the same value, the end of the RID list is found quickly.

Appending Data to an Indexed Data File

SAS provides performance improvements when appending a data file to an indexed data file. SAS suspends index updates until all observations are added, then updates the index with data from the newly added observations. See the APPEND statement in the DATASETS procedure in *Base SAS Procedures Guide*.

Recovering a Damaged Index

An index can become damaged for many of the same reasons that a data file or catalog can become damaged. If a data file becomes damaged, use the REPAIR statement in PROC DATASETS to repair the data file or recreate any missing indexes. For example,

```
proc datasets library=mylib;
   repair mydata;
run;
```

Indexes and Integrity Constraints

Integrity constraints can also use indexes. When an integrity constraint is created that uses an index, if a suitable index already exists, it is used; otherwise, a new index is created. When an index is created, it is marked as being "owned" by the creator, which can be either the user or an integrity constraint.

If either the user or an integrity constraint requests creation of an index that already exists and is owned by the other, the requestor is also marked as an "owner" of the index. If an index is owned by both, then a request by either to delete the index results in removing only the requestor as owner. The index is deleted only after both the integrity constraint and the user have requested the index's deletion. A note in the log indicates when an index cannot be deleted.

Compressing Data Files

Definition of Compression

Compressing a file is a process that reduces the number of bytes required to represent each observation. In a compressed file, each observation is a variable-length record, while in an uncompressed file, each observation is a fixed-length record.

Advantages of compressing a file include

□ reduced storage requirements for the file

□ fewer I/O operations necessary to read from or write to the data during processing.

However, disadvantages of compressing a file are that

□ more CPU resources are required to read a compressed file because of the overhead of uncompressing each observation

□ there are situations when the resulting file size may increase rather than decrease.

Requesting Compression

By default, a SAS data file is not compressed. To compress, you can use these options:

□ COMPRESS= system option to compress all data files that are created during a SAS session

□ COMPRESS= option on the LIBNAME statement to compress all data files for a particular SAS data library

□ COMPRESS= data set option to compress an individual data file.

To compress a data file, you can specify the following:

□ COMPRESS=CHAR to use the RLE (Run Length Encoding) compression algorithm.

□ COMPRESS=BINARY to use the RDC (Ross Data Compression) algorithm.

When you create a compressed data file, SAS writes a note to the log indicating the percentage of reduction that is obtained by compressing the file. SAS obtains the compression percentage by comparing the size of the compressed file with the size of an uncompressed file of the same page size and record count.

After a file is compressed, the setting is a permanent attribute of the file, which means that to change the setting, you must re-create the file. That is, to uncompress a file, specify COMPRESS=NO for a DATA step that copies the compressed data file.

For more information on the COMPRESS= data set option, the COMPRESS= option on the LIBNAME statement, and the COMPRESS= system option, see *SAS Language Reference: Dictionary*.

Disabling a Compression Request

Compressing a file adds a fixed-length block of data to each observation. Because of the additional block of data (12 bytes for a 32-bit host and 24 bytes for a 64-bit host per observation), some files could result in a larger file size. For example, files with extremely short record lengths could result in a larger file size if compressed.

When a request is made to compress a data set, SAS attempts to determine if compression will increase the size of the file. SAS examines the lengths of the variables. If, due to the number and lengths of the variables, it is not possible for the compressed file to be at least 12 bytes (for a 32-bit host) or 24 bytes (for a 64-bit host) per observation smaller than an uncompressed version, compression is disabled and a message is written to the SAS log.

For example, here is a simple data set for which SAS determines that it is not possible for the compressed file to be smaller than an uncompressed one:

```
data one (compress=char);
   length x y $2;
   input x y;
   datalines;
ab cd
;
```

The following output is written to the SAS log:

Output 28.7 SAS Log Output When Compression Request is Disabled

```
NOTE: Compression was disabled for data set WORK.ONE because compression overhead
      would increase the size of the data set.
NOTE: The data set WORK.ONE has 1 observations and 2 variables.
```

CHAPTER

29

SAS Data Views

Definition of SAS Data Views   **539**
Benefits of Using SAS Data Views   **540**
When to Use SAS Data Views   **541**
DATA Step Views   **541**
   Definition of a DATA Step View   **541**
   Creating DATA Step Views   **541**
   What Can You Do with a DATA Step View?   **542**
   Differences between DATA Step Views and Stored Compiled DATA Step Programs   **542**
   Restrictions and Requirements   **542**
   Performance Considerations   **542**
   Example 1: Merging Data to Produce Reports   **543**
   Example 2: Producing Additional Output Files   **543**
PROC SQL Views   **545**
Comparing DATA Step and PROC SQL Views   **545**
SAS/ACCESS Views   **546**

Definition of SAS Data Views

A *SAS data view* is a type of SAS data set that retrieves data values from other files. A SAS data view contains only descriptor information such as the data types and lengths of the variables (columns), plus information that is required for retrieving data values from other SAS data sets or from files that are stored in other software vendors' file formats. SAS data views are of member type VIEW. In most cases, you can use a SAS data view as though it were a SAS data file.

There are two general types of SAS data views:

native view
   is a SAS data view that is created either with a DATA step or with PROC SQL.

interface view
   is a SAS data view that is created with SAS/ACCESS software. An interface view can read data from or write data to a database management system (DBMS) such as DB2 or ORACLE. Interface views are also referred to as *SAS/ACCESS views*. In order to use SAS/ACCESS views, you must have a license for SAS/ACCESS software.

   Note: You can create native views that access certain DBMS data by using a SAS/ACCESS dynamic LIBNAME engine. See "SAS/ACCESS Views" on page 546, or the SAS/ACCESS documentation for your DBMS for more information. △

Benefits of Using SAS Data Views

SAS data views provide the following benefits:

- □ Instead of using multiple DATA steps to merge SAS data sets by common variables, you can construct a view that performs a multi-table join.
- □ You can save disk space by storing a view definition, which stores only the instructions for where to find the data and how it is formatted, not the actual data.
- □ Views can ensure that the input data sets are always current because data is derived from views at execution time.
- □ Since views can select data from many sources, once a view is created, it can provide prepackaged information to the information community without the need for additional programming.
- □ Views can reduce the impact of data design changes on users. For example, you can change a query that is stored in a view without changing the characteristics of the view's result.
- □ With SAS/CONNECT software, a view can join SAS data sets that reside on different host computers, presenting you with an integrated view of distributed company data.

The following figure shows native and interface SAS data views and their relationship to SAS data files:

Figure 29.1   Native and Interface SAS Data Views

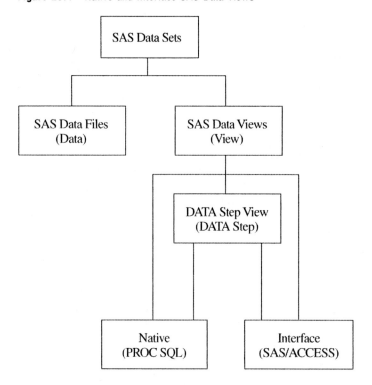

You can use views in the following ways:

- □ as input to other DATA steps or PROC steps
- □ to migrate data to SAS data files or to database management systems that are supported by SAS

□ in combination with other data sources using PROC SQL

□ as pre-assembled sets of data for users of SAS/ASSIST software, enabling them to perform data management, analysis, and reporting tasks regardless of how the data is stored.

When to Use SAS Data Views

Consider the following in order to determine whether a SAS data file or a SAS data view is better for your purposes:

□ Data files use additional disk space; data views use additional processing time.

□ Data file variables can be sorted and indexed prior to use; data views must process data in its existing form during execution.

DATA Step Views

Definition of a DATA Step View

A *DATA step view* is a native view that has the broadest scope of any SAS data view. It contains stored DATA step programs that can read data from a variety of sources, including:

□ raw data files

□ SAS data files

□ PROC SQL views

□ SAS/ACCESS views

□ DB2, ORACLE, or other DBMS data.

Creating DATA Step Views

In order to create a DATA step view, specify the VIEW= option after the final data set name in the DATA statement. The VIEW= option tells SAS to compile, but not to execute, the source program and to store the compiled code in the input DATA step view that is named in the option.

For example, the following statements create a DATA step view named DEPT.A:

```
libname dept 'SAS-data-library';

data dept.a / view=dept.a;
   … more SAS statements …
run;
```

Note that if the SAS data view exists in a SAS data library, and if you use the same member name to create a new view definition, then the old data view is overwritten.

Beginning with Version 8, DATA step views retain source statements. You can retrieve these statements using the DESCRIBE statement. The following example uses the DESCRIBE statement in a DATA step view in order to write a copy of the source code to the SAS log:

```
data viewname view=inventory;
   describe;
```

```
run;
```

For more information on how to create data views and use the DESCRIBE
statement, see the DATA statement in *SAS Language Reference: Dictionary.*

What Can You Do with a DATA Step View?

Using a DATA step view, you can do the following:
- directly process any file that can be read with an INPUT statement
- read other SAS data sets
- generate data without using any external data sources and without creating an
  intermediate SAS data file.

Because DATA step views are generated by the DATA step, they can manipulate and
manage input data from a variety of sources including data from external files and data
from existing SAS data sets. The scope of what you can do with a DATA step view,
therefore, is much broader than that of other types of SAS data views.

Differences between DATA Step Views and Stored Compiled DATA Step Programs

DATA step views and stored compiled DATA step programs differ in the following
ways:
- a DATA step view is implicitly executed when it is referenced as an input data set
  by another DATA or PROC step. Its main purpose is to provide data, one record at
  a time, to the invoking procedure or DATA step.
- a stored compiled DATA step program is explicitly executed when it is specified by
  the PGM= option on a DATA statement. Its purpose is usually a more specific
  task, such as creating SAS data files, or originating a report.

For more information on stored compiled DATA step programs, see Chapter 30, "Stored
Compiled DATA Step Programs," on page 547.

Restrictions and Requirements

Global statements do not to apply to a DATA step view. Global statements such as
the FILENAME, FOOTNOTE, LIBNAME, OPTIONS, and TITLE statements, even if
included in the DATA step that created the data view, have no effect on the data view.
If you do include global statements in your source program statements, SAS stores the
DATA step view but not the global statements. When the view is referenced, actual
execution may differ from the intended execution.

For information on using DATA step views created in an earlier release, see Chapter
35, "SAS 9.1 Compatibility with SAS Files From Earlier Releases," on page 583.

Performance Considerations

- DATA step code executes each time that you use a view. This may add
  considerable system overhead. In addition, you run the risk of having your data
  change between steps.
- Depending on how many reads or passes on the data are required, processing
  overhead increases.

□ When one pass is requested, no data set is created. Compared to traditional methods of processing, making one pass improves performance by decreasing the number of input/output operations and elapsed time.

□ When multiple passes are requested, the view must build a spill file that contains all generated observations so that subsequent passes can read the same data that was read by previous passes.

Example 1: Merging Data to Produce Reports

If you want to merge data from multiple files but you do not need to create a file that contains the combined data, you can create a DATA step view of the combination for use in subsequent applications.

For example, the following statements define DATA step view MYV9LIB.QTR1, which merges the sales figures in the data file V9LR.CLOTHES with the sales figures in the data file V9LR.EQUIP. The data files are merged by date, and the value of the variable **Total** is computed for each date.

```
libname myv9lib 'SAS-data-library';
libname v9lr 'SAS-data-library';

data myv9lib.qtr1 / view=myv9lib.qtr1;
   merge v9lr.clothes v9lr.equip;
      by date;
   total = cl_v9lr + eq_v9lr;
run;
```

The following PRINT procedure executes the view:

```
proc print data=myv9lib.qtr1;
run;
```

Example 2: Producing Additional Output Files

In this example, the DATA step reads an external file named STUDENT, which contains student data, then writes observations that contain known problems to data set MYV9LIB.PROBLEMS. The DATA step also defines the DATA step view MYV9LIB.CLASS. The DATA step does *not* create a SAS data file named MYV9LIB.CLASS.

The FILENAME and the LIBNAME statements are both global statements and must exist outside of the code that defines the view, because views cannot contain global statements.

Here are the contents of the external file STUDENT:

```
dutterono   MAT    3
lyndenall   MAT
frisbee     MAT   94
            SCI   95
zymeco      ART   96
dimette           94
mesipho     SCI   55
merlbeest   ART   97
scafernia         91
gilhoolie   ART  303
misqualle   ART   44
xylotone    SCI   96
```

Here is the DATA step that produces the output files:

```
libname myv9lib 'SAS-data-library';
filename student 'external-file-specification';  ❶

data myv9lib.class(keep=name major credits)
   myv9lib.problems(keep=code date) / view=myv9lib.class;  ❷
infile student;
   input name $ 1-10 major $ 12-14 credits 16-18;  ❸
select;
when (name=' ' or major=' ' or credits=.)
         do code=01;
            date=datetime();
            output myv9lib.problems;
         end;  ❹
when (0<credits<90)
         do code=02;
            date=datetime();
            output myv9lib.problems;
         end;  ❺
otherwise
      output myv9lib.class;
   end;
run;  ❻
```

The following example shows how to print the files created previously. The data view MYV9LIB.CLASS contains the observations from STUDENT that were processed without errors. The data file MYV9LIB.PROBLEMS contains the observations that contain errors.

If the data frequently changes in the source data file STUDENT, there would be different effects on the returned values in the SAS data view and the SAS data file:

□ New records, if error free, that are added to the source data file STUDENT between the time you run the DATA step in the previous example and the time you execute PROC PRINT in the following example, will appear in the data view MYV9LIB.CLASS.

□ On the other hand, if any new records, failing the error tests, were added to STUDENT, the new records would not show up in the SAS data file MYV9LIB.PROBLEM, until you run the DATA step again.

A SAS data view dynamically updates from its source files each time it is used. A SAS data file, each time it is used, remains the same, unless new data is written directly to the file.

```
filename student 'external-file-specification';
libname myv9lib 'SAS-data--library';  ❼

proc print data=myv9lib.class;
run;  ❽

proc print data=myv9lib.problems;
   format date datetime18.;
run;  ❾
```

❶ Reference a library called MYV9LIB. Tell SAS where a file that associated with the fileref STUDENT is stored.

❷ Create a data file called PROBLEMS and a data view called CLASS and specify the column names for both data sets.

❸ Select the file that is referenced by the fileref STUDENT and select the data in character format that resides in the specified positions in the file. Assign column names.

❹ When data in the columns NAME, MAJOR or CREDITS is blank or missing, assign a code of **01** to the observation where the missing value occurred. Also assign a SAS datetime code to the error and place the information in a file called PROBLEMS.

❺ When the amount of credits is greater than zero, but less than ninety, list the observations as code **02** in the file called PROBLEMS and assign a SAS datetime code to the observation.

❻ Place all other observations, which have none of the specified errors, in the SAS data view called MYV9LIB.CLASS.

❼ The FILENAME statement assigns the fileref STUDENT to an external file. The LIBNAME statement assigns the libref MYV9LIB to a SAS data library.

❽ The first PROC PRINT calls the data view MYV9LIB.CLASS. The data view extracts data on the fly from the file referenced as STUDENT.

❾ This PROC PRINT prints the contents of the data file MYV9LIB.PROBLEMS.

PROC SQL Views

A PROC SQL view is a PROC SQL query-expression that is given a name and stored for later use. When you use a PROC SQL view in a SAS program, the view derives its data from the data sets (often referred to as tables) or views listed in its FROM clause. The data that is accessed by the view is a subset or superset of the data in its underlying data set(s) or view(s).

A PROC SQL view can read or write data from:

- □ DATA step views
- □ SAS data files
- □ other PROC SQL views
- □ SAS/ACCESS views
- □ DB2, ORACLE, or other DBMS data.

For complete documentation on how to create and use PROC SQL views, see *Base SAS Procedures Guide*.

For information on using PROC SQL views created in an earlier release, see Chapter 35, "SAS 9.1 Compatibility with SAS Files From Earlier Releases," on page 583.

Comparing DATA Step and PROC SQL Views

To help you decide between a DATA step view and a PROC SQL view, consider the characteristics of each type of view:

- □ DATA step views
  - □ DATA step views are versatile because they use DATA step processing, including DO loops and IF-THEN/ELSE statements.
  - □ DATA step views do not have write capability; that is, they cannot directly change the data that they access.

□ There is no way to qualify the data in a DATA step view prior to using it. Therefore, even if you need only part of the data in your data view, you must load into memory the entire DATA step view and discard everything that you do not need.

□ PROC SQL views

□ PROC SQL views can combine data from many different file formats.

□ PROC SQL views can both read and update the data that they reference.

□ PROC SQL supports more types of WHERE clauses than are available in DATA step processing and has a CONNECT TO component that allows you to easily send SQL statements and pass data to a DBMS by using the Pass-Through Facility.

□ You can also use the power of the SQL language to subset your data prior to processing it. This saves memory when you have a large view, but need to select only a small portion of the data contained in the view.

□ PROC SQL views do not use DATA step programming.

SAS/ACCESS Views

A SAS/ACCESS view is an interface view, also called a *view descriptor*, which accesses DBMS data that is defined in a corresponding *access descriptor*.

Using SAS/ACCESS software, you can create an access descriptor and one or more view descriptors in order to define and access some or all of the data described by one DBMS table or DBMS view. You can also use view descriptors in order to update DBMS data, with certain restrictions.

In addition, some SAS/ACCESS products provide a dynamic LIBNAME engine interface. If available, it is recommended that you use SAS/ACCESS LIBNAME statement to assign a SAS libref to your DBMS data because it is more efficient and easier to use than access descriptors and view descriptors. The SAS/ACCESS dynamic LIBNAME engine enables you to treat DBMS data as if it were SAS data by assigning a SAS libref to DBMS objects. This means that you can use both native DATA step views and native PROC SQL views to access DBMS data instead of view descriptors.

See Chapter 33, "About SAS/ACCESS Software," on page 569 or the SAS/ACCESS documentation for your database for more information about SAS/ACCESS features.

For information on using SAS/ACCESS view descriptors created in an earlier release, see Chapter 35, "SAS 9.1 Compatibility with SAS Files From Earlier Releases," on page 583.

Note: Starting in SAS 9, PROC SQL views are the preferred way to access relational DBMS data. You can convert existing SAS/ACCESS view descriptors into PROC SQL views by using the CV2VIEW procedure, enabling you to use the LIBNAME statement to access your data. See the CV2VIEW Procedure in *SAS/ACCESS for Relational Databases: Reference.* △

CHAPTER

30

Stored Compiled DATA Step Programs

Definition of a Stored Compiled DATA Step Program **547**
Uses for Stored Compiled DATA Step Programs **547**
Restrictions and Requirements for Stored Compiled DATA Step Programs **548**
How SAS Processes Stored Compiled DATA Step Programs **548**
Creating a Stored Compiled DATA Step Program **549**
   Syntax for Creating a Stored Compiled DATA Step Program **549**
   Process to Compile and Store a DATA Step Program **549**
   Example: Creating a Stored Compiled DATA Step Program **549**
Executing a Stored Compiled DATA Step Program **550**
   Syntax for Executing a Stored Compiled DATA Step Program **550**
   Process to Execute a Stored Compiled DATA Step Program **551**
   Using Global Statements **552**
   Redirecting Output **552**
      Printing the Source Code of a Stored Compiled DATA Step Program **552**
   Example: Executing a Stored Compiled DATA Step Program **553**
Differences between Stored Compiled DATA Step Programs and DATA Step Views **554**
Examples of DATA Step Programs **554**
   Example of DATA Step Program: Quality Control Application **554**

Definition of a Stored Compiled DATA Step Program

A *stored compiled DATA step program* is a SAS file that contains a DATA step program that has been compiled and then stored in a SAS data library. You can execute stored compiled programs as needed, without having to recompile them. Stored compiled DATA step programs are of member type PROGRAM.

Note: Stored compiled programs are available for DATA step applications only. Your stored programs can contain all SAS language elements except global statements. If you do include global statements in your source program, SAS stores the compiled program but not the global statements, and does not display a warning message in the SAS log. △

Uses for Stored Compiled DATA Step Programs

The primary use of stored compiled DATA step programs is for executing production jobs. The advantage of using these DATA step programs is that you can execute them as needed without investing the resources required for repeated compilation. The savings are especially significant if the DATA step contains many statements. If you install a new version of SAS, you do not need to recompile your source code.

Restrictions and Requirements for Stored Compiled DATA Step Programs

The following restrictions and requirements apply for using stored compiled DATA step programs:

□ Stored compiled DATA step programs are available for DATA step applications only.

□ Stored compiled DATA step program cannot contain global statements. If you do include global statements such as FILENAME, FOOTNOTE, LIBNAME, OPTIONS, and TITLE in your source program, SAS stores the compiled program but not the global statements. SAS does not display a warning message in the SAS log.

□ SAS does not store raw data in the compiled program.

Operating Environment Information: You cannot move a compiled program to an operating environment that has an incompatible machine architecture. You must, instead, recompile your source code and store your new compiled program.

You can, however, move your compiled program to a different host machine that has a compatible architecture. △

How SAS Processes Stored Compiled DATA Step Programs

You first compile the SAS source program and store the compiled code. Then you execute the compiled code, redirecting the input and output as necessary.

SAS processes the DATA step through the compilation phase and then stores an intermediate code representation of the program and associated data tables in a SAS file. SAS processes the intermediate code when it executes the stored program. The following figure shows the process for creating a stored compiled DATA step program.

Figure 30.1   Creating a Stored Compiled Program

When SAS executes the stored program, it resolves the intermediate code produced by the compiler and generates the executable machine code for that operating environment. The following figure shows the process for executing a stored compiled DATA step program.

Figure 30.2   Executing a Stored Compiled Program

To move, copy, rename, or delete stored programs, use the DATASETS procedure or the utility windows in your windowing environment.

Creating a Stored Compiled DATA Step Program

Syntax for Creating a Stored Compiled DATA Step Program

The syntax for creating a stored compiled DATA step program is as follows:

DATA *data-set-name(s)* / PGM=*stored-program-name*
  <(<*password-option*><SOURCE=*source-option*>)>;

where

data-set-name
  specifies a valid SAS name for the output data set created by the source program. The name can be a one-level name or a two-level name. You can specify more than one data set name in the DATA statement.

stored-program-name
  specifies a valid SAS name for the SAS file containing the stored program. The name can be a one-level name, but it is usually a two-level name. Stored programs are assigned the member type PROGRAM in the SAS data library.

password-option
  assigns a password to a stored compiled DATA step program.

source-option
  allows you to save or encrypt the source code.

For complete information about the DATA statement, see *SAS Language Reference: Dictionary*.

Process to Compile and Store a DATA Step Program

To compile and store a DATA step program, do the following:

1 Write, test, and debug the DATA step program you want to store.

  If you are reading external raw data files or if you output raw data to an external file, use a fileref rather than the actual file name in your INFILE and FILE statements so that you can redirect your input and output when the stored program executes.

2 When the program runs correctly, submit it using the PGM= option in the DATA statement.

  The PGM= option tells SAS to compile, but not execute, the program and to store the compiled code in the SAS file named in the option. SAS sends a message to the log when the program is stored.

Note: The default SOURCE=SAVE or SOURCE=ENCRYPT options automatically save your source code. △

Note: If you move your application to another operating environment, you need to recompile your source code and store your new compiled program. △

Example: Creating a Stored Compiled DATA Step Program

The following example uses the information in the input SAS data set IN.SAMPLE to assign a plant type based on a plant code. Note that the global LIBNAME

statements are necessary to identify the storage location for your files, but are not part
of STORED.SAMPLE, the DATA step that SAS stores.

```
libname in 'SAS-data-library';
libname stored 'SAS-data-library';
```

```
data out.sample / pgm=stored.sample;
   set in.sample;
   if code = 1 then
      do;
         Type='Perennial';
         number+4;
      end;
   else
   if code = 2 then
      do;
         Type='Annual';
         number+10;
      end;
   else
      do;
         Type='ERROR';
         Number=0;
      end;
run;
```

Output 30.1   Partial SAS Log Identifying the Stored DATA Step Program

```
.
.
.
NOTE: DATA STEP program saved on file STORED.SAMPLE.
NOTE: A stored DATA STEP program cannot run under a different operating system.
NOTE: DATA statement used:
      real time        1.14 seconds
      cpu time         0.12 seconds
```

Executing a Stored Compiled DATA Step Program

Syntax for Executing a Stored Compiled DATA Step Program

The syntax for executing a stored compiled DATA step program, optionally retrieving
source code, and optionally redirecting input or output, is as follows:

global SAS statements

DATA PGM=*stored-program-name* <(*password-option*)>;
    <DESCRIBE;>
    <REDIRECT INPUT | OUTPUT *old-name-1 = new-name-1*<. . . *old-name-n =*
      new-name-n>;>

```
<EXECUTE;>
```

where

global SAS statements

specifies any global SAS statements that are needed by the program when it executes, such as a FILENAME or a LIBNAME statement that points to input files or routes output.

stored-program-name

specifies a valid SAS name for the SAS file containing the stored program. The name can be a one-level name or a two-level name.

password-option

specifies a password that you use to access the stored compiled DATA step program.

DESCRIBE

is a SAS statement that retrieves source code from a stored compiled DATA step program or a DATA step view.

INPUT | OUTPUT

specifies whether you are redirecting input or output data sets. When you specify INPUT, the REDIRECT statement associates the name of the input data set in the source program with the name of another SAS data set. When you specify OUTPUT, the REDIRECT statement associates the name of the output data set with the name of another SAS data set.

old-name

specifies the name of the input or output data set in the source program.

new-name

specifies the name of the input or output data set that you want SAS to process for the current execution.

EXECUTE

is a SAS statement that executes a stored compiled DATA step program.

For complete information about the DATA statement, see *SAS Language Reference: Dictionary*.

Process to Execute a Stored Compiled DATA Step Program

To execute a stored compiled DATA step program, follow these steps:

1 Write a DATA step for each execution of the stored program. In this DATA step, specify the name of the stored program in the PGM= option of the DATA statement and include an optional password. You can

 □ submit this DATA step as a separate program

 □ include it as part of a larger SAS program that can include other DATA and procedure (PROC) steps

 □ point to different input and output SAS data sets each time you execute the stored program by using the REDIRECT statement.

2 Submit the DATA steps. Be sure to end each one with a RUN statement or other step boundary.

Using Global Statements

You can use global SAS statements such as FILENAME or LIBNAME when you store or execute a stored compiled DATA step program. However, the global statements that you use to compile and store a DATA step program are not stored with the DATA step code.

Redirecting Output

You can redirect external files using filerefs. You can use the REDIRECT statement for renaming input and output SAS data sets.

You can use the REDIRECT statement to redirect input and output data to data sets you specify. Note that the REDIRECT statement is available only for use with stored compiled DATA step programs.

Note: To redirect input and output stored in external files, include a FILENAME statement at execution time to associate the fileref in the source program with different external files. △

CAUTION:
> **Use caution when you redirect input data sets.** The number and attributes of variables in the input SAS data sets that you read with the REDIRECT statement should match those of the input data sets in the SET, MERGE, MODIFY, or UPDATE statements of the source code. If they do not match, the following occurs:
> - If the variable length attributes differ, the length of the variable in the source code data set determines the length of the variable in the redirected data set.
> - If extra variables are present in the redirected data sets, the stored program will continue to execute but the results of your program may not be what you expect.
> - If the variable type attributes are different, the stored program stops processing and an error message is sent to the SAS log.
>
> △

Printing the Source Code of a Stored Compiled DATA Step Program

If you use both the DESCRIBE and the EXECUTE statements when you execute a stored compiled DATA step program, SAS writes the source code to the log. The following example executes a stored compiled DATA step program. The DESCRIBE statement in the program writes the source code to the SAS log.

```
data pgm=stored.sample;
   describe;
   execute;
run;
```

Output 30.2 Partial SAS Log Showing the Source Code Generated by the DESCRIBE Statement

```
    .
    .
    .
26
27   data pgm=stored.sample;
28      describe;
29      execute;
30   run;
NOTE: DATA step stored program STORED.SAMPLE is defined as:

data out.sample / pgm=stored.sample;
   set in.sample;
   if code = 1 then
      do;
          Type='Perennial';
          number+4;
      end;
   else
      if code = 2 then
         do;
             Type='Annual';
             number+10;
         end;
      else
         do;
             Type='ERROR';
             Number=0;
         end;
run;


NOTE: DATA STEP program loaded from file STORED.SAMPLE.
NOTE: There were 7 observations read from the dataset IN.SAMPLE.
NOTE: The data set OUT.SAMPLE has 7 observations and 4 variables.
NOTE: DATA statement used:
      real time          0.80 seconds
      cpu time           0.15 seconds
```

For more information about the DESCRIBE statement, see *SAS Language Reference: Dictionary*.

Example: Executing a Stored Compiled DATA Step Program

The following DATA step executes the stored program STORED.SAMPLE created in "Example: Creating a Stored Compiled DATA Step Program" on page 549. The REDIRECT statement specifies the source of the input data as BASE.SAMPLE. The output from this execution of the program is redirected and stored in a data set named TOTALS.SAMPLE. Output 30.3 shows part of the SAS log.

```
libname in 'SAS-data-library';
libname base 'SAS-data-library';
libname totals 'SAS-data-library';
libname stored 'SAS-data-library';


data pgm=stored.sample;
   redirect input in.sample=base.sample;
```

```
        redirect output out.sample=totals.sample;
    run;
```

Output 30.3 Partial SAS Log Identifying the Redirected Output File

```
        cpu time              0.00 seconds
   .
   .
   .
   6
   7   data pgm=stored.sample;
   8      redirect input in.sample=base.sample;
   9      redirect output out.sample=totals.sample;
  10   run;
NOTE: DATA STEP program loaded from file STORED.SAMPLE.
NOTE: The data set TOTALS.SAMPLE has 7 observations and 4 variables.
NOTE: DATA statement used:
      real time             0.67 seconds
```

Differences between Stored Compiled DATA Step Programs and DATA Step Views

Stored compiled DATA step programs and DATA step views are similar in function. They both store DATA step programs that can retrieve and process data stored in other files. Both have the same restrictions and requirements (see "Restrictions and Requirements for Stored Compiled DATA Step Programs" on page 548). For information about DATA step views, see Chapter 29, "SAS Data Views," on page 539.

Stored compiled DATA step programs and DATA step views differ in the following ways:

□ A stored compiled DATA step program is explicitly executed when it is specified by the PGM= option on a DATA statement. The stored compiled DATA step is used primarily in production jobs.

□ A DATA step view is implicitly executed when the view is referenced as an input data set by another DATA or procedure (PROC) step. Its main purpose is to provide data one record at a time to the invoking procedure or DATA step.

□ You can use the REDIRECT statement when you execute a stored compiled DATA step. You can not use this statement with DATA step views.

Examples of DATA Step Programs

Example of DATA Step Program: Quality Control Application

This example illustrates how to use a stored compiled DATA step program for a simple quality control application. This application processes several raw data files. The source program uses the fileref DAILY in the INFILE statement. Each DATA step that is used to execute the stored program can include a FILENAME statement to associate the fileref DAILY with a different external file.

The following statements compile and store the program:

```
libname stored 'SAS-data-library-1';
```

```
data flaws / pgm=stored.flaws;
   length Station $ 15;
   infile daily;
   input Station $ Shift $ Employee $ NumberOfFlaws;
   TotalNumber + NumberOfFlaws;
run;
```

The following statements execute the stored compiled program, redirect the output, and print the results:

```
libname stored 'SAS-data-library-1';
libname testlib 'SAS-data-library-2';

data pgm=stored.flaws;
   redirect output flaws=testlib.daily;
run;

proc print data=testlib.daily;
   title 'Quality Control Report';
run;
```

Output 30.4 Quality Control Application Output

```
                    Quality Control Report                        1

                                             Number     Total
        Obs     Station      Shift  Employee  OfFlaws    Number

         1      Cambridge      1      Lin        3          3
         2      Northampton    1      Kay        0          3
         3      Springfiled    2      Sam        9         12
```

Note that you can use the TITLE statement when you execute a stored compiled DATA step program or when you print the results.

CHAPTER

31

DICTIONARY Tables

Definition of a DICTIONARY Table   **557**
How to View DICTIONARY Tables   **557**
    How to View a DICTIONARY Table   **558**
    How to View a Summary of a DICTIONARY Table   **558**
    How to View a Subset of a DICTIONARY Table   **559**
    DICTIONARY Tables and Performance   **559**

Definition of a DICTIONARY Table

A DICTIONARY table is a read-only SAS data view that contains information about SAS data libraries, SAS data sets, SAS macros, and external files that are in use or available in the current SAS session. A DICTIONARY table also contains the settings for SAS system options that are currently in effect.

When you access a DICTIONARY table, SAS determines the current state of the SAS session and returns the desired information accordingly. This process is performed each time a DICTIONARY table is accessed, so that you always have current information.

DICTIONARY tables can be accessed by a SAS program by using either of these methods:

- □ run a PROC SQL query against the table, using the DICTIONARY libref

- □ use any SAS procedure or the DATA step, referring to the PROC SQL view of the table in the SASHELP library.

For more information on DICTIONARY tables, including a list of available DICTIONARY tables and their associated SASHELP views, see the *Base SAS Procedures Guide*.

How to View DICTIONARY Tables

You might want to view the contents of DICTIONARY tables in order to see information about your current SAS session, prior to actually using the table in a DATA step or a SAS procedure.

Some DICTIONARY tables can become quite large. In this case, you might want to view a part of a DICTIONARY table that contains only the data that you are interested in. The best way to view part of a DICTIONARY table is to subset the table using a PROC SQL WHERE clause.

How to View a DICTIONARY Table

Each DICTIONARY table has an associated PROC SQL view in the SASHELP library. You can see the entire contents of a DICTIONARY table by opening its SASHELP view with the VIEWTABLE or FSVIEW utilities. This method provides more detail than you receive in the output of the DESCRIBE TABLE statement, as shown in "How to View a Summary of a DICTIONARY Table" on page 558.

The following steps describe how to use the VIEWTABLE or FSVIEW utilities to view a DICTIONARY table in a windowing environment.

1 Invoke the Explorer window in your SAS session.

2 Select the SASHELP library. A list of members in the SASHELP library appears.

3 Select a view with a name that starts with V, for example, VMEMBER. A VIEWTABLE window appears that contains its contents. (For z/OS, type the letter 'O' in the command field for the desired member and press ENTER. The FSVIEW window appears with the contents of the view.)

In the VIEWTABLE window the column headings are labels. To see the column names, select

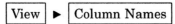

How to View a Summary of a DICTIONARY Table

The DESCRIBE TABLE statement in PROC SQL produces a summary of the contents of a DICTIONARY table. The following example uses the DESCRIBE TABLE statement in order to generate a summary for the table DICTIONARY.INDEXES. (The SASHELP view for this table is SASHELP.VINDEX).

```
proc sql;
   describe table dictionary.indexes;
```

The result of the DESCRIBE TABLE statement appears in the SAS log:

```
NOTE: SQL table DICTIONARY.INDEXES was created like:

create table DICTIONARY.INDEXES
  (
   libname char(8) label='Library Name',
   memname char(32) label='Member Name',
   memtype char(8) label='Member Type',
   name char(32) label='Column Name',
   idxusage char(9) label='Column Index Type',
   indxname char(32) label='Index Name',
   indxpos num label='Position of Column in Concatenated Key',
   nomiss char(3) label='Nomiss Option',
   unique char(3) label='Unique Option
  );
```

□ The first word on each line is the column (or variable) name, the name that you need to use when writing a SAS statement that refers to the column (or variable).

□ Following the column name is the specification for the type of variable and the width of the column.

□ The name that follows **label=** is the column (or variable) label.

After you know how a table is defined, you can use the processing ability of the PROC SQL WHERE clause in a PROC SQL step in order to extract a portion of a view.

How to View a Subset of a DICTIONARY Table

When you know that you are accessing a large DICTIONARY and you need to use only a portion of it, use a PROC SQL WHERE clause in order to extract a subset of the original. The following PROC SQL statement demonstrates the use of a PROC SQL WHERE clause in order to extract lines from DICTIONARY.INDEXES.

```
proc sql;
    title 'Subset of the DICTIONARY.INDEX View';
    title2 'Rows with Column Name equal to STATE';
    select * from dictionary.indexes
        where name = 'STATE';
quit;
```

The results are shown in the following output:

Output 31.1   Result of the PROC SQL Subsetting WHERE Statement

```
                                  Subset of the DICTIONARY.INDEX View
                                  Rows with Column Name equal to STATE


                                                                 Column
Library                           Member                         Index
Name       Member Name            Type      Column Name          Type        Index Name
  Position of
  Column in
Concatenated  Nomiss  Unique
      Key   Option  Option
------------------------------------------------------------------------------------------------
MAPS       USAAC                  DATA      STATE                COMPOSITE   SC000000
           0

MAPS       USAAC                  DATA      STATE                COMPOSITE   CS000000
           8

MAPS       USAAS                  DATA      STATE                SIMPLE      STATE
           .
```

Note that many character values in the DICTIONARY tables are stored as all-uppercase characters; you should design your queries accordingly.

DICTIONARY Tables and Performance

When you query a DICTIONARY table, SAS gathers information that is pertinent to that table. Depending on the DICTIONARY table that is being queried, this process can include searching libraries, opening tables, and executing views. Unlike other SAS procedures and the DATA step, PROC SQL can improve this process by optimizing the query before the select process is launched. Therefore, although it is possible to access DICTIONARY table information with SAS procedures or the DATA step by using the SASHELP views, it is often more efficient to use PROC SQL instead.

For example, the following programs both produce the same result, but the PROC SQL step runs much faster because the WHERE clause is processed prior to opening the tables that are referenced by the SASHELP.VCOLUMN view:

```
data mytable;
   set sashelp.vcolumn;
   where libname='WORK' and memname='SALES';
run;


proc sql;
   create table mytable as
      select * from sashelp.vcolumn
      where libname='WORK' and memname='SALES';
quit;
```

Note: SAS does not maintain DICTIONARY table information between queries. Each query of a DICTIONARY table launches a new discovery process. △

If you are querying the same DICTIONARY table several times in a row, you can get even faster performance by creating a temporary SAS data set (with the DATA step SET statement or PROC SQL CREATE TABLE AS statement) with the information that you desire and run your query against that data set.

CHAPTER

32

SAS Catalogs

Definition of a SAS Catalog   **561**
SAS Catalog Names   **561**
    Parts of a Catalog Name   **561**
    Accessing Information in Catalogs   **562**
Tools for Managing SAS Catalogs   **562**
Profile Catalog   **563**
    Definition   **563**
    How the Information Is Used   **563**
    How Sasuser.Profile Is Created   **563**
    Default Settings   **563**
Catalog Concatenation   **564**
    Definitions   **564**
    Example 1: Implicit Concatenation   **564**
    Example 2: Explicit Concatenation   **565**
    Rules for Catalog Concatenation   **567**

Definition of a SAS Catalog

SAS catalogs are special SAS files that store many different kinds of information in smaller units called catalog entries. Each entry has an entry type that identifies its purpose to SAS. A single SAS catalog can contain several different types of catalog entries. Some catalog entries contain system information such as key definitions. Other catalog entries contain application information such as window definitions, help windows, formats, informats, macros, or graphics output. You can list the contents of a catalog using various SAS features, such as SAS Explorer and PROC CATALOG.

SAS Catalog Names

Parts of a Catalog Name

SAS catalog entries are fully identified by a four-level name in the following form:

```
libref.catalog.entry-name.entry-type
```

You commonly specify the two-level name for an entire catalog, as follows:

```
libref.catalog
```

libref
> is the logical name of the SAS data library to which the catalog belongs.

catalog
> is a valid SAS name for the file.

The entry name and entry type are required by some SAS procedures. If the entry type has been specified elsewhere or if it can be determined from context, you can use the entry name alone. To specify entry names and entry types, use this form:

```
entry-name.entry-type
```

entry-name
> is a valid SAS name for the catalog entry.

entry-type
> is assigned by SAS when the entry is created.

Accessing Information in Catalogs

In Base SAS software, SAS catalog entries are generally accessed automatically by SAS when the information stored in them is required for processing. In other SAS software products, you must specify the catalog entry in various procedures. Because the requirements differ with the SAS procedure or software product, refer to the appropriate procedure or product documentation for details.

Tools for Managing SAS Catalogs

There are several SAS features to help you manage the entries in catalogs. The CATALOG procedure and the CEXIST function are two features of Base SAS software. Another tool is SAS Explorer, which enables you to view the contents of SAS catalogs. Many interactive windowing procedures contain a catalog directory window for managing entries. The following list summarizes the tools that are available for managing catalogs:

CATALOG procedure
> is similar to the DATASETS procedure. Use the CATALOG procedure to copy, delete, list, and rename entries in catalogs.

CEXIST function
> enables you to verify the existence of a SAS catalog or catalog entry. See the CEXIST function in *SAS Language Reference: Dictionary* for more information.

CATALOG window
> is a window that you can access at any time in an interactive windowing environment. It displays the name, type, description, and date of last update for each entry in the specified catalog. CATALOG window commands enable you to edit catalog entries. You can also view and edit catalog entries after double-clicking on a catalog file in SAS Explorer.

catalog directory windows
> are available in some procedures in SAS/AF, SAS/FSP, and SAS/GRAPH software. A catalog directory window lists the same kind of information that the CATALOG

window provides: entry name, type, description, and date of last update. See the description of each interactive windowing procedure for details about the catalog directory window for that procedure.

Profile Catalog

Definition

Profile catalog (Sasuser.Profile)
is a catalog that is available for customizing the way you work with SAS. SAS uses this catalog to store function key definitions, fonts for graphics applications, window attributes, and other information from interactive windowing procedures.

How the Information Is Used

The information in the Sasuser.Profile catalog is accessed automatically by SAS when you need it for processing. For example, each time you enter the KEYS window and change the settings, SAS stores the new settings with the KEYS entry type. Similarly, if you change and save the attributes for interactive window procedures, the changes are stored under the appropriate entry name and type. When you use the window or procedure, SAS then looks for information in the Profile catalog.

How Sasuser.Profile Is Created

SAS creates the Profile catalog the first time it tries to refer to it and discovers that it does not exist. If you are using an interactive windowing environment, this occurs during system initialization in your first SAS session. If you use one of the other modes of execution, the Profile catalog is created the first time you execute a SAS procedure that requires it.

Operating Environment Information: The Sasuser library is implemented differently in various operating environments. See the SAS documentation for your host system for more information about how the SAS user library is created. △

Default Settings

The default settings for your SAS session are stored in several catalogs in the Sashelp installation library. If you do not make any changes to key settings or other options, SAS uses the default settings. If you make changes, the new information is stored in your Profile catalog. To restore the original default settings, use the CATALOG procedure or the CATALOG window to delete the appropriate entries from your Profile catalog. By default, SAS then uses the corresponding entry from the Sashelp library.

During SAS sessions, you can make customizations, such as window resizing and positioning, and save them to Sasuser.Profile. If your Profile catalog is locked or corrupted, the customizations will be saved in Work.Profile instead of in Sasuser.Profile. The following notes will appear in the SAS log:

NOTE: Unable to open SASUSER.PROFILE. WORK.PROFILE will be opened instead.
NOTE: All profile changes will be lost at the end of the session.

The notes will appear at invocation and again the first time the SAS session writes a member to the WORK.PROFILE catalog.

Catalog Concatenation

Definitions

You can logically combine two or more SAS catalogs by concatenating them. This allows you to access the contents of several catalogs, using one catalog name. There are two types of concatenation, *explicit* and *implicit*.

Implicit catalog concatenation
: results from a concatenation of libraries through a LIBNAME statement. When two or more libraries are logically combined through concatenation, any catalogs with the same name in each library become logically combined as well.

Explicit catalog concatenation
: is a concatenation that is specified by the global CATNAME statement in which the catalogs to be concatenated are specifically (or explicitly) named. During explicit catalog concatenation, the CATNAME statement sets up a logical catalog in memory.

Example 1: Implicit Concatenation

This LIBNAME statement concatenates the two SAS data libraries:

```
libname both ('SAS-data-library 1''SAS-data-library 2' );
```

Members of library1	Members of library2
MYCAT.CATALOG	MYCAT.CATALOG
TABLE1.DATA	MYCAT2.CATALOG
TABLE3.DATA	TABLE1.DATA
	TABLE1.INDEX
	TABLE2.DATA
	TABLE2.INDEX

The concatenated libref BOTH would have the following:

Concatenated libref BOTH
MYCAT.CATALOG (from path 1 and 2)
MYCAT2.CATALOG (from path 2)
TABLE1.DATA (from path 1)

Concatenated libref BOTH
TABLE2.DATA (from path 2)
TABLE2.INDEX (from path 2)
TABLE3.DATA (from path 1)

Notice that TABLE1.INDEX does not appear in the concatenation but TABLE2.INDEX does appear. SAS suppresses listing the index when its associated data file is not part of the concatenation.

So what happened to the catalogs when the libraries were concatenated? A resulting catalog now exists logically in memory, with the full name BOTH.MYCAT.CATALOG. This catalog combines each of the two physical catalogs residing in 'library 1' and 'library2', called MYCAT.CATALOG.

To understand the contents of the concatenation BOTH.MYCAT, first look at the contents of both parts of the concatenation. Assume that the two original MYCAT.CATALOG files contain the following:

Contents of MYCAT.CATALOG in library1	Contents of MYCAT.CATALOG in library 2
A.FRAME	A.GRSEG
C.FRAME	B.FRAME
	C.FRAME

Then the combined catalog BOTH.MYCAT contains the following:

BOTH.MYCAT
A.GRSEG (from path 2)
A.FRAME (from path 1)
B.FRAME (from path 2)
C.FRAME (from path 1)

Example 2: Explicit Concatenation

The syntax of the CATNAME statement is:

```
CATNAME libref.catref
        (libref-1.catalog-1 (ACCESS=READONLY)
          libref-n.catalog-n (ACCESS=READONLY));
```

To disassociate a concatenated catalog the syntax is:

```
CATNAME libref.catref | _ALL_ clear;
```

In the following example, there must be a libref that is defined and named CATDOG. The libref CATDOG establishes the scope for the explicit concatenation definition.

Note: If a file in CATDOG named COMBINED.CATALOG already exists, it becomes inaccessible until the explicit concatenation CATDOG.COMBINED is cleared. △

Members of library1	Members of library2
MYCAT.CATALOG	MYDOG.CATALOG
TABLE1.DATA	MYCAT2.CATALOG
TABLE3.DATA	TABLE1.DATA
	TABLE1.INDEX
	TABLE2.DATA
	TABLE2.INDEX

If we issue the following statement,

```
CATNAME catdog.combined
        (library1.mycat (ACCESS=READONLY)
         library2.mydog (ACCESS=READONLY));
```

then the concatenated catalog CATDOG.COMBINED combines the following catalogs:

Concatenated catalog CATALOG.COMBINED
MYCAT.CATALOG (from library 1)
MYDOG.CATALOG (from library 2)

Note: In explicit concatenation only the named catalogs are combined. In implicit concatenation, any catalogs that have the same name in their respective libraries are concatenated when those libraries are concatenated. △

The previous CATNAME statement creates a catalog that exists logically in memory. This catalog, named CATDOG.COMBINED.CATALOG, combines the two physical catalogs residing in library1 and library2, called MYCAT.CATALOG and MYDOG.CATALOG respectively.

To understand the contents of the concatenation COMBINED.CATALOG, first look at the contents of both parts of the concatenation. The two original catalog files contain the following entries:

MYCAT.CATALOG library 1	MYDOG.CATALOG library 2
A.FRAME	A.GRSEG
C.FRAME	B.FRAME
	C.FRAME

The concatenated catalog COMBINED contains:

COMBINED.CATALOG contents
A.GRSEG (from MYDOG)
A.FRAME (from MYCAT)
B.FRAME (from MYDOG)
C.FRAME (from MYCAT)

Rules for Catalog Concatenation

The rules for catalog concatenation are the same, whether the catalogs are implicitly or explicitly concatenated.

☐ When a catalog entry is open for input or update, the parts are searched and the first occurrence of the specified entry is used.

☐ When an item is open for output, it will be created in the catalog that is listed first in the concatenation.

Note: A new catalog entry is created in the first catalog even if there is an item with the same name in another part of the concatenation. △

Note: If the first catalog in a concatenation that is opened for update does not exist, the item will be written to the next catalog that exists in the concatenation. △

☐ When you want to delete or rename a catalog entry, only the first occurrence of the entry is affected.

☐ Any time a list of catalog entries is displayed, only one occurrence of the catalog entry is shown.

Note: Even if a catalog entry occurs multiple times in the concatenation, only the first occurrence is shown. △

CHAPTER
33

About SAS/ACCESS Software

Definition of SAS/ACCESS Software   **569**
Dynamic LIBNAME Engine   **569**
 SAS/ACCESS LIBNAME Statement   **569**
 Using Data Set Options with SAS/ACCESS Librefs   **570**
 Embedding a SAS/ACCESS LIBNAME Statement in a PROC SQL View   **570**
SQL Procedure Pass-Through Facility   **571**
ACCESS Procedure and Interface View Engine   **572**
DBLOAD Procedure   **573**
Interface DATA Step Engine   **573**

Definition of SAS/ACCESS Software

SAS/ACCESS software
allows you to read and write data to and from other vendors' *database management systems (DBMS)*, as well as from some *PC file formats*. Depending on your DBMS, a SAS/ACCESS product might provide one or more of the following:

- a dynamic LIBNAME engine
- the SQL Pass-Through Facility
- the ACCESS procedure and interface view engine
- the DBLOAD procedure
- an interface DATA step engine.

These interfaces are described in this section. Each SAS/ACCESS product provides one or more of these interfaces for each supported DBMS. See Chapter 37, "SAS Engines," on page 597 for more information about SAS engines.

Note: To use the SAS/ACCESS features described in this section, you must license SAS/ACCESS software. See the SAS/ACCESS documentation for your DBMS for full documentation of the features described in this section. △

Dynamic LIBNAME Engine

SAS/ACCESS LIBNAME Statement

Beginning in Version 7, you can associate a SAS libref directly with a database, schema, server, or group of tables and views, depending on your DBMS. To assign a libref to DBMS data, you must use the SAS/ACCESS LIBNAME statement, which has syntax and options that are different from the Base SAS LIBNAME statement. For example, to connect to an ORACLE database, you might use the following SAS/ACCESS LIBNAME statement:

```
libname mydblib oracle user=smith password=secret
   path='myoracleserver';
```

This LIBNAME statement connects to ORACLE by specifying the ORACLE connection options: USER=, PASSWORD=, and PATH=. In addition to the connection options, you can specify SAS/ACCESS LIBNAME options that control the type of database connection that is made. You can use additional options to control how your data is processed.

You can use a DATA step, SAS procedures, or the Explorer window to view and update the DBMS data associated with the libref, or use the DATASETS and CONTENTS procedures to view information about the DBMS objects.

See your SAS/ACCESS documentation for a full listing of the SAS/ACCESS LIBNAME options that can be used with librefs that refer to DBMS data.

Using Data Set Options with SAS/ACCESS Librefs

After you have assigned a libref to your DBMS data, you can use SAS/ACCESS data set options, and some of the Base SAS data set options, on the data. The following example associates a libref with DB2 data and uses the SQL procedure to query the data:

```
libname mydb2lib db2;

proc sql;
   select *
      from mydb2lib.employees(drop=salary)
      where dept='Accounting';
quit;
```

The LIBNAME statement connects to DB2. You can reference a DBMS object, in this case, a DB2 table, by specifying a two-level name that is comprised of the libref and the DBMS object name. The DROP= data set option causes the SALARY column of the EMPLOYEES table on DB2 to be excluded from the data that is returned by the query.

See your SAS/ACCESS documentation for a full listing of the SAS/ACCESS data set options and the Base SAS data set options that can be used on data sets that refer to DBMS data.

Embedding a SAS/ACCESS LIBNAME Statement in a PROC SQL View

You can issue a SAS/ACCESS LIBNAME statement by itself, as shown in the previous examples, or as part of a CREATE VIEW statement in PROC SQL. The USING clause of the CREATE VIEW statement allows you to store DBMS connection information in a view by *embedding* a SAS/ACCESS LIBNAME statement inside the view. The following example uses an embedded SAS/ACCESS LIBNAME statement:

```
libname viewlib 'SAS-data-library';

proc sql;
   create view viewlib.emp_view as
      select *
         from mydblib.employees
```

```
        using libname mydblib oracle user=smith password=secret
           path='myoraclepath';
quit;
```

When PROC SQL executes the view, the SELECT statement assigns the libref and establishes the connection to the DBMS. The scope of the libref is local to the view and does not conflict with identically named librefs that might exist in the SAS session. When the query finishes, the connection is terminated and the libref is deassigned.

Note: You can also embed a Base SAS LIBNAME statement in a PROC SQL view. △

SQL Procedure Pass-Through Facility

The SQL Procedure Pass-Through Facility is an extension of the SQL procedure that enables you to send DBMS-specific statements to a DBMS and to retrieve DBMS data. You specify DBMS SQL syntax instead of SAS SQL syntax when you use the Pass-Through Facility. You can use Pass-Through Facility statements in a PROC SQL query or store them in a PROC SQL view.

The Pass-Through Facility consists of three statements and one component:

□ The CONNECT statement establishes a connection to the DBMS.

□ The EXECUTE statement sends dynamic, non-query DBMS-specific SQL statements to the DBMS.

□ The CONNECTION TO component in the FROM clause of a PROC SQL SELECT statement retrieves data directly from a DBMS.

□ The DISCONNECT statement terminates the connection to the DBMS.

The following Pass-Through Facility example sends a query to an ORACLE database for processing:

```
proc sql;
    connect to oracle as myconn (user=smith password=secret
       path='myoracleserver');

    select *
       from connection to myconn
          (select empid, lastname, firstname, salary
             from employees
             where salary>75000);

    disconnect from myconn;
quit;
```

The example uses the Pass-Through CONNECT statement to establish a connection with an ORACLE database with the specified values for the USER=, PASSWORD=, and PATH= arguments. The CONNECTION TO component in the FROM clause of the SELECT statement allows data to be retrieved from the database. The DBMS-specific statement that is sent to ORACLE is enclosed in parentheses. The DISCONNECT statement terminates the connection to ORACLE.

To store the same query in a PROC SQL view, use the CREATE VIEW statement:

```
libname viewlib 'SAS-data-library';

proc sql;
    connect to oracle as myconn (user=smith password=secret
       path='myoracleserver');
```

```
create view viewlib.salary as
   select *
      from connection to myconn
         (select empid, lastname, firstname, salary
            from employees
            where salary>75000);

   disconnect from myconn;
quit;
```

ACCESS Procedure and Interface View Engine

The ACCESS procedure enables you to create *access descriptors*, which are SAS files of member type ACCESS. They describe data that is stored in a DBMS in a format that SAS can understand. Access descriptors enable you to create SAS/ACCESS views, called *view descriptors*. View descriptors are files of member type VIEW that function in the same way as SAS data views that are created with PROC SQL, as described in "Embedding a SAS/ACCESS LIBNAME Statement in a PROC SQL View" on page 570 and "SQL Procedure Pass-Through Facility" on page 571.

Note: If a dynamic LIBNAME engine is available for your DBMS, it is recommended that you use the SAS/ACCESS LIBNAME statement to access your DBMS data instead of access descriptors and view descriptors; however, descriptors continue to work in SAS software if they were available for your DBMS in Version 6. Some new SAS features, such as long variable names, are not supported when you use descriptors. △

The following example creates an access descriptor and a view descriptor in the same PROC step to retrieve data from a DB2 table:

```
libname adlib 'SAS-data-library';
libname vlib 'SAS'-data-library';

proc access dbms=db2;
   create adlib.order.access;
   table=sasdemo.orders;
   assign=no;
   list all;

   create vlib.custord.view;
   select ordernum stocknum shipto;
   format ordernum 5.
          stocknum 4.;
run;

proc print data=vlib.custord;
run;
```

When you want to use access descriptors and view descriptors, both types of descriptors must be created before you can retrieve your DBMS data. The first step, creating the access descriptor, allows SAS to store information about the specific DBMS table that you want to query.

After you have created the access descriptor, the second step is to create one or more view descriptors to retrieve some or all of the DBMS data described by the access descriptor. In the view descriptor, you select variables and apply formats to manipulate the data for viewing, printing, or storing in SAS. You use only the view descriptors, and not the access descriptors, in your SAS programs.

The interface view engine enables you to reference your view with a two-level SAS name in a DATA or PROC step, such as the PROC PRINT step in the example.

See Chapter 29, "SAS Data Views," on page 539 for more information about views. See the SAS/ACCESS documentation for your DBMS for more detailed information about creating and using access descriptors and SAS/ACCESS views.

DBLOAD Procedure

The DBLOAD procedure enables you to create and load data into a DBMS table from a SAS data set, data file, data view, or another DBMS table, or to append rows to an existing table. It also enables you to submit non-query DBMS-specific SQL statements to the DBMS from your SAS session.

Note: If a dynamic LIBNAME engine is available for your DBMS, it is recommended that you use the SAS/ACCESS LIBNAME statement to create your DBMS data instead of the DBLOAD procedure; however, DBLOAD continues to work in SAS software if it was available for your DBMS in Version 6. Some new SAS features, such as long variable names, are not supported when you use the DBLOAD procedure. △

The following example appends data from a previously created SAS data set named INVDATA into a table in an ORACLE database named INVOICE:

```
proc dbload dbms=oracle data=invdata append;
  user=smith;
  password=secret;
  path='myoracleserver';
  table=invoice;
  load;
run;
```

See the SAS/ACCESS documentation for your DBMS for more detailed information about the DBLOAD procedure.

Interface DATA Step Engine

Some SAS/ACCESS software products support a DATA step interface, which allows you to read data from your DBMS by using DATA step programs. Some products support both reading and writing in the DATA step interface.

The DATA step interface consists of four statements:

□ The INFILE statement identifies the database or message queue to be accessed.

□ The INPUT statement is used with the INFILE statement to issue a GET call to retrieve DBMS data.

□ The FILE statement identifies the database or message queue to be updated, if writing to the DBMS is supported.

□ The PUT statement is used with the FILE statement to issue an UPDATE call, if writing to the DBMS is supported.

The following example updates data in an IMS database by using the FILE and INFILE statements in a DATA step. The statements generate calls to the database in the IMS native language, DL/I. The DATA step reads BANK.CUSTOMER, an existing SAS data set that contains information on new customers, and then it updates the ACCOUNT database with the data in the SAS data set.

```
data _null_;
   set bank.customer;
   length ssa1 $9;
   infile accupdt dli call=func dbname=db ssa=ssa1;
   file accupdt dli;
   func = 'isrt';
   db = 'account';
   ssa1 = 'customer';
   put @1   ssnumber $char11.
       @12  custname $char40.
       @52  addr1    $char30.
       @82  addr2    $char30.
       @112 custcity $char28.
       @140 custstat $char2.
       @142 custland $char20.
       @162 custzip  $char10.
       @172 h_phone  $char12.
       @184 o_phone  $char12.;
   if _error_ = 1 then
      abort abend 888;
run;
```

In SAS/ACCESS products that provide a DATA step interface, the INFILE statement has special DBMS-specific options that allow you to specify DBMS variable values and to format calls to the DBMS appropriately. See the SAS/ACCESS documentation for your DBMS for a full listing of the DBMS-specific INFILE statement options and the Base SAS INFILE statement options that can be used with your DBMS.

CHAPTER

34

Processing Data Using Cross-Environment Data Access (CEDA)

Definition of Cross-Environment Data Access (CEDA) **575**
Advantages of CEDA **576**
SAS File Processing with CEDA **576**
    What Types of Processing Does CEDA Support? **576**
    Behavioral Differences for Output Processing **577**
    Restrictions for CEDA **577**
Processing a File with CEDA **578**
    Understanding When CEDA Is Used to Process a File **578**
    Determining Whether Update Processing Is Allowed **579**
Alternatives to Using CEDA **580**
Creating New Files in a Foreign Data Representation **581**
Examples of Using CEDA **581**
    Example 1: Automatically Processing a Foreign File **581**
    Example 2: Creating a New File in a Foreign Environment **582**

Definition of Cross-Environment Data Access (CEDA)

Cross-environment data access (CEDA) is a Base SAS feature that enables a SAS file that was created in a directory-based operating environment (for example, UNIX, Windows, OpenVMS Alpha) to be processed as follows:

□ by a SAS session that is running in another directory-based environment. For example, if you move a file from one operating environment like Windows to a different operating environment like UNIX, CEDA translates the file, which eliminates the need for you to convert the file.

□ on a platform that is different from the platform on which the file was created. For example, CEDA is useful if you have upgraded to a 64-bit platform from a 32-bit platform.

□ by a SAS session in which the session encoding is incompatible with the encoding for the SAS file.

With CEDA, you do not need to create a transport file, use other SAS procedures, or change your SAS program. CEDA is available for files that are created with SAS 7 and later releases.

Here are a few terms and definitions to help you understand CEDA:

data representation
    is the format in which data is represented on a computer architecture or in an operating environment. For example, on an IBM PC, character data is represented by its ASCII encoding and byte-swapped integers.

encoding is a set of characters (letters, logograms, digits, punctuation, symbols, control characters, and so on) that have been mapped to numeric values (called code points) that can be used by computers. The code points are assigned to the characters in the character set by applying an encoding method. Some examples of encodings are Wlatin1 and Danish EBCDIC.

foreign refers to a file or an environment for which the data representation contrasts with the CPU that is processing the file. For example, the data representation that is created by an IBM mainframe is considered foreign to that of a Windows environment.

native refers to a file or an environment for which the data representation is comparable with the CPU that is processing the file. For example, a file that is in Windows data representation is native to a Windows environment.

Advantages of CEDA

CEDA offers these advantages:

☐ You can transparently process a supported SAS file with no knowledge of the file's data representation or character encoding.

☐ System performance is maximized, because a read operation requires a single translation between native and foreign representations, rather than a translation from native representation to transport file to native representation.

☐ No interim transport files are created.

☐ CEDA eliminates the need to perform explicit steps in order to process the file.

☐ The internal numeric representation that is provided by CEDA is more precise than that provided by the XPORT engine with PROC COPY. CEDA uses a one-step translation from the native representation of the source environment to the native representation of the target environment, whereas the XPORT engine uses a two-step transformation from a file's native representation to the target environment by means of a transport format.

SAS File Processing with CEDA

What Types of Processing Does CEDA Support?

CEDA supports SAS 7 and later SAS files that are created in directory-based operating environments like UNIX, Windows, and OpenVMS Alpha. CEDA provides the following SAS file processing for these SAS engines:

BASE default engine for Base SAS in SAS 9 (V9), SAS 8 (V8), and SAS 7 (V7).

SOCKET TCP/IP port engine for SAS/CONNECT.

TAPE sequential engine for SAS 9 (V9TAPE), SAS 8 (V8TAPE), and SAS 7 (V7TAPE).

Table 34.1 SAS File Processing Provided by CEDA

SAS File Type	Engine	Supported Processing
SAS data file	BASE, TAPE, SOCKET	input and output [1] processing
PROC SQL view	BASE	input processing
SAS/ACCESS view for Oracle or SYBASE	BASE	input processing
MDDB file[2]	BASE	input processing

1   For output processing that replaces an existing SAS data file, there are behavioral differences. See "Behavioral Differences for Output Processing" on page 577.
2   CEDA supports SAS 8 and later MDDB files.

Behavioral Differences for Output Processing

For output processing that replaces an existing SAS data file, there are behavioral differences regarding these attributes:

encoding

□ The BASE engine uses the encoding of the existing file; that is, the encoding is cloned.

□ The TAPE engine uses the current SAS session encoding.

□ For both the BASE and TAPE engines, the COPY procedure uses the encoding of the file from the source library (that is, the file being copied), regardless of whether the file existed in the target library.

data representation
The BASE and TAPE engines use the data representation of the native environment, except with the COPY procedure, which by default uses the data representation of the file being copied.

Restrictions for CEDA

CEDA has the following restrictions:

□ CEDA does not support DATA step views, SAS/ACCESS views that are not for SAS/ACCESS for Oracle or SYBASE, SAS catalogs, stored compiled DATA step programs, item stores, DMDB files, FDB files, or any SAS file that was created with a version of SAS prior to SAS 7.

□ Update processing is not supported.

□ Indexes are not supported. Therefore, WHERE optimization with an index is not supported.

□ CEDA is supported only for directory-based file systems. On OS/390 or z/OS, only HFS or zFS (UNIX file systems) libraries support CEDA. In particular, CEDA is not supported for bound libraries on z/OS. For additional information, see "Library Implementation Types for Base and Sequential Engines" in *SAS Companion for z/ OS*.

□ Because the BASE engine translates the data as the data is read, multiple procedures require SAS to read and translate the data multiple times. In this way, the translation could affect system performance.

□ If a foreign data set is damaged, CEDA cannot process the file in order to repair it. CEDA does not support update processing, which is required in order to repair a damaged data set. To repair the foreign file, you must move it back to its native environment. For information on how to repair a damaged data set, see the REPAIR statement in the DATASETS procedure in *Base SAS Procedures Guide*.

Processing a File with CEDA

Understanding When CEDA Is Used to Process a File

Because CEDA translation is transparent, you might not be aware when CEDA is being used. However, knowing when CEDA is used could be helpful, for example, because CEDA translation may require additional resources.

CEDA is used in these situations:

□ when the data representation of the SAS file differs from the data representation that is used by SAS for the operating environment and platform. This can occur, for example, if you move a file from one operating environment like Windows to a different operating environment like UNIX, or if you have upgraded to a 64-bit platform from a 32-bit platform.

Note: Processing a foreign file could result in numeric data loss during data translation. For example, if you move a file that contains a very large or small number from 64-bit UNIX to 32-bit z/OS, the value could lose precision or be significantly reduced in value due to differences in the data representation on the hosts. △

The following table groups (within a single cell) the compatible data representation values and environments. (Environments are named by the operating system and platform on which SAS is executed.) With the noted exception, CEDA is used if you access a SAS file with a data representation value in one group from an environment in another group.

Table 34.2 Compatibility Across Environments

Data Representation Value	Environment
ALPHA_TRU64	Compaq Tru64 UNIX
ALPHA_VMS_32	OpenVMS Alpha on 32-bit platform [1]
ALPHA_VMS_64	OpenVMS Alpha on 64-bit platform [1]
HP_IA64	HP UX on Itanium 64-bit platform
HP_UX_64	HP UX on 64-bit platform
RS_6000_AIX_64	AIX UNIX on 64-bit RS/6000
SOLARIS_64	Sun Solaris on 64-bit platform
HP_UX_32	HP UX on 32-bit platform
MIPS_ABI	ABI UNIX on 32-bit platform
RS_6000_AIX_32	AIX UNIX on 32-bit RS/6000
SOLARIS_32	Sun Solaris on 32-bit platform
LINUX_32	Linux for Intel Architecture on 32-bit platform
INTEL_ABI	ABI UNIX on Intel 32-bit platform

Data Representation Value	Environment
MVS_32	z/OS on 32-bit platform
OS2	OS/2 on Intel 32-bit platform
VAX_VMS	VAX VMS
WINDOWS_32	Microsoft Windows on 32-bit platform
WINDOWS_64	Microsoft Windows 64-Bit Edition

1 Although these 32-bit and 64-bit OpenVMS Alpha systems have different data representations for some compiler data types, SAS data sets that are created by the BASE engine do not store the data types that are different; therefore, CEDA is not required between these two groups.

□ when the encoding of character values for the SAS file is incompatible with the currently executing SAS session encoding.

Note: Transcoding could result in character data loss. For information about encoding and transcoding, see *SAS National Language Support (NLS): User's Guide.* △

Note: Starting in SAS 9, you can tell SAS to display a message when CEDA is being used by setting the SAS system option MSGLEVEL=I:

```
options msglevel=i;
```

Here is an example of the message:

```
INFO: Data file HEALTH.GRADES.DATA is in a format native to another
host or the file encoding does not match the session encoding.
Cross Environment Data Access will be used, which may require additional
CPU resources and reduce performance.
```

△

Determining Whether Update Processing Is Allowed

If a file's data representation is the same as that of the processing environment, and if the encoding is compatible with the currently executing SAS session encoding, then you can manually update the file, because CEDA is not needed in order to translate the file. For example, in a Windows environment, if a file was created in a Windows environment or if the OUTREP= option was used to designate the file in Windows data representation, then you can update the file.

Otherwise, if CEDA is used to translate the file, you cannot update it. If you attempt to update the file, then you will receive an error message that says that updating is not allowed. For example:

```
ERROR: File HEALTH.OXYGEN cannot be updated because its encoding does
not match the session encoding or the file is in a format native to another
host, such as SOLARIS_32, HP_UX_32, RS_6000_AIX_32, MIPS_ABI.
```

To determine the data representation and the encoding of a file, you can use the CONTENTS procedure (or the CONTENTS statement in PROC DATASETS). For example, the data set HEALTH.OXYGEN was created in a UNIX environment in SAS 9. The file was moved to a SAS 9 Windows environment, in which the following CONTENTS output was requested:

Output 34.1   CONTENTS Output Showing Data Representation

```
                                  The SAS System                                    1

                               The CONTENTS Procedure

Data Set Name        HEALTH.OXYGEN                    Observations           31
Member Type          DATA                             Variables              7
Engine               V9                               Indexes                0
Created              Wednesday, January 22, 2003 10:11:39   Observation Length  56
Last Modified        Wednesday, January 22, 2003 10:11:33   Deleted Observations 0
Protection                                            Compressed             NO
Data Set Type                                         Sorted                 NO
Label
Data Representation  SOLARIS_32, HP_UX_32, RS_6000_AIX_32, MIPS_ABI
Encoding             latin1  Western ( ISO )


                          Engine/Host Dependent Information

         Data Set Page Size          5120
         Number of Data Set Pages    1
         First Data Page             1
         Max Obs per Page            90
         Obs in First Data Page      31
         Number of Data Set Repairs  0
         File Name                   /u/xxxxxx/myfiles/health/\oxygen.sas7bdat
         Release Created             9.0100A0
         Host Created                HP-UX



                    Alphabetic List of Variables and Attributes

              #      Variable    Type    Len

              1      AGE         Num      8
              6      MAXPULSE    Num      8
              7      OXYGEN      Num      8
              4      RSTPULSE    Num      8
              5      RUNPULSE    Num      8
              3      RUNTIME     Num      8
              2      WEIGHT      Num      8
```

Alternatives to Using CEDA

Because of the restrictions, it might not be feasible to use CEDA. You can use the following methods in order to move files across operating environments:

XPORT engine with the DATA step or PROC COPY
In the source environment, the LIBNAME statement with the XPORT engine and either the DATA step or PROC COPY creates a transport file from a SAS data set. In the target environment, the same method translates the transport file into the target environment's native format. Note that the XPORT engine does not support SAS 7 and later features, such as long file and variable names.

XML engine with the DATA step or PROC COPY
In the source environment, the LIBNAME statement with the XML engine and either the DATA step or PROC COPY creates an XML document from a SAS data set. In the target environment, the same method translates the XML document into the target environment's native format.

CPORT and CIMPORT procedures
In the source environment, PROC CPORT writes data sets or catalogs to transport format. In the target environment, PROC CIMPORT translates the transport file into the target environment's native format.

Data transfer services in SAS/CONNECT software
Data transfer services is a bulk data transfer mechanism that transfers a disk copy of the data and performs the necessary conversion of the data from one environment's representation to another's, as well as any necessary conversion between SAS releases. This requires that a connection be established between two SAS sessions by using the SIGNON command and then executing either PROC UPLOAD or PROC DOWNLOAD to move the data.

Remote library services in both SAS/SHARE software and SAS/CONNECT software
This gives you transparent access to remote data through the use of the LIBNAME statement.

Creating New Files in a Foreign Data Representation

By default, SAS creates new files by using the native data representation of the CPU that is running SAS. For example, when using a PC, SAS creates a file that has ASCII characters and byte-swapped integers.

You can specify the OUTREP= option for flexibility when using CEDA. This option exists as both a SAS data set option and as a LIBNAME statement option. As a data set option, it applies to an individual file. As a LIBNAME statement option, it applies to the entire library.

To create new files in a foreign data representation, use the OUTREP= option. This option enables you to create a file within the native environment using a foreign data representation. For example, in a UNIX environment, you can create a SAS data set in Windows data representation. For a list of values, see the OUTREP= option for the LIBNAME statement or the OUTREP= data set option in *SAS Language Reference: Dictionary*.

Examples of Using CEDA

Example 1: Automatically Processing a Foreign File

This example shows how simple it is to move a SAS data set from one operating environment to another and to process the file in the new environment without any conversion steps.

First, the SAS data set is moved, using FTP, from an HP UNIX environment to a Windows PC.

```
C:\>ftp my.unix.node.com
FTP>binary
FTP>get unxdata.sas7bdat
FTP>quit
```

Then, using CEDA, SAS automatically recognizes the foreign data representation (which is HP UNIX) and translates it to the native data representation for the Windows environment. Because the SAS system option MSGLEVEL=I is specified, the log output displays a message that the file is being processed using CEDA.

```
options msglevel=i;
libname unx '.';

proc print data=unx.unxdata;
run;
```

Output 34.2   Log Output from Processing a Foreign File

```
INFO: Data file UNX.UNXDATA is in a format native to another host or the file
encoding which does not match the session encoding. Cross Environment Data Access
will be used, which may require additional CPU resources and may reduce
performance.
```

Example 2: Creating a New File in a Foreign Environment

In this example, an administrator who works in a z/OS operating environment wants to create a file on an HFS system so that the file can be processed in an HP UNIX environment. Specifying OUTREP=HP_UX_32 as a data set option forces the data representation to match the data representation of the UNIX operating environment that will process the file. This method of creating the file can enhance system performance because the file does not require data conversion when being read by an HP UNIX machine.

```
libname foreign v9 'HFS-file-spec';

data foreign.a (outrep=HP_UX_32);
    infile file-specifications;
    input student $ test1 test2 test3 final;
    total = test1+test2+test3+final;
    grade = total/4.0;
run;
```

CHAPTER
35

SAS 9.1 Compatibility with SAS Files From Earlier Releases

Introduction to Version Compatibility **583**
Comparing SAS System 9 to Earlier Releases **583**
    SAS 9 File Format **583**
        SAS 9 Filename Extensions **584**
Using SAS Library Engines **584**

Introduction to Version Compatibility

SAS recognizes that SAS 9 customers often have existing data and programs. You want to seamlessly process your existing files, and possibly to simultaneously operate both SAS 9 and an earlier release of SAS. In many cases, you can use SAS 9 to process SAS files that were created in versions 8, 7, and 6 of SAS without first converting the files; however, there are some limitations.

Compatibility between versions will vary depending on the type of SAS file, the SAS release that you are running, the operating environment in which the file was created, and the type of processing you need to do. Compatibility issues are generally handled automatically by SAS. However, there are situations that require you to specify an engine name or to migrate the file.

The additional information in this topic provides general, overview information regarding compatibility.

For specific processing information and guidelines for migration issues, see the Migration Community at **support.sas.com/rnd/migration**.

The Migration Community is your guide to migrating files from previous versions of SAS to SAS 9. Refer to this community for planning and cost analysis information, known compatibility issues and their resolutions, and step-by-step instructions. In addition, the Migration Community provides documentation for the MIGRATE procedure, which provides a simple way to migrate a library of SAS files from previous releases of SAS.

Comparing SAS System 9 to Earlier Releases

SAS 9 File Format

In order to provide longer file names and variable names, the file format used in SAS 7 and 8 is different from the file format used in SAS 6.

For SAS 9, the file format is basically the same as in SAS 7 and 8. The Base SAS engine is the same engine, except that for SAS 9, you can define and use longer format and informat names. You cannot use longer format and informat names in SAS 7 or 8.

SAS files created with SAS 7 and 8 are compatible with SAS 9. However, a SAS file that is created with a 32-bit version of SAS has a different data representation than a SAS file from a 64-bit version of SAS. The data representation is the format in which data is represented on a computer architecture or in an operating environment. Therefore, if you have SAS files that were created on a 32-bit version of SAS and you have upgraded to a 64-bit version of SAS, you will have processing limitations due to the different data representation.

SAS 9 Filename Extensions

A filename extension reflects the engine that was used to create both the file and the SAS file member type.

Because SAS needs to distinguish among the different file types and versions, SAS automatically assigns a specific extension to each file when the file is created. For example, in order to distinguish SAS 7 and 8 files from SAS 6 files, the extensions are different.

For SAS 9, the file extensions are the same as the file extensions in SAS 7 and 8.

The following table lists the file extensions for a SAS data file (SAS data set with member type DATA) in SAS 6, 7, 8, and 9 for different operating environments:

Table 35.1   File Extensions for a SAS Data File in Different Operating Environments

Engine Name	UNIX	OpenVMS Alpha	Windows	z/OS[1]
V6	.ssd01	.SASEB$DATA	.sd2	not available
V7	.sas7bdat	.sas7bdat	.sas7bdat	.sas7bdat
V8	.sas7bdat	.sas7bdat	.sas7bdat	.sas7bdat
V9	.sas7bdat	.sas7bdat	.sas7bdat	.sas7bdat

1   applies to SAS data sets that reside in the hierarchical file system of UNIX System Services.

Operating Environment Information: For a complete list of SAS member types and extensions, see the SAS documentation for your operating environment. △

Using SAS Library Engines

In order to access a SAS data library, SAS needs a libref and a library engine name. For example, you assign a libref to the SAS data library with the LIBNAME statement or the New Library window, but usually you do not have to specify an engine name because SAS automatically selects the appropriate engine.

If you do not specify an engine, SAS automatically assigns one based on the contents of the SAS data library. For example, SAS is able to differentiate between a SAS 6 library and a SAS 9 library. Note that in SAS 9, a SAS library containing SAS 7 and 8 files is the same as a SAS 9 library, because the engine that creates a SAS file determines its format, and the file format for SAS 7, 8, and 9 is the same.

For example, in a SAS 9 session, if you issue the following LIBNAME statement to assign a libref to a data library containing SAS 8 SAS files, SAS automatically uses the SAS 9 engine:

```
libname mylib 'v8-SAS-data-library';
```

In a SAS 9 session, if you issue the following LIBNAME statement to assign a libref to a data library that contains only SAS 6 files, SAS automatically uses the Version 6 compatibility engine:

```
libname mylib 'v6-SAS-data-library';
```

SAS automatically assigns an engine based on the contents of the data library as shown in the following table:

Table 35.2 Default Library Engine Assignment in SAS 9

Engine Assignment	Data Library Contents
V9	No SAS files; the library is empty
V9	Only SAS 9 SAS files
V9	Only SAS 8 SAS files
V9	Only SAS 7 SAS files
V6	Only SAS 6 SAS files
V9	Both SAS 9 SAS files and SAS files from earlier releases

Note: Even though SAS will automatically assign an engine based on the library contents, it is more efficient for you to specify the engine. For example, specifying the engine name in the following LIBNAME statement saves SAS from determining which engine to use:

```
libname mylib v6 'v6-SAS-data-library';
```

△

For more information about SAS engines, see Chapter 37, "SAS Engines," on page 597.

CHAPTER

36

File Protection

Definition of a Password   **587**
Assigning Passwords   **588**
   Syntax   **588**
      Assigning a Password with a DATA Step   **589**
      Assigning a Password to an Existing Data Set   **589**
      Assigning a Password with a Procedure   **589**
      Assigning a Password with the SAS Windowing Environment   **590**
      Assigning a Password Outside of SAS   **590**
Removing or Changing Passwords   **590**
Using Password-Protected SAS Files in DATA and PROC Steps   **590**
How SAS Handles Incorrect Passwords   **591**
Assigning Complete Protection with the PW= Data Set Option   **591**
Using Passwords with Views   **592**
   How the Level of Protection Differs from SAS Views   **592**
   PROC SQL Views   **593**
   SAS/ACCESS Views   **593**
   DATA Step Views   **593**
SAS Data File Encryption   **594**
   Example   **594**
      Passwords and Encryption with Generation Data Sets, Audit Trails, Indexes, and Copies   **595**

Definition of a Password

SAS software enables you to restrict access to members of SAS data libraries by assigning passwords to the members. You can assign passwords to all member types except catalogs. You can specify three levels of protection: read, write, and alter. When a password is assigned, it appears as uppercase Xs in the log.

Note: This document uses the terms *SAS data file* and *SAS data view* to distinguish between the two types of SAS data sets. Passwords work differently for type VIEW than they do for type DATA. The term "SAS data set" is used when the distinction is not necessary. △

read   protects against reading the file.

write   protects against changing the data in the file. For SAS data files, write protection prevents adding, modifying, or deleting observations.

alter   protects against deleting or replacing the entire file. For SAS data
                                     files, alter protection also prevents modifying variable attributes and
                                     creating or deleting indexes.

Alter protection does not require a password for read or write access; write protection
does not require a password for read access. For example, you can read an
alter-protected or write-protected SAS data file without knowing the alter or write
password. Conversely, read and write protection do not prevent any operation that
requires alter protection. For example, you can delete a SAS data set that is only read-
or write-protected without knowing the read or write password.

To protect a file from being read, written to, deleted, or replaced by anyone who does
not have the proper authority, assign read, write, and alter protection. To allow others
to read the file without knowing the password, but not change its data or delete it,
assign just write and alter protection. To completely protect a file with one password,
use the PW= data set option. See "Assigning Complete Protection with the PW= Data
Set Option" on page 591 for details.

Note: Because of the way SAS opens files, you must specify the read password to
update a SAS data set that is only read-protected.   △

Note: The levels of protection differ somewhat for the member type VIEW. See
"Using Passwords with Views" on page 592. △

Assigning Passwords

Syntax

To set a password, first specify a SAS data set in one of the following:

□ a DATA statement

□ the MODIFY statement of the DATASETS procedure

□ an OUT = statement in PROC SQL

□ the CREATE VIEW statement in PROC SQL

□ the ToolBox.

Then assign one or more password types to the data set. The data set may already
exist, or the data set may be one that you create. An example of syntax follows:

   password-type=password <... password-type=password>)

where *password* is a valid eight-character SAS name and *password-type* can be one of
the following SAS data set options:

   ALTER=

   PW=

   READ=

   WRITE=

CAUTION:
   Keep a record of any passwords you assign! If you forget or do not know the password,
   you cannot get the password from SAS. △

Assigning a Password with a DATA Step

You can use data set options to assign passwords to unprotected members in the DATA step when you create a new SAS data file.
This example prevents deletion or modification of the data set without a password.

```
    /* assign a write and an alter password to MYLIB.STUDENTS */
data mylib.students(write=yellow alter=red);
    input name $ sex $ age;
    datalines;
Amy f 25
… more data lines …
;
```

This example prevents reading or deleting a stored program without a password and also prevents changing the source program.

```
    /* assign a read and an alter password to the view ROSTER */
data mylib.roster(read=green alter=red) /
    view=mylib.roster;
    set mylib.students;
run;


libname stored 'SAS-data-library-2';

    /* assign a read and alter password to the program file SOURCE */
data mylib.schedule / pgm=stored.source(read=green alter=red);
    … DATA step statements …
run;
```

Note: When you replace a SAS data set that is alter-protected, the new data set inherits the alter password. To change the alter password for the new data set, use the MODIFY statement in the DATASETS procedure. △

Assigning a Password to an Existing Data Set

You can use the MODIFY statement in the DATASET procedure to assign passwords to unprotected members if the SAS data file already exists.

```
    /* assign an alter password to STUDENTS */
proc datasets library=mylib;
    modify students(alter=red);
run;
```

Assigning a Password with a Procedure

You can assign a password after an OUT= data set specification in PROC SQL.

```
    /* assign a write and an alter password to SCORE */
proc sort data=mylib.math
    out=mylib.score(write=yellow alter=red);
    by number;
run;
```

You can use a CREATE VIEW statement in PROC SQL to assign a password.

```
   /* assign an alter password to the view BDAY */
proc sql;
   create view mylib.bday(alter=red) as
      query-expression;
```

Assigning a Password with the SAS Windowing Environment

You can create or change passwords for any data file using the Password Window in the SAS windowing environment. To invoke the Password Window from the ToolBox, use the global command SETPASSWORD followed by the file name. This opens the password window for the specified data file.

Assigning a Password Outside of SAS

A SAS password does not control access to a SAS file beyond the SAS system. You should use the operating system-supplied utilities and file-system security controls in order to control access to SAS files outside of SAS.

Removing or Changing Passwords

To remove or change a password, use the MODIFY statement in the DATASETS procedure. For more information, see the DATASETS procedure in *Base SAS Procedures Guide*.

Using Password-Protected SAS Files in DATA and PROC Steps

To access password-protected files, use the same data set options that you use to assign protection.

□

```
      /* Assign a read and alter password
      /* to the stored program file*/ /*STORED.SOURCE */
      data mylib.schedule / pgm=stored.source
         (read=green alter=red);
         <... more data step statements ...>
   run;


      /*Access password-protected file*/
   proc sort data=mylib.score(write=yellow alter=red);
      by number;
   run;
```

□

```
      /* Print read-protected data set MYLIB.AUTOS */
         proc print data=mylib.autos(read=green); run;
```

□

```
      /* Append ANIMALS to the write-protected */
      /* data set ZOO */
   proc append base=mylib.zoo(write=yellow)
              data=mylib.animals;
   run;
```

□

```
      /* Delete alter-protected data set MYLIB.BOTANY */
   proc datasets library=mylib;
      delete botany(alter=red);
   run;
```

Passwords are hierarchical in terms of gaining access. For example, specifying the ALTER password gives you read and write access. The following example creates the data set STATES, with three different passwords, and then reads the data set to produce a plot:

```
data mylib.states(read=green write=yellow alter=red);
   input density crime name $;
   datalines;
151.4 6451.3 Colorado
… more data lines …
;

proc plot data=mylib.states(alter=red);
   plot crime*density;
run;
```

How SAS Handles Incorrect Passwords

If you are using the SAS windowing environment and you try to access a password-protected member without specifying the correct password, you receive a requestor window that prompts you for the appropriate password. The text you enter in this window is not displayed. You can use the PWREQ= data set option to control whether a requestor window appears after a user enters a missing or incorrect password. PWREQ= is most useful in SCL applications.

If you are using batch or noninteractive mode, you receive an error message in the SAS log if you try to access a password-protected member without specifying the correct password.

If you are using interactive line mode, you are also prompted for the password if you do not specify the correct password. When you enter the password and press ENTER, processing continues. If you cannot give the correct password, you receive an error message in the SAS log.

Assigning Complete Protection with the PW= Data Set Option

The PW= data set option assigns the same password for each level of protection. This data set option is convenient for thoroughly protecting a member with just one password. If you use the PW= data set option, those who have access only need to remember one password for total access.

□ To access a member whose password is assigned using the PW= data set option, use the PW= data set option or the data set option that equates to the specific level of access you need:

```
    /* create a data set using PW=,
        then use READ= to print the data set */
data mylib.states(pw=orange);
    input density crime name $;
    datalines;
151.4 6451.3 Colorado
… more data lines …
;


proc print data=mylib.states(read=orange);
run;
```

□ PW= can be an alias for other password options:

```
    /* Use PW= as an alias for ALTER=. */
data mylib.college(alter=red);
    input name $ 1-10 location $ 12-25;
    datalines;
Vanderbilt Nashville
Rice       Houston
Duke       Durham
Tulane     New Orleans
… more data lines …
;


proc datasets library=mylib;
    delete college(pw=red);
run;
```

Using Passwords with Views

How the Level of Protection Differs from SAS Views

The levels of protection for views and stored programs differ slightly from other types of SAS files. Passwords affect the actual view definition or view descriptor as well as the underlying data. Unless otherwise noted, the term "view" can refer to any type of view. Also, the term "underlying data" refers to the data that is accessed by the view:

read
□ protects against reading the view's underlying data.

□ allows source statements to be written to the SAS log, using DESCRIBE.

□ allows replacement of the view.

write
□ protects the underlying data associated with a view by insisting that a write password is given.

□ allows source statements to be written to the SAS log using DESCRIBE

□ allows replacement of the view

alter
- protects against source statements being written to the SAS log, using DESCRIBE.
- protects against replacement of the view.

An important difference between views and other types of SAS files is that you need alter access to DESCRIBE an alter-protected view. For example, to use an alter-protected PROC SQL view in a DESCRIBE VIEW statement, you must specify the alter password.

In most DATA and PROC steps, the way you use password-protected views is consistent with the way you use other types of password-protected SAS files. For example, the following PROC PRINT prints a read-protected view:

```
proc print data=mylib.grade(read=green);
run;
```

Note: You might experience unexpected results when you place protection on a view if some type of protection has already been placed on the underlying data set. △

PROC SQL Views

Typically, when you create a PROC SQL view from a password-protected SAS data set, you specify the password in the FROM clause in the CREATE VIEW statement using a data set option. In this way, when you use the view later, you can access the underlying data without re-specifying the password. For example, the following statements create a PROC SQL view from a read-protected SAS data set, and drop a sensitive variable:

```
proc sql;
   create view mylib.emp as
      select * from mylib.employee(pw=orange drop=salary);
quit;
```

Note: If you create a PROC SQL view from password-protected SAS data sets without specifying their passwords, when you try to use the view you are prompted for the passwords of the SAS data sets named in the FROM clause. If you are running SAS in batch or noninteractive mode, you receive an error message. △

SAS/ACCESS Views

SAS/ACCESS software enables you to edit view descriptors and, in some interfaces, the underlying data. To prevent someone from editing or reading (browsing) the view descriptor, assign alter protection to the view. To prevent someone from updating the underlying data, assign write protection to the view. For more information, see the SAS/ACCESS documentation for your DBMS.

DATA Step Views

When you create a DATA step view using a password-protected SAS data set, specify the password in the view definition. In this way, when you use the view, you can access the underlying data without respecifying the password.

The following statements create a DATA step view using a password-protected SAS data set, and drop a sensitive variable:

```
data mylib.emp / view=mylib.emp;
   set mylib.employee(pw=orange drop=salary);
run;
```

Note that you can use the view without a password, but access to the underlying data requires a password. This is one way to protect a particular column of data. In the above example, **proc print data=mylib.emp;** will execute, but **proc print data=mylib.employee;** will fail without the password.

SAS Data File Encryption

SAS passwords restrict access to SAS data files within SAS, but SAS passwords cannot prevent SAS data files from being viewed at the operating environment system level or from being read by an external program.

Encryption provides security of your SAS data outside of SAS by writing to disk the encrypted data that represents the SAS data. The data is decrypted as it is read from the disk.

Encryption does not affect file access. However, SAS honors all host security mechanisms that control file access. You can use encryption and host security mechanisms together.

Encryption is implemented with the ENCRYPT= data set option. You can use the ENCRYPT= data set option only when you are creating a SAS data file. You must also assign a password when encrypting a file. At a minimum, you must specify the READ= or the PW= data set option at the same time you specify ENCRYPT=YES. Because passwords are used in the encryption method, you cannot change *any* password on an encrypted data set without re-creating the data set.

The following rules apply to data file encryption:

□ To copy an encrypted SAS data file, the output engine must support encryption. Otherwise, the data file is not copied.

□ Previous releases of SAS cannot use an encrypted SAS data file. Encrypted files work only in Release 6.11 or in later releases of SAS.

□ You cannot encrypt SAS data views, because they contain no data.

□ If the data file is encrypted, all associated indexes are also encrypted.

□ Encryption requires roughly the same amount of CPU resources as compression.

□ You cannot use PROC CPORT on encrypted SAS data files.

Example

This example creates an encrypted SAS data set:

```
data salary(encrypt=yes read=green);
   input name $ yrsal bonuspct;
   datalines;
Muriel    34567   3.2
Bjorn     74644   2.5
Freda     38755   4.1
Benny     29855   3.5
Agnetha   70998   4.1
;
```

To print this data set, specify the read password:

```
proc print data=salary(read=green);
run;
```

Passwords and Encryption with Generation Data Sets, Audit Trails, Indexes, and Copies

SAS extends password protection and encryption to other files associated with the original protected file. This includes generation data sets, indexes, audit trails, and copies. When accessing protected or encrypted generation data sets, indexes, audit trails, and copies of the original file, the same rules, syntax, and behavior for invoking the original password protected or encrypted files apply. Data views cannot have generation data sets, indexes, and audit trails.

SAS Engines

Definition of a SAS Engine   **597**
Specifying an Engine   **597**
How Engines Work with SAS Files   **598**
Engine Characteristics   **599**
    Read / Write Activity   **600**
    Access Patterns   **600**
    Levels of Locking   **600**
    Asynchronous I/O or Task Switching   **601**
    Indexing   **601**
About Library Engines   **602**
    Definition of a Library Engine   **602**
    Native Library Engines   **602**
        Definition of Native Library Engine   **602**
        Default Base SAS Engine   **602**
        Remote Engine   **602**
        SASESOCK Engine   **603**
        SAS Scalable Performance Data (SPD) Engine   **603**
        Sequential Engines   **603**
        Transport Engine   **603**
        V6 Compatibility Engine   **603**
    Interface Library Engines   **603**
Special-Purpose Engines   **604**
    Character Variable Padding (CVP) Engine   **604**
    SAS Metadata LIBNAME Engine   **605**
    SAS XML LIBNAME Engine   **605**

Definition of a SAS Engine

An *engine* is a component of SAS software that reads from or writes to a file. Each engine enables SAS to access files that are in a particular format. There are several types of engines.

Specifying an Engine

Usually you do not have to specify an engine. If you do not specify an engine, SAS automatically assigns one based on the contents of the SAS data library.

However, even though SAS will automatically assign an engine based on the library contents, it is more efficient for you to specify the engine. In some operating environments, in order to determine the contents of a library, SAS must perform extra processing steps by looking at all of the files in the directory until it has enough information to determine which engine to use.

For example, if you explicitly specify the engine name as in the following LIBNAME statement, SAS does not need to determine which engine to use:

```
libname mylib v9 'SAS-data-library';
```

In order to use some engines, you must specify the engine name. For example, in order to use engines like the XML engine or the metadata engine, you must explicitly specify the engine name and specify specific arguments and options for that engine. For example, the following LIBNAME statement specifies the XML engine in order to import or export an XML document:

```
libname myxml xml 'c:\Myfiles\XML\Myxmlfile.xml' xmltype=generic;
```

You can specify an engine name in the LIBNAME statement, the ENGINE= system option, and in the New Library window.

How Engines Work with SAS Files

The following figure shows how SAS data sets are accessed through an engine.

Figure 37.1   How SAS Data Sets Are Accessed

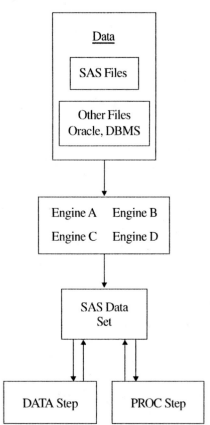

□ Your data is stored in files for which SAS provides an engine. When you specify a SAS data set name, the engine locates the appropriate file or files.

☐ The engine opens the file and obtains the descriptive information that is required by SAS, for example, which variables are available and what attributes they have, whether the file has special processing characteristics such as indexes or compressed observations, and whether other engines are required for processing. The engine uses this information to organize the data in the standard logical form for SAS processing.

☐ This standard form is called the *SAS data file*, which consists of the descriptor information and the data values organized into columns (variables) and rows (observations).

☐ SAS procedures and DATA step statements access and process the data only in its logical form. During processing, the engine executes whatever instructions are necessary to open and close physical files and to read and write data in appropriate formats.

Data that is accessed by an engine is organized into the SAS data set model, and in the same way, groups of files that are accessed by an engine are organized in the correct logical form for SAS processing. Once files are accessed as a SAS data library, you can use SAS utility windows and procedures to list their contents and to manage them. See Chapter 26, "SAS Data Libraries," on page 467 for more information about SAS data libraries. The following figure shows the relationship of engines to SAS data libraries.

Figure 37.2   Relationship of Engines to SAS Data Libraries

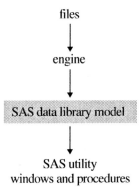

Engine Characteristics

The engine that is used to access a SAS data set determines its processing characteristics. Different statements and procedures require different processing characteristics. For example, the FSEDIT procedure requires the ability to update selected data values, and the POINT= option in the SET statement requires random access to observations as well as the ability to calculate observation numbers from record identifiers within the file.

The following figure describes the types of activities that engines regulate.

Figure 37.3 Activities That Engines Regulate

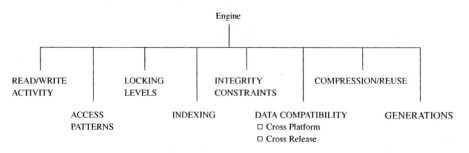

Read/Write Activity

An engine can

- □ limit read/write activity for a SAS data set to read-only

- □ fully support updating, deleting, renaming, or redefining the attributes of the data set and its variables

- □ support only some of these functions.

For example, the engines that process BMDP, OSIRIS, or SPSS files support read-only processing. Some engines that process SAS views permit SAS procedures to modify existing observations while others do not.

Access Patterns

SAS procedures and statements can read observations in SAS data sets in one of four general patterns:

sequential access
: processes observations one after the other, starting at the beginning of the file and continuing in sequence to the end of the file.

random access
: processes observations according to the value of some indicator variable without processing previous observations.

BY-group access
: groups and processes observations in order of the values of the variables that are specified in a BY statement.

multiple-pass
: performs two or more passes on data when required by SAS statements or procedures.

If a SAS statement or procedure tries to access a SAS data set whose engine does not support the required access pattern, SAS prints an appropriate error message in the SAS log.

Levels of Locking

Some features of SAS require that data sets support different levels at which update access is allowed. When a SAS data set can be opened concurrently by more than one SAS session or by more than one statement or procedure within a single session, the level of locking determines how many sessions, procedures, or statements can read and write to the file at the same time. For example, with the FSEDIT procedure, you can request two windows on the same SAS data set in one session. Some engines support this capability; others do not.

The levels that are supported are record level and member (data set) level. Member-level locking allows read access to many sessions, statements, or procedures, but restricts all other access to the SAS data set when a session, statement, or procedure acquires update access. Record-level locking allows concurrent read access and update access to the SAS data set by more than one session, statement, or procedure, but prevents concurrent update access to the same observation. Not all engines support both levels.

By default, SAS provides the greatest possible level of concurrent access, while guaranteeing the integrity of the data. In some cases, you might want to guarantee the integrity of your data by controlling the levels of update access yourself. Use the CNTLLEV= data set option to control levels of locking. CNTLLEV= allows locking at three levels:

☐ library

☐ data set

☐ observation.

Here are some situations in which you should consider using the CNTLLEV= data set option:

☐ your application controls access to the data, such as in SAS Component Language (SCL), SAS/IML software, or DATA step programming

☐ you access data through an interface engine that does not provide member-level control of the data.

For more information on the CNTLLEV= data set option, see *SAS Language Reference: Dictionary*.

You can also acquire an exclusive lock on an existing SAS file by issuing the LOCK global statement. After an exclusive lock is obtained, no other SAS session can read or write to the file until the lock is released. For more information on the LOCK statement, see *SAS Language Reference: Dictionary*.

Note: SAS products, such as SAS/ACCESS and SAS/SHARE, contain engines that support enhanced session management services and file locking capabilities. △

Asynchronous I/O or Task Switching

The Base SAS engine and other engines are able to process several different tasks concurrently. For example, you can enter statements into the Program Editor at the same time that PROC SORT is processing a large file. The reason that this is possible is that the engine allows task switching.

Task switching is possible because the engine architecture supports the ability to start one task before another task is finished, or to handle work "asynchronously." This ability allows for greater efficiencies during processing and often results in faster processing time. The ASYNCHIO system option controls this activity. For more information, see the ASYNCHIO system option in *SAS Language Reference: Dictionary*.

Indexing

A major processing feature of SAS is the ability to access observations by the values of key variables with indexes. See "Understanding SAS Indexes" on page 518 for more information on using indexes for SAS data files. Note that not all engines support indexing.

About Library Engines

Definition of a Library Engine

A *library engine* is an engine that accesses groups of files and puts them into a logical form for processing by SAS utility procedures and windows. A library engine also determines the fundamental processing characteristics of the library and presents lists of files for the library directory. Library engines can be classified as *native* or *interface*.

Native Library Engines

Definition of Native Library Engine

A *native library engine* is an engine that accesses forms of SAS files that are created and processed only by SAS.

Operating Environment Information: Engine availability is host dependent. See the SAS documentation for your operating environment. Also, specific products provide additional engines. △

Default Base SAS Engine

The default Base SAS engine writes SAS data libraries in disk format. The engine processes SAS 7, 8, and 9 files. If you do not specify an engine name when you are creating a new SAS data library, the Base SAS engine, which for SAS 9 is named V9, is automatically selected.

When accessing existing SAS data sets on disk, SAS assigns an engine based on the contents of the library. The Base SAS engine

- is the only engine that supports the full functionality of the SAS data set and the SAS data library.
- supports view engines.
- meets all the processing characteristics required by SAS statements and procedures.
- creates, maintains, and uses indexes.
- reads and writes compressed (variable-length) observations. SAS data sets created by other engines have fixed-length observations.
- assigns a permanent page size to data sets and temporarily assigns the number of buffers to be used when processing them.
- repairs damaged SAS data sets, indexes, and catalogs.
- enforces integrity constraints, creates backup files, and creates audit trails.

Note: SAS files created in SAS 7, 8, and 9 have the same file format. △

Remote Engine

The REMOTE engine is a SAS library engine for SAS/SHARE software. Using it enables a SAS session to access shared data by communicating with a SAS server. See *SAS/SHARE User's Guide* for more information.

SASESOCK Engine

The SASESOCK engine processes input to and output from TCP/IP ports instead of physical disk devices. The SASESOCK engine is required for SAS/CONNECT applications that implement MP CONNECT processing with the piping mechanisms. See *SAS/CONNECT User's Guide* for more information.

SAS Scalable Performance Data (SPD) Engine

The SAS Scalable Performance Data Engine (SPD Engine) provides parallel I/O, using multiple CPUs to read SAS data and deliver it rapidly to applications. The SPD Engine can process very large data sets because the data can span volumes but can be referenced as a single data set. The data in these data sets is also partitioned, allowing the data to be read in multiple threads per CPU. The SPD Engine is not intended to replace the default Base SAS engine for processing data sets that do not span volumes.

See *SAS Scalable Performance Data Engine: Reference* for details about this engine's capabilities.

Sequential Engines

A sequential engine processes SAS files on storage media that do not allow random access methods, for example, tape or sequential format on disk. A sequential engine requires less overhead than the default Base SAS engine because sequential access is simpler than random access. However, a sequential engine does not support some Base SAS features like indexing.

The sequential engine supports some file types for backup and restore purposes only, such as CATALOG, VIEW, and MDDB. ITEMSTOR is the only file type that the sequential engine does not support. DATA is the only file type that is useful for purposes other than backup and restore.

The following sequential engines are available:

V9TAPE (TAPE) processes SAS 7, 8, and 9 files.

V6TAPE processes SAS 6 SAS files without requiring you to convert the file to the SAS 9 format.

For more information, see "Sequential Data Libraries" on page 476.

Transport Engine

The XPORT engine processes transport files. The engine transforms a SAS file from its operating environment-specific internal representation to a transport file, which is a machine-independent format that can be used for all hosts. In order to create a transport file, explicitly specify the XPORT engine in the LIBNAME statement, then use the DATA step or COPY procedure.

For information about using the XPORT engine, see *Moving and Accessing SAS Files*.

V6 Compatibility Engine

The V6 compatibility engine processes SAS 6 files in SAS 9 without requiring you to convert the file to the SAS 9 format.

Interface Library Engines

An *interface library engine* is a SAS engine that accesses files formatted by other software. Interface library engines are not transparent to the user and must be explicitly specified, for example, in the LIBNAME statement.

The following are interface library engines:

SPSS

reads SPSS portable file format, which is analogous to the transport format for SAS data sets. The SPSS portable files (also called an export file) must be created by using the SPSS EXPORT command. Under z/OS, the SPSS engine also reads SPSS Release 9 files and SPSS-X files in either compressed or uncompressed format.

OSIRIS

reads OSIRIS data and dictionary files in EBCDIC format.

BMDP

reads BMDP save files.

In addition, a *view engine* is an interface library engine that is used by SAS/ACCESS software in order to retrieve data from files formatted by another vendor's software. These engines enable you to read and write data directly to and from files formatted by a database management system (DBMS), such as DB2 and ORACLE.

View engines enable you to use SAS procedures and statements in order to process data values stored in these files without the cost of converting and storing them in files formatted by SAS. Contact your SAS software representative for a list of the SAS/ ACCESS interfaces available at your site. For more information about SAS/ACCESS features, see Chapter 33, "About SAS/ACCESS Software," on page 569 and the SAS/ ACCESS documentation for your DBMS.

Operating Environment Information: The capabilities and support of these engines vary depending on your operating environment. See the SAS documentation for your operating environment for more complete information. △

Special-Purpose Engines

Character Variable Padding (CVP) Engine

The character variable padding (CVP) engine expands character variable lengths, using a specified expansion amount, so that character data truncation does not occur when a file requires transcoding. Character data truncation can occur when the number of bytes for a character in one encoding is different from the number of bytes for the same character in another encoding, such as when a single byte character set (SBCS) is transcoded to a double byte character set (DBCS) or a multibyte character set (MBCS).

The CVP engine is a read-only engine for SAS data files only. You can request character variable expansion by either of the following methods:

□ You can explicitly specify the CVP engine, for example, with the LIBNAME statement, and using the default expansion of 1.5 times the variable lengths.

□ You can implicitly specify the CVP engine with the LIBNAME statement options CVPBYTES= or CVPMULTIPLIER=. The options specify the expansion amount. In addition, you can use the CVPENGINE= option to specify the primary engine to use for processing the SAS file; the default is the default Base SAS engine.

For more information about using the CVP engine to avoid character data truncation and for details on the CVP engine options on the LIBNAME statement, see *SAS National Language Support (NLS): User's Guide.*

SAS Metadata LIBNAME Engine

The metadata engine accesses metadata that is stored on the SAS Metadata Server within a specific SAS Metadata Repository. The metadata is information about the structure and content of data, and about the applications that process and manipulate that data. The metadata contains details such as the location of the data and the SAS engine that is used to process the data.

The metadata engine works in a similar way to other SAS engines. That is, you execute a LIBNAME statement in order to assign a libref and specify an engine. You then use that libref throughout the SAS session where a libref is valid. However, instead of the libref being associated with the physical location of a SAS data library, the metadata libref is associated with specific metadata objects that are stored in a specific repository on the metadata server. The metadata objects define the SAS engine and options that are necessary to process a SAS data library and its members.

When you execute the LIBNAME statement for the metadata engine, the metadata engine retrieves information about the target SAS data library from the metadata. The metadata engine uses this information in order to construct a LIBNAME statement for the underlying engine and assigns it with the appropriate options. Then, when the metadata engine needs to access your data, the metadata engine uses the underlying engine to process the data.

You invoke the metadata engine by explicitly specifying the engine name META, along with specific arguments and options for the metadata engine, for example, in the LIBNAME statement or in the New Library window.

For information about how to use the metadata engine, see *SAS Metadata LIBNAME Engine User's Guide*.

SAS XML LIBNAME Engine

The SAS XML engine imports an XML document as one or more SAS data sets and exports a SAS data set as an XML document.

- □ The engine imports (reads from an input file) an external XML document by translating the XML markup into SAS proprietary format.
- □ The engine exports (writes to an output file) an XML document from a SAS data set by translating SAS proprietary format to XML markup.

To use the XML engine, you must explicitly specify XML as the engine name, along with specific arguments and options, for example, in the LIBNAME statement or in the New Library window.

For information about how to use the XML engine, see *SAS XML LIBNAME Engine User's Guide*.

SAS File Management

Improving Performance of SAS Applications **607**
Moving SAS Files Between Operating Environments **607**
Repairing Damaged SAS Files **607**
    Recovering SAS Data Files **608**
    Recovering Indexes **609**
    Recovering Catalogs **610**

Improving Performance of SAS Applications

SAS offers tools to control the use of memory and other computer resources. Most SAS applications will run efficiently in your operating environment without using these features. However, if you develop applications under the following circumstances, you may want to experiment with tuning performance:

- You work with large data sets.
- You create production jobs that run repeatedly.
- You are responsible for establishing performance guidelines for a data center.
- You do interactive queries on large SAS data sets using SAS/FSP software.

For information on improving performance, see Chapter 13, "Optimizing System Performance," on page 213.

Moving SAS Files Between Operating Environments

The procedures for moving SAS files from one operating environment to another vary according to your operating environment, the member type and version of the SAS files you want to move, and the methods you have available for moving the files.

For details on this subject, see *Moving and Accessing SAS Files.*

Repairing Damaged SAS Files

The Base SAS engine detects possible damage to SAS data files (including indexes, integrity constraints, and the audit file) and SAS catalogs and provides a means for repairing some of the damage. If one of the following events occurs while you are updating a SAS file, SAS can recover the file and repair some of the damage:

- A system failure occurs while the data file or catalog is being updated.

□ Damage occurs to the storage device where a data file resides. In this case, you can restore the damaged data file, the index, and the audit file from a backup device.

□ The disk where the data file (including the index file and audit file) or catalog is stored becomes full before the file is completely written to it.

□ An input/output error occurs while writing to the data file, index file, audit file, or catalog.

When the failure occurs, the observations or records that were not written to the data file or catalog are lost and some of the information about where values are stored is inconsistent. The next time SAS reads the file, it recognizes that the file's contents are damaged and repairs it to the extent possible in accordance with the setting for the DLDMGACTION= data set option or system option, unless the data set is truncated. In this case, use the REPAIR statement to restore the data set.

Note: SAS is unable to repair or recover a view (a DATA step view, an SQL view, or a SAS/ACCESS view) or a stored compiled DATA step program. If a SAS file of type VIEW or PROGRAM is damaged, you must recreate it. △

Note: If the audit file for a SAS data file becomes damaged, you will not be able to process the data file until you terminate the audit trail. Then, you can initiate a new audit file or process the data file without one. △

Recovering SAS Data Files

To determine the type of action SAS will take when it tries to open a SAS data file that is damaged, set the DLDMGACTION= data set option or system option. That is, when a data file is detected as damaged, SAS will automatically respond based on your specification as follows:

DLDMGACTION=FAIL
tells SAS to stop the step without a prompt and issue an error message to the log indicating that the requested file is damaged. This specification gives the application control over the repair decision and provides awareness that a problem occurred.

To recover the damaged data file, you can issue the REPAIR statement in PROC DATASETS, which is documented in *Base SAS Procedures Guide*.

DLDMGACTION=ABORT
tells SAS to terminate the step, issue an error message to the log indicating that the request file is damaged, and abort the SAS session.

DLDMGACTION=REPAIR
tells SAS to automatically repair the file and rebuild indexes, integrity constraints, and the audit file as well. If the repair is successful, a message is issued to the log indicating that the open and repair were successful. If the repair is unsuccessful, processing stops without a prompt and an error message is issued to the log indicating the requested file is damaged.

Note: If the data file is large, the time needed to repair it can be long. △

DLDMGACTION=PROMPT
tells SAS to provide the same behavior that exists in Version 6 for both interactive mode and batch mode. For interactive mode, SAS displays a requestor window that asks you to select the FAIL, ABORT, or REPAIR action. For batch mode, the files fail to open.

For a data file, the date and time of the last repair and a count of the total number of repairs is automatically maintained. To display the damage log, use PROC CONTENTS as shown below:

```
proc contents data=sasuser.census;
run;
```

Output 38.1   Output of CONTENTS Procedure

```
                        The CONTENTS Procedure

    Data Set Name       SASUSER.CENSUS              Observations         27
    Member Type         DATA                        Variables            4
    Engine              V9                          Indexes              0
    Created             10:06 Wednesday, January 22, 2003  Observation Length   32
    Last Modified       10:06 Wednesday, January 22, 2003  Deleted Observations 0
    Protection                                      Compressed           NO
    Data Set Type                                   Sorted               NO
    Label
    Data Representation WINDOWS
    Encoding            wlatin1  Western (Windows)


                      Engine/Host Dependent Information

      Data Set Page Size         4096
      Number of Data Set Pages   1
      First Data Page            1
      Max Obs per Page           126
      Obs in First Data Page     27
      Number of Data Set Repairs 0
      File Name                  c:\winnt\profiles\sasxxx\sasuser\census.sas7bdat
      Release Created            9.0000A0
      Host Created               WIN_NT


                    Alphabetic List of Variables and Attributes

              #     Variable      Type    Len

              2     CrimeRate     Num      8
              1     Density       Num      8
              4     PostalCode    Char     2
```

Recovering Indexes

In addition to the failures listed earlier, you can damage the indexes for SAS data files by using an operating environment command to delete, copy, or rename a SAS data file, but not its associated index file. The index is repaired similarly to the DLDMGACTION= option as described for SAS data files, or you can use the REPAIR statement in PROC DATASETS to rebuild composite and simple indexes that were damaged.

You cannot use the REPAIR statement to recover indexes that were deleted by one of the following actions:

☐ copying a SAS data file by some means other than PROC COPY or PROC DATASETS, for example, using a DATA step

☐ using the FORCE option in the SORT procedure to write over the original data file.

In the above cases, the index must be rebuilt explicitly using the PROC DATASETS INDEX CREATE statement.

Recovering Catalogs

To determine the type of action that SAS will take when it tries to open a SAS catalog that is damaged, set the DLDMGACTION= data set option or system option. Then when a catalog is detected as damaged, SAS will automatically respond based on your specification.

Note: There are two types of catalog damage:

□ *localized damage* is caused by a disk condition, which results in some data in memory not being flushed to disk. The catalog entries that are currently open for update are marked as damaged. Each damaged entry is checked to determine if all the records can be read without error.

□ *severe damage* is caused by a severe I/O error. The entire catalog is marked as damaged.

△

DLDMGACTION=FAIL
> tells SAS to stop the step without a prompt and issue an error message to the log indicating that the requested file is damaged. This specification gives the application control over the repair decision and provides awareness that a problem occurred.
>
> To recover the damaged catalog, you can issue the REPAIR statement in PROC DATASETS, which is documented in the *SAS Procedures Guide*. Note that when you use the REPAIR statement to restore a catalog, you receive a warning for entries that have possible damage. Entries that have been restored may not include updates that were not written to disk before the damage occurred.

DLDMGACTION=ABORT
> tells SAS to terminate the step, issue an error message to the log indicating that the requested file is damaged, and abort the SAS session.

DLDMGACTION=REPAIR
> for localized damage, tells SAS to automatically check the catalog to see which entries are damaged. If there is an error reading an entry, the entry is copied. If an error occurs during the copy process, then the entry is automatically deleted. For severe damage, the entire catalog is copied to a new catalog.

DLDMGACTION=PROMPT
> for localized damage, tells SAS to provide the same behavior that exists in Version 6 for both interactive mode and batch mode. For interactive mode, SAS displays a requestor window that asks you to select the FAIL, ABORT, or REPAIR action. For batch mode, the files fail to open. For severe damage, the entire catalog is copied to a new catalog.

Unlike data files, a damaged log is not maintained for a catalog.

CHAPTER

39

External Files

Definition of External Files   **611**
Referencing External Files Directly   **612**
Referencing External Files Indirectly   **612**
Referencing Many External Files Efficiently   **613**
Referencing External Files with Other Access Methods   **614**
Working with External Files   **615**
    Reading External Files   **615**
    Writing to External Files   **615**
    Processing External Files   **616**

Definition of External Files

external files

are files that are managed and maintained by your operating system, not by SAS. They contain data or text or are files in which you want to store data or text. They can also be SAS catalogs or output devices. Every SAS job creates at least one external file, the SAS log. Most SAS jobs create external files in the form of procedure output or output created by a DATA step.

External files used in a SAS session can store input for your SAS job as:

- records of raw data that you want to use as input to a DATA step
- SAS programming statements that you want to submit to the system for execution.

External files can also store output from your SAS job as:

- a SAS log (a record of your SAS job)
- a report written by a DATA step.
- procedure output created by SAS procedures, including regular list output, and, beginning in Version 7, HTML and PostScript output from the Output Delivery System (ODS).

The PRINTTO procedure also enables you to direct procedure output to an external file. For more information, see *Base SAS Procedures Guide*. See Chapter 10, "SAS Output," on page 161 for more information about ODS.

Note: Database management system (DBMS) files are a special category of files that can be read with SAS/ACCESS software. For more information on DBMS files, see Chapter 33, "About SAS/ACCESS Software," on page 569 and the SAS/ACCESS documentation for your DBMS. △

Operating Environment Information: Using external files with your SAS jobs entails significant operating-environment-specific information. Refer to the SAS documentation for your operating environment for more information. △

Referencing External Files Directly

To reference a file directly in a SAS statement or command, specify in quotation marks its physical name, which is the name by which the operating environment recognizes it, as shown in the following table:

Table 39.1   Referencing External Files Directly

External File Task	Tool	Example

Specify the file that contains input data.	INFILE	```data weight;```
		``` infile 'input-file';```
		``` input idno $ week1 week16;```
		``` loss=week1-week16;```

Identify the file that the PUT statement writes to.	FILE	``` file 'output-file';```
		``` if loss ge 5 and loss le 9 then```
		``` put idno loss 'AWARD STATUS=3';```
		``` else if loss ge 10 and loss le 14 then```
		``` put idno loss 'AWARD STATUS=2';```
		``` else if loss ge 15 then```
		``` put idno loss 'AWARD STATUS=1';```
		``` run;```

Bring statements or raw data from another file into your SAS job and execute them.	%INCLUDE	```%include 'source-file';```

Referencing External Files Indirectly

If you want to reference a file in only one place in a program so that you can easily change it for another job or a later run, you can reference a filename indirectly. Use a FILENAME statement, the FILENAME function, or an appropriate operating system command to assign a *fileref* or nickname, to a file.* Note that you can assign a fileref to a SAS catalog that is an external file, or to an output device, as shown in the following table.

---

*   In some operating environments, you can also use the command '&' to assign a fileref.

Table 39.2 Referencing External Files Indirectly

External File Task	Tool	Example
Assign a fileref to a file that contains input data.	FILENAME	`filename mydata 'input-file';`
Assign a fileref to a file for output data.	FILENAME	`filename myreport 'output-file';`
Assign a fileref to a file that contains program statements.	FILENAME	`filename mypgm 'source-file';`
Assign a fileref to an output device.	FILENAME	`filename myprinter <device-type> <host-options>;`
Specify the file that contains input data.	INFILE	```data weight; infile mydata; input idno $ week1 week16; loss=week1-week16;```
Specify the file that the PUT statement writes to.	FILE	```file myreport; if loss ge 5 and loss le 9 then put idno loss 'AWARD STATUS=3'; else if loss ge 10 and loss le 14 then put idno loss 'AWARD STATUS=2'; else if loss ge 15 then put idno loss 'AWARD STATUS=1'; run;```
Bring statements or raw data from another file into your SAS job and execute them.	%INCLUDE	`%include mypgm;`

Referencing Many External Files Efficiently

When you use many files from a single aggregate storage location, such as a directory or partitioned data set (PDS or MACLIB), you can use a single fileref, followed by a filename enclosed in parentheses, to access the individual files. This saves time by eliminating the need to type a long file storage location name repeatedly. It also makes changing the program easier later if you change the file storage location. The following table shows an example of assigning a fileref to an aggregate storage location:

Table 39.3   Referencing Many Files Efficiently

External File Task	Tool	Example
Assign a fileref to aggregate storage location.	FILENAME	`filename mydir 'directory-or-PDS-name';`
Specify the file that contains input data.	INFILE	```data weight; infile mydir(qrt1.data); input idno $ week1 week16; loss=week1-week16;```
Specify the file that the PUT statement writes to.[1]	FILE	```file mydir(awards); if loss ge 5 then put idno loss 'AWARD STATUS=3'; else if loss ge 10 then put idno loss 'AWARD STATUS=2'; else if loss ge 15 then put idno loss 'AWARD STATUS=1'; run;```
Bring statements or raw data from another file into your SAS job and execute them.	%INCLUDE	`%include mydir(whole.program);`

1   SAS creates a file that is named with the appropriate extension for your operating environment.

Referencing External Files with Other Access Methods

You can assign filerefs to external files that you access with the following FILENAME access methods:

□ CATALOG

□ FTP

□ TCP/IP SOCKET

□ URL.

Examples of how to use each method are shown in the following table:

Table 39.4   Referencing External Files with Other Access Methods

External File Task	Tool	Example
Assign a fileref to a SAS catalog that is an aggregate storage location.	FILENAME with CATALOG specifier	`filename mycat catalog 'catalog' <catalog-options>;`
Assign a fileref to an external file accessed with FTP.	FILENAME with FTP specifier	`filename myfile FTP 'external-file'     <ftp-options>;`

External File Task	Tool	Example

Assign a fileref to an external file accessed by TCP/IP SOCKET in either client or server mode.	FILENAME with SOCKET specifier	`filename myfile SOCKET 'hostname: portno' <tcpip-options>;`
		or
		`filename myfile SOCKET ':portno' SERVER <tcpip-options>;`

Assign a fileref to an external file accessed by URL.	FILENAME with URL specifier	`filename myfile URL 'external-file' <url-options>;`

See *SAS Language Reference: Dictionary* for detailed information about each of these statements.

Working with External Files

Reading External Files

The primary reason for reading an external file in a SAS job is to create a SAS data set from raw data. This topic is covered in Chapter 21, "Reading Raw Data," on page 357.

Writing to External Files

You can write to an external file by using:

□ a SAS DATA step

□ the External File Interface (EFI)

□ the Export Wizard.

When you use a DATA step to write a customized report, you write it to an external file. In its simplest form, a DATA step that writes a report looks like this:

```
data _null_;
   set budget;
   file 'your-file-name';
   put variables-and-text;
run;
```

For examples of writing reports with a DATA step, see Chapter 21, "Reading Raw Data," on page 357.

If your operating environment supports a graphical user interface, you can use the EFI or the Export Wizard to write to an external file. The EFI is a point-and-click graphical interface that you can use to read and write data that is not in SAS internal format. By using the EFI, you can read data from a SAS data set and write it to an external file, and you can read data from an external file and write it to a SAS data set. See the SAS online Help for more information on the EFI.

The Export Wizard guides you through the steps to read data from a SAS data set and write it to an external file. As a wizard, it is a series of windows that present simple choices to guide you through the process. See the SAS online Help for more information on the wizard.

Processing External Files

When reading data from or to a file, you can also use a DATA step to:

□ copy only parts of each record to another file

□ copy a file and add fields to each record

□ process multiple files in the same way in a single DATA step

□ create a subset of a file

□ update an external file in place

□ write data to a file that can be read in different computer environments

□ correct errors in a file at the bit level.

For examples of using a DATA step to process external files, see Chapter 21, "Reading Raw Data," on page 357.

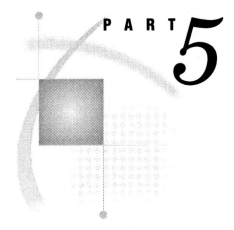

P A R T *5*

Industry Protocols Used in SAS

Chapter **40**. . . . . . . .The SMTP E-Mail Interface *619*

Chapter **41**. . . . . . . .Universal Unique Identifiers *621*

CHAPTER

40

The SMTP E-Mail Interface

Sending E-Mail through SMTP   **619**
System Options That Control SMTP E-Mail   **619**
Statements That Control SMTP E-mail   **620**
    FILENAME STATEMENT   **620**
    FILE and PUT Statements   **620**

Sending E-Mail through SMTP

You can send electronic mail programmatically from SAS using the SMTP (Simple Mail Transfer Protocol) e-mail interface. SMTP is available for all operating environments in which SAS runs. To send SMTP e-mail with SAS e-mail support, you must have an intranet or internet connection that supports SMTP. For more information on sending e-mail from SAS, refer to the SAS documentation for your operating environment.

System Options That Control SMTP E-Mail

Several SAS system options control SMTP e-mail. Depending on your operating environment and whether the SMTP e-mail interface is supported at your site, you might need to specify these options at start up or in your SAS configuration file.

Operating Environment Information: To determine the default e-mail interface for your operating environment and to determine the correct syntax for setting system options, refer to the SAS documentation for your operating environment. △

The EMAILSYS system option specifies which email system to use for sending electronic mail from within SAS. For more information about the EMAILSYS system option, refer to the SAS documentation for your operating environment.

The following system options are only specified when the SMTP e-mail interface is supported at your site:

EMAILAUTHPROTOCOL=
    specifies the authentication protocol for SMTP E-mail. For more information, see the "EMAILAUTHPROTOCOL= System Option" in *SAS Language Reference: Dictionary*.

EMAILHOST
    specifies the SMTP server that supports e-mail access for your site. For more information, see the "EMAILHOST System Option" in *SAS Language Reference: Dictionary*.

EMAILPORT
> specifies the port to which the SMTP server is attached. For more information, see the "EMAILPORT System Option" in *SAS Language Reference: Dictionary*.

The following system options are specified with other e-mail systems, as well as SMTP:

EMAILID=
> specifies the identity of the individual sending e-mail from within SAS. For more information, see the "EMAILID= System Option" in *SAS Language Reference: Dictionary*.

EMAILPW=
> specifies your e-mail login password. For more information, see the "EMAILPW= System Option" in *SAS Language Reference: Dictionary*.

Statements That Control SMTP E-mail

FILENAME STATEMENT

In the FILENAME statement, the EMAIL (SMTP) access method enables you to send e-mail programmatically from SAS using the SMTP e-mail interface. For more information, see the "FILENAME Statement, EMAIL (SMTP) Access Method" in *SAS Language Reference: Dictionary*.

FILE and PUT Statements

You can specify e-mail options in the FILE statement. E-mail options that you specify in the FILE statement override any corresponding e-mail options that you specified in the FILENAME statement.

In the DATA step, after using the FILE statement to define your e-mail fileref as the output destination, use PUT statements to define the body of the message. The PUT statement directives override any other e-mail options in the FILE and FILENAME statements.

CHAPTER
41

Universal Unique Identifiers

Universal Unique Identifiers and the Object Spawner   **621**
    What Is a Universal Unique Identifier?   **621**
    What Is the Object Spawner?   **621**
    Defining the UUID Generator Daemon   **621**
    Installing the UUID Generator Daemon   **622**
Using SAS Language Elements to Assign UUIDs   **623**
    UUIDGEN Function   **623**
    UUIDCOUNT= System Option   **623**
    UUIDGENDHOST System Option   **623**

Universal Unique Identifiers and the Object Spawner

What Is a Universal Unique Identifier?

A Universal Unique Identifier (UUID) is a 128-bit identifier that consists of date and time information, and the IEEE node address of a host. UUIDs are useful when objects such as rows or other components of a SAS application must be uniquely identified. For example, if SAS is running as a server and is distributing objects to several clients concurrently, you can associate a UUID with each object to ensure that a particular client and SAS are referencing the same object.

What Is the Object Spawner?

The object spawner is a program that runs on the server and listens for requests. When a request is received, the object spawner accepts the connection and performs the action that is associated with the port or service on which the connection was made. The object spawner can be configured to be a UUID Generator Daemon (UUIDGEND), which creates UUIDs for the requesting program. Currently, SAS can generate UUIDs only in the Windows operating environment. UUIDGEND generates UUIDs for SAS sessions that execute on hosts that do not have native UUID generation support.

Defining the UUID Generator Daemon

The definition of UUIDGEND is contained in a setup configuration file that you specify when you invoke the object spawner. This configuration file identifies the port that listens for UUID requests, and, in operating environments other than Windows, the configuration file also identifies the UUID node. If you install UUIDGEND in an

operating environment other than Windows, contact SAS Technical Support (http://
support.sas.com/techsup/contact/index.htm) to obtain a UUID node. The UUID node
must be unique for each UUIDGEND installation in order for UUIDGEND to guarantee
truly unique UUIDs.

Here is an example of a UUIDGEND setup configuration file for an operating
environment other than Windows:

```
#
##  Define our UUID Generator Daemon.  Since this UUIDGEND is
##  executing on a UNIX host, we contacted SAS Technical
##  Support to get the specified sasUUIDNode.
#
dn: sasSpawnercn=UUIDGEND,sascomponent=sasServer,cn=SAS,o=ABC Inc,c=US
objectClass: sasSpawner
sasSpawnercn: UUIDGEND
sasDomainName: unx.abc.com
sasMachineDNSName: medium.unx.abc.com
sasOperatorPassword: myPassword
sasOperatorPort: 6340
sasUUIDNode: 0123456789ab
sasUUIDPort: 6341
description: SAS Session UUID Generator Daemon on UNIX
```

Here is an example of a UUIDGEND setup configuration file for Windows:

```
#
##  Define our UUID Generator Daemon.  Since this UUIDGEND is
##  executing in a Windows NT operating environment, we do not need to specify
##  the sasUUIDNode.
#
dn: sasSpawnercn=UUIDGEND,sascomponent=sasServer,cn=SAS,o=ABC Inc,
c=US
objectClass: sasSpawner
sasSpawnercn: UUIDGEND
sasDomainName: wnt.abc.com
sasMachineDNSName: little.wnt.abc.com
sasOperatorPassword: myPassword
sasOperatorPort: 6340
sasUUIDPort: 6341
description: SAS Session UUID Generator Daemon on NT
```

Installing the UUID Generator Daemon

When you have created the setup configuration file, you can install UUIDGEND by
starting the object spawner program (objspawn), and specifying the setup configuration
file with the following syntax:

objspawn -configFile *filename*

The configFile option may be abbreviated as -cf.

filename specifies a fully qualified path to the UUIDGEND setup configuration
file. Enclose pathnames that contain embedded blanks in single or double
quotation marks. On Windows, enclose pathnames that contain embedded blanks
in double quotation marks. On z/OS, specify the configuration file as follows:

//dsn:*myid.objspawn*.log for MVS files.
//hfs:*filename*.ext for OpenEdition files.

On Windows, the objspawn.exe file is installed in the core\sasext folder in your installed SAS folder.

On UNIX, the objspawn file is installed in the utilities/bin directory in your installed SAS directory.

In the Alpha/VMS operating environment, the OBJSPAWN_STARTUP.COM file executes the OBJSPAWN.COM file as a detached process. The OBJSPAWN.COM file runs the object spawner. The OBJSPAWN.COM file also includes other commands that your site might need in order to run the appropriate version of the spawner, to set the display node, to define a process level logical name that points to a template DCL file (OBJSPAWN_TEMPLATE.COM), and to perform any other necessary actions before the object spawner is started. The OBJSPAWN_TEMPLATE.COM file performs setup that is needed in order for the client process to execute. The object spawner first checks to see if the logical name SAS$OBJSPAWN_TEMPLATE is defined. If it is, the commands in the template file are executed as part of the command sequence used when starting the client session. You do not have to define the logical name.

Using SAS Language Elements to Assign UUIDs

If your SAS application executes on a platform other than Windows and you have installed UUIDGEND, you can use the following to assign UUIDs:

☐ UUIDGEN function
☐ UUIDCOUNT= system option
☐ UUIDGENDHOST systems option.

UUIDGEN Function

The UUIDGEN function returns a UUID for each cell. For more information, see the "UUIDGEN Function" in *SAS Language Reference: Dictionary*.

UUIDCOUNT= System Option

The UUIDCOUNT= system option specifies the number of UUIDs to acquire each time the UUID Generator Daemon is used. For more information, see the "UUIDCOUNT= System Option" in *SAS Language Reference: Dictionary*.

UUIDGENDHOST System Option

The UUIDGENDHOST system option identifies the operating environment and the port of the UUID Generator Daemon. For more information, see the "UUIDGENDHOST System Option" in *SAS Language Reference: Dictionary*.

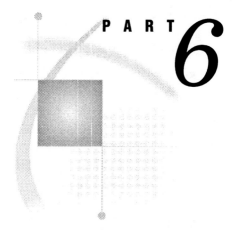

PART *6*

Appendices

Appendix 1 . . . . **Recommended Reading**   *627*

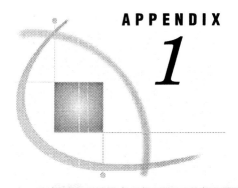

APPENDIX

1

Recommended Reading

Recommended Reading

Here is the recommended reading list for this title:

☐ *SAS Language Reference: Dictionary*

☐ *Base SAS Procedures Guide*

☐ *SAS Output Delivery System: User's Guide*

☐ *SAS National Language Support (NLS): User's Guide*

☐ *SAS Metadata LIBNAME Engine User's Guide*

☐ *SAS Scalable Performance Data Engine: Reference*

☐ *SAS XML LIBNAME Engine User's Guide*

The recommended reading list from *Books By Users* includes:

☐ *The Little SAS Book: A Primer, Revised Second Edition*

☐ *Output Delivery System: The Basics*

☐ *SAS Programming by Example*

For a complete list of SAS publications, see the current *SAS Publishing Catalog*. To order the most current publications or to receive a free copy of the catalog, contact a SAS representative at

SAS Publishing Sales
SAS Campus Drive
Cary, NC 27513
Telephone: (800) 727-3228*
Fax: (919) 677-8166
E-mail: **sasbook@sas.com**
Web address: **support.sas.com/pubs**
* For other SAS Institute business, call (919) 677-8000.

Customers outside the United States should contact their local SAS office.

Index

A

access descriptors 546, 572
ACCESS procedure
  interface view engine and 572
ALL name lists 88
alter protection 588, 593
AND operator 121
appending files 404
Application Response Measurement
  See ARM
applications
  ARM 226
  ARM and performance of 227
  ARM API objects 58
  peformance of 607
  threaded processing 224
arithmetic operators 118, 201
ARM 215, 225
  examples 231
  how it works 227
  need for 225
  performance and 227
  terminology 226
ARM agent 226
ARM API 226
ARM API function calls 56, 228
ARM API objects 58
ARM interface 226, 228
ARM log 226, 230
  internal SAS processing statistics 231
  post processing 234
ARM macro variables 57
ARM macros 55, 56, 226, 229
  ARM API function calls and 56
  %ARMEND 57
  %ARMGTID 56
  %ARMINIT 56
  %ARMSTOP 57
  %ARMSTRT 57
  %ARMUPDT 57
  complex call schemes 61
  conditional execution 66
  correlators in 64
  enabling execution 65
  enabling execution with SCL 66
  ID management with 58
  logging performance statistics 233
  macro variables with 57
  post-processing 68

setting macro environment 67
user metrics in 63
variables with 57
ARM subsystem 226
ARM system options 226, 228
  logging performance statistics 233
ARMAGENT= system option 228
%ARMCONV macro 68, 230
ARM_END function call 229
%ARMEND macro 57, 230
_ARMEXEC macro variable 65
ARM_GETID function call 229
%ARMGTID macro 56, 230
ARM_INIT function call 228
%ARMINIT macro 56, 229
%ARMJOIN macro 69, 230
ARMLOC= system option 228
%ARMPROC macro 68, 230
ARM_START function call 229
ARM_STOP function call 229
%ARMSTOP macro 57, 230
%ARMSTRT macro 57, 230
ARMSUBSYS= system option 228
ARM_UPDATE function call 229
%ARMUPDT macro 230
%ARMUPTD macro 57
array bounds 459
  determining 460
  HBOUND function 460
  HBOUND function vs. DIM function 460
  identifying upper and lower bounds 459
  LBOUND function 460
  two-dimensional arrays 460
array processing 449
  definition 450
  examples 461
  terminology 449
array reference
  definition 450
ARRAY statement 451
arrays
  action on all numeric variables 464
  assigning initial values to elements 462
  character variables in 461
  conceptual view of 450
  defining 451, 455
  defining quickly 456
  definition 449
  determining number of elements 456
  DO loops 453

DO loops for selected elements 453
DO UNTIL expressions 456
DO WHILE expressions 456
grouping variables, simple array 452
multidimensional 450, 457
one-dimensional 450
referencing 451
referencing, rules for 455
selecting current variable 453
temporary 463
two-dimensional 451
variable lists 456
assignment statement
  creating variables 81
asynchronous I/O 601
_AT*_ variables 491
ATOPCODE values 491
ATTRIB statement
  creating variables 83
  specifying formats 29
  specifying informats 31
audit trails 491
  capturing rejected observations 497
  considerations 493
  data file update 496
  definition 491
  description 491
  encryption with 595
  examples 495
  fast-append feature and 493
  in shared environment 493
  initiating 494, 495
  passwords with 595
  performance 493
  preservation by other operations 493
  programming considerations 493
  reading 494
  resuming 494
  status of 494
  suspending 494
  terminating 494
audit variables 491
autoexec files 9
automatic naming convention 485
automatic numeric-character conversion 116
automatic variables 85

B

base number   91
Base SAS
  concepts   10
  DATA step concepts   10
  overview   4
  SAS concepts   10
  SAS files concepts   10
Base SAS engine   602
base version   499
batch mode   9
  Universal Printing   274
BETWEEN-AND operator   203
bias   92
big endian platforms   32
binary data   369
binary informats   370
bit masks   114
bit testing constants   114
BMDP engine   604
Boolean numeric expressions   122
Boolean operators   121
buffers
  index requirements for   523
BUFNO= system option
  I/O optimization and   218
BUFSIZE= system option
  I/O optimization and   218
BY-group access
  engines   600
BY-group processing   195
  BY groups   377
  data grouped by formatted values   385
  data not in alphabetic or numeric order   384
  DATA step identification of BY groups   380
  definition   375
  in DATA step   383
  indexing for   379
  invoking   378
  preprocessing input data   379
  preprocessing needs   379
  sorting observations for   379
  syntax   376
  terminology   375
BY groups   377
  definition   376
  multiple BY variables   378
  processing conditionally   383
  processing observations in   380
  single BY variable   377
BY processing
  indexes for   532
  indexes for, with WHERE processing   533
BY values
  definition   376
BY variables
  definition   375
byte ordering   32

C

CALL routines   39
  PRX call routines   45
  random-number routines   43
  RX functions and CALL routines   45

syntax   40
catalog concatenation   564
  definition   564
  explicit   565
  implicit   564
  rules for   567
catalog directory windows   562
CATALOG window   562
catalogs   4, 561
  accessing information in   562
  catalog concatenation   564
  management tools   562
  names of   561
  Profile catalog   563
  recovering   610
  remote access and   12
CATCACHE= system option
  I/O optimization and   218
CEDA (Cross-Environment Data Access)   575
  advantages of   576
  alternatives to   580
  compatibility across environments   578
  creating files in foreign data representation   581
  examples   581
  file processing with   576, 578
  output processing   577
  restrictions   577
  update processing   579
cells
  editing values   320
character comparisons   120
  IN operator in   121
character constants   111
  compared with character variables   111
  in hexadecimal notation   112
  quotation marks with   111
character data
  reading raw data   360
CHARACTER name lists   88
character values   359
character variable padding (CVP) engine   604
character variables   78, 79
  compared with character constants   111
  converting to numeric variables   84
  in arrays   461
  missing values   104
characteristic (binary integer)   92
collating sequence
  character comparisons and   120
color values
  registry and   242
column-binary data   371
column-binary data storage   371, 372
column input   364
columns
  labeling   313
  moving   313
  sorting values   315
combining data sets   389, 391
  access methods   394
  concatenating   395, 402
  data relationships   391
  direct access   394
  error checking   400
  interleaving   395, 405
  match-merging   397, 416

methods for   395, 402
  one-to-one merging   396, 411
  one-to-one reading   396, 409
  preparing data sets   400
  procedures for   398
  sequential access   394
  statements for   398
  tools for   389, 398
  updating   397, 420
comparison operators   118, 201
compatibility
  See version compatibility
compilation phase (DATA step)   332
composite indexes   520
compound expressions   110
  order of evaluation   124
compound optimization   521, 528
COMPRESS= system option
  I/O optimization and   218
compressing data files   537
  definition of compression   537
  disabling compression requests   538
  requesting compression   538
concatenating catalogs   564
concatenating data libraries   471
concatenating data sets   395, 402
  efficiency   405
  examples   403
concatenation operator   123, 206
configuration files   9
console log   162
constants   110
  bit testing constants   114
  blank space in   115
  character constants   111
  date constants   113
  datetime constants   113
  in WHERE expressions   200
  misinterpretation of   115
  numeric constants   112
  time constants   113
constructors
  initializing hash objects   439
CONTAINS operator   203
copies
  encryption with   595
  passwords with   595
correlators
  in ARM macros   64
CPU-bound applications   224
CPU performance   220
  increasing memory   220
  parallel processing and   221
  reducing I/O   220
  search time for executables   220
  storing compiled programs   220
  variable lengths and   221
CPU time   214
Cross-Environment Data Access
  See CEDA (Cross-Environment Data Access)
customized output   189
  for output objects   191
CVP engine   604

D

D-floating format 93
damaged files 607
data components
　definition 178
data conversions 38
data errors 154
　format modifiers for reporting 156
data files 5, 481, 489
　as DATA step output 13
　audit trails 491
　compressing 537
　creating with DATA step 342
　definition 489
　encryption 594
　generation data sets 499
　indexes 518
　input to SAS programs 12
　integrity constraints 505
　recovering 608
　vs. data views 489
data libraries 4, 467
　accessing permanent files without libref 478
　copying files 307
　definition 467
　file types in 468
　library concatenation 471
　library directories 478
　library engines 469
　library names 469
　librefs 469
　logical names 469
　management tools 477
　managing with operating environment com-
　　mands 479
　permanent 473
　physical names 469
　SAS system libraries 474
　sequential libraries 476
　temporary 473
　utilities for 477
　viewing files 307
data relationships 391
　many-to-many 393
　many-to-one 392
　one-to-many 392
　one-to-one 392
data set names 482
　how and when assigned 483
　one-level 484
　parts of 483
　two-level 484
　where to use 482
data set options 25
　compared with system options 76
　controlling index usage 531
　interaction with system options 26, 75
　SAS/ACCESS librefs with 570
　syntax 25
　with input data sets 25
　with output data sets 25
data sets 5, 481
　assigning passwords to 589
　automatic naming convention 485
　calculating size 221
　combining 389, 391

concatenating 395, 402
copying to Excel 312
copying with Explorer window 293
creating for I/O optimization 217
default data sets 485
definition 481
descriptor information for 481
editing 486
generation data sets 499
importing data into 321
input to SAS programs 12
interleaving 395, 405
labeling columns 313
management tools 485
match-merging 397, 416
missing values when reading 105
modifying 389
moving columns 313
names for 482
null data sets 484
one-to-one merging 396, 411
one-to-one reading 396, 409
reading 346, 389, 390
SAS files and 4
saving as HTML 312
saving hash object data in 444
sorted data sets 485
sorting column values 315
updating 397, 420
viewing 310, 486
writing observations to 335
DATA step 6, 329
　assigning passwords 589
　changing default execution sequence 338
　checking for missing values 108
　concepts 10
　creating data files 342
　creating data views 342
　creating HTML reports 352
　generating data from programming state-
　　ments 346
　identifying BY groups 380
　input data 343
　ODS and 354
　output 13
　processing BY groups in 383
　reading from data sets 346
　reading raw data 343
　report writing with 347
　SAS processing and 13
　setting values to missing 107
DATA step Component Interface 437
DATA step debugger 4, 159
DATA step objects 437
　hash iterator object 445
　hash object 438
DATA step processing 330
　altering flow for given observation 339
　compilation phase 332
　concatenating data sets 402
　default execution for statements 337
　execution phase 332
　flow of action 330
　interleaving data sets 406
　match-merging 417
　one-to-one merging 412
　one-to-one reading 410

sample DATA step 333
step boundaries 340
troubleshooting execution 341
updating data sets 421
DATA step statements 69
　declarative 69
　executable 69
DATA step views 541
　additional output files 543
　creating 541
　definition 541
　examples 543
　merging data for reports 543
　passwords 593
　performance 542
　restrictions and requirements 542
　uses for 542
　vs. PROC SQL views 545
　vs. stored compiled programs 542, 554
data values 5, 334, 358
data views 481, 539
　benefits of 540
　creating with DATA step 342
　DATA step views 541
　PROC SQL views 545
　SAS/ACCESS views 546
　vs. data files 489
　when to use 541
DATASETS procedure
　creating indexes 526
　creating integrity constraints 511
date constants 113
date intervals 137
　boundaries of 141
　by category 138
　multiunit 142
　multiweek 143
　shifted intervals 144
　single-unit 142
　syntax 138
date values 127
　as recognizable dates 136
　calculating 137
　formats/informats and 131
　integrity of 130
　reading 137
　tools by task 131
　writing 137
　year 2000 and 128
　year digits 128, 129
datetime constants 113
datetime intervals 137
　boundaries of 141
　by category 138
　multiunit 142
　multiweek 143
　shifted intervals 144
　single-unit 142
　syntax 138
datetime values 128
　as recognizable dates and times 136
　formats/informats and 131
　integrity of 130
　tools by task 131
　year 2000 and 128
　year digits 128, 129
DBLOAD procedure 573

DBMS files 6
debugging 147
    logic errors 159
declarative statements 69
default Base SAS engine 602
default data sets 485
depreciation functions 41
descriptive statistic functions 41
descriptor information 332
    for data sets 481
destination-independent input 181
DICTIONARY tables 557
    performance 559
    viewing 557
    viewing subset of 559
    viewing summary of 558
DIM function
    determining number of array elements 456
    vs. HBOUND function 460
direct access
    combining data sets 394
directory of library members 478
disk space
    index requirements for 523
DO loops 453
    nested 457
    processing selected array elements 453
DO UNTIL expressions 456
DO WHILE expressions 456
DOCUMENT destination 182
    definition 178
drop-down menus 285
DROP statement
    I/O optimization and 216
dropping variables 88
    examples 90
    input or output data sets for 88
    order of application 89
    statements vs. data set options 88
duration integer 137, 140

E

e-mail
    sending through SMTP 619
encodings 38
encryption 594
    audit trails with 595
    copies with 595
    example 594
    generation data sets with 595
    indexes with 595
engines
    access patterns 600
    asynchronous I/O 601
    characteristics of 599
    CVP engine 604
    data set access 598
    definition 597
    files and 598
    I/O optimization and 218
    indexing 601
    interface DATA step engine 573
    levels of locking 600
    LIBNAME engine 569
    library engines 602

metadata LIBNAME engine 605
    read/write activity 600
    SAS XML LIBNAME engine 605
    specifying 597
    task switching 601
entries 468
ERROR automatic variable 85
error checking
    combining data sets 400
    examples 429, 432
    indexes and 428
    KEY= option and 432
    tools for 428
error processing 147, 156
    log control options 159
    multiple errors 157
    return codes 159
    syntax check mode 156
    system options for 158
ERROR statement
    writing to log with 165
errors
    data errors 154
    execution-time errors 151
    format modifiers for error reporting 156
    logic errors 159
    macro-related errors 156
    semantic errors 150
    summary of 147
    syntax errors 148
    types of 147
Excel
    copying data sets to 312
exclusion lists 190
    destinations for output objects 191
executable files
    reducing search time for 220
executable statements 69
execution phase (DATA step) 332
execution-time errors 151
    out-of-resources condition 152
explicit catalog concatenation 564
Explorer
    backing up SASUSER registry 240
    configuring with registry 246
Explorer window 291
    assigning filerefs 292
    copying data sets 293
    creating and saving programs 297
    opening files 296
    renaming files 295
    sorting files 296
    viewing file details 295
exponent 91
Export Wizard 324
exporting data
    Export Wizard for 324
expressions 110
    automatic numeric-character conversion 116
    Boolean numeric expressions 122
    character comparisons 120
    compound expressions 110
    constants in 110
    examples 110
    functions 117
    logical (Boolean) operators and 121
    operators in 117

order of evaluation 124
regular expressions (RX) 45
simple expressions 110
variables in 116
WHERE expressions 110
external files 5, 611
    as DATA step output 13
    input to SAS programs 12
    processing 616
    reading 615
    reading raw data 362
    referencing directly 612
    referencing indirectly 612
    referencing multiple files 613
    referencing with FILENAME access methods 614
    writing 615

F

file formats
    SAS 9 583
file protection
    See also passwords
    assigning with PW= data set option 591
    complete protection 591
    encryption 594
file shortcuts
    configuring with registry 247
File Transfer Protocol (FTP) 12
filename extensions
    SAS 9 584
filerefs
    assigning with Explorer window 292
    configuring with registry 247
files 4
    accessing without librefs 478
    moving between operating environments 607
    opening with Explorer window 296
    renaming 295
    repairing damaged files 607
    sorting 296
financial functions 41
FIRSTOBS= data set option
    I/O optimization and 217
    segmenting a subset 209
FIRST.variable 376, 380
floating-point representation 90
    double-precision vs. single-precision 98
    fractions 94
    IBM mainframes 91
    IEEE standard 94
    minimum number of bytes 97
    numeric comparisons 95
    OpenVMS 93
    precision vs. magnitude 94
    storing numbers with less precision 95
    transferring data between operating systems 98
    troubleshooting 91
    truncating numbers 97
foreign key integrity constraints 505
format modifiers
    for error reporting 156
FORMAT statement
    creating variables 82

specifying formats 28
formats 27, 79
    byte ordering for integer binary data 32
    data conversions 38
    date values and 131
    datetime values and 131
    encodings 38
    packed decimal data 34
    permanent 29
    specifying 28
    specifying with ATTRIB statement 29
    specifying with FORMAT statement 28
    specifying with PUT functions 28
    specifying with PUT statement 28
    specifying with %SYSFUNC function 28
    syntax 27
    temporary 29
    time values and 131
    user-defined 32
    zoned decimal data 34
formatted input 365
fractions
    floating-point representation 94
FTP (File Transfer Protocol) 12
FULLSTIMER system option 214
fully-bounded range condition 202
functions 38
    argument restrictions 40
    changing DATA step execution sequence 339
    depreciation functions 41
    descriptive statistic functions 41
    file manipulation 42
    financial functions 41
    in expressions 117
    in WHERE expressions 200
    PRX functions 45
    random-number functions 43
    syntax 39
    Web application functions 55
    within macro functions 42

G

general integrity constraints 505
generation data sets 499
    base version 499
    definition 499
    deleting 504
    encryption with 595
    generation numbers 499
    generaton groups 499
    GENMAX= data set option 499
    GENNUM= data set option 500
    historical versions 500
    invoking 500
    maintaining 500
    oldest version 500
    passwords with 595
    rolling over 500
    terminology 499
    youngest version 500
generation groups 499
    appending 503
    copying 503
    deleting versions 504
    displaying data set information 503

managing 502
    modifying number of versions 503
    passwords in 505
    processing specific versions 502
    renaming versions 504
generation numbers 499
GENMAX= data set option 499
GENNUM= data set option 500
Ghostview previewer 276
global statements 70
    executing stored compiled programs 552

H

hash iterator object 445
    declaring and instantiating 445
    retrieving hash object data 446
hash object 438
    declaring and instantiating 438
    defining keys and data 440
    initializing with constructor 439
    replacing and removing data 442
    retrieving data with hash iterator 446
    saving data in data sets 444
    storing and retrieving data 441
HBOUND function 460
    vs. DIM function 460
help
    from toolbar 288
Help menu 287
hexadecimal notation
    character constants in 112
    numeric constants in 113
historical versions 500
HTML
    saving data sets as 312
HTML destination 183
HTML output
    sample 173
HTML reports
    creating with ODS and DATA step 352
HTML version setting 188

I

I/O
    reducing for CPU performance 220
    threaded I/O 223
I/O-bound applications 223
I/O optimization 215
    BUFNO= system option 218
    BUFSIZE= system option 218
    CATCACHE= system option 218
    COMPRESS= system option 218
    creating data sets 217
    DROP statement 216
    engine efficiency 218
    FIRSTOBS= data set option 217
    indexes 217
    KEEP statement 216
    LENGTH statement 216
    OBS= data set option 217
    SASFILE statement 219
    views for data access 217

WHERE processing 216
IBM mainframes
    floating-point representation 91
ID management
    ARM macros for 58
IEEE standard
    floating-point representation 94
illegal operations
    missing values and 105
implicit catalog concatenation 564
importing data
    into data sets 321
IN= data set option
    creating variables 83
IN operator 202
    in character comparisons 121
    in numeric comparisons 120
INDEX= data set option
    creating indexes 526
index files 519
index type 80
indexed data files
    adding observations to 536
    appending data to 537
    copying 535
    sorting 536
    updating 536
indexes 518
    benefits of 518
    buffer requirements 523
    BY processing with 532
    composite indexes 520
    compound optimization 521
    costs of 522
    CPU cost 522
    creating 524, 525
    creating with DATASETS procedure 526
    creating with INDEX= data set option 526
    creating with SQL procedure 526
    data file considerations 524
    definition 518
    disk space requirements 523
    displaying data file information 534
    encryption with 595
    engines and 601
    error checking 428
    for BY-group processing 379
    I/O cost 522
    I/O optimization and 217
    index files 519
    integrity constraints and 508, 537
    key variable candidates 524
    maintaining 534
    missing values 521
    multiple occurrences of values 536
    passwords with 595
    recovering 537, 609
    simple indexes 520
    specifying with KEY= option 534
    taking advantage of 534
    types of 520
    unique values 521
    updating data sets 422, 428
    use considerations 524
    WHERE and BY processing with 533
    WHERE processing with 527

INFILE statement
  data-reading features   366
infix operators   117
INFORMAT statement
  creating variables   82
  specifying informats   31
informats   29, 80
  binary informats   370
  byte ordering for integer binary data   32
  data conversions   38
  date values and   131
  datetime values and   131
  encodings   38
  packed decimal data   34
  permanent   31
  specifying   30
  specifying with ATTRIB statement   31
  specifying with INFORMAT statement   31
  specifying with INPUT functions   30
  specifying with INPUT statement   30
  syntax   29
  temporary   31
  time values and   131
  user-defined   32
  zoned decimal data   34
input buffers   332
  creating   333
input data sets
  data set options with   25
  dropping variables   88
  keeping variables   88
input data sources   12
INPUT functions
  specifying informats   30
input pointer   334
INPUT statement
  column input   364
  data-reading features   366
  defining variables when reading raw data   82
  formatted input   365
  input style   362
  list input   363
  modified list input   363
  named input   365
  reading raw data   362
  specifying informats   30
input style
  choosing   362
  column input   364
  formatted input   365
  list input   363
  modified list input   363
  named input   365
instream data   361
  input to SAS programs   12
  semicolons in   362
INTCK function
  interval boundaries and   141
integer binary data
  byte ordering   32
integer binary notation   33
integrity constraints   505
  creating with DATASETS procedure   511
  creating with SCL   513
  creating with SQL procedure   512
  definition   505
  examples   511

foreign key constraints   505
general constraints   505
indexes and   508, 537
listing   511
locking   508
overlapping primary key and foreign key constraints   506, 517
passwords and   508
preservation of   507
reactivating   517
referential constraints   505
rejected observations   511
removing   516
specifying   511
interactive line mode   8
interface data files   489
interface DATA step engine   573
interface library engines   603
interface view engine   604
  ACCESS procedure and   572
interface views   539
interleaving data sets   395, 405
  comments and comparisons   409
  examples   406
  sort requirements   406
internal SAS processing transactions   231
interval   137
INTNX function
  interval boundaries and   141
invalid data   367
IORC automatic variable   428
  error-checking with   159
IS MISSING operator   204
IS NULL operator   204
iterative DO loops   453
  processing selected array elements   453

J

Julian dates
  packed   35

K

KEEP statement
  I/O optimization and   216
keeping variables   88
  examples   90
  input or output data sets for   88
  order of application   89
  statements vs. data set options   88
KEY= option
  error checking and   432
  MODIFY statement   534
  SET statement   534
key variables   520, 524
keys
  registry and   237
Keys window   304

L

LABEL= option
  ODS TRACE statement   190
labels   80
LAST.variable   376, 380
LBOUND function   460
LENGTH statement
  creating variables   82
  I/O optimization and   216
LIBNAME engine   569
LIBNAME statement
  associating librefs   470
  clearing librefs   470
library concatenation   471
library directories   478
library engines   469, 602
  definition   602
  interface library engines   603
  native library engines   602
  version compatibility and   584
  view engines   604
librefs   469
  accessing files without   478
  assigning   470
  associating with LIBNAME statement   470
  clearing with LIBNAME statement   470
  configuring with registry   247
  fixing libref problems with registry   249
  reserved names   471
  SAS/ACCESS   570
LIKE operator   204
links
  registry and   238
list input   363
LIST statement
  writing to log with   165
LISTING destination   182
  definition   178
Listing output
  sample   171
literals   16, 110
little endian platforms   32
log   162
  altering contents of   165
  as DATA step output   13
  changing destination of   170
  console log   162
  customizing   165, 166
  structure of   163
  suppressing parts of   165
  writing to   165
log control options   159
Log window   299
logic errors   159
logical names   469
logical operators   121
  combining WHERE expressions   207
  syntax for WHERE expressions   207

M

macro environment
  ARM macros   67
macro facility   6

macro functions
    DATA step functions within 42
macro-related errors 156
macro variables
    ARM macros with 57
    _ARMEXEC 65
macros
    ARM macros 55
mantissa 91
many-to-many relationships 393
many-to-one relationships 392
MARKUP destination 183
    definition 178
markup languages 178
master data set 420, 427
match-merging data sets 397, 416
MAX operator 123, 206
memory
    increasing for CPU performance 220
    optimizing usage 220
menus
    drop-down menus 285
    pop-up menus 286
MERGE statement
    match-merging 416
    one-to-one merging 412
merging
    match-merging 397, 416
    one-to-one 396, 411
metadata LIBNAME engine 605
metrics
    user metrics in ARM macros 63
MIN operator 123, 206
    in WHERE expressions 206
missing values 5, 101
    automatically set by SAS 104
    character variables 104
    checking for, in DATA step 108
    generated by SAS 105
    illegal character-to-numeric conversions
        and 105
    illegal operations and 105
    in raw data 107, 368
    indexes 521
    numeric variables 103
    order of 103
    printing in output 169
    propagation of 105, 106
    representing 368
    setting values to missing in DATA step 107
    special missing values 102, 106
    special values in numeric data 368
    updating data sets 422
modified list input 363
MODIFY statement
    updating data sets 420
modifying data sets 389
    tools for 389
multidimensional arrays 450, 457
    grouping variables in 457
    nested DO loops 457
Multiple Engine Architecture 469
multiple-pass access
    engines 600
multiweek intervals 143

N

_N_ automatic variable 85
name literals 21
name prefix lists 87
name range lists 87
named input 365
names 16
    data set names 482
    reserved names 18
    SAS names 18
    user-supplied 18
naming conventions
    automatic, for data sets 485
    SAS names 18
    variable names 20
native data files 489
native library engines 602
    default Base SAS engine 602
    definition 602
    REMOTE engine 602
    SAS Scalable Performance Data Engine 603
    SASESOCK engine 603
    sequential engines 603
    transport engine 603
    V6 compatibility engine 603
native views 539
nested DO loops 457
New Library window 302
nibbles 34
noninteractive line mode 8
nonstandard data 359
NOT operator 122
NOTEPAD 297
null data sets 484
numbered range lists 86
numbers 16
numeric-character conversion 116
numeric comparisons 119
    IN operator in 120
numeric constants 112
    hexadecimal notation 113
    scientific notation 113
    standard notation 112
numeric data
    reading raw data 359
    special missing values in 368
NUMERIC name lists 88
numeric precision 78, 90
numeric values 358
numeric variables 78, 79
    converting to character variables 84
    missing values 103
    precision 78, 90
    storing values 90

O

object spawner 621
OBS= data set option
    I/O optimization and 217
    segmenting a subset 209
observations 5
    position of variables in 80
    processing in BY groups 380
    reading data sets 390
    sorting for BY-group processing 379
    writing to data sets 335
ODS destinations
    categories of 181
    changing default settings 189
    definition 178
    destination-independent input 181
    exclusion lists 190
    SAS formatted destinations 182
    selection lists 190
    system resources and 185
    third-party formatted destinations 183
ODS output
    definition 179
ODS (Output Delivery System) 4, 170
    customized output 189
    DATA step and 354
    how it works 179
    processing 179
    registry and 187
    samples 171
    summary of 192
    terminology 178
    Universal Printing and 253
ODS TRACE statement
    LABEL= option 190
    purpose 190
oldest version 500
one-dimensional arrays 450
one-level data set names 484
one-to-many relationships 392
one-to-one merging 396, 411
    comments and comparisons 416
    examples 413
one-to-one reading 396, 409
    comments and comparisons 411
    examples 410
one-to-one relationships 392
OpenVMS
    floating-point representation 93
operands 110
    in WHERE expressions 199
operating environment commands
    managing data libraries with 479
operators 110, 117
    AND 121
    arithmetic operators 118, 201
    BETWEEN-AND 203
    comparison operators 118, 201
    concatenation operator 123, 206
    CONTAINS 203
    fully-bounded range condition 202
    IN 202
    in WHERE expressions 201
    infix operators 117
    IS MISSING 204
    IS NULL 204
    LIKE 204
    logical (Boolean) operators 121
    MAX 123, 206
    MIN 123, 206
    NOT 122
    numeric comparisons 119
    OR 122
    prefix operators 117, 206
    SAME-AND 205
    sounds-like 205

OR operator   122
OSIRIS engine   604
out-of-resources condition   152
output   162
   See also log
   centering   168
   changing destination of   170
   console log   162
   date and time values   168
   default destinations   163
   footnotes   168
   formatting characters for   169
   labels   169
   line size   169
   page breaks   169
   page numbering   169
   page size   169
   printing missing values   169
   program results   162
   reformatting values   169
   routing   163
   titles   169
   traditional listing output   167
output data sets
   data set options with   25
OUTPUT destination   182
   definition   178
output objects
   customized output for   191
   definition   178
   determining destinations for   190, 191
Output window   300

P

packed decimal data   34
   definition   369
   languages supporting   35
   platforms supporting   35
packed Julian dates   35
parallel processing   223
   CPU performance and   221
password-protected files   590
passwords   587
   See also passwords, assigning
   audit trails with   595
   changing   590
   copies with   595
   DATA step views with   593
   definition   587
   generation data sets with   595
   in generation groups   505
   incorrect   591
   indexes with   595
   integrity constraints and   508
   level of protection   587, 592
   PROC SQL views with   593
   removing   590
   SAS/ACCESS views with   593
   views with   592
passwords, assigning   588
   outside of SAS   590
   syntax   588
   to data sets   589
   with DATA step   589
   with procedures   589

   with SAS windowing environment   590
pattern matching
   LIKE operator   204
   RX and PRX for   45
PDF output
   sample   175
PDV (program data vector)   332
   input buffer and   333
performance
   ARM and   227
   audit trails   493
   DATA step views   542
   DICTIONARY tables   559
   of applications   607
   system performance   213
performance statistics   213
   Application Response Measurement
     (ARM)   215, 231
   collecting   214
   FULLSTIMER system option   214
   interpreting   214
   STIMER system option   214
Perl regular expression (PRX) functions and
   CALL routines
   license agreement   46
   pattern matching and   45
   syntax   47
permanent data libraries   473
permanent files
   accessing without libref   478
permanent formats   29
permanent informats   31
physical names   469
pop-up menus   286
position in observations   80
PostScript output
   sample   173
   Universal Printing   276
prefix operators   117, 206
Preview command box   269
previewers   266
print previewers   266
PRINT procedure
   style definitions with   187
Print Setup window   255
PRINTER destination   184
   definition   178
printers
   See Universal Printing
PROC SQL views   545
   embedding SAS/ACCESS LIBNAME state-
     ment in   570
   passwords   593
   vs. DATA step views   545
PROC steps   6, 14
   output   14
procedures   4
   assigning passwords with   589
   combining data sets with   398
   style definitions with   187
Profile catalog   563
program data vector (PDV)   332
   input buffer and   333
Program Editor window   298
program results   162
programming statements
   generating data from   346

propagation of missing values   105
Properties window   303
PRTDEF procedure
   Universal Printing and   274
PRX functions and CALL routines
   license agreement   46
   pattern matching and   45
   syntax   47
punched cards   372
PUT functions
   specifying formats   28
PUT statement
   specifying formats   28
   writing to log with   165
%PUT statement
   writing to log with   165
PW= data set option
   assigning complete file protection   591

Q

quotation marks
   character constants with   111

R

radix point   92
random access   428
   engines   600
random-number CALL routines   43
random-number functions   43
raw data
   definition   357
   input to SAS programs   12
   missing values in   107
   missing values when reading   104
raw data, reading   357
   binary data   369
   character data   360
   column-binary data   371
   DATA step for   343
   data types   358
   external files   362
   INPUT statement for   362
   instream data   361
   instream data with semicolons   362
   invalid data   367
   methods for   358
   missing values   368
   numeric data   359
   sources of raw data   361
read protection   587, 592
reading data sets   389, 390
   multiple data sets   390
   reading/writing observations   390
   reading/writing variables   390
   single data set   390
   tools for   389
reading raw data
   See raw data, reading
real binary representation   90
real time   214
records
   DATA step processing of   334, 336

recovering catalogs 610
recovering data files 608
recovering indexes 609
referential integrity constraints 505
registry 236
    adding values or keys to 244
    backing up SASUSER registry 239
    changing default HTML version setting 188
    changing ODS destination default set-
        tings 189
    color control with 242
    configuring 246
    configuring file shortcuts 247
    configuring libraries 247
    configuring SAS Explorer 246
    configuring Universal Printing 246
    creating values in 243
    deleting items from 245
    displaying 237
    editing 236
    finding data in 243
    fixing libref problems with 249
    managing 238
    ODS and 187
    recovering from failure 241
    restoring 241
    storage location 236
    terminology 237
Registry Editor 242
    adding values or keys 244
    backing up SASUSER registry 240
    changing the view 245
    creating values in registry 243
    deleting items from registry 245
    exporting registry files 246
    finding data in registry 243
    importing registry files 245
    renaming items in registry 245
    saving registry files 246
    starting 242
    when to use 242
registry files
    exporting 246
    importing 245
    in SASHELP library 236
    in SASUSER library 236
    saving 246
REGISTRY procedure 246
regular expressions (RX)
    pattern matching and 45
remote access
    input to SAS programs 12
REMOTE engine 602
renaming files
    with Explorer window 295
renaming variables 88
    examples 90
    input or output data sets for 88
    order of application 89
    statements vs. data set options 88
repairing damaged files 607
REPORT procedure
    style definitions with 187
reports
    as DATA step output 13
    creating with DATA step 347
reserved librefs 471

reserved names 18
resource usage 214
Results window 301
return codes 159
rolling over 500
routing output 163
    changing destination 170
    default destinations 163
RTF destination 184
    definition 178
RTF output
    sample 174
RX (regular expressions)
    pattern matching and 45

S

SAME-AND operator 205
SAS
    Base SAS and 3
    concepts 10
SAS/ACCESS LIBNAME statement 569
    embedding in PROC SQL views 570
SAS/ACCESS software
    definition 569
SAS/ACCESS views 546
    passwords with 593
SAS ARM interface 226, 228
SAS catalogs
    See catalogs
SAS data files
    See data files
SAS data libraries
    See data libraries
SAS data sets
    See data sets
SAS data views 5, 481
    See also data views
    as DATA step output 13
    input to SAS programs 12
SAS Explorer window
    list of available styles 186
SAS file types 468
SAS files 4
    concepts 10
SAS formatted destinations 181, 182
SAS indexes
    See indexes
SAS language 4
    components of 4
    data sets 5
    DBMS files 6
    elements 6, 25
    external files 5
    files 4
    macro facility 6
SAS log
    See log
SAS name lists 88
SAS output
    See output
SAS processing 11
    DATA step 13
    input data sources 12
    PROC steps 14
SAS registry

    See registry
SAS regular expression (RX) functions and
    CALL routines 45
SAS Scalable Performance Data Engine 603
SAS sessions 7
    batch mode 9
    customizing 9
    customizing windowing environment 10
    default system option settings 9
    executing statements automatically 9
    interactive line mode 8
    noninteractive line mode 8
    starting 7
    types of 7
    windowing environment 7
SAS statements
    See statements
SAS system libraries 474
SAS utilities
    for data libraries 477
SAS windowing environment 7, 283, 307
    assigning passwords with 590
    customizing 10
    drop-down menus 285
    Explorer window 291
    features 284
    help 287, 288
    keyboard equivalents, z/OS 284
    Keys window 304
    Log window 299
    New Library window 302
    Output window 300
    pop-up menus 286
    Program Editor window 298
    Properties window 303
    Results window 301
    toolbars 287
    window commands 288
    windows 288, 290
SAS XML LIBNAME engine 605
SASESOCK engine 603
SASFILE statement
    I/O optimization and 219
SASHELP library 476
    registry files in 236
SASUSER library 476
    registry files in 236
SASUSER registry
    backing up 239
Sasuser.Profile catalog 563
SASXREG file 238
scientific notation 90
    numeric constants in 113
SCL
    creating integrity constraints 513
    enabling ARM macro execution 66
search time
    reducing for executables 220
seed values 43
selection lists 190
    destinations for output objects 191
semantic errors 150
sequential access
    combining data sets 394
    engines 600
sequential data libraries 476
sequential engines 603

SET statement
  concatenating data sets 402
  interleaving data sets 405
  one-to-one reading 409
shifted intervals 144
sign bit 92
simple expressions 110
simple indexes 520
SMP machines 223
SMTP e-mail 619
  statements for controlling 620
  system options for 619
sorted data sets 485
sorting column values 315
sorting files 296
sorting indexed data files 536
sorting observations
  for BY-group processing 379
sounds-like operator 205
SPD Engine 603
special characters 16
special missing values 106
special SAS name lists 88
SPSS engine 604
SQL
  concatenating data sets 404
SQL procedure
  creating indexes 526
  creating integrity constraints 512
  list of available styles 186
SQL Procedure Pass-Through Facility 571
standard data 359
statements 69
  changing DATA step execution sequence 338
  combining data sets with 398
  DATA step statements 69
  declarative 69
  default execution in DATA step 337
  executable 69
  executing automatically 9
  global, definition 70
  options compared with system options 76
  step boundaries 340
  word spacing in 17
statistics
  performance statistics 213
step boundaries 340
STIMER system option 214
stored compiled programs 4, 547
  CPU performance and 220
  creating 549
  examples 549, 553, 554
  executing 550
  global statements for execution 552
  printing source code 552
  processing 548
  quality control application 554
  redirecting output 552
  restrictions and requirements 548
  uses for 547
  vs. DATA step views 542, 554
style attributes 184
  definition 186
style definitions
  definition of 185
  procedures with 187
  SAS-supplied 186

style elements
  definition 185
subkeys
  registry and 237
subsetting IF statement
  vs. WHERE expression 211
syntax check mode 156
  enabling 157
syntax errors 148
%SYSFUNC function
  specifying formats 28
SYSRC autocall macro 428
system libraries 474
  SASHELP 476
  SASUSER 476
  USER 475
  WORK 474
system options 71
  altering log contents with 166
  ARM 226, 228
  changing settings 73
  compared with data set options 76
  compared with statement options 76
  customizing log appearance with 166
  default settings 9, 71
  determining how value was set 72
  determining settings in effect 71
  duration of settings 74
  for error handling 158
  getting descriptive information about 73
  interaction with data set options 26, 75
  order of precedence 75
  restricted options 72
  syntax 71
  Universal Printing 273
system performance 213
  calculating data set size 221
  CPU performance 220
  memory usage 220
  optimizing I/O 215
  performance statistics 214

T

table attributes
  definition 185
table definitions
  definition of 178, 185
table elements
  definition 185
TABULATE procedure
  style definitions with 187
tagsets 183
  list of 179
task switching 601
TCP/IP socket 12
TEMPLATE procedure
  list of available styles 186
temporary data libraries 473
temporary formats 29
temporary informats 31
third-party formatted destinations 183
  definition 181
  formatting control and 184
threaded application processing 224
threaded I/O 223

threads 223
time constants 113
time intervals 137
  boundaries of 141
  by category 138
  multiunit 142
  shifted intervals 144
  single-unit 142
  syntax 138
time values 128
  as recognizable times 136
  formats/informats and 131
  tools by task 131
tokens
  See words
toolbars 287
  help from 288
traditional listing output 167
transaction classes 58
transaction data set 420
transaction instances 58
transaction monitoring
  See ARM
transaction records 230
transactions
  ARM 226
  internal SAS processing 231
transport engine 603
two-dimensional arrays 451
  bounds in 460
two-level data set names 484

U

unexpected conditions 429
Universal Printing 252
  changing default printer 255
  configuring 273
  configuring with registry 246
  defining printers 256
  defining printers for batch mode 274
  forms printing 279
  Ghostview previewer 276
  multiple printers 274
  multiple users 275
  ODS and 253
  page properties 270
  previewers 266
  previewing Postscript output 276
  print output formats 252
  printer definitions 275, 277
  printer for current SAS session 264
  printer properties 259
  printing 264
  printing a test page 264
  printing window contents 264
  PRTDEF procedure for 274
  removing printer from selection list 255
  setting up printers 255
  system options for 273
  turning on/off 252
  windows 254
Universal Unique Identifiers
  See UUIDs (Universal Unique Identifiers)
UPDATE statement
  updating data sets 420

updating data sets 397, 420
  error checking 428
  examples 424
  indexes with MODIFY statement 422
  missing values 422
  new variables 422
  nonmatched observations 422
  sort requirements for UPDATE statement 422
  UPDATE vs. MODIFY with BY 422
URLs
  remote access and 13
user-defined formats 32
user-defined informats 32
USER library 475
  assigning USER libref 475
  relation to WORK library 476
user metrics 63
user-supplied SAS names 18
utilities
  for data libraries 477
UUID Generator Daemon 621
  installing 622
UUIDCOUNT= system option 623
UUIDGEN function 623
UUIDHOST system option 623
UUIDs (Universal Unique Identifiers) 621
  assigning 623
  object spawner 621

V

V6 compatibility engine 603
values
  registry and 238
variable attributes 78
  format 79
  index type 80
  informat 80
  label 80
  length 79
  name 79
  position in observation 80
  type 79
variable labels 80
variable length 79
  CPU performance and 221
  not explicitly set 81
variable lists 86, 456
  name prefix 87
  name range 87
  numbered range 86
  special SAS name 88
variable names 79
  naming conventions 20
variable types 79
  converting 84
  not explicitly set 81
variable values 334
variables 5, 78
  aligning values 85

ARM macros with 57
automatic variables 85
character variables 78
creating 80
creating with assignment statement 81
creating with ATTRIB statement 83
creating with FORMAT statement 82
creating with IN= data set option 83
creating with INFORMAT statement 82
creating with LENGTH statement 82
defining with INPUT statement 82
dropping 88
in expressions 116
in WHERE expressions 199
keeping 88
maximum number of 78
numeric variables 78
reading data sets 390
renaming 88
setting values to missing in DATA step 107
version compatibility 583
  comparing SAS 9 to earlier releases 583
  library engines and 584
  SAS 9 file format 583
  SAS 9 filename extensions 584
view descriptors 546, 572
views
  I/O optimization and 217
  level of protection 592
  passwords with 592
  WHERE expessions and 209
VIEWTABLE window 486
  clearing subsetted data 321
  creating WHERE expressions 317
  editing cell values 320
  labeling columns 313
  moving columns 313
  sorting column values 315
  viewing data set contents 310

W

Web applications
  functions for 55
WHERE-expression processing 197
WHERE expressions 110, 198
  combining with logical operators 207
  compound expressions 198
  compound optimization 528
  constants in 200
  creating with VIEWTABLE window 317
  efficient expressions 208
  functions in 200
  operand specification 199
  operators in 201
  optimizing 527
  order of evaluation 208
  processing compound expressions 207
  processing views 209

  segmenting a subset 208
  simple expressions 198
  syntax 199
  variables in 199
  vs. subsetting IF statement 211
  where to use 198
WHERE processing
  comparing resource usage 530
  compound optimization 528
  controlling index usage 531
  displaying index usage information 531
  estimating qualified observations 529
  I/O optimization and 216
  indentifying available indexes 527
  indexes for 527
  indexes for, with BY processing 533
  indexes with views 532
windowing environment
  See SAS windowing environment
words 15
  literals 16
  name literals 21
  names 16
  numbers 16
  spacing in statements 17
  special characters 16
  types of 16
  variable names 20
WORK library 474
  copying files to 307
  relation to USER library 474
write protection 587, 592

X

XML LIBNAME engine 605
XML output
  sample 176

Y

year 2000 128
YEARCUTOFF= system option
  year 2000 and 128
  year digits and 128, 129
years
  four-digit 128, 129
  two-digit 128, 129
youngest version 500

Z

z/OS
  keyboard equivalents 284
zoned decimal data 34
  definition 370
  languages supporting 35
  platforms supporting 35

Your Turn

If you have comments or suggestions about *SAS® 9.1 Language Reference: Concepts*, please send them to us on a photocopy of this page, or send us electronic mail.

For comments about this book, please return the photocopy to

SAS Publishing
SAS Campus Drive
Cary, NC 27513
email: yourturn@sas.com

For suggestions about the software, please return the photocopy to

SAS Institute Inc.
Technical Support Division
SAS Campus Drive
Cary, NC 27513
email: suggest@sas.com

Printed in the United States
19437LVS00001B/77-90